THE YALE EDITIONS OF

The Private Papers of James Boswell

Boswell's London Journal, 1762–1763

Boswell in Holland, 1763–1764

Portraits, BY SIR JOSHUA REYNOLDS

Boswell on the Grand Tour: Germany and Switzerland, 1764

Boswell on the Grand Tour: Italy, Corsica, and France, 1765–1766

Boswell in Search of a Wife, 1766–1769

Boswell for the Defence, 1769–1774

*Boswell's Journal of a Tour to the Hebrides
with Samuel Johnson,* LL.D., 1773

Boswell: The Ominous Years, 1774–1776

Boswell in Extremes, 1776–1778

Boswell, Laird of Auchinleck, 1778–1782

Boswell: The Applause of the Jury, 1782–1785

AUCHINLECK HOUSE, as it appeared in 1968. Photograph by Morton Lustig.

Boswell:

THE APPLAUSE OF
THE JURY

1782-1785

EDITED BY IRMA S. LUSTIG

SENIOR RESEARCH ASSOCIATE IN ENGLISH

YALE UNIVERSITY

AND FREDERICK A. POTTLE

STERLING PROFESSOR OF ENGLISH EMERITUS

YALE UNIVERSITY

McGRAW-HILL BOOK COMPANY

NEW YORK   TORONTO   LONDON

Boswell: The Applause of the Jury, 1782–1785. Copyright © 1981 by
Yale University. Copyright 1932 by Yale University. Copyright
renewed 1960. All Rights Reserved. Printed in the United States
of America. No part of this publication may be reproduced, stored
in a retrieval system, or transmitted, in any form or by any means,
electronic, mechanical, photocopying, recording, or otherwise,
without the prior written permission of the publisher.

Library of Congress Cataloging in Publication Data

Boswell, James, 1740–1795.
  Boswell: The Applause of the Jury, 1782–1785.

  (The Yale editions of the private papers of James Boswell)
  Bibliography: p. 371.
  Includes index.
  1. Boswell, James, 1740–1795—Diaries. 2. Authors, Scot-
tish—18th century—Biography. I. Lustig, Irma Spritz, 1921—
II. Pottle, Frederick Albert, 1897— III. Title. IV. Series:
Yale editions of the private papers of James Boswell.

PR3325.A799 1980   828'.603 [B]   79-28144
ISBN 0-07-039114-9

    123456789 DODO 898765432 1

Christine Aulicino designed this book; Sally Fliess supervised the
production. It was set in Baskerville with display lines in Stationer's
Semiscript by Photo Data, Inc.
Printed and bound by R. R. Donnelley and Sons, Inc.

The preparation of *Boswell: The Applause of the Jury* was generously supported by the Editing Program of the National Endowment for the Humanities. We are also deeply grateful for timely gifts of matching funds from the Andrew W. Mellon Foundation and the following individuals.

PATRONS

Curtis Carroll Davis   William Peyton May
Wilmarth S. Lewis   Warren H. Smith

FRIENDS

Richard N. Berry   Jean and Maurice Jacobs
Bertrand H. Bronson   Arthur M. Kaplan
John Brooke   Sheila Lambert
Chester F. Chapin   Louis A. Landa
James L. Clifford   Martha and Victor Laties
Ben Cohen   Charles W. Loeb
Irene Dash   John R. Mapel
Damian O. Desmond   John N. Morris
Frank H. Ellis   David F. Musto
David A. Garrick   William B. Ober
Sidney L. Gulick   Guy J. Pevtchin
Nellie P. and John E. Hankins   Arthur G. Rippey
Charles Beecher Hogan   Arthur H. Scouten
Mary Hyde   Nonna and René Wellek

Margaret H. Wimsatt

The Yale Editions of the Private Papers of James Boswell consists of two independent but parallel series. One, the "research" edition, gives a complete text of Boswell's journals, diaries, and memoranda; of his correspondence; and of the *Life of Johnson,* from the original manuscript. It preserves the spelling and capitalization of the original documents and is provided with extensive scholarly annotation. A large group of editors is engaged in this comprehensive undertaking. The first three volumes of at least thirty appeared in 1966, 1969, and 1976, respectively. The other series, the reading or "trade" edition, selects from the total mass of papers those portions that appear likely to be of general interest and presents them in modern spelling and with appropriate annotation. The publishers have also issued limited de luxe printings of some of the trade volumes, with extra illustrations and special editorial matter, but neither the trade volumes nor the de luxe printings include matter from Boswell's archives that will not appear in the research edition.

The present volume is the eleventh in the trade edition of the journals, the twelfth in the entire trade series.

CONTENTS

ILLUSTRATIONS

following page 228

Auchinleck House, as it appeared in 1968. Photograph by Morton Lustig.

Henry Home, Lord Kames, painting by David Martin. Reproduced by permission of the Scottish National Portrait Gallery, Edinburgh.

Henry Dundas, first Viscount Melville, painting by John Rising. Reproduced by permission of the Duke of Buccleuch and Queensberry, K.T.

The Wreck of the *Centaur.* Engraving by Thomas Gaugain, 1784, after a painting by James Northcote. Reproduced by permission of the Trustees of the British Museum.

Samuel Johnson, LL.D., painting by Sir Joshua Reynolds. Reproduced by permission of the Haverford College Library.

Anna Seward, painting by George Romney A gift of the Lucy Hanes Chatham Library Fund, the portrait is reproduced by permission of the Forsyth County Public Library, Winston Salem, North Carolina.

John Lee, painting by Sir Joshua Reynolds. Reproduced by permission.

The Aerial Travellers. Engraving by F. Bartolozzi, 1785, after a painting by J. F. Rigaud. Reproduced by permission of the Trustees of the British Museum.

Edmond Malone, painting by Sir Joshua Reynolds. Reproduced by permission of the National Portrait Gallery, London.

James Boswell, painting by Sir Joshua Reynolds. Reproduced by permission of the National Portrait Gallery, London.

INTRODUCTION

The Applause of the Jury begins with a modest success and ends in triumph. Boswell's serene and patient efforts to become a model laird were only fleetingly successful; his *Journal of a Tour to the Hebrides*, prepared for the press amidst distraction and anxiety, has stood for two centuries. But no matter how success came and what pleasure it gave, it was owing to a trait Boswell has been too little credited with: will-power, emerging as tenacity and inventiveness.

Boswell's succession to the estate of Auchinleck was an accident of birth, but he was willing to earn his inheritance. Loyal, patient despite provocation, and determined during the protracted years of his dependence, he displayed the same attributes in his first months as laird. From late September 1782 until mid-January 1783 he attended systematically to his duties and discovered that being laird was as gratifying as he had dreamed it would be. Few other experiences in life matched Boswell's fantasies. His position as laird, the ninth in a succession established by royal gift, was infused with romance and responsibility. Both the land and the people who worked it depended upon his stewardship, and he was shown in turn the respect traditionally accorded his rank. Status solaced Boswell when he knew himself outdistanced by men of humble family or, as he thought, lesser ability. "An ancient baron may pull up when he pleases; and his pride may prevail over his gaiety," he writes loftily. He is so aware of himself as example that he also becomes rather pompous in his insistence on forms like prayers at home and keeping the Sabbath.

The fault is minor, and more than compensated for by Boswell's efforts to overcome his ignorance of country affairs. Lord Auchinleck had reserved the management of the estate to himself despite Boswell's wish to help, and Boswell had been sufficiently self-protective not to offer himself repeatedly as pupil to so overbearing a teacher. His own master now, he put himself to school with James Bruce, his overseer, took arithmetic lessons from Alexander Millar, assistant minister, and made a companion of Alexander Fairlie, the distinguished agricultural improver, on his rounds of the Auchinleck farms. For a while, at least, learning when to plant, to lime, to leave the land fallow was a challenge and a pleasure as well as a duty. He is very well, Boswell tells his friend Dempster, "not by a strong anchor ... but by riding before a brisk

gale." He was also "very well" because regular and productive work following the rhythm of nature gave solidity to his existence, which was
haunted by fears of evanescence. Pleased with his own conduct, he
acknowledges that it would also have pleased his father and grandfather. When he took care of Lord Auchinleck's improvements upon
the estate, he writes, "I thought I was doing what he approved; and
I wished always to preserve the notion of his seeing what I was about."
The need to satisfy his father's expectations persists beyond Lord
Auchinleck's death; only then, we note, can Boswell attain and enjoy a
pattern of behaviour that might have won his approval. "Felt a steadiness as Laird of Auchinleck which I never before experienced in
London," he observes happily on the first jaunt after his accession. But
he has already felt the irresistible pull southwards.

We are dismayed to read less than a week after Boswell removed
to Edinburgh for the winter term of the Court of Session, "Began to
have a little return of bad spirits," and, on the next day, "not as I could
wish . . . the enamel of my sound mind was a little broken." The chronic
depression of Boswell's middle years has resurfaced. As usual, his mood
flutters erratically in Edinburgh, to historians the "Athens of the
North," to Boswell "provincial obscurity." He had always been in the
shadow of his father's eminence in that city. Self-consciousness returns,
and he languishes for London, Parliament, or "any state of animated
exertion." From the onset of the depression early in 1783 almost to
the end of *The Applause of the Jury* the journal reverberates with a
ground note of uncertainty and despair (we shall return to that subject).
Boswell never again enjoyed the sustained pleasure in Auchinleck that
he experienced as the new laird. He cannot gratify Bruce's "well-meant"
wish that he bid adieu to London for seven years, he tells him in 1783,
but he will do all the good he can as laird consistent with his love of
that "great city."

The pledge was as important as the qualification. Boswell never
abandoned his stewardship of Auchinleck, though he spent long periods in London and finally made it his home. Without the exemplary
loyalty and diligence of his overseers the estate might have been ruined,
but Boswell was a watchful administrator even though at a distance.
He responded closely to the weekly letters he exacted from Bruce
and scrutinized the journal of events on the estate that Bruce kept at
his direction. "When you mark a burial in your journal let me know
whose it is," he requested, and added the commendation, "Your journal
pleases me much."

The concern that Boswell showed for the people of Auchinleck is
the noblest feature of his performance as laird. Abundant entries in

his journal, expense accounts, and other papers document his kindness, deliberate and spontaneous. The cost to him was not always trifling. He reserved grain for his tenants when it was in short supply and other landowners were selling it for malt at high prices; he did not raise rents though his calculations showed increased costs; and he withheld eviction indefinitely when payments were long overdue. He would contract his operations rather than that Bruce be "stressed." He drew a will in 1785 that made specific provision for the overseer, housekeeper, and ancient tenants. A postscript reads, "I do beseech all the succeeding heirs of entail to be kind to the tenants and not to turn out old possessors to get a little more rent."

A feeling heart may conceal a shrewd mind: charity is cheaper than an increased share of the crops, and a judicious benevolence forestalls barn burnings. But Boswell was neither calculating nor far-seeing enough to sustain our scepticism about his motives, though he complained when he was low in spirits and easily vexed that his tenants were not sufficiently attentive to his interests. On the whole, his gestures were innocent. The most observant of reporters, his eye was on the specimen not the species, the immediate rather than the abstract. He ignored the social implications of the events in Ayrshire that he described so vividly in these journals, the cruel winters of 1782 to 1784, the grain riots, the hunger. Not a word about the accelerated consolidation of farms resulting from the catastrophes, natural and manmade. The agricultural revolution of the later eighteenth century is a series of discrete incidents in *The Applause of the Jury*.

Boswell was the very model of feudal paternalism because ideology was bonded to him emotionally by a romantic attachment to Auchinleck and its traditions and by his own insatiable need for a wise and loving father. What he desired for himself he yielded instinctively to others. As late as 1785 he had not overcome his personal need for a moral guide who would cherish him despite his failings. Johnson gone, he turned to Sir Joshua Reynolds, who catered to his comfort and his taste for elegance but rebuked him plainly for associating with Margaret Caroline Rudd. There was no living friend thereafter whom Boswell revered more than Sir Joshua. So the dedication of the *Life of Johnson* attests.

The separate paper on which he preserved an anecdote about George III is also instructive. Boswell clearly adored the King for sparing the life of the convict Patrick Madan, whom the courts had doomed for escaping the ship transporting him to Africa. Burke had recently described in the Commons in the most graphic terms the deaths from disease and starvation, if not massacre by natives, which threatened prisoners in Africa. By waiving Madan's death sentence but transporting him to Australia the King proved himself compassionate yet protective of all his subjects. The juxtaposition of his charity with the relentless procession to the gallows recorded in these journals eluded Boswell. He was horrified by the casual taking of life, but he did not perceive that the occasional royal gift of mercy was essential to maintaining a system of official brutality. Hope of relief beyond the frigid authority of the law seduced most of the propertyless into accepting their condition. To Boswell also the King was the best of fathers, just such a father as he had yearned for, and his adoration was complete.

The wonder is that the deprived and fearful son was himself a loving father. Children and adults, we commonly vow that we will not commit as parents the errors we detect in our own upbringing, but we discover all too often that the imprint is indelible. Boswell, however, did indeed welcome fatherhood in every form and practised it generously not despite his experience but because of it. Having suffered the tyranny of power, he felt instant empathy with the helpless whom he recognized as any way kin with himself, and when he gave pain to his dependents, as he did to his wife Margaret, he was tormented by guilt and by fear. The later conduct of his children, who loved him deeply, suggests that Boswell's fault was over-indulgence as well as exaggerated family pride. With his tenants, as with his children, he *was* his father in one, at least, of Lord Auchinleck's major roles, but he was such a father as he himself had desired.

For Boswell as an individual we regret the lost peace of mind when he was no longer satisfied by rural life and resumed his pursuit of a public career. For Boswell as writer and ourselves as his beneficiaries we are relieved. The journal he kept in the first months of his accession is engaging because of his "extraordinary metamorphosis," as he called it, but as a specimen it suggests that a pastoral journal kept to the end of his life would have been interesting chiefly to antiquarians. Had Boswell not been impelled to visit London and finally to live there, we might also have been deprived of the *Journal of a Tour to the Hebrides* and the *Life of Johnson,* both of which Edmond Malone catalysed to publication by a balance of encouragement, discipline, and attention to Boswell's well-being: measured wine as well as work.

§ II

Boswell's steady practice of his literary skills, both publicly and privately, the decision recorded at least as early as 1772 to write a life

of Johnson, and the enthusiastic, even dogged, collecting of biographical materials point to his masterworks as the satisfaction of his deepest
instincts. Yet they were jeopardized by the difficulty he himself recognized of distinguishing between "noble ambition and foolish, restless,
conceited aspiring." Like most of his contemporaries, Boswell was cap-
tivated by the political spectacle. Avid for acclaim, he fancied himself
in Parliament, a Burke in defence of the King, or commanding the
sinecure necessary to maintain a family home in London as well as at
Auchinleck. The numerous applications to great men, the political
pamphlets, manoeuvrings at county meetings, and addresses to the
King were all futile means to prizes he was neither wealthy nor prudent
enough to obtain. Sometimes a shrewd strategist with an eye on the
main chance, he was also an impetuous and outspoken independent.
A patriotic but privileged Scotsman, an Anglophile with a romantic
attachment to the Stuarts, his ambivalence made him reckless when his
country's traditions or his nationalism seemed threatened.

It was clear even to Boswell by 1785 that the power-brokers were
shunning him. His gamble at winning office outside the usual alliances,
through a *Letter to the People of Scotland* opposing the bill to reduce the
Court of Session, was likewise doomed to failure. Populist techniques
require organization, a large independent or disaffected electorate,
patience, and more nerve than Boswell possessed. He hesitated in
writing the pamphlet, changed it repeatedly, and feared that he would
be challenged to a duel. That Boswell risked his future despite his
obvious anxiety about the *Letter* is evidence of his panic as he approached his forty-fifth year without prospects. The poor wretch that
he dreamed of lying naked on a dunghill in London, complaining
woefully as he was flayed by a ruffian—who could that have been but
the dreamer himself?

Though Boswell's noisy public activities in his mid-forties were
avowedly practical, they may be likened, as General Paoli observed, to the
frenzy of the Curetes protecting the infant Jupiter: the clamour drew
attention from the cries deep in the hiding-place. The growing terror
was not just the lack of significant position well into middle age but
later middle age itself. "I did not feel at Hamilton the fine sensations
I once had at that place," Boswell observes. "I *must* submit to life losing
its vividness." To a greater or lesser degree, depending upon fortune
and one's involvement in the world, the experience is universal. But
the sensationalist, unsatisfied by faded colours, strives restlessly to
restore the brilliance. He is not only staving off death (we shall come
to that subject); he is striving for the intensity he experienced when
the world was new. Physical pleasures alone did not exhilarate Boswell,

though they became increasingly the means of escaping loss and regret. The truly glorious experiences had an intellectual core. Even London paled after Johnson's death, and in the midst of his abandoned whirl there in the spring and summer of 1785 Boswell lamented its spiritual emptiness.

The difficulty with which Boswell sat to the *Journal of a Tour to the Hebrides* suggests that resurrecting even the best of the past could not fill the vacuum. It was not the expectation of reliving experience that compelled him to journalize, but the need to fix it verbally, and therefore permanently. "I should live no more than I can record," he had written in 1776, but he hungered to extend both life and journal. It was of himself that Boswell wrote, surely, when he generalized in the *Life of Johnson* that man was willing to take an addition to his life because he clung to the "deceitful hope" that the next part would be free from pain and anxiety. From adolescence at least, the rhythm of Boswell's life was between struggle—determined and imaginative effort—and torpidity. But as it grew harder to experience a genuine delight in a less vivid world, the hidden terrors surfaced and the periods of overt depression and physical abandonment were more frequent and longer lasting. "I said to Sir Alexander Dick, 'Between ourselves, it is happier to be a young laird than an old one.' 'Because' (said he very well) 'the one lives in hope, the other in fear.' "

The resurfacing of metaphysical doubts which threatened Boswell all his life—free-will versus predestination; death and the after-life—signalized depression and also deepened the gloom. The spiritual debate is interwoven with the material, Boswell's apparent powerlessness to control his own fate. We note that in February 1784, when he could recollect "nothing remarkable" in his daily existence, drank only water, and suffered from nervous headaches, he was distressed for the first time after a long interval by the irreconcilability of fate and free-will. He worried the problem on at least four days within the week, and disclosed at the last entry that his reason was weighted against what he wished to believe: "While I *half apprehended* that all was *irresistible fate,* I *half hoped* that there was *free volition and agency,* though I could not understand it." Soon afterwards, he proved *his* effectuality at least by moving the Edinburgh Address in support of the King. Boswell also suffered and was inactive from the summer through the winter of 1784, because his scheme of removing to the English bar was more reckless than even he could justify as yet. Those who would pay for it were before his eyes. He might rationalize transplanting the children: they were young and flexible (so people argue), and an English education would profit them. But Margaret Boswell, who he himself had said could not live in the smoke of London because of her weak lungs—how could he justify uprooting her? When reason supplanted fantasy, Margaret's loyalty—she would follow wherever his best interests lay—was a rebuke rather than a release. Frustration confirmed the spectres of Calvinism and paralyzed him.

We discover with a start as the middle years advance that death has become more familiar than birth. Between 1782 and 1785 Boswell suffered the incomprehensible, the death of Johnson, and many losses from his family and circle of friends, young and old. Every end reminds Boswell of his own mortality. What is it like to die? How do men endure it? He needs evidence, from this world and the next, as his dream of Johnson in the night between 6 and 7 February 1785 reveals. He attends Newgate compulsively, as if it were a school or a rehearsal for eternity ("Thinking of Newgate and violent deaths hardened me," he wrote when he feared a challenge from Sir Adam Fergusson). Boswell, in the forefront of the crowd, pushes close to the gibbet so as to observe the victim and overhear his last words, a voice, perhaps, from mid-passage. He cross-examines his friends of distinguished intellectual power as each one approaches his end. Hume's tranquil insistence on his scepticism when he knew that he was dying terrified Boswell. Seven and a half years later he dreams in 1784 of learning from Hume's diary that he was really a Christian. Lord Kames's pedestrian replies to Boswell's questions disappoint him: "nothing edifying, nothing pious." He is reassured only by Johnson's Christianity, which Johnson applies rigorously to himself but more charitably (in private) to others. When his mentor is gone, Boswell attempts to live by his precepts and example.

That is Boswell's way when he is consciously proper, but when death surprises him or occurs before his eyes he is frantic to assert his animal vitality. At the age of twenty-six he had gone to a Parisian brothel "as in fever" after learning from a newspaper of his mother's death in Edinburgh. Almost twenty years later he hurries from Newgate to Betsy Smith, a prostitute, while the ten convicts he saw hanged are not yet cut down, and directs her to take out the "shocking sight in my head." After another execution Boswell looks at the victim's face and is struck by the "quick transition from life to death." He breakfasts at Baldwin's, but still "very uneasy. Visited Chelmsford," almost certainly a place-name under which he concealed the identity of a woman. When Boswell is depressed by his mortality he also drinks excessively, without effect, he persuades himself, but he is sick the next day. A pattern of dissipation is *his* "signal of distress." As Boswell descends to the pit he lets all controls go. His "philosophical impression of the nothingness of all things in human life" has been confirmed; he himself is contemptible, he will surely suffer eternal damnation. At his worst Boswell is neither drunkard nor fornicator; he is nothing. Stupified, he is unable to rise from his bed.

The ascent from the depths is slow and erratic. He lives abstemiously—eats little, drinks only water—as if to avert physical shock and lighten his body against buffetings. Purging restores Boswell's equilibrium; the world, where it pulsates with life and substantial conversation, restores his spirits. Public life engages him in the living moment and requires nimble wits as well as nimble footwork. He tries it again.

§ III

This is the last volume of journals in which we shall enjoy the conversation of Samuel Johnson, a period hardly to be closed silently. Although *The Applause of the Jury* is rich in Johnson's late wit and wisdom, it contains less of it than we should like. Boswell's pursuit of his own advancement and pleasure aside, his opportunities to converse with Johnson in the final years were limited. Johnson was weakened by a stroke, advanced asthma, probably emphysema, congestive heart failure, and cutting and bleeding to relieve its symptoms. Confined to the house for three months in the previous winter, he was still only as entertaining at a meeting of The Club on 22 June 1784 "as his indisposition allowed him breath to be." Through how many nights of penetrating dampness and polluted air was he forced to sit upright to draw his breath? Small wonder that he was sometimes napping when Boswell called upon him and irritable when he was awake. It is also understandable that Boswell was relieved to escape the contrariness all of Johnson's friends expected when he was short of sleep or in pain. Boswell himself was tense with unresolved debate about his future, the carping of a sick and testy father was all too vivid in his memory, and he could not endure to be checked now by the counsellor whose approval of his plans he was the most anxious to obtain.

The strains engendered by mutual uneasiness, which Boswell makes no effort to conceal in the journal or even in the *Life of Johnson*, are counterbalanced by a mutual affection. Boswell's solicitude as well as his vivacity roused Johnson out of his torpor; the extraordinary efforts to extend his life by a winter in Italy rendered him almost speechless. Johnson displays in turn the tenderness that marks their friendship. Relief of human need was always more important to him than abstract principles. If a man who has led a good life for seven years dies after a wrong act, will the good he has done be weighed in his favour, Boswell asks during an earnest conversation. "Sir, if a man has been seven years good and afterwards is by passion hurried to commit what is wrong, he'll have the reward of his seven years," Johnson assures him. "GOD won't take a catch of him." Johnson understood Boswell's need for opinions which justified his desires and allayed his apprehensions, and though he feared that the scheme of removing to England was impractical, he approved it at last, but with conditions which Boswell could meet. He also spared Boswell the burden of a vow, though Johnson bound himself repeatedly with the resolutions he wrote out at the beginning of each year.

The most remarkable of Johnson's kindnesses is the patience and candour with which he responded to Boswell's probing of his behaviour and his expectations of the after-life. These conversations pregnant with the unspoken acknowledgement of Johnson's approaching end are now part of common memory. To the last meeting, Johnson's intellectual powers are undiminished. His command of his learning and his audience is sure, his arguments pithy, his judgements decisive. Occasionally Boswell or another companion—even the "amiable Dr. Adams"—prolongs too personal an argument and touches a nerve. Johnson's anger at their insensitivity, and his anguish as he faces his own imperfections and the imminence of judgement ("Let me alone, let me alone, I am overpowered"), are among the most moving scenes in our literature. I use the word "scenes" deliberately: whether made directly after the event, ten days or ten years afterwards, Boswell's transcriptions of experience employ all of the novelist's skills except fable. He is no less an artist because he is constrained by fact, which is sometimes more wonderful than invention.

The most dramatic evidence of his genius in this volume of journals is the "Extraordinary Johnsoniana—*Tacenda* [to be kept silent]," now published in their entirety for the first time. The *Tacenda* make two biographical points: the first that Johnson was sexually potent, the second that on occasion he permitted himself to encourage sexual appetite without intention of gratifying it. The first point was very much to Boswell's purpose for his life of Johnson but required that it be made casually, briefly, and within the bounds of Boswellian decorum. The other incidents which humanized his hero were set amidst a prevailing impression of dignity. Only one of Mrs. Desmoulins's reports of Johnson's virility could be adapted to Boswell's standard, Garrick's anecdote of playing the spy upon his schoolmaster through the keyhole of the Johnsons' bedroom. The story did not damage Johnson's char-

acter. His prancing around Tetty's bed, no doubt displaying the proof
of his aroused manhood, is exquisitely comic and undignified, but it is
innocent and active. Boswell translated the anecdote to the *Life of
Johnson* (anno 1736), but he muted the details. Though he appears to
have violated his own injunction to suppress Mrs. Desmoulins's account,
if Garrick had indeed spread his mischief all over town, as she reported
and as seems likely, Boswell doubtless felt freed from the need of
censorship.

The frustrated temptation of Mrs. Desmoulins was not such a story,
however, as Boswell could repeat. Modern readers may think Johnson's
struggle between scruples and desire poignant rather than shocking.
Readers in the late eighteenth century did not have so relaxed an
attitude. Johnson's statements on infidelity were reported in the biography; his attempt to seduce a young woman of his household while
the aging wife who kept him from her bed lay nearby would have
branded him a hypocrite and a lecher. Most men would have thought
him a fool for banishing Mrs. Desmoulins when she was obviously
yielding. Admirers of Johnson were sure to be disillusioned or dis-
believing; the hostile would discover additional proof that he was un-
worthy of a biography. In any case Boswell was certain to be abused,
as he learned from the angry responses to the failings he had disclosed
in the *Tour to the Hebrides*. The quotations from reviews and letters in
the press which we print at the close of the journal are a sampling of
what he suffered for aiming at truth in fact and spirit. The world was
not yet wise enough, Boswell discovered, for his explicit biographical
method.

Up to the highpoint of Mrs. Desmoulins's cross-examination, the
Tacenda could be a scene from Restoration comedy, all forward strain-
ing action, an interplay of characters through dialogue, gestures, asides;
nothing superfluous. The sexual tension of the immediate drama, the
tête-à-tête, mirrors in comic fashion the scene-within-the-scene, yet it
heightens rather than diminishes the earnestness and integrity of Johnson's struggle. Boswell and Lowe seduce Mrs. Desmoulins into confession by flattery and sexual suggestion; she holds the limelight and lures
them on by both a real and artful reluctance. (If Boswell reports her
right, she was herself an accomplished raconteuse.) A hint of slyness or
flirtation in the behaviour of Johnson or the youthful Mrs. Desmoulins
would have corrupted the anguish we believe each of them to have
endured. Boswell's vision of man's moral aspirations and of the *comédie
humaine* is seldom blurred, and his tact in keeping them distinct is most
refined when he writes about Johnson. Like other potentially vulgar
scenes involving him, the *Tacenda*, which were written spontaneously

and for Boswell's eyes alone, skirt the danger without sacrificing either humour or pathos. The concentric spheres of action, comic and serious, are harmonized by elegance of language and gesture, as they are in the best of Restoration drama.

Boswell, subtle advocate, reveals himself also as he questions the star witness. Johnson's unhandsome figure blinds him, but not Mrs. Desmoulins, to the sexual attractiveness of Johnson's commanding mind. At the close of the *Tacenda* Boswell muses: "Strange." Does that final word apply to the whole of the document or to the last topic only? Mrs. Desmoulins reports that Johnson spent hundreds of pounds supporting Betty, Mrs. Johnson's Scotch maid, "an abandoned, diseased creature." He demurred when it was proposed to send her to a workhouse. "No—her feelings as delicate as yours." Is Boswell baffled by Johnson's sensibility or by his generosity to a profligate woman? Boswell himself gave token sums to the women he used (they are surely some of the "sundries" listed among his expenditures). He was genuinely fond of Betsy Smith, it appears: he paid the fee admitting her to St. Thomas's Hospital, gave her 10*s*. 6*d*., and proposed rescuing her from her profession, not, however, at his own expense. Lordly man, he would place her as a lady's-maid, and rebukes her good-naturedly for her wickedness in rejecting his offer. She would be "her own mistress," she says. Boswell does not understand Betsy's preference for casual exploitation to perpetual enslavement to a single employer. Like the journal throughout, the *Tacenda* give repeated evidence that Boswell had little access to a woman's mind and to her desire for independence.

"Strange": a chorus also on an entire scene, the perplexity of a narrator who gratifies his sensuality directly. The word reverberates as we contemplate what we have read.

§ IV

It is not appropriate to comment in this essay on the *Journal of a Tour to the Hebrides*, but the journal in which Boswell recorded its preparation makes a point about the book that may interest its admirers. Methodical entries, day by day, record the time, place, associates, and approximate duration of his work, manuscript to bound books. "In almost all forenoon . . . long with Malone . . . corrected a little," etc. We know, or are pretty certain, that Boswell "did something" on the *Tour*, chiefly with Malone but sometimes alone, on a total of sixty-one days. Interpreting his descriptions as nearly as one can, and allowing generously for ambiguous entries, oversights, and a week of missing journal, it seems that Boswell edited his journal of the Hebridean tour, composed the additional passages, and saw the book through the press in the equivalent of about thirty full working days.

This "quantification" of Boswell's art reveals the speed and deftness with which he produced the *Tour to the Hebrides*, his ready and confident application to the material. The book gives no hint, moreover, of the distraction amidst which Boswell prepared it for publication. It has the freshness and verve of the journal kept when he and Johnson were animated by the adventure in 1773. The spontaneity of that rich journal is evidence of a natural gift fully matured. That Boswell could preserve the charms of the immediate record when he shaped it in 1785 is testimony to the finely honed skills on which he drew even in low spirits. The lifelong journal which itself gives us so much pleasure was the practice ground for a master-work which still evokes the applause of the jury.

STATEMENT OF EDITORIAL PRACTICES

The index to this volume is intended to serve not merely as a finding tool but also as a supplement to the annotation. Readers should normally consult the index for Christian names, professions, and titles of persons whom Boswell mentions only casually.

Spelling, capitalization, and punctuation of text and notes (including quotations in the notes from all sources) have been brought close to modern norms, Boswell being allowed to retain a few idiosyncrasies. The standard of spelling for all but proper names is *The Concise Oxford Dictionary* 5th ed., 1964. For place names, F. H. Groome's *Ordnance Gazetteer of Scotland*, J. G. Bartholomew's *Survey Gazetteer of the British Isles*, and *London Past and Present* by Peter Cunningham and H. B. Wheatley have been followed. Family names have been conformed to the usage of the *Dictionary of National Biography*, Mrs. Margaret Stuart's *Scottish Family History*, George F. Black's *Surnames of Scotland*, G. E. Cokayne's *Complete Baronetage* and *Complete Peerage*, Sir James Balfour Paul's *Scots Peerage*, and various other special books of reference.

Abbreviations and contractions have been silently expanded at will. Names of speakers in conversations cast dramatically are set in small capitals. Names of speakers which Boswell failed to provide in conversations cast dramatically are supplied silently when there is no doubt as to who is speaking. A few clear inadvertencies of various sorts have been put right without notice. Otherwise, all words whatever added by the editors where the documents show no defects are enclosed in square brackets. Words or parts of words missing from the manuscripts through crumbling are restored silently when the sense (not necessarily the exact words or order of words) seems certain; restorations involving any considerable degree of conjecture are enclosed in angular brackets.

Omissions, apart from those resulting from the conflation of duplicate entries, are indicated by ellipses. Omissions so indicated in the documents from which the text is composed are always slight, and usually mean that transcription at that point is highly uncertain or that the 'omitted words would require a forbidding amount of annotation to make them intelligible. Ellipses in the text of the manuscript of the *Life of Johnson* as Boswell first drafted it mark the deletion of editorial passages which ring of 1788, the year of composition.

References to the *Life of Johnson* are made by date so that the reader can use any edition at hand. A text complete in one volume and the scholar's edition are listed in the selected bibliography under Documentation, section C.

ACKNOWLEDGEMENTS

The preparation of a book in the trade series of the Yale Boswell Editions is in many ways a collective enterprise, although the individual editors alone are responsible for the structure, the content, and the deficiencies. Both text and annotation owe much to earlier studies in Boswell and Johnson, most of which are described in the bibliography at pp. 371–372. A great deal of unpublished research is available in the Boswell Office, which was established at Yale University in 1931. Mrs. Pottle's forthcoming *Catalogue* of Boswell's Papers at Yale, a multivolume work incorporating bibliographical descriptions and minutes of content of the many papers of the entire enlarged collection, served us for many years in typescript and recently in galley proofs. The late Dr. Charles H. Bennett, a scholar of exceptional resourcefulness and accuracy, from 1933 to 1943 reviewed the text and prepared systematic annotation for all the journal in the present volume except for the sections reported as previously unpublished in Documentation, sections A and B. Between 1937 and 1945 Professor Pottle drew on Bennett's collection of notes and his own researches for a trade or reading edition of all the fully written journal, to be published as a set in several volumes. Lt.-Colonel Isham's acquisition in 1948, by judicial award and by purchase, of the Fettercairn and further Malahide papers, and the sale of his collection to Yale University the next year led to a radical reorganization and change of editorial policy. In 1950 the Yale Editions of the Private Papers of James Boswell and the McGraw-Hill Book Company began serial publication of a trade edition of the journal. *Boswell: The Applause of the Jury,* like the ten volumes which have preceded it, was raised on a foundation of Pottle's unpublished manuscript and Bennett's findings, but they had to be revised extensively to incorporate the "newer" Boswell papers and to extend the annotation, not merely to take recent scholarship into account but also to fit each volume to appear as a separate, self-contained work.

Frank Brady, Herman W. Liebert, and Martin Price of the Editorial Committee and Alan S. Bell, Bertrand H. Bronson, and Sheila Lambert of the Advisory Committee read galley proofs and returned valuable suggestions. We are indebted to Mr. Bell, in addition, for advice on a broad range of Scottish matters, law to literature, and to Marshall Waingrow of the Editorial Committee and Professor Bronson, Walter J. Bate, John Brooke, the late James L. Clifford, the late Sir James Fergusson, Bt., Mary Hyde, David F. Musto, and Fred C. Robinson of the Advisory Committee for answers to particular queries. Mrs. Hyde also responded with unfailing kindness to our requests for access through photocopy to documents in the Hyde Collection. Mrs. Pottle helped the editors unstintingly with difficult transcriptions and with identifications of persons and places named in Boswell's manuscripts, and Dr. Jean Munro conducted important research for us in Edinburgh. Anthony E. Brown's unpublished checklist of Boswell paragraphs in the Burney Collection of eighteenth-century newspapers at the British Library was invaluable to Dr. Lustig throughout her search there in the papers for 1782–1785. Mr. Nicholas Barker graciously expedited matters for her both at the Library and in obtaining microfilm copies of the newspapers for the Boswell Office.

We welcome the opportunity to acknowledge publicly the versatile staff, past and present, of the Boswell Editions, and the extraordinary range and quality of its assistance. Our sincere thanks to Rachel McClellan, assistant research editor; Maura Shaw Tantillo, chief copy editor from October 1977 to March 1980; Caterina Kazemzadeh, former secretary to the Boswell Office, now its manager; Carolyn Cott, copy editor; Harriet Chidester, chief copy editor to 1977; and three student assistants, Barbara Hurwitz, Yale College 1977, and Marcia Wagner, Cornell 1978, both presently candidates in the Graduate School, Yale University, and Roger S. Kohn, Yale College 1979, who began work modestly as a volunteer. Glorieux Dougherty, New York City, and Mrs. McClellan prepared the comprehensive index, with the assistance of the office staff. Diane Weinstock, Penn Wynne, Pennsylvania, typed Dr. Lustig's original manuscript with interest and care.

We also acknowledge various kinds of expert assistance from G. F. Archer, Myrtle M. Baird, Peter S. Baker, David Bissett, Derk Bodde, Edwin B. Bronner, William Burns, Sir Harold Cassel, Bt., Mrs. I. W. Charles, John R. G. Comyn, the late Thomas W. Copeland, Thomas Crawford, Marlies K. Danziger, Robert Donaldson, J. G. Dunbar, Barrows Dunham, Francis Edwards, Ltd., Leigh Ehlers-Telotte, James F. Elms, Elspeth A. Evans, Ruth Fiesel, Joseph Foladare, Hans Frankel, W. E. H. Fuller, Holden Furber, J. A. Gere, the late Edith Lady Haden-Guest, John W. Hanes, Mrs. Ralph P. Hanes, Catherine Itzin Hawkes, the late Alan Hazen, John Herington, D. L. Hill, Charles Beecher Hogan, Robert Hume, Jonathan T. Isham, Coral Lansbury, Morton Lustig, Emily B. Lyle, Andrew L. McClellan, Edward H. Milligan, Earl Miner, Kathleen J. Moretto, Donna Moseman, A. L. Murray, Eva W. Myer, Robert Manson Myers, Stephen Parks, Henry Pettit, Henri Peyre, Nicholas Phillipson, Michael R. Raymer, Brian Rees, John C. Riely, William H. Roberts, Ian S. Ross, T. L. A. Samuel, Arthur H. Scouten, Henry Sefton, Francis H. W. Sheppard, R. N. Smart, Glenn Sonnedecker, John Sunderland, H. T. Swedenberg, Malcolm Thomas, Peter Adam Thrasher, Frederick B. Tolles, and William P. Williams.

To our publisher, Thomas H. Quinn, representative of McGraw-Hill on the Editorial Committee, we express our deep gratitude for maintaining the quality of the Boswell Editions at a time of high costs. We acknowledge also the cooperation of Michael Hennelly, editorial supervisor, who managed the book at McGraw-Hill with Mr. Quinn.

A grant from the Penrose Fund of the American Philosophical Society was very helpful to Mrs. Lustig in the earlier stages of this work. For assistance beyond recounting, she also gives heartfelt thanks to Samuel Spritz and the late Paula Euster Spritz, Alice and Barrows Dunham, Arthur H. Scouten, Judith Leah Lustig, and Morton Lustig, whose contribution was unique.

I.S.L.

New Haven, Connecticut
20 June 1980

BOSWELL:
THE APPLAUSE OF THE JURY

1782-1785

The great difficulty is to distinguish between noble ambition and foolish, restless, conceited aspiring.

[23 MARCH 1783]

I must here remark a curious circumstance in my own character at present, which is a consciousness of having, if I choose to indulge it, a total insensibility to what others may think of me in point of decorum. I am indifferent as to all censure of my mode of living. To feel thus gives one a wonderful feeling of independence. But too much of it is not right. The late Lord Eglinton regretted to my father my want of the sense of shame. It has been owing partly to a vain idea of my own talents; partly to a kind of philosophical impression of the nothingness of all things in human life.

[21 JANUARY 1784]

Boswell: The Applause of the Jury

1782–1785

SKETCH OF BOSWELL'S LIFE TO 30 AUGUST 1782. James Boswell was born at Edinburgh 29 October 1740 into a proud and ancient landed family with connexions by marriage to the nobility. His father's line was linked to the House of Stuart, and his mother was directly descended from the grandfather of Lord Darnley. On both sides Boswell could claim some share of the blood of the Bruces. He was heir male, moreover, to the extensive barony of Auchinleck in Ayrshire, which James IV had presented to Thomas Boswell in 1504 for faithful service. The first laird of Auchinleck fell with his king at Flodden Field and added not a little to the romanticized feudal ideal which Boswell proclaimed from his youth and in later years tried seriously to practise.

Boswell's father, Alexander Boswell (by judicial custom styled Lord Auchinleck), was an impressive model and a formidable parent. One of the fifteen justices of the Court of Session, the highest tribunal in Scotland for civil causes, he enjoyed the additional distinction of serving with five other Lords on the High Court of Justiciary, the supreme court for criminal causes. Himself upright, industrious, self-disciplined, a good classicist, convinced Whig and Presbyterian, Lord Auchinleck was impatient and piercingly critical of deviation from these norms. Boswell, a timid and imaginative child, clung to his mother, and in after years remembered her tenderly, though her Calvinist piety helped implant a morbid and ineradicable fear of the afterlife. Lord Auchinleck engendered conflicting needs for independence and approval, neither of which he ever gratified.

Boswell was educated according to his station at a private school, by domestic tutors, and as a student in Arts and in Law at the Universities of Edinburgh and of Glasgow (where, by a happy conjunction of time and place, he heard the lectures of Adam Smith). Emerging robust and gregarious at the age of seventeen from a severe mental depression, he acquired a more worldly education by associating with players and writing for the theatre. He became infatuated with a married actress, exalted her talents in a pamphlet, *A View of the Edinburgh Theatre* (1759),

1

his first independent publication, was converted to Roman Catholicism after his father whisked him to Glasgow, and at twenty ran away to London determined to become a monk or a priest. His intention was frustrated at Lord Auchinleck's request (though not by such means as he would have approved) by the tenth Earl of Eglinton, an Ayrshire neighbour residing in London. He introduced Boswell into the circles of "the great, the gay, and the ingenious" (the words are Boswell's) and converted him for life to both the high and the low pleasures of the metropolis.

Within three months Boswell was back in Edinburgh quarrelling with his father over a new ambition. In 1762 they finally struck a bargain which Boswell thought would fulfil it: if he passed the examination in Civil Law, as he did in July of that year, he might go to London to seek a commission in the Foot Guards. Lord Auchinleck quietly and effectually made *his* wishes known to persons of influence in London, but Boswell, while he fruitlessly pursued the one dream, lived another. Alert and irrepressible, he savoured the conversations of citizens in their coffee-houses and of peers and countesses ensconced in splendour. He attended theatres and exhibitions, took delight in the entertainments of Ranelagh, encountered a surprise ending to a carefully plotted liaison with an actress, and by his resilience and likeability extended a bruising introduction to Samuel Johnson into an enduring friendship. The sustained journal which Boswell kept during those nine months in 1762–1763 is the prime exemplar of his finest style and of a lifetime practice.[1]

In August 1763 Johnson escorted Boswell to the packet-boat to Holland, where by agreement with Lord Auchinleck he continued his study of Civil Law at Utrecht and was rewarded by a tour of the German courts. During his ten months in Holland Boswell applied himself methodically to his purpose and also improved in Latin, Greek, and conversational French. He remained chaste, mingled in prominent but stolid society, and suffered the acute depression that customarily followed such routine. Towards the end of the Dutch sojourn he courted Belle de Zuylen (because of Boswell, better known in English-speaking countries as Zélide), the daughter of a noble family. As independent as she was brilliant, she declined the uneasy offer of marriage he later tendered her by post. The elegant profusion of the German courts pleased Boswell, but his sensibilities vibrated most exquisitely in the interviews he won in Switzerland with Rousseau and Voltaire. Having probed their souls and committed his own, unsolicited, to their care, he proceeded in 1765 to Italy, extracting a greater indulgence from his

[1] *Boswell's London Journal, 1762–1763*, ed. Frederick A. Pottle (McGraw-Hill Book Company, 1950). For the other volumes in the series, see p. [i].

father, as usual, than Lord Auchinleck had intended. In Italy Boswell systematically studied the remains of classical civilization, part of the time as companion to Lord Mountstuart, the eldest son of Lord Bute. He shared the various pleasures of the British colony, which included artists, Jacobites, and the dissolute exile, John Wilkes, laid siege to various noble ladies, and in Siena won Girolama Piccolomini, wife of the Capitano del Popolo, the head of a leading family. "Moma," as Boswell called her, was genuinely grieved by his departure. In October and November 1765 he climbed the mountain fastnesses of Corsica to interview General Pasquale Paoli, the leader of the resistance against the Genoese and later, the French. That meeting, too, led to a lifelong friendship, and to international fame for Boswell when his *Account of Corsica, the Journal of a Tour to that Island, and Memoirs of Pascal Paoli* was published in 1768.

In 1766 Boswell read in a Paris newspaper of his mother's death and returned to Edinburgh, by way of London. He passed advocate and began a law practice of more than average competence and success: his many legal papers thus far recovered are shrewdly argued and well written; and he was co-counsel in a respectable number of causes with lawyers of distinction at the Scottish bar and in the House of Lords (the supreme Court of Appeal in Great Britain). Boswell's practice, like most advocates', dealt chiefly with matters of property, but occasionally, and by choice, his spirits were animated by defending the poor and the disinherited, often without fee. Self-appointed pamphleteer for the defendant in the Douglas Cause, he was later overjoyed at being named one of the counsel in Douglas's appeal. In 1774 he became so desperate at the judgement against John Reid, a sheep-stealer (his first criminal client, on an earlier charge), that he plotted to snatch Reid's body after it was cut down and to resuscitate him. Avowedly for King and Church, in his younger and middle years Boswell was also flexible, generous-minded, and independent. He worshipped in Quaker meeting-houses occasionally, as well as in Anglican cathedrals, harangued at considerable risk an Edinburgh crowd burning a Roman Catholic chapel, challenged the deals by which county elections in Ayrshire were controlled, and defended the American colonists, on constitutional grounds, against adversaries as unyielding as Dr. Johnson. Had Boswell stuck discreetly to the law he might ultimately have worn the robes of a Lord of Session. But that ambition was second to his heart's desire, a seat in Parliament or other high office that assured him residence in London as well as in Scotland. An Anglophile *and* a Scots patriot, every year that he could he hurried south when the law courts rose (12 March) and returned to duty, and invariable melancholia, at the opening of the new session (12 June).

His extravagant native urge to publication he exercised wherever he was. He wrote songs, verses, dedications; he published broadsides and pamphlets on a variety of contemporary subjects and made voluminous contributions, signed, unsigned, and pseudonymous, to both English and Scottish newspapers and magazines, where his ephemera are still being uncovered. The monthly series of essays Boswell began in 1778 for the *London Magazine,* of which he was part-proprietor, he appropriately called *The Hypochondriack.*

After pursuing a succession of heiresses Boswell yielded to a deep attachment to an almost penniless cousin, Margaret Montgomerie, a handsome woman of quick intelligence and great strength of character. They were married, by his choice both dressed in white, 25 November 1769, the day that Lord Auchinleck was remarried, also to a cousin, Elizabeth Boswell. When this book opens Boswell is the devoted father of five children. In the first years of his marriage he was also a contented and proper husband, but the tedium of his work, a narrow sphere (by his terms), and the galling checks and tight-fistedness of Lord Auchinleck, who treated Margaret Boswell shabbily, made him increasingly restless. The jaunts to London and with Johnson to Ashbourne, Oxford, Lichfield, and even, in 1773, to the Hebrides provided only intermittently the intensity of experience which he craved. The urge for wine and for sexual adventures grew compulsive, and though his remorse on discovery was terrible, Margaret's loyal support was tried to the limit.

On 30 August 1782 Lord Auchinleck died after prolonged ill health, and Boswell, who was in the room, wept, "for alas! there was not affection between us." He buried his father with traditional splendour (4 September) and at the age of forty-two assumed responsibility for the family estate. These climactic events he recorded in notes for his journal which were published in the volume previous to this one, *Boswell, Laird of Auchinleck.* But in the summer of 1782 Boswell also kept a separate, almost clinical journal devoted to Margaret Boswell and her alarming symptoms of consumption, which had troubled her, with periodic remissions, for some time. He attended his wife anxiously, read the Bible and *Tom Jones* to her (and gave up *Roderick Random* when she expressed her dislike of it). Fielding's *Amelia* they read together. Gradually the single-minded record of Margaret's illness gave way to other events and took the form of his regular journal. We print it beginning the day after they had hastened to Edinburgh, on a warning of Lord Auchinleck's approaching death, from Valleyfield, where they had been visiting attentive relations, the Prestons.

Journal in Scotland and England

30 August 1782–28 September 1785

FRIDAY 30 AUGUST. From the hurry of her journey the day before and the agitation on account of my father's death, she spit some blood. After that, she grew better. On the 9, 10, and 11 September, π.[1] Dined at Prestonfield[2] on the 12, looking very well. On the 13, Raasay, his daughter and son-in-law, Lady Margaret Macdonald, and Dr. Young dined and drank tea with us.[3] She stood the fatigue very well. Her spirits were better now.

From the 30 of August she continued pretty well, and on the 17 September we set out for Auchinleck, where we arrived on the 18 to dinner. She stood the journey very well, and walked to the Old House[4] that evening.

THURSDAY 19 SEPTEMBER. A fine day. She walked to the Old House. Mr. Dun came to us in the garden. He and Mr. John Boswell[5] dined. The house was dampish, and she had catched cold.

[1] Boswell's common symbol for conjugal intercourse. The Greek character actually stands for the English word "pleasure."

[2] The estate near Arthur's Seat of Sir Alexander Dick, an eminent physician, one of the elderly friends for whom Boswell felt a special respect and affection.

[3] John MacLeod, ninth Laird of Raasay, endeared himself to Boswell by his exemplary hospitality when Johnson and Boswell toured the Hebrides, 1773; which of MacLeod's eight living daughters this is we do not know. Lady Margaret, daughter of the ninth Earl of Eglinton and the widow since 1746 of Sir Alexander Macdonald of Macdonald, like MacLeod, helped manage the escape of Prince Charles Edward after Culloden. Dr. Thomas Young, Professor of Midwifery at the University of Edinburgh, attended Mrs. Boswell at the birth of at least three of her children.

[4] The second of three mansions on the estate, erected in the first half of the sixteenth century and occupied until the noble house which Lord Auchinleck built in the Adam style was completed in 1762. A walk of about a quarter-mile brought one to a very fine garden at the Old House, which is now only picturesque ruins.

[5] The Rev. John Dun, Boswell's first tutor, minister of the parish of Auchinleck since 1752; and John Boswell, a collateral Boswell from the Craigston line and the heir through his grandmother to the ancient property of Knockroon, which was south-east of Auchinleck House and once part of the estate. Knockroon (as he was also called: see below, 3 October 1782) was a solicitor and Clerk to the Commissioners of Supply in Ayr.

5

FRIDAY 20 SEPTEMBER. Craigdarroch[6] breakfasted. A wet day. Lord and Lady Dumfries called. Mr. Millar dined.[7] She had a cough.

SATURDAY 21 SEPTEMBER. I had walked to Stevenston.[8] A wet day. Fingland[9] dined. She had tried horse a little; would not do. Still a cough. π.

SUNDAY 22 SEPTEMBER. Wet morning. Sandy and I church, Old John Boswell and Dernconner with us.[10] Mr. Dun came home with us. Still a cough. I was sorry to go.[1]

MONDAY 23 SEPTEMBER. Wet day. I was quite ill. Mr. Millar dined and stayed all night. Her cough troublesome. As she played at backgammon, seized with spitting blood. Alarmed. Some nights had omitted laudanum, yet slept. I was sadly agitated. I was to set out next morning.

TUESDAY 24 SEPTEMBER. I proposed staying till next week. She thought better go now and be back for business. I parted with her sorry. But Dr. Johnson's wisdom was highly requisite.

WEDNESDAY 25 SEPTEMBER. W. Lennox[2] had come in the night express that she had a violent fit of spitting of blood. I rode home in agitation. Found her in bed. My return calmed her. Lord Justice Clerk,[3] etc., called.

THURSDAY 26 SEPTEMBER. She was rather better. Mr. Bruce Campbell dined.[4]

FRIDAY 27 SEPTEMBER. She was still easier. I got a letter from Dr. Johnson which settled me not to go.[5] This affected her agreeably. π.

SATURDAY 28 SEPTEMBER. She was comfortable. Weather so all these days she did not go out. π. This day I went to visit Lord Dumfries.

[6] Andrew Howatson of Craigdarroch, a small property in New Cumnock; one of Boswell's tenants in Dalblair.

[7] Patrick Macdowall-Crichton, fifth Earl of Dumfries, and his Countess, Margaret Crauford, were making a courtesy call on Boswell's accession as laird. The families had not been on good terms since 1777 (see below, 14 October 1782). The Rev. Alexander Millar, Mr. Dun's assistant, was later immortalized (not, however, as he would have wished) in Burns's *Holy Fair*.

[8] A farm on the estate.

[9] James Chalmers of Fingland, a property in Kirkcudbright. He leased the Auchinleck farm of Braehead.

[10] Boswell's eldest son, Alexander, now seven years old; the father of John Boswell of Knockroon, whom Boswell also calls "Old Knockroon" though only his son was heir to the property; and John Lennox of Dernconner in the parish of Auchinleck.

[1] To London, to see Samuel Johnson.

[2] The coachman.

[3] Thomas Miller. The Lord Justice Clerk was professional head of the High Court of Justiciary, the supreme court of Scotland for criminal actions.

[4] Boswell's second cousin.

[5] Not recovered. The one paragraph which Boswell published in the *Life of Johnson*, urging him to spare no expense to preserve Mrs. Boswell ("she is the prop and stay of your life"), implies that Johnson disapproved the expense of a jaunt to London at this time.

SUNDAY 29 SEPTEMBER. I very gloomy. She pretty well.

MONDAY 30 SEPTEMBER. I wonderfully well. Viewing Turnerhill. Visit at Barskimming.[6] π. Showery.

TUESDAY 1 OCTOBER. Viewing farms with James Bruce.[7] She walked to Old House. Pretty well.

WEDNESDAY 2 OCTOBER. She had got bad sleep from there being a storm. But was pretty well all day. Mr. John Erskine dined.[8]

THURSDAY 3 OCTOBER. She was better. I went to Lord Justice Clerk's and with him to Ayr. Was quite sound. Dined with the Judge[9] and was sober. Tea Lady Cunninghame's.[1] Called Knockroon's. Rozelle at night. Company there. Lady Crawford said, "This is a lost night."[2]

FRIDAY 4 OCTOBER. Knockroon came early, and we went through moor to Craigengillan's. Breakfast and dined there. Hearty conversation and some farming instruction.[3] Weary ride home by Cumnock. π. Chaise set a-going.

SATURDAY 5 OCTOBER. Good day. Walked about. Knockroon and Miss Chalmers[4] dined.

SUNDAY 6 OCTOBER. Veronica, Phemie, and Miss Campbell in chaise to kirk. Sandy and I rode, young Duncanziemuir[5] and ——— McCormick, a son of Dornell's, with us. I perfectly as I could wish.

MONDAY 7 OCTOBER. Amused taking measurement of principal

[6]Turnerhill was a farm on the Auchinleck estate. Barskimming, the seat of Thomas Miller, Lord Justice Clerk, was situated near Auchinleck on the River Ayr.
[7]The overseer of the estate. His father had also worked at Auchinleck.
[8]Probably John Erskine of Cambus, advocate, eldest son of James Erskine of Alva, Lord Barjarg.
[9]The Lord Justice Clerk, who was holding the autumn circuit court as sole judge. There was no criminal business.
[1]Margaret Fairlie, the widow, now about sixty years old, of Sir William Cunninghame of Robertland. She was a warm friend of Mrs. Boswell.
[2]Rozelle was the seat outside Ayr, near Robert Burns's birthplace, of Jean Hamilton, the widow of George Lindsay-Crawford, twenty-first Earl of Crawford, and Margaret Boswell's dear friend.
[3]John McAdam, Laird of Craigengillan, had made a fortune as a drover, and improved and enlarged his property extensively. He and his three children were immortalized in Burns's verse epistle, *To Mr. McAdam of Craigengillan.*
[4]Probably Margaret Chalmers, daughter of James Chalmers of Fingland, whom Burns courted and to whom a dozen of his surviving letters are addressed.
[5]Veronica is Boswell's eldest child, aged ten, and "Phemie" his daughter Euphemia, aged eight. The other two of his five children were James, aged four, and Elizabeth ("Betsy"), two. Jean Campbell was the daughter by his first wife of James Campbell of Treesbank, deceased, a first cousin to Boswell's father and Margaret Boswell's mother. Young Duncanziemuir's family name was Reid. His father had recently acquired Duncanziemuir.

trees. Fingland dined. My wife, Miss Campbell, Sandy, and Jamie visited Mr. George Reid.[6]

TUESDAY 8 OCTOBER. Went out in chaise with my wife and paid visit at manse;[6a] Sandy and Jamie with us. Quite comfortable. Home by Brackenhill. Colonel Craufurd[7] dinner and all night. Wife walked and was much better.

WEDNESDAY 9 OCTOBER. I went to Barskimming with Colonel Craufurd, and Sandy with us. Paid a forenoon's visit there and at Fingland's, who together with Mr. and Mrs. Dun and their son dined with us, it being Sandy's birthday. I was comfortably happy. The chaise was sent for Mr. and Mrs. Dun, and took them home. At night I walked home with old John Wylie[8] to the Burnhouse. Was convinced of his good plain sense and contentment. Promised him wood to make a brace[9] for his fire to vent, and to root out some ash-trees which hurt his garden. Found Sir Walter M. C. and his brother Sandy when I came home.[1]

THURSDAY 10 OCTOBER. Sir Walter accompanied me to a meeting of the trustees on the turnpike roads at Mauchline. I felt myself rational and active. Came home soon to meet Countess of Crawford and Lady Mary Lindsay. Sundrum also and Mr. Robert Chalmers dined.[2] I was easy and happy. All but Mr. Chalmers stayed all night. Mr. Alexander Millar, assistant to Mr. Dun, had for several weeks been with us five days a week to read with Sandy and say prayers at night. I felt a little embarrassment as to prayers when I had great company. I was resolved to have them, but thought they should be in another room from that in which the company sat, and everybody that pleased might attend.

[6]The minister of Ochiltree, now eighty-seven years old. He had been chaplain to Boswell's paternal grandfather and domestic tutor to Lord Auchinleck. Boswell enjoyed his stories about them and was always very attentive to him. An entry in his accounts for 12 October 1783 reveals one shilling "given Jean Murdock, who read to my grandfather and now reads to Rev. Mr. George Reid."

[6a]The residence of the minister (the Rev. John Dun) in Auchinleck.

[7]John Walkinshaw Craufurd of Craufurdland, ancient and extensive lands in Kilmarnock parish.

[8]A servant on the estate.

[9]"A screen made of stakes interwoven with twigs and covered with prepared clay, used to conduct the smoke from the hearth to an aperture in the roof" (*English Dialect Dictionary*).

[1]Sir Walter Montgomerie-Cuninghame, Bt., of Corsehill, and Alexander, the second of four younger brothers, were nephews of Mrs. Boswell and second cousins to Boswell himself. Sandy had served as captain in the 76th (Highland) Foot during the American war and returned home consumptive in April 1782.

[2]John Hamilton of Sundrum was an important landed proprietor and Vice-Lieutenant of Ayrshire. He and Boswell had been college-mates at the Universities of Edinburgh and Glasgow. Chalmers was a "writer," or solicitor.

This shall be my plan. This night the Countess readily agreed to prayers. We had not singing psalms and reading a chapter as usual. I am pleased with family devotion. But I wish in time to introduce the prayers of the Episcopal Church.

FRIDAY 11 OCTOBER. Prevailed on the ladies to walk with me to the grotto and the Old House, and had a pride and pleasure in showing them my fine Place. Had a high admiration of the Countess. All left us before dinner. My wife has for many days been charmingly.

SATURDAY 12 OCTOBER. A very good day. My wife went in the chaise to Mauchline. Sir John Whitefoord[3] dined and drank tea with us. I was pleased with his neat, genteel conversation. I had almost broke through my sober scheme of life, as we were tête-à-tête and it was the first time he had been in my house since my succession. But I checked myself. Indeed my wish to drink with him was not from love of wine and intoxication, as has frequently been the case with me, but from a desire to be cordial. He excused me, and drank claret easily while I took wine and water.

SUNDAY 13 OCTOBER. I thought it proper to go once after my succession to each parish church where I am an heritor, except to Ochiltree, where my right is suspended by the *locality* of my *noverca*.[4] I this day went to Mauchline, and took Sandy with me. It was a delightful day. I had all the comfort of recollecting former occasions of piety here with my dear mother, and feeling myself now Laird of Auchinleck. I gave a guinea to the poor. I sat in front of the loft belonging to my family, and looked with satisfaction on my tenants ranged behind me. Was at worthy Mr. Auld's between sermons.[5] Upon the whole an excellent day. Fine association of early ideas. In the evening Mr. Millar came. W. Lennox at a burial kept my wife at home.

MONDAY 14 OCTOBER. My wife and I paid a forenoon visit to Lord and Lady Dumfries. It was a showery day. Our visit was a little awkward, as there had been no communication between the families for several of the last years of my father's life, and as I was resolved not to grant the favour the refusal of which had occasioned the difference.[6] I however wished to live on civil terms with such near neighbours; and as

[3]Of Ballochmyle, a near neighbour. Sir John was an early patron of Burns, and is mentioned in his verse. He was also an intimate of Boswell's friend, Andrew Erskine, with whom he walked in company so frequently that Erskine being tall, and Whitefoord short, they were called the "gowk and the titling": the cuckoo and the meadow pipit (John Kay, *Original Portraits*, 1877, iii. 59).

[4]Farms from which Lady Auchinleck enjoyed the liferent. *Noverca* means stepmother.

[5]The Rev. William Auld, the minister at Mauchline.

[6]Lord Auchinleck had in 1777 refused the Earl's request to run a grand road almost due north from Dumfries House through the Auchinleck farm of Glenside to the Auchinleck Church road.

they had made very polite advances to us, I thought we should show a proper attention.

TUESDAY 15 OCTOBER. My wife and I went in the chaise to Ayr. She was wonderfully well now, and walked about Ayr as lively as when Miss Peggie Montgomerie. I had engaged to be at the general meeting of the high road trustees this day, and I spoke as well as I wished. We dined at Lady Cunninghame's, where I had the pleasure of seeing my wife, now mistress of Auchinleck, under the roof of a worthy friend who had always shown the greatest regard for her. Fairlie and Craufurdland, etc., were here. I had some solid conversation with Fairlie.[7] After tea, I carried my wife to visit Mrs. Boswell of Knockroon, and I visited Bailie Neill. In the evening, we went to Rozelle and had a most agreeable evening with Lady Crawford. I was quite happy to find my dear wife now so well and in so respectable a situation. It was as much as I suppose humanity has ever enjoyed. π.

WEDNESDAY 16 OCTOBER. Awaked well. Walked out. Was charmed with the Countess and Lady Mary. We drove into Ayr to order bread. Then came home to dinner. It was comfortable. Wettish weather.

THURSDAY 17 OCTOBER. For some days had been occupied in writing *The Hypochondriack* No. 61.[8] Did not write so well as I have sometimes done. Still bad weather. My wife paid a visit in the forenoon at Barskimming.

FRIDAY 18 OCTOBER. Wettish day. But time passed easily. One of these days had a letter from Sir Joshua Reynolds which agitated me a little by renewing my eagerness for London.[9] But I felt myself so comfortable and of such consequence at Auchinleck that I doubted if London could, upon the whole, make me enjoy life more.

SATURDAY 19 OCTOBER. A very wet and windy day. Knockroon and his son came. Knockroon's cheerful contentment pleased me. They stayed all night. Veronica was not very well.

SUNDAY 20 OCTOBER. A better day. I was out early and saw an ass

---

[7] Alexander Fairlie, whose estate in Ayrshire bore the family name, was a leader of agricultural improvement, and advised Boswell generously in his first months as Laird. He was the brother of Lady Cunninghame, who inherited Fairlie upon his death in 1803.

[8] The second of two essays on dedications. See below, p. 24, n. 3.

[9] "If I felt the same reluctance in taking a pencil in my hand as I do a pen, I should be as bad a painter as I am a correspondent. Everybody has their taste. I love the correspondence of viva voce over a bottle with a great deal of noise and a great deal of nonsense. Mr. Burke dined with me yesterday. He talked much of you and with great affection. He says you are the pleasantest man he ever saw, and sincerely wishes you would come to live amongst us. All your friends here, I believe, will subscribe to that wish" (From Reynolds, 1 October 1782).

brought in to give milk for my wife. My wife went to Auchinleck Church for the first time since she was *Lady*. Phemie and Sandy and Miss Campbell, Knockroon and son made good appearance in loft. Mr. Millar preached two excellent discourses on Providence from Psalm 113:5 and 6. There was no intermission today. My wife thought Mr. Millar preached as well as Dr. Blair.[1] It was really a good day's sacred employment. Mr. Millar came home with us, and the evening went on agreeably. I retired with Sandy to the library and we said together part of the Evening Prayer, and I prayed particularly. I wrote to Mr. Rae as my honoured father's successor in the Court of Session.[2]

MONDAY 21 OCTOBER. Knockroon and his son went away early. I have for some time risen easily between six and seven, which braces my frame; and every morning before breakfast I read a portion of the sacred scriptures and of Thomas à Kempis, by which my mind is calmed and sanctified. I read in the dressing-room of the family apartment; and it seems a *chapel* from this daily celestial habit. It was a wet day again. I need not mark every airing my wife takes in the chaise. I read some now from time to time in Felltham's *Resolves*.[3] But I should lament that I neglect study shamefully. I find myself at present sufficiently occupied without it. The occupations of the *estate*, even in speculation, content me. I this day began to take lessons in arithmetic from Mr. Millar.

TUESDAY 22 OCTOBER. It was a mixed day of sunshine and rain. I took Sandy with me to Mr. Dun's, left him there, and rode on to Ridge, where Mr. Dun was overseeing his shearers.[4] I walked with him completely along his marches, and was in the best frame, and pleased to see him so happy in the consciousness of having an estate (though small) of his own. He said "Who would have thought it?" was his reflection. I dined comfortably at the manse, full of sound thoughts and pleasingly wondering at being quite free from the melancholy

[1] The Rev. Hugh Blair, minister of the New Church, Edinburgh, and Regius Professor of Rhetoric and Belles-Lettres in the University of Edinburgh, famous for his sermons.
[2] David Rae, who lived to 1804 and whose mannerisms were the delight of youngsters like Walter Scott and Henry Cockburn, assumed the style of Lord Eskgrove on his elevation to the bench in 1782. He was appointed a Lord of Justiciary in 1785, succeeded Robert Macqueen, Lord Braxfield, as Lord Justice Clerk in 1799, and was made a baronet a few months before his death.
[3] *Resolves, Divine, Moral, Political*, one hundred short essays first published in 1620, when Owen Felltham was eighteen, and so popular among the middle classes that it ran to four editions and eleven printings before 1700.
[4] Scots for "reapers." Boswell has anglicized the form of Rigg, the farm on the estate which Mr. Dun had purchased. See the entry below, 31 October 1782.

clouds which used to hang upon my mind, peculiarly about the kirk and manse in the end of the year. They appeared to me *dreary realities*. I was now convinced they were mere *shadows*. I am lost when I think intensely of the course of things, and especially of the operations of my own mind. But I avoid that kind of thinking, and have some notion of the kind of existence which my father had all his life till his faculties decayed. I now prayed for him with delicate awe, that in case he was not yet received into a state of happiness, he might be soon received.

WEDNESDAY 23 and THURSDAY 24 OCTOBER. I recollect nothing.

FRIDAY 25 OCTOBER. Logan dined.[5]

SATURDAY 26 OCTOBER. I expected the Laird of Fairlie. I rode out and met him and his nephew, Mr. Cunninghame, near the turn-off to Brackenhill, and took them to Dernlaw, which Fairlie thought a good farm, and to the village. He was against letting small parks to the feuars[6] unless at a high rent. I brought him home by the kirk road. He thought the land much better than he expected. Fingland dined, and was so engaged by Fairlie he stayed supper. In the country there is no having an arranged party. I was quite sober, and listened with avidity to his excellent instruction in farming.

SUNDAY 27 OCTOBER. Fairlie rode with us to church. It was today a collegiate charge.[7] Both Mr. Dun and Mr. Millar preached. In our way home we looked at Lord Dumfries's gate and the famous road. Fairlie was satisfied that the road would be a great favour, which no neighbour was entitled to take amiss that he was refused. I showed him that granting it would make the Auchinleck improvements appear part of the Earl of Dumfries's domains. I said I should make Fairlie understand it at once. If Lord Eglinton—if *my* Earl—were Earl of Dumfries and living at Dumfries House, he should have the road, but not to him and his *heirs*. Each Earl should accept of it as a favour from each Laird, and behave himself accordingly.

MONDAY 28 OCTOBER. Before breakfast Fairlie rode with me and looked at Turnerhill, James Bruce walking. It came on a heavy rain, but this was not to stop us. So after breakfast he and I and Sandy with us in the chaise viewed Stevenston, James Bruce faithfully attending. He advised me to let all I could in grass for some years, then lime a

[5]Hugh Logan, whose racy humour was celebrated in a nineteenth-century collection of anecdotes called *The Laird of Logan*.

[6]Strictly speaking, a feuar held a perpetual grant of land in return for a fixed periodic payment, but in popular usage a feu was a long-term lease.

[7]In Scotland a collegiate church is one served by two or more joint incumbents or pastors. Boswell is making a joke, which he explains in his next sentence.

third of each farm, and thus get a good rent. Mr. Bruce Campbell was with us today. We considered leases. We were quite as I could wish.[8]

TUESDAY 29 OCTOBER. Being your birthday, at Ayr;[9] came home in company with Mr. Bruce Campbell, and found Mr. Johnston[1] from Edinburgh arrived.

WEDNESDAY 30 OCTOBER. Very rainy; not abroad.

THURSDAY 31 OCTOBER. Forenoon, went with Mr. Johnston to visit Mr. Dun and your farm at Cumnockbridge-end; returned to dinner and brought Mr. Dun and young *Rigg*[2] with you, who stayed all night.

FRIDAY 1 NOVEMBER. Took Mr. Johnston through part of the barony of Trabboch. Called upon the Rev. Mr. George Reid, and viewed the House of Ochiltree;[3] there entertained by a droll conversation with the old housekeeper. Came home to dinner at a late hour when everybody was crying, *"Essurio."*[4]

SATURDAY 2 NOVEMBER. Miserably confined to the house by storm of snow, the most remarkable in the memory of man at this season of the year.[5] Mrs. Montgomerie came.[6]

SUNDAY 3 NOVEMBER. At church; heard sermons from Romans, 12 ch., 3rd v., "not to think more highly of himself than he ought to think."

[8]The entries from 29 October to 8 November were written at Boswell's request by Mr. Millar.

[9]Where he attended a meeting of the freeholders of the county and got a resolution passed declaring that certain of the votes of Sir Adam Fergusson, the M.P. whom he had long and unsuccessfully opposed, were "nominal and fictitious" (see below, 18 November 1782, p. 21, n. 4).

[1]John Johnston, Boswell's intimate friend since their university days. Boswell usually calls him "Grange," the name of his small landed property in Dumfriesshire. The style "Mr. Johnston" is no doubt due to Millar. Johnston, a "writer," lived in the apartment below Boswell's in James's Court, Edinburgh. Like Boswell, he was a hypochondriac, a Tory, and a sentimental Jacobite, passionately interested in the history of Scotland.

[2]Alexander Boswell Dun. See above, 22 October 1782, n. 4.

[3]The manor house, property of the Dowager Countess of Glencairn. It was now vacant and in ruinous condition. See below, 17 October 1783.

[4]"I'm hungry."

[5]"From the beginning of the year 1782 to the end, there was something dreary and judgement-like in the weather. It was one of those memorable seasons which baffle the skill and labour of the husbandman, and which, happily for mankind, do not occur above twice or thrice in a century. It seems to have resembled the worst years of King William's dearth" (John Ramsay, *Scotland and Scotsmen in the Eighteenth Century*, ii. 255–256).

[6]The widow of James Montgomerie of Lainshaw, Mrs. Boswell's brother.

MONDAY 4 NOVEMBER. Breakfasted at Coilsfield.[7] Upon return met with Lord Justice Clerk and Mr. Miller just leaving Auchinleck House on a forenoon's visit, or rather "vis," according to the style of the author of the *World*.[8] Found Mr. and Mrs. and Miss Chalmers and Old Knockroon, which two gentlemen were very cosh[9] from a similarity of circumstances in their life. Miss was made happy by being allowed to sing and speak French; the old men with claret and strong beer. The talent of making people with whom we converse each pleased with himself is possessed by few, but is what every man owes to his guests, and ought to be cultivated as much as possible, because it leaves an agreeable reflection, and gains for the person who practises it an advantageous situation in the minds of those upon whom it is practised.

TUESDAY 5 NOVEMBER. Dined at Lord Justice Clerk's, and came home at night. Laughed, sang, and said a great many funny things of Lord Cassillis,[1] but made no figures. I mean, neglected your arithmetic.

WEDNESDAY 6 NOVEMBER. Went to a meeting of trustees upon the roads at Mauchline, and dined there. Heard Mr. Wallace of Cessnock say that he had seen Lady Crawford in an attitude which her most intimate friends of this country had no access ever to see her in— sucking a black.[2]

THURSDAY 7 NOVEMBER. Walked to the village of Auchinleck and rouped[3] the farm of Stonebriggs; dined with Mr. Dun, and came home pleased with self and everybody. Found Mr. and Mrs. Hamiltons (Sundrum). Was glad to see them, and spent the night in agreeable mirth, towards which an extempore verse of a song upon the Earl of Cassillis and Miss Coopers greatly contributed.[4]

[7]The residence of Alexander Montgomerie, heir male presumptive to the Earl of Eglinton.

[8]"When a fine gentleman chooses to signify his intention of making a short visit . . . I am for an abridgement of the word, and only calling it a vis" (No. 62). Edward Moore, playwright and poet, was the editor of the *World*, a weekly periodical published 1753–1756, which satirized the vices and follies of fashionable society. William Miller, only son of the Lord Justice Clerk, was later also a Lord of Session.

[9]"Cosh" means friendly, comfortable. The word is probably Mr. Millar's, not Boswell's.

[1]David Kennedy, the tenth Earl; advocate, M.P. for Ayrshire 1768–1774, and Scottish Representative Peer since 1776. Boswell thought him devoid of talent for public life, and complained because Cassillis failed to employ him or to benefit his family and friends.

[2]That is, that he had seen her being suckled by a black nurse. She was no doubt born in Jamaica, where her father had an estate.

[3]Auctioned the rental, for another period of eighteen or nineteen years.

[4]*The Scots Musical Museum*, ed. James Johnson, 1853, iv. 410*:

The Coopers they came to Lord Cassillis at Colzean,
    With their hoops all tight and ready,

FRIDAY 8 NOVEMBER. Walked from breakfast till dinner laying out a new road from Sorn. Was at the Holm Catrine; eat bread, supped cream, drank brandy, and admired Dernconner's daughters. Missed a visit of Lord Cassillis, Lady Dumfries, and Mrs. Fullarton, who stayed just one hour. Met with Dr. Deans, who stayed all night, and Fingland and Logan, who went away before tea.

SATURDAY 9 NOVEMBER.[5] A little dispute between my wife and me to be settled by Lady Crawford. Rode to Rozelle to breakfast without a servant, and pair of partridges[6] in my pocket. Her Ladyship found both in the wrong. She was in sad anxiety about her son.[7] But I dissipated the gloom. Home to dinner; Rev. Mr. Miller (Cumnock) and James Johnston. Busy afternoon with tenants.

SUNDAY 10 NOVEMBER. At church, comfortable.

MONDAY 11 NOVEMBER. Bid adieu to Mrs. M. in bed. Set out with wife, Ve, and Sandy after a good Auchinleck breakfast. Chaise broke at Bellow Water. Soon mended. Dined Douglas Mill; drove by change of horses in good time to town.

MONDAY 11 NOVEMBER.[8] (Writing on Friday the 29.) Came to Edinburgh from Auchinleck in a day; my wife and Veronica in the chaise with me, the rest of our children to follow. Found myself in steady vigour of mind, which I experienced next morning when I waited on the Lord President[9] and saw him and his brethren at the beginning of a session. Lord Covington's death, of which I had notice

---

From London they came down, baith the black and the brown,
   And they wanted to give him a lady.

"Your Lordship, we pray, may not say us nae,
   For it's now full time you was girded" [hooped];
Quoth the Earl, "Faith my dears, so great are my fears,
   In conscience I'd rather be yearded" [buried].

(To the tune of *Johnnie Faa, or The Gipsie Laddie*.) Cassillis died a bachelor in 1792. The "Miss Coopers" may have been daughters of Sir Grey Cooper. If so, their mother was a Kennedy.

[5]Here Boswell resumed the pen.

[6]The manuscript has "patridges," a dialectal form still in use in parts of Great Britain and the United States.

[7]News reached Great Britain late in October that several ships in the Jamaica fleet and its convoy had been lost in a hurricane off Newfoundland. Lady Crawford's third son, Bute Lindsay, captain in the 92nd Foot, was known to be aboard the *Centaur*, which was reported "entirely dismasted, her rudder gone and stern drove in" (*Scots Magazine*, October 1782, xliv. 550).

[8]This is really a review of the rest of November.

[9]Robert Dundas, Lord Arniston, who had held the office since 1760 and administered it with exceptional firmness and efficiency. He was the fourth generation of his family in a straight line to serve the Court of Session.

by a burial-letter, made an impression upon my mind not deep but pensively grave. I attended his funeral on Wednesday from the Coates, where he died.[1] He was buried in the floor of the Greyfriars Church.[2] There was a wonderful indifference in the appearance of all who did him the last honours, except Lord Justice Clerk, whom I observed saying twice with an agitation which pleased me, "There lies all his eloquence." I felt myself quite reconciled to the course of nature, without any gloom; but by looking forward was sensible that Mr. Alexander Lockhart was in his progress of being, and had only made a great move. I felt myself quite as I could wish in the Court of Session. I applied to business with independent avidity, from love of occupation rather than love of money, and I with pleasure found that I was still employed, though Laird of Auchinleck. I did what I should not have done when I was in a dependent state: I challenged an attempt of Lord Eglinton's agents to give Wight my place as Counsel in Ordinary to his Lordship. I spoke to Cumming, whom I in my own mind blamed less than Wauchope. I told him both the Earl and Fairlie had told me I was to be Counsel in Ordinary.[3] The pecuniary consideration was nothing to me. But there was a credit in it to which I thought myself entitled, unless there had been different instructions given. But I had observed Mr. Wight was oftener enrolled for the Earl than I was, though I understood he was only to be an occasional counsel. Cumming admitted a wrong; and the consequence was, a cause was in a day or two brought to me which had been enrolled with Mr. Wight's name. I thought it wrong that the Earl's obliging intention should be defeated by his agents in favour of one of their cronies; and I had spoke of it to Fairlie. They now saw that I was not so simple or so weakly delicate as to permit it.

[EDITORIAL NOTE. Boswell appears to have kept no systematic record of his life from 12 to 30 November 1782. On two days of that period, 18 and 29 November, he called on Henry Home, Lord Kames, judge in the Courts of Session and of Justiciary, known for his severity in criminal trials and for the range of his voluminous publications on

[1]The Coates was the area to the west of Princes Street; Lord Covington (Alexander Lockhart) had his residence there. Boswell once resolved to write the life of Lockhart, who became a Lord of Session after fifty-two years at the bar.

[2]At the south-east end, "under a through-stone" (a flat gravestone) which no longer remains. There is a blank in the journal before the name of the church, Boswell apparently having forgotten whether Lord Covington was buried in the Old or the New Greyfriars. His lapse is understandable, because the "new church," completed 1721, was added to the west end of the old.

[3]George Cumming and John Wauchope were "writers," or solicitors, who in Scots Law prepared and managed the causes which the advocate they engaged pleaded before the court. Fairlie was Eglinton's factor.

metaphysics, literary criticism, agriculture, and law. Boswell had been collecting notes of Kames's conversation intermittently since 1775 for a life of him which he never wrote. He had last interviewed him in February 1782. Now in his eighty-sixth year, Kames was failing rapidly, and in the last months of his life Boswell was assiduous in relieving his isolation and recording as much of his conversation as Kames's health permitted. Though Boswell kept the notes separate for his biographical project, the give and take of dialogue shows that he was in fact journalizing—the very reason, probably, that the journal proper is brief. We therefore print the entries from the Kames materials for 18 and 29 November below, and interweave the notes taken in December with Boswell's journal for that month. Where bits duplicate each other one of the versions has been silently expunged.]

MONDAY 18 NOVEMBER. [Lord Kames] had been so ill, was said to be dead; had come to town night before. Went to him at night. His clerk was reading *Cecilia* to him.[4] "My Lord, I am happy to see you. How do ye do? Are you here?" "Yes, I am here. I know I am here, as Descartes that he existed." BOSWELL. "*Cogito, ergo sum.* I am sure you are here, for I've shaken hands with you. Well, what news from the other world?" KAMES. "They told me it was not time for me yet." BOSWELL. "We're much obliged to them. We shall take as good care of you as we can." I talked of my father's easy death. He said, "Some men die very easily." The thought did not seem to strike him deep, nor did he seem to be affected when I spoke of Lord Covington's death. I asked him if he was writing anything for us. KAMES. "No, I shall write no more. I shall leave that to men who have more vigour of mind." BOSWELL. " 'Spectatum satis et donatum iam rude.' "[5] KAMES. "I have done very well." BOSWELL. "You have 'done the state some service.' "[6] KAMES. "I have hung up my ——— in the temple of ———."[7] BOSWELL. "You have hung up many dresses: your farmer's coat, your philosopher's—" KAMES. "You are puzzled to describe them all." BOSWELL. "Your antiquarian's rough cap. Ha! ha! ha! Did you ever think of a splendid edition of your works?" KAMES. "No." BOSWELL. "I think it is very agreeable. It is a grand equipage. But all your works could not be put into

[4] Fanny Burney's second novel, published just this past summer.
[5] "Well tested in the fray and already presented with the foil" (Horace, *Epistles,* I. i. 2, trans. H. R. Fairclough, Loeb ed., 1961). Horace alludes to the wooden staff used by gladiators in their exercises which they received upon honourable discharge.
[6] *Othello,* V. ii. 339.
[7] Horace, *Odes,* I. v. 13–16: "As for me, the temple wall with its votive tablet shows I have hung up my dripping garments to the god who is master of the sea" (trans. C. E. Bennett, Loeb ed., 1960).

it. The *Dictionary of Decisions* could not.[8] Yet that is an excellent work, and we are much obliged to you for it." KAMES. "Nor all my law papers could not be put into it." BOSWELL. "No. But we have the portable soup of them in your books. Pray, how long time did the *Dictionary* cost you?" KAMES. "I don't like to recollect." BOSWELL. "I have heard your Lordship tell that the scheme of it was thought of by MacEwan the bookseller, and he employed poor Bruce, who blocked it out."[9] KAMES. "Yes. And after he had advanced a great deal of money from time to time, it was like to stop, by which he would have lost much. So he applied to the Faculty to see if they would authorize its being published. Some of us were appointed to consider it,[1] and really from compassion I undertook to smooth it over so as it might pass. But when I came to set about it attentively, I found it was like taking down an old ruin: I should bring it about my ears. So I had to begin it anew. I employed Peter Haldane, Archie Murray, and William Grant to abridge Durie's *Decisions* for me, as I could not trust to Bruce there. But what they did was so short, I was obliged to do it all over again. Pitfour did some which were well done.[2] The difficulty was to trace the steps which led to each decision, find out a *ratio decidendi*,[3] and place it under a head." BOSWELL. "Ay, there was the genius." KAMES. "I have been ten hours studying one decision to fix its proper principle and place." "But, my Lord, there is some difficulty in finding out the head under which a decision is placed unless one is acquainted with the *Dictionary*. A man must be a good lawyer to be able to consult it." KAMES. "No doubt it is of no use but to one acquainted with it."

[8] *The Decisions of the Court of Session, from Its Institution to the Present Time . . . in Form of a Dictionary* was published at Edinburgh in two volumes in 1741. The entries, collected from many unpublished manuscripts as well as from printed decisions, were abridged and classified alphabetically under appropriate headings. Kames published four other collections of decisions between 1728 and 1780.

[9] James MacEwan, who in 1718 founded the *Edinburgh Evening Courant*, the voice of the Whigs, in 1752 became immediate successor to the poet Allan Ramsay as proprietor of the principal bookshop in Edinburgh and of the first lending-library in Scotland. Alexander Bruce, admitted advocate December 1702 and the author of two legal works by 1714, six years later brought out the abridged *Decisions of the Lords of Council and Session* for late 1714 and four months in 1715. Kames acknowledged in his *Dictionary* that in compiling it he used both Bruce's printed *Decisions* and his manuscript collection for 1716–1717.

[1] The Faculty of Advocates appointed a committee to revise Bruce's collection 2 January 1722.

[2] *Decisions of the Lords of Council and Session* between 1621 and 1642, reported by Sir Alexander Gibson of Durie, favourite of King James VI and Lord of Session, was brought out in 1690. Pitfour was James Ferguson, named Lord of Session in 1764.

[3] The ground of decision, that is, the point in a case which determines the judgement.

I told him that I had experienced a wonderful change upon myself this autumn. I had felt a high relish of the country, of actual farming; had looked with eagerness on ploughed land, and upon a dunghill with as much pleasure as upon Lady Wallace.[4] "I am glad of it," said he. "But take care lest, like a fit of enthusiasm in religion, it go off and leave you as you were." I said I hoped not. But I was only mentioning it as an extraordinary metamorphosis. I had acquired a new sense.

Lord Monboddo was spoken of by one of us.[5] I said he was not well. He had a bad cough notwithstanding all his exercise. And I had told him it brought to my mind a passage in our translation of the Psalms:

> An horse for preservation
> is a deceitful thing.[6]

KAMES. "I met him at Gordon Castle[7] lately. I never argue with him except now and then throwing out a sly joke" (or some such expression to denote his playing with him). "He took it into his head to praise Milton's prose. I could not agree with him. 'Who writes better?' said he. 'I'll tell you who writes better,' said I; 'Lord Monboddo.' He was down in the mouth. He found fault with Tacitus. Now I admire the concise and beautiful expression of Tacitus. I think there is as much pleasure in reading Tacitus as Horace." BOSWELL. "Lord Monboddo says it is not history, but notes for history." KAMES. "But are they not fine notes?"

Speaking of the sale of books, I told him it was very limited in Scotland, for a London bookseller told me he sold more to York than to all Scotland. My Lord controverted this, and said there were more readers in Scotland in proportion than in England, and more books sold in proportion to the two countries, London not excepted. "Well,"

---

[4] Eglinton Maxwell, beauty, playwright, and wit, the former wife of Thomas Dunlop-Wallace, self-styled baronet of Craigie, whom she divorced in 1778 on grounds of various adulteries. Boswell had "tasted her delicious lips," and found her amusing as well as decorative, but he also criticized her for "indelicate effrontery," objecting, no doubt, to the independence and abandon with which she held her own in society (Journal, 29 September 1778, and 11 May 1780).

[5] James Burnett, judge in the Court of Session and a prolific writer on linguistics, anthropology, and philosophy. He was jeered at for studying man as one of the animals.

[6] The passage continues:

> And by the greatness of his strength
> can no deliv'rance bring.

Psalm 33, ll. 53–56 in the Scottish Psalter.

[7] The ancient seat in Moray which Alexander Gordon, fourth Duke of Gordon, was rebuilding around the six-storied tower of Bog-of-Gight Castle, founded 1498.

said I, "you should know something of this. But 'non concessere columnae':[8] the booksellers must determine." He said he was obliged to me for a reading of Dr. Johnson's *Lives of the Poets*, which had given him some hours of entertainment. He was pleased with Miss Burney's *Evelina*, in particular with the characters of a disagreeable City family, well diversified; equal, he thought, to *Tom Jones*.

I shall mark detached passages of conversation as I recollect them. He seemed much satisfied with his son's marriage to Miss Jardine,[9] and said it was rare that a match so rational happens; for a woman, when she knows there is an intention of it, puts on a mask, and there is not a fair opportunity of being well acquainted with her. He approved of Sibbald's circulating library,[1] as it gave him a sight of books and let him judge if he should buy them. In talking of the sale of books, I told him John Balfour[2] said very few Greek and Latin books were now sold. "Because," said my Lord, "people are stocked with them. I have not bought a classic for many years, except a particular fine edition which has come out, such as the Glasgow Homer or the Edinburgh Horace.[3] There is another kind of books which do not sell at all: the commentators on Civil Law, of which I have a great number purchased by my father-in-law while he studied in Holland. Nobody reads them now." BOSWELL. "The study of Civil Law is much gone out. In the Session papers when your Lordship first began to collect decisions, there is a great deal of Civil Law. Every case is illustrated by it. Whereas now we seldom see it." KAMES. "Because then there were many points to settle. But a man would be laughed at were he to quote Civil Law now that they are settled." BOSWELL. "One should think, then, that as many points

[8]Horace, *Ars Poetica*, l. 373 (Loeb ed., 1961).
[9]It had been solemnized the month previous, 11 October 1782. George Home Drummond was Lord Kames's only son and Janet Jardine the daughter of the Rev. John Jardine, D.D., leader of the Moderate Party in the Church of Scotland.
[1]The library formed by Allan Ramsay in 1725 to diffuse plays and other works of fiction (see above, p. 18, n. 9) and purchased in 1781 by James Sibbald, antiquarian, bookseller, and founder of the *Edinburgh Magazine*, 1783. The magistrates tried to suppress the library in 1728 because of complaints about the effects of its holdings on the minds of the young.
[2]Bookseller and printer in Edinburgh.
[3]Kames clearly alludes to the folio edition of Homer's works edited by James Moor and George Muirhead, Professors of Greek and Latin respectively at the University of Glasgow, published in two volumes by the Foulis Press, 1756 and 1758, and to the works of Horace published at Edinburgh by Robert Freebairn, 1731. Each volume of the Homer was awarded in its turn the medal of the Select Society of Edinburgh for the best printed and most accurate Greek book. The copy of the *Odyssey* apparently submitted for judgement (now at The University Library, Cambridge) is endorsed for the prize by Lord Auchinleck and Lord Monboddo.

are settled, the papers should now be shorter. Yet they are much longer." KAMES. "Because there are more points to settle. At first there is a very gross view of a subject. Refinement sees with a more piercing eye, and a variety of questions appear."

I told him I had been today at a meeting to consider freehold qualifications. I stated the two principles of men (numbers) and property (quantity). He thought with me that if property was the principle, a man should have a number of votes in proportion to it; and he thought men of large property less liable to be bribed. He would not admit of men and numbers, because the people in general are not judges of a proper representative, as we see how ill they judge in a popular election of a minister. He coincided with me in thinking that the technical terms of "superiority" and "property" should be abolished, and that whoever had a permanent estate, or revenue out of land belonging to him and his heirs, should have a vote, the value of it only to be fixed, no matter by what species of tenure.[4]

He asked me to stay and sup. I said I was afraid it would be inconvenient for him. He said, "If it were so, I would not ask you." Mrs. Drummond came into the room and introduced ludicrous mirth, describing Lord Monboddo dancing the Groningen Minuet at Gordon Castle,[5] Baron Stuart's awkward, stammering vanity, Lord Braxfield's getting himself drunk on the Circuit with the Laird of Udny and kissing her in the coach, Annie Lockhart's putting on weeds as the posthumous widow of Charles Boyd, etc., etc., etc.[6] Before supper he called for a

[4] A "freeholder" in Scots usage of the time can be defined quite simply as a man qualified to vote for or to be elected a Member of Parliament at a county election. "Superiority" and "property," however, as Boswell says, are highly technical terms of feudal tenure. All land was vested in the King, who granted it to his barons to be "held" subject to the payment of dues or rendering of services. A baron who "held" of the King could grant a subordinate estate to a "vassal" to be "held" of himself as "superior," again subject to certain feu duties which were sometimes considerable but were generally nominal or whimsical. The ultimate "proprietor" of the estate, whether "superior" or "vassal," leased the land to tenants and collected rents. Power to vote, however, was restricted to "superiors." But it was possible by a complicated legal manoeuvre to sell or make a gift of the "superiority" while retaining the "property." The holder of the bare "superiority" of qualifying lands qualified for a vote no less than a man holding both "superiority" and "property" of similar lands. Boswell is saying in effect that the sole qualification for the franchise should be landed "property" of a certain value. The conversation reflects the widespread concern of the time over nominal and fictitious votes, which Boswell had long opposed.

[5] Mrs. Drummond is Lady Kames. See p. 24, n. 8. "The Groningen Minuet" may be the title of a piece of music rather than a dance-form supposedly imported from Holland.

[6] The other victims of Mrs. Drummond's mimicry are Andrew Stuart, W.S., agent for the Duke of Hamilton in the Douglas Cause and since 1770 King's Remembrancer in the Court of Exchequer (the title "Baron" is jocular); Alexander Udny, advocate,

glass of port and asked me to pledge him, which I did. I declare his judgement, memory, and vivacity were the same as ever, except that there was some failure of animal spirits, as he had for some time been weakened by a looseness. It was truly a pleasant scene, and as I was in sound cheerfulness, I relished it egregiously. It was agreeable to see a man who had been tortured by Liberty and Necessity and other metaphysical difficulties sitting at his ease by the fireside. I spoke of the difference between Sir John Pringle and my father on the subject of a future state. Sir John was anxious and uneasy about it; my father quite firm and never speculating. "Because," said he, "Sir John was once a Deist, though he afterwards returned so far as to believe the Christian revelation of immortality. But a man who had wavered was very naturally uneasy. Your father had never doubted of Christianity, and as he was conscious he had done his duty to God and man, he was sure he would be well in another world."

My Lord, on my inquiry and gently urging him on, gave me an account of his acquaintance with Butler, author of the *Analogy*,[7] which he had formerly given me, but I had not marked it down. He had read his *Sermons* and *Analogy,* and formed a high opinion of him. One year when he was in London, he was very desirous of being introduced to him. But time passed on till he was afraid he should go to Scotland without seeing him. So one morning he knocked at his door. He was then Clerk of the Closet to the Queen. A great big fellow of a porter, like a Swiss, opened the door and desired to know the gentleman's name. He told him, "Dr. Butler would not know me by my name. Just tell him a gentleman wants to wait upon him." He was shown in. The Doctor came sailing out of another room in a long gown like Hamlet's ghost (an erroneous comparison, for Hamlet's ghost appears in a coat of mail—"in complete steel."[8] But however). "He asked me what were my commands. I was obliged to do the honours of the house, and said, 'If you'll please to sit down, I'll tell you.' I then told him I had read

---

Commissioner of Excise for Scotland, and proprietor of Udny Castle, a fortress in Aberdeenshire dating from the thirteenth century; and Annie Lockhart, daughter of Lord Covington, whose marriage to Charles Boyd seems not to have been revealed until after Boyd's death, 3 August 1782, aged fifty-four. He was married first to a Frenchwoman during his exile for Jacobitism.

[7] Joseph Butler, D.C.L., successively Bishop of Bristol (and Dean of St. Paul's) and Bishop of Durham, published in 1726 his *Fifteen Sermons Preached at the Rolls Chapel* and in 1736 the *Analogy of Religion, Natural and Revealed, to the Constitution and the Course of Nature.* He served in that same year as Clerk of the Closet to Queen Caroline, who died in 1737.

[8] I. iv. 52. Kames may be remembering the Ghost's appearance "in his habit as he lived" (III. iv. 135).

his *Sermons* and *Analogy*, and had a great desire to pay my respects to him. I saw he seemed to imagine that I was one come to dispute with him, which he did not like, and I said, 'I now see, Sir, the incongruity, the impropriety, of my visit. But I can assure you I did not come in this manner till I had first endeavoured to be properly introduced. I applied to Lord Ilay,[9] who said, "I know not how to get you introduced but by introducing you to the Queen, and she will introduce you to her favourite chaplain." ' And I told him I was afraid I should be obliged to leave London without seeing him. He was pleased with Lord Ilay's compliment, and finding I was connected with the great, 'Sir,' said he, 'will you walk into the next room? I was drinking a dish of chocolade. Will you drink one with me?' He was very courteous, and I sat with him two hours and had very good conversation. I asked him particularly as to a passage in his ———,[1] where he seems to say he would show the Deists that their objections against Christianity are weak. I found he meant that though there are cogent objections, they may be overcome. He had a very decent manner." I told my Lord I had heard a story which I had formerly found from his Lordship was a lie: that he had seen Butler on his deathbed and Butler had owned to him that he did not believe what he had written. My Lord said tonight he was convinced Butler wrote what he thought, and that his *Analogy* was not *a professional book*—a phrase of mine in questioning him. He visited him again and was politely told by him he had been endeavouring to find out his lodgings, which my Lord said he had not told, that he might not take the trouble of inquiring. He afterwards corresponded with him on some points of his sermons, and when he was Bishop of Durham, was preparing to go and visit him when he heard of his death.[2]

Lord Kames supped well tonight on oatmeal porridge and cream and rice and milk, and drank a glass of water. He said the President had no conversation and very little reading. We talked a very little of farming. He could not tell what is the effect of lime upon land besides instigating vegetation. But he maintained that by a proper course of labour and rest, limed land might be preserved much better than it was before.

[9]Archibald Campbell, Earl and Viscount of Ilay and from 1743 the third Duke of Argyll, was a mainstay of the Hanoverian Royal Family. He managed Scottish affairs with so much authority during the Walpole administration that he was called the King of Scotland.
[1]A gap in the manuscript indicates that Boswell either did not recall the title of Butler's work or that he was uncertain of it.
[2]He was appointed to the bishopric 16 October 1750 and died 16 June 1752.

FRIDAY 29 NOVEMBER. Went to him in the evening. His clerk was with him. He had been dictating I know not what. His clerk went away. He put me in mind of finishing the reading of my *Hypochondriack* No. 61, in which I had been interrupted one forenoon.[3] "But," said he, "begin it." I read it all to him, and he was much pleased with it. I then read him my paper on this age being better than former ones, to which he listened with seeming satisfaction and said I was right.[4] I told him I was sending up anecdotes to Dr. Kippis for Sir John Pringle's life.[5] I mentioned his[6] anxious care not to offend any person or body of men of any consequence. My Lord said he had a specimen of it when he sent him the Dedication of his *Gentleman Farmer* to revise ("for," said he, "I would not dedicate to any man without consulting him"). There was a sentence saying that the Royal Society had applied themselves too much to abstract questions. He was happy they were of late turning their attention more to practical matters. Sir John wrote, "You must not find fault with the Royal Society," and the sentence was left out.[7]

I said my never having been at Blair-Drummond[8] was really incredible. I would put it into a book which I had called *Poleatus de Incredibilibus*.[9] He asked me how I met with so many curious books. I told him I was a great wanderer amongst books. I spoke to him of a

[3]Essay No. 61, on dedications, published October 1782, in which Boswell reasons that though there is no meanness in dedication, there is more dignity in not dedicating at all. "For my own part," he adds, "I own I am proud enough. But I do not relish the stateliness of not dedicating at all. I prefer pleasure to pride, and it appears to me that there is much pleasure in honestly expressing one's admiration, esteem, or affection in a public manner, and in thus contributing to the happiness of another by making him better pleased with himself" (*The Hypochondriack*, ed. Margery Bailey, 1928, ii. 221). Boswell's major works were dedicated to intimate friends, the *Account of Corsica* to Gen. Pasquale Paoli, the *Journal of a Tour to the Hebrides* to Edmond Malone, and the *Life of Johnson* to Sir Joshua Reynolds.

[4]*The Hypochondriack* No. 52, "On Past and Present," published January 1782.

[5]Andrew Kippis, biographer and Presbyterian minister, was preparing a life of Pringle for his edition of Pringle's *Six Discourses*, published in 1783. Sir John, physician to the King, President of the Royal Society, and reformer of military medicine and sanitation, had been a good friend to both Lord Auchinleck and Boswell. He had died in January of this year. A copy of Boswell's notes for Kippis, which include anecdotes furnished by his father, is among the Papers at Yale.

[6]Pringle's.

[7]*The Gentleman Farmer*, a practical guide to husbandry subtitled "An attempt to improve agriculture by subjecting it to the test of rational principles," was published at Edinburgh in 1776.

[8]Kames's actual country residence after 1766, about six miles from Stirling. It belonged to his wife, who inherited it from her brother. As a landed proprietor in her own right, she was usually styled Mrs. Drummond.

[9]Obviously an author and book of Boswell's own invention but with an allusion he

Process of Reduction[1] which had been before the Lords this week to set aside a deed because the maker of it was excessively addicted to brandy and the man in whose favour it was made had with cunning art prevailed on him to disinherit his brother. My Lord was of opinion that the majority of the Lords were right in not setting aside the deed. "For," said he, "if it could be erased from the records and never be a precedent *this* deed might be reduced. But it would be very dangerous to set aside a man's Will if it really be his Will, though very bad influence has been employed to produce such a Will." I agreed that this would lead deep into the consideration of cause and . . . .[2]

He said very well that a man of a vigorous mind has many degrees of failure to pass through before he is worse than a man of ordinary understanding. I took down the words from his dictating, for I made him repeat them again. "A man of great vigour of mind has many degrees to sink through and yet at last be equal in capacity to many a man who is a tolerable manager of plain affairs." I thought the remark applied well to my father. I said this was a comfortable night when I had him just alone. He said I was very kind to him. He had never seen Felltham's *Resolves*.[3] I promised to send the ⟨book⟩ to him. I read to him a little of the notes I had taken of his conversation. He had mistaken something, which he corrected. He frankly promised me his vote for Peter Miller to succeed Mitchell in a small office under the Trustees for Fisheries and Manufactures at Ayr.[4] We were truly easy and cordial

---

expected Kames to recognize to Palaephatus, *De Incredibilibus*, a treatise probably dating in its original form from the fourth century B.C. which attempts to rationalize the Greek myths. Boswell's copy of the book with his signature in it, dated 1779 and with Greek and Latin on facing pages, is at Yale. What Boswell meant by "Poleatus" is uncertain.

[1] An action to rescind or annul.

[2] Manuscript defective for most of three lines, a total of about twenty words lost without trace.

[3] In the *Hypochondriack* essay on dedications which Boswell had just read to Lord Kames he cited the *Resolves* ("a book of singular merit") for its dedication in the eighth edition to Felltham's patron, in this case Mary, Countess Dowager of Thomond, whose beneficence enabled him to write the book.

[4] The Board of Trustees for Encouragement of the Fisheries, Arts, and Manufactures of Scotland, an unsalaried commission of twenty-one members, was established with a substantial revenue by an act of 1727. It awarded premiums for inventions and improvements, furnished equipment and seed to the poor, founded schools of spinning and weaving, and hired local inspectors and stamp-masters for enforcing regulations to ensure uniform high quality in Scottish cloth. Boswell probably wanted to get an office of this kind for Peter Miller, who, with Mitchell, remains unidentified. Kames, a benevolent and conscientious Trustee since 1755, generally chaired the meetings of the Board.

tonight. He seemed to be a good deal better. I was struck with wonder while I thought of his great age, and at the same time perceived he was so clear in his judgement and memory.

We supped with Mrs. Drummond. He took sowans[5] and cream. She said they had gone to England in 1745 on account of the disturbance. He said to me, "Her memory is failed. She's mistaken, as I shall convince her.—Our going to England was with a party with whom we had agreed to go a year before." "Very true," said she. "Sir Robert Stewart of Tillicoultry and his Lady. We were some time at Durham, some time at York." Lord Kames said, "It is true we went from home some time, because I was unwilling to meet with some good friends who were along with the Highland army that I might not be called as a witness against them." This was very accurate. Both he and she were pleased with my attention in waiting upon them so often. She said of me tonight at supper, "This is a good man. He's very good to us." He went to bed about eleven. She insisted on my sitting longer.

She told me she was sixty-nine last May. I mentioned that it was now two-and-twenty years since I was introduced to Lord Kames. "Ay," said she, "since you and my poor daughter were first acquainted." This was a strange subject. I kept myself steady, and expatiated on that unfortunate lady's many engaging qualities.[6] Mrs. Drummond said Mr. Heron was a most unfit husband for her, a good-natured, weak man. She should have had a man who would have held her in with bit and bridle. She was not seventeen when she married him. Everybody about her paid her such compliments on her superiority she despised him. She told me how Lord Kames and she were first informed of their daughter's ruin. He had gone in to the Winter Session leaving his wife and son and Mrs. Heron at Blair-Drummond. Mr. J. R. Mackye[7] put

[5]A kind of porridge made by steeping oatmeal hulls in water, allowing the infusion to ferment slightly, and then boiling it down.

[6]Boswell's wariness almost certainly arises from a passionate intrigue with Jean Home, the Kameses' only daughter, shortly after her youthful marriage in 1761 to Patrick Heron of Kirroughtrie. Boswell, then twenty-one, suffered deep remorse over the adultery because Lord and Lady Kames had been very kind to him when he and his own father were on poor terms, and Heron, an amiable man, had insisted that he make extended visits to his country-seat near Dumfries. In 1764 Boswell put this problem of conscience before Rousseau. Heron divorced Jean Home in 1772, presenting evidence publicly of adultery with a young army officer. Strong-willed and independent, she did not deny the charge.

[7]John Ross Mackye, advocate, one of the guardians of the young Duke of Hamilton and counsel for him in the Douglas Cause (see below, 12 December 1782, n. 10). Mackye also had an active political career in England, summarized below, 26 March 1783, n. 3.

into his hands in the lobby of the Parliament House a letter from Heron to this purpose: "My Lord, I have discovered such circumstances in your daughter's conduct that I shall not be two nights in the same place for some months. I am resolved to take legal measures to be separated from her for ever. Make no opposition, for I am confident of success." He put the letter in his pocket, went upon the bench, and did his duty. She complained of this letter as cruel. Said it was like shooting him with a pistol. He went home and wrote to her that he wished to see them all in town, the sooner the better. Before this the affair had become public. His relation, Mrs. Walkinshaw, had written to her daughter, then at Blair-Drummond, to come home directly, she would not allow her to stay another day. This seemed odd. But there was no accounting for a mother's taking a positive fit.[8] Little did she suspect what was the real cause.

They arrived at Edinburgh to tea. Miss Carres of Nisbet[9] were with my Lord and them that evening. Mrs. Heron laid her hand on her father's knee and said, "Papa, for all the faults that follow me I believe you was right sorry for me when I was ill." "Yes," said he. Nothing transpired that night. Next morning Mrs. Drummond herself received a letter from Mr. Heron. One of the Miss Carres was with her. "Oh," said she, "what is this?" Was in great distress. My Lord came into the room. "There is something wrong," said he. "Yes," said she. "My dear, can you explain it?" Said he, "Mr. Heron is jealous." Said she, "I shall never again see my daughter's face." He flew into a passion. "What!" said he, "would you abandon your daughter because a man is suspicious?" Said she, "She must be guilty since he condemns her." He stood petrified, then said, "It is very hard, but there's no help for it. Inquire for somebody to go abroad with her." Drummond the French teacher was going to France with a daughter.[1] He agreed to take her. Mrs. Drummond saw her. Was not minute upon the subject. She did not deny it. But said she despised him. Was not much affected. Said to Grace, the faithful maid, the morning of her departure, "It's time for

[8]Probably Kames's cousin, Lyonella, one of ten daughters of his mother's older brother, John Walkinshaw of Barrowfield. Lyonella was married to her cousin William Walkinshaw, but we have found nothing concerning their offspring. Lyonella's younger sister was the renowned Clementina Walkinshaw, sometime mistress of Prince Charles Edward and mother of his only child, the Duchess of Albany.

[9]George Carre, Lord Nisbet, judge in the Court of Session 1755–1766, had three unmarried daughters: Margaret, Grizel, and Anne. They were Mrs. Drummond's cousins, her mother having been half-sister to Lord Nisbet.

[1]Alexander Drummond, a private tutor. French did not become a part of the official curriculum of the schools in Edinburgh until 1834.

me to learn to do without an Abigail."[2] Lord Kames said, "She is not tear-eyed." "I never knew him[3] cry but once. It was not many years ago, when I was ill."

She gets no money but by asking it of himself. He thinks a small sum will last for ever. He likes to see a genteel table, but were he told the cost, he would sit down to a withered cabbage. She attempted to maintain he was not fond of money. "Why, Madam," said I, "he is unwilling to part with it. He lends it out and he's very rich." She said he had really enriched himself considerably by farming. She said Mr. Orr, the agent for Heron, had laid all the accusations against her daughter before her at her desire. I wondered if she had read the Precognitions,[4] but did not ask. She never hears from Mrs. Heron, but sends her every year £10 in addition to £80 from her father, also linens, etc. She shed some tears tonight as she talked of this distressing history. I sat with her till half an hour after twelve, amazed at my present vigour of mind.

I had the satisfaction this evening of making both Lord Kames and Mrs. Drummond apparently satisfied that our family was not in the wrong in refusing the road asked by the family of Dumfries, that it was a great favour, and a point of vanity on the one hand to make the grounds without the gateway appear part of the Earl's domains and on the other hand to have them appear ours, as they really are.

SUNDAY 1 DECEMBER. (Writing the 4.) Rose well. Heard Dr. Blair in the forenoon on keeping from "my iniquity."[5] He said a man's iniquity was the sin which he would be most unwilling his enemies should know, the sin which he would wish to be excepted from his duty. But that an exception would rather be given for any other sin than that to which a man is most inclined. To give it up is a test of sincerity. I walked in the Meadow with Grange. Met Lord Monboddo, who told me he was sunning himself like a fly, which, when laid in the sun, will revive. I was in such spirits that everything gave me agreeable feelings. Miss Semple dined with us between sermons. I heard Mr. Walker in the afternoon. I do not remember the subject. I rode out

[2] A lady's-maid, from the name of the "waiting gentlewoman" in Beaumont and Fletcher's popular play, *The Scornful Lady*, or perhaps from the expression "thine handmaid" so frequently applied to herself by Abigail the Carmelite, I Samuel 25: 24–31.

[3] Lord Kames. Lady Kames is comparing father and daughter.

[4] The preliminary examination of possible witnesses in order to ascertain the evidence which they can give at a trial.

[5] II Samuel 22: 24.

and drank tea at Commissioner Cochrane's; Hon. James Cochrane there. Neglected the children this evening. Supped at Dr. Webster's.[6]

MONDAY 2 DECEMBER. (Writing the 4.) Got up early. Was *robust*. Wrote notes for Sir John Pringle's life, which I sent to Dr. Kippis by this evening's post. Attended for a little in the forenoon a committee of the presbytery of Edinburgh taking evidence against Affleck, the preacher. Dined with them at Walker's Tavern, John Tait, Junior, entertaining there for the heritors of Carsphairn.[7] Was quite sober and as I could wish to be. I never before experienced constitutional sobriety. What a happy change to be free of the rage of drinking!

TUESDAY 3 DECEMBER. (Writing the 4.) Was in full health and spirits. Pleaded with force, ease, and pleasure. Delighted in the practice of the law. Drank tea at Lady Auchinleck's, whom I had not visited since Sunday sennight. Only she and her sister. Both in most complaisant frame. Curious to observe such a difference in their behaviour to me now from what it was when they had influence and I was dependent. Not in favour of human nature.[8] Sat a long time, and talked much—perhaps with too little reserve. My father's picture, which hung in the room, affected me with an awful tenderness.[9] I came home and sent Dr. Kippis some additional notes for Sir John Pringle's life. Then went in cheerful spirits to Lord Kames's. Found him weaker and somewhat fretful. Found Mr. Craig the architect showing him plans of the New Town,[1] which he looked at with a keen eye. I mentioned a monument which Craig had sketched at his desire (he had not said for himself but Craig understood so and had put his medallion on it),[2] and

[6]Basil Cochrane, Commissioner of Customs, was an uncle of Boswell's mother and of the Rev. and Hon. James Atholl Cochrane, vicar of Mansfield. Dr. Webster, minister of the Tolbooth Church, was Boswell's uncle by marriage and one of his convivial older friends.

[7]Boswell was counsel for the heritors of Carsphairn in their cause against Robert Affleck, their probationary minister, who was accused of ante-nuptial fornication, fraud, and simony. The General Assembly revoked his licence as a probationer in 1783.

[8]Boswell had violently opposed Lord Auchinleck's marriage to his cousin, Elizabeth Boswell of Balmuto. He blamed his stepmother, who was openly critical of his behaviour, for much of the coldness between his father and himself. Lady Auchinleck's sister was Miss Margaret Boswell.

[9]This is presumably the portrait now in the possession of James W. Irvine-Fortescue, Esq., of Kingcausie, the descendant of Lady Auchinleck's brother, Claud Irvine Boswell of Balmuto.

[1]Craig designed it on plans inspired by lines in the poem *Liberty*, written by his uncle, James Thomson.

[2]It is not certain that Craig's design was ever used. The present Gothic monument to Lord and Lady Kames, which forms part of the Blair-Drummond memorial in Kin-

that I had differed with Craig, who, as my Lord had said he disliked death's head and bones, had thrown a veil upon the skeleton. "This," I said, "made it look like an old woman's skeleton. Besides death is a figure well known. We must not alter emblematical figures which are once established, such as Death a skeleton, Time with wings, scythe, and sandglass, Justice with scales." My Lord was not clear as to this. "Somebody," said he, "first invented an emblem. Why should not another man invent a new one?" "But it is a universal sign," said I, "when once established, and a new one would not be understood." Miss Home of Ninewells,[3] Craig, and I supped. My Lord was so weak it not only was difficult for him to rise but to sit down. Yet he had his old spirit to a surprising degree. As his length went suddenly down on the settee he said to Miss Home, "I just fall like a sack of dross" (grains). Mrs. Drummond said he would not take any help in rising or sitting down should she be ever so earnest, and she was afraid he would hurt himself. Most old people were hurt from their feebleness. When I came home, found my wife uneasy with a cold. She coughed severely.

WEDNESDAY 4 DECEMBER. (Writing 5.) Whether a sort of damp from seeing Lord Kames last night as a dying man, as I thought, or something in my stomach had hurt my spirits, I know not. But I felt myself somewhat fretted this morning, and spoke angrily to my clerk for being late and looking sulky when I found fault with him. I was vexed to feel any return of bad spirits.

In the forenoon I visited Lord Kames, whom I found weak and not in good humour. But he talked tolerably well, and I grew better.[4] My Lord said he [David Hume] had no settled character—I think that was the phrase. He said it was unaccountable how he should be easy when he knew he had laboured in vain. He had laboured to free mankind from the fear of futurity. He had convinced nobody but his brother and his nephew David.[5] My Lord said to him, "You and I may differ as to the question of a future state. No help for it. But why will

cardine churchyard, replaces an earlier monument about which nothing is known. The mural monument erected in Kincardine Church about 1815 is also Gothic.

[3]Miss Catherine Home, David Hume's elderly sister (he changed the spelling of the family surname some time before he was twenty-three). The Homes of Ninewells and the Homes of Kames had an ancestor in common around 1400.

[4]In the Kames materials dated 3 and 4 December 1782 (actually 4 and 5 December) Boswell wrote, "Saw him both these days in the forenoon. I forget on which of them we talked of David Hume." Because of their lengthy conversation on the 5th we think it likely that the dialogue on Hume belongs here.

[5]John Home of Ninewells, Hume's only brother, and John's second son, David, Professor of Scots Law in the University of Edinburgh 1786–1822 and Baron of Exchequer 1822–1834. Hume supervised his nephew's education and virtually adopted him.

you endeavour to take the belief of it from people to whom it is a comfort?" David said he wished to relieve them from false terror, which made them miserable. My Lord said, "David's atheism was owing to his want of sensibility. He did not perceive the benevolence of the Deity in His works. He had no taste, and therefore did not relish Shakespeare. His criticism was in the lump, all general. He could not see the beauties. He could see the want of order in Shakespeare's dramas because that is obvious. But could not see the fine poetry in his works."

I kept Mr. Lawrie to dinner today, that I might not seem to "keep my anger."[6] I dictated a good deal of law after dinner. Grange drank tea with us. I was much better in the evening, though troubled with a slight cold, which I suppose had fretted me. Got my feet washed.

THURSDAY 5 DECEMBER. (Writing the 9.) Was well again this morning. Sat awhile with Lord Kames in the forenoon. Found Mr. Baron Norton[7] sitting with him. He was violent·against the people at large having the choice of their representatives in Parliament because they in his opinion were not proper judges, and much riot is occasioned by popular elections. I spoke keenly on the other side. Put him in a passion by not agreeing that his running off from Inveraray the third day of a circuit was proper. I mark the debate.[7a] After the Baron went away I spoke of narrowness, which I owned I often felt but said he would not own it, mentioning as a proof of his having it his savings at circuits. He grew really angry and asked how I could believe infamous falsehoods of him? I said a very good man might have the disease of narrowness, but "I see, my Lord, you think it a very bad thing." He said such reports of him might be raised because when he first came to be a Lord of Justiciary he found the judges were grossly imposed upon at the circuits, there being no regularity or order in their expense; and it had cost him much exertion to get the better of this. "There was," said he, "an innkeeper at Inveraray who would not agree to my terms of three shillings a head for dinner. Very well. I called for his bill the first day and paid it. I did the same the second day. The third day I ordered my horses and left the town. The innkeeper had provided provisions for five days, so he suffered from his attempt to impose upon me." "So" (said I with a sarcastical smile), "you put the expense of three days in your pocket." Growing serious, "My Lord, I'm glad you have mentioned this. It made a great deal of noise, and I shall be

[6]A paraphrase of Jeremiah 3: 12: "For I am merciful, saith the Lord, and I will not keep anger for ever."
[7]Fletcher Norton, Baron of Exchequer.
[7a]In his notes for a life of Lord Kames, which now follow to the end of the next paragraph.

glad to have it explained. Did not the man prosecute you and get damages?" "No, Sir," said he. "The consequence was, he was ever after most reasonable and obliging." "But," said I, "was it not too severe a punishment? The poor man had provided provisions for five days upon the faith of an Act of Parliament, by which your Lordship was obliged to stay so long in the place." Said Lord Kames, "Everybody thought me in the right." "My Lord," said I, "I cannot help being of a different opinion." "What would you have done?" said he, angrily. BOSWELL. "I would have said, 'Very well, Sir. You won't furnish dinner on my terms. Go on, and let me have your bill at the end.'" KAMES. "What, Sir, and pay what he pleased? Since he refused to agree for three shillings a head he might have charged three pounds, and I am clear in law I would have been obliged to pay it." BOSWELL. "No, my Lord, you would have been obliged to pay only what was reasonable; and if he would not take that let him prosecute you for his bill, and a court of justice would settle it." KAMES. "But he would have arrested me and my horses." BOSWELL. "Your Lordship would have found bail." KAMES. "What, Sir, a supreme judge find bail!" BOSWELL. "Better find bail than go away, and, as I am informed, have the bellman going through the town calling a sale of the judge's provisions. But, my Lord," said I, "I'll tell you what I would have done, had I been to go away. I would have sent for the minister of the parish and said, 'Sir, this fellow wanted to impose upon me. I am going to punish him by leaving his house. If I had been three days more with him and he had charged me reasonably, I should have spent so much. Here is the money for the poor of the parish.' People could not then have said your motive was saving money. And, my Lord, if I was a Lord of Justiciary I would give to the poor of each of the three towns what of the King's money remained after entertaining. It is the King's money. My father always said so." I insisted on the genteel behaviour of the English judges at the circuit. He was quite enraged and hurt and said, "Are you come to distress me?" I asked his pardon and said there was no help for difference of opinion. He grew calm. It was really amazing how he could be so blindly partial to himself or imagine I could be so blind as to think he was in the right in this shabby piece of injustice. I made a happy transition to the first volume of my Hebrides journal, which I had in my pocket, and read him passages of it concerning Lord Monboddo, etc. He was much pleased and said it would sell better than Dr. Johnson's *Journey*.

I mentioned today that Lord Gardenstone told me Lord Elchies[8]

---

[8] Francis Garden of Gardenstone (1721–1793; see below, 19 February 1783) and Patrick Grant of Elchies (1691–1754), both Lords of Session and of Justiciary.

said it would be wrong to have the bench filled with great lawyers. They would speak too much. It was better to have the judges in general plain, sensible, honest men with a few great lawyers to whom they might trust in difficult cases. Said Lord Kames with ready smartness, "Because he himself was a great lawyer and did not wish to have rivals. I remember him a great man for the Crown. But being disappointed, first when Duncan Forbes was made President, and then again when Arniston succeeded, he became a patriot, and canted to the day of his death."⁹ "I observe, my Lord," said I, "you quote him often in your *Remarkable Decisions.* You don't quote the Earl of Leven or Lord Monzie."¹

The Countess Dowager of Dundonald and her sons James and Andrew, Dr. Webster and his daughter and son-in-law, and Grange dined with us.² I was in good sound spirits.

FRIDAY 6 DECEMBER. (Writing the 9.) Visited Mr. Andrew Lumisden and finished the reading of his excellent account of Rome.³ He and I walked to Prestonfield and dined; Mr. Bennet there.⁴ Felt my independence fully. Mr. L. was of opinion I might pass some years in London and try my fortune there, and afterwards return. He came home with me to tea. Relished his conversation.

SATURDAY 7 DECEMBER. (Writing the 11.) Nothing particular to mark during the day. At night called on Lord Kames. He was so ill he could not see me. Supped with Mrs. Drummond, Dr. Roebuck,⁵ his wife and daughter. π.

⁹Lord Elchies, a Whig, was a great lawyer of harsh and overbearing manner but unquestioned probity. John Ramsay of Ochtertyre added the qualification "where party dislikes were out of the question," but he also said that Elchies was not a promotion-hunter (*Scotland and Scotsmen*, 1888, i. 94). The Arniston Kames mentions was the father of the Lord President then in office.
¹Alexander Leslie, fifth Earl of Leven and fourth Earl of Melville, raised to the bench July 1734 and named a Representative Peer in 1747; and Patrick Campbell of Monzie, one of the committee appointed to revise Bruce's collection of decisions (see above, 18 November 1782, p. 18), raised to the bench June 1727.
²Jean Stuart, the widow of Boswell's maternal great-uncle, the eighth Earl of Dundonald, was thirty years younger than her late husband, and very beautiful when she married him. The Rev. James Cochrane, vicar of Mansfield (see above, 1 December 1782, n. 6), was the fourth surviving son of twelve; Andrew was the youngest. Dr. Webster's daughter and her husband were Captain and Mrs. Mingay.
³*Remarks on the Antiquities of Rome and Its Environs*, which was not published until 1797. Boswell first read portions of the manuscript in 1765, when he met Lumisden, then private secretary to the Old Pretender, in Rome. Lumisden returned to Scotland in 1773 and was pardoned five years later.
⁴William Bennet, minister of the parish in which Prestonfield lies.
⁵John Roebuck, a physician who experimented in chemistry and its application to

SUNDAY 8 DECEMBER. (Writing the 11.) Had Grange with me at the Old English Chapel,[6] the first day of an organ playing there. Dr. Bell preached. We were very comfortable. He dined with me. We went back to prayers in the afternoon. But being too late, walked in the Meadow and Bruntsfield Links, and then drank tea cordially with Miss Scott and Monsieur Dupont, who in his eighty-fourth year was quite distinct, and talked of the resurrection with spirited orthodoxy.[7] Sandy had gone to bed before I came home. My two eldest daughters and James said divine lessons. π.

MONDAY 9 DECEMBER. (Writing on the 11.) I breakfasted at Belleville with the Countess of Dundonald and her sons James and Andrew very agreeably, being in fine spirits. Visited Sir George Preston's sisters. Dictated some today. In the evening had a message from my friend the Hon. A. Gordon to come and read the King's Speech. Went, and was truly hurt that my sovereign should be so humiliated.[8] Supped and was sober. No company there. No card-playing. This day, after much consulting about it, Veronica went a day-boarder to Mrs. Billingsley.[9]

TUESDAY 10 DECEMBER. (Writing the 12.) Was well in the Court of Session. Only was angry to observe the Lord President attempt to hurry a Petition of mine to inconsiderate refusal, trusting to the chance of the Lords not having read it, or not having spirits at the time to oppose him. A trick he plays too often. Lords Justice Clerk, Gardenstone, Eskgrove spoke for the Petition (Isobel Bruce's), and it was appointed to be answered. Mr. Donaldson, the painter, came at two

---

industry, revolutionized the manufacture of sulphuric acid, and founded the Carron ironworks above the Firth of Forth.

[6] A Church of England chapel in Blackfriars Wynd.

[7] The Rev. Pierre Loumeau Dupont was in his fifty-sixth year as minister of the French church in Edinburgh, which his father, a Huguenot refugee, had founded. The flock was now largely dispersed or absorbed into the Scottish congregations. Magdalen Scott, youngest daughter of the Professor of Moral Philosophy in the University of Edinburgh, was the minister's housekeeper and his legatee. Boswell was fond of Dupont from an early age.

[8] The speech, which had been delivered before Parliament on 5 December, announced that provisional articles of peace had been concluded, in which the American colonies were recognized as "free and independent states." "In thus admitting their separation from the Crown of these kingdoms, I have sacrificed every consideration of my own to the wishes and opinion of my people." Though Boswell was hurt at the concession of royal authority, he had long supported the colonists' cause. "Sandy" Gordon, a younger son of the second Earl of Aberdeen, was born in 1739, one year before Boswell, admitted advocate in 1759, and made Sheriff-depute of Kirkcudbrightshire in 1764.

[9] Of St. James's Square. Her name suggests that she was English or had been married to an Englishman, and that Veronica, and later Euphemia, were placed with her to correct the Scotch accent.

and helped his miniature picture of my wife.[1] He dined with us. I was firm in spirit, so that his infidel nibbling only made me smile. He stayed tea, and made the children happy by drawing little things to them. I went to Lord Kames and had, I think, the most agreeable interview of any. Had not seen him since Friday[2] forenoon. He was so ill on Saturday night he could not see me. I had sent every day to inquire for him. His clerk told me today in the forenoon, when I was on my way to call on him, that he was out taking an airing in his carriage, and I might see him. I called about five. He was then taking a nap. I told his servant I would probably call again. I did so about eight. He was sitting on the settee in the parlour. Miss Walkinshaw was with him. She left him when I came in. He seemed to be very low at first. I sat down on the settee by him. I said I was afraid of disturbing him. I would stay only six minutes. Said he: "If you'll let me draw my breath sometimes, you may stay the evening." He asked me how the President was. I said, very well. I mentioned a curious question in law which occurred in a cause of mine before the Court in a Petition this day. A man pursued by a woman as the father of her bastard child, upon a reference to his oath, depones *negative*. He afterwards is seized with remorse when dying. He calls witnesses, and in their presence acknowledges the child, and gives it under his hand. Will not this after-acknowledgement make the man's representatives liable in aliment[3] of the child? Lord Justice Clerk thought it would. Said Lord Kames: "I differ from him. For after a negative oath, the claim is at an end by the agreement of parties. It cannot be revived." "But, my Lord," said I, "it occurs to me this moment that the acknowledgement may be considered in the light of a new obligation." "Yes," said he. "That will do." (I next day stated the case to old Mr. David Graham,[4] who said my Lord and I were wrong, for there could not arise a new obligation out of the same fact, which was finally out of the way by the oath. Upon talking over the equity of the case with him, and the hardship of making it impossible for a man to repent and do justice, he came to be of opinion that the claim might be effectual, for the oath did not operate *ipso jure*[5] as an ex-

[1]Boswell may mean that Donaldson mended or repaired the miniature, which was painted on tile or porcelain. It seems more likely, however, that he now asked Donaldson to improve the portrait, which had been completed in 1776. At any rate, a little over a year later Mrs. Boswell sat to Donaldson again, "for a better miniature, for his own credit." See below, 4 February 1784. The whereabouts of the miniatures is unknown.
[2]Probably a mistake for "Thursday."
[3]Support.
[4]David Graham of Newton, admitted advocate 1727. He died Father of the Bar 26 March 1785.
[5]By the law itself; did not operate automatically expressly to exclude further consideration.

tinction. It was only an exception, and might be renounced by an after-acknowledgement.)

I know not how Lord Kames and I got upon the subject of a future state, or rather how I introduced it. I said it was hard that we were not allowed to have any notion of what kind of existence we shall have. He said there was an impenetrable veil between us and our future state, and being sensible of this, he never attempted to think on the subject, knowing it to be in vain. And he applied his mind to things which he could know. "But," said I, "we may conjecture about it." Said he with that spring of thought, that kind of sally for which he was ever remarkable, "You'll not go to hell for conjecturing."

I told him how Maclaurin had pushed Sir John Pringle at Lord Monboddo's upon the subject, and had asked him what we were to have that could make us wish for a future state: "Shall we have claret, Sir John?" "I don't know but you may, Mr. Maclaurin." "Well," said my Lord, "it is true this body is put into the grave. But may we not have another film, another body, more refined? The ancients," said he, "all describe a future state as having enjoyments similar to what we have here. Let us lay aside the prejudices which we have been taught. Suppose we have other bodies. Why may we not have all the pleasures of which we are capable here? For instance, the pleasure of eating. Why not that, in a more delicate manner?" I mentioned, before he spoke of eating, our being told we are to have music. "And," said he (raising himself with an earnestness while I was all attention, and coming closer to me), "and there is another pleasure"; (I thought, though I divined what he meant clearly enough, that he should speak it out plainly, so waited in silence till he proceeded) "why not have the pleasure of women?" "Why not," cried I, with animation. "There is nothing in reason or revelation against our having all enjoyments sensual and intellectual." I mentioned advances in knowledge, and seeing our friends again and eminent men. He was calm and kindly tonight and seemed to acquiesce quietly in the course of Providence, without any of the enthusiasm of *O praeclarum diem!* [6]

I know not how *evil* was introduced. Said he, "Mandeville was a man of a narrow mind. He maintains private vices to be public benefits. [7] But he might have seen that all evil tends to good." (Here he uttered the superficial wild doctrine upon this which I have read in his *Sketches*,

---

[6] "O glorious day!" (Cicero, *On Old Age*, c. 23. 84). Speaking in the character of the elder Cato, Cicero goes on, "when I shall set out to join that heavenly conclave and company of souls, and depart from the turmoil and impurities of this world" (trans. E. S. Schuckburgh).

[7] In *The Fable of the Bees, or, Private Vices, Public Benefits*, 1714, a poem with extensive prose commentary, Bernard Mandeville represented man as innately selfish and im-

saying that to exist happily without evil man must be a different being from what he is.[8]) I said this kind of thinking was apt to make a man careless of his conduct; at least I could say for myself that when I had got myself drunk or infected venereally I had been apt to think all tended to a greater good. Yet surely it ought to be our study to diminish and prevent vice. He said, "Yes." But the notions of a fatalist must be ever inconsistent.

I told him my father's death had relieved me of the horror I used to have at the act of dying, yet there was something discouraging that one could see no appearance of transition in death. "None to our senses," said he. He seemed to be firm in his belief of future existence. I said to him, "It is curious what a propensity there is in the mind of man to listen to anything like information as to the particulars of a future state. I was all attention to your Lordship just now, as if you had been there and had returned again. And yet you can tell no more about it than I can." I laughed a little at this.

There was in his appearance tonight something that put me in mind of my father when in a calm, serious frame. He quieted me somehow. I told him I frequently could not help thinking my father was alive and that I might go and consult him; and when I was taking care of his improvements at Auchinleck I thought I was doing what he approved; and I wished always to preserve the notion of his seeing what I was about. My grandfather was introduced into the conversation. He repeated to me the pretty story of asking his assistance and how my grandfather came to him and said, "I helped you when you was young. You must help me now when I am old." "And this," said he, "without a blush, quite frank." He also told me again how my grandfather thought it heroism to restore his family, and how he travelled home for sevenpence.[9]

I was so intent on his conversation tonight I let the candles be long without snuffing. So there was a dim, solemn light, which increased

---

moral, but concluded (some few have thought ironically) that his vices, which are hopeless of reform, were essential to public prosperity:

> Millions endeavouring to supply
> Each other's lust and vanity;
> While other millions were employ'd,
> To see their handiworks destroyed (ll. 33–36).

[8]Probably the end of Sketch 1, "Appetite for Society—Origin of National Societies," in *Sketches of the History of Man*, Bk. II, 1774.
[9]From Edinburgh to Auchinleck. James Boswell, the seventh laird (d. 1749), inherited an estate seriously embarrassed by the fifth laird. An advocate educated at Glasgow and Leiden, he built up one of the largest practices of his day, lived frugally, and freed the barony of encumbrance. He also bought back alienated portions of the estate and made additions to it.

my feelings as sitting with a dying man. Yet he was as much Mr. Henry Home, as much Lord Kames as ever. Sometimes death is like a fire going out gradually. Sometimes like a gun going off, when the moment before the explosion all is as entire as ever.

He put to me this curious question, "It is said in the Bible 'GOD created man in His own image, in the image of GOD created He him.'[1] What's the meaning of that?" "I really do not know," said I. "It has often puzzled me. I never read any of the commentators upon it which I might have done. I have no notion what it means. I wish to know your Lordship's interpretation of it." "Why," said he, "you'll think it very simple when you hear it." "What is it?" said I. "It is," said he, "that He has a head, two arms, and two legs." "Do you mean that the Deity has the human form and figure?" "Yes, I do. Plato and Aristotle and the ancient philosophers represented Him so, and we find this in many places of the Bible. For instance, when He appears to Moses He says, 'You may behold my back parts, but nobody ever saw my face but he died.'"[2] "Why," said I, "I like the notion and I have frequently wished it were true, for an aggregate of abstract qualities of extension and light and power and so on cannot be the object of regard and affection. There must be a person. But I am afraid it is not a philosophical idea, for we are told GOD is a spirit extending over all." "He does not extend as space does, and therefore GOD is not space." "But," said I, "if He be of a form and figure, how is He omnipresent?" "He is not omnipresent," said my Lord. "In what manner, and with what rapidity He darts from one part of the universe to another, I cannot tell." This was curious and new to me. I have since learnt that there was a sect of Christian heretics called Anthropomorphites, from ἄνθρωπος (man), and μορφή (figure), who held this notion.[3]

Mrs. Drummond joined us. She talked in metaphor of something very humorously. My Lord said he knew a lady with whom he has talked for two hours at a time, and not a word plain but all figure, and quite clear and lively. I got him to tell who the lady was: Lady Jean Hume, afterwards Nimmo, sister to this Earl of Marchmont, but, my Lord said, much cleverer.[4] I made him laugh really heartily by a droll image. Speaking of a certain lady's excellent conduct in all situations,

[1] Genesis 1: 27.

[2] "And I will take away mine hand, and thou shalt see my back parts: but my face shall not be seen" (Exodus 33: 23).

[3] A sect of Christians, followers of Audius, a Mesopotamian layman, which arose in Syria in the fourth century and spread into Scythia when Audius was banished there in his old age.

[4] The only characterization of Lady Jean that we have found. The younger sister of Hugh, third Earl of Marchmont, she married James Nimmo, Receiver-General of the Excise in Scotland, and died without issue at the age of sixty.

I took particular notice of it. While married to an old, clumsy husband, whose appearance, I said, was a sign hung out stronger than the Saracen's Head or the Turk's Head to invite young men to entertainment, yet she was perfectly free from suspicion.[5] The idea of the Saracen's Head was truly comical. My Lord took sowans and milk. Mrs. Drummond and I supped. I paid him a fine compliment tonight on his variety of writing, from sublime metaphysics to practical farming. I said he was like the poet as described by Shakespeare: "The poet's eye with a fine frenzy,"[6] etc. Mrs. Drummond told me tonight that she was not acquainted with him more than half a year before their marriage. It was never suspected. She was out of his line.[7] The late Countess of Dundonald, who lived in Bishopsland, used to observe him going to visit her in Dickson's Close. He used to go down the next close and come up it to come unperceived.

WEDNESDAY 11 DECEMBER. (Writing the 16). Was very well. Had Colonel Preston, Mr. Richard Lake, etc. to sup. Received an excellent letter from Dr. Johnson.[8]

THURSDAY 12 DECEMBER. (Writing the 16.) My practice at the bar this session seemed much better than expectation. I talked a little insolently. "Now that I don't want money," said I, "I'm determined to

[5]Boswell almost certainly alludes to Lady Elizabeth Erskine, widow successively of two men much older than herself: Walter Macfarlane of Macfarlane, an eminent antiquary, and Vice-Admiral Alexander Colville, seventh Lord Colville of Culross. In his journal for 2 December 1762 Boswell had written of the "absurd" union of an "old clumsy dotard" (Macfarlane) with a "strong young woman of quality" (Lady Elizabeth). In the year of her marriage to Macfarlane, her brother, the sixth Earl of Kellie, had sold all the family estates except the mansion-house. She undoubtedly entered into both unions in order to provide a home for her other brothers and for her unmarried sisters. Boswell at one time thought seriously of marrying Lady Elizabeth; they had remained close friends.

[6]*A Midsummer Night's Dream*, V. i. 12.

[7]Kames was the eldest son of a small, improvident landowner burdened with debts, and he himself, though forty-five and well known, had not yet won preferment at the law. Agatha Drummond's family had a fine estate in Perthshire and wintered in Edinburgh, where she was one of the most charming women in fashionable society. On 29 July 1782 she told Boswell that she probably would not have married Kames if she had known she would inherit Blair-Drummond, but at the time she had a fortune of only £1,000 and he was a rising man. Alexander Fraser Tytler reports her saying on the other hand that she truly loved Kames, who was a tall and animated man, very attractive to women. The best observation of their relationship appears to be Boswell's: "Seldom have I seen a stronger picture of conjugal felicity. I have observed with pleasure the mutual confidence and affection which subsists between them, after having lived together upwards of twenty years. Could I see many more such instances I should have a higher idea of marriage" (Journal, 16 October 1762).

[8]Reporting some improvement in Johnson's health, it counsels Boswell to economy and attention to practical matters. "Let me know the history of your life since your

have it." I meant that I could more easily refute[9] any attempts of agents
to make me labour gratis in causes where it was not charity. I paid a
visit to Lady Auchinleck this forenoon, and was rather pleased with
her conversation; perhaps by contrasting my present independent state
with my former uneasy one. I also sat some time with Sir Philip Ainslie.
DOUGLAS was in town for a day or two. He and I, Sir Alexander Don,
and Sir John Scott dined at Bayle's elegantly.[10] I drank a glass or two
and then port and water. It was genteel company. But I felt it insipid
for want of stronger talk. The Hon. A. Gordon made a very good
remark to me next day, that "sitting in such company is pleasing for
a while; but as when one is sitting with whores, there comes a thought,
'What have I to do here?'" We went and drank tea with Douglas at
Walker's Hotel. I then came home and read law papers.

FRIDAY 13 DECEMBER. (Writing the 19.) Sir Walter Montgomerie-
Cuninghame and his brother Sandy dined with us. In the evening I
met Young Tytler by appointment at Lord Kames's, and supped there.[1]
I had sent my Lord Felltham's *Resolves*. He said, "I wonder how you
could discover from whence you get all your knowledge" (or good
things, or some such phrase, I know not whether ironically or not).
We talked of second sight. He was very dull and fretful tonight. He
told a story of Sir H. Campbell's son being seen before his birth to be
drowned, and that he *was* drowned.[2] I asked him what we were to infer
from this. He gave the common answer of the incredulous, that it was

accession to your estate," Johnson wrote. "How many horses, how many cows, how much
land in your own hand, and what bargains you make with your tenants."

[9] Refuse, a rare usage.

[10] Archibald Douglas was the hero of the great legal action, the Douglas Cause. Fifteen
years earlier Boswell had roused popular sympathy for him by songs, pamphlets, and
newspaper paragraphs, and had been rewarded by being made one of Douglas's counsel
in the latter stages of the action. In two judgements the House of Lords had now
declared Douglas to be really the nephew of the Duke of Douglas and heir to his vast
properties, not a French child stolen or purchased by the Duke's sister and her husband
to impose upon the Duke. The capital letters Boswell assigns to Douglas attest to the
veneration he felt for the antiquity and nobility of that family line. Bayle's was a tavern.

[1] Alexander Tytler, a fellow advocate of long acquaintance raised to the bench in 1802
as Lord Woodhouselee, is styled "Young Tytler" in order to distinguish him from his
father, William Tytler, Writer to the Signet (a solicitor of superior standing), man of
letters, and friend of Lord Kames. Alexander Tytler had published a supplement in
1778 to Kames's digest, *The Decisions of the Court of Session*, and in 1807 brought out
Memoirs of his life and writings. According to his own account, he had declined a
request which Lord Kames made long before this evening to write his life while he
lived and under his own inspection. The appointment for supper suggests that Kames
nevertheless wished to furnish Tytler as well as Boswell with materials.

[2] There can be little doubt that the person actually meant was Sir *James* Campbell of
Ardkinglass. He had nine children but only one son, who was drowned when a boy.

by *chance* the *seer* was right; for that a hundred prophecies which do not come to pass are forgotten; one that does is remembered. I said that where one simple fact happens when foretold, it may be imputed to chance. But when there is a group of circumstances, there *must* be something more. I did not push the argument, as he was quite languid tonight. We supped. He was almost quite silent, and dozed away by us.

SATURDAY 14 DECEMBER. Though it was a cold, frosty morning, he was in the Outer House and called a roll of seven causes, not judging, I believe, but only going through little forms. He looked miserably. I mentioned to him his not being very well last night. He did not like the observation, and I think said he was wearied in the evening. (Writing the 19.) The Rev. Mr. John Macaulay, who had attended Dr. Johnson and me at Inveraray, Mr. Adam Bell, Dr. Gillespie, and Grange dined with us.[3] It was a dinner of duty.

SUNDAY 15 DECEMBER. (Writing the 19.) Heard Dr. Blair in the forenoon and Mr. Walker in the afternoon.[3a] Drank the last of Sir John Pringle's coffee in the afternoon. The children said divine lessons. I supped at Dr. Webster's.

MONDAY 16 DECEMBER. (Writing the 19.) Read a little in Hippocrates in the Advocates' Library for a motto to *The Hypochondriack* No. 63.[4] Lt. David Cuninghame dined with us. In the evening, after a meeting with Sir Walter and Mr. Blane about Sir W.'s affairs,[5] they and Lieutenant David supped with us. It was a tiresome evening.

TUESDAY 17 DECEMBER. (Writing the 23.) Dictated some law and wrote the best part of *The Hypochondriack* No. 63.

WEDNESDAY 18 DECEMBER. (Writing the 23.) John Hud in Hudston had come in last night in the fly to see about James Samson, his brother-in-law, who had deserted from General Gordon of Fyvie's regiment. I assured him I would get him prevented from being sent away till a man was found in his place, on which condition the General had agreed to discharge him. He was now apprehended and on his road to Edinburgh Castle. I dined at the Hon. A. Gordon's with the Earl of Selkirk, his lady, two daughters and son, Miss Mackenzie Hum-

[3]"Poor Macaulay," Lord Macaulay's grandfather, had come under fire from Johnson for audible protest while Johnson held the floor. " 'Mr. Macaulay! Mr. Macaulay! Don't you know it is very rude to cry eh! eh! when one is talking?' " (Journal, 25 October 1773.) Adam Bell was a legal writer, or agent, with whom Boswell was sometimes associated; Dr. Thomas Gillespie had been physician by retainer to Lord Auchinleck in his last years. He also attended Mrs. Boswell.
[3a] The New Church was a collegiate charge (see above, p. 12, n. 7); the Rev. Robert Walker was the other minister.
[4]On hypochondria; the motto, "When the brain is quiet, then is a man wise."
[5]Because of inherited debts and his own mismanagement, Sir Walter appealed to Boswell frequently both for advice and for money.

berston, and Sir James and Miss Hall.[6] All sobriety and genteel manners. I liked it much.

THURSDAY 19 DECEMBER. I do not recollect whether I saw him [Lord Kames] since Saturday. This (I recollect that last night I sat with Mrs. Drummond a good while in her own room. Russell, the surgeon,[7] had told her he was losing ground daily, and she was satisfied there was no hope. She cried, and talked much of his good qualities) forenoon I called and found Mrs. Drummond. A Miss Pringle, niece to Mr. John Pringle, was shown into the room. In a little he came. She rose and met him. He took her by the hand, looked her in the face, and said ludicrously, "Shake not thy hairy locks at me."[7a] She sat down by him. He took her hand again, and said, "Will you not *greet*" (cry) "for me?" She said, "I hope it shall be long before I have to greet for your Lordship." She asked him how he was today. He said, "Very ill this day and every day." He said something which I did not hear distinctly, but heard these words, "Prepare me for the other world." He said I would see her to her carriage, which I did. When I came back, he bid me take a chair and sit opposite to him and Mrs. Drummond, who were on the settee, and close by them. She and I talked. She asked if it disturbed him. He said, "On the contrary." He lay back and seemed feeble and spiritless.

(Writing the 23.) Pleaded with extempore vivacity for the College of Physicians against Dr. Hunter before Lord Justice Clerk and Mr. Swinton, Lord Probationer.[8] Was pleased to find my *Burkeish* talents in vigour. Finished No. 63. Little Jamie's rush[9] pained him much. My practice was better this winter than the last at this time.

FRIDAY 20 DECEMBER. (Writing the 26.) Had Sir Walter and his brothers David and Alexander at dinner, to see the three together. Grange was with us. To see their aunt well recovered was most comfortable. Supped at Lord Kames's. Was shown into his room. He was sitting in his armchair. His clerk was with him, but soon went away.

[6]The Earl and Countess of Selkirk had five living sons and five daughters, one of whom, Helen, was married in 1786 to Sir James Hall, Bt., of Dunglass, later an eminent geologist. Miss Isabella Hall was the niece of the late Sir John Pringle, Bt., and Sir James's cousin once removed. Miss Mackenzie Humberston is Frances, the eldest of four sisters of the Chief of the Clan Mackenzie.

[7]James Russell, Fellow of the Royal College of Surgeons, Edinburgh; later Professor of Clinical Surgery in the University of Edinburgh.

[7a]*Macbeth*, III. iv. 49–50; "never shake/ Thy gory locks at me."

[8]The Royal College of Physicians of Edinburgh claimed payment of ten guineas which Dr. James Hunter had promised towards the building of a library and museum, and £20 of expenses. Decreet was given against Hunter by interlocutor of the Lord Justice Clerk on 24 February 1783.

[9]Rash.

He seemed very spiritless from bodily weakness. I wished much to hear him say something as a dying man. It was unsatisfactory to be with a very old man, and a judge, and perceive nothing venerable, nothing edifying, nothing solemnly pious at the close of life. I mentioned how comfortable my father had been in never having an anxious fear of death, as also how Sir Alexander Dick was perfectly easy, and how Sir John Pringle had been quite different in that respect. I hoped this would have led him to speak of his own way of thinking. He sat silent. I then fairly said, "I believe, my Lord, you have been lucky enough to have always an amiable view of the Deity, and no doubt of a future state." He said nothing. I said the doctrine of the eternity of hell's torments did harm. "No," said he. "Nobody believes it." I could make nothing out of him tonight. I rose to go away. He asked me to stay supper. I said I was afraid of intruding (or being troublesome, or some such expression). He cried with keenness, "O GOD!" I went into the parlour and was a little with Mrs. Drummond. When he came, he said to her with his usual vivacity, "My dear, Mr. Boswell was going away because you did not come to him." He spoke, I think, nothing, till, after trying some sago[1] at a little table set by the settee, he said, "Tell Hannah to make me a little porridge." He had that, and took as small a tasting as of the sago. He then called for rusks and put some into milk and eat a very little. He said, "I have made out a supper *put* and *row*."[2] It was a dreary novelty to see Lord Kames sitting silent.

SATURDAY 21 DECEMBER. Just saw him in the Court of Session like a ghost, shaking hands with Lord Kennet in the chair, and Lords Alva and Eskgrove patting him kindly on the back as if for the last time. (Writing the 26.)[3] The session rose for the Christmas recess. My wife and I dined and drank tea at old Lady Grant's.[4] I paid a visit to Lady Auchinleck. I called [on Lord Kames] in the evening. Mrs. Drummond told me he had been very weak since he came in from his airing and had been in bed. She desired I would go in and see him. I first sent in the servant to tell I was there. He desired I would wait half a minute and he would come into the parlour. Mrs. Drummond came there and was with me till he was supported by his servant, Samuel, while he moved along like a spectre and was set down on the settee. He looked miserably ill. I sat down by him. He sat silent. I felt no power to speak. At last I said, "My Lord, you show a remarkable instance of philosophy, as it is called; practical philosophy—patience."

[1] A pudding made of a starch by that name and commonly fed to the sick.
[2] With difficulty, with much ado.
[3] The journal is resumed for three sentences.
[4] The widow of Sir Archibald Grant of Monymusk.

"Oh," said he, with a fretful tone, "I cannot bear you; flattering me when I'm ———." I did not hear what followed, he spoke so indistinctly. I told him I was very sincere. I went to the opposite settee and sat by Mrs. Drummond. He seemed to be very uneasy. He bid the bell be rung, and when his servant came, had his legs laid up on the settee, and remained in a listless state till I went away, which I did in a few minutes, after shaking hands with him and saying, "Good night, my Lord. GOD bless you." His servant told me Dr. Cullen said tonight he should not be surprised if he was dead in the morning.[5]

SUNDAY 22 DECEMBER. (Writing the 26.) Passed the forenoon with Mr. Blane and Mr. Alexander Mackenzie[6] about Sir Walter, who was in danger of being apprehended for debt. In the afternoon heard Dr. Blair preach to Lady Derby.[7] Dined and drank tea at Lady Dundonald's. I called [on Lord Kames] between three and four. Mrs. Drummond said he was weak as yesterday, and in bed, and she desired I would go in and inquire for him. He liked it. I went to his bedside and said, "As I was passing by, I just called to inquire for you, my Lord. I am going to dine with your old friend Lady Dundonald." "Not at that time of day!" said he. "Yes," said I, "it is after three o'clock. How are you, my Lord?" "Oh, dinna' ask foolish questions. I hope to be better in the evening." "Then in the evening I will have the honour to attend you." I then went and dined and drank tea at Lady Dundonald's, with whom I talked of him, and begged she would give me something to tell that would divert him. She did so. I called again on him and was shown to his bedside. "How are you now, my Lord?" He recollected clearly his having desired I would not ask him, and catching me at it again, he said, "Have you been debauching with Lady Dundonald?" "No," said I, and immediately gave him *un précis,* as the French say, of what had passed. "She says she used to get suppers from Mr. Harry Home when you and Succoth lived together in James's Court"[8] ("These are old

---

[5] William Cullen, a kind and attentive physician distinguished by acute perception and sound judgement. He was successively Professor of Medicine in the University of Glasgow, Professor of Chemistry and of the Theory of Physic in the University of Edinburgh, President of the Edinburgh College of Physicians, and Fellow of the Royal Society.

[6] Both Writers to the Signet.

[7] Boswell is being playful. See below in this paragraph, "I told him that I had heard Dr. Blair preach this afternoon to a very crowded audience, Lady Derby being in church." "Lady Betty Hamilton" of the *Tour to the Hebrides* (Journal, 24, 25 October 1773) married the Earl of Derby in 1774, but he had turned her out because of an intrigue with the Duke of Dorset. The prominence of the families concerned and the notoriety of the separation made her a marked figure in any audience.

[8] A fashionable "land" or multiple tenements of flats erected in Edinburgh between 1725 and 1727, still occupied by persons of good position (Boswell and his wife had

stories," or, "That is an old story," said he), "and you gave her the finest Hermitage wine[9] she ever tasted. When you opened the bottle, it scented the room. She says you used to have her mother[1] there and her cousin Betty Dalrymple and Jenny Craufurd, a very pretty woman. Does your Lordship remember giving any present to Lady Dundonald?" He said no. "But she tells me she has two presents which she got from you: Dryden's *Fables*, which she will keep as long as she lives, and a set buckle for a girdle.[2] I said to her, 'It seems there has been more courtship between you and him than the world knows. It was coming close to come to the girdle.' " (This tickled his fancy. He put out his cold right hand and chucked me under the chin, as if he had said, "You're a wag.") "She bid me tell you that now when you are not able to attend the Board of Trustees, you must give them your directions or they will go all wrong. You know she is a great manufacturer, especially of linen." All that I told him was literally reported from my conference with the Countess. He did not speak to me any more. He lay with the same countenance which he has had for several years, though somewhat emaciated; and while I looked at him, I could not help wondering why he did not answer me as usual. To perceive Lord Kames, who used to be all alive, now quite quiescent, was a change to which my mind could not easily agree. I told him that I had heard Dr. Blair preach this afternoon to a very crowded audience, Lady Derby being in church, and that he gave us an excellent sermon on our years being as a tale that is told. I sat a little longer by him. He twice put out his hand and took mine cordially. I regretted that he did not say one word as a dying man. Nothing edifying, nothing pious. His lady told me he had not said a word to her of what he thought of himself at present. I sat a long time with her. Mr. Sandilands, his agent,[3] came. And soon after, my Lord to my surprise was supported into the room and sat down on a settee. But he did not speak and seemed to be very

---

made it their city residence since 1771). Kames and his cousin John Campbell, younger of Succoth, another aspiring advocate, were among the earliest if not the original inhabitants. Kames withdrew from the "pretty riotous and expensive" fellowship of the Court when he was faced with debts of £300 (*Private Papers of James Boswell from Malahide Castle*, 1932, xv. 272), but he continued to live there privately, probably until his marriage.

[9]A French wine produced from vineyards on the Hill of Hermitage (twelve miles north of Valence), so called from a ruin on the summit supposed to have been a hermit's cell.

[1]Elizabeth Myreton, daughter of Sir Andrew Myreton, Bt., of Gogar, in the county of Midlothian, and wife of Archibald Stuart of Torrance.

[2]A buckle set with stones.

[3]Matthew Sandilands, Writer to the Signet. He had been an apprentice to Walter Scott, the novelist's father.

uneasy, so in a few moments he made a sign to his servant and was led away. I came home. The children said divine lessons in the evening.

MONDAY 23 DECEMBER. Breakfasted and dined with Sir Thomas Dundas.[4] Drank more wine than for some months, but not too much. Evening had Sir W. and Lady Forbes,[5] etc., at cards and supper. Was very pleasant.

TUESDAY 24 DECEMBER. (Writing the 26.) I visited M. Dupont and Miss Scott. Grange and I dined at Prestonfield. I drank tea at Mr. Robert Boswell's, and then paid a visit to Miss Gray.[6]

WEDNESDAY 25 DECEMBER. (Writing the 26.) Breakfasted doubly after lying comfortably in bed, quite in Christmas frame, as with Temple in youth.[7] Had a message from Mr. Drummond,[8] who had come last night. Went to him. Was pleased to see him in tears for his dying father. Was confidentially consulted as to his funeral.[9]

FRIDAY 27 DECEMBER.[1] West in fly.

SATURDAY 28 DECEMBER. Dernconner breakfasted. Walked much, and took note of trees in farmyards. Lady Crawford's.

SUNDAY 29 DECEMBER. To Auchinleck Church.

MONDAY 30 DECEMBER. Planting limes,[2] etc. Fingland and Bruce Campbell dined. Sir John's.

TUESDAY 31 DECEMBER. Laying out new dike, Mains roading. Coilsfield.

[4] M.P. for Stirlingshire since 1768.

[5] Sir William Forbes, Bt., of Pitsligo, was head of the most distinguished banking-house in Edinburgh, Forbes, Hunter and Company. A long-time friend and confidant as well as Boswell's banker, Forbes was later named executor of his estate and one of the three executors given charge of his manuscripts. A significant batch of them, including the *London Journal*, was found at Fettercairn, which had been the home of Forbes's son.

[6] Boswell's cousin, son of the late Dr. John Boswell, and a Writer to the Signet; and Miss Jane Gray, like Miss Hall one of the late Sir John Pringle's "dull women" (Journal, 13 June 1781).

[7] William Johnson Temple, an Englishman from Berwick upon Tweed, Boswell's class-mate in Edinburgh College, had introduced him to Anglican worship by taking him to the English chapel in Carrubber's Close, Christmastide, 1755. Boswell had been charmed. Temple was now vicar of St. Gluvias, Cornwall, where he remained the rest of his life. Boswell still considered him his most intimate friend, though they seldom met.

[8] Lord Kames's only son, George Home Drummond (see above, p. 20, n. 9).

[9] Kames died on the 27th, on which day Boswell set out for Auchinleck. He did not return for the funeral; indeed, as the burial was in the graveyard of the parish church of Blair-Drummond, Perthshire, there may have been no service in Edinburgh.

[1] No record has survived for 26 December.

[2] Linden-trees.

1783

WEDNESDAY 1 JANUARY. (Writing the 14.) Rose early; a fine frosty morning. Left Coilsfield with youthful ideas of that social family, and rode briskly to Rozelle. Found there Lord Crawford, whom I had not seen for seven years, and his brother Bourtreehill.[3] Talked of going home after breakfast. But the Countess and Lady Mary asked me to stay in so obliging a manner that I passed all New Year's Day there, and was really happy; only when alone with the Countess, was hurt by perceiving her distress on account of her son Bute, who, it was feared, was lost in the *Centaur*.[4] Was sober and just as I could wish. Knockroon and Bailie Neill were both with me about business, of which I found myself sufficiently capable.

THURSDAY 2 JANUARY. (Writing the 14.) Rode home to breakfast; still a fine frost. Had James Bruce along with me, while I (writing 15 January) took a note of trees round my farmyards, marking what were to grow and what to be cut. This amused me much. I this day finished my survey of them in that part of the barony which lies to the south of the *via sacra*, as my father used to call the kirk road. I then sat as preses of a meeting of heritors and farmers in the church which had been very properly called by Mr. Dun to consider of securing meal for the people, particularly of the village, as an apprehension had been taken that it would be carried out of the parish and sold at a distance. He suggested that each of us, according to our stock of it, should engage to have a certain number of bolls[5] kept to be sold at the market price, which was then 15*d*. I subscribed for forty bolls; and the subscription in all amounted to above eighty. I had three bolls ready at Brigend Mill, which I ordered to be sold out directly at 14*d*., but declaring publicly that this was not to be any rule to the farmers, who were to have the market price. There was something comfortable in

[3]Between 1776 and 1779 Lord Crawford had been an officer in the 51st Foot, commanded by Lord Eglinton and on duty in Minorca. He and his brother Bute Lindsay then served as captains in the 92nd Foot, which was on duty between 1780 and 1782 in Ireland, the West Indies, and England. It was disbanded at the peace in 1783. Bourtreehill, who took his style from the Countess's family estate, is her second son, Robert Lindsay.
[4]See above, 9 November 1782, and the account of the wreck, below, 8 May 1783.
[5]A measure in Scotland generally equivalent to six imperial bushels of grain and 140 pounds or ten stone English of oatmeal.

thus quieting the minds of the people. I then rouped my farm of Dernlaw for a year in grass, at Lapraik's,[6] and got within a few pounds of the rent paid for it in the ordinary state of a farm. Then the Laird of Logan, Old Mr. John Boswell, some others, and myself dined at Mr. Dun's. After tea Mr. Halbert, the session-clerk, came and I revised his register. Then I walked home, accompanied by Mr. Millar; and the evening was concluded as usual most decently with family worship and a sober supper.

FRIDAY 3 JANUARY. (Writing the 15.) Mounted early, rode to Fairlie; the Laird not at home. Went on to Eglinton, where he was, and where I was to dine. Reached it about ten—excellent alertness. Found Fairlie, Captain Peebles, and Williamwood,[7] whom I had never seen before. I liked him much. The Baron of Lochrig[8] also appeared. Captain John Fergusson arrived and paid a forenoon visit. The Earl made his appearance about noon. He and I and Fairlie walked near to Irvine. His Lordship was very glad to see me. I had a plain conversation with him on the politics of the county. I told him he might depend upon my assistance in (writing 19 January) his interest, and I desired to know if he was again to set up Col. Hugh Montgomerie.[9] He said the Colonel was to stand. He said he was much obliged to me, and he really seemed to be keen. I told him that though his Lordship were not to support my friend Hugh, I would stand by him if he had but a wish for being Member. But in case of his not choosing it, I intended to offer myself. I told the Earl that since I had the influenza last summer I really was not able to drink; and if it was disagreeable to him that a man should sit by him without drinking, I would take my horse and go away. He said I should do just as I pleased. I paid a visit before dinner to my old acquaintance, Mrs. Reid the housekeeper. At dinner there was quite a comfortable company; just the Earl, the Laird of Fairlie, the Baron of Lochrig, and Knockroon and myself; neither grandees, nor numbers to make his Lordship hold himself up in state. He was quite cheerful and easy, and at my request sung *Sheriffmuir*, "Coming through the broom," and "Row me o'er the lea-rig."[1] I had some old

[6] Probably a public house in Auchinleck village.
[7] James Maxwell, whose seat was in Lanarkshire.
[8] Matthew Arnot Stewart, whose seat was a "goodly old mansion . . . well sheltered by plantations" in Ayrshire (James Paterson, *History of the Counties of Ayr and Wigton*, 1866, III, ii. 604).
[9] Cousin to the Earl, and later his successor. Montgomerie won election to Parliament in 1780 with Boswell's active support, but his opponent, Sir Adam Fergusson (the candidate of Henry Dundas, Lord Advocate and political manager of Scotland), appealed to the Court of Session and a Select Committee of the House of Commons, and was declared elected.
[1] There are several songs on Sheriffmuir, the best known being one that Burns imitated

Malaga; and finding I really had liberty to drink as I pleased, my heart dilated, and I drank two bottles all but three glasses. We then played *vingt-et-un* till supper, at which I did my part decently enough; but being sleepy with my potion, went to bed as soon as the cloth was taken away.

SATURDAY 4 JANUARY. (Writing the 19.) Awaked very ill, and was somewhat vexed that I had not been able to maintain my sobriety even at Eglinton.[2] It was a wet morning. Fairlie and Knockroon went away before I got up. I had some tea, and then followed them to Fairlie, where I breakfasted; then went to Riccarton to a meeting of the tutors and curators of Treesbanks;[3] dined at Mr. Bruce Campbell's, and then went to Loudoun, where I found the excellent Earl, and the Laird of Dunlop and the Major with him.[4] Was comfortable here, and much pleased to see little Lady Flora, a fine, healthful child.[5] Miss Bell MacLeod and Mrs. Vernon were here.[6] After tea I played whist, and after supper drank very little. Was glad to find no continuation of a drinking disposition. Thought I should be often at this good Place, where I was truly happy.

SUNDAY 5 JANUARY. (Writing the 19.) Being resolved to appear at my own parish church, I had chocolade early and set out in good

---

in *The Battle of Sherramuir*. "Coming through the broom at e'en" is the first line of *The Silken-Snooded Lassie*. The old song with the refrain "Row me o'er the lea-rig, my ain kind dearieo" (row = roll; lea-rig = the unploughed ridge between two cultivated fields) is now known in the respectable version by Robert Fergusson, "Will ye gang o'er the lea-rig?" Three years before this Boswell had written in his journal that he would almost have been willing to suffer a headache if he could hear Lord Eglinton sing "Row me o'er the lea-rig" again.

[2]Notorious as a "den of drunkenness," to quote Boswell (Journal, 10 November 1778).

[3]"Tutors": legal guardians of girls under twelve and of boys under fourteen; "curators": legal guardians of children beyond those ages but under twenty-one. David and George Campbell, twelve and fifteen years old respectively, were the orphaned sons of James Campbell of Treesbank, and of Mrs. Boswell's sister, Mary. Boswell was warm and attentive to his charges.

[4]James Mure Campbell, fifth Earl of Loudoun, had succeeded within the year to the title and debt-ridden estates of his cousin, John Campbell, the fourth Earl, Commander-in-Chief for one unsatisfactory year of all the British forces in North America. Major Alexander Dunlop was a guardian of the young Campbells.

[5]Her mother, the former Flora MacLeod (the elegant, good-humoured daughter of the Laird of Raasay, in whom Johnson found no fault except that "her head was too high-dressed"—Journal, 11 September 1773), died after giving birth to her, 2 September 1780. Mrs. Boswell had gone to a village ten miles west of Edinburgh to get a nurse for the infant, and even lent her own daughter Betsy's nurse during the emergency.

[6]Isabel, the late Mrs. Mure Campbell's younger sister; of Mrs. Vernon we know only that Flora MacLeod had lodged with her in Edinburgh in 1775.

time; a fine morning. Called on Mr. Auld at Mauchline and engaged him to be with me at four o'clock. Alighted when I had passed the Howford bridge, and having ordered my horses home, walked to Willockstown, which I had never seen, and conversed with William Murdoch, the tenant, whom I found to be a sensible, candid man. Then went by the Tenshillingside and visited old John Colville,[7] whom I had placed in a good house there in his eighty-ninth year. He was lying in bed and conversed very distinctly, and told me it was the best house he had ever been in. I also looked in upon Quintin Dun, who was not well. My heart was calmly benevolent. I went by the turnpike and the Old House, and was happy as in my early years, with the addition of the loftiness of being Laird. I called on James Bruce, who walked so far[8] with me. Then had breakfast, shifted, and was made happy with an agreeable letter from my dear wife. Then took fresh horses (old Browning for myself) and rode to church. Mr. Millar preached. Had a cordial short conversation with Mr. Dun; and Mr. John Boswell, Senior, and Mr. Millar rode home with me. Mr. Auld arrived; and we passed the evening in most decent and agreeable sociality, quite in the style of the family. Mr. Auld said prayers, and mentioned those of this family in former generations. I was just as I wished to be. I was quite satisfied with my character and conduct at present. It was what would have pleased my father and my grandfather. May I ever behave in like manner at the seat of my ancestors!

MONDAY 6 JANUARY. (Writing the 19.) Let me write shorter. I had received so polite a card from Lord Dumfries, I wished to breakfast with him today. But so many of my tenants came about me, I did not get away till about eleven. I paid him and the Countess a short visit; then called on Mr. George Reid, whom I must see every time I am in the country; then rode to Ayr and dined at Knockroon's with Dr. Campbell.[1] Visited Lady Cunninghame; drank tea with John Webster. Met on business with Garallan and Mr. James Fergusson.[2] Then went to Lady Crawford's. But found she had received sad accounts of her son Bute being lost, and was confined to her room. Would not go in to Lord Crawford, etc., who were there, but went back to Ayr quite dreary, and resolved to sit all night by myself till bedtime. Next morning

[7] A retired servant on the estate.

[8] A considerable distance. This usage, which appears frequently in the journals, was hardly idiosyncratic, but we have not found it reported in any historical dictionary or history of the English language.

[1] The Ayrshire physician who attended Mrs. Boswell in her last illness and outlived her by only nine days.

[2] Patrick Douglas of Garallan was a surgeon and neighbour, and Fergusson a "writer" at Ayr. For Boswell's business with them, see below, 18 and 25 February 1783.

early Dr. Campbell was to go with me by Straiton to Craigengillan's. I tried a bottle of perry,[3] which put some spirit into me; then sat an hour with Lady Cunninghame, who had Miss Whitefoord of Dunduff with her. Was a little relieved. But returned to the King's Arms to indulge melancholy. Luckily for me, Knockroon joined me, and his contentment, and saying our own distresses were enough for us, and some good veal cutlets and warm port with spice, made me very comfortable. Unnecessary sadness is irrational. My melancholy could do Lady Crawford no good. She did not see me, to be soothed by it.

TUESDAY 7 JANUARY. (Writing the 21.) It was a rainy morning. But Dr. Campbell and I rode briskly along. It soon faired, and I had a most agreeable ride with him, quite new to me after we passed Dalrymple bridge, up the Water of Girvan by Glencaird.[4] One purpose I had this morning was to view Sir John Whitefoord's old family seat, Blairquhan.[5] I was much pleased with my ride, and the ancient house and large plane- and ash-trees at this Place delighted my ancient baron soul. We breakfasted at Straiton, and I viewed the church and churchyard, which is uncommonly spacious and has several old trees in it. Got to Berboth to dinner. Craigengillan huzzaed when he saw me, and I returned the jovial shout. The day passed heartily, and I had the happiness to be assured that his beautiful daughter should go with me to Auchinleck, as I was to conduct her to our house at Edinburgh.

WEDNESDAY 8 JANUARY. (Writing the 21.) Dr. Campbell went away betimes. I passed the forenoon in taking down from Craigengillan's dictating a number of particulars of his life, which for good sense, activity, and prosperity is truly remarkable. I had formerly taken down some anecdotes of it. Captain McAdam[6] came before dinner. The day passed as heartily as yesterday. I was in sound, cheerful spirits, just as I could wish to be.

THURSDAY 9 JANUARY. (Writing the 21.) A terrible morning; wind, hail, thunder, and lightning. It grew better, and I set out with Miss McAdam on horseback through the moors. Captain McAdam went with us till the road to New Cumnock struck off. Wind and rain came on, and we were wet to the skin. Craigengillan's servant Gilbert, a Cumnock man, was so excellent a guide that there seemed no difficulty in the moor road. I sent forward William Lennox. We passed through

---

[3] A beverage resembling cider made from the juice of pears.
[4] An alternative form of Cloncaird Castle, a seat on Girvan Water, near Maybole.
[5] Sir John later lost it (as Dr. Campbell had lost Wellwood, his family estate at Muirkirk) as a consequence of the crash in 1772 of Douglas, Heron and Company, the Ayr bank, in which he was a partner.
[6] Identity uncertain. Quintin McAdam, Craigengillan's only son, was now about fifteen years old.

Lord Dumfries's Place to have a short road, and when we got to Auchinleck, things were pretty comfortable, so that my beautiful charge and I passed the afternoon and evening very agreeably. I was vain of such a trust. I recollect this as one of the most pleasing days of my life: the certainty of being undisturbed by company; looking at books, medals, etc., with a sweet creature; in short a group of good ideas. She told me since she had also such a recollection.

FRIDAY 10 JANUARY. (Writing the 21.) After an early breakfast, had a chaise from Cumnock which drove us there. I was detained by several of my tenants a good while. We then had all the fly secured, and after a very good journey got to my house in Edinburgh about eleven at night. It was comfortable to me to be with my wife and children again.

SATURDAY 11 JANUARY. (Writing the 21.) The day passed I know not well how. Grange and several of our young friends dined with us.

SUNDAY 12 JANUARY. (Writing the 21.) At home in the forenoon waiting till it should fair, that I might go to Duddingston; but the rain continued. Heard Dr. Blair in the afternoon. Paid a visit to Lady Auchinleck. Supped at Dr. Webster's. Nobody there but old Mr. John McLure.[7]

MONDAY 13 JANUARY. (Writing the 21.) Dr. Webster and I dined at Lady Dundonald's. Mr. Callender from Quebec there, who talked a great deal, and gave us very distinct information about Canada. Dr. Webster and Grange supped with us.

TUESDAY 14 JANUARY. (Writing the 21.) Dr. Webster and I dined at Commissioner Cochrane's, where we again met Mr. Callender, as also his father, Mr. Callender, Clerk of Session. The Commissioner's gentlemanly good sense pleased me. But I was sorry to think he was so old, and when he shivered a little, he said it was a coldness before death.

WEDNESDAY 15 JANUARY. (Writing the 21.) Grange dined with us. I began to have a little return of bad spirits.

THURSDAY 16 JANUARY. (Writing the 21.) After making my appearance in the Court of Session, where I had nothing to do today, I went to Lady Colville's and took a second breakfast, Lord Kellie, who was come from Fife, having called on me.[8] My spirits were pretty good. But the enamel of my sound mind was a little broken. I paid a visit at Mr. Wellwood's. Missed Sir Charles Preston and Miss Preston.[9] Visited

[7] A writing-master and accountant, now eighty years old.
[8] Archibald, seventh Earl of Kellie, made his home with his sister, Lady Colville (see above, p. 39, n. 5).
[9] Robert Wellwood of Garvock, advocate, was married to Mary, sister of Sir Charles Preston, Bt., of Valleyfield, Fife. Boswell held the Valleyfield family in special esteem

Colonel Montgomerie. Wrote a part of *The Hypochondriack* No. 64.[1] Dined at Mr. George Wallace's. Not as I could wish.

FRIDAY 17 JANUARY. (Writing the 21.) Finished, I think, No. 64. The Court of Session was irksome to me. Old Mar[2] came to me in the afternoon and absurdly opposed my writing Dr. Johnson's life, against whom he had the most ignorant Scotch prejudice. He and the Rev. James Cochrane drank tea with us. I waited by invitation on Mrs. Drummond, who was anxious about my scheme of writing her husband's life, which I however resolved should not be done in a hurry. I could not sup with her, as I was busy with law. There was a dreariness in the thought that Lord Kames was gone, while I sat in his house. Miss McAdam is so sweet and amiable a part of our family that I cannot sufficiently express my happiness at having her with us. My wife is now in as good health and looks as I ever saw her. Poor little James is miserably distressed with a scorbutic disorder, but Mr. Wood[3] declares it not dangerous. Veronica is a day-boarder with Mrs. Billingsley. I am pleased in assisting her to learn French.

SATURDAY 18 JANUARY. (Writing the 21.) To what purpose waste time in writing a journal of so insipid a life? I had a cold and hoarseness, but would not be absent from the annual dinner of Mundell's scholars, at which I got into better spirits than I could have imagined. I sat by Mr. Ilay Campbell, who had in the most obliging manner given me his opinion in writing upon my father's settlements.[4] I half resolved to drink pretty freely on so merry an occasion, but found my constitution so altered in that respect, I really could not. Ilay Campbell said this meeting grew better every year. I came home about nine.

SUNDAY 19 JANUARY. (Writing on the 23.) Had a hoarseness and sore throat, having been troubled with a cold some days. Lay in bed

---

and affection. Sir Charles's parents had protected his mother (Lady Preston was her aunt), and had treated Boswell himself with parental solicitude when relations with Lord Auchinleck were strained. Miss Preston, who also figures frequently in the journals, was Sir Charles's sister.

[1] On change.

[2] James Erskine of Mar, advocate and Knight Marischal of Scotland, now in his sixty-ninth year, was Boswell's third cousin once removed.

[3] "Lang Sandy" Wood, Boswell's friend as well as medical practitioner to his family, was also a friend of Robert Burns. Wood was consulted when Sir Walter Scott became lame in his early childhood.

[4] Although Boswell had hated James Mundell's school, and left it at the age of eight, the journals record almost perfect attendance from 1772 to 1786 at the annual dinner-meeting of the association formed after the schoolmaster's death in 1762. Many prominent men attended the reunion. Ilay Campbell was appointed Solicitor-General in the spring of this year, Lord Advocate in 1784, and Lord President of the Court of Session in 1789, when he assumed the style of Lord Succoth.

all forenoon. Was not in a good frame, but kept myself quiet. Rose at dinner-time. Miss Preston and Sir William Augustus Cunynghame sat awhile with us. I read today two of Mr. Carr's sermons[5] and the first volume of Miss Burney's *Cecilia*. In the evening the children said divine lessons. Sir Charles and Colonel Preston and Sir W. A. Cunynghame supped with us.

MONDAY 20 JANUARY. (Writing the 23.) Dictated some law tolerably, but with no relish. Supped by earnest invitation with Mrs. Drummond; read her a part of my notes for her husband's life, and was shown his and her settlements. Had visited the Hon. A. Gordon before I went to her. Was sadly impressed with a conviction of the transient nature of human life with all its concerns and occupations.

TUESDAY 21 JANUARY. (Writing the 23.) Had little to do. Lady Colville, Lady Anne Erskine, Lord Kellie and the Hon. Andrew dined and drank tea with us.[6] I was not in high spirits, and did not much enjoy the day.

WEDNESDAY 22 JANUARY. (Writing 1 February.) Nothing to mark but that Miss Christy Hart[7] supped with us, which amused me.

THURSDAY 23 JANUARY. (Writing 1 February.) Grange dined with us. I was pretty well.

FRIDAY 24 JANUARY. (Writing 1 February.) Drank tea with Mrs. Mingay at her particular request. Had no animation such as I could wish. Have this week visited several times the Hon. A. Gordon, confined by a sore leg.

SATURDAY 25 JANUARY. (Writing 1 February.) Could not refuse an invitation to dine with poor Crosbie, with whom I had passed many a jovial and instructive hour in his better days, but who was now ruined in his circumstances and married to a strumpet.[8] We had with us a

[5] Two volumes of the sermons of the late Rev. George Carr, senior clergyman at the Episcopal Chapel, Edinburgh, had been brought out by Sir William Forbes in 1778. Moderate and charitable, though they preached regulation of all the appetites, they went into eight editions by 1796.

[6] Andrew Erskine, a former army officer and a poet, of Boswell's own age and hypochondriac disposition, had been a close friend since 1761, but they had drifted apart in recent years. Like Lord Kellie and their sister, Lady Anne, Erskine was unmarried and made his home with Lady Colville.

[7] The daughter of the minister of Kirkinner, Wigtownshire.

[8] Andrew Crosbie, the brilliant, fearless, and witty advocate supposed by some to have been the prototype of Counsellor Pleydell in *Guy Mannering*, was a partner in Douglas, Heron, and one of the principal hands, it was believed, in the speculative transactions which ruined him and many others. Always an independent but dissipated man, he became an alcoholic, and as his practice declined, he estranged himself from many of his old friends. After his fall he married a woman "of more than dubious character" (*Scotland and Scotsmen*, 1888, i. 450–451, 458). Though dunned on all sides, Crosbie

Major Poynton who could tell us about the North American Indians,[9] Mr. John Donaldson, the painter, and Mr. Anderson, Remembrancer of Exchequer. It was awkward and humiliating to see Crosbie in this state. Dr. Brown (Joannes Bruno)[1] came after Poynton went away, and we talked away tolerably. I drank tea at Princes Street Coffee-house. Lord Crawford, Colonel Montgomerie, and Mr. John Hunter supped with us.

SUNDAY 26 JANUARY. (Writing 2 February.) Grange and I heard the Hon. and Rev. James Cochrane preach in the Old English Chapel. I heard Dr. Webster in the afternoon on "I will be to them a father,"[2] etc. I drank tea at Mrs. Preston's with Veronica. The children said divine lessons. I supped at Dr. Webster's.

MONDAY 27 JANUARY. (Writing 2 February.) Breakfasted with Baron Gordon. Heard him read my first *Hypochondriack* on saving money, of which he highly approved. I left him it and the next, and the three on death, to read.[3] Found Lord Cassillis at Dunn's Hotel, Lord Dumfries with him. Was glad to find him easy with me as usual, having heard that he was offended at a little jocular song I had joined with Sundrum in making upon his Lordship and the Miss Coopers, of which indeed I was the inventor.[4] But it would have been weak in him to be seriously angry, and I should have been really sorry. I called at Lady Auchinleck's, she out. Sat a little with Miss Boswell.[5] Sat a little at Miss Ords'.[6] Then visited Lady Glencairn, with whom I had a good conversation (had called at Lord Alva's, who was not at home), then visited Commissioner Cochrane, who had been ill, but was better. Felt

---

fitted up and occupied his magnificent house in St. Andrew Square, which had barely been roofed-in when Douglas, Heron stopped payment.

[9] He had served with General Wolfe at the Battle of Quebec and was now a major in the army and a captain in the 21st Regiment of Foot.

[1] The author of *Elementa Medicinae* and founder of the famous Brunonian system, which convulsed the medical schools for decades and caused him to be ostracized and impoverished. Brown maintained that diseases indicated debility rather than excessive strength and condemned the "lowering" treatment then in vogue.

[2] Hebrews 1: 5.

[3] Nos. 56 and 57; 14–16. Cosmo Gordon was a Baron (judge) in the Court of Exchequer, which tried cases relating to customs, excise, and other matters concerning crown revenue.

[4] See above, 7 November 1782.

[5] Lady Auchinleck's sister Margaret.

[6] Possibly "Miss Ord's." Boswell omitted the apostrophe. The sentence is a cramped interlinear addition. The late Robert Ord, Chief Baron of the Scottish Exchequer, had six daughters. Two of them, Margaret and Elizabeth (usually called "Betsy"), were certainly unmarried at this time. Nancy, with whom David Hume was reported to be deeply smitten, may also still have been at home.

that the exercise of walking and variety of visiting cleared my mind of the gloom and languor which had for some time distressed me. My table was now clear. I had not one paper to write. In the evening Sir Walter Montgomerie-Cuninghame supped with us.

TUESDAY 28 JANUARY. (Writing 2 February.) My mind was again cloudy and listless. I looked back with wonder and wishfulness on my healthful state of mind last autumn and this winter till after my return from Ayrshire, which I had flattered myself was to be permanent. Sir Walter, Grange, and Mr. James Loch[7] dined with us. Sir Walter stayed tea and then came the Hon. and Rev. James Cochrane, whom I kept to supper, though I was in such want of spirits that I not only had difficulty to speak a little, and affect attention, but was obliged to go for a little and lie down on my bed, just for a kind of relief from teasing pain.

WEDNESDAY 29 JANUARY. (Writing 2 February.) My wife and I and Miss McAdam and Sir Walter dined at Lady Auchinleck's; Miss Preston, etc., there. I was dull, but conducted myself sufficiently well. I was tenderly affected while I viewed the furniture which I had used to see in my honoured father's time; and when I passed the door of the room where he died, my heart was touched with a tremulous awe. My client Killantringan[8] supped with us. Sir Walter and his brother David came in late and also supped, and assisted in entertaining him, for which I was not very fit. During this hypochondria *Cecilia* entertained me.

THURSDAY 30 JANUARY. (Writing 2 February.) Called on Lord Eglinton, who had been two nights in town. He walked to my house with me and saw my wife. I then called with him at Lord Chief Baron's;[9] not at home. My wife and I, Miss McAdam, and Colonel Montgomerie dined at Lord Justice Clerk's; Lord Kellie, Lady Colville, etc., there. A great feast, and his conversation hearty and animated. Sir Walter supped with us. Had some regret at not keeping the day. But thought it rather long.[1]

---

[7]Writer to the Signet, in 1786 made H. M. Remembrancer to the Court of Exchequer (the officer who collected debts due to the sovereign). Boswell and he had been well acquainted at least since 1768.

[8]John MacMikin, Laird of Killantringan, of whom we know only that he was one of the original partners of Douglas, Heron and that he died in August 1789.

[9]Sir James William Montgomery, called the "Father of the County" (Peeblesshire) because of his outstanding agricultural improvements. The Lord Chief Baron headed the Court of Exchequer.

[1]Rather long, that is, to continue a fast on the anniversary of the execution of Charles I. Johnson thought the observance might be allowed to lapse after a decent period of time.

FRIDAY 31 JANUARY. (Writing 10 February.) My wife and I and Miss McAdam dined and drank tea at Lady Colville's. Her Ladyship was ill and did not appear. Sir William and Lady Forbes were there. I drank more than was necessary. I supped at Maclaurin's with Baron Gordon, Cullen, Drimnin, and Corrimony.[2] Cullen's mimicry entertained us so much that we did not part till near three in the morning. I had a bad cold and drank a good deal of Madeira to keep out the night air, so that I was heated.

SATURDAY 1 FEBRUARY. (Writing the 10.) Awaked so ill that I could not rise, but was obliged to lie in bed till near three. Was somewhat vexed that I had allowed myself such an indulgence last night. But it could not well have been avoided. Rose and entertained Killantringan, his wife and daughter and son, and Matthew Dickie[3] at dinner and tea. Was quite sober.

SUNDAY 2 FEBRUARY. (Writing the 10.) My cold continued. I kept the house in the forenoon. Heard Dr. Blair in the afternoon. The children said divine lessons. I was in a dull state of mind.

MONDAY 3 FEBRUARY. (Writing the 10.) I breakfasted at Lady Colville's. Lord Kellie had gone for London on Saturday. The Hon. Andrew walked with me to town. It was curious to hear from him that he had not at any time even a wish to distinguish himself. He just acquiesced in a consciousness of want of spirits and activity. The Earls of Crawford, Eglinton, and Cassillis, and Colonel Hugh Montgomerie supped with us. I drank negus, and was quite calm.

TUESDAY 4 FEBRUARY. (Writing the 10.) Sir Charles and Miss Preston, Baron Gordon, Miss Leslie, Dr. Webster, Mr. George Wallace, Mr. Maclaurin, Mr. Robert Dundas dined with us; a good creditable day. Dr. Webster, the Baron, and Mr. Wallace drank tea with me, my wife having gone out, after the ladies had drank tea, to Corri's concert[4] with Miss McAdam. Sir Walter and Grange supped with us.

WEDNESDAY 5 FEBRUARY. (Writing the 10.) Sat awhile with Lord Eglinton. His Lordship, Lady Colville, and Mr. Hamilton of Grange supped with us. I drank some rum punch from social inclination. Was sober though. Dr. Young died suddenly this afternoon.

THURSDAY 6 FEBRUARY. (Writing the 10.) Grange dined with us. I recollect nothing else except that I had the satisfaction of being

[2]All advocates. John Maclaurin and Robert Cullen (renowned as an acute but good-humoured mimic) were raised to the bench as Lord Dreghorn (1788) and Lord Cullen (1796) respectively. Drimnin was Charles Maclean and Corrimony was James Grant.

[3]A writer (solicitor), formerly Boswell's law clerk, though twenty-two years older than he and an established solicitor when Boswell came to the bar.

[4]Domenico Corri, music-master, composer, and publisher, a native of Italy who spent most of his life in Edinburgh and London.

actively benevolent and getting James Samson, a Trabboch deserter, set at liberty.[5]

FRIDAY 7 FEBRUARY. (Writing the 10.) Felt myself restless and uneasy after dinner. Went down to my worthy friend Grange, and he and I drank one bottle of good old mountain[6] and eat some toasted hard biscuit, and were cordial, and I soon grew well. I experienced clearly that *mental* distress may be removed by *material* applications.

SATURDAY 8 FEBRUARY. (Writing the 10.) Awaked with a rheumatism in my right shoulder. Attended a Faculty meeting of my brethren, where we had a debate for two hours whether we should oppose the granting of a royal charter to the Society of Scottish Antiquaries. Only eleven of us were against opposing. Thirty-seven were for opposing. I was vexed that there was such a majority on the illiberal side.[7] I was very uneasy with the rheumatism all day. My good friend the Hon. A. Gordon came and took a share of our family dinner and a bottle of claret cordially. I took very little wine, not to inflame my blood. He drank tea with us. In the evening I received a letter from Dr. Johnson so rigorous against my drinking wine at all, and so discouraging to my settling in London, that I was a good deal hurt.[8]

SUNDAY 9 FEBRUARY. (Writing the 19.) My rheumatism pained me much. I kept at home and heard the children say divine lessons till after church hours (except being at Dr. Young's funeral), and then went in a chair and dined (for the first time) with the Hon. Henry Erskine;[9] the Hon. Alexander Gordon, Mr. David Erskine, and his brother Archibald there. I drank Teneriffe negus and was comfortably warmed in body, but my mind roved on London, and was discontent, though we had good social talk.

MONDAY 10 FEBRUARY. (Writing the 19.) I recollect nothing.

TUESDAY 11 FEBRUARY. (Writing the 19.) Paid a visit to Lady Auchinleck in the forenoon, and I think drank tea with Mr. Nairne.[1] I am sure I did so one day this week.

[5]Boswell's Register of Letters seems to show that he had obtained a pass for Samson to return home and was negotiating for his discharge with General William Gordon in London. The discharge appears to have cost him ten guineas. See above, 18 December 1782 and below, 27 March 1783.
[6]A variety of Malaga wine, made from grapes grown on the mountains.
[7]The petition for a charter was granted 29 March 1783.
[8]Boswell printed extracts from the letter in the *Life of Johnson*, suppressing the parts that had hurt him.
[9]"Harry," the brother of the eleventh Earl of Buchan, a close legal associate of Boswell's, and an eloquent pleader at the bar. He served as Lord Advocate later this year, during the brief Coalition government of Fox and North. See below, 12 November 1783.
[1]One of Boswell's close friends in the Faculty of Advocates (he figures in the journals from the beginning). Nairne was quiet, regular, and prudent—virtues that Boswell

WEDNESDAY 12 FEBRUARY. (Writing the 19.) It was a very long time since I had paid a visit to Sir Alexander Dick. There is no accounting for such eclipses. It vexed me to think of them. I at once resolved to go out to him. Worthy Grange accompanied me, and we found him as happy as ever. But I had not such a relish of anything as I could wish. Grange both drank tea and supped with me.

THURSDAY 13 FEBRUARY. (Writing the 19.) Was weary and fretful. Sir Walter dined with us. His thoughtless conduct and wretched circumstances hurt me. In the evening I felt all at once a flow of good spirits, and with great ease wrote several letters for next night's post, one of which was to the Bishop of Killaloe, a correspondence which I had delayed to begin for almost two years after we had cordially settled it in London.[2] I *must* believe that man is in many respects subject to influence quite unknown to him. I have day after day resolved to write to the Bishop, yet it has been deferred, though I was vexed at the delay and loss of real pleasure from his correspondence. On a sudden I have written to him, and now cannot imagine *how* it was put off or *where* was the difficulty. Father of Spirits! I implore thy benignant influence!

FRIDAY 14 FEBRUARY. (Writing the 19.) Paid a visit to Mr. Crosbie, and found with him a son of Paul Sandby's, a young officer in the army, whom I asked to dine with me, that I might show some civility to the son of so fine an artist.[3] The rest of the company were Capt. William Dick, the Rev. Mr. William Bennet, and Grange. I was not at my ease. I viewed all things with a sad indifference. Phemie had been tried as a complete boarder at Mrs. Billingsley's. But she was so unhappy at not coming home at night that she was made only a day-boarder as well as Veronica. Little James and Betty were still distressed with a scorbutic eruption.

SATURDAY 15 FEBRUARY. (Writing the 19.) Was very feeble-

---

aspired to—and according to Sir Walter Scott, a man of punctilious good manners, scrupulous integrity, and unmatched dulness. He was elevated to the Court in 1786, and assumed the style Lord Dunsinnan (pronounced Dun*sin'*nin, the cause of an obvious and well-worn pun).

[2]Dr. Thomas Barnard, previously Dean of Derry, later Bishop of Limerick, had been a member of The Club since 1775, though he lived much of his life in Ireland. Boswell praised him as "a Christian and a Tory" (*Verses on Thomas Barnard's Promotion to the See of Killaloe*, a draft, 1781), and by the time he wrote the *Life of Johnson* presumed to call him "not only my Right Reverend, but my very dear friend" (see between 30 March and 10 April 1783). The Bishop provided both religious comfort and a generous table adorned with the choicest literati. Boswell wrote in this first letter to Barnard that he languished for residence in London.

[3]Paul Sandby, Jr., lieutenant in the 97th Regiment of Foot, Gibraltar. His father, a water-colourist, was the pioneer of topographical art and "acquatinta" in England.

minded. Looked into books in the Advocates' Library for a motto to *The Hypochondriack* No. 65. Found one on time[3a] in Josephus. Put down some hints, but was indifferent whether I should write well or ill. Went with the Hon. Alexander Gordon and Grange to Hall's Cellar, near Nicolson Street, and tasted some claret. Was in a dissipated frame. Grange dined with me. In the evening I was quite in the humour of London life, and wished to go to Princes Street Coffee-house and sup. But was persuaded to stay at home, and indulged myself with a broiled bone and some rum punch, which I seldom choose. I was hearty at home.

SUNDAY 16 FEBRUARY. (Writing the 19.) Was at the New Church all day, and felt a satisfaction in decent regularity. Heard Mr. Hardy at Ballingry lecture well in the forenoon and Mr. Walker preach as usual in the afternoon. Visited the Hon. Alexander Gordon between sermons. Then he called and eat a bit of veal with us; Mr. Grant of Monymusk at dinner. At Gordon's pressing request I went to him in the afternoon, after hearing my children say divine lessons, and tasted different kinds of claret, and then drank tea with him. Tasting heated me a little and made me wish if possible to be a pure water-drinker. Sir Charles and Colonel Preston, Mr. William Nairne, Hon. Alexander Gordon, and Hon. Andrew Cochrane supped with us; a good cheerful evening.

MONDAY 17 FEBRUARY. (Writing the 19.) Had a visit of Colonel Montgomerie. Was in poor spirits, but wrote an *Hypochondriack* with curious ingenuity of thinking. I wrote chiefly to please myself, and with a view to make out a couple of proper volumes of that periodical paper; for my partners of the *London Magazine* did not relish it much. I was not in the least affected by this, because I had no opinion of their taste in writing, for they wished rather for a *merry essay*. I wrote to Dilly that I wished to continue it to No. 70, the years of man's life.[4] But if the partners really thought they could find a variety of materials all better, I should close it next month. It is wonderful how the spur of engagement makes me write.

TUESDAY 18 FEBRUARY. (Writing the 19.) Was rather better, but quite dissatisfied with the narrow sphere here, and perpetually languishing for London eminence. Dined at Commissioner Cochrane's; Dr. Webster there. They both approved much of my continuing to apply to business as a lawyer. My mind however was so clouded and so broken that I could not feel with clearness and strength the dis-

[3a] The subject of the essay.
[4] This plan was followed, and the monthly series, which was begun October 1777, ended August 1783.

tinction between doing well and doing ill in this uncertain and short life. Strange that one should think so differently at different times. For upon some occasions I am quite animated with good ambition. I however this day wrote an able Petition for Garallan in support of a Decreet Arbitral which a majority of the Lords had very erroneously reduced.[5] I was pleased with my own powers, while I at the same time did not *feel* that it was of much consequence to have talents. Such was the state of my mind.

WEDNESDAY 19 FEBRUARY. (Writing the 20.) Felt all at once in the Court of Session a happy state of mind which made me view it with complacency instead of disgust. I wondered, while I experienced how little reality there is in external things. (Writing the 21.) I went and visited Lord Gardenstone, who was confined to the house, this forenoon. I had not visited him for many years, I know not why. I found his conversation both substantial and animated; and as we are prone to look at objects with the eyes of those with whom we are at the time, if we have any respect for their faculties, I was the better for hearing him give an account of his views of life. He told me he never had higher views than to be a judge in Scotland, and he was made a judge in his forty-second year. I asked him if he never had high ambitious views, which make me unhappy. He said never. Nay, he had his mind prepared for being disappointed of a judge's place, and was to have retired to the country. He said he never had five minutes' uneasiness at a time except from a bad hand at whist or a bad partner.[6] All this (if true) was sound philosophy, and I thought I might have it. But it was being contented with a lower state than what my keen and constant wishes for years have prompted, and which I have an impression I ought not to despair of obtaining. The great difficulty is to settle between foolish fancy and spirited ambition; and probably I shall dream and balance till it is too late to exert.

[5]The late Robert and William Alexander in 1778 had exercised their privilege of mining coal at Dalmelling, that portion of the estate of Blackhouse, Ayr, which Patrick Douglas of Garallan held on a long lease. Eight of the ten enclosures were so affected that the subtenants would not pay rent to Douglas. Compensation for damages went to arbitration, but the Alexanders appealed the award to the Lords of Session. They decided for the appellants 7 February 1783. Boswell asserted in his Petition for Douglas that only the arbiters were empowered to set damages, and that their settlement was just because waste from the mines had damaged farms and crops on which the mines did not actually sit. For the outcome, see below, 25 February 1783, n. 6.

[6]Francis Garden, styled Lord Gardenstone, was an acute and eloquent advocate raised to the bench in 1764 and to the Court of Justiciary twelve years later. Contented, but by no means phlegmatic, he had a considerable knowledge of literature, both ancient and modern, and was so contemporary in outlook as to develop a thriving village around the estate he had purchased in 1768 at Laurencekirk, Kincardineshire.

THURSDAY 20 FEBRUARY. Sir Walter and Grange dined with us. I called a little on Maclaurin after dinner. Went to the Pantheon in the evening to hear a debate on this curious question: whether it was most culpable for a young woman to marry an old man or for an old woman to marry a young man. But it was so crowded and blackguard, I soon left it in disgust.[7] Grange supped with us. I was now happy in the consciousness that I had written every letter which I had any call to write, and in short that I was upon very even terms with my duty in life in small or in great things. I had not much practice in the Court of Session. But I did well what was entrusted to me. I had a regular weekly return of work and weather from Mr. James Bruce, my faithful overseer at Auchinleck, and I wrote to him as regularly.

FRIDAY 21 FEBRUARY. (Writing on the 26.) My wife and I and Miss McAdam dined at Dr. Webster's with Sir Charles and Miss Preston, etc. I was pleased with the manners of Mr. Watson of Saughton, a man against whom there is a general prejudice.[8] I drank some claret with His Holiness,[9] which pleased me at the time and did me no harm afterwards. I was in a good manly frame. The Laird of Fairlie, who came to town yesterday, Mr. Matthew Dickie, and Captain Trotter, Mortonhall's son, supped with us. I was cheerful and moderate.

SATURDAY 22 FEBRUARY. (Writing on the 26.) I took a walk to Leith and paid a visit to David Boswell and his wife. Poor man, though he be a dancing-master, he is a branch of the family of Auchinleck, and gets his bread honestly. I regret that my wife will not receive him and his wife to dine with us privately.[1] She is wrong. I am however to have him to dine with me soon. I met Colonel Montgomerie a little before dinner in Princes Street, and engaged him to dine with us

[7] Boswell was made an honorary member of the Pantheon Society in 1773, the very year it was founded to improve public speaking and give relief to the "meriting poor" from the profits of the debates (*Edinburgh Advertiser*, 7 March 1783). The society gradually fell into decay and disrepute because of debts, the treasurer's perfidy, and the discomfort of St. Andrew's Chapel in Carrubber's Close, where numerous Edinburgh clubs held their meetings.

[8] Charles Watson was the representative of an ancient Midlothian family. We have not been able to find the reasons for this prejudice.

[9] Dr. Webster. The style was invented by Boswell's cousin, Patrick Preston (Journal, 6 January 1777).

[1] David Boswell of Leith was the impoverished representative of the Boswells of Craigston, who were descended from the second son of John Boswell, third Laird of Auchinleck (d. 1609). James Boswell was descended from James, the first son and heir. David's grandfather had sold Craigston, heavily burdened with debt, to Boswell's grandfather. Lord Auchinleck's entail, which carried male succession no farther back than heirs male of his own grandfather, excluded David with all the rest of the Craigston line. Like Margaret Boswell, he also shunned David personally because he considered his profession disgraceful.

without ceremony. We had also the Laird of Fairlie, Mr. Thomas Smith, Craigengillan's agent (first time), young Craigengillan and his tutor, and the young Campbells. I was quite sober, and was truly happy to find that the rage for strong liquor, which used to vex me, had ceased. Such is the agreeable change which I have experienced in my constitution within these seven or eight months. In the evening I accompanied Colonel Montgomerie to Fortune's, where he was engaged with a party, all of my acquaintance but one, to sup and hear MacLauchlan, the excellent fiddler, play Highland tunes. The company with us was Colonel John Macdonell, Colonel Wemyss, Sir John Scott, and Mr. MacNeill of Colonsay, whom I had never seen before. He is proprietor of one of the Hebrides, twelve miles long and I think four broad, and I believe of another island also. I loved him at once; for he told me there was in his island an ancient building raised by St. Columba before he went to Iona; that it never had a roof, for that the Saint had vowed not to settle anywhere from whence he could see Ireland; and having descried Ireland from Colonsay after the walls of his building were up, he stopped and left it, and Mr. MacNeill said he himself had built a stone wall round it to secure it from being hurt.[2] He also spoke with admiration of Dr. Johnson's *Journey*, repeated some passages of it, and said he was angry at his countrymen for imagining that it was unfavourably intended. I was surprised with this gentleman. I expected to have found him a rough Highlander. But he proved to be a well-informed man of the world. He knew the most fashionable people. He spoke French well. I drank a little weak gin punch without souring, and relished the fiddler's music and the company so well that I did not get home till about two in the morning. But I was not in the least inflamed. I thought in my chair coming home of Dr. Johnson's observation that no society is so agreeable as that in a tavern.[3] My rheumatism was now gone. But a large pimple on one of my hands had turned to a sore which was painful and troubled me. I am too easily troubled.

SUNDAY 23 FEBRUARY. (Writing the 26.) Was at the New Church both forenoon and afternoon, but attended indifferently. Dr. Carlyle preached in the afternoon.[4] I was in that kind of frame in which I believe a great many men are during the course of their lives: I was

[2] The traditional account, but the ruins now remaining on Colonsay are considered to be of much later date than the time of Columba. Archibald MacNeill's grandfather purchased Colonsay and Oronsay from the tenth Earl (later first Duke) of Argyll in 1701, and a line of capable and energetic lairds brought great prosperity to the islands during the two centuries the MacNeills held them.

[3] *Life of Johnson*, 21 March 1776.

[4] The only reference in Boswell's journal to Alexander Carlyle (because of his impressive good looks known as "Jupiter" Carlyle), minister of Inveresk near Edinburgh from 1748 to his death in 1805 and author of the well-known *Autobiography*.

well enough, without any lively sensation at all. The children said divine lessons in the evening. Grange supped with us. I fell into a fretful fit. The Hon. A. Gordon drank tea with us.

MONDAY 24 FEBRUARY. (Writing the 28.) Breakfasted at Lady Colville's. Was "pressed with the load of life."[5] But when I got home, dictated law papers pretty well. Was at a meeting of proprietors of land to consider of an application to Parliament to improve the rights of voting in our counties; was in such low spirits that it seemed to me a matter of indifference. There was a fire in the close next to our court just before dinner, which gave some alarm but was extinguished. Grange dined with us. Mr. George Wallace and the Hon. Alexander Gordon, who came to inquire how we were, drank some wine.

TUESDAY 25 FEBRUARY. (Writing the 28.) Had a large company at dinner: Lord Gardenstone, who had never before been with me, Lord Eskgrove, the successor of my father on the bench, Commissioner Cochrane, etc. Had no vivid enjoyment, but in a discontented frame speculated on every man's situation who was at table compared with my own, but relished none of them. Languished for London, Parliament, or any state of animated exertion. Was vexed this forenoon by hearing the Lord President and several others of the judges give what I thought most erroneous opinions against my client Garallan, though Lords Braxfield, Monboddo, Hailes, and others were for him.[6] Perhaps it is a weakness to be hurt like Heraclitus at observing the faults of human nature. But I cannot help it.

WEDNESDAY 26 FEBRUARY. Mr. R. Mackintosh, who after an absence of many years appeared at our bar today to support the Earl of Crawford against Lady Mary Campbell's claim for the family estate,[7] interested me as an able unfortunate man. His stately appearance too

---

[5] The beginning of Johnson's Prologue to Goldsmith's *Good-Natur'd Man*.

[6] On 29 July 1783 the Lords of Session adhered to their decision reducing the award for damages made in the Decreet Arbitral.

[7] On the death in 1749 of John, twentieth Earl of Crawford, a distinguished soldier, it was questioned whether the estate had passed to the heir male, George, Viscount Garnock, a second cousin once removed, or to Lady Mary Campbell, the Earl's sister and the heir of line. Viscount Garnock was retoured heir in 1757, and in 1781 was succeeded by his eldest son, George Lindsay-Crawford. (Boswell was an intimate of the Rozelle family, as we have seen.) Lady Mary brought an action against the twenty-second Earl to recover ancient marriage contracts and other papers which she asserted would shed light on her claim to the estate of Crawford. On 8 August 1783 the Court of Session decided for her by a large majority, on the principle that the holder of particular documents could not withhold them by an oath that they were of no benefit to the pursuer. The House of Lords affirmed the interlocutor, without prejudice to any other question, 24 July 1784. The papers must have proved useless to Lady Mary, because the Earl of Crawford retained possession of the estate.

had influence upon me. I had been very keen against him in his contest with my friend Dempster, and knew not how he might think of me. Yet I wished to show him attention. He addressed himself to me very politely, and I sat down by him and had some good talk. There was something curious in seeing him in the Court again after so long an absence, and something humbling to think that it was much diminished in dignity and abilities since he left it.[8] (Writing 2 March.) I dictated a great deal today, having several law papers to write. I was sensible that I was not fit to go through a great deal of business. Yet I repined that I had too little; though I considered that a gentleman of good fortune never gets much practice at our bar, and that I had more than anyone in that situation ever had. Grange and Mr. Lawrie dined with us. Formerly Mr. Lawrie used to eat almost constantly at my table, but it being disagreeable to my wife and indeed to myself to have him constantly since he had a family of his own, I invite him rarely. Veronica continues to be a day-boarder at Mrs. Billingsley's. Phemie was fixed as a boarder both day and night. But she cried so much that after persisting for a week, we allowed her to come home every evening as well as her sister.

THURSDAY 27 FEBRUARY. (Writing 2 March.) I went in the forenoon and paid a visit to Mr. R. Mackintosh at Paterson the stabler's in the Pleasance;[9] found him surrounded with law books and papers and quite like a man immersed in business. He talked in a style much above common, with a force and a command of expression and a manly manner which I admired, while I felt for him on account of the state of his affairs, which I was told was bad. I paid him much attention, partly from benevolence, partly from my never-failing wish to know distinguished men. Clerk Matthew and some more secondary company

[8]Robert Mackintosh, indeed an able but an unpopular man, had quitted the Scottish bar almost twenty-two years before. During a long residence in London he was associated successively with the Duke of Queensberry, Earl Temple, and the first Lord Clive, under whose patronage he challenged the incumbent, George Dempster (Boswell's friend for more than twenty years), as M.P. for the Perth Burghs. Mackintosh lost both the election and an action for bribery. The Court of Justiciary granted Dempster's plea of Parliamentary privilege, and the House of Lords, to which Mackintosh took an appeal, ruled that attempts to bribe the electorate had not been proved successful. Everyone knew that both candidates had been guilty of the same tactic. Mackintosh had returned to Scotland as Governor and principal shareholder of the troubled York Buildings Company to salvage the Company's investments in Scottish estates forfeited after the rebellion of 1715.

[9]A narrow, quaint, and straggling street going south from the Canongate. It took its name from the convent of St. Mary of Placentia, Pleasance being an old corruption of the Italian place-name (now the modern city of Piacenza). The quarter was now decayed and squalid.

dined with us. In the evening I was sadly shocked by a visit of Mr. Crosbie's clerk, Mr. Maule, who with tears in his eyes showed me a letter to his master telling him that if he did (writing 7 March) not pay fifteen guineas, he should be apprehended next day. I had been put upon my guard against applications for money from that quarter, and told what was true: that I had at present no money but what I borrowed; and so waived the demand at the time, but said I should endeavour to get the affair settled next morning, which indeed I hoped to do with the assistance of others at the bar. How wretched a change was it for a man of uncommon knowledge, abilities, and spirit to be thus in danger of imprisonment for a small sum!

FRIDAY 28 FEBRUARY. (Writing 7 March.) Maclaurin accosted me in the Court of Session thus: "You would do nothing last night for an old friend," and told me that Mr. Ilay Campbell had paid ten and he five guineas to relieve Crosbie. I was uneasy a little to think that my benevolence might be suspected. Yet I was conscious how sincerely I felt for Crosbie, and that in case of necessity, I should have advanced the fifteen guineas for him, though I doubted if it would be right to contract more debt while in reality I as yet owed more than my funds could discharge. And Maclaurin observed that it was wrong in Crosbie to take money from one of us and give to any other person. It would be better for him to clear himself by a *cessio bonorum*,[1] and then take aids from his friends. I had this evening Mr. R. Mackintosh, Mr. Ilay Campbell (appointed Solicitor-General),[2] Mr. George Wallace, the Laird of Fairlie, and Grange at supper. I drank almost a bottle of claret, as we sat till near three in the morning. Mackintosh harangued fluently but with too much vanity. Mr. Campbell was as usual silent and indifferent. But he gave a wonderful testimony of his confined Scottish views. He said Sir Gilbert Elliot[3] and Lord Advocate, he thought, would have done better to have continued at the bar here. I exclaimed, "I would rather have vital motion in the House of Commons than be Lord President of the Court of Session." Mackintosh seemed to think of

[1] A voluntary surrender by a debtor to his creditors of his whole property heritable and movable, by which action he escaped arrest and imprisonment. We do not know how Crosbie managed his plight in this instance, but as there are no further references to him in the journals, we report that after his untimely death in 1785 (he was in his forty-ninth year), the Faculty of Advocates granted his widow an annuity of £40. Just the previous December they had elected Crosbie Vice-Dean of the Faculty, evidence that he was still popular and respected despite some diminution of his powers.
[2] Alexander Murray, Solicitor-General since 1775, had succeeded to both of Lord Kames's judgeships and was now serving on the bench as Lord Henderland.
[3] The late baronet, of Minto, who entered Parliament in 1753, and rose to be successively Lord of the Admiralty, Lord of the Treasury, and Treasurer of the Navy. He was a special confidant of George III.

returning to the practice of the law here, as there was now a great opening for one of his seniority and abilities. The Solicitor encouraged him to return. I secretly dreaded that he might be mortified by neglect.[4]

SATURDAY 1 MARCH. (Writing the 7.) I dined at the Hon. A. Gordon's with Baron Gordon, Maclaurin, the Solicitor, Harry Erskine, Cullen; a party settled a fortnight before. The Solicitor's lady and Miss McAdam were there. My wife had a bad cold and could not go. We had some merriment, and sat till ten over claret, I drinking little. But upon the whole, it was not a good day.

SUNDAY 2 MARCH. (Writing the 7.) Stayed at home in the forenoon. Heard Mr. Walker in the afternoon. The children said divine lessons. Sir Charles Preston and the Hon. and Rev. James Cochrane supped with us. I have for some time been in a state of mind not so bad as miserable, but insipid and uneasy, having no pursuits that animate me, and viewing life as hardly worth being in earnest. I am lamentably indifferent to religion. It is amazing how very different I am at different times.

MONDAY 3 MARCH. (Writing the 12.) Had Mr. James Donaldson at dinner. His petulance was displeasing. But I take notice of him on his father's account.[5] Was at Barnard's ball at night and saw my daughters dance. First time of my being at a public place since my father's death, and this was a kind of duty. My wife got a fright with a carriage coming near a chair in which were two of our children, which made her spit blood.

TUESDAY 4 MARCH. (Writing the 12.) My wife kept the house. Miss McAdam and I and the children dined at Lady Auchinleck's; Commissioner Cochrane, Dr. Webster, and Balmuto[6] there.

WEDNESDAY 5 MARCH. (Writing the 13.) My wife still kept the house. Miss McAdam and I dined with Mr. Gilbert Innes (my first time there).[7] A decently good day.

THURSDAY 6 MARCH. (Writing the 13.) Dictated a paper of forty pages for the proprietors of the Edinburgh and Dumfries Fly against

[4] Boswell's fears were realized, because former colleagues had established new connexions, and those who might have given Mackintosh business remembered his egotism and the uncouth manners of his early years. He withdrew into seclusion at his house.

[5] Alexander Donaldson, bookseller and publisher, had published Boswell's early verses. James Donaldson, the son, proprietor and editor of the *Edinburgh Advertiser*, which his father had founded, doubled the fortune he inherited and left the bulk of it for the maintenance and education of three hundred poor children at the hospital in Edinburgh which bears his name.

[6] Claud Boswell, Lady Auchinleck's brother and Boswell's first cousin once removed. Boswell had a low opinion of Balmuto and decried his lack of family spirit.

[7] Innes, a very rich man, had a house in St. Andrew Square. He was later made Deputy Governor of the Bank of Scotland and held the office for thirty-eight years.

a judgement obtained against them by Dalziel, one of their number.[1]
Was pleased with my abilities.

FRIDAY 7 MARCH. (Writing the 13.) I recollect nothing.

SATURDAY 8 MARCH. (Writing the 13.) I dined at Lord Eskgrove's
with Lord Alva and son, Maclaurin, etc. Drank so much as to be a little
heated. But our conversation was pretty good. Lord Eskgrove made
a pretty just remark which was new to me: that decisions of the courts
in England are not found fault with as in Scotland, because *there* a
number of lawyers who are not in a cause attend to it and form an
impartial opinion. Whereas here, except in a very few instances, no
lawyers attend to a cause except those interested in it, so that in every
case there is one side to rail from prejudice or bias.

SUNDAY 9 MARCH. (Writing the 13.) Heard Mr. Walker in the
forenoon and Dr. Blair in the afternoon. The children said divine
lessons. Grange and I supped at Dr. Webster's. Little James, who had
been very ill from the effects of mercury given him for his scorbutic
complaint, was now a good deal better. His mother and I had a sad
alarm about him. She had no return of the spitting of blood. Dr.
Gillespie dined with us today.

MONDAY 10 MARCH. (Writing the 13.) I dined at Lady Colville's
with Lord Kellie, who returned from London last night. His steady
sense and preferring a creditable private life to the bustle of Court or
Parliament struck me to meditation.

TUESDAY 11 MARCH. (Writing the 13.) The Lords of Session disregarded my paper for the fly proprietors.[2] I was so much hurt by
what I thought gross injustice that I really inclined never to enter the
Court again. Grange and I paid a visit to Sir Alexander Dick, and
Grange dined with me. I thought of setting out for London next morning, but resolved to stay two days quietly and write *The Hypochondriack*
No. 66.

WEDNESDAY 12 MARCH. (Writing the 13.) After much search
among books in the Advocates' Library, found a good motto for keeping
a diary, the subject of No. 66.[3] Grange dined with us.

[1]We know nothing about the cause except the identity of the litigants. Boswell's clients
were Hugh Cameron, innkeeper and stabler at the Cowgate Head, from which the
fly to London by way of Dumfries and Carlisle set out, and John McVities, innkeeper
of the George, at Dumfries. George Dalziel kept a famous posting establishment and
inn at Noblehouse, Peeblesshire, seventy miles south-west of Edinburgh.

[2]This is the last day of the Session, and in the next year or so there is no notice of the
cause in the Minute-Book or in the legal processes, further evidence that the Lords
declined to reconsider it.

[3]"Perutile fuerit ante somnum notare quaecunque luce ea peracta sunt" (which he
translated, "It will be of great use to mark down every night, before going to sleep,

THURSDAY 13 MARCH. Sat calmly incog. at home. Wrote most part of No. 66. It was the Fast Day before the Sacrament. Sir W. Forbes paid me a private visit. I was somewhat hurried, notwithstanding two days of preparation. Grange dined and supped with us.

FRIDAY 14 MARCH.[4] (Writing the 22.) Got into the Dumfries diligence at four in the morning, and with two other gentlemen reached Moffat about six in the evening. They went on to Dumfries. I sent for my brother John, who was glad to see me, and seemed in so cordial a frame that I resolved to stay a day here, though I risked the fly to Carlisle being full next day.[5] Moffat has a very agreeable place in my mind, as I there first saw the gaiety of genteel company, and as I there have meditated much when my fancy was finer than it now is.[6] We drank tea comfortably, and I invited Mr. Little, the landlord, to sup with us, which he did. He is my old acquaintance and my client.

SATURDAY 15 MARCH. (Writing the 22.) I breakfasted with John at his room, by invitation. I wished to pay him all proper attention, and I submitted to continual restraint in conversation with him, as he is proud and irritable. We walked to the well and about the village on all quarters. His recovery of reason to the degree which he now has

---

what you have done during the day"), from the first sentence of Chapter 33 of *Liber de Ratione Studii*, by the sixteenth-century Dutch scholar Joachimus Fortius. Boswell found the treatise in a seventeenth-century collection of essays. *The Hypochondriack* No. 66 is of greater autobiographical interest than any other in the series. It shows that Boswell's principal reason for keeping a journal was to enable him to review his own life. He makes veiled reference to his materials for the *Life of Johnson*, and remarks that "if a diary be honestly and judiciously kept, it will not only be immediately useful to the person who keeps it, but will afford the most authentic materials for writing his life, which, if he is at all eminent, will always be an acceptable addition to literature; and in some instances it will give the most genuine view of many of the events and characters of the time." Keeping a journal he thought not possible "unless one has a peculiar talent for abridging." His own notes were "like portable soup, of which a little bit by being dissolved in water will make a good large dish; for their substance by being expanded in words would fill a volume."

[4]This entry opens another notebook devoted entirely to the London jaunt of 1783.
[5]John Boswell, three years younger than James and a retired lieutenant in the army, had suffered periodically since the age of nineteen from violent or morose insanity. Boswell visited him frequently at the towns where he boarded or was hospitalized when his conduct at home became intolerable. John left Edinburgh this time late in 1782 or early in 1783, probably by choice: his funds were slight, and Moffat, where he had lived before, provided cultured society at a modest cost.
[6]He was sent to Moffat in his twelfth year and again in his seventeenth to recover from melancholy and illnesses of nervous origin. It was then only a small and unsophisticated village with a sulphur-spring and a natural setting of great beauty, but the modest activity Boswell remembers was doubtless more effective than the mineral waters in restoring his health.

it, after being several years in confinement, is remarkable. But he (writing the 24) told me he had been drinking hard of late, which alarmed me, and I counselled him against it. We saw Lord Hopetoun's house here.[7] The landlord dined with us. Then we had coffee, and a little after seven I got into the diligence from Glasgow to Carlisle, in which was only a son of Mr. Gillespie at Douglas Mill, who was going out to Canada. The weather was cold, and I felt it disagreeable and somewhat mean to travel in a stage-machine. But I considered that it was wise for me to be rigidly economical till at least my funds should be quite sufficient to pay all my debts.

SUNDAY 16 MARCH. (Writing the 24.) Arrived at the Bush Inn, Carlisle, about four in the morning. Lay down without throwing off my clothes, having bad accommodation, as fly passengers are looked upon as low people. Rose between eight and nine. Went to the deanery, where my friend Dr. Percy, formerly Dean, now Bishop of Dromore, was ready to receive me, as I had engaged on his invitation to be with him. Was sorry to hear from him that his only son, who had gone to Italy for the recovery of his health from an asthmatic complaint, was given over.[8] But as I perceived that the Bishop could be social not-withstanding, I did not affect to dwell long upon the melancholy subject. We talked as usual of Dr. Johnson. I regretted that there was not somebody continually to collect his sayings. "Why," said the Bishop, "you collect." "But I have little opportunity," said I. "You all collect some. But I venture more than any of you. I am like the man 'who gathers samphire, dreadful trade.'[9] I gather upon the face of the rock while there is a storm." "True," said the Bishop. "Others will pick up a flower in the meadow." The allusion was not amiss to the difference between conversing with the Doctor when mild and when passionate. Mrs. Percy and the Bishop's two daughters[10] appeared at breakfast. He ordered my baggage to be brought from the inn, that I might be his guest at the deanery in full hospitality. We went to the cathedral in the forenoon. Mr. Archdeacon Paley preached uncommonly well.[1] There was a very good organist. I had not the exquisite sensations from being

---

[7]Not the family seat, which was in Linlithgowshire, but Moffat House, a plain but stately structure built by his father in 1751.

[8]Thomas Percy, member of The Club, editor of the important *Reliques of Ancient English Poetry* (1765), had been elevated to the bishopric 22 May 1782, but continued to reside at Carlisle until the new episcopal palace at Dromore was completed in June 1783. His only son, Henry, aged twenty, died at Marseilles eleven days after this entry.

[9]*King Lear,* IV. vi. 15.

[10]Barbara, and Elizabeth, who later married the Rev. Pierce Meade, archdeacon of Dromore. Three other daughters died in infancy.

[1]The author (1794) of the famous *Evidences of Christianity.*

in England which I had in my youth, but was steady as a laird. I was somewhat cold and uneasy after last night's fatigue. The Bishop took the ladies and me out an airing in his coach. It pleased me to see him enjoying such a respectable situation, in which he seemed to be easier than I could have imagined, considering how humble his original state was.[2] He told me that he was with Shenstone soon after Toldervy, a London rider[3] (who while he took orders for linen, I believe, was at the same time employed by some London booksellers to compile a Tour), had been catched by him copying some of his inscriptions to insert; and his purpose being discovered, Shenstone had prevailed with him to show him his notes, in which he found all the absurdities which circulated concerning him in the neighbourhood; how Maria was a lady in love with him who broke her heart because he refused her, and such stuff. He coaxed Toldervy to leave his notes of the Leasowes to have additions made to them, and put him off from time to time till the first volume of the *Tour* was published, and an account helped by Mr. Shenstone himself was promised in the second volume. But the first not having succeeded, it never appeared.[4] So Shenstone escaped what his extreme sensibility was frightened to think might come out. The Bishop was led to tell me this anecdote from my mentioning Pennant, whose *Tour* he said was written in the style of a rider. We went to evening prayers, after which we had a very good dinner, the archdeacon and Counsellor Clark with us. Our conversation turned chiefly on the strange state of politics. The Bishop however enlivened it with literary anecdote. He told us that Morell, S.T.P., who is an excellent Greek scholar and is supposed to have helped Dr. Gregory Sharpe, who was very ambitious to appear a scholar, used to compose words for Handel's music, and Handel used to carry him down with him to ———, where he entertained him.[5] Morell could not live without his wife. So he had her conveyed down and lodged in a garret, the window of which looked

[2]Percy was the son of a Shropshire grocer.
[3]A travelling salesman.
[4]The Leasowes, the family estate of the poet William Shenstone, was widely known because of Shenstone's feats of landscape-gardening. His cousin, Maria Dolman, died of smallpox in 1756 and he erected an urn to her memory in "Lover's Walk" at the Leasowes. William Toldervy's *England and Wales Described* was published in London in 1762.
[5]Thomas Morell, Sacrae Theologiae Professor (D.D.), supplied libretti for eight of Handel's oratorios. The place-name Boswell failed to get is almost certainly Tunbridge Wells, Handel's favourite spa in his later years, when Morell was his lone collaborator. He retired there up to the summer before his death, both for his general health and for a pointless eye operation and continued treatment by Dr. John ("the Chevalier") Taylor, the itinerant oculist who also attended King George II, and unfortunately, Johann Sebastian Bach.

into the room where Handel and he dined. Handel had always a good
dinner; and as he was blind, Morell used to make signs to his wife most
significantly, pointing to a fowl or veal or whatever dishes were upon
the table, that she might choose what she liked, which she did by a nod;
and Morell, having a waiter in his confidence, had it carried to her. I
was much satisfied with the Bishop's having repaired the deanery and
preserved the old Gothic style with modern elegance. Mr. Clark stayed
supper, after which the Bishop assembled his family and read prayers,
partly from the evening service, partly by the Bishop of Man.[6] It was
very agreeable to me to be present at this decent family devotion. I
had a very excellent apartment, which I enjoyed much after last night's
uneasiness.

MONDAY 17 MARCH. (Writing the 24.) The Bishop showed me the
correspondence between him and Drs. Blair and Ferguson concerning
Ossian, in which I thought my countrymen made but a shabby figure;
though I also thought the Bishop insisted too much upon the evidence
of minutes kept by him, which he showed me, and I saw were very
curt and did not mention having heard Erse poetry repeated at Dr.
Ferguson's, but only fixed the date of his drinking tea there. The
Bishop was very keen and violent upon the subject. This was a fresh
instance of the uncertainty of literary friendship.[7] But to own the truth,
my mind was now in such an indifferent frame that I looked on all
human concerns as scenes in a drama, and it did not seriously affect
me. I paid a visit to the Miss Waughs and to Dr. Carlyle, an old con-

[6]Probably Thomas Wilson, Bishop of Sodor and Man, 1698–1755, who composed
many widely-used prayers both in English and Manx.

[7]According to Bishop Percy, when he visited Hugh Blair in Edinburgh in 1765 he
there heard a student, John Macpherson (later Sir John Macpherson, Governor-General of India), recite passages in Gaelic at the home of Adam Ferguson, Professor of
Moral Philosophy. Percy did not understand the language, but Macpherson's translations convinced him of the authenticity of Ossian. He gave an account of the incident
in the second edition of his *Reliques of Ancient English Poetry* (1767), but later came to
believe that he had been deceived and quietly withdrew the note from the third edition
(1775). Others, however, turned the matter into a public controversy, and the principals
then conducted a protracted and sometimes ruthless warfare in the magazines and
newspapers. Ferguson repeatedly denied that he had been present at Macpherson's
performance, and after so many years, Blair could not recollect it at all. Percy then
turned up two letters to him from Blair mentioning the recitation, and though he did
not publish them, Blair himself reported the relevant passages in a letter to Dr. Alexander Carlyle, 22 April 1782. The extracts prove that Macpherson did indeed recite
and translate Gaelic verse to Percy and Blair, but as Boswell observes in this entry (he
was trained, after all, in weighing evidence), they do not clearly make Ferguson present
or place the event at his home.

nexion of our family.[8] I walked with the Bishop, and dined well again with him. He gave me hopes of a visit at Auchinleck. About five o'clock I got into the post-coach for London, which travelled on night and day till it arrived at the Bell Savage Inn upon Ludgate Hill on Thursday evening the 20. I group the days of this journey together, as nothing happened worth recording. I was absolutely distressed with the fatigue, and thought this mode of travelling a punishment to which I would never again submit. I made the most of what companions I had in the coach that my humour inclined me to do. But that was not much. I took a hackney-coach and drove to Mr. Dilly's, my constant landing-place, where I found a cordial reception.

FRIDAY 21 MARCH. (Writing the 24.) My brother David break-fasted with us.[9] I called at Dr. Johnson's, and was told he was at Mrs. Thrale's. Went to Nerot's and got my hair dressed, so as to appear decently well. Felt a steadiness as Laird of Auchinleck which I never before experienced in London. Went to Mrs. Thrale's in Argyll Build-ings. Was shown into Dr. Johnson's room.[10] He said, "I am glad you are come. I am very ill." I was disagreeably surprised to find him looking very pale, and afflicted with a difficulty of breathing. For in his last letter to me he said nothing of his being ill again. I shall collect his conversation as well as I can.

He said the superiority of a country gentleman over the people on his estate was very agreeable, and that whoever says he does not feel it agreeable, lies. For it must be agreeable to have a casual superiority over those who are by nature equal with us. I objected great proprietors of land preferring living in London. "Why, Sir," said he, "the pleasure

[8]Dr. George Carlyle was the nephew of a great friend of Boswell's paternal grandfather and himself the companion of Boswell's uncle, Dr. John Boswell, when they were both studying medicine at Leiden.

[9]Boswell's youngest brother had gone out to Spain at the end of 1767 as a merchant, but had returned in 1780 because of the outbreak of war between the two countries and settled in London as a banker. Boswell was overjoyed by David's homecoming but disappointed by his cold reserve. He often refers to him now as "T. D.," David having prefixed the name Thomas to his own because of Spanish prejudice against Old Testament names.

[10]For many years a room was reserved for Johnson at both the town and country residences of the wealthy brewer, Henry Thrale. Hester Thrale, educated and viva-cious, ministered to Johnson's comforts and drew a brilliant circle around him. Johnson vested in the Thrales and their children a familial love unsatisfied until his fifties, and whatever house they lived in to him was home. On 4 April 1781 Thrale died of an apoplectic stroke; in the autumn of 1782 his widow let the villa at Streatham Park to Lord Shelburne, turned her back on the house in Southwark, and rented winter quarters in Argyll Street.

of living in London and the intellectual superiority to be enjoyed there may counterbalance the other. Besides, a man may prefer the state of the country gentleman upon the whole, and yet there may never be a moment when he is willing to make the change." He said, "It is better to have five per cent out of land than out of money, because it is more secure; but the readiness of transference and promptness of interest make many people prefer the funds." He said, "A man is not so much afraid of being a hard creditor as of being a hard landlord." "Because," said I, "there is a sort of kindly connexion between a landlord and his tenants." "No, Sir," said he. "Many landlords here never see their tenants. It is because if a landlord drives away his tenants, he may not get others; whereas the demand for money is so great it may always be lent."

He imputed the present anarchy in Government in a good measure to the Revolution. "For," said he, "this Hanoverian family is *isolée* here. They have no friends. Now the Stuarts had friends who stuck by them so late as 1745. When the right of the King is not reverenced, there will not be reverence for those appointed by the King."

He said he had no objection to my coming to reside at London, provided I passed half the year, or four months of it, at Auchinleck. But that I ought not to come unless I could secure a place the salary of which would pay the additional expense of living here.

He repeated to me some very fine verses which he had made on the death of his old attendant, Mr. Levett, and repeated them with an emotion which made them have full effect. He said, "You must be as much with me as you can. You have done me good. You cannot think how much better I am since you came in."

He sent to Mrs. Thrale that I was there. She came, and I saluted her with gladness. I had not seen her since Mr. Thrale's death till now. She promised me a copy of the verses on Levett.[1] She asked me to stay dinner. We had no company but her three eldest daughters. She said she was very glad I was come, for she was going to Bath and should have been uneasy to leave Dr. Johnson till I came. He had told me of her going to Bath, and said they had driven her out of London by attacks upon her which she had provoked by attacking everybody.[2] I

[1]We should no doubt recognize this as the copy of the verses (they are indeed very fine) in the hand of Hester Maria ("Queeney") Thrale, Mrs. Thrale's eldest daughter, which is among the Boswell Papers at Yale. Boswell used it as printer's copy when he inserted the verses in the *Life of Johnson* immediately after a memorandum of Johnson's dated 20 January 1782. Robert Levett, the self-educated medical practitioner who lived with Johnson, had died 17 January 1782.

[2]A memorandum in Boswell's hand, now in the Hyde Collection, clarifies the entry: "Dr. Johnson said of Mrs. Thrale, 'I am glad she is gone to Bath, to some place where

had called on Mr. Burke, who was gone out.[3] Little was said by Dr. Johnson at dinner, and he went to sleep after it. I went to the drawing-room where the ladies were, and tea and coffee were brought. I felt myself quite easy; and I know not how, the mysterious kind of peculiarity of feeling which used to fill my mind in London was gone. I rather foolishly regretted this. For surely it is better to have a more rational and a stronger frame of mind than before.

When the Doctor joined us, he was more disposed to talk. Of conversation he said, "There must in the first place be knowledge; there must be materials. In the second place, there must be a command of words. In the third place, there must be imagination to place things in such views as they are not commonly seen. And in the fourth place, there must be presence of mind and a resolution which is not to be overcome by failures. This last is an essential requisite. For want of it, many people do not excel in conversation. Now I want it. I throw up the game upon losing a trick." "I don't know," said I, "you beat other people's cards out of their hands." I doubt whether he heard this. While he went on talking triumphantly I was all admiration, and said, "Oh, for shorthand to take this down!" Said Mrs. Thrale: "You'll carry it all in your head. A long head is as good as shorthand." I have the substance, but the felicity of expression, the flavour, is not fully preserved unless taken instantly.

He said Fox never talked in conversation, not from any determination not to talk, but because he had not the first motion.[4] "A man who is used to the applause of the House of Commons has no wish for that of a private company. A man accustomed to throw for a thousand pounds, if set down to throw for sixpence, would not be at the pains

---

her head may cool. Sir, they have fairly driven her from London. Sir, she has made innumerable enemies by her tongue.' L[?Langton] said to me, '*Who* has helped her to it?' 'Dr. Johnson,' said I. 'He knocks them on the head, and she cuts their throats. They butcher it fairly between them.'" Johnson and Boswell had talked previously about Mrs. Thrale's sharp and candid remarks in company. But the "attacks" from which she suffered almost daily at this time were gossip and indecent squibs in the newspapers about her relations with Gabriel Piozzi, the music-master whom she loved but had now given up. (They were reunited and married in 1784.) Johnson, like her daughters, opposed the "misalliance" strenuously.

[3]Edmund Burke, the statesman and author, whose oratorical powers Boswell admired greatly, though he thought them more dramatic than persuasive. This is the first time that Boswell has called on him since he appealed for a political appointment through Burke the previous spring. See below, 22 March 1783, p. 76.

[4]The impulse. Fox appears to have been modest in mixed groups of company, and restrained in the presence of Johnson, as Boswell reports at this point in the *Life of Johnson.* With intimate friends, however, he was open and vivacious.

to count his dice. Burke's talk is the ebullition of his mind. He does not talk from a desire of distinction, but because his mind is full."

He said, "Sheridan is a good man.[5] But Sheridan is a vain man and a liar. But he only tells lies of vanity; of victories, for instance, in conversation which never happened." He said, "I wonder how I should have any enemies. For I do harm to nobody." "In the first place, Sir," said I, "you set out with attacking the Scotch. So you got a whole nation for your enemies." He owned that by his definition of oats he meant to vex them.[6] I asked him if he could trace the cause of his antipathy to them. He said he could not. I told him that Old Mr. Sheridan says it was because they sold Charles I. "Then," said he, "Old Mr. Sheridan has found out a very good reason." I sat till ten, and then sauntered to Dilly's.

SATURDAY 22 MARCH. (Writing the 24.) Mr. Dilly and I breakfasted at my brother David's, whose cold formality displeased me. I called at Mr. Burke's, and found him and his lady and son[7] all glad to see me. He was in high glee from a belief that an Administration to his mind was by that time settled. I seriously regretted the situation of the King, overwhelmed by a faction.[8] Burke laughed, I thought with too insolent a *laetitia*.[9] He had some gentlemen at breakfast with him. He and his son and I went for a while into his study, where I most heartily thanked him for his friendly behaviour to me. I enjoyed the consciousness of independence. But I hoped that by his influence I might obtain the pleasurable lot of an employment in London.[1] I found

[5]Thomas Sheridan, actor, elocutionist, lexicographer, and the father of the famous dramatist. This sentence in the journal and the next were later additions written on the blank side facing that on which Boswell was writing. Hence the oddity of calling Sheridan "Old" after he had been introduced without the epithet.

[6]"A grain which in England is generally given to horses, but in Scotland supports the people."

[7]Richard, his only living son, elected to The Club in 1782, where he was known as "the whelp."

[8]On 21 February, Charles James Fox, who had been Lord North's principal opponent during North's ministry, formed a coalition with him which succeeded in passing in the House of Commons a vote of censure against the articles of peace concluded with the Americans by Lord Shelburne's government. Shelburne resigned three days later. The famous Coalition Ministry of Fox and North, under the nominal leadership of the Duke of Portland, was about to come into office. The King struggled desperately for six weeks—at one period even resolving to abdicate and retire to Hanover—against appointing an administration which would be controlled essentially by Fox, the man he most hated.

[9]Pleasure, joy.

[1]Burke had held the post of Paymaster of the Forces during the brief Rockingham ministry, March to July 1782. On hearing of his appointment, Boswell had begged him by letter to recommend him for appointment as Judge Advocate of Scotland.

General Paoli at home, looking remarkably well, and as good to me as ever. I engaged to dine with him next day, and found that my room was in readiness for me.

I found Dr. Johnson rather better. I told him General Paoli said I need not be uneasy about the King—he laughed at them all. He played them one against another. "Don't think so, Sir," said the Doctor. "He is as much oppressed as a man can be. If he plays them one against another, he wins nothing." I am not sure whether it was yesterday or this day that he made the remark on the present royal family being *isolée*. I think yesterday. Mrs. Thrale and Dr. Pepys, his physician, came into the room. He seemed to be an unruly patient. Dr. Pepys, who was a genteel little man, said, "If you were tractable, Sir, I should prescribe so and so."

I had visited General Oglethorpe in my way from General Paoli's, whom I found the same man as ever.[2] He told me Dr. Johnson saw company on Saturday evenings, and he would meet me there tonight. When I mentioned it to the Doctor, his anger kindled, I know not why, and he said, "Did not you tell him not to come? Am I to be hunted in this manner?" I satisfied him that I could not take upon me to forbid the General. Dr. Pepys told me at the street-door that some little time ago he was afraid Dr. Johnson would have died.

I called at Dempster's in Percy Street, and was very sorry to hear he was ill, and lived in Brompton Row, Hyde Park, for better air. Then called at Squire Godfrey Bosville's. Nobody at home. Left word I should dine there today. Walked round by Clerkenwell Green all the way to Rood Lane, Fenchurch Street, to Dobbins's, my brother David's tailor, to get a suit of clothes tried on. A man's dress is really a considerable part of him, both in his own idea and in that of others. I resolved to take the full year of mourning for my father, according to the old fashion. I wore full mourning six months. I now wore second mourning, which was shabby, so I ordered it new: a dark raven-grey frock, black cassimere vest and breeches for common wear, and silk for genteeler

---

Burke, warning Boswell that he had very little power in such matters, had recommended him immediately to General Conway, but the post had gone to another. In his recent letter to the Bishop of Killaloe (see above, 13 February 1783), Boswell had remarked of Burke's application that it "contained a character of me which I prefer to the office which I did not get" (14 February 1783).

[2]Oglethorpe, now eighty-seven years old and senior general in the army, had founded the colony of Georgia as a refuge for paupers, forbidding slavery there. He had initiated a warm friendship with Boswell in the spring that *An Account of Corsica* came out (1768) by calling on him in his rooms in Piccadilly to shake the hand of its author. On several occasions Boswell took notes for Oglethorpe's life, but he is not known to have gone beyond the stage of collecting materials.

occasions. In the mean time I walked about in an old dark-grey frock, satin vest, and stocking-breeches. I went back to Great Russell Street and had a hearty plain dinner with Squire Godfrey, his lady, and Captain Thomas, their son.[3] My heart warmed, and I drank rather more wine than I should have done, but only to heat a little. Was tired with walking so much, being not yet used to the hard exercise of London. I sauntered in Covent Garden piazzas, where I met Ross, the player, and renewed a friendly acquaintance; then paid a visit to Tom Davies and his wife.[4]

Then sauntered along to Dr. Johnson's in Bolt Court, Fleet Street, who was at tea and coffee with Mrs. Williams and Mrs. Desmoulins, who were both ill.[5] It was a sad scene. He was not in very good humour. He said if you should search all the madhouses in England, you would not find ten men who would write such a Martial as Elphinston had done, and think it sense.[6]

General Oglethorpe came, and the Doctor and I went to the parlour to him. He said he was busy reading the writers of the Middle Age. The Doctor said (I think) they were the most curious. General Ogle-

[3]Under a standing invitation which had held since 16 February 1776, when the Squire had invited him "to come at any time and eat his family dinner" (Journal). Godfrey Bosville, at this time nearly sixty-six years old, owned extensive properties in Yorkshire, his manor of Gunthwaite, in the West Riding, having come to his family through marriage in 1375. He believed himself to be Chief of the Bosville-Boswell clan, a claim that Boswell heartily accepted, though present-day genealogists find it unsupported and improbable. Thomas Bosville, Godfrey's younger son, was a captain in the army and lieutenant in the Coldstream Guards.

[4]Boswell wrote the Prologue to *The Earl of Essex*, the play with which David "Royal" Ross, actor and manager, opened the Theatre Royal in Edinburgh in 1767. It was the first legal theatre there, and Ross suffered much criticism and incurred heavy debts. In 1770 he leased the theatre to Samuel Foote, and returned to the London stage. Thomas Davies was the actor, author, and bookseller in whose back parlour Boswell first met Samuel Johnson, 16 May 1763.

[5]Anna Williams, a learned poet long blinded by cataracts, had managed Johnson's household since the death of his wife in 1752. She was unmarried, but she was addressed by the eighteenth-century courtesy title of "Mrs." Mrs. Williams died later this year, 6 September, at the age of seventy-seven. Mrs. Elizabeth Desmoulins was the widow of a writing-master, and daughter of Johnson's improvident godfather, Dr. Samuel Swynfen. She too had been an occupant in the household for some time, and told Boswell five years earlier that Johnson gave her a half-guinea a week.

[6]The translation by James Elphinston, author and former schoolmaster, had been universally ridiculed when it appeared just the year before. In less troubled moods, however, Johnson spoke kindly of Elphinston, who in 1750 brought out an elegant Edinburgh edition of *The Rambler*, with his own translations of the mottoes. The two authors had corresponded thereafter, and became acquainted in London, but Johnson did not feel himself so intimate with Elphinston as to dissuade him from publishing the Martial, as Garrick told Johnson he himself had tried to do.

thorpe said the House of Commons had usurped the power of the nation's money and used it tyrannically, and that government was now carried on by corrupt influence, instead of the inherent right in the King. He[7] said, "The want of inherent right in the King occasions all this disturbance. What we did at the Revolution was necessary. But we broke our Constitution." "Um!" said the General. "My father did not think it necessary."[8] I came off with the General and sauntered to Mr. Dilly's, having walked twice from the City and back again today.

SUNDAY 23 MARCH. (Writing the 24.) Called on Captain Robert Preston;[9] gone to the country. Breakfasted with Dr. Johnson, who was better, having taken opium last night. But he declaimed against it. I mentioned the Turks taking it. He grew warm and said, "Turks take opium and Christians take opium. But Russell in his *Account of Aleppo* tells us that it is as disgraceful for a Turk to take too much opium as it is with us to be drunk.[1] It is amazing how things are exaggerated. A gentleman was lately telling where I was that in France as soon as a man of fashion marries, he takes an opera-girl into keeping. 'Pray, Sir,' said I, 'how many opera-girls may there be?' 'About fourscore.' 'Well, then, you see there can be no more than fourscore who do this.' "

Mrs. Desmoulins made tea. She and I talked before him of his not complaining of the world because he was not called to some great office, or was not richer. He flew into a violent passion and commanded us to have done; for nobody had a right to talk in this manner, to bring before a man his own character and the events of his life, when he did not like it should be done. He said he never had sought the world. The world was not to seek him. It was rather wonderful that so much had been done for him. He said all the complaints of the world were unjust. He never knew a man of merit neglected. It was generally by his own fault that he failed of success. "A man may hide his head in a hole; he may go into the country and publish a book now and then which nobody reads, and complain he is neglected." (This was too close a description of my friend Temple.) "There is no reason why anybody should exert himself for a man who has written a good book. He has not written it for any individual. I may as well make a present to the

[7]Johnson.

[8]Oglethorpe's father, Sir Theophilus Oglethorpe, was an active Jacobite until 1696, when James II's policy of purging his court at St. Germain of Protestants caused him to take the oath of loyalty to William III.

[9]Sir Charles Preston's youngest brother, a former East India captain, now a "ship's husband" or owner-manager of various East Indiamen. He and Boswell were the same age, though he was a first cousin of Boswell's mother.

[1]Alexander Russell had served for thirteen years at Aleppo as physician to the representatives of English merchants. Johnson had reviewed *The Natural History of Aleppo* in the *Literary Magazine* the year it was published, 1756.

postman who brings me a letter. When patronage was limited, an author expected to find a Maecenas, and complained if he did not find one. Why should he complain? Maecenas has others as good as he, or others who have got the start of him." "But, Sir," said I, "many men of merit at the bar never get practice." "Sir," said he, "you are sure that practice is got from an opinion that the person employed deserves it best; so that if a man of merit at the bar does not get practice, it is from error, not from injustice. He is not neglected. A horse that is brought to market may not be bought, though a very good horse. But that is from ignorance, not from intention."

He maintained that a man could not make a bad use of his money, so far as regards society, if he did not hoard it. For if he either spends it or lends it out, society has the benefit. He said it was in general better to spend money than to give it, for that industry was more promoted by the former than the latter. "A man who spends his money is sure he is doing good with it. He is not so sure when he gives it away. A man who spends £10,000 a year will do more good than a man who spends two thousand and gives away eight."

I went to the Bavarian Chapel and worshipped.[2] Called at Sir Joshua Reynolds's. Neither he nor Miss Palmer at home. Called at the Turk's Head, Gerrard Street; looked at the list of our club, and saw five new members had been elected since I was in London.[3] Felt The Club and everything else wonderfully approximated to Auchinleck in my imagination. The feeling of independence, of coming to London whenever I choose it, makes the difference. Called on Mr. Dance; found him and his wife, a very genteel woman whom I had not seen before, and his mother, Mrs. Love.[4] Engaged to dine with him next Sunday. Found Lord Eglinton; also General Oglethorpe. Time was borne up on a thousand wings. Drank chocolade at the Mount Coffee-house. Found General Paoli at home, and Dempster, who had inquired for me, sitting with him. Accompanied Dempster to Grosvenor Gate, where his horses waited for him. He had brought me a letter from James Bruce, with a week's journal of weather and work at Auchinleck. I walked in Hyde Park, the sun shining bright, and an infinity of company in carriages and on horseback dazzling my sight, and read my *return* as a steady

[2] Boswell first heard the Roman service at the Bavarian Chapel, which was nominally the private chapel of the Bavarian Envoy. Like the chapels of other official representatives of Catholic monarchs, however, it was in fact a mission church for English Catholics in London, and mass was said publicly.

[3] Edward Eliot, M.P., later Lord Eliot, Edmond Malone, Thomas Warton, Lord Lucan, and Edmund Burke's son Richard.

[4] Boswell had an affair with Mrs. Love, the wife of his actor-friend, James Dance, alias Love, and herself a comedienne, when he was twenty-one and she about forty. He seems to have renewed it in the springs of 1776 and 1778, in London.

laird; and thought highly of my state in life, so that I did not see it insipid, even when compared with London in all its glory. Called on Lord Mountstuart; not at home. Would fain have asserted a lofty independence of all aid from him and his family; as I am (though perhaps unreasonably) somewhat mortified at the want of warmth towards me which I experience in them.[5] But wisdom made me resolve to pursue my purpose of at last obtaining some good office by his interest, which he has promised me. I however pleased myself with determining not to go near Col. James Stuart and his fair spouse till I should have a pretty strong invitation, as they had neglected me of late.[6] I even thought of first answering their invitation by a very polite formal card, evading them till I should see them fully sensible of their being in the wrong to me. An ancient baron may pull up when he pleases; and his pride may prevail over his gaiety. Called at Sir Thomas Dundas's. The porter said he was very busy. Met Ross, the player, in Hyde Park and walked with him. Dined at General Paoli's; a numerous company, mostly foreigners. Showed myself quite moderate in wine, and was in perfect good spirits. Langton, who was just come up from Rochester, had called on me at the General's this forenoon.[7] I hastened to him and drank tea with him and Lady Rothes at Faulder's in Bond Street.[8] We were most comfortably social.

[5] Lord Mountstuart, the eldest son of George III's favourite, the Earl of Bute, invited Boswell (who was four years older than he) to be his companion when they were both travelling in Italy in 1765. Boswell had regarded him as his patron ever since. Lord Mountstuart allowed Boswell to interpret his remarks as promises, but the journals show a record of practical indifference.

[6] He had reason to expect cordiality from Lord Bute's second son and from Margaret Stuart, the daughter of Sir David Cunynghame of Milncraig and niece of Lord Eglinton. At Colonel Stuart's invitation he had accompanied him on an extended jaunt to London and Chester in the autumn of 1779 (effecting for the worse both the violence of Boswell's temper and his consumption of alcohol). Mrs. Stuart was Margaret Boswell's intimate friend and Boswell's confidante also, but the numerous sentimental letters he exchanged with her suggest nothing irregular.

[7] Bennet Langton, familiar to readers of Boswell's journals and of the *Life of Johnson* as the gangling "stork on one leg" (Henry Beste, *Personal and Literary Memorials*, 1829, p. 62) whom Johnson loved but ridiculed for a mismanaged household and the doting indulgence of his children. (There were already eight of ten.) Langton was an original member of The Club, and Boswell was acquainted with him at least as early as 1768. Boswell found Langton attractive because of his learning, his piety, and his descent from an ancient, landed Lincolnshire family. He had been working since the early summer of 1780 as a military engineer repairing and augmenting the fortifications around the naval arsenal and shipyards at Chatham. In 1781 he moved his family to the adjacent town of Rochester.

[8] Langton's wife retained the style of her former marriage to an elderly Scots peer, John Leslie, tenth Earl of Rothes. She had been left a widow at twenty-four. Faulder seems to be the bookseller in New Bond Street (an extension of Bond Street) who later

I then sauntered to Dr. Johnson's. Found him with one Lowe, an inferior painter, sitting by him. I asked him if he had been abroad today. "Don't talk so childishly," said he. "You may as well ask if I hanged myself today." This was churlish. I mentioned politics. He said, "I'd as soon have a man break my bones as talk to me of public affairs, internal or external. I have lived to see things all as bad as they can be."

Lowe went soon away. The Doctor told me he was a bastard son of Lord Southwell's.[9] He said Lord Southwell was the highest-bred man, without insolence, he ever was in company with; the most *qualified* [1] (I suppose from *quality*) he ever saw. Lord Orrery was not dignified. Lord Chesterfield was, but he was insolent. He never was at table with him.[2] "Lord Shelburne is a man of coarse manners, but a man of abilities and of information. I don't say he is a man I would set at the head of a nation, though perhaps he may be as good as the next prime minister that comes. But he is a man to be at the head of a club. I don't say our club. For there's no such club. He talks himself out of breath till he howls, from which he was called Malagrida. You know the meaning of the word." "Yes," said I, "crying harshly." "Well, Sir," said he, "he was called Malagrida on that account. Goldsmith's blundering speech, which he really did make to him, was only a blunder in expression: 'I wonder they should call your Lordship Malagrida, for Malagrida was a very good man,' meant, 'I wonder they should use Malagrida as a term of reproach.' "[3] "But, Sir," said I, "was not Lord Shelburne a factious man?" "O yes, Sir; as factious a fellow as could

published Boswell's scurrilous *Ode by Dr. Samuel Johnson to Mrs. Thrale upon Their Supposed Approaching Nuptials* (1788) and his verse pamphlet, *No Abolition of Slavery* (1791).

[9] So the *Gentleman's Magazine* reported in its obituary of him, but he himself claimed a connexion with an ancient Bishop of Rochester. Mauritius Lowe was quarrelsome, conceited, and not a very good painter, but his poverty and wretchedness secured him Johnson's protection. Johnson stood godfather to two of his children, recommended him as a portrait-painter to anybody who he thought could pay for a picture (he offered to accept the pictures as a gift if the sitters did not wish them), and left him a small legacy.

[1] "Belonging to the upper classes of society; 'of quality' " (OED), an obsolete usage except in dialect by the later nineteenth century. In the manuscript and the first edition of the *Life of Johnson* the word is also *qualified*; it was changed to *qualitied*, without comment, in the second edition.

[2] Affirmation of the statement Johnson had made some years before, that the "respectable Hottentot" in Lord Chesterfield's *Letters* was not meant for him because Lord Chesterfield had never seen him eat or drink (Journal, 28 March 1775).

[3] Malagrida was an Italian Jesuit executed in Portugal in 1761, ostensibly for heresy but actually because he had not divulged a plot to assassinate the king which he had learned of through the confessional. His trial was long and notorious, and his name

be found; one who was for sinking us all into the mob." "How then, Sir, did the King choose him to be his Prime Minister?" "Because, Sir, I suppose he promised the King to do whatever he pleased."

I told him how this day in Hyde Park by reading my overseer's letter I had found I had an anchor. He said, "I am sorry you should want an anchor. I doubt if your fondness for London is so great as you talk." "Sir, a man must know himself if it be so." "I am not sure of that." He was in that kind of humour tonight that he had no allowance to make for anything but the rational part of our nature, nothing for fancy, nothing for inclination, nothing for the *nescioquae dulcedo* which may be experienced from a variety of causes as well as the *natale solum*.[4] I spoke of building on the old situation at Auchinleck.[5] He raged against this, and said, "It is too late to indulge fancy. It may do in a young man, but not at your age; not in a man with a wife and five children." He even checked every ambitious wish which started from me, and wanted to beat me down to dull content with my present state. He said, "Talk no more in this way. People will only laugh at you, or be vexed, as I am." In short he was in a very disagreeable frame tonight; and amidst all my admiration of his great talents, I recollected how Sir John Pringle objected that he had not wisdom for giving counsel. He meant that sagacity or common sense which is practically of more consequence than all the genius of the first writers. And I recollected also how roughly he discouraged me from my exertions in favour of the Corsicans, by which, as I myself foresaw, I raised myself twenty degrees higher in fame and in general advantage as a social man than I should have been had he been successful in repressing my generous ardour. The great difficulty is to distinguish between noble ambition and foolish, restless, conceited aspiring. In my coolest moments, and after employing the powers of judgement and reflection which GOD has given me, with a fair wish to be well-informed, I am clearly persuaded that a man of my family, talents, and connexions may reasonably

---

became symbolic of the duplicity popularly associated in Protestant countries with the Jesuit order. So Johnson makes clear when he explains Goldsmith's blunder (an example, according to Sir Joshua Reynolds, of intended humour which others took seriously). But Johnson is also making the point that the name Malagrida can be etymologized as "harsh cry" or "he cries harshly," and that in the beginning Shelburne was being arraigned not for duplicity but for a disagreeable way of speaking. He was called Malagrida "on *that* account" (italics ours). This is one of the rare instances where Boswell wrote a really private journal, that is, where he omitted information which any reader except himself and Johnson would need.

[4]"Nescioqua natale solum dulcedine cunctos/ducit et inmemores non sinit esse sui: I know not by what sweet charm the native land draws all men nor allows them to forget her" (Ovid, *Epistolae ex Ponto*, I. iii. 35–36).

[5]On the site of the old castle.

endeavour to be employed in a more elevated sphere than in Scotland, now that is in reality only a province. But if I find after some time that there is little hope of being so employed, I shall set my mind to be satisfied with a judge's place in Scotland.

I sauntered home to Mr. Dilly's, where I found Mr. Braithwaite of the Post-Office.[6] I eat a crust of bread and drank some glasses of Madeira; was very well, and went quietly to bed.

MONDAY 24 MARCH. (Writing the 30.) Sat at Mr. Dilly's quietly all the morning and wrote journal. Then took a hackney-coach and drove with my baggage to General Paoli's. Found myself at home in my room in his house, just as formerly. Two Corsicans, Masseria, who had been at Gibraltar, and Colle, who had served at Minorca and lost an arm there, were with the General every day at dinner.[7] I find that if I neglect to make memorandums at the time, I cannot bring up my journal with any accuracy. I dined at the General's today. I then called on Tom Davies and sat a little with him and his wife. Then called on Dr. Johnson. He was asleep, and I would not disturb him or wait till he should awake. In truth I was not displeased that he was asleep, being not disposed to bear any checks. Such was my humour at the time. I sauntered home. Sat awhile with General Oglethorpe.

TUESDAY 25 MARCH. (Writing the 30.) Breakfasted with the General. Called on Lord Mountstuart. The porter said he was not stirring yet, but after asking if my name was Boswell, seemed authorized to let me in. So I told him I would return. I went and paid a visit to Lord Cassillis, drank some tea, and was cordial with him. Took an opportunity to tell him that I was very sorry my song about him and the Coopers had displeased him; that I would not offend him a moment for five hundred songs. He mumbled something. But all offence was removed, and he asked me when I was not engaged to send in a friendly way and ask if he dined at home, and come to him. I then was admitted at Lord Mountstuart's. He shook hands with me. But was strangely cold and distant. The Rev. Dr. Douglas[8] and another clergyman were with him, which prevented me from talking freely to him of such a manner. They went away. He then talked of the state of politics, and

[6]Daniel Braithwaite, clerk to the Postmaster-General, whom Boswell described as "a well-behaved man, but modest and silent among *us*" (Journal, 15 April 1779).

[7]Since Paoli's exile in 1769, after the French crushed the Corsican struggle for independence, he had maintained followers in England and in Italy from the pension of £1,200 awarded him by the British government. Pietro Colle was one of Paoli's bravest and most trusted captains throughout the fighting. Filippo Masseria later acted as Paoli's emissary to Paris when Corsica declared loyalty to the French revolutionary government and Paoli was recalled to the island.

[8]Dr. John Douglas, canon residentiary of St. Paul's, later Bishop of Carlisle and a member of The Club.

with his admirable calm clearness showed how the whole range of the Party striving to get into Administration were needy men. One of the clergymen returned to him; and I saw there was business, so went away. This was a poor crop of old friendship. But there is no help for his way. I found Lady Mountstuart in her coach at the door. She was very affable, and said she was come from countries where they never talk of liberty and never feel slavery.[9] I made some calls, and sat awhile with Dr. Johnson. (Writing 3 April from short notes.) I do not recollect any of his sayings. I dined at the Literary Club. There were present Dean Marlay, Sir Joshua Reynolds, Dr. Fordyce, Mr. Colman, Sir William Jones, Mr. Steevens, Mr. Gibbon, who came late, and myself;[10] in all eight. We were well enough. But I find nothing in our conversation to pickle or preserve (to use a metaphor of General Paoli's). I went home with Sir Joshua and drank tea; found Miss Palmer as agreeable as ever.[1] We intended to have gone and visited Dr. Johnson. But a heavy rain came on. So we sat still where we were, and I read to him and Miss Palmer a good part of a poem called *The Village* by a Mr. Crabbe, which had been revised by Dr. Johnson. The Doctor had made some alterations and added some lines.[2] I got the poem home with me and copied all the Doctor's fragments. Sir Joshua, who always makes just and delicate remarks, observed that all young writers tried pastoral because it is a species of composition for which no knowledge of life is requisite. His nephew, Mr. Palmer, a clergyman in Ireland, and his niece, Mrs. Salkeld, and her husband came from the play, and we had some supper. I was quite gay and happy, having drank little wine at The Club. I have no merit in my present sobriety. There is nothing moral in it, but merely a fortunate physical state. I have no inclination to drink much, as I used to have; no irritation that urges me to it.

WEDNESDAY 26 MARCH. (Writing the 3rd April from short notes.)

[9]Lord Mountstuart was Envoy to Turin from 1779 to 1783.

[10]Dr. Richard Marlay, Dean of Ferns, later Bishop of Clonfert and of Waterford; Dr. George Fordyce, F.R.S., physician and lecturer on medicine and chemistry; George Colman the elder, dramatist and manager of the Haymarket Theatre; Sir William Jones, jurist and orientalist, knighted just six days previous to this meeting; George Steevens, editor of Shakespeare, an intimate of Samuel Johnson's; and Edward Gibbon, the great historian of Rome.

[1]Mary Palmer, the eldest daughter of Sir Joshua's sister Mary, lived with him from 1773 until his death in February 1792, when she inherited most of his estate. Five months later, at the age of forty-two, she was married at Beaconsfield to the Earl of Inchiquin, a widower then almost seventy.

[2]When Boswell transcribed this information into the manuscript of the *Life of Johnson* he wrote in the margin, "This must be touched very delicately." In response to his memorandum he added a note which praised Johnson but assured the reader that his contributions to Crabbe's poem "were so small as by no means to impair the distinguished merit of the author." *The Village* was published in May 1783.

I breakfasted with Mr. John Ross Mackye, as my father's only surviving friend in London, and listened to him with a conscientious, a pious, patience, from parental duty at second-hand.[3] Went with General Paoli and paid a visit to Dempster at Brompton Row. Dined at Mr. Dilly's; my brother David, Dr. Mayo, Sir Charles Field there. Sauntered along homewards. But I should have observed that Henry Sampson Woodfall was there, who being an old publishing acquaintance, and a fine hearty fellow, and one who loves a bottle, I, to give him an opportunity of being as he could wish, called for another bottle of port and drank rather more than usual.[4] I went to Mrs. Thrale's and sat awhile with Dr. Johnson in his own room, and then went up to the drawing-room and saw Mrs. Thrale, Mr. Cambridge, Dr. Burney, Miss Burney,[5] etc. They were just parting. But I was glad to shake hands with Miss Burney after the great fame of her *Cecilia*.

THURSDAY 27 MARCH. (Writing 3 April.) Breakfasted with General William Gordon, who was very pleasant and friendly, and delivered me a discharge of James Samson, one of my Trabboch people, who had deserted from his regiment.[6] Either yesterday or today Lord Marchmont paid me a visit and sat a quarter of an hour.[7] It was very agreeable to see him animated as ever. He said this country had been governed by great men, and people had no notion how much mischief fools could do. I went this forenoon to Mr. Burke's, and to my regret found him cajoling the blackguard mad publican, Sam House, because he has a considerable influence in Westminster, and at Fox's election

[3] He could have learned much from Mackye, a Scots advocate, M.P. (1742–1768), private secretary to Lord Bute, Treasurer of the Ordnance (1763–1780), and since 1780 Receiver General of Stamp Duties. He held the last office until 1794, and died three years later, aged ninety.

[4] Woodfall had published letters, verses, and essays by Boswell in the *Public Advertiser* as early as 1763. A group of occasional essays by him signed "Rampager" had appeared there from 1770 to 1782.

[5] Common friends, now at the high point of their intimacy. Richard Owen Cambridge, wit, verse satirist (*The Scribleriad*), and essayist, attracted eminent figures from the political world as well as the arts to his beautiful villa at Twickenham. The attention he was now showing Fanny Burney led her concerned friends to question whether it was he rather than his son, the Rev. George Owen Cambridge, who had a romantic interest in her. Miss Burney's friendship with Mrs. Thrale had become so close that she resided with the Thrales for considerable periods of time. Dr. Charles Burney, Fanny's father, a fashionable musician, composer, conductor, and teacher, is best known for his four-volume *History of Music*.

[6] See above, 6 February 1783.

[7] He doubtless called because Boswell was now Laird. No other visit to Boswell is reported in the journal. The old statesman, Keeper of the Great Seal of Scotland and since 1750 a Representative Peer, was now in his seventy-fifth year. His reminiscences of Pope and Bolingbroke, who had been his intimate friends, and his connexion by marriage with Boswell's grandfather had endeared him to Boswell.

gave porter gratis and carried a number of voters for him. The fellow was sitting in the middle of Mr. Burke's breakfasting-room with a head close-shaved, without a wig, without a coat, the knees of his breeches loose, a pair of white silk stockings and slippers; and he had a large glass of brandy or brandy and water with some pieces of bread for his regale. A hackney-coach waited at the door for him. I was vexed to think that Burke, "fraught with all learning" and a good Tory, I do believe, should from party keenness debase himself thus.[8] Mrs. Burke, my Lord Templetown, and several gentlemen formed a circle round the animal. I walked with Mr. Burke to the House of Commons, and he took me to the committee then sitting on India Affairs. The volumes of information, and the neat gentlemanlike manner in which business appeared to be carried on here, pleased me much. I dined at my Chief Godfrey Bosville's, a large company there to celebrate Sir Thomas Blackett's birthday.[9] I did not drink too much. In the evening was Mrs. Bosville's rout. I played a pool at commerce and a rubber at whist, and lost at both, which vexed me a little. I should never play at all. I felt myself wonderfully steady in London now, and had lost the idea of great distance between it and Auchinleck. My brother David dined here today and passed the evening. But neither he nor I stayed supper. I went home with General Paoli and Mr. Gentili[1] quietly.

FRIDAY 28 MARCH. (Writing 3 April.) Breakfasted pleasingly with Sir Joshua Reynolds. Then found Mrs. Thrale at breakfast, and drank some chocolade. Dr. Johnson appeared, and was better and more agreeable. I made many calls. My brother David dined with us at General Paoli's comfortably. I passed the evening cordially with Langton.

SATURDAY 29 MARCH. (Writing 3 April.) Sat a little with Lord Mountstuart; then was at home all the forenoon writing letters, and in a settled good frame. Had visits of the Earl of Galloway, Mr. Johnston of Carnsalloch, and Mr. Hunter Blair,[2] who told me an admirable saying of the Attorney-General (Kenyon's), who complained of Burke's

[8] Boswell is quoting Goldsmith's mock epitaph on Burke, in *Retaliation*, ll. 31–34. The rest of the passage exactly summarizes Boswell's feelings:

> Who, born for the universe, narrow'd his mind,
> And to party gave up what was meant for mankind;
> Though fraught with all learning, yet straining his throat
> To persuade Tommy Townshend to lend him a vote.

[9] Sir Thomas Wentworth, Mrs. Bosville's brother, had added his mother's surname to his own when he succeeded to her family estates in 1777.

[1] Paoli's trusted friend and his secretary in London. He had taken part in the Corsican struggle against the Genoese when he was only sixteen years old.

[2] All Scots friends. John Stewart, seventh Earl of Galloway, was a Representative Peer and a Knight of the Thistle. James Hunter Blair, whom Boswell met when they were

wildness. He said, "I never could *cage* his opinions." Lord Pembroke
had with his usual very flattering kindness called on me, and then sent
an obliging pleasant note inviting me to dine with him today. I was
happy to be there. The company: Lady Pembroke, Lord Herbert, Sir
George Metham, Mr. Hinde, a clergyman, and the Irish Lord Fitzwilliam, my Lord's cousin, whom I had seen here before, and who
talked to me of Temple and Nicholls, with whom he had been at college
at Cambridge;³ and when I talked flashily of ambition, and being discontent if I had not something . . .⁴ great Earl of Pembroke, the British
peer of high respect. I loved and admired, but did not reverence him.
I went to Lord Eglinton's, with intention to sup with him. But though
it was eleven at night, he had not risen from dinner; so, luckily enough
for me, I went home quietly, and had my bit of dry toast with warm
port and water and sugar, which I take at night, and had some agreeable
conversation with the General and Messrs. Gentili and Masseria, I
think.

SUNDAY 30 MARCH. (Writing 4 April.) Went to high mass in the
Portuguese Chapel; was calm and elevated. Then paid a visit to the
Duke of Montrose, with whom I sat some time. He talked easily and
well, and asked me to dinner. But as I had made a resolution never
to break an engagement, I refused an invitation from his Grace, as I
had done one from Lord Advocate, that I might keep my appointment
with Mr. Dance, the musician. Walking down Lower Grosvenor Street,
I was accosted by three Yorkshire sailors who wanted to find Sir Charles
Turner's house, and told me it was in Davies Street. I found it for
them; and on the strength of having pleaded ten days before him on
the Ayrshire election, I paid him a visit.⁵ He knew me at once, said he
was glad to see me, presented me to his lady, raved awhile on politics,
and when I went away, said he was obliged to me, and asked where
I lived. I am confirmed by Dr. Johnson in the notion that the more a
man extends and varies his acquaintance, the better. It was a wet day.

---

both students at the University of Edinburgh, was a wealthy banker (senior co-partner
of Sir William Forbes) and M.P. for Edinburgh.
³ The Rev. William Johnson Temple, Boswell's intimate friend, and the Rev. Norton
Nicholls, a close friend of Temple's, who was at this time in Boswell's bad graces
because of what Boswell considered his foppery and his flippancy about religion.
⁴ Two leaves (three pages) were here torn out and removed from the notebook. The
missing leaves may have contained scandal about the Earl of Pembroke, with whose
name the journal is resumed. What follows gives no indication of improper behaviour
on Boswell's part.
⁵ Sir Charles, M.P. for York from 1768 until his death later this year, had been a
member of the Parliamentary committee before which Boswell had argued unsuccessfully in March and April 1781 on the disputed Ayrshire election of 1780.

I sat awhile with Lord Ankerville and awhile with Tom Davies; then dined at Dance's. My old acquaintance his mother, Mrs. Love; his wife (a pleasing girl of Lymington); and Miss Reynolds, a teacher of music from Oxford, all contributed to entertain me. I had a deliberate enjoyment of that species of life which the middle ranks have in London. Dance played a little on the harpsichord, and so did Miss Reynolds. I was well entertained. I had nothing to vex me. I then went to Dr. Johnson's; found him with his two ladies and a Mr. Ryland, a good-talking man enough.[6] Then the Doctor and I went to his own room. Dr. Brocklesby came, and roused us by that flow of spirits just supplied by an active bustling through life. He took to me agreeably, and we had much conversation about Sir John Pringle. He praised him as a very worthy man, and said that his being President of the Royal Society had given him an opportunity to display a much greater variety of literature than he was supposed to possess. He mentioned his sad failure and narrowness in the latter part of his life. Dr. Johnson said there must have been a degree of madness about him. Dr. Brocklesby said his judgement was entire. But when he mentioned his being worth £27,000 yet unwilling to keep a carriage because he feared he should die of want, "Nay, Sir," said Dr. Johnson, "when the judgement is so disturbed that a man cannot count, that is pretty well."

I should have mentioned that one day last week I paid a visit to Lady Diana Beauclerk at No. 19 in Sackville Street. She (writing 8 April) was exceedingly agreeable; and she owned herself a true hypochondriac. She said she was sometimes quite miserable, and could paint nothing but what was hideous. She said she believed she should die mad, melancholy mad. Our conversation was fine raving. She told me that her melancholy never took the turn of fear of a future state. She thought there were many good things about her, and any follies she had committed were sufficiently punished in this world.[7] The Hon. Andrew Erskine is another instance of one afflicted with melancholy who never dreads "something after death."[8] This is amazing to me whose imagination, when gloomy, stretches itself beyond the grave into unlimited extent of conjecture.

MONDAY 31 MARCH. (Writing 11 April.) Breakfasted with Mr. Burke most agreeably. He alluded pleasantly to my attending execu-

[6] A West India merchant in London, the last surviving friend of Johnson's early life in the city. Oddly enough, this is Boswell's only reference to him in the journal.
[7] Lady Diana, the eldest daughter of the third Duke of Marlborough, was married to Beauclerk two days after her divorce from Viscount Bolingbroke by Act of Parliament. Beauclerk turned out to be a very difficult husband, and her second marriage was also troubled.
[8] *Hamlet*, III, i. 77.

tions, and said, "You have seen more life and more death than any man." "Well," said I, "and I hope I shall see immortality: *Night Thoughts on Life, Death, and Immortality*. I hope I shall be Dr. Young when I grow old." This was playing with words and ideas in his own style. Mr. Francis came and sat awhile with Mr. Burke and me in his study.[9] I at Mr. Burke's desire gave him Lord Chatham's harangue to me.[1] Mr. Francis had lived in his family and acted, I believe, as a private secretary to him. He said he used to harangue to him, and was proud and despotic, and he had no books or papers about him, but used to sit and meditate, and work it all out of his own mind. Mr. Burke read us his character of Lord Chatham, which he said Lord Chatham did not like, for he clearly saw the defects and bad parts which it hinted at. Lucan was his favourite author, and what follows the quotation from that author is against him.[2] After Francis went away, Burke kept me sitting by him a long time. He would not let me go. I talked to him of my removing to London. He gave the subject only a superficial, cursory view; for at first he seemed to encourage my coming, and thought my estate, with the profession of the law in aid of it, might support me very well in London. Then again he said I enjoyed London more by coming to it two or three months every year than if I lived in it. I resolved to obtain his attentive opinion in writing. I chatted a little with him easily, so that there is not much to register. I dined at Langton's with Mr. Windham of Norfolk and Dr. Parr, the celebrated Greek scholar, whom

[9]This is also Boswell's sole reference to Philip Francis, reputed author of the Junius letters, and another man who might be expected to make a larger figure in the journals.
[1]In a private interview on 23 February 1766, when Boswell, recently returned from Corsica, attempted to convey a verbal message from Paoli which Pitt refused to hear because he was a member of the Privy Council and was committed by oath to report the message to the King and the Council (see Journal, 23 February 1766).
[2]"Lord Chatham, a great and celebrated name, a name that keeps the name of this country respectable in every other on the globe. It may truly be called
'clarum et venerabile nomen
gentibus, et multum nostrae quod proderat urbi'
['A name which the nations account glorious and venerable, a name that did much good to our city'—Lucan, Cato's eulogy on Pompey, *Pharsalia*, ix. 203–204.] Sir, the venerable age of this great man, his merited rank, his superior eloquence, his splendid qualities, his eminent services, the vast space he fills in the eye of mankind, and more than all the rest, his fall from power, which, like death, canonizes and sanctifies a great character, will not suffer me to censure any part of his conduct. . . . But what I do not presume to censure, I may have leave to lament. . . . He made an Administration so checkered and speckled, he put together a piece of joinery so crossly indented and whimsically dovetailed, a Cabinet so curiously inlaid . . . patriots and courtiers, King's friends and republicans, Whigs and Tories, treacherous friends and open enemies, that it was indeed a very curious show, but utterly unsafe to touch, and unsure to stand on" (*Speech on American Taxation*, 19 April 1774).

I had not seen before.[3] His learning, and I may say, eloquence, pleased me, though I was not quite easy under the consciousness of my own ignorance, and though there was something odd in his manner and rather lax in his way of thinking; I do not mean immoral, but not quite orthodox. I said a pretty good thing today at Burke's of Parr and Langton: "Langton himself is *above par*—in Greek."

I sat some time with Dr. Johnson in the forenoon. He said that increasing the wages of day-labourers was injudicious, for it did not make them live better but only be idler; and that idleness is a very bad thing for human nature.

Mrs. Buller, the learned lady, and Lady Scarsdale and her daughter, Miss Curzon, drank tea at Langton's. The conversation was agreeable. I was quiet, and sat the remainder of the evening with him and his lady. Mrs. Buller pointed out the economy by which living in London may be managed, and Langton and I, who are both exceedingly fond of that life could we afford it, listened eagerly. Said he: "This will put you again in the humour of it, and you'll have Dr. Johnson scolding you." "Ay," said I. "It is setting up the poor cock to be thrown at again."

TUESDAY 1 APRIL. (Writing the 11.) Col. James Stuart having called on me and a card having come from his fair lady that "they were shocked at my neglect," I drove this morning to Richmond Park. The General went with me in his chariot till we were near to it. Then he mounted his horse, and I took on the chariot. The Colonel was gone to London. But I found Mrs. Stuart, got breakfast from her and was kindly received, and any suspicion of my being neglected by them vanished. It was, as she called it in a letter to my wife, an earthly paradise. She walked with me a little, and then I came in and had cold ham and veal and ale, quite hearty and rural. I had engaged to return and dine with the General. But I engaged to be at Colonel Stuart's on Friday, to dine and stay till next day.

I went to Dr. Johnson's in the evening. But I recollect nothing. So much do I lose by being less assiduous in recording his sayings than

---

[3]William Windham, friend of Johnson and a member of The Club, a classicist and mathematician of outstanding abilities and considerable personal charm. In 1784 he entered the House of Commons, where his changeable views during a long tenure earned him the sobriquet "Weathercock Windham." Dr. Samuel Parr, schoolmaster and divine, was generally described as learned, sociable, and kindly, but verbose and pompous. He held somewhat ambiguous religious views: an outspoken Whig with many friends among the dissenters, at this time he still upheld the Test Act and subscription to the Thirty-nine Articles, which he interpreted liberally. Just the week before Boswell met him Parr was inducted as prebendary of Wenlock Barnes in St. Paul's Cathedral at the request of his patron, the second Earl Dartmouth. Not surprisingly, however, he failed to rise in the church.

I have been. I may however put down here, though I am not sure of the time, that he one of these days approved of keeping a journal for a man's own use, and said that one may write upon a card a day all that is necessary to be written after one has had experience of life. At first there is a great deal to be written, because there is a great deal of novelty. But when once a man has settled his opinions, there is seldom much to be set down. He said there was nothing wonderful in the journal which we see Swift kept in London; for it contains slight topics, and it might soon be written. I thought it sophistry in him to maintain, as he did, that keeping accounts was of no use when a man is spending his own money and has nobody to whom he is to account. I had praised the accuracy of Mrs. Stuart's household book. "Sir," said he, "you won't eat less beef today because you have written down what it cost yesterday. Let people take only what is necessary, and spend only what they can afford." I told him my wife maintained the same doctrine with him upon this subject, and I could not get her to keep an account. "Sir," said he, "it is fit she should keep an account because you wish it, but I do not see its use." I said that it may be of use to satisfy a man that his money has not been lost or stolen, which one would sometimes be apt to imagine were no account kept of one's expense; and besides, a calculation of economy so as not to exceed one's income cannot be made without a view of the different articles in figures. One may see how to retrench in some particulars less necessary than others.

There was next morning to be a meeting of the partners of the *London Magazine* to breakfast at the Chapter Coffee-house to hold a consultation what we should do, as our publication, instead of being profitable, was of late become a loss to us.[4] So I went this night to my City quarters at Mr. Dilly's. I should have mentioned that I this afternoon drank tea at Lord Mountstuart's.

WEDNESDAY 2 APRIL. (Writing the 12.) Let me begin this day with recording some sayings of General Paoli. He said, "Wisdom prevents unhappiness, but does not give pleasure. Lord Stormont is so stately and walks so erect because he is full of wind, and were he to stoop, would f—t."[5] (An excellent ludicrous image of the wind of the Murrays.) "Sir Joshua Reynolds paints so very naturally that his colours fade as fast as those in the natural face. Do not put down the good things you

[4]The other partners were Henry Baldwin, Robert Baldwin, Thomas Becket, Edward Dilly, and John Rivington. Boswell had contributed to the magazine and been part-owner since 1770.

[5]David Murray, seventh Viscount Stormont and later second Earl of Mansfield, this day accepted the office of Lord President of the Council in the Duke of Portland's Coalition ministry. He had been a Representative Peer since 1754, and was Lord Justice General (nominal head of the Court of Justiciary).

hear. You will forget them. You cannot have the same thing in two places." I this morning called again on Mr. Robert Preston. Not at home. Visited Mr. and Mrs. Forbes, and was pleased to see all their six children. [6] Took some breakfast with them. Then went to the Chapter and took a hearty breakfast with the partners of the *London Magazine*. Was vexed a little to find there was a considerable loss of the capital. But liked the animation of endeavouring to raise it again, for which purpose we resolved to take in more partners and have a new plan. [7] I sat a little with Dr. Johnson. Do not recollect anything. Dined at home. Went again to Lord Mountstuart's, and found old John Ross Mackye with him. Was a little hurt that he should never send for me while he had such a man with him. I said I had thoughts of trying to dine with him today. Instead of kindly saying, "I should have been glad to see you," he formally and coldly said, "I did happen to dine at home today." I drank a dish of tea; then went to Burke's. He was not at home. [8] But I drank some tea with Mrs. Burke and his son. Sauntered home.

THURSDAY 3 APRIL. (Writing the 16 from notes.) Lord Ankerville breakfasted with us, or rather indeed sat by us while we breakfasted, and was pleased with being introduced to the General. I sat a little with Miss Palmer. Had called on Lord Advocate and been asked to dine with him, but was unluckily engaged. Called again today. He sent his servant after me to bring me back. Was open, frank, and hearty. [9] Read me Lord Shelburne's letter to him pressing him to join his administration, his letter to Lord Shelburne pressing the appointment of Mr. Pitt as First Lord of the Treasury, to disappoint the factious coalition, and Mr. Pitt's letter to him declining to accept after having deliberately weighed all circumstances. These were important and animated State papers; and though I might see a lofty vanity working in the Advocate's breast, I was highly gratified in having them communicated to me. He said he avowed his having attached himself to Pitt, whose abilities

[6] John Forbes was a merchant and banker in Aldermanbury. Boswell claimed Mrs. Forbes as his nearest relation in London before his brother David settled there, but their exact relationship is not certain. She was probably of the family of Douglas of Kelhead.

[7] The "new plan" of an enlarged and improved publication in ten "departments" or sections was adopted, and the price of each issue raised to one shilling, but the *London Magazine* survived only to June 1785. Boswell withdrew as a partner 7 December 1784.

[8] The arrangement of a coalition government was announced in Parliament this day, and though not all the appointments were officially concluded, it was known that the Duke of Portland would be First Lord of the Treasury, the former adversaries Lord North and Charles Fox Principal Secretaries of State, and Edmund Burke Paymaster of the Forces.

[9] Henry Dundas, of the famous Arniston legal family, was made Lord Advocate for Scotland in 1775, and in 1782 given official management of all places falling vacant

and high virtue were most distinguished. He said he wished Burke might keep his place, for he was a virtuous man. I consulted him on my own schemes. He was against my purchasing a seat in Parliament and encumbering myself with £3,000 of debt which I might find it difficult ever to discharge. He said, "The first thing for a man is to be round in himself."[1] He was for my continuing assiduously at my profession, and said that this, and being a man of family, would give me a claim to a judge's place. That this was a time quite improper for coming into Parliament upon purchase, everything being in uncertainty. But that I might dash into Parliament afterwards if a good opportunity should offer. He engaged to be friendly to me, should I apply some time hence for a judge's place in Scotland. I called at Mrs. Boscawen's, Sir George Baker's, Lord Cathcart's, Mr. Paradise's, Sir John Dick's, Lord Thurlow's; all not at home.

I called at Lord Mansfield's,[2] not expecting to find him at home; but as I had written to him from Scotland and taken occasion to observe that I had been honoured with less of his Lordship's notice than others whom I did not think better entitled to it, I was resolved to leave my card to let him know where I lived, and if he did not send to me, would not go near him.[3] To my surprise, a *maid* who opened the door said my Lord was at home; and then a footman, having got my name, announced me to the Earl, who had just come home and was sitting in his study in a bob-wig. He received me with a courteous smile; bid me sit down, and said, "I am glad I happened to be come in when you called. What are you doing in Scotland?" BOSWELL. "Cursing Lord North." MANSFIELD. "Ay? ha! ha!" BOSWELL. "Why, my Lord, you know

---

there. Almost two years older than the Lord Advocate, Boswell was jealous of his abilities and his success, and although presently on good terms with him, had opposed him openly in certain of the elections by which Dundas consolidated his power over Scottish politics.

[1] An allusion to Horace, *Satires*, II. vii. 83–86: "Who then is free? The wise man, who rules himself . . . and in himself is whole, smooth, and rounded."

[2] Lord Chief Justice of the King's Bench. William Murray, first Earl of Mansfield, a Scot educated at Westminster and Oxford, was a member of the Privy Council and twice held the seals of the Exchequer. He deeply influenced the development of English common law.

[3] "MY LORD,—I reckon myself unlucky in having had less of your Lordship's attention than others not better entitled to it. I have been informed that I gave you offence several years ago, by speaking too favourably in your presence of the gay and classical John Wilkes. 'Nihil est ab omni parte beatum' ['Nothing is completely happy'—Horace, *Odes*, II. xvi. 27–28]. I regret never having been invited to Caen Wood, or to share any of the social hours of Pope's Murray, which few could have relished more than myself" (14 February 1783).

they worshipped him there for a long time like the Golden Calf. But
if he has mixed himself with baser metal, it is fair to curse him."
MANSFIELD. "No inconsistency, Sir." I mentioned Lord Kames's death
and my having seen much of him in his last days, and I mentioned the
good situation into which my friend Mr. Murray, now Lord Henderland, had got.⁴ "That is according to a man's disposition," said the Earl.
"The Advocate would not like it." He took no notice of the letter I had
written to him. But I perceived it had operated favourably, for upon
Single-speech Hamilton's coming in, I rose to go away, and the Earl
was again smilingly courteous, and said, "I shall be glad to have the
favour" (or "pleasure," or some such polite expression) "of your company to dine here one day."⁵ General Oglethorpe told me he had mentioned to Lord Mansfield my being in town, and my Lord said, "Why,
I han't seen him." This was a little hint of good reception. I mentioned
General Oglethorpe to him today. He said, "He does me the favour
to come sometimes on Sunday." The truth is I had no interested view
in waiting on Lord Mansfield. I wished only to be with him as a man
of great eminence.

I paid a visit to Lady Margaret Macdonald, who was by no means
pleased that I would not put money into her hands to be ready to
answer any future bill of Henry Cuninghame.⁶ She had advanced £30
for him, and I suspected she might reimburse herself. I told her she
was richer than I. But if a future bill came, my brother had my authority
to answer to the extent of £30. I dined at Mr. Windham's in Queen
Anne's Street West. It was agreeable to be on an easy footing with the
Norfolk Windham, a scholar and a Brooks's man, whose *name* is to me

⁴By clever phrasing in the *Journal of a Tour to the Hebrides*, Boswell hinted that Murray's
marriage to a niece of Lord Mansfield was helpful to his promotion. No doubt it was,
but custom permitted the Solicitor-General to nominate himself for a vacancy in the
Court of Session and the High Court of Justiciary.
⁵William Gerard Hamilton (Boswell's second cousin) when a young man of twenty-six
made a maiden speech in Parliament so remarkable as to attract general attention.
Because it was "full of antithesis," and these antitheses "full of argument," as Horace
Walpole wrote to General Conway (London, 15 November 1755, *Yale Walpole Correspondence*, 37. 416), it has been suggested (but also vigorously denied) that Samuel
Johnson was the author. Though it was not literally true that Hamilton never spoke
again, his silence by 1783 had lasted so long that the legend of a single speech was
justified. Hamilton was an early patron of Burke, who, according to contemporary
testimony, helped write his speeches when Hamilton sat in the Irish Parliament,
1761–1768.
⁶The youngest of Boswell's impecunious Cuninghame cousins. Boswell had no doubt
appealed to Lady Margaret as a distant relation. She was a Montgomerie (half-sister
of the tenth Earl of Eglinton), of which family the Montgomeries of Lainshaw (Henry
Cuninghame's mother's family) were ultimately cadets.

highly classical from Pope.[7] Langton and Dr. Parr were the company. The comfortable house, good library, and good entertainment, both for the mouth and the mind (to use Dr. Johnson's phrase), gave me much satisfaction. Yet I have nothing to record except the general pleasure of our conversation, checked a little by my perceiving in Parr less of orthodox acquiescence than in my opinion is becoming in a clergyman. I am reconciled to Hurd by finding it in his sermons. Dr. Johnson however said, "I am glad he is not made Archbishop of Canterbury, for I suspect he is a Whig in his heart."

After drinking coffee and tea, Langton and I went and sat awhile with Dr. Johnson at Mrs. Thrale's. I was easier with him in Langton's company, and talked again of my coming to settle in London. He was in a more agreeable frame than the Sunday evening when I have complained of him in this journal. He said, "I am unwilling to repress your ambition. But it appears to me that as you would be obliged to maintain your family in some dignity here, you would find yourself embarrassed. When you come to London now and leave it because you cannot afford the expense of living in it constantly, people applaud your wisdom. Were you to settle here, they'd despise you as a man ruining himself." This was strong sense, and it *did* repress my ambition. We went upstairs a little to Mrs. Thrale and her daughters. I then called at Mr. Burke's, who was not at home; so I walked quietly to General Paoli's, took my warm port and water with sugar and a bit of dry toast, had some good conversation with the General, who agreed with Dr. Johnson, and then went to bed.

FRIDAY 4 APRIL. (Writing the 16.) Breakfasted with Dempster at his country-lodgings at Brompton Row; intended to walk to Richmond Lodge. But he gave me one of his horses, and he and I rode cheerfully to Putney, where his servant, upon getting a shilling from me, waited, having walked on; and then my amiable friend made me take the horses and servant to Richmond Park gate while he walked about with somebody of his acquaintance. He was also of opinion that considering the state of my income and my having a wife and five children, it would be wrong to risk settling in London. But that I should come up every spring and enjoy it. I was glad to find his servant much attached to him; and though I had not boots on, I galloped with animated pleasure

---

[7]Sir William Wyndham (1687–1740; no relation of William Windham) is mentioned several times by Pope in a strain of adulation. Boswell probably remembered especially the lines that couple him with Marchmont:

> Where British sighs from dying Wyndham stole,
> And the bright flame was shot through Marchmont's soul

(*Verses on a Grotto by the River Thames at Twickenham*, ll. 11–12). Brooks's is the famous Whig club in St. James's Street.

along the wonderfully fine road, through a rich country in charming weather. I walked agreeably from the gate to the Lodge, having wandered a little, not unpleasingly, out of the road. I found a truly kind reception from my good friend Col. James Stuart, who was become an honest, sagacious farmer, and what is truly most remarkable, was cured of the two most baneful vices, gaming and drinking. Yet today he and I, having our hearts warmed by meeting again after an absence of near two years, drank a good deal of ale and a bottle apiece of claret. I positively refused another, and was happy to find I was above wine— master of my bottle. No company but Mrs. Stuart, the two young ladies,[8] and Madame ———, their Swiss governess. His excellent characters of different people, his humorous account of Lord Eglinton passing some time with him when he could drink very little with his Lordship and the weather was rainy, and the Earl's attempts to read, diverted me exceedingly; and his firm, sensible remarks pressed down my foolish imaginations as lead or marble does fluttering leaves of paper. I should be ashamed now to acknowledge having foolish imaginations. But I still have some. Nay, I am not yet settled as to my choice of life. We sat tête-à-tête till after nine o'clock. We supped and drank a little mulled wine. I was uneasy with what I had drank, and went to bed not quite satisfied with myself. My dissatisfaction was produced by the uneasiness I felt in my head and stomach; for surely my judgement could not much condemn a *little* occasional excess with an old and honourable friend.

[EDITORIAL NOTE. No journal entries survive for 5 to 10 April, and it may well be that none ever existed. On Saturday 5 April Boswell walked the eight miles from Richmond Lodge, exhilarated (he wrote to James Bruce) by another idyllic spring day. On the 10th he visited Johnson at Bolt Court, and made both a rough note of the conversation and an expansion of the note which was fully enough written to serve after revision as printer's copy for the *Life of Johnson*. The copy was not recovered until some time after Colonel Isham's initial collection of Boswell manuscripts was privately published (1928–1934), and consequently it is now printed for the first time, as it stood before revision. Some passages of the rough note not incorporated into the more fully written entry are reported in footnotes. On the same paper as the rough notes Boswell recorded two addresses, one of an upholsterer in Wood Street, the other "Little Polly Bond, No. 9, Brewer's Court, Great Wild Street, Lincoln's Inn Fields." He later inked over the words "Little Polly."]

[8]Mary and Charlotte. Charlotte died two years later; Mary married William Dundas, son of the Lord President.

THURSDAY 10 APRIL. I presented the Rev. and Hon. William Stuart to Dr. Johnson.[9] I shall endeavour to write down what passed pretty exactly. MR. STUART. "Sir, you'll forgive the curiosity of a very young man who wishes to see you." DR. JOHNSON. "Sir, you do me honour." MR. BOSWELL. "I hope you are better today, Sir." DR. JOHNSON. "Why, yes." BOSWELL. "This fine weather will do you good. But we must have a jaunt somewhere. We make it out together exceedingly well. Our journey to the Hebrides was very curious." JOHNSON. "I got an acquisition of more ideas by it than anything that I remember. I saw quite a different system of life." BOSWELL. "You would not like to make the same journey again." JOHNSON. "Why, no, Sir. Not the same. It is a tale told. Gravina, an Italian critic,[1] observes that every man desires to see that of which he has read, but no man desires to read an account of what he has seen. So much does description fall short of reality. Description only excites curiosity. Seeing satisfies it. Other people may go and see the Hebrides." STUART. "Your book, Sir, has diffused a general knowledge of that system of life." BOSWELL. "I should wish to go and see some country totally different from what I have been used to, such as Turkey, where religion and everything else are different." JOHNSON. "Yes, Sir. There are two objects of curiosity: the Christian world and the Mahometan world. All the rest may be considered as barbarous." BOSWELL. "Pray, Sir, is *The Turkish Spy* a genuine book?" JOHNSON. "No, Sir. Mrs. Manley in her *Life* says that her father wrote the two first volumes; and in another book, Dunton's *Life and Opinions*, we find that the rest was written by one *Sault*."[2]

BOSWELL.[3] "This has been a very factious reign owing to too much

[9]The third son of Lord Bute, vicar of Luton in Bedfordshire and later Archbishop of Armagh.

[1]Gian Vincenzo Gravina, 1664–1718, who wrote voluminously in both Latin and Italian.

[2]*The Turkish Spy*, an essay-series which ran through twenty-six English editions between 1691 and 1770 and inaugurated the *genre* of pseudo-foreign letters, purported to be secret reports written in Arabic to the Sultan by a Turk in Paris, but it was totally fabricated. Scholars are satisfied that Mrs. Manley deserves no credence, and that the letters corresponding to the first volume of the English edition were written in Italian by Giovanni Paolo Marana, an Italian journalist living in France. The remaining seven volumes of the English edition were written in English by an author not certainly identified. John Dunton, *Life and Errors*, 1705 (the book which Johnson cites inaccurately), thought he was a hack writer named William Bradshaw. Boswell's notes for this day show that he has dropped the discussion of another spurious book with which the subject was probably opened: "Herbert Croft wrong to call *Love and Madness* Hackman's. We have many [such impostures]." (The Rev. James Hackman's murder of Martha Ray and his trial and execution are dealt with in *Boswell, Laird of Auchinleck, 1778–1782*, 1977.) Herbert Croft had fabricated most of what he published in 1780 as the correspondence between Hackman and Miss Ray.

[3]Boswell passed over three sentences in his note for the day that could have served

indulgence by Government." JOHNSON. "*I* think so, Sir. What at first was lenity then grew timidity. Yet this is reasoning *a posteriori*, and may not be just. Supposing a few had at first been punished, I believe faction would have been crushed; but it might have been said that it was a sanguinary reign. A man cannot tell *a priori* what will be best for Government to do. This reign has been very unfortunate. We have had an unsuccessful war. But that does not prove that we have been ill-governed. One side or other must prevail in war, as one or other must win at play. When we beat Louis we were not better governed; nor were the French better governed when Louis beat us."

[EDITORIAL NOTE. No record for 11 April has survived. For 12 April we are printing the manuscript of the *Life of Johnson* as Boswell first drafted it. A Johnsonian anecdote not of that date and a slur at Mrs. Piozzi expressive of Boswell's attitude in 1788 have been deleted, as is indicated by ellipses.]

On Saturday 12 April I visited him in company with Mr. Windham of Norfolk, whom, though a Whig, he highly valued. . . . He talked today a good deal of the wonderful extent and variety of London, and how men of curious inquiry might see in it such modes of life as very few could even imagine. He recommended to us to *explore Wapping*.[4]

Mr. Lowe the painter was with him, very much distressed that a large picture which he had painted was refused to be received into the Exhibition of the Royal Academy. . . . He[5] now gave Mr. Lowe the letters [to Sir Joshua Reynolds and James Barry], of which I was diligent

---

here as matter for another paragraph: "[BOSWELL]. 'Russians, roving barbarians with no policy, conquered nation that had nothing else.' JOHNSON. 'Sir W. Temple said all this. Head heated; did not know he lied, as Voltaire [did].'" The reference is to a passage in Temple's *Of Heroic Virtue*: "There is no part of the world that was ever subject to Assyrian, Persian, Greek, or Roman empires (except perhaps some little islands) that has not been ravaged and conquered by some of those northern nations whom they reckoned and despised as barbarians" (*Works*, 1757, iii. 348–349).
[4]Nine years later, Windham let himself "foolishly be drawn by Boswell to explore, as he called it, Wapping," instead of going to a prizefight 23 October 1792 (*Diary of the Rt. Hon. William Windham,* ed. Mrs. Henry Baring, 1866, p. 265). "Wapping-in-the-Wose, or Wash" (according to Stow) was the hamlet of St. Mary, Whitechapel, established on land on the north bank of the Thames which was reclaimed from the flooding river in the era of Elizabeth. In the seventeenth century pirates were hanged there in chains in low water and their bodies left to be washed three times by the tides. Seafaring men and their suppliers occupied the small tenements and cottages which developed along a narrow, mile-long street, and brewing-houses later multiplied there. Boswell, like Windham, was disappointed in modern Wapping.
[5]Johnson.

enough to take copies at the next coffee-house while Mr. Windham was so good as to wait for me.[6]

[EDITORIAL NOTE. No journal or notes survive for 13–18 April. The *Life of Johnson* contains a lengthy record of that last date, which we print from the manuscript as Boswell first drafted it. Since he later cut the draft considerably, much of the entry for 18 April is now printed for the first time.]

On Friday 18 April (being Good Friday), I found him at breakfast in his usual manner upon that day, taking tea without milk and eating a cross-bun merely to prevent faintness. He said, "My last long walk was from Miss Monckton's.[7] I would not have a coach called, as I thought I should find one in my way. There were none at the head of St. James's Street, where I never before missed them. There were none at Charing Cross. When I came to the New Church in the Strand[8] I found them there. 'Nay', said I, 'I won't take one now, I'm so near home.'" BOSWELL. "I think you don't love walking, Sir. Did you ever walk for walking's sake?" JOHNSON. "I once walked a good deal. I left it off at two-and-twenty, when I grew melancholy."[9] We went to St. Clement's Church, as formerly, and there was something of an agreeable permanency in having the same curate to read prayers, the same Mr. Burrows to preach.[1]

He told me that within these few months his old friend Edwards met him in the street, and said, "'I am told you have lately published a very ingenious book called *The Rambler*. Is it true?' I was not willing he should leave the world in total darkness, so I sent him a set."[2]

[6]Johnson had written to Sir Joshua, President of the Royal Academy, and to Barry, Professor of Painting, asking them to procure a reversal of the decision and to give the public an opportunity to judge Lowe's canvas. "Such intercession was too powerful to be resisted," Boswell wrote in the *Life of Johnson*, where he printed the two letters, and the painting of the Deluge, which represents the water verging to the top of the last mountain, was hung at Somerset House—alone, in an empty room. Northcote, Reynolds's assistant and his biographer, described it as "execrable beyond belief" (*Memoirs of Reynolds*, 1813, p. 297).

[7]Charles Street, Berkeley Square, where the charming blue-stocking, daughter of the first Viscount Galway, conducted celebrated conversaziones at her mother's house.

[8]St. Mary-le-Strand, designed by James Gibbs and consecrated 1723.

[9]In the *Life of Johnson* Boswell reported under the date 1729 that Johnson frequently walked from Lichfield to Birmingham and back (thirty-two miles) in order to conquer melancholy.

[1]He was rector from 1773 to his death in 1786.

[2]The *Rambler* essays, first printed between 1750 and 1752, were about to go into the tenth English edition. Oliver Edwards is the retired London solicitor, by his own

When we came home from church he placed himself on one of the stone seats at his garden door, and I took the other, and thus in the open air and in a placid frame he talked away very easily. JOHNSON. "Were I a country gentleman I should not be very hospitable. I should not have crowds in my house." BOSWELL. "Sir Alexander Dick tells me that he remembers having at the rate of a thousand people in a year to dine at his house; that is, reckoning each person one each time that he dined there." JOHNSON. "That is three a day." BOSWELL. "How your statement lessens the notion." JOHNSON. "That is the good of counting. It brings everything to a certainty which before floated in the mind indefinitely." BOSWELL. "But 'Omne ignotum pro magnifico habitur.'[3] One is sorry to have this diminished." JOHNSON. "Sir, you should not allow yourself to be delighted with falsehood." BOSWELL. "Three a day seem but few." JOHNSON. "Nay, Sir, he who entertains three a day does very liberally. And if there is a large family, the poor entertain those three; for they eat what the poor would get. There must be superfluous meat.[4] It must be given to the poor, or thrown out." BOSWELL. "I observe in London that the poor go about and gather bones, which I understand are manufactured." JOHNSON. "Yes, Sir. Of the best pieces they make a mock ivory, which is used for hafts to knives, and various other purposes. The coarser pieces they burn, and pound them and sell the ashes." BOSWELL. "For what purpose, Sir?" JOHNSON. "Why, Sir, for making a furnace for the chemists for melting iron. A paste made of burnt bones will stand a stronger heat than anything else. Consider, Sir, if you're to melt iron, you cannot line your pot with brass because it is softer than iron and would melt sooner; nor with iron; for, though malleable iron is harder than cast, yet it would not do. But a paste of burnt bones will not melt." BOSWELL. "Do you know, Sir, I have discovered a manufacture to a great extent of what you only piddle at— scraping and drying the peel of oranges.[5] At a place in Newgate Street there is a prodigious quantity done, which they sell to the distillers." JOHNSON. "Sir, I believe they make a higher thing out of them than a

definition too cheerful to be a philosopher, who recognized Johnson on the street, 17 April 1778, though they had not seen each other since they were both students at Pembroke College, Oxford, forty-nine years before.

[3]"Omne ignotum pro magnifico est: The unknown is ever magnified" (Tacitus, *Agricola*, ch. xxx, trans. Sir William Peterson, Loeb ed., 1914).

[4]Food in general.

[5]Despite artful questioning Boswell never learned from Johnson what use he made of these scrapings. He reported in the *Life of Johnson* for this date that Johnson recommended finely powdered dried orange-peel to Mrs. Thrale as a medicine, a use to which it has been put at least from the Renaissance to the present time. The powder was commonly mixed in wine or another liquid and taken as a stomachic.

spirit. They make what is called orange-butter, the oil of the orange inspissated, which they mix perhaps with common pomatum and make it fragrant.[6] The oil does not fly off in the drying."

BOSWELL. "I wish to have a good garden with walls." JOHNSON. "I don't think it would be worth the expense to you. We compute in England a park-wall at a thousand pounds a mile. Now a garden wall must cost at least as much. You intend your trees should grow higher than a deer will leap. Now let us see;—for a hundred pounds you could only have forty-four square yards, which is very little. For two hundred pounds you may have eighty-four square yards,[7] which is very well. But when will you get the value of two hundred pounds off walls in your climate? No, Sir, such a contention with Nature is not worth while. I would plant an orchard, and have plenty of such fruit as ripen well in your country. My friend, Dr. Madden, of Ireland, said that in an orchard there should be enough to eat, enough to lay up, enough to be stolen, and enough to rot upon the ground.[8] Cherries are an early fruit. You may have them; and you may have the early apples and pears." BOSWELL. "We cannot have nonpareils."[9] JOHNSON. "Sir, you can no more have nonpareils than you can have grapes." BOSWELL. "We have them, Sir. But they are very bad." JOHNSON. "Nay, Sir. Never try to have a thing merely to show that you *cannot* have it. For ground that would let for forty shillings you may have a large orchard; and you see it costs you only forty shillings. Nay, you may graze the ground when the trees are old. You cannot while they are young." BOSWELL. "Is not a good garden a very common thing in England?" JOHNSON. "Not so common, Sir, as you would imagine. In Lincolnshire there is hardly an orchard; in Staffordshire very little fruit." BOSWELL. "Has Langton no orchard?" JOHNSON. "No, Sir." BOSWELL. "How so, Sir?" JOHNSON. "Why, Sir, from the general negligence of the county. He has it not, because nobody else has it." BOSWELL. "A hothouse is a certain thing. I may have that." JOHNSON. "A hothouse is pretty certain; but

[6] Inspissated: thickened, condensed. The only example of orange-butter in the OED is an edible product made of whipped new cream, orange-flower water, and red wine. The OED calls the essential oil obtained from the rind of the orange "orange oil." Orange-butter does not appear in Johnson's *Dictionary*.

[7] Correctly, eighty-eight yards square. The errors in these calculations are almost certainly Boswell's, whose arithmetic was always shaky.

[8] Samuel Madden, D.D., of co. Fermanagh, who devoted both mind and money to promoting learning, manufacture, and agriculture in Ireland. A writer in various forms, he paid Dr. Johnson ten guineas when that sum seemed generous for improving *Boulter's Monument* (published 1745), a panegyric in 2,034 lines which he had written on the late Archbishop of Armagh.

[9] A variety of apple.

you must first build it; then you must keep fires in it, and have a gardener to take care of it." BOSWELL. "But if I have a gardener at any rate?" JOHNSON. "Why, yes." BOSWELL. "I'd have it near my house. There is no need to have it in the orchard." JOHNSON. "Yes, I'd have it near my house. I would plant a great many currants. The fruit is good, and they make a pretty sweetmeat."

I record this minute detail, which some may think trifling, in order to show clearly how this great man, whose mind could grasp such large and extensive subjects as he has shown in his literary labours, was yet well-informed in the common affairs of life, and loved to illustrate them.

Mr. Walker, the celebrated master of pronunciation and elocution, came, and then we went upstairs into the study.[1] I asked him if he had taught many clergymen. JOHNSON. "I hope not." WALKER. "I have taught only one, and he is the best reader I ever heard, not by my teaching but by his own natural talents." JOHNSON. "Were he the best reader in the world I would not have it told that he was taught." Here was one of his peculiar prejudices. Could it be any disadvantage to him to have it known that he was taught an easy and graceful delivery? BOSWELL. "Will you not allow, Sir, that a man may be taught to read well?" JOHNSON. "Why, Sir, so far as to read better than he might do without being taught, yes. Formerly it was supposed that there was no difference in reading, but that one read as well as another." BOSWELL. "It is wonderful to see Old Sheridan as enthusiastic about oratory as ever." WALKER. "His enthusiasm as to what oratory will do may be too great. But he reads well." JOHNSON. "He reads well, but he reads low, and you know it is much easier to read low than to read high; for when you read high you are much more limited.[2] Your loudest note can be but one, and so in proportion to loudness. Now some people have occasion to speak to an extensive audience, and must speak loud to be heard." WALKER. "The art is to read strong though low."

Talking of the origin of language, JOHNSON. "It must have come by inspiration. A thousand, nay, a million of children, would not invent a language. While the organs are pliable, there is not understanding enough to form a language. When there is understanding enough, the organs are become stiff. We know that after a certain age we cannot

[1]John Walker, who dedicated two of his many works on elocution to Johnson: *Elements of Elocution*, 1781, and *Rhetorical Grammar*, 1785. His *Critical Pronouncing Dictionary*, published 1791 and revised many times, was regarded as the chief authority on British pronunciation until the publication of the great Oxford dictionary.

[2]Johnson invariably derided Sheridan's enthusiasm for elocution. He had criticized Sheridan's theories and his teaching as early as 28 July 1763.

learn to pronounce a new language. No foreigner who comes to England when advanced in life ever pronounces English tolerably well; at least instances of it are rare." WALKER. "Do you think that there are any perfect synonyms in any language?" JOHNSON. "Originally there were none, but by using words negligently or in poetry, one comes to be confounded with another."

He talked a little of Dr. Dodd,[3] and told us that in his last speech he put in "dreadfully erroneous" instead of some harsher epithet which Dr. Johnson had applied to his life.[4] "A friend of mine came to me and told me that a lady wished to have Dodd's picture in a bracelet, and asked me for a motto. I said I could think of no better than *currat lex*.[5] I was very willing to have him pardoned, that is, to have the sentence changed to transportation. But when he was once hanged, I did not wish he should be made a saint."

Mrs. Burney came to visit Dr. Johnson, and seemed to be very easy with him, and to entertain him very well with her conversation.[6] The fashion of giving genteeler names to places was mentioned, and as an instance was given Hog Lane changed to Worship Street,[7] which I observed was like the change of Tommy Townshend to Lord Sydney.[8]

Garrick's funeral was talked of as prodigiously expensive, upon which Johnson, from his violent antipathy to exaggeration, lowered it,

[3]The popular but high-living preacher, chaplain-in-ordinary to the King, had been convicted of forging the name of the Earl of Chesterfield, his former pupil, to a bond for £4,200. He appealed to Johnson for help in obtaining a royal pardon, though they had met only once many years before, in 1750. Johnson's magnanimous efforts failed, however, and Dodd was hanged 27 June 1777.

[4]"Hypocritical" had been Johnson's word, but Dodd said he could not make the charge of hypocrisy against himself. This was not news to Boswell, for Johnson on 15 September 1777, at Ashbourne, had put in his hands a collection of the pieces he had written for Dodd and had allowed Boswell to take it to his room to study.

[5]Let the law run its course.

[6]Mrs. Elizabeth Allen, Dr. Burney's second wife, and Fanny's stepmother. A wealthy widow with three children, she married Charles Burney in 1767, and added two children by him to the accomplished family.

[7]Changed in the 1760's, perhaps because it was an avenue of approach to Wesley's place of worship in the Old Foundry in Windmill Hill, Shoreditch.

[8]A recent event. As Home Secretary and chief Government spokesman in the Shelburne administration, July 1782–April 1783, Townshend had led an able defence of the peace preliminaries in the debate in the Commons, 17–18 February 1783. On 4 March the *London Gazette* announced that the King had created him Baron Sydney of Chislehurst. The nickname by which Townshend's contemporaries knew him was fixed by Goldsmith in *Retaliation* (see above, p. 87, n. 8). "Tommy" is not an "ungenteel" name; Boswell's parallel is rather between a patronizing style that implies contempt and a style recalling the heroic virtues of Sir Philip Sidney. Boswell later struck through the sentence on "genteeler" names in the manuscript.

I thought, too much. "Were there not six horses in each coach?" said Mrs. Burney. JOHNSON. "Madam, there were no more six horses than six phoenixes." I observed that upon those mournful occasions every article was charged very high, from a notion, probably, that people being in great grief would not examine into the prices with such attention as at other times. Mrs. Burney gave an instance of cool precaution in a gentleman of her acquaintance, who, when his wife died, had her lead coffin weighed, and then refused to pay the common exorbitant charge, but insisted that no more could be exacted but the value of the lead and workmanship. The plumber was resolute, and told him, "I will have the usual price or nothing. You shall pay me that, or be in my debt to eternity." And the gentleman was shamed out of his economy. "His attention," said I, "not to be imposed upon might be wise, but it was not amiable. One cannot love such a man. It is not amiable not to feel grief for the loss of a near relation." JOHNSON. "He had no more or less grief than another. He only had wit to have the lead weighed."[9]

Mrs. Burney wondered that some very beautiful new buildings should be erected in Moorfields, in so shocking a situation as between Bedlam and St. Luke's Hospital, and said she could not live there.[1] JOHNSON. "Nay, Madam, you see nothing to hurt you. You no more think of madness by having windows that look to Bedlam than you think of death by having windows that look to a churchyard." MRS. BURNEY. "Sir, we may look to a churchyard; for it is right that we should be put in mind of death." JOHNSON. "Nay, Madam, if you go to that— it is right we should be kept in mind of madness, which is occasioned by too much indulgence of imagination. I think a very moral use may be made of these new buildings. I'd have those who have heated imaginations live there and take warning." MRS. BURNEY. "But, Sir, many of the poor people that are mad have become so from disease, or from distressing events. It is therefore not their fault but their misfortune, and their condition is a melancholy thought."

[9]Boswell also cancelled in manuscript all that follows Johnson's exchange with Mrs. Burney on Garrick's funeral. He probably feared that readers would attribute the complaints of exorbitant funeral charges to him, even if he introduced them generally, because all attentive readers would remember that his father had died in the previous year.

[1]The new dwellings on the west side of Finsbury Square were the only ones in the area until 1789. St. Luke's served the same purpose as Bedlam, and faced it from Windmill Hill, the northern margin of the vast green space where citizens took their recreation and Whitefield and Wesley had preached. George Dance, Jr., the architect and clerk of the City Works, had laid out Finsbury Square in 1777, and James Peacock, his assistant for over forty years, designed the houses.

Time passed on in conversation till it was too late for the service of the church at three o'clock. I took a walk and left him alone for some time;[2] then returned, and we had coffee and conversation again by ourselves.

I stated the character of a friend of mine as a case to him for his opinion. "He is the most inexplicable man to me that I ever knew. Can you explain him, Sir? He is, I really believe, noble-minded, generous, and princely. But his best friends may be separated from him for years, without his ever corresponding with them. He will meet them with a formality, a coldness, a stately indifference. But when they come close to him and engage him in conversation, they find him as entertaining, easy, pleasant, and friendly as they could wish. One then supposes that what is so agreeable will soon be renewed. But stay away from him for half a year, and he will neither call nor send."[3] JOHNSON. "Why, Sir, I cannot ascertain his character exactly, as I do not know him. But I should not like to have such a man for *my* friend. He may love study, and wish not to be interrupted by his friends. 'Amici fures temporis.'[4] He may be a frivolous man, so much occupied with petty pursuits that he may not want his friends. Or he may have got a notion that there is a dignity in appearing indifferent, while he may not be more indifferent at his heart than another."

We went to evening prayers at St. Clement's at seven, and then parted.

SATURDAY 19 APRIL. Brother breakfasted with us. He said I had too many ideas; went too rapidly from one to another. I said, "I am a tree which produces much fruit." "But," said he, "better a few that ripen than a quantity green." Called Lord Mountstuart; in country. Called Sundrum with brother. Coach at Charing Cross. Felt really affection again. Home with him a little. Then Dilly's and wrote notes of journal, or diary of life.[5] With him to H. S. Woodfall's. His daughter, sweet girl, and son George, fine boy, Hamilton, printer, and son, George Robinson, Paternoster Row, Mr. Wyatt, architect.[6] Old Hamilton quite hearty. Said he'd show me in David Hume honesty good with some

[2]Boswell first wrote "I left him for a little while and called on friend." He struck it through at once, and on the same line substituted the sentence we print.
[3]Boswell doubtless alludes to Lord Mountstuart, of whom he made the same complaint 30 April 1783. See below, p. 121. Mountstuart may be the "friend" of the preceding note.
[4]"Friends are thieves of time." Quoted in Bacon's *Advancement of Learning*, Bk. II, ed. J. Spedding, 1870, iii. 446.
[5]Script ambiguous. Perhaps "Notes of journal or diary or life."
[6]Except for Wyatt, the entire company were printers and booksellers. George Woodfall, now sixteen, became his father's partner and was esteemed as a typographer. Archibald

deviations.[7] "Courtney Melmoth greatest puffer. His mother a bellows-blower.[8] Glover like Sir J. Falstaff. Has nothing now militia broke; wife and ten children. Eats and drinks unconcerned—let world take care of them. Drummed out of *Ledger* and several papers. Blown up in a magazine—the *Universal Magazine of Knowledge and Pleasure*.[9] Bullock kind to him. Song, best line, 'Bullock's a man.'[10] Absurd complaints of age. Better tables, and not waste, for a perennial supply, 'So plain we fare.'"[1]

[EDITORIAL NOTE. There are three entries for 20 April, two of them previously unpublished. The second and third will be described at the proper places in the text. The first, which now follows, is a leaf bearing on one side a series of memoranda, directions for things to be done, written early in the day, and on the other a collection of Boswelliana, pointed and witty remarks made by Boswell.]

20 APRIL. EASTER SUNDAY. After the Holy Solemnity in St. Paul's and swearing at the altar neither too much drinking nor. . . .[2] While now in London go to brother and recollect *eating a pear* and *Spain* at once.[3] Walk calm. Go to Dilly's and put Nelson in pocket.[4] Be excellent

---

Hamilton, Jr., like "Old Hamilton" was a printer, near St. John's Gate. George Robinson, "the king of booksellers," had a large wholesale trade. James Wyatt, dubbed "The Destroyer" by archaeologists of his own time, restored Salisbury, Lincoln, Hereford, and Lichfield cathedrals, and was surveyor of Westminster Abbey. He is considered founder of the great revival of interest in Gothic architecture.

[7] We have not found any specific passage in Hume corresponding to Hamilton's description, which appears to be a variation on Hume's theory that virtue and self-interest are not necessarily incompatible.

[8] Samuel Jackson Pratt (Melmoth was a pseudonym), prolific author of poems, plays, novels, essays, and travel books. He imitated renowned authors like Goldsmith and Sterne and also celebrated them in print.

[9] A pun on *magazine*, which down to the founding of the *Gentleman's Magazine* in 1731 meant only "a store of arms, ammunition, or provisions"; hence "drummed out, blown up." William Frederick Glover, during the American war an ensign and surgeon of the East Essex Militia, was later a poverty-stricken assistant to booksellers as translator, compiler, and journalist. A gifted anecdotist widely courted for his wit and congeniality, at his death in 1787, aged fifty, the *Gentleman's Magazine* reported that he had devoted the last twenty years of his life to the entertainment of his friends.

[10] John Bullock was Colonel of the East Essex Militia. The song is untraced.

[1] Quotation unidentified.

[2] Boswell has carefully inked out everything from "neither" to the end of the sentence. Three words remain undeciphered.

[3] See above, p. 73, n. 9. We have not found a convincing explanation of this association of ideas.

[4] Robert Nelson's very popular *Companion for the Festivals and Fasts of the Church of*

with Dr. Johnson. Ask if you should associate with Adam Smith as formerly friendly to you. Lord Kames's life. Letter to King's Librarian characterizing you may be perhaps of capital service.[5] Will he write history of family?[6] Then Sundrum and rebuke him gently.[7] Boast of your vivacity. General's and get linens. Lord Eglinton's a moment.

Call Langton. Deliver book. Promise to study under him and mention you're *behooved*.[8] Make out memorial of choice of life for Burke.[9] Mem: raise family by your talents if you can.

When Burke, as I thought, had neglected to fix a day for my coming to his country-seat, I was vexed and uneasy, but excused him from his hurry of business. Said my brother David: "He is just in a fever." BOSWELL. "Was afraid in ague, *cold* fit."

I an electrical eel to Dr. Johnson.[1] Also the boy in the bowling-green who gives him the bowls.[2] Langton said it was a great deal to do this, to be always ready. And he plays with no common bowls. His the

---

England (1704), a catechism with appropriate prayers which Boswell praised in the *Life of Johnson* as a "most valuable help to devotion" (22 March 1776). His own copy of the 24th edition, printed in 1782 for twenty-five publishers, is inscribed in his hand "London 1783." It is now in the Hyde Collection.

[5] Boswell thinks that a letter of recommendation from Johnson may help him to obtain access to a long letter which Johnson had written, 28 March 1768, to Frederick Augusta Barnard, the King's Librarian, giving him advice on the acquisition of books and manuscripts. Barnard later printed the letter himself, faultily, in the introduction to his *Bibliothecae Regiae Catalogus* (1820).

[6] Though Boswell's obvious hopes for a tête-à-tête were destroyed by finding the painter Mauritius Lowe with Johnson, he must have got in his request for a family history. He reports in the *Life of Johnson*, at the end of the collection of undated Johnsoniana preceding 10 April 1783, that Johnson agreed to write it in both Latin and English. (See below, 7 February 1784.)

[7] Because he did not fall in readily enough with Boswell's current desire to suppress the song on Lord Cassillis? See above, 27 January and 25 March 1783.

[8] More likely the Scotticism meaning that he is under obligation, it is incumbent upon him, than the English expression documented through the seventeenth century and meaning "to be in need of." Boswell had probably sworn at the altar that morning to study the *Festivals and Fasts* under Langton, who was known for his piety and would provide discipline as well as instruction.

[9] Boswell is counselling himself to draw up the case for his removing to London, which he had resolved to put in writing so as to get Burke's full attention (see above, 31 March 1783). Boswell could not have used the phrase "choice of life" without thinking of Johnson's *Rasselas*.

[1] He stimulated him to talk by the shocks he administered: the provocative topics he started, and the questions he asked about Johnson's behaviour and such matters as death and futurity.

[2] "The choosing of the bowl is the greatest cunning," wrote a seventeenth-century writer quoted by Joseph Strutt, *The Sports and Pastimes of the People of England*, 1830, p. 270.

long bullets. Great rubs. Often *rides*. Seldom *draws* a cast. But gets to the jack better than anyone.[3] Sometimes not quite safe to give him the bowls. If not in humour will toss them away or throw them at your head. Even Argyll's bowling-green.[4]

[EDITORIAL NOTE. No general record for 20 April has been found, but Boswell kept a special record ("paper apart") of the conversation before dinner at Dr. Johnson's which was fully enough written to serve, after revision, as printer's copy for the *Life of Johnson*. We print it for the first time as Boswell originally wrote it. He prefaced it in the *Life* with a sentence saying that after the solemn service at St. Paul's he came to Johnson's.]

Mr. Lowe, sitting with him, mentioned Foley Place,[5] etc., the great number of new buildings, yet that the Doctor had observed the number of inhabitants not increased. JOHNSON. "Why, Sir, the bills of mortality prove that no more people die now than formerly. So no more live. Births are nothing. For not one tenth of the people of London are born there." BOSWELL. "I believe, Sir, a great many of the children born in London die early." JOHNSON. "Why, yes, Sir." BOSWELL. "But those who do live are as stout and strong people as any. Dr. Price says they must be naturally stronger to get through." JOHNSON. "That is system, Sir. A great traveller observes that it is said there are no weak or deformed people among the Indians; but that the reason is that the hardship of their life as hunters and fishers does not allow weak or diseased children to grow up. Now, had I been an Indian I must have died early. My eyes would not have served me to get food. I indeed now could fish, give me English tackle. But had I been an Indian, I

---

[3] A sustained allusion to the game of bowls played with biased balls on a smooth green, the aim being to roll the bowls closest to the jack, a stationary target-ball previously thrown into position. To "fire" the bowl, or "cast a long bullet," means to deliver the bowl straight at the jack hard enough to overcome the bias. The player "draws a cast" when he employs the bias of the bowl and delivers it in an arc. In a "rub," a bowl arrives at a winning position by striking and glancing off bowls already on the field. To "ride" or drive the jack is to strike the jack with a bowl which follows after it. Boswell's metaphor for Johnson's conversation when he was in company and most likely to talk for victory implies that he knew all the tricks of the game, though his attack was frontal, and he always won.

[4] Mrs. Thrale's dwelling, where Johnson had his usual room, was now in Argyll Buildings. See above, 21 and 26 March 1783.

[5] Formerly Queen Anne Street East (today Langham Street), off Regent Street, it had recently been renamed after Lord Foley, whose mansion stood nearby. Edmond Malone's house is marked now with a plaque on No. 40.

should have starved. Or they'd have knocked me on the head when they saw I could do nothing." BOSWELL. "Perhaps they'd have taken care of you. We are told they are fond of oratory. You'd have talked to them." JOHNSON. "Nay, Sir. I should not have lived long enough to be fit to talk. And depend upon it, Sir, a savage when he is hungry will not carry about with him a looby of nine, who cannot help himself. They have no affection, Sir." BOSWELL. "I believe natural affection, of which we hear so much, is very small." JOHNSON. "Sir, natural affection is nothing. But affection from principle and established duty is sometimes wonderfully strong." LOWE. "A hen, Sir, will feed her chickens in preference to herself." JOHNSON. "But we don't know that the hen is hungry. Let the hen be fairly hungry and I'll warrant she'll peck the corn herself. A cock, I believe, will feed hens instead of eating himself. But we don't know that the cock is hungry." BOSWELL. "And that, Sir, is not from affection, but gallantry. But some of the Indians have affection." JOHNSON. "Sir, that they help some of their children is plain; for some of them live, which they could not do without being helped."

[EDITORIAL NOTE. The first draft of the manuscript of the *Life of Johnson* continues, "I dined with him, with Mrs. Williams, Mrs. Desmoulins, and Mr. Lowe. He seemed not to be well, talked little, grew drowsy soon after dinner, and retired, upon which I went away." That this was not strictly true is shown by five more pages, clearly not a part of the conversation just recorded, though they must have been written about the same time. Boswell has headed these "Extraordinary Johnsoniana—*Tacenda*"; that is, Johnsoniana to be kept secret. And *tacita* they remained, except perhaps for one sentence considered below. Even that sentence, if Boswell did indeed except it from his general injunction, was paraphrased and given without a direct source. We now for the first time print Boswell's five pages, much the most extensive and intriguing of the accredited Johnsoniana he passed over.]

After dinner, when the Doctor had retired to take a nap, I believe, and Mrs. Williams also was gone, Mrs. Desmoulins, Lowe, and I remained. Said Lowe: "Now, Ma'am, let us be free. We are all married people. Pray tell us, do you really think Dr. Johnson ever offended in point of chastity? For my own part I do not believe he ever did. I believe he was chaste even with his wife, and that it was quite a Platonic connexion" (grinning a smile with his *one* eye to me). MRS. DESMOULINS. "Ah, Sir, you are much mistaken. There never was a man who had stronger amorous inclinations than Dr. Johnson. But he conquered them. Poor Logie, who was very intimate with him, knew this, and has talked to me of it.[6] It has been said there was a criminal connexion between him and Mrs. Williams; and I remember a lady observed that no woman could behave so impudently[7] if she did not know she had this awe over his head." BOSWELL. "But why an awe? What need he care?" MRS. DESMOULINS. "Sir, he would not like it. But I do not believe it." BOSWELL. "Nor I, indeed. I have heard people joke about it, and talk of Dr. Johnson's seraglio, which included you as well as her, Madam. But nobody had a serious belief of anything for a moment." LOWE. "I do still think the Doctor never has had any inclination for women." MRS. DESMOULINS. "But he has." LOWE. "I do not believe his marriage was consummated." BOSWELL. "Do you know, Ma'am, that there really was a connexion between him and his wife? You understand me." MRS. DESMOULINS. "Yes, yes, Sir. Nay, Garrick knew it was consummated, for he peeped through the keyhole, and behaved like a rascal, for he made the Doctor ridiculous all over the country by describing him running round the bed after she had lain down, and crying, 'I'm coming, my Tetsie, I'm coming, my Tetsie! ph! ph!' (blowing in his manner).[8] She was near fifty when the Doctor married her, and he was only two-and-twenty,[9] and I believe she never had any love for him but only to get money from him. They did not sleep together for many years. But that was her fault. She drank shockingly and said she was not well and could not bear a bedfellow. And I remember once when at Hampstead a young woman came on a visit.[1] I lay in the room with Mrs. Johnson in a small bed. She said, 'It will not hold you both. So if you will promise not to tell Mr. Johnson, you shall sleep with me. But if he should know this, he'd say, "If you can bear a bedfellow, why not me as well as another?"'" LOWE (waggishly). "He has been so bad a bedfellow she could not bear him, and this has made her take to

[6] We have done everything we can think of to identify "Logie," but have come up with no plausible suggestion.

[7] The last two words were cancelled immediately, and the sentence continued as "behave to Dr. Johnson in the manner she does."

[8] "His oddities of manner and uncouth gesticulations could not but be the subject of merriment to them [Johnson's pupils at Edial]; and in particular the young rogues used to listen at the door of his bed-chamber, and peep through the key-hole, that they might turn into ridicule his tumultuous and awkward fondness for Mrs. Johnson, whom he used to name by the familiar appellation of *Tetty* or *Tetsey*" (*Life of Johnson*, ann. 1736). Boswell in this passage gives the impression that he had his information from David Garrick, but it is our opinion that the immediate source of the anecdote was the account from Mrs. Desmoulins. The matter is discussed more fully in the introduction to this volume.

[9] Mrs. Porter was forty-six and Johnson almost twenty-six.

[1] In 1748, if not earlier, Mrs. Johnson went for her health to Hampstead, a popular resort, but Johnson stayed in London to earn their livelihood.

drinking. He has had no passion." MRS. DESMOULINS. "Nay, Sir, I tell you no man had stronger, and nobody had an opportunity to know more about that than I had." LOWE. "I am sure, Madam, were I to indulge that passion, I should think you a very agreeable object." BOSWELL. "You'll forgive me, Madam. But from what you have said, I beg leave to ask you if the Doctor ever made any attempt upon you?" MRS. DESMOULINS (Lowe and I closing in upon her to listen). "No, Sir, I have told you he commanded his passion. But when I was a young woman and lived with Mrs. Johnson at Hampstead, he used to come out two or three days in a week, and when Dr. Bathurst lived there, he'd go and stay with him till two or three in the morning. The maid went to bed, as she could not be kept up, and I used to sit up for him; and I have warmed his bed with a pan of coals and sat with him in his room many an hour in the night and had my head upon his pillow." BOSWELL. "What, when he was in bed, Madam?" MRS. DESMOULINS. "Yes, Sir. He'd desire me to go out of the room, and he'd go to bed; but to come back in a little while and talk to him—and I have come and sat on his bedside and laid my head on his pillow." BOSWELL. "And he showed strong signs of that passion?" MRS. DESMOULINS. "Yes, Sir. But I always respected him as a father." BOSWELL. "What would he do? Come now" (Lowe like to jump out of his skin), "would he fondle you? Would he kiss you?" MRS. DESMOULINS. "Yes, Sir." BOSWELL. "And it was something different from a father's kiss?" MRS. DESMOULINS. "Yes, indeed." LOWE (approaching his hand to her bosom). "But would he? eh?" MRS. DESMOULINS. "Sir, he never did anything that was beyond the limits of decency." LOWE. "And could you say, Madam, upon your oath, that you were certain he was capable?" MRS. DESMOULINS. "Y-yes, Sir." BOSWELL. "But he conquered his violent inclination?" MRS. DESMOULINS. "Yes, Sir. He'd push me from him and cry, 'Get you gone.' Oh, one can see." BOSWELL. "So you saw the struggle and the conquest." MRS. DESMOULINS. "I did."

What a curious account. That he should bring himself to the very verge of what he thought a crime. Mr. Burke, to whom I afterwards told it, thought there was nothing very curious—just common human nature. But it *was* certainly curious in so eminent a man. She said, "I have many times considered how I should behave, supposing he should proceed to extremities—and as I told a lady who once put the question to me, I do own that such was my high respect for him, such the awe I felt of him, that I could not have had resolution to have resisted him." BOSWELL. "But you never felt any inclination for him as a woman does for a man?" MRS. DESMOULINS. "O no, Sir." BOSWELL. "I cannot imagine it of any woman. There is something in his figure so terribly disgusting."

MRS. DESMOULINS. "Yet, Sir, one cannot tell. His mind is such. Now Mrs. Thrale has been exceedingly fond of him, and I am convinced now that he is in some way vexed about her. Either she has made a proposal to him which he has thought improper and has declined, or he, presuming on her great fondness, has made a proposal to her, which she has rejected. But I am convinced one or other is the case." I mentioned the dispute between Sir Joshua Reynolds and me whether the Doctor would yield to the amorous solicitations of the Duchess of Devonshire.[2] Mrs. Desmoulins said he would not. He would instantly feel such a contempt and indignation that he would treat her with disdain. "I believe, Madam," said I, "if the contempt and indignation rose at once, as I think it would do, he would spurn her from him. But if he at all hesitated—as the woman who deliberates is lost—it would be the same with him." "Yes, Sir," said she, "were he to deliberate, I allow he might yield." She told us how he had spent hundreds of pounds in supporting Betty, her[3] Scotch maid, afterwards with Mrs. Williams, an abandoned, diseased creature; and when the workhouse was proposed, said, "No—her feelings as delicate as yours." Strange.

[EDITORIAL NOTE. For 21 April we have memoranda, journal, and an expansion of the journal made on a separate occasion. We print the memoranda first, and follow with a conflated text of the journal.]

21 APRIL. EASTER MONDAY. [Memoranda.] Away in coach. Be powdered near Gregories.[3a] Mem.: you're going to enjoy as much as can be had on earth perhaps. Write to Grange and wife there. Learn farming. Write memorial on choice of life as well as you can. Write to Sir W. Forbes.[4] Learn farming. Be sober. When you return, call Sheridan. Cultivate Lord Somerville as son of your first noble patron or encourager.[5] Mem.: a *little* more *retenue*.[6] Have Drs. Douglas and Kippis

---

[2]"The most charming duchess in all His Majesty's dominions," Boswell wrote in the *Life of Johnson* (May 1781), employing the very adjective that Fanny Burney thought "might have been coined for her" (*Journals and Letters*, ed. Joyce Hemlow, 1972, i. 60).

[3]Mrs. Johnson's.

[3a]The name of Burke's estate at Beaconsfield.

[4]Boswell did write to him from Gregories describing his happiness "in this southern region," but burned the letter because he feared that to Forbes "in Edinburgh" it would seem "so hyperbolical" (Register of Letters, 5 May 1783).

[5]The twelfth Lord Somerville (1698–1765), a friend of Pope and of Allan Ramsay, reviewed and encouraged Boswell's first writing at his private apartments in Holyrood House. He was an alluring figure to Edinburgh youth: his estate near the city was the resort of authors and actors, and the illegal theatre in Edinburgh was tolerated under his protection.

[6]Reserve, restraint.

and Swinburne to a dinner. Mem.: know who you are and what you are. Hire troop of horse. "What images he has!" This imagination raise troop of horse in a minute.[7] Giurate far vedere che potete[8] govern tongue. Franks wife, Grange, and Sir A. Dick. Call Mrs. Reynolds. Be sure directly to get brush and powder for teeth.

[Journal]. Rose pretty well. Got into Oxford coach at Old Bailey. A coachman talked what an excellent woman Mrs. Jachir,[9] who keeps the inn at Beaconsfield, was. My companions sweet young woman, architect (ugly; builder, I believe),[1] jolly, good-humoured man, I know not who. Quite hearty and lively all the way. Only sudden fever of love. Quite sentimental. Pretty riding-clothes, fine hair, sweet voice. Gave her my[2] cheap nosegay: a tulip, a white lily, three sprigs of myrtle. Charming creature. Stoand,[3] the architect, when I wondered what she was, said, "Lady's-maid," and wondered I did not perceive the *style*. He was right. I asked Mrs. Smith, mine hostess:[4] Mrs. Foley's woman, Mrs. Foley of Aisley Park. Harangue by Stond on party, abusing Fox, praising Lord Shelburne. "King good man. Is he not, Ma'am?" SHE. "Obstinate man, Sir." HE. "Why should a man have honour of perseverance if successful, reflection of obstinacy if unlucky, as in American war?" BOSWELL. "If one can show a man *ought* to have seen a thing won't succeed, obstinate." Old age sad, he said. I talked strongly of it, and mentioned pretty woman changed to old decrepit creature. *She* had no dread of old age. Did not think it horrid. "Ah," said I, "when in full spirits, we brave dismal things at a distance. *She* cannot think

[7] This cryptic passage no doubt refers to Johnson's assertion (Journal, 3 June 1781) that he knew of only one example of a great use of money, and that was when James ("Jamaica") Dawkins, an amateur archaeologist of exceptional wealth, hired a troop of Arab horse to protect his party from robbers while on an excursion in Palmyra. Boswell probably implies that his own wealth consists in his power of imagination.

[8] "Swear to show that you can." The two words in English which follow are characteristic of Boswell's lapses into his native tongue when he was writing quickly and the Italian did not come to him readily.

[9] Boswell's spelling could be "Jackir" (for "Jacquier"), "Jackin," or "Jacken," but "Jagger" is the only related local name we find in a list of Beaconsfield inhabitants published late in the eighteenth century.

[1] Boswell means, "He called himself an architect, but I fancy that he was a builder" (the equivalent of a modern contractor).

[2] The word is uncertain.

[3] Later in the entry Boswell wrote *Stond* and *Ston'd*. We have not found this surname, and believe that the spellings indicate a colloquial pronunciation of *Stone*. The addition of final *d* after final *n* is common in English speech. (Johnson is reported in the *Life of Johnson* October 1783 as having heard the actress Mrs. Pritchard say *gownd* for *gown* off stage.) Edward Stone, builder, Fetter Lane, is listed in a London directory published a few years after Boswell wrote this entry.

[4] Probably the landlady of the inn where they stopped for breakfast.

of old age as connected with herself 'in flower of youth and beauty's pride.' "[5] *She* said, "It is according as we have spent younger years; if no uneasy reflections." Said he, "Now I'll take t'other side. Old age agreeable if a man can look back on his former life with pleasure. Now there's General Eliott.[6] He's an old man, and I dare say very happy." BOSWELL. "That is a particular instance where the dreariness of old age is counteracted by particular favourable circumstances. It is only saying the bitter cup may sometimes be sweetened. His red-hot balls are sugarplums to him for this."[7] At ——— she showed finest cedar in England. At breakfast said, "Most gentlemen drink sugar." "They who do not," said I, "are very *fine* gentlemen." "But not *refined*," said Ston'd. He read newspapers drolly: "Public Office Bow Street taken up two *suspicious* persons." Looking at her and me, between whom he sat, he said, "I shall be destroyed between them." "Yes," said I, "annihilated. You're space and time: 'Ye Gods, destroy. . . .'[8] I'd level mountains or drain seas." "Yes," said he. "Take vinegar."[9] I declared upon my honour in love, and a great deal passed. When Beaconsfield, "Now," said he, "for a speech: 'My heart is bursting.' 'Mine too breaks.' " Strange that I should still be *so tindery.* Bid her farewell. Squeezed her hand and kissed it. To inn, back again. Stood on step; again the same, "God bless you." She told me she returned to town after the holidays. I said I knew the Park,[1] "and—well, we shall meet."

Beaconsfield tea and barber, who had many trades. "Shave, grind razors, bleed, draw teeth, and play fiddle." BOSWELL. "Mr. Burke as many. Shaves Ministry, grinds state razors (and good sharp ones and good metal to last so long), pulled old Ministry's teeth (Lord North's teeth), and bleeded them." When I told this to Burke, he said, "But Lord North's teeth are grown again." Said I: "You've given him teeth.

[5] John Dryden, *Alexander's Feast,* ll. 9–11:
> The lovely Thais by his side,
> Sat like a blooming Eastern bride
> In flow'r of youth and beauty's pride.

[6] Governor and hero of Gibraltar. He defended the fortress successfully during a siege and blockade of three years. Reynolds in one of his most famous portraits represents him in his red coat against the Rock of Gibraltar, holding the huge key of the fortress in his hand.

[7] The Spanish fired red-hot shot at the garrison.

[8] "Martinus Scriblerus" (Alexander Pope), *On the Art of Sinking in Poetry,* ch. xi:
> Ye Gods! annihilate but space and time,
> And make two lovers happy.

[9] Evidently an allusion to the account in Livy (XXI. xxxvii) of Hannibal's soldiers pouring vinegar over heated rocks, which caused them to crumble and cleared the passage over the Alps.

[1] We have not been able to locate Aisley Park.

You've transplanted patriotic ones into his mouth." "Ay," said he. "We've given him some *tusk*ulan questions."[2] Had barber to carry my coat. Little boy of three crying for one who took care of him having left him. That one was but five. I said this like Mr. Pitt being Prime Minister too young. "Nay," said Burke, "that is child of three taking care of one of five." As we approached, said barber: "There's his windmill, Sir." "I knew," said I, "he had windmills in his head, but did not know anywhere else." "You see," said he, "has one in his park."

The place looked most beautiful. He was at window with scratch-wig. Let me in. His hall admirable busts. I was struck. Mr. Curzon, his neighbour, Lord Curzon's[3] brother, and Mr. Vane, Lord Darlington's brother, with him. Introduced me to them. Administration mentioned. Burke said, "We must have a strong Government." "Ay," said I, "there it is. We must always come to Toryism. There is so much good sense, so much practical sense in it, that we find it the true system of government." Mr. Vane said he was of a different opinion. But we laughed pleasantly on our different political notions. We then saw Mrs. Burke and Mrs. Champion. I was affected with wonder by seeing a suite of rooms hung with valuable pictures in rich gilded frames: seven landscapes of Poussin which Sir Joshua values at £700, a fine Titian, a ———; in short, a great many. Mr. Burke purchased the place anciently called Butler's Hall, as having belonged to the family of Ormond, afterwards Gregories, from a branch of the celebrated Waller's family which took that name; and he got house, busts, pictures, and furniture all at once, for ———.[4] He has done a good deal to the place himself. The two gentlemen took their horses to go to Mr. Curzon's. Mr. Burke and I accompanied them to the extremity of his domain on that quarter, and then he and I walked round almost the whole of his Place. He said I would find the occupations of a country-place very comfortable in old age. The soil here is gravelly and bears a beautiful verdure; and the ground is formed into swells and hollows as if in a mould by an exquisite artist. He begins his husbandry course by dunging his land well, and then sowing barley with clover and rye-grass. Next year it is in hay, of which he takes one crop or two, according as the season is. He then fallows and sows turnips, or takes a crop of. . .

[EDITORIAL NOTE. The entry was carried no further. Boswell was recalled from Beaconsfield on 22 April by an express with the news that Lt. David Cuninghame, Mrs. Boswell's nephew, had killed his

[2] A pun on Cicero's *Tusculanae Disputationes.*
[3] He should have said "Lord Scarsdale's."
[4] £20,000.

antagonist in a duel and was himself dangerously wounded. David had long been a source of worry to Boswell. He was reckless and improvident, like his elder brother, Sir Walter Montgomerie-Cuninghame, and Boswell had expended considerable effort getting him settled in the army. Some years before, when he was an officer in the Scots Greys, he had differed at cards with a fellow officer, George James Riddell, second son of Sir James Riddell of Ardnamurchan and Sunart. A persistent enmity resulted, and Riddell finally sent Cuninghame a challenge, which he declined. The other officers regarded his behaviour as disgraceful, and Riddell treated him with contempt. Cuninghame then called Riddell out and, when he learned that his opponent felt no obligation to meet him, forced him to action by spitting in his face. The duel was fought at eight paces. Riddell won the toss for first fire and shot Cuninghame in the breast. Cuninghame, believing himself mortally wounded, insisted on his right to fire, and after a pause of two minutes gave Riddell a fatal wound above the left hip. Riddell, like David, twenty-four years old, was buried in Westminster Abbey; six general officers appeared as pall-bearers.

No journal survives for 22–27 April, and we know little of Boswell's activities in London during that period. He attended David, who was in "a fair way of recovery"[5] by 24 April, when Boswell wrote two letters on his behalf to his superior officers in the Greys. The journal for 28 April is fragmentary at the beginning, although there was no doubt once a fairly full record of the entire Johnsonian conversation for that day. We substitute for the missing portion the draft of the manuscript of the *Life of Johnson* as it stood before revision.]

I saw little of Dr. Johnson till Monday 28 April, when I was with him a considerable time. JOHNSON. "I do not see, Sir, that fighting is forbidden in Scripture. I see revenge forbid but not self-defence." BOSWELL. "The Quakers say it is. 'Unto him that smiteth thee on one cheek offer also the other.'"[6] JOHNSON. "But stay, Sir, the text is meant to have the effect of moderating passion. It is plain that we are not to take it in a literal sense. We see this from the context, where there are other recommendations which I warrant you the Quaker will not take literally, as, for instance, 'From him that would borrow of thee turn thou not away.'[7] Let a man whose credit is bad come to a Quaker and say, 'Well, Sir, lend me a hundred pounds,' he'll find him as unwilling as any other man. No, Sir, a man may shoot another who

---

[5] Boswell to Sir Walter Montgomerie-Cuninghame, requesting £30 or £40 for David (Register of Letters).
[6] Luke 6: 29.
[7] "Turn not thou away" (Matthew 5: 42).

invades his character as he may shoot one who attempts to break into his house. So in 1745 my friend, Tom Cumming the Quaker, said, 'I would not fight, but I'd drive an ammunition cart';[8] and we know that the Quakers have sent flannel waistcoats to soldiers to enable them to fight better." BOSWELL. "When a man is the aggressor and by ill usage forces on a duel in which he is killed, have we not little ground to hope that he is gone into a state of happiness?" JOHNSON. "Sir, we are not to judge determinately of the state in which a man leaves this life. He may in a moment have repented effectually and been accepted by GOD. There is in Camden an epitaph upon a very wicked man who was killed by a fall from his horse, in which he is supposed to say,

> Between the stirrup and the ground
> I mercy asked, I mercy found."[9]

BOSWELL. "Is not the expression in the burial-service 'in the *sure* and *certain* hope of a blessed resurrection'[1] too strong to be used indiscriminately, and indeed, sometimes when those over whose bodies it is said have been notoriously profane?" JOHNSON. "It is sure and certain *hope*, Sir, not *belief*." I did not insist farther; but cannot help thinking that less positive words would be more proper.

He said of an eminent politician, "Considering his origin and situation in life, he has done more for himself than anybody has done. But how has he done it? By means that an honest man cannot approve; by disturbing Government and fomenting faction as much as he could. His talents no doubt entitle him to promotion. In a regular government he might have had a thousand a year."[2]

Talking of a man who was grown very fat so as to be incommoded by corpulency[3] he said, "He eats too much, Sir." BOSWELL. "I don't

[8] He did considerably more. Cumming, a private merchant in the African trade who came to be known as the "fighting Quaker," devised a plan to wrest control of South Barbary (Senegal) from the French, persuaded the Government to send a military expedition against them, and actually directed the successful conquest, though not, as he had hoped (he said), without bloodshed. He took all the blame in explaining his actions to the Society of Friends, which did not disown him.

[9] Camden's *Remains*, 1623, p. 341:
> Betwixt the stirrup and the ground,
> Mercy I asked, mercy I found.

[1] "In sure and certain hope of the resurrection to eternal life" (*Book of Common Prayer*).

[2] This entire paragraph was cancelled before the manuscript was sent to the printer, no doubt because Johnson refers to Edmund Burke, their Irish-born friend of a middle-class family, Roman Catholic parentage on his mother's side, and little or no personal fortune. Johnson is obviously roused by Burke's appointment at £4,000 per annum (plus unofficial perquisites) in the new Administration which had wrested power from the King's ministers.

[3] He remains unidentified.

know, Sir. You will see one man fat who eats moderately and another lean who eats a great deal." JOHNSON. "Nay, Sir, whatever may be the quantity that a man eats, it is plain that if he is too fat, he has eat more than he should have done. One man may have a digestion that consumes food better than common. But it is certain that solidity is increased by putting something to it." BOSWELL. "But may not solids swell and be distended?" JOHNSON. "They may swell and be distended; but that is not fat."

We talked of the prosecution against Sir Thomas Rumbold.[4] JOHNSON. "What foundation there is for the accusation I know not, but they will not get at him. Where actions are committed at so great a distance, a delinquent can obscure the evidence till the scent becomes cold. There is a cloud between, which cannot be penetrated. Therefore all distant power is bad. I am clear that the best plan for the government of India is what your Lord Advocate Dundas proposed, a despotic governor;[5] for if he be a good man it is clearly the best government; and supposing him to be a bad man, it is better to have one plunderer than many. A governor now lets others plunder that he may be allowed to do it. But if despotic he sees that the more he lets others plunder the less there will be[6] for him; so he restrains it; and though he plunders himself, the country is a gainer compared with being plundered by numbers. It would be better were Rumbold despotic than now." He had before him *English Review*, which he called "an irregular review" (in opposition to the regular established ones).[7] Doubted if it could be established. The others, he said, were done well. I mentioned writers in them being well paid; Shebbeare's getting six guineas a sheet. "He might," said he, "get six guineas for a particular sheet. But not *communibus sheetibus*." I asked, "What is meant by a sheet?" HE (hastily). "Why, don't you know what a sheet is?" and was going to show me. "I mean," said I, "is it a sheet all of the writer's own composition? Are extracts deducted?" "No,

[4]Governor of Madras 1778–1781, and the object of a bill of penalties and pains introduced by Henry Dundas for corrupt and oppressive dealing with native Indian rulers. The bill had passed a second reading in Commons 23 January 1783, but it was allowed to expire, as a consequence, it has been alleged, of bribery and collusion. Boswell deleted Rumbold's name when he revised the manuscript of the *Life of Johnson* for publication.

[5]Boswell painstakingly obliterated the clause "what your Lord Advocate proposed" when he revised the manuscript for publication. On 14 April 1783 Dundas brought in a bill which vested control of Bengal in a governor and council, but gave the governor power to override the council, with full responsibility for the consequences.

[6]The text of the journal follows from this point.

[7]The *English Review*, a monthly first issued in January 1783, was continued until December 1796. The "regular" or established reviews were the *Monthly Review* and the *Critical Review*, also published monthly.

Sir," said he. "It is a sheet, no matter of what." I objected this not reasonable. He said, "A man would easier write a sheet of his own than read an octavo volume to get extracts." (Here I fancy he was not quite right.) He said David Cuninghame as a duellist did right to fire. A man who fights means to prevail.

TUESDAY 29 APRIL. Breakfasted comfortably at home. Then went with the General to Langton's. By the way, while he restrained my vivacity, he said, "You're like my mare; when I put on the curb, she dance."[8] We got into a hackney-coach and drove to Westminster Bridge. There a Trinity barge was waiting for us, and away we sailed to Blackwall, a delightful day.[9] Langton and I had incessant talk. But I remember none of it, though at the time it was very agreeable. We had a good walk viewing Mr. Perry's dockyard. Then to dinner: Captain Cotton, whom he called "Commodore," Mr. Grindall, Mr. Cooper, also an Indian medical man, Mr. Bicheno, Preston's honest superintendent.[1] Excellent entertainment in a large place like a ship. Liquors briskly flowing. Then to the other room with bow-window to the Thames, light and cool. Dessert and wine. I was exceedingly happy, roaring outwardly and comfortable inwardly. Preston talked a little with me confidentially on the ingratitude of some people to him, and expressed warm sense of my attachment. I pressed his marriage. He promised to talk of it in a morning, and gave me hopes he would keep up the family of Valleyfield.[2] In the evening got into hackney-coach, he with us. He harangued on the importance of East India Company. "Wealth of this nation afloat; landed interest nothing compared with it." (Langton hurt curiously.[3]) "Every shilling I have afloat." Defended Lord Shelburne's peace ably. Made us stop at Lime Street. One glass of old

[8] A rare example in Boswell's journal of a grammatical slip in General Paoli's spoken English. Fanny Burney's diary for 1782 reports numerous inaccuracies in his speech.
[9] The barge belonged to Trinity House, the headquarters (now on Tower Hill, but at that time in Deptford) of a society founded in 1514 for the improvement of navigation. Robert Preston was an Elder Brother of Trinity House, an important marine office he held for more than fifty years, and he doubtless had sent the barge for Boswell and the other two guests.
[1] Joseph Cotton had been captain of the *Queen Charlotte*, an East Indiaman. Boswell suggested in an earlier journal that Richard Grindall, a surgeon at the London Hospital, had prospered by treating East India people.
[2] He married in 1790, but had no children. In 1830 Preston roused the envy of Sir Walter Scott (already sadly broken in health) by his vigour: "In his ninety-second year he has an ample fortune, a sound understanding, not the least decay of eyes, ears, or taste; is as big as two men, and eats like three" (*Journal*, 19 June 1830, ed. W. E. K. Anderson, 1972, p. 599). He outlived Scott, dying in 1834 at the age of ninety-four.
[3] The Langtons of Langton by Spilsby, Lincolnshire, were an ancient landed family. They traced their male line in the same place back to the twelfth century.

Madeira. All along most polite. I would stop at H. Baldwin's to correct No. 67.[4] Not in. Away to David Cuninghame's a little. Supped George's[5] with Sir Thomas Wallace and Major Mackay. Sir A. Cathcart sat by awhile. Sauntered home by park.

WEDNESDAY 30 APRIL. Found Lord Mountstuart at home, Rev. Mr. —— and a young clergyman with him. I talked away pretty well. There came in a slender, swarthy, pock-pitted, smart-eyed officer, with whom I entered into conversation. I again complained to Lord Mountstuart of seeing him so little, and asked if he'd be at home in the afternoon. He said, "I shall be at home about eight o'clock. I dine at John Ross Mackye's." "Strange," said I, "that he has not asked me. I'll go call on him and endeavour to be of the party." "I dare say he'll ask you if you call on him," said my Lord loftily and coolly. The officer and I walked along Hill Street and Grosvenor Street, on to Swallow Street. He was frank and communicative. I lamented Lord Mountstuart's indifference. He comforted me by telling me he had been always so in his manner (he had been at school with him at Harrow), but that he was a kind, affectionate creature. The officer had heard my name and addressed me by it. I begged to know his. And who was he but the distinguished Colonel Capper, who has gone to the East Indies by land and returned the same way so often.[6] I asked where he lived. He told me Margaret Street, Cavendish Square, and said he should be glad to see me. I said Lord Mountstuart was a bond of union between us, and was happy at the acquisition of so agreeable an acquaintance. Lord Mountstuart told me afterwards this day that Capper was his very particular friend, and that they had a long correspondence. It was indeed only of one side, for he never answered his letters, which were full of information. At length Capper wrote to him, "My dear Lord, has any malicious person prejudiced you against me? What have I done to offend you?" Upon this he wrote, "My dear Capper, you force me to do a thing which is very disagreeable to me. I dislike writing. I am very much obliged to you for your letters, and I continue to have a very great regard for you." This is a most curious instance of character—that my Lord should not feel that a friend must be uneasy who gets no return to his letters but a cool silence. Capper observed to me that our nobility are many of them excellent men as individuals, but

[4] Of *The Hypochondriack*. The subject is memory.
[5] Of the four coffee-houses with this name, it is probably George's at the top of the Haymarket, No. 6, Coventry Street. Boswell could have walked home to South Audley Street afterwards by way of Piccadilly and the Green Park.
[6] James Capper later in this year published *Observations on the Passage to India, through Egypt and across the Great Desert.*

that they are apt to think a distant state to be kept up at times is a duty not only to themselves but to their order, and therefore he did not like to be with them in company. I said they were in the right; and one ought to attend to this, and though in friendly terms with them, not to be too familiar, especially before others, to lessen their respect. I called at Mr. R. Mackye's, resolved to risk pride against pleasure. He was gone out. I left a note, like putting in a baited hook and line in a pool, and then walked away upon my morning active rounds. Called on David Cuninghame. Was somewhat hurt to find him still foolishly impatient for preferment, and wanting to apply to the Commander-in-Chief directly, when he ought to keep quiet for some time and do his duty steadily. I spoke to him warmly as a friend. I then went a little to Paterson's auction of "Bibliotheca Croftsiana," where I have been once or twice, and am always pleased. [7] It is being touched with literature as with a feather. There I had some talk with Steevens of Dr. Johnson. I have marked down some anecdotes which I got at this interview. [8] I then sat awhile with Tom Davies and his wife.

Then went to Dr. Johnson's. Found him in his study in good health and spirits. Seward with him. [9] He was pleased with my Auchinleck brier, [1] and said none like it grew in England. I said there did. He bid me cut him one. "I will," said I, "and then you'll be Briareus." [2] He laughed a little. "This," said I, "would please Burke"; and I told his definition of a manor. The Doctor analysed it, and said "Est modus in rebus" (a modus in tithes) was very well. But "certi denique fines" (certain fines) was poor. [3] I was not so nice. I said Horace had much thinking in him. "One finds there, I think, almost everything except

[7] The sale of the library of the late Rev. Thomas Crofts, A.M., Chancellor of the Diocese of Peterborough and Fellow of the Royal and Antiquarian Societies, was begun at Paterson's Great Room, No. 6, King Street, Covent Garden, on Monday, 7 April 1783, and continued for forty-two days. The one book Boswell is known to have bought, the Marchese Spolverini's *La coltivazione del riso* (1758), was offered for sale by the Brick Row Bookshop, 1927.

[8] They were no doubt included in the *Life of Johnson*, but no separate manuscript of them has been identified among the Boswell Papers.

[9] William Seward, whom the *Gentleman's Magazine* at his death politely called "a great gleaner of information," published *Anecdotes of Distinguished Persons* in five volumes in 1795 and *Biographiana* in two volumes in 1799. He was a great favourite of the Thrales.

[1] A branch of the white heath which he was using as a walking-stick.

[2] The mythical monster of one hundred arms. The strained pun is typical of Boswell.

[3] The Latin is Horace, *Satires*, I. i. 106, and is properly translated "There is a measure of things; there are, in short, fixed limits." In Burke's pun, made at dinner at Sir Joshua Reynolds's 30 March 1781, a modus was a moderate fixed sum paid instead of a tithe, and a certain (as opposed to an uncertain) fine was a fixed payment made to the lord of the manor on the admission of a new tenant.

religion. He seems to have been quite without any sentiment of that kind." Seward mentioned his confession of returning to it: "Parcus deorum," etc.[4] Dr. Johnson said, "He was not in earnest. It was merely poetical." I said there were many people without any religion at all. "Yes," said the Doctor. "And sensible people too," said Seward. "Why, Sir," said the Doctor, "not sensible in that respect. There must be either a natural or a moral stupidity" (or some such word) "if one lives in a total neglect of so very important a concern." Seward wondered how there should be people without religion. "Sir," said the Doctor, "you need not wonder when you consider how large a proportion of almost everyone's life is passed without thinking of it. I myself was many years totally without religion. It had dropped out of my mind." "When was that, Sir?" said Seward. "Why, Sir, I think from ten till two-and-twenty. Sickness brought it back, and I hope I have never lost it since." "Dear!" said I, "what a terrible man" (or some such expression) "must you have been without religion. Why, you must have gone on drinking and swearing!"[5] Said he with a sort of smile, "I drank enough and swore enough, to be sure."

I mentioned Langton as a very religious man, but too ready to introduce serious subjects upon all occasions. Seward listened then *arrectis auribus*.[6] "Why, Sir," said the Doctor, "he will introduce religious discourse without seeing whether it will end in instruction and improvement or produce some profane jest. He'd introduce it in the company of Wilkes and twenty more such." He then told how he had introduced the Trinity in a mixed company at Dilly's, and how he had reproved him.[7] Said I: "He will not own it. But he was in the wrong." "I hope you tell him so," said the Doctor. "I do," said I.

I mentioned the Doctor's excellent distinction between liberty of conscience and liberty of teaching. He said today, "If you have children and educate them in the principles of the Church of England, and there comes a Quaker who tries to pervert them to his principles, you'd drive away the Quaker. You would not trust to the predomination of right which you believe is in your opinions. You'd keep wrong out of their heads. The vulgar are the children of the State. If anyone attempts to teach them doctrines contrary to what the State approves, the mag-

[4]"Parcus deorum cultor et infrequens: I, a chary and infrequent worshipper of the gods" (Horace, *Odes*, I. xxxiv, trans. C. E. Bennett, Loeb ed., 1960). In this ode, Horace goes on to admit the power of Jupiter to govern the lives of men.

[5]The *Life of Johnson* reads "drinking, and swearing, and ———," but the suggestive "and ———" was not in the sentence as Boswell first wrote it.

[6]"With ears pricked up" (Ovid, *Metamorphoses*, xv. 516).

[7]Reported in the *Life of Johnson*, 7 May 1773.

istrate may and ought to restrain him." Seward asked if he would restrain private conversation. "Why, Sir," said he, "it is difficult to say where private conversation begins and where it ends. If we three should discuss even the great question concerning the existence of a Supreme Being sitting by ourselves, we should not be restrained; for that would be to put an end to all information and improvement. But if we should discuss it in the presence of ten boarding-school girls and as many boys, I think the magistrate would do well to put us in the stocks to finish the debate there."

I brought to him two of my law cases, that of Garallan's Arbitration, on which he agreed with me that in so far as the land yielded less to the tenant, there was damage; and Duff and Mercer against the Justices, in which he thought the master had a claim for damages. I shall get him to dictate to me on both. I told him I had got but three guineas for writing the long paper for Duff and Mercer, "You were ill paid," said he. But when I had told him how much the Lord President had praised it, "Then you were well paid," said he.[8] So lively, so ready is he on all occasions!

I showed him verses by *Malloch* in imitation of *Donaides, a Poem*, which Lord Hailes had sent to him. I asked to have this as a curiosity which I would preserve and he would not. He gave it me. But asked me to get him information from Lord Hailes *who* was Donaus of whom Donaides was the son.[9] He read some of the first lines of this poem

[8] For Garallan's Arbitration, see above, 18 February 1783. Charles Mercer and John Duff, his servant, had in 1781 won damages of £40 and expenses in a suit brought against the Justices of the Peace for Perth for impressing Duff during the corn-harvest of 1778 and sending him to America. The law specifically limited impressment to persons who were disorderly or a burden to the community. Duff died, presumably in action or in a prison camp in America, and Mercer authorized Robert Boswell, W. S., to appeal to the House of Lords for increased damages. James Boswell, moved by the spirit of justice, wrote to Mercer that he would be proud to conduct the appeal (see below, 8 June 1785, n. 7). The "long paper," Boswell's successful Answers to the Petition by the Justices appealing the award of 1781, is printed, abridged, in *Boswell, Laird of Auchinleck*, 1977, Appendix B.

[9] Boswell may have put the question to Hailes, but we have no record of an answer. "Donaides" does not mean "son of Donaus," as Johnson supposed, but "daughters (or children) of Dona," the River Don, at the mouth of which the city of Aberdeen is situated. The Donaides are the Aberdonian Muses, and represent allegorically all the scholars, past and present, of King's College, Aberdeen. James Fraser, first Secretary of Chelsea Hospital, having made a timely bequest to the college, was created J.U.D., 29 March 1725, on which occasion John Ker, Professor of Greek, read his Latin eulogy, a history of King's entitled *Donaides*. When *Donaides* was published in November 1725 it was accompanied by a professed "imitation" in English heroic couplets by David Malloch. Johnson had pilloried him in the abridged edition of his *Dictionary* for changing his name after he had settled in England (Alias: "Mallet, *alias* Malloch; that is

and observed how false it was to talk of in ancient times learning not being as now a disgrace to a peer.[1] "Why," said he, "a peer then was as ignorant as anyone else. He'd have been angry to have it thought he could write his name. Men in ancient times dared to stand forth with a degree of ignorance with which nobody would dare now to stand forth. I am always angry when I hear ancient times praised at the expense of modern times." He said, "There is now a great deal more learning in the world. For it is universally diffused. You have perhaps no man who knows as much Greek and Latin as Bentley, no man who knows as much mathematics as Newton. But you have many more people who know Greek and Latin and who know mathematics."

Seward had observed that he wondered sickness and the view of death did not make more men religious. "Sir," said the Doctor, "they do not know how to go about it. They have not the first idea. A man who has not had religion before, no more grows religious when he is sick than a man who has never learnt figures can count when he has need of calculation." Tom Hervey's son came, and Seward and I went.

I called at H. Baldwin's and got a copy of the *London Magazine* containing my *Hypochondriack* No. 67, which pleased me much. Home. Found kind card of invitation from Mr. Ross.[2] Went; just Lord Mountstuart, Colonel James, Lord Denbigh. I was in great spirits and roared down Lord Denbigh. Lord Mountstuart whispered at last not to let him have a word.[3] Lord Mountstuart said some people thought me like Charles Fox. I said I had been told so before. "Why, you're much uglier," said Col. James Wortley Stuart with sly drollery. [BOSWELL.] "Does *your* wife think so, Colonel James?" Lord Mountstuart gave an account of Lord Weymouth. More information than any man. Won't speak before anybody he does not like. My Lord sits up with him till seven. He sips wine slowly. His information not only State affairs (*that* his situation gave him), not ordinary learning taught at school, but everything. [Will] dispute on passage in Bible. Quoted many authors.[4]

---

otherwise Malloch"), and Lord Hailes had sent Johnson the imitation as evidence that the early poems, published in Scotland, bore the name Malloch. The copy of the imitation of *Donaides*, with inscriptions by Hailes and Boswell, is now in the Dyce Collection, Victoria and Albert Museum, London.

[1]   In ancient times, ere Wealth was Learning's foe
      And dar'd despise the worth *he* would not know,
      Ere Ignorance look'd lofty in a peer
      And smil'd at Wit cast back in Fortune's rear,
      The pious PRELATE [Bishop Elphinstone], truly good and great,
      Courted the muses to this happy seat.

[2] John Ross Mackye.

[3] We interpolate at this point four sentences from another leaf headed "30 April 1783."

[4] A generous appraisal of Weymouth. Horace Walpole described him as "in private a

My Lord and Lord Denbigh went to White's; my Lord determined to sit up with Lord Weymouth. Colonel James and I sat on awhile. Then to Mount Coffee-house. Aberdein and Governor Dalling, with whom I soon became quite hearty. He said, "You have written so well of mountains, I wish you saw ours in Jamaica."[5] Balgowan, Balweary,[6] and several more passed in succession before my heated optics.

THURSDAY 1 MAY. Breakfasted at home (heated a good deal), and afterwards drank some tea at Aberdein's in Park Lane with Col. James Stuart and him, having been a little first with Lord Cassillis. Was in capital spirits. Walked with Colonel Stuart to Mr. Burke's door, where I went in, having an appointment to go with Mrs. Burke and her son to see Sion House. Mr. Hickey was with them.[7] Mr. Burke came to us a little.[8]

[I repeated my riposte to Colonel Stuart: "Does *your* wife think so, Colonel James?"] YOUNG BURKE. "I suppose here *less* is meant than meets the ear." BOSWELL. "'Tis fine to fight with a wooden sword and have your antagonist and the spectators think it a real one." [I remarked that] Langton [was] sometimes sportive. YOUNG BURKE. "Yes, he wreathes himself." BOSWELL. "Curious to make him a snake."[9] [YOUNG BURKE.] "'A needless alexandrine,' etc."[1] BOSWELL. "Yes, alexandrine from Alexander, as a great warrior. After all company named, [I] mention Langton. [You say] 'What! a needless, etc.'" Burke repeated part of Dryden's *Ode on Music* on your alleging he had done it before

---

close and sound reasoner," but believed it extraordinary that he was master of himself or of "what little he knew" considering Weymouth's hard gaming and drinking (*Memoirs of the Reign of George III*, 1894, iii. 97).

[5] Where Dalling had been governor from 1777 to 1782.

[6] Thomas Graham of Balgowan, later M.P. and a celebrated military commander in the Peninsular War, created Baron Lynedoch in 1814; and Sir John Scott, Bt., of Ancrum, descendant and representative of the Scotts of Balweary.

[7] Sion House, the seat of the Duke of Northumberland and Robert Adam's "greatest commission" (John Fleming, *Robert Adam and His Circle*, 1962, p. 266), is on the Thames near Isleworth; John Hickey was a young Irish sculptor patronized by Burke.

[8] We here interpolate some remarks which Boswell recorded on the supplementary leaf mentioned above, p. 125, n. 3. The date on that leaf, 30 April, was presumably meant to apply only to the first four sentences.

[9] Young Burke's "he wreathes himself" alludes to Satan disguised as a serpent in *Paradise Lost*, ix. 517:

> So varied he, and of his tortuous train
> Curl'd many a wanton wreath in sight of Eve,
> To lure her eye.

[1] Alexander Pope, *Essay on Criticism*, ll. 356–357:

> A needless alexandrine ends the song,
> That, like a wounded snake, drags its slow length along.

in allusion to himself.[2] Told him he was mad: elephants in his brain, nabobs, etc. "Will you frank [a letter for me]?" was the match that kindled and produced the explosion. He folded paper like Ophelia with the straws. BOSWELL. "Port Eliot[3] is sometimes entertaining." YOUNG BURKE. "If you let him go on his own way, like a drunk man reeling along," etc.

I said I professed to flatter; "I am Professor of Flattery in *grease him* (like Gresham) College." I mentioned Dr. Johnson against toleration. He said it was always erroneous to argue on Government as a private family. There is no defining and drawing exact limits. The very case of the Quaker occurred to himself. He was educated in the Church of England, yet was at a Quaker school, heard all their arguments, and sometimes went to their meetings, yet was not perverted. Mrs. Burke, her son, Mr. Sainte-Marie, and I went in Mr. Burke's coach pleasantly to Sion House.[4] I was exceedingly struck with the costly elegance of the rooms which are shown, and felt an *immensa cupido* for wealth. The gilding was certainly not *aurea mediocritas*. There was truly *invidenda aula*.[5] We walked in the pleasure-ground. Young Burke, Rev. Dr. Douglas, Langton, General Rainsford, my brother, ———— all dined. Dr. Johnson was ill and could not come. Very well, though not brilliant. I went with Young Burke and drank tea with Langton, and was entertained with his various knowledge of books.

Then Young Burke and I went to Dr. Johnson's; sat with him in his bedroom. He was mild and communicative. He said that in general people do not read willingly if they can have anything else. "There must be an external impulse: emulation or vanity or avarice. The progress which the understanding makes through a book has more pain

---

[2] Perhaps Part IV of *Alexander's Feast*, subtitled "The Power of Music," ll. 66–72, where the King, having been humoured by a song which celebrated soldiers and wine,

> Fought all his battles o'er again;
> And thrice he routed all his foes; and thrice he slew the slain.
>> The master saw the madness rise;
>> His glowing cheeks, his ardent eyes,
>> And while he Heav'n and Earth defied,
>> Chang'd his hand, and check'd his pride.

[3] Edward Eliot, whose seat was at Port Eliot, near St. Germans, Cornwall.

[4] Jean-Edmé Parisot de Ste.-Marie was the second son of a family in Auxerre with whom young Burke had stayed in 1773 and 1774. He in turn lived with the Burkes at Beaconsfield for about six months late in 1782 and in the first part of 1783. He was later a language-teacher at Chester.

[5] *Immensa cupido* ("boundless longing") is Virgil, *Aeneid*, vi. 823; the other phrases (*auream mediocritatem*, "golden mean," and *invidenda aula*, "a palace exciting envy") are from the second stanza of Horace's ode "Rectius vives, Licini" (II. x. 8–11).

than pleasure in it. Language is scanty and inadequate to express the nice gradations and mixtures of our feelings. We say we are pleased when there is more pleasure than pain, but we do not tell how much there is of one and of t'other. No man reads a book of science willingly; that is to say, from pure inclination. What we do read with pleasure are light performances which contain a quick succession of events." He said he this year had read all Virgil through. He read a book of the *Aeneid* every night, so it was done in twelve nights, and he had great delight in it. The *Georgics* did not give him so much pleasure, except the fourth book. The *Eclogues* he has almost by heart. Mr. Burke said the story of the *Aeneid* was interesting. The Doctor did not think it much so. He preferred the story of the *Odyssey*. "More wonderful things in it," said Burke. "Nay, Sir," said the Doctor. "There are wonderful things enough in the *Aeneid*: the ships of the Trojans turned to sea-nymphs, the tree at Nisus's[6] grave dropping blood. The story of the *Odyssey* is interesting, as a great part is domestic." He said, "It seems strange there should be so little reading in the world and so much writing," which he explained as above. Burke talked of curiosity, and said, "It is a principle which grows in the mind." He said there was pleasure in writing; in verses particularly. "Why, Sir," said the Doctor, "you may have pleasure from writing after it is over, if you have written well. But you don't go willingly to it again. When I have written verses, I know I run my finger down the margin to see how many I had made and how few I had to make."

He took this visit very kind, and bid Young Burke give his compliments to all at home. He spoke in a kind tone of courtesy. Young Burke did exceedingly well. I just lay by and let him play the great organ. The Doctor said to me afterwards, "He did very well indeed. I have a mind to tell his father." We walked home each. Young Burke said, "If a man kept his mind in exercise as Dr. Johnson does, he would retain his faculties."

[EDITORIAL NOTE. No journal has survived for the period from 2 to 7 May, and in the *Life of Johnson* Boswell expressly says that he had no Johnsonian notes between the 1st and the 15th. He did jot down a programme of activities for Sunday and Monday, 4 and 5 May, in an inimitable mixture of English and Italian, which he wrote with abandon. ("*Domenica*. Chocolado e dolce. Messa momento. Poi Temple. Siete calmo se sia possibile. Dr. Johnson con lui. Lunedi[7] devote to

---

[6] Corrected to "Polydorus's" in the *Life of Johnson*.
[7] "*Sunday*. Chocolate and sweet rolls. Mass a moment. Then Temple. Remain calm if possible. Dr. Johnson with him. Monday . . ."

write letters. Inquire in Chancery about Mitchells' money.[8] Commons Monday, etc.") Much of what Boswell actually did is preserved in the diary of his old friend William Johnson Temple, who was in London from 2 to 30 May in company with Christopher Hawkins. (Hawkins, whom Temple served as chaplain, took a seat in the Commons in 1784 which he held consecutively for various Cornwall constituencies a total of forty-four years.) Whether Boswell went to mass on Sunday 4 May we do not know, but he did indeed call on Temple, whom he had not met since 1775. Temple had prior engagements, and does not report the visit to Johnson that Boswell had planned. On Monday 5 May Boswell, Temple, and Hawkins walked to Knightsbridge to call on the Rev. Christopher Wyvill, the Yorkshire leader of radical Parliamentary reform and Temple's friend since their Cambridge days. The three companions met again that evening to enjoy the pleasures of Ranelagh, where Boswell introduced the others to Burke. On the 6th he and Temple dined at General Paoli's and went to Drury Lane to see Mrs. Siddons's affecting performance in *Isabella, or The Fatal Marriage*, Garrick's adaptation of the play by Southerne. The friends apparently went their separate ways on the 7th, but on the 8th Boswell breakfasted with Temple and Hawkins and took them to call on General Oglethorpe, whom Temple found "a surprising character at his age . . . though near ninety quoted several of the Latin poets."]

THURSDAY 8 MAY. Met Mr. Burke as I was walking towards the City. He wanted to have me with him to Betty's fruit-shop to laugh. But I was hurried and had not time. He talked of the debate the night before on reformation of Parliament, and how the Advocate had spoke in direct contradiction to what he had formerly held forth.[9] He said, "He is a dirty dog." I resolved to keep this violent expression concealed, as it might exasperate the Advocate, who has a favourable opinion of Burke as a private man, and who may have it in his power to hurt him or to ward off ill from him. I said the Advocate's change was too sudden. It was a child born in the fifth month after marriage. It was clearly illegitimate. Burke was highly pleased with this allusion, and said he'd take care it should circulate.

[8] He was trying to locate for Ayrshire clients unclaimed funds reported to have been left many years before by William and James Mitchell of Tarbolton parish.
[9] Dundas had spoken against Pitt's motion of 7 May 1782 to appoint a committee to inquire into the need for reform. He now supported his proposals for increasing the representation from the counties and extinguishing boroughs where the majority were notoriously guilty of bribery and corruption. Burke believed that Dundas was trimming to maintain Pitt's support.

When I got to Mr. Alexander Donaldson's, about three o'clock, I was introduced to Captain Inglefield, a tall, genteel man between thirty and forty, and to the Master of the *Centaur*, Mr. Rainy, a steady-looking, stout Aberdeenshire man, I suppose about forty.[1] The Captain was dressed in a light-grey frock and I forget what waistcoat and breeches (I think white waistcoat and black silk or satin breeches); the Master in his Navy uniform. As I walked along, I had read over again Captain Inglefield's *Narrative*, which I bought at Murray's on purpose to have the particulars fresh in my head so as to talk with him to the greatest advantage. I had asked Burke to suggest to me questions to ask. But he could not take the trouble. I said I had insatiable curiosity. "And he" (Captain Inglefield), said Burke, "had an insatiable hunger." I inquired particularly about Bute Lindsay. They told me he had been ill, but was much recovered. He, however, though quite well could not have escaped in the boat; for in the rolling of the sea it required the particular agility of a seaman to jump from the ship into the boat. Lt. George Crawford, a natural son of the late Earl's, a fine young fellow, was very attentive to Bute, and gave him up his cabin (or place, whatever it was). The forenoon of the last day in the ship, Captain Inglefield told me Bute said to him, "We are all just convicts in a condemned hole." In the afternoon he sent his servant for Mr. Rainy. He was lying in his cot. He asked Mr. Rainy if there was no hope. "Sir," said he, "it is in vain to flatter you. I think there is none; and that the next jump" (or spring) "the ship makes, we shall all go to the bottom." He held Mr. Rainy by the hand. He burst into tears, turned away from him, and said, "It is very hard that at my age, and having the rank I have in the army, and going home, I should be cut off."[2] Mr. Rainy

[1] Boswell had written to the Countess of Crawford 1 May that he was to dine in company with Inglefield and Rainy. Obviously one of his motives was to get what report he could of Bute Lindsay (see above, 6 January 1783). The *Centaur*, a ship of the line (seventy-four guns), had fought off Chesapeake Bay and the West Indies in the concluding engagements of the American war, and late in the summer of 1782 sailed for England as part of a convoy of nearly one hundred vessels. On 16 September, off the New-foundland Banks, she was overtaken by a hurricane and dismasted. She was kept afloat with great difficulty until 23 September, when she went down with all on board except Inglefield, Rainy, a midshipman, and nine seamen, who managed to escape in the pinnace. Without compass or quadrant and with no sail except a blanket, they managed sixteen days later to reach Fayal in the Azores, one of the seamen dying from hunger and exposure the day before land was sighted. According to Inglefield's estimate, they had travelled upwards of nine hundred miles. Of the seven ships of the line which accompanied the convoy, five (including the flagship) perished. Many of the most vivid portions of Byron's account of the shipwreck in *Don Juan* are versified from Inglefield's *Narrative*, 1783.

[2] He was twenty-one.

then left him and went upon deck. And just at that instant the Captain proposed to him to get into the boat, which they both did. There was no struggling, no fighting for place in it, though both of them fairly said that in case of competition they should have killed others to save their own lives. The only struggle was beating off the young man Baylis two or three times, as he swum and held by the boat. At last the Captain thought it a pity to have him sunk, and let him get in.[3]

They both told me the same subordination was kept up in the boat as on board the ship. The Captain was still Captain, the Master, Master. The seamen were told that whoever rebelled should be thrown overboard. And the Master once flogged one of them pretty severely. Sullivan, it seems, had been born with a cap on, which had been superstitiously preserved and given to him. He wore it in his bosom, and used to clap his hand upon it and cry, "I have it here." The Captain said, "Sullivan believes now, and ever will believe, that it preserved him."[4] ("And you believe so, too," said Lord Mountstuart to me, knowing my superstition. I would not positively deny all influence to it.) Sullivan is as good a seaman as ever existed. But is quite a drunken profligate at land. Hutchins, an Englishman, is the firmest fellow, indeed to a wonderful degree. During the whole time they were in the boat he never changed countenance, never uttered the least complaint or desponding word, did his duty, took his scanty bit of bread and allowance of water without ever saying it was little, and slept sound; for they kept watches as regularly as in the ship. Once when they were making a lamentation on their wretched fate as he was going to take his nap, he called to them, "Damn your eyes, be quiet and let me sleep. Why do you whine so? We are not so bad yet as we may be. We are not begun to eat one another." And then he fell asleep. (General Paoli thought this an instance of the greatest strength of mind that can almost be conceived.) It was Hutchins who broke out into the "swearing fit of joy" mentioned in the *Narrative*. Gregory, a Scotsman from Dundee,

[3] The sea was running so high that the great majority of the officers and men believed there was no hope of living on a raft or in boats (of which there were only two) and had gone to their berths and hammocks, preferring to go down with the vessel, which now "appeared little more than suspended in the water" (Inglefield's *Narrative*, 1783, p. 24). Some, however, refused to die without a last trial. Inglefield, coming on deck, found that several seamen had forced the pinnace, and that unless someone in authority took charge, the boat would be swamped by numbers. He immediately decided that as he could do nothing more for the ship or those on board, he would make the desperate attempt of the pinnace. Baylis was the midshipman, mentioned in the last note but one. He was fifteen years old.

[4] A caul enveloping the head of an infant at birth is still believed to be a good omen. It is supposedly a protection against drowning.

a steady, good seaman, first spied land, and very calmly announced it. But when Hutchins was certain he saw it, he swore in the most violent and extraordinary manner, inventing many strange oaths for the occasion.

The Captain told me he just humoured the men in all their variations. Sometimes they were all religious, praying and confessing their sins, sometimes telling droll stories, sometimes singing songs. I begged as a favour he would sing one of the songs he himself sung in the boat, I having first sung, "Today let us never be slaves, nor the fate of tomorrow inquire," from *The Jovial Crew*.⁵ He very obligingly complied, and gave us "A bottle's the mistress I mean," which he sung exceedingly well. It was the first time I heard it. I have since got it, words and music, and it will always bring Captain Inglefield to my lively remembrance.⁶ I told him I expected a feast from him, but had got a dessert too. He told me Mr. Rainy sung. But I could not prevail on him to do it today. I said he would not sing but when in danger. He was a swan that sings only when dying. While in this dreadful state of

⁵   Today let us never be slaves,
              Nor the fate of tomorrow inquire:
          Old wizards and gypsies are knaves,
              And the Devil, we know, is a liar.

          Then drink off a bumper whilst you may,
          We'll laugh and we'll sing though our hairs are grey;
              He's a fool and an ass,
              That will baulk a full glass,
          For fear of another day.

The Jovial Crew is a comic opera of unknown authorship adapted from Richard Brome's comedy, with additional songs by Edward Roome, Matthew Concanen, and Sir William Yonge.

⁶Boswell's copy of *The Bottle* is not among his papers at Yale. The words of the first stanza, which follow, are from a copy in the British Library:

          What'er squeamish lovers may say,
              A mistress I've found to my mind,
          I enjoy her by night and by day
              Yet she grows still more lovely and kind.
          Of her beauties I never am cloy'd,
              Though I constantly stick by her side,
          Nor despise her because she's enjoy'd
              By a legion of lovers beside;
          For though thousands may broach her,
              May broach her, may broach her,
          By Jove I shall feel neither envy nor spleen,
              Nor jealous can prove of the mistress I love,
          For a bottle, a bottle, a bottle's the mistress I mean;
              Nor jealous can prove of the mistress I love,
          For a bottle, a bottle, a bottle's the mistress I mean.

distress, Captain Inglefield had a wife and three daughters at home. He told me he drove them from his thoughts. To think of them would have been too severe. He owned to me that still in some states of his spirits, the recollection of his situation was too much for him. I said he might comfort himself that he could not feel distress in the future part of his life; for, compared with what he had suffered, all other distresses must appear nothing. He had an insurance against suffering: not the Sun *Fire* Office, but *Water*.[7] This was playing on words like Burke, rather with too much levity. And upon reflection the thought is not true. For present evils, though slighter, will be felt compared with great ones past. Even a kind of pleasure is felt from *acti labores*.[8] 'Tis not so with horrible imaginings of the future. I said I was very happy to meet him, and we shook hands. He said, "I was acquainted with you, Sir, many years before I had the pleasure of seeing you." How *much* has that *Corsica* done to make me known! I observed he drank wine very gently. Rainy seemed to take it more heartily. Albert Innes[9] sung two Scots songs to us, and my brother T. D. was a very attentive listener, and spoke some too.

The Captain said he told the men when they were confessing their sins and expressing themselves as if they'd never do so again, "If you escape, you will not be long at land till you're as bad as ever." Accordingly they had not been long at Fayal till they were all as drunk as they could be. Nay, Gregory, the solid man who first saw the land, was just like the rest. The Captain had promised a six-and-thirty-shilling piece to the man who should discover it. When they were pretty well recovered at Fayal, Gregory sent to the Captain begging to have his six-and-thirty, for he was now well enough to get drunk. He and what companions he chose drank it all in two days, though they had wine for sixpence a bottle; seventy-two bottles in all. Both he and Mr. Rainy had remarkable good large gold watches with compasses in them, which they showed me. The Captain said he wished to send the blanket which served as the sail to the British Museum, if he knew how.[1] I undertook to inform myself and let him know. (I did so of Sir Joseph Banks, who is one of the Trustees, and promised to take care of it if sent to his house.) Both Captain Inglefield and Mr. Rainy told me that all of them,

[7] The Sun Fire Office was a London fire-insurance company established in 1710. It was acquired in 1959 by the Sun Alliance and London Insurance, Ltd.
[8] "Iucundi acti labores: Past labours are pleasant" (Cicero, *De Finibus*, II. xxxii. 105).
[9] A navy agent.
[1] "It was now five o'clock in the evening, and in half an hour we lost sight of the ship. Before it was dark, a blanket was discovered in the boat. This was immediately bent to one of the stretchers, and under it as a sail we scudded all night" (Inglefield's *Narrative*, p. 27). The blanket does not appear to be in the British Museum at present.

even the wickedest, believed that Providence had interfered to preserve them. The clearness of their passage to Fayal in the midst of darkness around was truly wonderful. [2]

After Hutchins had made his remarkable speech about their not yet eating one another, the Captain and Rainy retired to one end of the boat, and the Captain asked Rainy in a low voice what they should do if it should be proposed to kill some of their number and eat them, as has been done on many such occasions of horrible distress. Rainy said he never would agree to such a thing. He'd rather jump overboard. The Captain said, "I am glad you think so. It is my own resolution." Just after this they wanted to have an iron crow with which one of the seamen was working near them, and called to him to give them it. The poor fellow, imagining that the result of their conversation was to kill some of the crew, and that he was to be the first victim, delivered it with evident fear, and slunk away to the other end of the boat.

I do not recollect where I passed this evening.

[EDITORIAL NOTE: He had passed at least part of the evening of the 8th with Temple, whose diary also furnishes some particulars of Boswell's life for the next two days missing from his journal, 9 and 10 May. On the 9th they called together on Johnson, with Hawkins and Bennet Langton, and they afterwards dined at Dilly's, where the other guests included R. B. Sheridan, dramatist, M.P., and new joint Secretary to the Treasury (with Richard Burke, Sr., Edmund's brother); Major John Cartwright ("Father of Reform"), founder of the Society for Constitutional Information and agitator for annual parliaments, universal suffrage, and the ballot; Isaac Reed, Shakespearean editor; and "Mr. Scott," presumably Dr. William Scott, Camden Professor of Ancient History at Oxford, Johnson's friend, and a member of The Club. Of Boswell's activities on 10 May we know only that he breakfasted with Temple and that he responded as conscientiously as usual to the weekly report from his overseer at Auchinleck. Bruce had enclosed a document which we reprint below as an example of Boswell's *penchant* for ritual and tradition, much of it of his own making. We are reminded of his ceremonial farewell to his native land *en route* to London 15 November 1762, when he stopped the carriage and bowed thrice to the Abbey and Palace of Holyrood and thrice in the direction of Arthur's Seat.

[2] "In every part of the horizon, except where land was discovered [at a distance of seventy miles], there was so thick a haze that we could not have seen anything for more than three or four leagues. Fayal by our reckoning bore E. by N., which course we were steering, and in a few hours, had not the sky opened for our preservation, we should have increased our distance from the land, got to the eastward, and of course missed all the Islands" (Inglefield's *Narrative*, p. 34).

He had even induced his sober brother David to swear an oath of loyalty to the ancient family of Auchinleck upon the crumbling walls of the Old Castle before he emigrated to Spain in 1767, and when David returned to Scotland got him to ratify the oath, 17 August 1780. Boswell played out his commitment to a feudal ideal as imaginatively and as seriously as a child enacting a fairy-tale and drawing others into its fantasy.]

[Bruce to Boswell]

At Auchinleck Place, Saturday the third day of May, one thousand seven hundred and eighty-three years, betwixt the hours of twelve and one o'clock at noon.

Assembled in my dwelling-house at Auchinleck Place my son, Alexander Bruce, gardener at Auchinleck, and Isobel Ronald, his wife, with their son James Bruce, my grandson, being this day five months and eight days old. AND by special order from James Boswell, Esq., of Auchinleck, and as a present from him put into each hand of the said James Bruce my grandson ONE GUINEA of gold. And by these two guineas as per order he is hereby Nominated in Succession to be Gardener and Overseer at Auchinleck Place. All this being done in presence of Rebecca and Jean Bruces, my daughters.

JAMES BRUCE.

[EDITORIAL NOTE: "I am pleased that you have *engaged* your grandson," Boswell wrote to Bruce 10 May 1783. On 11 May he was to accompany Robert Preston on an overnight excursion into Essex, to the home of Charles Foulis, Director of the Sun Fire Insurance Company, the owner of extensive properties in the East Indies, and Preston's warm friend. But Boswell missed his escort, and had to make his way to Woodford, some ten miles distant, as best he could.]

SUNDAY 11 MAY. General, fine spirits. [He called Preston] "floating Bob [who thinks] landed interest pinch of snuff"; [spoke of] "Langton's geese fluttering, and [he] reed shaken with wind."[3] Lord Mountstuart's. Dear.[4] Lady Mountstuart and sons. Story of Jamie and "God's fly."[5] [MOUNTSTUART]. "Does you credit. Teach 'em one religion;

[3] See above, the end of the entry for 29 April 1783, Preston's depreciation of the landed interest. "Langton's geese fluttering" is probably Paoli's version of "flutter Langton's dove-cote."

[4] Perhaps Mountstuart addressed Boswell as "my dear Boswell," an unwonted note of cordiality which Boswell thought deserving of mention.

[5] The story is not recorded as far as we know.

you know you [have] good many." Lord Eglinton's, dry, dry. Hon. John Cunningham's, David Cuninghame. Chapel[6] a moment. Dilly's. Lime Street, [Preston] gone. Away. Footman refused. Hearse and two coaches; [thought] grief [might be] kindly, asked leave, box up to burying-ground. Thought of hearse like Baron Dalrymple.[7] Then along. Hackney-coach, "Come inside." Away to Stratford. Lady to go on to Bell, Leighton Stow,[8] good *sign*. But coachman stopped. Reverse of Macfarlane's geese; meat better than play.[9] Hurried on. Came up with Mr. Fogg, carpenter, Malton near Chippen Ongley.[1] Told me at once how many miles from each known place. Had been to release debtor in King's Bench, £48, let him off for twelve. [Debtor] promised more if in power, but that power probably never come. BOSWELL. "And will not if it should." Told [I was invited to] good dinner; "'t'will be over, but I shall get something. Always solid dinner." FOGG. "Ay, you'll do well on the ruins." Distance from two brewers[2] two miles; still two, though [we had gone] a mile further. FOGG. "Ay, we must rub on and endure. But a working man, and not so able to do such things to debtors as I have done [to] several, now with a family and growing old. Eighteen daughters and three sons by one wife, as jolly a woman as in England." Thus I had *comes iucundus*.[3] Foulis wished I had brought him in. When I arrived, table-cloth shaking a flag of distress; all over. Entered room. Foulis out from the table, ill. Old Major Forbes, seventy and hearty, Grindall, Martin, Constable (old friend of Temple's), Bob [Preston].

[6]The Portuguese Ambassador's chapel: see above, 30 March 1783 and below, 18 May 1783. This chapel was in South Audley Street, only a step from Paoli's house.

[7]Perhaps Boswell thought of composing an account of his ride on the hearse burlesquing the style and manner of Sir John Dalrymple's *Memoirs of Great Britain and Ireland*. Johnson had ridiculed Dalrymple's practice of inventing thoughts and speeches for characters of the past, and had himself made such a burlesque (Journal, 20 November 1773).

[8]Leytonstone, Essex.

[9]Macfarlane of that ilk had a house on an island in Loch Lomond which a brood of wild geese also frequented. King James VI(I) visited Macfarlane. "His Majesty had been previously much amused by the geese pursuing each other on the loch. But when one which was brought to table was found to be tough and ill fed, James observed 'that Macfarlane's geese liked their play better than their meat,' a proverb which has been current ever since" (Sir Walter Scott, *The Monastery*, ch. xiii, note). Boswell implies that *he* preferred a good dinner to the possibility of amorous intrigue with the "lady," who he thought had signalled encouragement.

[1]Malden Ashes, near Chipping Ongar. Here and in Leighton Stow Boswell may be recording a local pronunciation.

[2]The brewers are named farther on in the entry. Apparently they had country-houses near Woodford.

[3]"Comes iucundus [*or* facundus] in via pro vehiculo est: A pleasant companion on the road is as good as a carriage" (No. 116 in the collection from Publilius Syrus).

He took me to hall,[4] boiled beef, young cabbages, French beans. Madeira first, beer, ale, cider. Clean shirt, well. Then port and claret jovially. Hudson and Gordon, the two brewers of Bow, came. Jurymen of Stratton, etc. They'd have fined £10,000 apiece. Damned Lord Mansfield, bribed to be sure.[5] Bob *would* have [it that] Foulis very ill. [BOSWELL]. "It *won't* do."[6] GRINDALL. "No Providence."[7] Bob at him with sun and moon instead of throwing a bottle at his head. [BOSWELL]. "Bottle *in* it." Tea. Walk in garden: hothouse, greenhouses, etc. I quite happy. Shrub and water. Foulis to bed. Supper. Madeira. Shrub and water again. All hearty, never minding Foulis. Such is life. To bed in elegant comfort. Had lively thoughts. Sheridan and Cartwright [putting] reform of Parliament before education.[8] *Cart* before horses. Not an argument *ad hominem* but argument *ad nominem*. Last night by Bob's good sense, resolved [to aim at appointment as] Lord of Session.

MONDAY 12 MAY. Confused a little. Delightful view. Soon well. Captain Sutton. Bob walked so far; lame man rode his horse. "Good horseman," said I, "because lame." Then Bob mounted and joined Captain Sutton. Away they rode. John Taylor, servant to Mr. Taylor, formerly builder in London, now living on fortune at Leytonstone,[9] with two horses, one from grass, four shillings a week. Gave me the saddle-mare he rode, and took master's mare without saddle. Overtook Bob, etc., with a holla. We rode on cheerfully. I mentioned Grindall's denying a Providence. "Why," says Bob, "He does not believe there's a GOD." "GOD's wounds!" cried Captain Sutton. Said Bob: "He believes in nothing but a good dinner. That's his creed. Why, he has not been in a church these thirty years unless when he goes to the anniversary sermon for the London Hospital, to which he is surgeon, that he may dine after." "Lord, have mercy upon us!" said Sutton, with a fat voice.

[4]The servants' hall.

[5]A violent conflict having developed between Lord Pigot, Governor of Madras, and his council (one of whom was named George Stratton), the council seized Pigot and put him in confinement, where he died (11 May 1777). The coroner's jury declared a verdict of wilful murder against those concerned in his arrest. At a later trial in King's Bench before Lord Mansfield and a special jury, Pigot's opponents were found guilty merely of a misdemeanour, and were fined £1,000 each (10 February 1780).

[6]He *was* very ill. He died on 10 July following.

[7]Boswell had no doubt reported the testimony of Inglefield and his companions (above, 8 May 1783, near the end).

[8]Sheridan had spoken in the Commons on 7 May in support of Pitt's motion for Parliamentary reform, though he himself advocated more stringent measures.

[9]Pretty certainly Sir Robert Taylor, architect to the Bank of England, Sheriff of London, and donor of the Taylorian Foundation at Oxford, though it is odd that Boswell should not have known him by reputation. "Mr. Taylor" is not so surprising, for he had been knighted only a few months previously.

I left them, and stopped at Stratford. I went to the Bell and had ale and brown bread, and wrote a little journal. Then walked a little till there came Will Kettlewell, carter to Mr. Hurst, schoolmaster at ————. He took me up, put a board for a seat, and covered it with his frock. Three large horses. Had been once in London and back with dung today. Was going for another carriage; had it at a shilling a cart. I sang "Gee-ho, Dobbin."[10] I continued till we got to the end of Whitechapel. Out of town nobody seemed surprised. In town nobody laughed but a boy (foolish of course), a seller of teeth-powder, and a Whitechapel butcher. Bought in Leadenhall Street some songs with music, etc. Called at Bob's a little and left message Doctors not to come.[1] Called Dr. Knowles's. Saw him a little; she not in.[2] Then Dilly's. Found him and his brother John. Had a large glass lemon, Seville orange, China orange, water and sugar, and was refreshed. Wrote some journal and several letters. Put off time too long. Was engaged a week before to dine at Aberdein's with Col. James Stuart and Sir John Dalling. Was hurried dressing and late. But they waited for me. The company was of *my* settling, a *partie quarrée*. But Aberdein took upon him to add Mr. Foster, Commissary-General of Jamaica, who proved to be Temple's next neighbour, and Dalling's son, a spoiled boy of thirteen or fourteen who was in a few days to go to an academy in France. We had really a good dinner. The hock was to my mind and the claret superexcellent. I was in amazing spirits. Dalling and I had taken much to each other at the *Mount*, the night of J. R. Mackye's day,[3] and this day we were truly jovial. Only I was too violent against a certain *mason* in Parliament whom he likes. My rage was merely at a low man being so much raised, and being so vulgar and impudent and the bravo of a party. And when Stuart defended him, I said it was Scots partiality, the oatmeal in the blood, and some more such stuff.[4] We supped, drank a great deal of

[10] Unidentified.

[1] That is, that John Douglas and Andrew Kippis, both of them eminent clergymen and authors, were not coming. On 21 April Boswell had made a memorandum to ask them to dinner with Henry Swinburne, the traveller.

[2] Thomas Knowles, the physician, and his wife Mary, the witty and talented Quaker so steadfast in argument with Johnson, according to the *Life of Johnson*, that she even won his praise by an apposite scriptural reference 15 April 1778.

[3] See above, 30 April 1783 (last paragraph), the day that Boswell successfully managed an invitation to dine at Mackye's in company with Lord Mountstuart.

[4] Boswell's rage was almost certainly directed against William Adam, whose father, John Adam of Blair-Adam, like his father before him was architect and master mason to the Board of Ordnance in Scotland. William Adam was known as a "bravo" because of his intrepid baiting of Fox and others in the House of Commons. He had challenged Fox, moreover, to a celebrated duel in which he had wounded him slightly. At the formation of the Coalition ministry in April Adam was named Treasurer of the Ord-

wine, and sat till about two. Stuart, Aberdein, and I a little by ourselves. I was somewhat hurt by their expressing some doubts of my getting a Lord of Session's place. The only thing that disgusted me a little was Dalling's son, little impudent urchin, sitting by us.

[EDITORIAL NOTE. There are no notes for 13 and 14 May. At the beginning of the next entry Boswell appears to be at Colonel Stuart's, in Richmond Park.]

THURSDAY 15 MAY. Restless. Rose half past four. Could not open bars of door or of windows. Chink in library window gave me light to read in Dalton's *Egypt*, Pennant's *Wales*, and *Adventurer*. Was pretty well entertained. Then hit on knack of opening door bolt. Away through park. All beautiful and gay with birds. Walked to Kew Bridge. Had tea and agreed with Landlord Crisp on the hardship of quartering soldiers on innkeepers. Went in a stage-coach to Turnham Green. Called on Mr. Umfreville, the coroner. Not up. Walked in his garden till he came. Very courteous. Told him I was uncle to Cuninghame, who had the misfortune to kill Mr. Riddell; that I was a friend of Dr. Johnson, from whom I might have had an introduction to him, but thought I might do without it. He praised Dr. Johnson's worth and abilities, and said, "He is older than me. I am eighty-one"; and he had been coroner of this county thirty years. I told him the Doctor was not so old. He said he would show me everything concerning Cuninghame. So he went to his study (I believe) and brought me the verdict of the inquest, the depositions of the seconds, and his warrant to commit Cuninghame to Newgate, which he told me he would keep in his possession, so that Cuninghame should not be obliged to find bail before Lord Mansfield, which would cost £10, but should just surrender himself next Sessions.[5] He said he must have an attorney, and he (Mr. Umfreville) would give him all the information necessary. I asked what dues were to be paid. He said, "I have no demands." He praised our judges in Scotland and our deliberate proceedings in our courts of justice. I talked of them intelligibly to him for some time. I asked

nance, an office he had first held in the North administration. It was fully expected that he would displace Dundas in at least part of the control of Scottish patronage. Colonel Stuart after much wavering supported the new government.

[5] The coroner's jury had brought in a verdict of manslaughter. Cuninghame appeared at the next session of the Old Bailey, 4–11 June, but his trial was postponed on the last day. On 26 July 1783 the *General Evening Post* reported having been assured that Captain Cuninghame would surrender himself to the court and that the principal witnesses were summoned.

him if he was not of the old *Um*fravilles (as we pronounce it),[6] the
Earls of Angus. He said he was of that family. His pedigree was as long
as *that* (stretching out his arm to some distance from his body).[7] But
it would not get him a dinner at market. I said, "Sir, your politeness
proves your pedigree." I asked him if the duty of a coroner was to be
found in print. He said he had published a book upon it in two octavo
volumes.[8] (Dr. Johnson, who said to me afterwards he was a very good
man, said, "It is a silly book, I think." This may be a rash saying. I shall
read the book.) He was mild and civil, though formal and speaking in
an old man's voice.

I then drove in another stage-coach to Piccadilly. Came to the
General's. He and Mr. Gentili out. Found letters from my dear wife
so kind and interesting, resolved at once with a generous affection not
to go to Mrs. C.[9] Then found Hawkins and Temple at breakfast, and
had some. Was sunk a little with over-heat and want of sleep. Was
dressed by Hawkins's servant. Then we three drove in an excellent
post-chaise by Croydon to Mr. Claxton's at Shirley.[1] Good rooms. Good
land; twenty-five acres, none arable. Rich verdure and woods, and on
one quarter Shirley Common, brown heath rising from the house so
high that a woman in a red cloak passing along seemed on a level with
the high branches of the elms through which I saw her from the
window, and "Streamed like a meteor through the troubled air."[2] I
began to flag. There was no earnest talk, no brilliancy, no flash, no
vives secousses.[3] I drank little. I grew drowsy. I was miserable. We walked
out after dinner upon the common. I was quite sunk. I had not even
hope of happiness. I was in dreary hypochondria. We had coffee and
tea. Then away for London. I revived a little as I approached it. But
my mind was black and sore. I told Temple. He could not clearly
understand my feelings.[4] At Charing Cross I jumped out of the chaise,

[6]The coroner stressed the second syllable of his name; the Scotch Umfravilles stressed
the first.
[7]He could trace his descent back twenty generations to the founder of his family, Sir
Robert de Umfreville, or back twenty-seven generations to Egbert, King of the West-
Saxons.
[8]*Lex Coronatoria: or the Office and Duty of Coroners*, 1761.
[9]"Mrs. C." cannot certainly be connected with any other entry in the journal.
[1]A barrister at Lincoln's Inn and another of Temple's Cambridge friends. Boswell and
Claxton were also old friends, Temple having introduced them in London in the
summer of 1763.
[2]Gray's *The Bard*, ll. 19–20:
> (Loose his beard, and hoary hair
> Stream'd, like a meteor, to the troubled air).
[3]"Lively shocks."
[4]Temple was as "black and sore," but for the opposite reason: London provided too

resolved to try if this wretchedness *could* be relieved. Called Thomas Erskine about Cuninghame.⁵ Not at home.

Hasted to Dr. Johnson's. It was better for me I was afraid to own my melancholy to him, though I said I was over-fatigued. In a very little I felt a return of animation, of manly spirit. I said I wished to be in Parliament. "Sir," said he, "unless you come, like your countrymen, resolved to support any administration, you'd be the worse for being in Parliament, because you'd be obliged to live more expensively." "Sir," said I, "I never should sell my vote. And it would vex me if things went wrong." JOHNSON. "That's cant, Sir. It would not vex you more in the House than in the gallery. Public affairs vex no man." BOSWELL. "Have not they vexed yourself a little, Sir? All the turbulence of this reign, and the House of Commons voting that the influence of the Crown has increased, etc.?" JOHNSON. "Sir, I have never slept an hour less or eat an ounce less meat. I'd have knocked 'em on the head, to be sure. But I was not vexed." BOSWELL. "I declare, Sir, upon my honour, I did imagine I was vexed, and I took a pride in it. But I see it *is* cant, for I neither eat less nor slept less." JOHNSON. "Nay, my friend, clear the bottom of your mind of cant.⁶ You may talk as other people do. You may say, 'I'm your most humble servant.' You're not his most humble servant. You may say, 'These are sad times. It is a melancholy thing to be reserved to such times.' You don't mind the times. You tell a man, 'I'm sorry you had such bad weather the last day of your journey, and were so much wet.' You don't care sixpence whether he was wet or dry. You may *talk* in this manner; it is a mode of talking in society. But don't *think* foolishly."

I mentioned living in the country. He said, "Don't set up for what is called hospitality. It is a waste of time and a waste of money. You are eat up and no more minded. If your house is like a coffee-house,

---

many "*vives secousses.*" "Found myself incapable of doing anything: should never go from home: no enjoyment elsewhere. . . . Highly nervous for want of riding and good air and composure. . . . Not amused. . . . No pleasure here. Nothing but noise and madness. O for my wife and quiet parsonage!" (*Diaries of William Johnston Temple*, ed. Lewis Bettany, 7, 8, 25 May 1783.)

⁵The most brilliant and affluent courtroom counsel at the English bar, later Lord Chancellor (1806) and Baron Erskine of Restormel. Though the fee in this case could have been merely nominal, the client would have interested Erskine because of his profession, nationality, and the crime with which he was charged. Erskine himself had been an army officer and had fought a duel only six months before. On 2 June Boswell sent a letter to Erskine "reminding him of his generous promise to appear at the Old Bailey for Lt. David Cuninghame" (Register of Letters).

⁶Boswell has bracketed "the bottom of," and written above, "I am not sure." The *Life of Johnson* reads, "clear your *mind* of cant."

nobody cares for you. A man who stays a week with another makes him a slave for a week." "But," said I, "some people make their houses a home to their guests and are themselves quite easy." "Then," said he, "home must be the same to them, and they need not come." He said, "I would not be a stranger in my own county. I would visit my neighbours and receive their visits. But I would not be in a hurry to return visits. If a gentleman comes to see me, I tell him he does me a great deal of honour. I do not go to see him perhaps for ten weeks. Then we are very complaisant to each other" (or words to that effect). "You will have much more influence by giving or lending money where it is wanted than by hospitality."[7]

SATURDAY 17 MAY. Rose pretty well. Had hair cut, dressed, and powdered by ———, one of Nerot's men, which refreshed me. Drank chocolade at home. Then to Hawkins's; tea with him and Temple. Then Duke of Argyll's. He assured me he could do nothing for the poor soldier in whose favour I solicited his Grace.[8] I hoped he'd excuse my troubling him. He said he was glad to see me upon every occasion. He said the emigrations from the Highlands were no loss to the proprietors unless manufactures were established. For where the country is incapable of improvement, a few men are sufficient to take care of the cattle, and all the rest only consume what would be rent to the proprietor; so that unless for soldiers, they are no advantage. This was a new thought to me. But I recollected Goldsmith's lines:

> Ill fares the land, to hastening ills a prey,
> Where wealth accumulates, and men decay.[9]

I asked about Inveraray, and mentioned General Paoli's intention to be there this year. The Duke said he should be glad to see him. Told me the horse Dr. Johnson rode had been rode by himself, though then used for the cart. That manufactures went on pretty well at Inveraray. That sheep took fewer men to keep them than black cattle. I then called Lady Oughton. Not at home; but saw Miss Ross and Mrs. Symmers, Mrs. and Miss Green.[1] General Skene came. Walked with him. Called several places. Met Major Farquhar, Gilmillscroft's nephew. Saw Mrs. Love and No. 5 Cumberland Court.[1a] Disgusted. Miss Burney long time. Then Dr. Johnson's. He dressing. Sat with Mrs. Williams.

[7] There is no entry for 16 May, and Temple's diary for that day contains no mention of Boswell.
[8] Not identified. The Duke of Argyll had the rank of general in the army.
[9] *The Deserted Village*, ll. 51–52.
[1] Anne Catherine Green, whom Thomas David Boswell married at the end of the year. T. D. later charged Lady Oughton with forcing him into an imprudent match.
[1a] Unexplained.

Had heard at Miss Burney's Mrs. Desmoulins eloped. Heard an indictment against her.[2] Then to Doctor. He said, "I'll show you what I have for some time concealed" (or "refrained," or some such word). He took out a letter from a drawer. "There's a letter from Mrs. Thrale which you may read." I imagined upon my honour it was some *tender* epistle; something of love, perhaps of marriage. But it was writing him that if he chose to scold me, I had one night come to her house . . ."[3]

[EDITORIAL NOTE. A leaf of the manuscript, probably written on both sides, has been removed. Boswell says in the *Life of Johnson* that his visit to Johnson on 17 May was brief, and he reported only one bit of conversation. We print it from the manuscript of the *Life* as it stood before revision.]

Having mentioned that I had that morning been with Old Mr. Sheridan he remembered their former intimacy with a cordial warmth, and said to me, "Tell Mr. Sheridan I shall be glad to see him and shake hands with him." BOSWELL. "It is to me very wonderful that resentment should be kept up so long."[4] JOHNSON. "Why, Sir, it is not altogether resentment that he does not visit me. It is partly falling out of the habit, partly disgust as one has for a drug that has made him sick. Besides, he knows that I laugh at his oratory."[5]

[2] Boswell means only that Mrs. Desmoulins had unexpectedly departed the house. She seems to have returned by the end of 1783, and was certainly back in the next year. See below, 3 June 1784, p. 226. The quarrelling of the two sick ladies, reflected in Mrs. Williams's indictment, may account for Mrs. Desmoulins's departure. Johnson wrote to Mrs. Thrale 5 June 1783 that he now had "more peace at home, but I remember an old savage chief that says of the Romans with great indignation, 'ubi solitudinem faciunt, pacem appellant' " ("Where they make a wilderness they call it a peace" — Tacitus, *Agricola*, ch. xxx).

[3] The next word would no doubt have been "drunk." The occasion cannot be identified with certainty, but it must have been before Henry Thrale's death. Boswell's record for 21 March 1783 shows that it was the first time he had met Mrs. Thrale since she was widowed.

[4] James Macpherson had maliciously reported to Sheridan in 1762 that when Johnson heard of his getting a pension he had exclaimed, "What, have they given *him* a pension? Then it is time for me to give up mine." Johnson complained that Macpherson had not also transmitted his addendum, "However, I am glad that Mr. Sheridan has a pension, for he is a very good man" (*Life of Johnson*, 1763). To Sheridan the insult was compounded with ingratitude: it was at his suggestion, he told Boswell, that Alexander Wedderburn, whom he taught pronunciation, had prompted Lord Bute, his intimate friend, to pension Johnson in July 1762. Wedderburn, now Lord Loughborough, Chief Justice of the Court of Common Pleas, agreed that Old Sheridan had "rung the bell" (Journal, 16 May 1781).

[5] The journal for 17 May is resumed at this point.

Called Hairs's, and ordered seeds of different kinds. Then David Cuninghame a little. Then home. Large company to dinner: Dempster, Colonel Fothringham, Bishop of Killaloe, Bob Preston, Lord Provost of Glasgow, [6] Sir Joshua Reynolds, my brother T. D., General Rainsford, Masseria, Colle, General Paoli, Mr. Gentili, and myself. Jovial and happy. After coffee, brother came up to my room, and we talked of business calmly. I then called a few minutes on Temple, who was fatigued and would not come home with me. Mr. Liston came by appointment, and we had a *diplomatique petit souper*, the General and Mr. Gentili with us. [7] Mr. Gentili went to bed. The General and Liston talked of European politics with respect to Corsica. I firmly resolved I *would* enjoy wine. But not to excess. Liston's asking to pass an evening with me was a real compliment. I told him, "It is a sign you have a strong head that you are not intoxicated with your promotion." [8]

SUNDAY 18 MAY. Up pretty well. Lemonade, chocolade, tea. Rainy morning composed me. Went to high mass in Portuguese Chapel. Was devout as I could wish; heavenly and happy. Vowed before the altar no more *filles* while in London. A memorable moment. Then Temple and Hawkins, quite gay and placid. Then Lord Mountstuart. Fine laugh at story of printer from New Street. [9] Told him I was to be with Duke of Portland, and should talk of management of Scotland. "Why always an agent, a salesman for us like cattle? Archibald Duke of Argyll drove us up like bullocks for an age. Then came Dundas, the same. Why not let us speak ourselves, every duke, every peer, every baron?" Lord Mountstuart said Archibald Duke of Argyll was not so great as he made us believe. "Duke of Newcastle kept him hanging on. And his way was, when he found Duke of Newcastle for a different man than one whom

[6] Patrick Colquhoun, founder of the Chamber of Commerce of Glasgow, later police magistrate in London. Colquhoun wrote numerous pamphlets on relief of the poor and of labouring people in addition to the work for which he was chiefly known, *Treatise on the Police of the Metropolis,* 1795.

[7] Robert (later Sir Robert) Liston, who had been private secretary to the British Minister at Munich and Berlin, had been commissioned Secretary of Embassy to Madrid on 14 May, and on the same day given credentials as Minister Plenipotentiary until Lord Mountstuart, Ambassador Extraordinary, should arrive.

[8] "Mr. Liston, supping at General Paoli's, said he was afraid to go to Dr. Johnson because he understood he was rough and insolent. 'Not at all,' said I, 'if you do not oppose him. His principle is "Parcere subiectis et debellare superbos" ["To spare the lowly and vanquish the proud" — Virgil, *Aeneid,* vi. 853].' Liston acquiesced in being ranked with *subiectis.* Said General Paoli, 'If you are a *brebis* [sheep] in the cave of Polyphème, he will not hurt you' (alluding to Ulysses and his companions)" (Detached note for this day, perhaps intended for a collection of Paoli's witty remarks).

[9] William Strahan's printing-house was 10, Little New Street, near Gough Square. The end of the entry for this date suggests that the story concerned Strahan's awkwardness.

he recommended, he gave up his own and recommended that one. So he prevailed. As it is notorious Lord Mansfield has always assembled the judges of the King's Bench and heard their opinions; and if they would not submit to his, he did to theirs, so that in this way his judgements have always been adopted by the Court." My Lord said it was better for Scotland to have a Minister, one man to act, provided he was a man of great consequence and a good man. "Dundas very improper. You talk of Duke of Gordon. Were I a Minister, I should not care for Duke of Gordon, who has not a word to say. What is it to me that a man has seventy miles of estate? There are but three ways in which a man can have weight with a Minister: talents, Parliamentary interest, or a great deal of money to buy Parliamentary interest. Duke has it not."

I came home and dressed and went to Lord Advocate's to dinner. Disappointed a little at first to find just a company of Scots lawyers (Pitfour and Sinclair, whom I disliked), with his nephews William and the Colonel.[1] Thought of being almost silent, very abstemious, and going away soon. But thought better, and found I could display my London spirits. Repeated to Lord Advocate my question to Lord Mountstuart about salesman for Scotland; added the phrase "topsman," and called his Lordship "a Craigengillan."[2] He said it was better for the country, a salesman, as I called him; better for individuals not. For when all could scramble, they would have a chance [to] get more for themselves and their friends, without regard to merit. Whereas an agent for Government must distribute to the best purpose. He has a trust. He maintained against his nephew William that to speak English was a slight advantage, not worth expense and risk of estranging your son from his own country by educating him in England. As a proof he showed more Scotsmen in proportion well heard in House of Commons. And he maintained ably that the forty-five Scots Members were as independent in proportion to numbers as the English. Talking of Douglas, he said Thurlow said, "Be what he will, he has taken care to bring good blood into the family: Montrose and Buccleuch." "Ay," said I. "If it be *glass*, 'tis well *stained*."[3] A good dinner: burgundy, cham-

[1] Sons of Lord President Dundas. William Dundas, now twenty-one years old, was later M. P., Secretary at War, and a Lord of the Admiralty. Francis Dundas had fought in the American war and surrendered with Cornwallis at Yorktown. He became lieutenant-colonel in the army April 1783 and rose to general by 1812.

[2] A topsman was the chief drover in charge of a herd of cattle on the road. The reader may remember that Boswell's Ayrshire friend Craigengillan had acquired considerable wealth by droving.

[3] The Dundases had maintained that Douglas was really the son of a French glassblower. But they had to admit that his *sons* had or would have noble blood, for his first

pagne, deal of excellent claret. Had sense not to go to Miss Monckton's. Called Sir Joshua: to bed.[4] Then Lord Mountstuart; merry for a little. He humorously assimilated me to Strahan, as my sword hung awkward. Called it "that New Street affair." Home. Lemonade.

[EDITORIAL NOTE. There are no notes or journal for 19, 20, and 21 May. The dates in Temple's journal are confused, and he made matters worse by recording some events twice, on different days. But it was probably on Monday the 19th that he and Boswell dined at Wilkes's and called on Dr. Johnson, and on the 20th that Boswell took him to Richmond Lodge to dine with Colonel Stuart. (General Dalling and John Ross Mackye were among the guests. "Much wine and little agreeable conversation," Temple wrote—*Diaries*, p. 40.) The next day, by our reckoning the 21st, Boswell, Temple, Hawkins, the Bishop of Killaloe, and Sir Francis Drake went to see Charles Townley's fine collection of Roman sculpture, which was later acquired by the British Museum. Boswell probably suggested the visit, for he had gone twice to Townley's in the spring of 1781, and his enthusiasm for classical marbles, which was stimulated by a Grand Tour of Italy in 1765, appears not to have been quenched. After viewing the sculptures he and Temple dined with General Paoli and had tea at Bennet Langton's, where they found Dr. Johnson. The following conversation, which Boswell reported in the *Life of Johnson* between his entries for 17 and 26 May 1783, must have occurred on either the 19th or the 21st. We are printing it from the manuscript of the biography, first draft. The gentleman of whom Johnson had a very high opinion was obviously Burke, as was also the "eminent person then in place." The gentleman who "talked of retiring to a desert" was undoubtedly Boswell himself.]

On another day I spoke of a gentleman of whom he had a very high opinion. "But, Sir," said he, "he is a cursed Whig, a *bottomless* Whig, as they all are now."

I mentioned my expectations from the interest of an eminent person then in place, adding, "But I have no claim but the claim of friendship. However, some people will go a great way for that." JOHNSON. "Sir, they will go all the way from the world."[4a] A gentleman talked of retiring

---

wife was a daughter of the Duke of Montrose, and his second (whom he had married only a few days before this) a sister of the Duke of Buccleuch. Thurlow had been counsel for Douglas in the appeal to the House of Lords.

[4] Reynolds, that is, had gone to bed.

[4a] The expression, which was probably Johnson's own, is not without difficulty, but may be taken to mean, "They will go completely counter to the world's usage." Boswell changed it in the proofs to "they will go all the way from that motive."

to a desert. "Never think of that," said Johnson. The gentleman urged, "I shall then do no ill." JOHNSON. "Nor no good either. Sir, it is a civil suicide."

THURSDAY 22 MAY. Was at the House of Lords in due time.[5] Messrs. Morthland and Solicitor and Lord Advocate spoke. Temple, Hawkins, my brother T. D. attended. I was in no uneasiness. Dined with Blane and Anderson and brother at Spring Garden Coffee-house *pretty hearty*. Then Hughes's Circus[6] with Blane and brother. Then, *as a coarse day*, and as I had not been with him for several weeks, supped with Lord Eglinton, Lord Crawford, and Barker, who both went away before I had finished my second bottle of claret. Talked to my Lord of his want of belief of a future state. He persisted. I was shocked. I was going away. He sent for me wickedly, and made me finish bottle. Staggered home.

FRIDAY 23 MAY. Was at House of Lords in proper time, having first drank tea with Lord Graham, who refreshed my head "sicut mos est,"[7] and said I drank a great deal with him and with Lord Eglinton, though different liquids. Was in flow of spirits. Drank coffee and had some soup at a coffee-house in Court of Requests. Appeared at the bar quite easy, and spoke distinctly and as I could wish. And when Lord Advocate perceived by a question that Lord Mansfield was satisfied, and whispered to me, "Finish," I did so in a very little, which was being perfectly master of myself. Then after affirmance with costs,[8]

[5]On the appeal brought by the partners in John McDowall and Company, Glasgow traders, against a unanimous decision of the Court of Session for Mrs. Jane Ferguson, the widow of Gilbert Macmikin and residuary legatee of her son, Hugh Macmikin, late partner in the Company and its representative at Portsmouth, Virginia. Mrs. Ferguson had been trying since 1775 to recover the £630. 12s. 10d. sterling which she claimed the company owed her son, chiefly for salary, at the time of his death the year previous. McDowall and partners argued that the present American factor was obligated for whatever debt there might be, and that if they were compelled to assume it, they should make payment at the current depreciated rate of the American currency. Boswell, Henry Dundas, and George Fergusson were counsel for Mrs. Ferguson; counsel for appellants were John Morthland and Ilay Campbell, Solicitor-General and the most successful advocate in Scotland. The House of Lords continued the appeal to a second day.
[6]The Royal Circus and Equestrian Philharmonic Academy in St. George's Fields, Surrey, which Charles Hughes and Charles Dibdin founded in 1782 for the exhibition of feats of horsemanship.
[7]"Sicut meus est mos: After my fashion" (Horace, *Satires*, I. ix. 1, trans. H. R. Fairclough, Loeb ed., 1961).
[8]£100, four times the amount in costs Lord Kennet had decreed, which the entire Court of Session had finally reduced on a Reclaiming Petition to three guineas plus the cost of the extract.

drove to Nerot's and was dressed. Then Le Telier's:[9] Lord Pembroke, Lord Herbert, General Stopford, Major Skeffington, Dean Marlay. I was in highest spirits, and called out, "I am as happy as a prince. I resolved to be happy and I *am* happy." But I drank too much wine and too fast, and was intoxicated, and talked too openly of *myself* and my licentious indulgences, and my wife's goodness. And how if I was to have but *one* woman, I'd rather have her than anyone in the world. And joked Lord Pembroke about his licentiousness. Talked of the great era to which we looked forward: his Lordship's being Lord Lieutenant of Ireland, and how we should all have good places. They were all vastly gay too. Only Lord Herbert was more sedate. I said, "I see the Prime Minister in your face," and called him "my grave and good Lord of Sunderland."[1] His father seemed to stand a little in awe of him. He won my heart by saying with a proper dignity that he was shocked to hear Beauclerk talk profanely.[2] I was not quite at my ease till I had called them all by their names: "Stopford," etc., except the lords. I make it a principle never to encroach on their rank. We had an excellent dinner, good port, sherry, and claret and iced water. A magnificent upper room. All quite in high tavern style. We parted, I believe, near ten. I went back and wrote letters to my wife, Craigengillan,[3] and Killantringan. Then called up Baxter, the landlord, son of a Yorkshire farmer, but always ambitious. Would not go to plough. Became waiter. Was at Lady's Club, etc. Paid 2,750 guineas for an eighteen and a half years' lease of Le Telier's at 246 of rent. Had one club once, 200 [members] at five guineas only for the house. Some drunkards amongst them broke it up. He had done well upon whole. Told him all my situation as laird. We had four bottles of claret. I sallied forth shockingly drunk, and picked up a girl in St. James's Street. Went into park; sat on bench and toyed, but happily had sense enough left not to run risk.

[9] A tavern in Dover Street of which Baxter, below, was the proprietor. The Club later met here, from 14 December 1784 until 17 May 1791.
[1] Charles Spencer, third Earl of Sunderland, Prime Minister 1718–1721, excited great hopes by his youthful promise. Lord Herbert was Sunderland's great-grandson, his mother, Lady Elizabeth Spencer, being daughter of the third Duke of Marlborough, who was Sunderland's son. Sunderland had been the political patron of Addison. Boswell's flattery was intended to put Lord Herbert in mind of his own ardent wish for preferment.
[2] Topham Beauclerk (who had died in 1780) was his uncle by marriage. In 1787 Lord Herbert married Beauclerk's second daughter, Elizabeth.
[3] This letter is registered in Boswell's Letter-Book as follows: "Craigengillan, . . . I am now happy for three reasons: first, I have dined most agreeably with Lord Pembroke and some more distinguished friends; secondly, I recollect your saying that if I had the misfortune to lose my excellent wife, you would give me your charming daughter; to whom, *take her for all in all*, I have not seen an equal here (some more warm things about her); thirdly, that I have this day won Mrs. Macmikin's cause, with £100 costs."

However, when we rose and walked along, missed watch. She denied. Grew sober; said she should go to watch-house. She broke off in St. James's Street. Watchman, two chairmen, and a soldier catched her, and we marched to St. James's watch-house.

[EDITORIAL NOTE. The journal breaks off here at the bottom of a page with a blank reverse, the entry probably never having been completed. The lapse extends, in fact, to 29 May 1783. Temple reported in his diary under the date of Saturday the 24th that "Boswell came in intoxicated from the Duke of Montrose's; had his pocket picked of his gold watch." At first sight it looks as though he had mistaken both the date and the place where Boswell had dined, but it is by no means impossible that Boswell was drunk on Friday night and again on Saturday, the first time he saw Temple after the incident. The watch was not recovered as late as 20 June, when Boswell sent his brother David information concerning the number and the maker's name, presumably so that the loss could be advertised.

Temple had been very unhappy during most of his stay in London and was fretting because Boswell was delaying their departure for the north. Temple's destination was his boyhood home near Berwick-upon-Tweed, where he had property. He attended church with Boswell on Sunday 25 May, and indulged in severe reflections: "Boswell irregular in his conduct and manners, selfish, indelicate, thoughtless, no sensibility or feeling for others who have not his coarse and rustic strength and spirits. Sorry I came to town to meet him. Detaining me here to no purpose. Seems often absurd and almost mad, I think. No composure or rational view of things. Years do not improve him. Why should I mortify myself to stay for him?" In the evening Boswell came to Temple and Hawkins "in his usual ranting way and stayed till twelve, drinking wine and water glass after glass" (*Diaries*, p. 41).

The only surviving record of Boswell's activities on Monday 26 May is the conversation with Johnson in the *Life of Johnson*, which we print from the draft of the manuscript.]

On Monday 26 May I found him at tea, and the celebrated Miss Fanny Burney, the writer of *Evelina* and *Cecilia*, with him. I asked if there would be any speakers in Parliament if there were no places to be had. JOHNSON. "Yes, Sir. Why do you speak here? Either to instruct and entertain, which is a benevolent motive; or for celebrity, which is a selfish motive." I mentioned *Cecilia*. JOHNSON (with an air of animated satisfaction). "If you talk of *Cecilia*, talk on."

Of Mr. Barry's exhibition of his pictures he said, "Whatever the hand may have done the mind has done its part. There is a grasp of mind there which is not in the other."⁴ In Mr. Barry's printed analysis or description of these pictures he speaks of Johnson's character in the highest terms.⁵

A learned and amiable friend being mentioned, JOHNSON. "Sir, he has no rest abed or up—at home or abroad. At home he has his wife; abroad the Americans.⁶ She fairly turned Sir William Jones out of the house for breaking a china cup, and asked her husband if he brought him there to insult her.⁶ᵃ She has always behaved well to me; gives me good words and pleasing looks; and I am very careful to return my best words and most pleasing looks."

I asked whether a man naturally virtuous or one who has overcome wicked inclinations is the best. JOHNSON. "Sir, to *you* the man who has overcome wicked inclinations is not the best. He has more merit to *himself*. I'd rather trust my money to a man who has no hands, and so a physical impossibility to steal, than to a man of the most honest principles. Foote had a small bust of Garrick upon his bureau. 'You may be surprised,' said he, 'that I allow him to be so near my gold; but you will observe he has no hands.'"

⁴Changed in the manuscript of the *Life of Johnson* to "a grasp of mind there which you find nowhere else." Boswell must have recognized in revising that the statement as he originally cast it implied a contrast between two of Barry's paintings, whereas his notes showed that Johnson alluded to another painter. Boswell's generalization makes one wonder whether that painter was not Reynolds. "Barry's exhibition" was the public viewing of the Great Room of the Society of Arts at the Adelphi, which Barry had decorated with six pictures eleven feet six inches high and a total of 140 feet in length illustrating the development of human culture. He began the work in July 1777 on his own suggestion and with only sixteen shillings in his pocket, expecting no payment except the cost of materials and models. The Society accepted the paintings 26 April, just a month before this conversation, and voted Barry a total of 250 guineas and a gold medal.

⁵One of the paintings at the Society of Arts showed Johnson between the two beautiful duchesses of Rutland and Devonshire, pointing to Mrs. Montagu, the blue-stocking, as an example to them. In featuring Johnson as mentor, Barry wrote in *An Account of a Series of Pictures in the Great Room of the Society of Arts, at the Adelphi*, published in 1783, he was expressing his "reverence for his consistent, manly, and well-spent life."

⁶The harried husband is almost certainly John Paradise, the linguist, whose wife, Lucy Ludwell, an American heiress, was notoriously erratic. She was officially declared insane two years before her death (nineteen years, it must be added, after his). Paradise was also troubled financially. His father had excluded him from his will after a violent quarrel; Mrs. Paradise's estates had been temporarily confiscated by the Commonwealth of Virginia in 1778; and the payments of indemnities to British and American subjects that had been stipulated in the peace treaty were indefinitely postponed because of a serious post-war depression.

⁶ᵃSir William Jones was the extraordinary linguist, reputedly master of thirteen languages and proficient in twenty-eight, who pioneered in Sanskrit learning. Boswell deleted this whole paragraph from the manuscript of the *Life of Johnson*.

[EDITORIAL NOTE. Of Boswell's activities during the next two days we know only that Temple called on him on the 27th and on the 28th dined with him at General Paoli's ("Much good conversation with the General," Temple noted—*Diaries*, p. 42). The journal is resumed with Boswell again at Dr. Johnson's.]

THURSDAY 29 MAY. I soon announced to him that I was to set out for Scotland next day. JOHNSON. "Langton, Sir, is as good a man as lives." BOSWELL. "But ridiculous." JOHNSON. "It will do him no harm in the next world. But it makes him be laughed at in this." BOSWELL. "He is a man of great knowledge." JOHNSON. "Yes, Sir. But it never lies straight. There is never one idea by the side of another. 'Tis all entangled. And then he drives it in so awkwardly upon conversation." (I had said, "Sometimes I think of being a grave, solid man, who keeps his mind to himself; sometimes a fine, gay, flashy fellow as in the county,"[7] upon which it was that he introduced Langton as a foolish instance of studied behaviour: that he was first grave and silent and then gay and talkative. I said he was the reverse of the insect which is first snail then butterfly, for he was first butterfly then snail. JOHNSON. "*Who* said this of him?" BOSWELL. "I say it now." JOHNSON. "It is very well said." BOSWELL. "I say very good things sometimes." And then I said, "But he is a worthy man," after which followed what is above.)

"Sir," said I, "It is incredible how absurd and weak I am, with talents—I mean in conduct and in speculative opinions; for I do very well when I come to an argument in law. I have not force of mind." "Sir," said he, "endeavour to get as much force of mind as you can. Live within your income. Always have something saved at the end of the year. Let your imports be more than your exports, and you'll never go far wrong." I said I would. "But," said I, "what hurts me sometimes is the question how it is to be with us. Is not the last part of our conduct of most weight? What I mean is, if there be such a thing as balancing accounts, suppose a man has been seven years good and then acts wrong, will his former good have any effect in his favour?" "Sir," said he, "if a man has been seven years good and afterwards is by passion hurried to commit what is wrong, he'll have the reward of his seven years. GOD won't take a catch of him. So Richard Baxter says a suicide may be saved. 'If' (says he), 'this should encourage suicide, I am not to tell a lie to prevent it.' " I said, "But it is said, 'As the tree falls,' etc." "Yes, Sir, as the tree falls. But" (here a little embarrassment) "it is meant as to the general state of the tree, not a sudden blast." In short,

[7]The meaning probably is, "as fine, gay, flashy a fellow as there is in the county of Ayr," but "county" should perhaps be emended to "country."

he meant not position. So Shenstone wrong.[8] Burke afterwards wisely observed we should not take off any restraint such as this or eternity of hell torments. One may be silent.

The Doctor asked me *how many* trees I had sold for £70. I could not tell, and said it was not our way to count. He said he was sorry for it; he'd have them counted and their girths measured. I said, "I shall do so, and learn the value of wood." When I objected to the trouble and time measuring would take, he said, "I hope you have not sold more than 100 trees for £70, and 100 may be measured in a day."

I asked him to come to Auchinleck. He said, "I cannot come this year. But when I grow better, as I hope I shall, I should gladly come. I should like to totter[9] about your Place, and live mostly on milk, and be taken care of by Mrs. Boswell. We're good friends now, are we not?"[1] I told him yes. I said to him that in the range of various people whom he had known, none had a more sincere respect and affection for him than I had. He said he was persuaded of it, and added, "If I were in distress, there is no man I would come to so soon as you. I should come to you and have a cottage in your park."

He advised me to set my mind on practice as a lawyer in Scotland. Every new cause would teach me more law, and the more causes I had, the less surprising it would be that I was made a judge. I should court employment by all honest and liberal means, be still more civil to agents than before, as they naturally suspect a rich man to be proud. "Have them to dine and show them you are desirous of practice." I was animated by his manly conversation. I told him I was persuaded there was a transfusion of mind, like Hermippus Redivivus in body.[2] I had experienced it from him. Talking of cutting my large wood, he said, "You are to consider whether the value of its yearly growth or the interest of the price is most, and then either cut or delay."

[8] Boswell himself expands this cryptic jotting (a crowded marginal addition) later in the entry.

[9] In revising the manuscript of the *Life of Johnson* Boswell changed this to "toddle." As a matter of fact, the dictionaries give "toddle" as a synonym for "totter" and *vice versa*.

[1] Mrs. Boswell had objected to Boswell's making the tour to the Hebrides, and doubtless believed Johnson the chief magnet in London. According to Boswell's own report she thought that Johnson had too much influence over him. When heated once she remarked "with more point than justice . . . 'I have seen many a bear led by a man; but I never before saw a man led by a bear'" (*Life of Johnson*, note to Johnson's letter of 27 November 1773). Johnson had also aroused Mrs. Boswell's antipathy by his irregular hours and uncouth habits when he visited the Boswells in Edinburgh in 1773. He later won her, however, by his courtliness and solicitude, especially when she was ill late in 1782.

[2] Dr. Cohausen of Coblenz maintained in the work *Hermippus Redivivus* (1742) that life might be prolonged to 115 years by breathing the breath of healthy young women.

When he had talked of Richard Baxter's opinion as to a suicide, I said, "What a shocking instance was this of Powell![3] And, Sir, I am really uneasy about Burke. They take advantage of this to attack him. Some impute Powell's death to him from his having restored him, and put him in a situation to be driven out." "Sir," said he, "it is no more to be imputed to Burke than to you or me." "But," said I, "they represent him as actually mad." "Sir," said he, "if a man will appear extravagant, as he does, and cry, can he wonder that he is represented as mad?" I said he was unhappy. "Sir," said he, "that is the cant of statesmen from age to age." "But," said I, "he says he has not had an hour of peace since he came into the Pay Office." "That may be true," said he. "If a man will restore rascals, he may not have peace." "But," said I, "not only Burke, but Lord Mountstuart assure me Powell had no dishonest intention." "Depend upon it, Sir," said he, "Lord Shelburne would not have moved it again in the House of Lords if he had not known there were good grounds."

I asked him what works of Richard Baxter I should read. He said, "Read any of them. They are all good." (I have written the short dispute concerning the text, "As the tree falls, so shall it lie," so ill that it is hardly legible. I shall therefore write it over again. I objected: "But it is said, 'As the tree falls, so shall it lie.'" DR. JOHNSON. "Yes, Sir, as the tree falls. But" (after a little embarrassment) "that is meant as to the general state of the tree, not of what is the effect of a sudden blast." In short, he meant to interpret it as referring to condition, not to position. Therefore the general notion must be wrong. And Shenstone's witty remark on divines trying to give the tree a jerk upon death-bed, to make it lie well just as it falls, is not well founded.)

When I told him that Mrs. Strange assured me their family was kept in London for £500 a year, "Sir," said he, "it may be so. But *your* family would not be kept in London for £500 a year, nor £1,000 neither. You would wish to make a figure suitable to your rank. Your lady would wish to do it." "Oh, Sir, she has nothing of that turn. I believe she has cost me less for clothes than any woman, not only of her rank, but really in any decent style." JOHNSON. "Ah, Sir, were she here, it would be different. And you would not be satisfied if, when she went about to the conversaziones, she were not as well dressed as other ladies."

[3] John Powell was one of two clerks in the Pay Office who had been dismissed for malversation by Burke's predecessor as Paymaster, Isaac Barré. Burke, mistakenly believing them innocent, reinstated them while they were still under indictment, and was severely criticized for doing so. Powell resigned. Before his case came to trial, he committed suicide.

He was mild and cordial this morning. I felt a tender concern at parting with him, as it was very uncertain if I should see him again. I complained of not having him near me to consult upon all occasions of any difficulty. He said, "Write." "Then," said I, "you will not be unwilling" (or "slow," or some such phrase) "in answering my letters?" He said, "No." I got up to part from him. He took me in his arms, and said with solemn fervour, "GOD bless you for Jesus Christ's sake." I then hastened away. He called after me, "You'll see" (or "you'll call on") "Mrs. Williams." "Yes, Sir," said I. "I intended to see her." I did so, and sat down a little by her. She said Dr. Johnson would not allow he had been very ill whenever he got pretty well again. But when his complaints returned, he was very dreary, or some such phrase. I told her he had said he would leave me my letters in case he should die before me. But I doubted he would neglect it. For he had told me since I came last to London that he had not made his will. I regretted this, and said he should be spoke to about it. She thought I ought to speak. I said it was a delicate subject. But I would write to him about it. [4] I bid her adieu. I then gave Frank a crown and bid him drink his master's health, or take good care of him. I walked away from Dr. Johnson's door with agitation and a kind of fearful apprehension of what might happen before I returned.

The day was now fair. I walked along till I came to a barber's shop near the New Church in the Strand. And there I was shaved and had my hair dressed and my clothes brushed. It began to rain again. I took a hackney-coach and drove to the *Paymaster's*. There was a card from him to me requesting my being with him this day at two to go to Chelsea College, which had not yet been sent and was delivered to me; so that I found there was no wavering about my having the anniversary feast of King Charles II's restoration with him in his official capacity, for which I had stayed in London some days. [5] I was apprehensive his uneasy state of mind on account of Powell's melancholy exit might have prevented him from attending. I found him very well today. A Mr. Burgh from Ireland, a near relation of Dr. Burgh's at York, was with him, as was his son. [6] He talked of Delany's *Life of King David*, which

[4] Boswell's Register of Letters shows that after this date he made numerous anxious inquiries of Johnson about his health but no references to a will.

[5] As Paymaster General of the Forces Burke was also Treasurer of the Royal Hospital for old and disabled soldiers, which was founded by King Charles II, designed by Sir Christopher Wren, and erected (1682–1690) on the site of Chelsea College, a theological college founded by James I but soon abandoned. The Governor and officers dined together at an elaborate feast on 29 May (Oak Apple Day) and the pensioners were given a double allowance of food and beer.

[6] William Burgh, of Ireland, Parliamentary reformer rewarded by Oxford with a D.C.L. for a book which refuted Unitarian doctrines against the Holy Trinity. He had long

I took down from a shelf in the library where we sat, and read the curious passage where it is maintained that it was a point of honour and indeed humane in David to get Uriah killed rather than let him live under the disgrace of having his wife debauched. Upon which Dowdeswell, a friend of Mr. Burke's, had humorously remarked, "Dr. Delany shall never lie with my wife, since he thinks it a point of honour to cut my throat afterwards." Mr. Burke said he had laughed more reading Delany's *King David* than ever he did in his life; that Delany was a good man, a learned man, and (I think) an eloquent man, but a weak man. And in that book there were the strangest passages. He pointed out the account of Naboth's[7] wife as an accomplished woman, and the account of Abishag the Shunammite.[8] I read several passages which truly confounded me by the mixture of excellent writing and absurdity. There was a fine sentence which Mr. Burke praised. It was comparing the conduct of man in this state to St. Peter walking upon the sea: one step firm, the next sinking, etc.[9] Mr. Burke told us as a curious fact that although there had been reading men before him in the Pay Office (Lord Holland and Mr. Rigby),[1] there were no shelves for books till he put them up. He showed us the house, which is an admirable one.[2] I felt a longing after such an Office with its appurtenances. Yesterday he had expressed some uneasiness that Mrs. Burke was not returned from their country-seat. She came this forenoon while I was with him. It was truly agreeable to observe their conjugal affection. They had not met since Powell's death. She showed no womanish extravagancies, but spoke of it with calm concern. Mr. Burgh engaged to dine with her.

The Paymaster, his son, Mr. Ste.-Marie, and I drove in a hackney-

lived in York though he owned large estates in his native land. His relation is probably Thomas Burgh of Chapelizod, Member for Athy in the Irish House of Commons, the seat William Burgh had held from 1769 to 1776.

[7]*Read* Nabal's: that is, Abigail (I Samuel 25).

[8]The fair damsel who cherished David in her bosom when he was very old and "gat no heat" (I Kings 1:1). Delany says that she had to be fair (1) as an indication of health; (2) "as David was very beautiful himself, they sought for some person of complexion and constitution likest to his own; and of consequence best suited, and most congenial to it" (Patrick Delany, *An Historical Account of the Life and Reign of David, King of Israel*, 3rd ed., 1745, ii. 286).

[9]"It is melancholy to observe, that whilst we are tossed upon the waves of this world, the boisterous waves of passion and appetite, the very best men are but too much in the condition of St. Peter in the sea; they walk one step upright, and sink the next" (Delany, ii. 86).

[1]Lord Holland had been Paymaster General from 1757 to 1765, in the administrations of the Duke of Newcastle, the Earl of Bute, and George Grenville; and Richard Rigby from 1768 to 1782, in the administrations of the Duke of Grafton and Lord North.

[2]In Whitehall, next to the Horse Guards.

coach to Chelsea College. Mr. Burke's own horses were ill. As we drove along, I mentioned Dr. Johnson's observation today upon a man who has lived a good life seven years being afterwards criminal, together with Richard Baxter's opinion as to a suicide. Mr. Burke said there were articles he might think which he would not publish. I mentioned the eternity of hell's torments. He said we could not be sure they were not eternal, yet GOD was not obliged to put his threatenings in execution. He talked of the inconsistency of some people's religious principles. He told me of a curious Irish gentleman, who, when he was in the Temple and about three-and-twenty,[3] left his seat in a remote part of Ireland, where he lived in a course of rigid religious discipline, and came all the way to London to fight another gentleman who had a lawsuit with him and had used some slighting expression concerning him. The gentleman very properly answered his challenge with my Lord Chief Justice's warrant. He was in great indignation at this. One day when with Mr. Burke, he was talking violently against the wickedness of the age, particularly some of the slighter vices of young men. Mr. Burke took him up, and said, "Here are you so severe upon these things, yet you are come all the way from Ireland with that little brasshilted sword deliberately to commit murder.[4] Does religion permit that?" The gentleman said he could not believe GOD Almighty meant that we should bear to be insulted, or would be angry at a man's taking revenge if he did it like a gentleman. So curiously does every man plead for his own propensity. The gentleman was obliged to return home to his strict religious life unrevenged. Mr. Burke said the Christian religion imposes no duty at all hard except a little fasting. He compared something (I forget what) to a work of supererogation. "So," said I, "you admit works of supererogation." Said he: "I shall not quarrel with you about a word. But we all know there may be more done than what we are strictly obliged to do. A man may live upon very little and give all the rest of his fortune to the poor." (This I think was his instance.) Talking of the eternity of future punishment, Mr. Burke said he hoped much from the mercy of GOD, who was not obliged to fulfil his threatenings. But we were not *sure* but it might be so.

Sir George Howard was very courteous to me at Chelsea College during the whole repast, and after it was over asked me to dine there every anniversary as long as he was Governor.[5] I sat between Mr. Burke

[3] That is, when Burke was at the Middle Temple, about 1752.
[4] Carrying a sword in Ireland identifies the gentleman as a Protestant.
[5] Boswell's journal shows that he attended all the dinners celebrating Oak Apple Day from 1783 to 1790 except in 1788, when he was in Scotland because of an alarming

and Dr. Monsey, physician to the College, who in his eighty-ninth year was quite entire in his mind. I had a good deal of conversation with him. He professed his belief in a future state.[6] He told me brandy was very pernicious to the stomach. I asked him how one might attain to such an old age as his. He referred me to Celsus, who advises not to observe any constant regimen. Mr. Burke was very attentive to old Captain Grant, son of the minister of Auchinleck in my grandfather's time, who is adjutant to the College; so that the Captain, who has the old-fashioned enthusiastic attachment to *the Laird*, was much pleased to see him so intimate with Mr. Burke. We had an excellent dinner and a great deal of good wines. I drank liberally and was in high spirits and very happy in my talk, being much encouraged by Mr. Burke. I got acquainted with General Trapaud. He[7] and I, his son, and Mr. Ste.-Marie drank tea at Mr. Champion's.[8] We drove home well, and then I had a close conversation with Mr. Burke, in which he counselled me to fix my mind on an employment in Scotland, and to come only for a visit to London. I was satisfied at the time.

I hastened home to Mr. Dilly's, whom I found sitting with my friend Temple and my brother David, and after making an apology for coming late, I eat a hearty supper of cold meat, was in high spirits, and sat up and wrote many letters and cards. At Dr. Johnson's in the forenoon, talking of devotion, he gave it as his opinion that although GOD dwelleth not in temples made with hands, yet that in this state of being our minds are more solemnly affected in places appropriated to divine worship than in others. "Some people," said he, "have a particular room in their house where they say their prayers." I told him I had

---

turn in Mrs. Boswell's illness. After 1790 the journal (which is very fragmentary) furnishes no evidence one way or the other. General (later Field Marshal) Sir George Howard, Governor of Chelsea Hospital 1768 to 1795, was a pompous but good-humoured man, according to Fanny Burney. He was Commander of the Buffs at Fontenoy, Falkirk, and Culloden and, except for two years as Governor of Minorca, Member of Commons from 1762 to his death in 1796.

[6] A famous eccentric, something like Swift in temperament, he lived to be ninety-four. Boswell's note that he believed in a future state contradicts the popular accounts, which are no doubt largely legendary. It is certain, however, that Monsey directed in his will that no funeral ceremony should be held over his body, but that it should be dissected and the "remainder of his carcass . . . put into a hole, or crammed into a box with holes, and thrown into the Thames" (C. G. T. Dean, *The Royal Hospital, Chelsea*, 1950, p. 221).

[7] Burke. The preceding sentence is an interlinear addition.

[8] The porcelain-maker of Bristol whom Burke in 1782 had made joint-deputy Paymaster General. He later emigrated to South Carolina.

one at Auchinleck. He bid me keep it for that purpose. I intend to do so. It is the dressing-room of the family apartment. There I every morning pray and read a part of the Holy Scriptures and a part of Thomas à Kempis; and I never fail to find myself calmed and elevated. My evening prayers I say at my bedside.

[EDITORIAL NOTE. Boswell and Temple left London on the morning of Friday 30 May. Boswell, as usual, relished the varieties of life along the road. Twelve miles north of London he purchased a copy of *Select Original Letters on Various Subjects*, 1781, twenty-two hortatory essays to reform the age written by James Ripley, the ostler at the Red Lion Inn for over thirty years. Boswell's endorsement reads, "This book I bought from its author at Barnet, 30 May 1783. He seemed to be a sagacious old man" (*Catalogue of the Auchinleck Library* . . . sold at auction by Sotheby, Wilkinson, and Hodge, London, 23–25 June 1893, p. 38). From dinner on Friday through the weekend the travellers stayed at Southill, the Bedfordshire home of Squire John Dilly. There Boswell wrote the following memorandum, which is printed for the first time.]

FRIDAY 30 MAY. You are now fixed both by Dr. Johnson and Mr. Burke, the first of whom hath told you there is a patriarchal duty in residence at Auchinleck, and that you may take as much of London as you can purchase. The latter that your situation is very desirable. Not a great but an ancient and respectable family. Fine Place. Something added to your fortune would make you vastly well. This country now in an unsettled state. But suppose you were to get £1,000 a year? £200 in Scotland better considering expense of family in London and going backwards and forwards. And depend on it, were I to get into a line here I must keep close to it. It would not do to be fidgeting. It is not like having a place near London, as Langton's.[9] I must not think of going home except once in two or three years. "Then, Sir, I am settled. But you would not banish me from my friends here?" "GOD forbid—on their account."

I am then to be steady to the great point of being of consequence in my own country and having my wife and children comfortable and creditable—with the addition of London, The Hague, Paris, to enlarge and enliven. And keep up the piety of your family.

[EDITORIAL NOTE. On Monday 2 June Boswell and Temple continued north by way of York (where William Burgh took them to his

[9] The reference is almost certainly to Langton, although the name is concealed by a large ink blot except for the first and last letters. He and his family were living at Rochester. See above, 23 March 1783, p. 81.

house and showed them his drawings and paintings), Durham, and
Newcastle-upon-Tyne. Boswell's money gave out, and Temple had to
pay most of his bills on the road. On the 5th they reached Berwick-
upon-Tweed, and the next morning went to see Allerdean, Temple's
farm. Boswell remained at Berwick some days, taking Temple to dine
at Blackadder on the 9th with Nabob Boswall (so called because he had
been medical adviser to the Nawab of Arcot). He seems to have intended
an even longer stay, for on that day he wrote to Lord Eglinton proposing
a visit to his regiment, then at Berwick, and asking Eglinton to set the
day. His dallying at this time is unusual, for in previous years Boswell
felt impelled to be present at the opening of the Session 12 June. But
his return was hastened after all, probably by news that Jamie was ill,
for on the 12th he wrote to Temple that Jamie was better. After a brief
visit to Auchinleck, where the children were, Boswell returned to
Edinburgh. There on 27 June he received the news from his brother
T. D. that Johnson had suffered a paralytic stroke. He wrote to Johnson
the next day, and on 7 July received a reassuring reply, although his
respected friend had temporarily suffered a loss of speech. The journal
is resumed with 1 August.]

FRIDAY 1 AUGUST. (Writing the 8.) I was in very bad spirits. Yet
I went and supped at Lord Justice Clerk's with Mr. Ross Mackye and
a large company.

SATURDAY 2 AUGUST. (Writing the 8.) I just appeared in the Court
of Session, and then drove in my chaise with Grange, by special invitation, to the Hon. A. Gordon's at Rockville. My spirits were bad. But
viewing the ruins of Seton and particularly the chapel did me some
good.[1] Before dinner, got some good instruction in farming; then dined
cordially and drank freely till Sir Hew Dalrymple and Mr. Swinton
of North Berwick came. Sir Hew invited us to dine with him next day.
We drank tea and played at cards. Sir Hew rode home after supper.

SUNDAY 3 AUGUST. (Writing the 8.) It was a rainy day. We went
to North Berwick Church to afternoon service and heard Professor
Hill of St. Andrews preach. Then went to Sir Hew Dalrymple's, where
I had never been before. He had ironically described to me an elegant
new house he had built[1a] as if no better than a hut. I put Mr. Gordon

[1] Seton Palace, in Haddingtonshire, was damaged by the English in 1544, and the
nearby church of St. Mary and Holy Cross, founded late in the fourteenth century
but never completed, was burned and destroyed. The Palace was restored magnificently
and occupied periodically by Mary Queen of Scots (to whose reign the rebuilt south-
east front was attributed), James VI, and Charles I. After the rebellion of '45 Seton
was confiscated and sold to a company of estate agents. The palace was razed in 1790.
[1a] Leuchie House.

and some more in the secret, and affected to take Sir Hew at his word, commending his good sense in making a plain, cheap house in an extravagant age. He was fairly taken in, and desired me to look, and was almost angry. I burst out a-laughing and was joined by the rest; owned my fighting him with his own weapons. And then, having really admired the house, drank his health by the title of Sir Inigo Jones, walked out with him after dinner, and agreed in a taste for squares and straight lines. We became great friends. He liked Grange much. I was a little entertained in thinking of this as a law Place, it having been acquired by that profession.² At night we were quietly social at Rockville.

MONDAY 4 AUGUST. (Writing the 8.) Walked out with Mr. Gordon in the morning; a fine day. Drove well to Edinburgh. Found Mr. Boswall of Blackadder and Mrs. Thomas Boswall just set down to dinner with my wife. Grange and I joined them. He went away. Lady Auchinleck drank tea with us.

TUESDAY 5 AUGUST. (Writing the 8.) Lord Mountstuart and his lady had come to town last night in their way to Bute. I waited on them this morning and found a numerous levee and not a warm reception. My wife called afterwards, but Lady Mountstuart was not at home. I called on my Lord for a little before dinner and asked them to supper. But they were to set out next morning, and would not sup abroad. I dined at Bayle's, a party made for Mr. Ross Mackye; Hon. A. Gordon at the head, I at the foot. Sir William Erskine was very good company. I drank very liberally, just to dissipate dreary dulness. I came home somewhat intoxicated.

WEDNESDAY 6 AUGUST. (Writing the 8.) My wife and I dined at Lady Colville's; the Hon. A. Gordon and Lady Dumfries,³ Sir William and Lady Forbes the company. I was in such miserable spirits that I resolved to drink a great deal of wine. I did so, and afterwards played ill at cards. In short, it was a day not to be remembered with satisfaction. I went to bed immediately on my getting home. In the forenoon we had a visit of David and Henry Cuninghames, who came last night.

THURSDAY 7 AUGUST. (Writing the 8.) Was still in bad spirits. I indeed was sensible that drinking was a bad remedy. Yesterday the dismission of Mr. Dundas from the office of Lord Advocate was announced. It did not agitate me much, as it was expected, and as my spirits were so wretched.⁴ David and H. Cuninghames dined with us.

²Sir Hew was the fourth generation in a line of advocates. His great-grandfather and grandfather had been successively Lord President of the Court of Session.

³Gordon's wife, the widow of the Earl of Dumfries and Stair.

⁴Dundas had been turned out of his office as Treasurer of the Navy in the previous April on the formation of the Coalition government. Though Boswell was too dull to

In the evening Captain Cuninghame,[5] who had been David's second, paid us a visit. I felt a woeful difference upon myself from what I was in London. I was quite discontented. Worthy Grange endeavoured to soothe me, and to persuade me that I should reconcile my mind to living in Scotland. At night I felt some relief from gloom.

I was kept in Edinburgh till Tuesday the 12, though the Session rose on the 9th, because I was engaged to plead a cause before the Commissaries, my first appearance in that Court.[6] I liked it very well. We sent our own horses to Little Vantage on the 11, and with the aid of two Edinburgh hacks for that stage, got to Auchinleck at night. At Douglas Mill we found my old friend Mr. Ross, patentee of the Edinburgh Theatre, in his way to his nephew's house at Kerse. He dined with us. For some days I was pretty well. But a fit of low spirits came upon me, which distressed me much for some time. On the 27 August Miss Young came to be governess to my daughters. Her brother, the Rev. Mr. Young, minister at Erskine, came with her. Next day was the Fast Day (as they call it) before the Sacrament at Auchinleck. I was better than I expected to be during the whole of the sacramental ceremonies.[7] On Sunday the 24 August my friend Mr. Charles Dilly, bookseller in London, arrived at Auchinleck from Dublin. He stayed with us till Monday the 1 September, on which day Commissioner Cochrane and Dr. Webster came. On Thursday they left us and went by Ayr to Craigengillan's. I rode through the moors by Little Mill and was there before them. Lord Justice Clerk and his lady and Dr. Hugh Blair

12 AUG.

27 AUG.

28 AUG.

24 AUG.

1 SEPT.

4 SEPT.

---

be very hopeful, he wrote to Burke the next day complaining that he languished "in provincial obscurity" and stating his pretensions for preferment as Lord Advocate or even joint Solicitor-General.

[5] John Cuninghame, Laird of Caddell and Thornton, twenty-seven years old and a veteran of extensive service in America as captain of a company in the 69th Regiment. He was put upon the half pay at the reduction of the forces this year.

[6] Both the original court for Edinburgh and the Supreme Court of Scotland for probate and divorce, absorbed by the Court of Session in 1836. The judges were appointed by the Crown and chosen from the Faculty of Advocates.

[7] The Church of Scotland at this time generally observed the Sacrament once a year, in a summer month, the Sacrament for Auchinleck parish regularly falling in August. (Burns's *Holy Fair* satirizes the Mauchline Sacrament of 1785.) The preparation was strenuous: on 26 August 1780 Boswell wearily calculated that the preaching had lasted four hours. The crowd, which was much too large for the church, sat in the open air in the churchyard while several ministers in succession exhorted them from a covered pulpit or "tent." Boswell no doubt listened from a comfortable room in the family "aisle" (see below, 10 January 1785, n. 3).

3 SEPT.	and his wife dined with us on Wednesday 3 September. I
6 SEPT.	returned from Craigengillan's on Saturday the 6, a wet, stormy day. Was wet to the skin and went to bed. On Friday
12 SEPT.	the 12 my amiable old friend Sir Alexander Dick, in his eightieth year, paid us a visit most cordially, accompanied by his son Robert and his brother-in-law, Captain Butler. My
10 SEPT.	wife and I paid a visit at Eglinton on Wednesday the 10 and
11 SEPT.	returned Thursday the 11. I was pleased with his new-married Countess as much as I could at this time be pleased with anything.[8] For though the uneasiness of low spirits went off, my mind was affected with a kind of dull indifference, a sort of callous stupor. The promotion of Harry Erskine to be King's Advocate while I thought myself more deserving of that office, vexed me, especially as a kind and candid letter from Mr. Burke gave me faint hopes of any promotion by his influence.[8a] All my lively ambition was mortified. I had no object, and indolence seemed to overwhelm me. I read none at all but a chapter of the Bible and one of Thomas à Kempis every morning. But it was without unction and only from a habit of duty. I said to Sir Alexander Dick, "Between ourselves, it is happier to be a young laird than an old one." "Because" (said he very well) "the one lives in hope, the other in fear." His company cheered me a good deal. On Saturday
13 SEPT.	the 13 Commissioner Cochrane and Dr. Webster returned to us. That day I had at my table three old gentlemen whose ages together amounted to about 236 years; viz., they two
15 SEPT.	and Sir Alexander Dick. They left us on Monday, Sir Alex-
16 SEPT.	ander on Tuesday. Dr. Webster preached in our parish
21 SEPT.	church on Sunday, and I was comfortably pleased. A great variety of other company was at Auchinleck. I felt the entertaining of them in general as a laborious and anxious task. I several times drank too much wine, and suffered severe distress after it. I was quite averse to writing. I was exact only in keeping my Book of Company and Liquors, in which I marked with more regularity than I supposed possible for

---

[8] Lord Eglinton's first countess, the lovely daughter of Lady Crawford, whom Boswell had reserved in fancy as his own second wife, died in 1778 in her twenty-second year. Frances, daughter of Sir William Twisden, the new Countess, engaged in an intrigue with the Duke of Hamilton and was divorced in 1788.

[8a] Weak from illness and dispirited, Burke wrote on 13 August that he would lay Boswell's letter of 8 August before the Prime Minister, with his best recommendation, but that he would be "little consulted about the arrangements of Scotland, or any other places." Erskine was appointed Lord Advocate 23 August.

me all the company with us at dinner in one column, and all
night in another, with the different liquors drank each day
in separate columns.[9] I also marked down my letters sent,
which were very few, and kept my Account-Book pretty well.[1]
But upon the whole I led a life of wretched insignificance in
my own estimation, though indeed it was perhaps no worse
than that of many gentlemen of fortune. My valuable wife
and agreeable children were constant objects of satisfaction.
But my mental eye was often too dim or confused to relish
them sufficiently. I began to despair of acquiring any knowledge in country affairs, and apprehended that my affairs
would go into confusion. I had a sudden relief on Friday the
10 October when the Laird of Fairlie paid me another visit   10 OCT.
and in the most friendly manner instructed me as he did last
year. Sometimes I thought of appointing a faithful trustee
and going to reside in London or in France. My Book of
Company will remind me of clusters of ideas which it would
take me much time to register. I had letters from many
friends, but deferred from day to day answering them. I had
one early in October from Dr. Samuel Johnson. I thought
of his death with dreadful gloom. It appeared to me that if
he were gone, I should find life quite vapid and myself quite
at a loss what to do, or how to think.

Part of this summary was written, I think, in September;
the rest on the 16 of October, when I felt myself a good deal   16 OCT.
better. I had the day before dined at Logan, where I had not   15 OCT.
dined for fifteen years.[2] I was in agreeable expectation of a
visit of the Valleyfield family. (Writing on Friday 31 October.)

[9] The Book of Company and Liquors, which is now in the Hyde Collection, was begun
at Boswell's accession and kept up to his last visit to Auchinleck in January 1795. Since
he records his absences from home as well as the list of his company, it furnishes an
exact chronicle of his movements while in the country. For example, we learn from
it that on 16 and 17 September he and Mrs. Boswell were at Rozelle, and on 18
September at Sundrum.

[1] Both records for this period survive, the Register of Letters from 1 January 1783 to
September 1785, and the Account-Book from 12 June 1783 to 15 March 1785. The
latter includes among many spontaneous acts of charity ("a sailor"; "a blind beggar") one
shilling on 16 October 1783 "To Tibby Pagan the poetess." This is the only direct
evidence that Boswell knew the lame and whimsical friend of Burns, who conducted an
illicit traffic in whisky at her hut near Muirkirk. *The Laird o'Glenlee,* Boswell's satire on
John Miller, elder brother of the Lord Justice Clerk, was included anonymously in her
Collection of Songs and Poems, published in 1803.

[2] Boswell thought the Laird of Logan clownish and double-dealing, and disliked the
fact that he was compared with him. The Laird characterized their relationship when,

Sir Charles, Colonel George, Captain Robert, and Miss Prestons, with Captain Cotton, a jolly old East Indian captain,

16 OCT.   came to us on Thursday the 16 October to dinner. I had that day a sudden relief from hypochondria, and entertained them in the heartiest manner; and what is curious, I drank a great deal of wine without feeling any bad effect.[3] My friend Mr. George Wallace came and joined us in the afternoon. I was so well that, while I kept the highest pitch of jollity, I at the same time maintained the peculiar decorum of the family of Auchinleck, and had family prayers in the library, which Miss Preston attended, while we left the gentlemen at cards.

17 OCT.   On Friday we took a walk to the Old House, etc., and Captain Robert Preston and I rode out by Cumnock and Ochiltree, at which last place (the seat of his grandfather,[4] long ago sold) he said, "Memento mori." The house seemed quite different when so cheerfully inhabited; and it was pleasant to see a goodly band parading before breakfast upon the gravel in front of the house, which Captain Cotton called a good quarter-deck. I was as sound and happy while this company

18 OCT.   was with me as I could wish. On Saturday morning Captain Preston and Captain Cotton set out for London by Carlisle. Old John Boswell came on Friday to dinner by my special invitation, to partake of the excellent cheer and society, and stayed till Sunday. On Saturday Sir Charles, the Colonel, and he and I and Mr. Wallace took a long walk round the Hern and Tenshillingside. I relished much Mr. George Wallace's knowledge and philosophical speculation. He went with me into the grotto which I dug at the Corbiecraighead. I was so well now that I wrote several letters with satisfaction, and in

19 OCT.   particular one to Dr. Johnson.[5] On Sunday Miss Preston and

---

"very drunk and very good-humoured," he remarked to Boswell, " 'I would do anything to serve you. I court you. But you winna court me' " (Journal, 4 June 1779).

[3] The company consumed, at dinner and supper, seven bottles ("and two pints") of claret, three of port, one of Lisbon, two of Madeira, one of mountain, and one of rum (Book of Company and Liquors).

[4] Boswell's great-grandfather, William Cochrane. Old James Boswell had purchased many of the farms of the Ochiltree estate, and in 1819 Boswell's son Alexander bought the mansion house and some farms lying near the Old Castle of Auchinleck.

[5] According to the Register of Letters, Boswell described a sudden relief from the bad spirits of the autumn, inquired affectionately after Johnson, and asked again, "Why should I not venture in London?" He sent the letter the next day, 19 October 1783, but both the original and the copy he made have disappeared, like most of Boswell's other correspondence with Johnson.

Mr. Wallace went to church with us. On Monday morning
Sir Charles, the Colonel, and Miss Preston left us, as did Mr.
Wallace, whom I accompanied to the old castle of Craigie,
which he had a curious desire to see. He was to go to Kilmarnock and Ayr, never having seen them before. The day
turned out very wet. I came home. Next day I found my
spirits somewhat flat. I set out on horseback, not fixed where
to go. I went to Rozelle, and was pleased to find Lady Crawford and Lady Mary Lindsay, with little company. Next day
I resolved to visit the Laird of Fairlie. I got John Boswell at
Ayr to accompany me. It rained much. But I did not mind
it, and was delighted with the prospect from the Clavin hills,
above the Loans, which I had never before seen. Was disappointed that Fairlie was not at home. Dined at Kilmarnock.
Sent to know if Craufurdland was at home. [6] He was gone to
Auchinleck and Lord Dumfries's. Left Kilmarnock about
seven and got home about nine. Craufurdland had been at
Auchinleck the day before. He returned on Thursday. I
should have mentioned that on Saturday the Earls of Cassillis
and Dumfries and Sir Andrew Cathcart offered me the honour of a visit to dinner on Sunday. I had decent firmness
enough to let them know that Sunday was a day on which
I did not expect company, and therefore unless Lord Cassillis
and Sir Andrew were in such a hurry that they could not stay
another day, so that it would be *a work of necessity*, I politely
declined the honour. [7] I was glad that I had thus taken such
an opportunity of showing my family regard to Sunday that
I should probably ever after be free of temptations to deviate
from the good example which I sincerely wished to give.

During this autumn I had by no means the same activity
and ardour in country affairs as last year. I was lazy every
morning and indulged in bed. But that was an enjoyment.
I was active in small matters: in collecting fern and rushes
for dung, and such things. My ignorance in the management
of ground vexed me, and I was fretted at the cunning of the
country people and the little regard which appeared to me
to be felt for my prosperity. Mr. Stobie came on Friday the

[6] John Walkinshaw Craufurd of Craufurdland.
[7] The correspondence is preserved. Boswell has endorsed the reply, "Exemplary instance of my keeping holy the Lord's day, to be attended to by those who come after
me. It effectually prevented visits to me on that day. The two earls and Sir Andrew
did not come."

24 OCT.   24 to collect the remaining arrears of rent. His ungrateful conduct to me when he owed so much to my mother, and his vile partiality for the woman who took advantage of my father in his old age, revived most disagreeable feelings.[8] I twice had visited the Rev. Mr. George Reid. I was pleased with his just liberality of thinking one of the days, when speaking of Mr. Grant, minister at Auchinleck, who preached with fervour yet was very licentious in his conduct with women; and I heedlessly said (against my considerate opinion) that he must have been a great hypocrite. "I don't know,"

28 OCT.   said Mr. Reid. "He had strong passions." On Tuesday 28 October I went to Ayr in my chaise and qualified as a Justice of Peace. I was then chosen preses of the Quarter Sessions, and thought I did very well in the chair. I was pleased to find this mark of respect shown to the Laird of Auchinleck; yet I could not have as high a feeling of it when realized in my own person as when imagined. I dined at Lady Cunninghame's, and went at night to Lady Crawford's, where I am

29 OCT.   always happy. Next day[1] dined at Coilsfield. Nobody there but his lady and sister. He had been so very ill that it was supposed he could not recover, and was yet very weak. But his spirit never failed him, and I found him genteel and social as ever.[2]

30 OCT.   On Thursday the 30 I was not at ease. I know not what had affected me. But I was irritable in a sad degree; and upon some careless expression of my dear wife's which hurt my pride, I burst into a paroxysm of horrible passion, of which I feel (31 October) a most painful recollection. I put some shirts in my greatcoat pocket, got upon my horse, and rode out in a hurried dubiety which way I should go to be from home. Luckily I met Mr. Dun in the road to the church, and returned with him and entertained him with tolerable decency. It is shocking to be subject to such fits of violence. I was harsh to the most valuable of wives, and at the same time shuddered at the apprehension of the dismal uneasiness it would give me to reflect on this, should I be unhappy enough to have her taken from me by death. I regretted that

[8] John Stobie, former law clerk to Lord Auchinleck, now collected Lady Auchinleck's rent from her locality lands. Boswell's resentment of Stobie was long-standing, for Stobie had behaved impudently towards him while Lord Auchinleck was alive.
[1] Boswell's forty-third birthday.
[2] Alexander Montgomerie lingered until 28 December of this year, but his lady, whom Boswell does not mention as having been ill, died three weeks after this visit.

she had not more acquaintance with the various workings of my mind. Yet I thought it was better that she was not so troubled herself, without which she could not have much acquaintance with hypochondria. I was ashamed and humbled, and passed the rest of the day in dejected vexation. I prayed to GOD, and was in some degree quieted. It has been usual every evening since Miss Young came to have music and sometimes a little dancing in the library, for the improvement and diversion of my daughters. This night I could not bear to be present. It is amazing how much everything depends on the state of our minds at the time, and how little the state of anyone's mind is known to others. On the 31   31 OCT. October Mr. Beatson of Redhouse came from Fife to breakfast, being chosen on the part of Lady Auchinleck to inspect the houses and fences on the locality lands and make a report of their state and condition.[3] Mr. James Johnston, merchant in Cumnock, was named on my part. He came after breakfast, and they went this day and inspected the lands in Auchinleck parish. Mr. Beatson came back at night. Next day they in-   1 NOV. spected the barony of Trabboch. Sandy and I dined cordially at Mr. Dun's. In the evening Mr. Beatson and Mr. Johnston came to Auchinleck. Mr. Beatson's intelligent conversation upon improving of land pleased me much. I learnt several things of him. He stayed till Monday morning. At the meeting   3 NOV. of the Quarter Sessions at Ayr on Tuesday 28 October, when a new Commission of the Peace was read, and I along with a good many more took the oaths as a Justice for the first time, I was chosen preses, which was a real satisfaction to me as Laird of Auchinleck. I have, I see, mentioned this before. At a general meeting of the landholders of the county on the 7 November I had again the honour of being chosen preses.[4]   7 NOV. I felt this very sensibly as a mark of regard from the real gentlemen of the county. I sincerely wished to do them every service in my power, and to have power to do a good deal. I dined at Wharton's with Mr. Mure of Caldwell, Mr. Ross

---

[3] Doubtless Robert Beatson, LL.D., who wrote practical agricultural papers as well as extensive reference works on military and political history. The elaborate *General View of the Agriculture of the County of Fife, with Observations on the Means of Its Improvement* which he drew up for the Board of Agriculture was published in 1794.
[4] The movement for Parliamentary reform which had originated in England was now arousing Scotland as well, and Boswell had the satisfaction of presiding over a meeting held to press for the abolition of nominal and fictitious votes. For his objection to them, see above, 29 October 1782, n. 9.

of Kerse, his uncle, my old friend David Ross, and John Boswell, the Clerk of Supply. We were very jolly. Mr. Mure went to Eglinton. The rest of us went to a Mason lodge in the house. Then at supper we were joined by Mr. John Ballantine, merchant, Mr. Robert Aiken, writer, and Mr. Mackenzie, late master of the inn where we were, whom Kerse introduced as his friend. Soon after supper Kerse appeared so much in liquor and so changed into a harsh and abusive companion that the company must have broke up had not I fallen upon a most extraordinary contrivance, which was to get it agreed by the company (Kerse being silent) that whatever any gentleman might say should not be taken amiss, so that we might have full licence. This private specimen of *Saturnalia* succeeded wonderfully, all of us except Kerse seeing the design. The effect was that whatever he threw out was admitted and laughed at, and "rascal" and "liar" and such epithets flew about in high jocularity, so that he was quite bamboozled and was obliged to be quiet. We sat till four in the morning and had many good songs. Though I drank

8 NOV. liberally, I was not a bit the worse; and next day rose in good time and got home well, though *then*, as I cooled, the late sitting and wine affected my nerves. Lord Loudoun dined with us, and I drank cordially with his Lordship, which did me good. Lord Eglinton had been seized with the gout, which prevented him and my Lady from coming to us this year. Lady Crawford and Lady Mary Lindsay had been with us

9 NOV. this week for a day. On Sunday Mr. Auld preached at Auchinleck, and was comfortably with us at night.

10 NOV.   On Monday the 10 my wife and I, with our two eldest daughters and their governess, set out for Edinburgh. We left the other three children. Sandy seemed sorry at parting, though he liked to stay. I was afraid little James would have been very sorry, and perhaps have made a noise. But he looked bold and steady; and when I asked him if he was not going to cry, he said briskly, "I'm too good a bairn." I insisted we should go the Hamilton road, which pleases me as the road of my youth. I rode, as I used to do in early years, and we paid a visit at Mr. Bruce Campbell's, as my father and his family used to do at his father's. When we got to Hamilton, my wife grew very uneasy about the children we had left, as the dairymaid was ill, and she feared it might be a fever which had been fatal in the country. She wrote to Bell Bruce[5] to

[5] Nurse and housekeeper for the Boswells.

come to town with them if the surgeon thought it dangerous for them to stay. I did not feel at Hamilton the fine sensations I once had at that place. I *must* submit to life losing its vividness. We got to Edinburgh on Tuesday evening the 11.

WEDNESDAY 12 NOVEMBER. (Writing the 21.) The Court of Session sat down. The Hon. Henry Erskine and Mr. Wight were received as Lord Advocate and Solicitor-General.[6] I was sadly vexed that I had not been promoted to either of these offices. I paid a visit to Mr. George Wallace, who was sitting quietly at home. I was in bad spirits. The weather was cold.

THURSDAY 13 NOVEMBER. (Writing the 21.) The weather was exceedingly cold, and I much upon the fret. While I sat dull by the fire before dinner, the Hon. A. Gordon came and cordially asked if I would give him a dinner. I made him heartily welcome, and by drinking some wine with him I was cheered.

FRIDAY 14 NOVEMBER. (Writing the 21.) Worthy Sir Alexander Dick paid me a visit in the forenoon. But I was insipid. The vulgarity and bustle of the Court of Session was very disgusting after my consequence at Auchinleck. I drank tea at Lady Auchinleck's.

SATURDAY 15 NOVEMBER. (Writing the 21.) Waited on Lord President while at breakfast. Found him as hearty as ever, though parted from his lady.[7] But I was shocked at such an instance of the instability of human connexions. Dined at Prestonfield rather dully. We had an alarm today that the dairymaid at Auchinleck had really a fever. By Mr. Wood's advice, we ordered our three younger children to come to us directly.

SUNDAY 16 NOVEMBER. (Writing the 21.) Was at New Church forenoon and afternoon. Two strangers preached. In the evening the children said divine lessons.

MONDAY 17 NOVEMBER. (Writing the 21.) Breakfasted at Lady Colville's. The conversation of her Ladyship, Lady Anne, and the Hon. Andrew had much the same effect on me it has had for some years. My views of life were dim. I drank tea at Mr. George Wallace's.

[6]"On the morning of the appointment he [Erskine] had an interview with Dundas in the Outer House; when, observing that the latter gentleman had already resumed the ordinary stuff gown which advocates are in the custom of wearing, he said gaily that he 'must leave off talking, to go and order his silk gown' (the official costume of the Lord Advocate and Solicitor-General).—'It is hardly worth while,' said Mr. Dundas drily, 'for the time you will want it—you had better borrow mine.' Erskine's reply was exceedingly happy—'From the readiness with which you make the offer, Mr. Dundas, I have no doubt that the gown is a gown made to *fit any party*; but however short my time in office may be, it shall ne'er be said of Henry Erskine that he put on the *abandoned habits* of his predecessor'" (John Kay, *Original Portraits*, 1877, i. 125).

[7]There seems to be no other record of this separation. They had been married since 1756.

TUESDAY 18 NOVEMBER. (Writing the 21.) Nothing to be marked except that the children arrived at night, Mr. Millar with them.

WEDNESDAY 19 NOVEMBER. (Writing the 21.) It was a great comfort to their mother to have the children again with her. She had yesterday a slight return of spitting of blood, owing, I believe, to anxiety about them. She had a little more today. It was a thick, wet day as I ever remember. I had a dreary struggle against it. I was helped somewhat by Mr. Millar's company, and by the children. Mr. Millar and I drank tea at Dr. Webster's. Col. George Preston and Captain Trotter supped with us.

THURSDAY 20 NOVEMBER. (Writing the 25.) Mr. Millar and I went in my chaise and dined at Sir Alexander Dick's; a fine clear day. I was but tolerably well.

FRIDAY 21 NOVEMBER. (Writing the 25.) Mr. Millar set out for Auchinleck in my chaise. I hoped that the house there might be so free of infection against Christmas that the three children might return to it. So I resolved to try to carry on Sandy in Latin myself till then. One of these days I had a serious conversation with the new Lord Advocate. He could make but awkward excuses for my not being appointed Solicitor-General; and I plainly saw that Scotland was in the hands of understrapping managers, of which I wrote to Mr. Burke in strong terms.[8] Erskine however professed much willingness to serve me. I did not trust too much to what he said. I was impatient and fretful, and revolved various schemes for having some better share of wealth and distinction.

SATURDAY 22 NOVEMBER. (Writing 8 December.) Dined at Mr. Maclaurin's with Sir Philip Ainslie, etc. Played cards and supped, and sat late.

SUNDAY 23 NOVEMBER. (Writing 8 December.) At home all day. The children said divine lessons.

MONDAY 24 NOVEMBER. (Writing 8 December.) Visited Lord Eglinton, who came to town yesterday, ill of the gout.

TUESDAY 25 NOVEMBER. (Writing 8 December.) Balmuto and his young wife and Miss Menie and Mr. Nairne dined with us. My wife and I had paid our visit of compliment duly.[9] This being my wedding-day, I most sincerely renewed my most affectionate vows to my valuable

[8] The letter, which survives, is entered in Boswell's Register as "an indignant manifesto upon my being totally neglected by Administration." He congratulated Burke on his election as Lord Rector of the University of Glasgow; and expressed the hope that he would come to Scotland and give Boswell the honour of his company at Auchinleck.
[9] The marriage of Claud Boswell, aged forty-one, to Anne Irvine, heiress of Kingcausie in Kincardineshire, occurred late in April or early in May of this year. "Miss Menie" is Balmuto's sister.

spouse. I had warmed myself rather too much with wine at dinner.
But I believe it was necessary.

[EDITORIAL NOTE. Boswell's renewal of his vows was followed with
ironical swiftness by a relapse (see below, 14 February 1784). Six pages
containing the entries from 26 November to 12 December have been
removed from the manuscript. No notes survive for the period, and
the only social activity reflected in Boswell's account of expenditures
is one shilling to the collection at the New Church on 30 November
and sixpence to the collection the following Sunday, 7 December. The
Register of Letters shows that political ferment, local and national, was
stimulating him to advance his own interests. He had written to Dr.
Johnson on 22 November about peers interfering in county elections
(and just as soberly inquired in his role as laird what was to be done
with old horses.) On 29 November he wrote to Knockroon (John Boswell the younger) that all "decent landholders" and all the Commissioners of Supply (to whom Knockroon was Clerk) should sign the
petition to Parliament against nominal and fictitious votes which had
been initiated at the meeting of the Ayrshire landholders 7 November
1783. It was Boswell's duty as preses, and undoubtedly his pleasure,
to present that petition to Sir Adam Fergusson, whom he still hoped
to supplant as Member for Ayrshire.]

SATURDAY 13 DECEMBER. (Writing the 16.) This day I had ten
processes upon my table, so that my practice as a lawyer made a goodly
appearance. I had a bad cold, which added to my uneasiness. I have
it to remark that during my wretchedness on this occasion, I have given
my son Sandy pretty regular lessons in Latin and Miss Young in Italian,
and have dictated several law papers very well. But I at present thought
of keeping clear of society as disgusting, or at least insipid. I *felt* how
easily I could do with very little of it, and I wondered how people could
be animated to so much exertion in carrying it on.

SUNDAY 14 DECEMBER. (Writing the 16.) Lay in bed all day and
took a sweat for my cold. Was quite indifferent to everything. Had a
kind of false *pride* in this. But surely I had not *pleasure*. Rose at night.
The children said divine lessons. Sandy read the Bible to me while I
was in bed.

MONDAY 15 DECEMBER. (Writing the 23.) Lady Frances Montgomerie and Sir Walter M.-C. dined with us. During the next three days
of this week nothing happened worth remarking except that on Thursday, I think, my wife and I visited poor Sandy Cuninghame, who was

now in town, very ill of a consumption. I had a kind of dead indifference of mind. [1]

FRIDAY 19 DECEMBER. (Writing the 23.) I experienced now how well I could do without going into company. In the evening, however, we had at cards and supper Sir William and Lady Maxwell of Springkell and their two daughters, Lady Frances Montgomerie, Sir Walter M.-C., Mr. Robert Mackintosh. There had been an unlucky difference between my cousin Sir William's family and me for several years, which was this evening happily over. [2] It was a very agreeable party.

SATURDAY 20 DECEMBER. (Writing the 23.) News had come by express that the House of Lords had made a noble stand against Fox's East India Bill, which would have overwhelmed the Crown. [3] This rejoiced my Tory soul; and in the forenoon I went down to the library and drew up an Address to His Majesty from the Dean and Faculty of Advocates to congratulate him on it, and I moved for our addressing at our anniversary meeting this day. The dastardly fellows, afraid to

[1] He was able, nevertheless, to write to William Strahan this day, inquiring about Dr. Johnson's health, and asking for "good materials" and a title for a collection of compliments other writers had paid their great friend. Three weeks later, 8 January 1784, he asked Charles Dilly to "go halves" with him in publishing "The Praises of Dr. Samuel Johnson by Contemporary Writers" (Register of Letters).

[2] We have found nothing indicating the nature of this "unlucky difference." When Boswell visited Sir William Maxwell at his seat in Dumfriesshire many years before he described him as a sensible man "of handsome figure and genteel air," who carried in his external appearance "the character much talked about and seldom found, a gentleman" (Journal, 7 October 1762). Boswell's grandfather, Colonel John Erskine, was Sir William's great-grandfather by an earlier marriage.

[3] On 18 November Fox, as Secretary of State for Foreign Affairs, had brought in a bill for reforming the East India Company, which had come into existence and long operated as a private commercial corporation under a royal charter, with the right to acquire territory, coin money, make war and peace, and exercise both civil and criminal jurisdiction. When Clive's victory over the French in 1757 made the Company the ruling power over the enormous territory of India, it became essential that the British government should have some control. By Lord North's Regulating Act of 1773 a governor-general (Warren Hastings) and council were appointed, and a supreme court of judicature established: the governor-general was nominated by the directors of the Company, but his appointment was subject to the approval of the Crown, which also appointed the judges. Fox sought essentially to vest a greater power of control in the legislature: he proposed a supreme council, appointed by Parliament, with complete control over government, patronage, and commerce. Though the bill provided that at the end of four years the power of nomination should rest in the Crown, it was held by the Tories to be an attack on chartered rights and the royal prerogative; worse, to give the Whig majority in the House of Commons the virtual sovereignty of India. The bill passed the Commons but was rejected in the House of Lords on 17 December 1783 through the personal influence of the King, who dismissed the Coalition ministry and appointed Pitt Prime Minister.

take an open part, were all against it. I despised them, and felt myself an ancient constitutionalist. Messrs. Robert Boswell, Matthew Dickie, and Alexander Walker dined with us. My best amusement at present is playing at draughts. My health is much as it was. But starving has calmed my spirits.

SUNDAY 21 DECEMBER. (Writing the 23.) At home all day. The children said divine lessons.

MONDAY 22 DECEMBER. (Writing the 30th.) Nothing to mark but that Dr. Webster drank tea with us,[4] and I went to a puppet-show with my children.

TUESDAY 23 DECEMBER. (Writing the 30th.) Nothing to mark.

WEDNESDAY 24 DECEMBER. (Writing the 30th.) Attended an examination by Lord Hailes in the cause, Spence against Spens.[5]

THURSDAY 25 DECEMBER. (Writing the 30th.) There was snow on the ground, and the weather was very cold.[6] I and my three eldest children read devoutly in the prayer-book. The comfortable family dinner on this holy festival was held as usual. I did not take the children to the New English Chapel, but Grange and I went. The rigour of the season chilled my good feelings, and the consciousness of disease vexed me. I began tonight to write again to my friend Temple, which I had not done for many months.[7]

FRIDAY 26 DECEMBER. I had resolved to write and publish a *Letter to the People of Scotland on the State of the Nation*, to endeavour to rouse a spirit for *property* and the *Constitution* in opposition to the East India Bill, and I read in the Parliamentary journals and debates with attention, which amused me. The present fluctuation of Councils in the kingdom agitated my mind, while I at the same time had a wonderful philosophical power of indifference. I could view objects with as much

---

[4] Some time after 25 January 1784 Boswell added the following note: "N.B. This was the last day Dr. Webster was in my house."

[5] We have found nothing concerning this cause.

[6] From 24 December through the greater part of January the country experienced very heavy snowfalls, high winds, and a degree of frost that in Edinburgh exceeded even that of January 1780. Roads were blocked, many vessels wrecked, and "the post-boy with the mail from Dumfries to Thornhill . . . frozen to death upon his horse" (*Scots Magazine*, January 1784, xlvi. 54).

[7] "Rev. Mr. Temple, that I was angry he did not come to Scotland [in the previous July, after finishing his business at Berwick], and resolved to hold out against writing to him. His second letter came to meet my feelings, as I would not let the holy season of Christmas pass without renewing our correspondence. Complaints, and reasonings against complaints. The quantity of evil we *see* is so great that he who does not take in a future state must be an atheist or a Manichean, etc., etc. Begging payment of what he owes me. That the *Spectator* puts us in good humour [blotted word or words]. We should read it more" (Register of Letters: the letter itself is lost).

light as others do, and at once let down a curtain and shade them.

SATURDAY 27 DECEMBER. (Writing the 30.) I dictated my *Letter to the People* with animation, and advanced a good way in it.[8] Time passed better than one would imagine in my situation.

SUNDAY 28 DECEMBER. (Writing the 30.) The weather continued inclement. I stayed at home all day. Sir William Forbes called for a little while. I wrote some more of my *Letter to the People*, which I did not scruple to do on Sunday, considering it as labouring for sacred monarchy. I read two of Carr's sermons to my wife and children and Miss Young. The children said divine lessons.

MONDAY 29 DECEMBER. (Writing 7 January 1784.) Finished my pamphlet, and had my calm friend Nairne to revise it. Sir William Forbes, who drank coffee with us in the evening, also heard a good part of it read. Both of them approved of it. I had this evening a delicate hint from Sir William that my credit with his house was exhausted.[9] This gave me a kind of sensation which I had never before experienced. My valuable spouse and I talked together and resolved on strict frugality till I should be easier.

TUESDAY 30 DECEMBER. (Writing 7 January 1784.) The printing of my pamphlet entertained me, and I was really animated about public affairs, but still was conscious of indifference when I chose it.

WEDNESDAY 31 DECEMBER. (Writing 7 January 1784.) Was kept busy about my pamphlet, and had it advertised as published *this day*. But it could not be in the shops till next morning. I sent the first copy tonight to Sir Charles Preston for the ancient burgh of Culross. I had yesterday or today (the post coming very irregularly by reason of the frost) an excellent letter from Dr. Johnson. I flattered myself he might live some time yet.

[8] The pamphlet, a brief, and on the whole temperate, document, begins with characteristic references to the American war, General Oglethorpe, and Dr. Johnson, proceeds to attack the East India Bill as undermining property rights and the Constitution in general, continues with a historical account of the influence and prerogative of the Crown, and concludes with an exhortation to the Scottish people to address the King on this occasion.

[9] On 22 January 1784, Forbes, Hunter and Company gave Boswell a financial statement balanced to 31 December 1783 showing £1,310. 2s. 6d. in its favour. The bank placed the debit in a new account.

1784

THURSDAY 1 JANUARY. (Writing the 8th.) Began the new year with no peculiar emotion. I found that keeping the house and tasting no fermented liquor kept me calm to a great degree. Yet I had spirited sentiments of monarchy. I thought my pamphlet might, at least ought, to do me good with a Tory administration, and surely with the King himself. And if it did not, I had the satisfaction of standing forth as a loyal gentleman, which would all my life give me better feelings than any preferment could do without the consciousness of that character. I went out in a chair and visited poor Sandy Cuninghame. The severe weather affected me so that I resolved not to go abroad soon again. Grange dined with us. In the evening I wrote letters with copies of my pamphlet to several eminent persons.[1]

FRIDAY 2 JANUARY. (Writing the 8.) I was really very well content upon the whole. Wrote more letters with my pamphlet.

SATURDAY 3 JANUARY. (Writing the 9.) This day passed much in the same way with yesterday.

SUNDAY 4 JANUARY. (Writing the 9.) Was at home all day. In the evening read two of Mr. Carr's sermons to my wife, etc. The children said divine lessons.

MONDAY 5 JANUARY. (Writing the 9.) No diversity to mark except that Lady Colville and the Hon. Andrew Erskine drank tea with us and praised my pamphlet most agreeably.

TUESDAY 6 JANUARY. (Writing the 9.) I awaked in horror, having dreamt that I saw a poor wretch lying naked on a dunghill in London, and a blackguard ruffian taking his skin off with a knife in the way that an ox is flayed; and that the poor wretch was alive and complained woefully. How so shocking a vision was produced I cannot imagine.

[1]Between 2 January and 10 February he sent letters and pamphlets to T. D. Boswell for the King's Librarian, to General Oglethorpe, Dundas, Burke, Pitt, W. J. Temple, the Marquess of Graham, John McAdam of Craigengillan, Wilkes, Johnson, Dempster, and Charles Macklin. On this day he wrote to Dilly requesting him to reprint the pamphlet in London and offering to "go half risk, half profit." Anxious inquiries as to the rate of the English sale followed on 15 and 19 January; on the latter date he asked Dilly to send copies to Henry Sampson Woodfall, Capell Lofft, and Dr. Towers. Dilly gave a "dull" account of the pamphlet in a letter which Boswell received on 28 January, but on 14 February he received another in which Dilly reported that they "would not be losers" by having republished it (Register of Letters).

But its impression was such that I was dismal the whole day. Worthy Grange dined with us. His sensible, friendly talk did me good.

WEDNESDAY 7 JANUARY. (Writing the 9.) During this confinement I declare my life has been happier than in many portions of it when I was going abroad. I have shunned all the inconveniencies of a most severe season. I have had visits of Sir William Forbes, Mr. Hunter Blair, Sir John Henderson, Sir James Pringle, Sir Charles Preston, Col. George Preston, Col. Christopher Maxwell, Major Andrew Frazer. I have felt the comfort of doing well and at my leisure all that I had to do. So that my mind has had, as it were, ease and elbow-room. It hurt me a little that I did not get out to Auchinleck to receive my rents myself and have my tenants about me, and, as Dr. Johnson advised me in an excellent letter, "wrap myself up in my hereditary possessions,"[2] which I should have done in my good house, with a wood fire. But I gave a commission to James Bruce to receive money from the tenants *to account of rents*, and remit it to me. The consciousness of being Laird of Auchinleck was a *constant* support. The applause my pamphlet got pleased me for a time.[3] Nothing particular this day.

THURSDAY 8 JANUARY. (Writing the 12.) Had a visit of Sir Alexander Dick, after having been in the chair at Mr. Henry Dundas's election for Midlothian.[4] Mr. James Donaldson drank tea with us. His petulance disgusted me.

FRIDAY 9 JANUARY. (Writing the 12.) This day was kept in Edinburgh as a thanksgiving day for peace and plenty by the last good harvest. Sir Charles and Col. George Preston visited me. I read one of Mr. Carr's sermons to my wife, etc. After this I shall say "my family." But servants are not included.

SATURDAY 10 JANUARY. (Writing the 13.) Awaked after a very agreeable dream that I had found a diary kept by David Hume, from which it appeared that though his vanity made him publish treatises of scepticism and infidelity, he was in reality a Christian and a very pious man. He had, I imagined, quieted his mind by thinking that whatever he might appear to the world to show his talents, his religion was between GOD and his own conscience. (I cannot be sure if this thought was in sleep.) I thought I read some beautiful passages in his diary. I am not certain whether I had this dream on Thursday night or Friday night. But after I awaked, it dwelt so upon my mind that I

[2] From the letter of 24 December 1783, printed in the *Life of Johnson*.
[3] He had congratulatory letters in the succeeding months from the Marquess of Graham, Dempster, Robert Preston, Pitt, Alexander Millar, and Johnson.
[4] Having been made Treasurer of the Navy in the new Administration, Dundas had to resign his seat and stand again.

could not for some time perceive that it was only a fiction. Sir Charles and Col. George Preston, Lady Frances Montgomerie, Henry Cuninghame, and Grange dined with us. I was in a comfortable frame, and did worthy Grange's spirits good. My book of letters is in effect a part of my journal, as it shows how my mind was occupied. I read nothing regularly just now. Revising my *Hypochondriack* pleased me.[5] I had a little agitation as to the effect which my *Letter* on the East India Bill might have on my future fortune in life. I thought it might perhaps seriously offend my friend Burke.[6] And yet I trusted that he was of too liberal a mind to be angry because I, who had always avowed my Tory principles, should stand forth for the King when an attempt was making to create a power greater than that of His Majesty. I also thought it might offend Lord Mountstuart, as it with a generous warmth supported the cause of royalty, from which, to my astonishment, he had retired, and associated himself with Opposition. I had written a letter of congratulation to him in the full belief of his being *against* the East India Bill; and after my letter was sent off, I received the newspaper mentioning him in the list of Lords *for* it. I next night wrote to him again, anxious to have this explained to me as an old Tory friend. I have as yet had no answer from him, and probably will have none, he is so indifferent.[7] I made up my mind as to both his Lordship and Burke being offended, as I was fully conscious I was in the right, and had even reason to glory in my zeal. I at the same time, without allowing myself to indulge sanguine hopes, pleased myself with fancying that perhaps the Sovereign or Lord Temple or some other of the great men to whom my congenial sentiments and good talents might recommend me, would call me into a respectable employment, and not improbably

[5] Among the Malahide papers were found three incomplete collections of *The Hypochondriack* taken from the monthly numbers of the *London Magazine* (where they were published anonymously) and revised in Boswell's hand. Johnson himself was to revise the series, Boswell wrote to Temple on 8 July 1784, for he admired the essays that Boswell had read to him and would have Boswell publish them with his name. There are no signs of Johnson at work, but four essays show corrections by James Beattie. The Malahide papers also include fifty assorted manuscript leaves of "additions," supplementary materials which Boswell had gathered from his reading. Preserved with this packet are an index of the authors of Boswell's mottoes and two specimen printed pages, one small octavo, the other duodecimo, in different sizes of type. Despite these labours, Boswell never published the collected essays.
[6] Burke, who had made a special study of Indian affairs, was the virtual author of Fox's bill.
[7] There is no record of a reply. On 23 December 1783 Boswell had written letters to Lord Mountstuart and Lord Pembroke asking them to use their influence to get him appointed Solicitor-General or at least joint Solicitor.

bring me into Parliament. I brought to my recollection such things having sometimes happened; and why might not I have the same success which others had experienced without deserving it better? At any rate, by proper economy I could certainly never fail to be an independent baron.

SUNDAY 11 JANUARY. (Writing the 15.) My health was now so much better that I might have gone abroad. But I was afraid, kept the house, and took physic. The weather was become pretty mild. During my confinement I had amused myself with the curious lawsuit between Sir John and Lady Houston. It was shocking to find how bad humour and conceit may operate.[8] I read today two of Mr. Carr's sermons to my wife, etc. The children said divine lessons.

MONDAY 12 JANUARY. (Writing the 15.) Nothing to be recorded.

TUESDAY 13 JANUARY. (Writing the 15.) The Session sat down again. Felt a reluctance to renew the bustle of life. Went out in a chair and had two causes before the Lords. Had some weak uneasiness lest I might meet with some coarse jokes from my brethren upon my *Letter* on the East India Bill. But I soon was firm, and indeed got such compliments as pleased me.

WEDNESDAY 14 JANUARY. (Writing the 15.) Got six guineas in fees, which animated me. My mind was at present in a good tranquil state, for which there is no accounting. My children delight me. I tell my valuable spouse that we should be sensible of the immediate happiness which we enjoy from them. Sandy has for some days had sore eyes, which prevents him from reading and attending Mr. Morton's writing-school. I make him say a little of his Latin lessons from memory.

THURSDAY 15 JANUARY. (Writing the 20.) Nothing to be recorded.

FRIDAY 16 JANUARY. (Writing the 20.) Walked to the Court of Session, the first time of my being upon the street (I should have said in good English *in* the street, I believe) since the 20 of December last. Grange supped with us.

SATURDAY 17 JANUARY. (Writing the 20.) I had last night an excellent letter from the Marquess of Graham upon my pamphlet, and upon the present political contest. It gave me fresh spirit. I had this

[8] Lady Houston had married Sir John in 1744, though she was aware that he was impotent. They quarrelled constantly, and in 1750 Lady Houston was granted a decree of separation and aliment, the text of which extended to 2,000 pages. Sir John's "bad humour" took the form of bringing animals into the house: dogs, a monkey, a jackass, and even a snake. The "conceit" was probably the lady's, who fancied herself an author. Boswell (a very distant relation of Lady Houston) had brought one of her plays on the stage in his teens, and had written a prologue for it. *The Coquettes, or the Gallant in the Closet* was damned on the third night; as presumed author, Boswell had to endure the mockery of the town.

forenoon a visit of Mr. Hamilton of Bargany, who as an old, sly politician sounded me as to my engagement in the Ayrshire election. I with perhaps too much frankness told him that I rather thought I was engaged to support Lord Eglinton's interest, independent of my friend Hugh Montgomerie being the candidate; and therefore I must vote for the Devil if his Lordship should set him up. But I was very sorry I was engaged, and would take care again. He put on an air of friendly regard and bid me say nothing till Lord Eglinton applied to me; and that as I had been one of his Lordship's steadiest friends, I or my friends should insist with him that the Administration he supported should promote me in the law. Bargany himself would insist. I told him I did not like the Coalition party, and that I thought the Constitution in danger. He kept himself very quiet upon that subject. Little did I suspect that he was a keen partisan of the *late* Administration. He asked me if I would accept of being Sheriff of Ayrshire; for that the present Sheriff had behaved so that it would not do long with him (or words to that purpose).[9] I said it was an office I did not desire, but I believed I should not refuse it if it were offered to me. "Very well," said he with an air of significancy. I said too much to Bargany as to my thinking myself engaged to Lord Eglinton. My impression is from what is marked in this volume on the 3 January 1783. But I think it may be understood as not to "bind me in all cases whatsoever." I mean that I am bound to support Lord Eglinton's interest against any other, merely as interest in the county. But if the interest of the State comes to be at stake, the private obligation is absorbed. And at this important moment when the King's just prerogative is attacked, it appeared to me that my oath of allegiance should prevail. I had written to Dr. Johnson to consult him on the question, before thinking on it sufficiently myself; for I stated that a positive promise of a vote must be kept; otherwise any scoundrel might plead *principle* for breaking his word. But I now saw it in a different light, though I could not settle my mind. I had altered my opinion as to the right of peers to influence the election of commoners, and had been confirmed by Dr. Johnson in thinking it usurpation.[1] But this could not set me free from my promise to Lord Eglinton, because I might give up my own right as

[9] William Wallace, who held the office until his death in 1786. Bargany, an advocate, was accused in the House of Commons of transmitting an offer of a place worth £500 a year to his nephew, Hew Dalrymple, M.P. for Haddingtonshire, to support the Coalition. He denied the charge and the matter was dropped.
[1] "The usurpation of the nobility, for they apparently usurp all the influence they gain by fraud and misrepresentation, I think it certainly lawful, perhaps your duty, to resist. What is not their own they have only by robbery" (*Life of Johnson*, letter of 24 December 1783).

a commoner. It is exceedingly difficult to have it believed that a man is honest in altering a political opinion. I dined today with Mundell's scholars, and was allowed to drink only water. I was the merriest man there, such command of spirits had I. Dr. Webster, as the father of several scholars, was entertained by us today, and invited to be with us at every meeting.

SUNDAY 18 JANUARY. (Writing the 22.) My health was now almost quite restored. But with Mr. Wood's approbation I resolved to take medicine twelve days more to be quite secure. I was at home all day. The children said divine lessons. I read two of Mr. Carr's sermons to my wife, etc.

MONDAY 19 JANUARY. (Writing the 27.) I recollect nothing but that I think I visited Sandy Cuninghame. Grange and Miss Wardrop of Auldhouse dined with us.

TUESDAY 20 JANUARY. (Writing the 27.) In the evening the Earl of Dundonald unexpectedly paid me a visit. His Lordship had not done me that honour for some years. My heart warmed to him from remembrance of his father and other relations. Blood is blood. [1a] He wished I would hear him read over something which he had drawn up for preventing smuggling and improving the revenue in Scotland. I fixed next day, and he promised to dine with me.

WEDNESDAY 21 JANUARY. (Writing the 27.) My spirits had now been for some time calm and steady, owing, I really believe, to my living abstemiously. My life, I am certain, was happier upon the whole than when in a state of more fermentation. Lord Dundonald read his paper to me, which was very well done. Either yesterday or today I read over a little account of his coal-tar and varnish, which he had printed. I was struck with his knowledge and ingenuity and perseverance, but sorry to perceive his wildness of project and hot-headed positiveness. [2] He dined and drank tea with us. I must here remark a curious circumstance in my own character at present, which is a consciousness of having, if I choose to indulge it, a total insensibility to

[1a] The eighth Earl of Dundonald (d. 1778), father of the Earl here mentioned, had been Boswell's grand-uncle; Boswell had always maintained very close relations with him.

[2] Archibald Cochrane, ninth Earl of Dundonald, had tried scheme after scheme to recoup the family fortune by applying to commercial processes the recent chemical discoveries of Cavendish, Priestley, and Black. He now proposed using coal-tar for protecting ships' bottoms from worms, and designed and built retorts for distilling the tar. His views were correct, and he was close to discovering the other important substances to be derived from coal-tar, but the Admiralty adopted copper sheathing and declined to try his process. Unlucky in all his ventures, he wasted what remained of the family fortune, and died abroad in poverty.

what others may think of me in point of decorum. I am indifferent as to all censure of my mode of living. To feel thus gives one a wonderful feeling of independence. But too much of it is not right. The late Lord Eglinton regretted to my father my want of the sense of shame. It has been owing partly to a vain idea of my own talents; partly to a kind of philosophical impression of the nothingness of all things in human life. I was at present much pleased with my fame on account of my late pamphlet, which Mr. Dundas had quoted in the House of Commons.[3] I thought I might have much reputation as a writer were I but more concealed in a large society; and therefore wished to settle in London, at least to be a good deal there. But indeed I keep myself wonderfully abstracted here.

THURSDAY 22 JANUARY. (Writing the 28.) One of the days of this week, I am not sure which, I met my Lord Kellie at Sir William Forbes's counting-house. His Lordship walked home with me, and to my surprise and concern I found that notwithstanding the late monstrous attempt of the Coalition, he was still a friend to Lord North, and (writing the 3 February) did not feel the generous indignation I expected against the late attempt to injure the royal prerogative. I saw that *interest* is a heavy bias on every mind. Grange and Mr. James Loch supped with us.

FRIDAY 23 JANUARY. (Writing 3 February.) The Earl of Dundonald drank tea with us.

SATURDAY 24 JANUARY. (Writing 3 February.) Grange and I paid a visit to poor Sandy Cuninghame. He looked quite like death. Miss Betty Boswell and Miss Cuninghame of Robertland, a fine stout girl,

[3] In the debate (8 December) on the East India Bill in the House of Commons, John Lee, Attorney-General under the Coalition ministry, had defended the proposed changes and pointed out several instances in which charters had been infringed for the good of the public. He concluded by asking what a charter was but a piece of parchment with a bit of wax dangling at the bottom. This unfortunately blunt remark (which was more innocent in its context than in isolation) was immediately seized upon by the Opposition, whose tactics generally were to make out that Fox and his associates were a gang of desperate adventurers willing to subvert the entire Constitution in order to keep themselves in power. Boswell, in his pamphlet, had countered by asking what great harm there would be in hanging an attorney-general, since it could be said that a hanged attorney-general was only a carcass dangling at the end of a rope. A satirical print of Lee with this label seems to have been issued. On 12 January, Dundas, in censuring a strong expression of Lord North's as to "scarecrow prerogative," had referred to Lee's unlucky figure, and had quoted the rejoinder "in a public letter by his friend Mr. Boswell" (*Parliamentary History*, xxiv. 292). Boswell was personally on good terms with Lee, and made amends in his second *Letter to the People of Scotland* (1785): "I love Mr. Lee exceedingly though I believe there are not any two specific propositions of any sort in which we exactly agree" (p. 75).

not fifteen, dined with us. Sir Walter M.-C., Grange, and his old client and mine, Mr. Borland from Jamaica, supped with us.[4] I had met him in the morning at Grange's. I was in admirable spirits today. But in the evening was suddenly informed that Dr. Webster was dying.

SUNDAY 25 JANUARY. (Writing 3 February.) Grange, who went up to inquire how Dr. Webster was, informed me about ten o'clock that *it was all over.* Both he and I were struck with the removal of so eminent a man, and regretted that we had not been more with him of late. Commissioner Cochrane paid us a visit. In the evening, divine lessons and two of Mr. Carr's sermons.

MONDAY 26 JANUARY. (Writing 3 February.) Visited Mrs. Mingay in the forenoon and Captain Webster in the evening, when he arrived from Ayr. I dictated well today. I think I visited Sandy Cuninghame. I visited the Lord President, who was confined by the gout.

TUESDAY 27 JANUARY. (Writing 3 February.) Mr. Stobie and Mr. Lawrence Hill dined with us.

WEDNESDAY 28 JANUARY. (Writing 3 February.) Visited Captain Webster. Miss Annie Boswell dined with us.

THURSDAY 29 JANUARY. (Writing 3 February.) The weather had all this time been very severe. This day was uncommonly so. Yet a most numerous company attended the funeral of Dr. Webster. I was affected with a dreary impression of mortality, but not with tenderness. For Webster was a man more to be admired for his talents and address than to touch the heart with affection. Grange dined with us. After the funeral I visited poor Sandy Cuninghame, who was in bed, and so ill that it distressed me to see him. It was the last time. My present indisposition was an excuse for my having been but little with him. I was somewhat uneasy that I had not been more.

FRIDAY 30 JANUARY. (Writing 3 February.) My practice went on very well at present, though I did not get much money. But I had a creditable appearance, was useful to many people, and hoped I might be better in time. This forenoon Dr. Webster's repositories were opened, and it appeared he had appointed six trustees, of whom I was one, and had settled all his property on his daughter and her children, except a mother-of-pearl cabinet and silver tureen given to his son John, who was miserably vexed to find himself unjustly used, as he thought. I resolved to think a little before accepting of the trust.[5] I

[4] Boswell was counsel for him (Grange was the agent) in a cause, Grieves against Borland, that goes back to at least 1771. The dispute appears to have concerned a note. The decision of the Lords of Session was favourable to Grieves; whether Borland appealed, as seems to have been expected, we cannot now determine.

[5] Boswell did accept appointment as one of Dr. Webster's trustees; Sir Charles Preston declined, because he thought the settlement unjust.

should have mentioned that I found there was no service performed in the chapel in Blackfriars Wynd today,[6] where I have a seat. So I went down to my worthy friend Grange and read the best part of it from my Oxford Prayer-Book, and he said amen. In the evening John Webster was with me, quite disturbed. He and Sir Walter and Lady Frances Montgomerie supped.

SATURDAY 31 JANUARY. (Writing 13 February.) Mr. Stalker, my son Sandy's English-master, Grange, and Mr. Donaldson, the painter, who had not been with me for a long time, dined.

SUNDAY 1 FEBRUARY. (Writing the 13.) About ten o'clock in the morning, I got a note from Henry Cuninghame that poor Sandy, his brother, was just dead. I went to him and saw the dead body. I was not much shocked. I paid a visit to Mrs. Jefferies, an officer's widow who lodged in the house with the Cuninghames (Zeigler's in Alison's Square), and had been humanely attentive to them. Sir Walter and Henry dined and supped with us; and their presence prevented the usual divine lessons in my presence. But Veronica and Phemie said some to their governess. In the forenoon I paid a visit to Mr. R. Mackintosh and heard him harangue consequentially.

MONDAY 2 FEBRUARY. (Writing the 13.) Nothing particular recollected.

TUESDAY 3 FEBRUARY. (Writing the 13.) Nothing particular recollected.

WEDNESDAY 4 FEBRUARY. (Writing the 13.) My health was now almost quite restored. My wife sat to Painter Donaldson for a better miniature, for his own credit, than one he had done for her.[7] While she sat, Lord Chief Baron and Mrs. Montgomery paid us a visit. Miss Young described my wife's agreeable countenance when she is in good humour exceedingly well. She said, "Mrs. Boswell has at times the pleasantest look I ever saw. Her eye glistens." Mr. Donaldson dined with us. I would give a great deal could I have but the look described by Miss Young preserved by painting. I have neglected to mention that Col. Hugh Montgomerie was in town and paid me a visit, which I did not return. But indisposition was my excuse; also that Lord Eglinton was in town and paid us a visit on Sunday forenoon last. Also that Grange and I and Sir Walter M.-C. and his brother Henry searched poor Sandy Cuninghame's papers one forenoon, and saw him put into his coffin one evening. The corpse was by his earnest desire to be carried to the family vault. Grange and I this forenoon paid a visit to M. Dupont.

[6] In commemoration of the death of Charles I.
[7] This miniature, like the earlier one (see above, 10 December 1782), has dropped out of sight.

THURSDAY 5 FEBRUARY. (Writing the 13.) Nothing recollected except a visit from Sir William Forbes.

FRIDAY 6 FEBRUARY. (Writing the 13.) Lady Colville, her sister and brothers, Sir William Forbes and Lady, and Lady Frances Montgomerie dined and drank tea with us. I was in good spirits, but (for the first time this fit of sobriety) felt my not drinking wine somewhat awkward.

SATURDAY 7 FEBRUARY. (Writing the 13.) Dr. Gillespie, Mr. James Baillie, and Grange dined. While we sat at table, I received letters from Dr. Heberden and Dr. Brocklesby, in answer to my anxious inquiries about Dr. Johnson, and had such accounts as comforted me and made me hope I should have the happiness of having some more of his admirable counsel in this world, and perhaps get him to put the memoirs of the family of Auchinleck into the permanent form of his noble style, both in Latin and English. I was impatient to be in London and attend upon him with respectful affection.

SUNDAY 8 FEBRUARY. (Writing the 16.) I awaked with a severe nervous headache. Rose and called on Grange. But was so ill I was obliged to go to bed again. Lay all day in great distress. Sent for Mr. Wood. He bid me just lie still. Mr. Boswall of Blackadder came and sat by me as a kindly medical friend. I mentioned to him the system of Dr. Brown as very simple.[8] He said it might do very well if man was a machine, like a piece of leather. But that there was a *mind*, the effects of which we did not understand. I was pleased with his reasoning. He was calm. He returned in the evening. Mr. Nairne also sat by my bedside awhile. I grew better, and they both supped. I was able to sup with them. This day's illness gave me a striking impression of my own frailty.

MONDAY 9 FEBRUARY. (Writing the 16.) Walked out and breakfasted at Lady Colville's. I was free from the headache. I attended some part of the Justiciary trial, the Rev. Dr. Bryden against Murray of Murraythwaite. I was vexed by the partiality of *some*, at least, of the judges against Dr. Bryden.[9] I received tonight a letter from the Prime

[8] See note above, 25 January 1783, p. 55.
[9] The heritors of the parish of Dalton, Dumfriesshire, had brought their minister, the Rev. Dr. William Bryden, before the church courts in 1782 on charges of fornication, adultery, seduction, and profanity. At a meeting of the presbytery on 5 August 1783 Dr. Bryden denounced John Murray of Murraythwaite, a heritor and Justice of the Peace, in inflammatory terms ("impertinent puppy"), and charged that Murray retaliated by striking him over the head. Murray denied the charge and the presbytery censured both parties without deciding whose account of the altercation was correct. Bryden brought a private prosecution against Murray for assault and battery aggravated by having been committed upon a minister in church. The jury found Murray not guilty, and the Court directed Dr. Bryden to pay him expenses of £77 sterling.

Minister applauding my East India *Letter*. This raised my mind.[1]

TUESDAY 10 FEBRUARY. (Writing the 16.) I recollect nothing particular. My practice as a lawyer made a decent show. My domestic
happiness was more relished than usual.

WEDNESDAY 11 FEBRUARY. (Writing the 18.) I recollect nothing
remarkable.

THURSDAY 12 FEBRUARY. (Writing the 18.) I paid a visit before
dinner to Lady Auchinleck. Sir Charles Preston, Grange, and Mrs.
Mingay dined with us. I was calm and well.

FRIDAY 13 FEBRUARY. (Writing the 18.) Henry Cuninghame
dined with us. As I keep an exact Company Book,[2] I shall not mark
in my journal *who* dined or supped unless when there is something to
record.

SATURDAY 14 FEBRUARY. (Writing the 18.) I recollect nothing remarkable except feeling myself perplexed with a cause, Malcolm against
Malcolm, in which I had a paper to write.[3] My health was now clear.
———.[4]

SUNDAY 15 FEBRUARY. (Writing the 18.) Intended to have gone
to church. But there was such a fall of snow I stayed at home. Went
down and sat part of the forenoon with my worthy friend Grange,
whose faithful friendship and mild manners are my never-failing consolation. I have observed with satisfaction that his religious principles
have of late grown stronger, and it pleases me that by having a seat
for myself by the year in the Old English Chapel I accommodate him,

---

In 1788 the General Assembly cleared Dr. Bryden of all the heritors' charges except
that of profanity, which he admitted and was rebuked for.

[1] He published in the *Life of Johnson* (footnote to Johnson's letter of 27 February 1784)
an extract from his own letter to Pitt and the greater part of the Prime Minister's reply.
(He did commend Boswell's "zealous and able support" of the cause of the public, and
Boswell cherished the phrase.) It should be pointed out that Pitt usually did not answer
letters.

[2] The Company Book for Edinburgh has not been recovered.

[3] What Boswell *should* have recollected was that he received a mourning-ring this day
from William Bosville in remembrance of his father, Squire Godfrey Bosville, who
died Sunday morning, 25 January, at his house in Great Russell Street, London, aged
sixty-six. As to the paper Boswell had to write, it appears from the Minutes of the
Court of Session for 19 February 1784 that the Court issued a Decreet (final judgement)
in the cause James Malcolm of Balbedie against Sir Michael Malcolm of Lochore and
others (James Malcolm was Sir Michael's cousin and succeeded him as baronet in 1793),
but the Decreet was not recorded, and no papers or process of the cause have been
found.

[4] This dash at the end of an entry, which appears occasionally in the manuscript after
17 May 1780, is another private symbol for conjugal intercourse.

so that his attendance upon public worship is more frequent. The children said divine lessons, and I read two of Carr's sermons to my family, by which is to be understood my wife and children and Miss Young. Sir Charles Preston, etc., supped with us. ——.

MONDAY 16 FEBRUARY. (Writing the 18.) I recollect nothing remarkable except breakfasting at Mr. Alexander Wood's. ——.

TUESDAY 17 FEBRUARY. (Writing the 18.) My wife had been troubled for two days with a bad cold, Veronica with a sore throat, and little James with a complaint which we supposed might be worms. My mind was at this time so healthful that I could think with philosophic serenity of the evils which *might* befall me, and imagined I could counterbalance them by recollecting the good I had actually enjoyed. I thought of my happiness from my dear wife and children, and that if I should lose them, still that happiness might soothe me. "O gracious GOD, be pleased to preserve them to me!" was my constant prayer; and I also prayed often for Dr. Johnson, that his health might be restored, and that at least he and I might still have a comfortable meeting in this world. Since Dr. Webster's death, Dr. Erskine paid me a visit.[5] I started a curious thought: that we wish much that we may know one another in a future state. But alas! how seldom are people who have a sincere regard for each other in company in this life, where we are sure of personal knowledge, and have it certainly in our power to meet. How seldom do he and I meet. He did not see the force of the remark. For he said, "Ay, but when they have an eternity!" Indeed we may consider that everything in a future state will be amazingly different from what we experience in the imperfection of this. Sir Walter M.-C. and his brothers David and Henry, and Mr. Cummyng, the painter, etc., dined. Cummyng's curious variety of knowledge entertained me.[5a] The state of the nation was now wavering. I feared that Mr. Pitt might yield to at least a coalition with the factious opposers of the Crown. Several of my brethren at the bar were of the factious party. I endeavoured to maintain a composed elevation as a royalist, and to rest upon my pamphlet. ——.

WEDNESDAY 18 FEBRUARY.[6] (Writing the 24.) My wife and I dined

[5] John Erskine, son of the author of the *Institutes of the Law of Scotland*, was for twenty-six years the colleague at Old Greyfriars of Principal Robertson, though he was devoted to the evangelical party and Robertson was leader of the "moderates." Erskine was a modest and amiable man, a preacher of unprepossessing appearance but fine style, and a prodigious writer with a widespread correspondence at home and abroad. He is depicted in Sir Walter Scott's *Guy Mannering*, chapter sixteen.

[5a] Herald-painter and Lyon Clerk Depute, he satisfied Boswell's interest in heraldry and genealogy.

[6] On this day, at Ayr, Boswell was served heir to his father. On 8 January he had recorded as follows a letter to Knockroon: "Mr. John Boswell, Junior, sending him

at Balmuto's, the first time of our dining or supping abroad this year. General and Miss Leslie were there, and we did very well.

THURSDAY 19 FEBRUARY. (Writing the 24.) Sir Walter M.-C. was apprehended for a debt of £20. I thought a *cessio bonorum* the best thing to keep him easy, and was against relieving him. But his brother David, with tears in his eyes, was so earnest, I yielded to his request and paid the money. This affair agitated me sadly, as I hesitated between humanity and prudence—I may add, strict honesty, as my own affairs are as yet embarrassed.

FRIDAY 20 FEBRUARY. (Writing the 24.) Sir Walter was apprehended for another debt of £30. I was quite determined not to interfere again. He was all day detained in a private house. In the evening poor David and Thomas Baillie, his agent, became bound to present him on the 6 of March. He went to the Abbey.[7] I dined at Mr. Nairne's, where I had not dined for two years, so that he insisted on my coming. I still drank only water, and [as] there was no conversation to my mind I wearied and came home soon. There was this night a disagreeable domestic affair, of which I forbear to record the particulars.[8]

SATURDAY 21 FEBRUARY. (Writing the 24.) I awaked in vexation on account of what I allude to last night, and I had a severe nervous headache and sickness. I took a little cognac brandy, which did me some good, so that I was able to do my duty in the Court of Session. I starved myself all day, and was in a sort of desperation. It is enough that my mind may recall why. It ought not to be registered. Lord and Lady Eglinton, Lord Chief Baron, his lady and daughter, and Colonel Macdonell supped with us. I grew better and got through the evening easily, and the domestic affair was wonderfully quieted. ——.

SUNDAY 22 FEBRUARY. (Writing the 27.) Awaked in fine spirits. ——. Stayed at home in the forenoon and had all my five children sitting round a table with me in the drawing-room most agreeably,

---

a brieve for serving me heir to my father. I choose to have it before the sheriff of my own county, and the jury to be tenants of the family of Auchinleck, of whom I shall send a list to James Bruce, to be in readiness at a call, a day or two of notice to be given. Not one but them to be on the jury. I am resolved to have it according to my own fancy. Their names and farms must be mentioned, and then 'All tenants of the foresaid Alexander Boswell, and now of the said James Boswell.' I mean to be frugal. So let them have a steady dinner of beef and greens and plenty of punch at Dunn's or some private house. He may invite the sheriff-substitute and clerk if they will condescend to dine with plain countrymen" (Register of Letters).

[7] Holyrood Abbey had been for centuries a sanctuary for debtors.

[8] This "domestic disturbance," which was renewed on 12 and 21 March, remains unexplained; for a guess as to its nature, see below, Editorial Note for 2 July 1784, p. 256. Boswell's rough notes for his journal reveal that on 2 April 1784 he "had *éclaircissement* of domestic disturbance. Was ashamed and clear."

while I read the first chapter of the *Revelations*, which I do every Sunday, and heard them say divine lessons. It was a mild thaw. I called on Lord Eglinton, who was gone abroad, but I sat a little with the Countess. I went to the New Church in the afternoon, the first time for many Sundays, and heard a Mr. Singer; poor entertainment. Sir Walter had come out of the Abbey and was to go home next day, as he trusted no messenger could seize him there, and he believed he could raise money to clear the debt for which he was last apprehended. I visited him at Wallaces's Inn.[9] I then drank tea with Mrs. Drummond of Blair-Drummond tête-à-tête, and had so much conversation that I sat almost three hours and thought the time much shorter. I was not melancholy when I reflected on her husband, Lord Kames, being gone. My spirits were so good I took everything well. In the evening I was happy to be sure that the domestic *trouble* was over. ——.

MONDAY 23 FEBRUARY. (Writing the 29.) Breakfasted with Baron Gordon and had a good flow of conversation. I mentioned how Lord Monboddo denied to me that there was any contradiction between any action of mine being *certain from all eternity*, and *human liberty*. The Baron said he also thought there was none. "For," said he, "it is certain from all eternity that everything is to be either one way or another. Yet there is liberty of determination." I was now for the first time again after a long interval brought into the distressing perplexity of fate and free will. I suffered for laughing at what I thought, and still think, an absurd obstinacy in Lord Monboddo not to perceive that previous *certainty* is a contradiction to *liberty*. I paid a visit to Miss Gray. I was disturbed by the vile metaphysical perplexity during the day. ——.

TUESDAY 24 FEBRUARY. (Writing the 29.) I dined at Belleville with Lady Dundonald, and had in some degree the same ideas there as in early years. A Mr. Fenwick, Fellow of University College, Oxford, was there. He talked highly of Dr. Johnson, and pleased me. ——.

WEDNESDAY 25 FEBRUARY. (Writing the 29.) I drank tea with Lord Eskgrove. His daughter and her governess were with us. I had inquired of his clerk and been informed that I could be with my Lord at that time. I wished to pay him respect as my father's successor on the bench, and I found his conversation instructive and entertaining. He stated to me some causes which he had lately decided. We joined in regretting that the custom of a drawing-room and tea-table was gone out, and we thought that kind of society much better than what we now have at laborious dinners and suppers. In the evening we had a

---

[9]The George, on Bristo Street. Sir Walter had left the Abbey because debtors could not be arrested on Sunday.

visit of Shawfield.¹ My vile perplexity was dissipated by variety of ideas.

———

THURSDAY 26 FEBRUARY. (Writing 2 March.) William Lennox came to town last night with my chaise to carry out our three youngest children. This had a curious effect upon my *metaphysicized* mind. I recollect nothing particular today except being at Corri's concert with my wife and daughters.

FRIDAY 27 FEBRUARY. (Writing 2 March.) My wife and I went in our own chaise and dined at Lady Auchinleck's; Balmuto and his wife, Commissioner Cochrane, and the Rev. Dr. Andrew Hunter there. I was inwardly thoughtful; and as I passed the door of the room where my father died, I prayed for his soul. We drank tea. It was really a decent and pretty comfortable day. ———.

SATURDAY 28 FEBRUARY. (Writing the 2 March.) My practice in the Court of Session, though not very profitable (yet more so than last winter) was pretty extensive at present, and I did it easily and well. We had the young Campbells and young Craigengillan at dinner. My wife and I drank tea very agreeably at Mrs. Young's; nobody with her but her sister. I had not seen her before since her husband's death, having called once this winter but missed her. I was however still disturbed by *poring* with *my mind's eye* on the *machinery* of *Necessity*, which I was not *sure* was not the true condition of man. ———.

SUNDAY 29 FEBRUARY. (Writing the 2 March.) Heard Dr. Blair preach on "Take no thought for the morrow,"² etc. He gave us some plausible declamation, but one part of his discourse contradicted another; for he talked of everything being ordered by GOD, and yet that our fanciful discontents were against his designs. This was the import of what he said in fine language. I went to him to his *vestry*³ afterwards, and he owned to me that too much *acquiescence* would make us poor members of society. Visited Old Mar between sermons. I sat at home in the afternoon and looked at some old letters and other papers. The children said divine lessons. The three youngest seemed dearer to us that they were to leave us next morning. My wife and I paid a visit this evening to old Lady Grant.

MONDAY 1 MARCH. (Writing the 2.) We rose early and saw our three youngest children set out for Auchinleck. I had an abhorrence at metaphysical speculation, while I perceived that it sickened my perceptions of real life. I paid a visit to Mr. Boswall of Blackadder, who

¹Walter Campbell of Shawfield and Islay, advocate.
²Matthew 6: 34.
³Boswell underlined the word to indicate that Blair, or perhaps he himself, was using Anglican terminology for one of the lesser apartments in St. Giles's.

talked to me in a kind, friendly manner about my health, as I was now thin, and advised me to ride. He said bad spirits was as real a disease as any; and that the mind and body mutually affected each other. I asked him if the Asiatics of better rank were serious in religion, or only appeared to be so from a regard to decency. He said they were serious, as the people of this country were formerly. He said it was the fashion in India to be religious, and that the Nabob of Arcot was really so. He said that a plurality of women did not hurt men there. But that in every country there is a difference of constitutions, upon which more or less communication with women being hurtful or not depended. I sounded him on predestination, which is a Mahometan doctrine. He did not enter far into the subject. My spirits were raised by moving about, and talking with one who had been long in Asia, for which I have a warm fondness in my imagination. I dined by pressing invitation at Lady Colville's; a good deal of company there. Sir John Whitefoord and I talked to one another pleasantly as opposing candidates against the next election for Ayrshire. While conversation and wine circulated, I sat calm on my water regimen, and while I *half apprehended* that all was *irresistible fate*, I *half hoped* that there was *free volition and agency*, though I could not understand it. I was not well here. I was not animated. It was a labour to me to do my part tolerably. When I came home, I felt myself exhausted. But I bathed my feet in warm water and grew easier both in body and mind.———.

TUESDAY 2 MARCH. (Writing the 5.) Was rather better in mind. Lady Dundonald and her son Andrew, Old Mar, and Captain John Webster dined with us. Mar was so insolent after the ladies were gone that I was obliged to give him a pretty strong check. I commended Tod's pamphlet on hospitals,[4] and said Dr. Webster had commended it. Said he: "I shall read it on his opinion; I would not read it on yours." This was really impertinent. I said calmly, "You pay me a great compliment," with an ironical look, and thought of saying no more. "I do not pay you a great compliment," said he. It then instantly occurred to me to reply, "Yes, you pay me a great compliment in supposing my understanding to be so different from yours." This had some effect upon him, and no more passed. I was sorry to have said such a thing to an old gentleman of his blood, and who in my younger days had shown me kindness. But there was no bearing his rudeness. Metaphysical clouds were broken by variety of conversation.

[4] Thomas Tod, a merchant, treasurer to the Orphan Hospital, had defended the Edinburgh system of hospitals and poor-houses in *Observations on Dr. McFarlan's Inquiries Concerning the State of the Poor*, published 1783.

WEDNESDAY 3 MARCH. (Writing the 5.) Lady Auchinleck dined with us today for the first time since my father's death. We had Balmuto and his wife, etc., a creditable company, and all was decent and indeed comfortable. ——.

THURSDAY 4 MARCH. (Writing the 31.) My wife and I dined at Commissioner Cochrane's; Lady Auchinleck there. Also the Laird of Fairlie and Capt. John Webster.

FRIDAY 5 MARCH. (Writing the 31.) Dined at Mr. Matthew Dickie's with the Laird of Fairlie, etc.

SATURDAY 6 MARCH. (Writing the 31.) Drank tea and eat *whigs* [5] with old Mr. James Spence, Treasurer of the Bank of Scotland, who had been at the same class in the College with my father. Got from him many anecdotes for a life of Dr. Webster. Wrote them down afterwards. [6] I was calmly pleased with the family scene of him, his wife, and daughter; neat, worthy people.

SUNDAY 7 MARCH. (Writing the 31.) Went down to Grange's and in a steady frame wrote to Drs. Cullen, Monro, and Hope for advice upon Dr. Johnson's case. The letter to each was verbatim the same. Dr. Johnson had desired me to talk to our physicians. I thought writing would do better; and this writing I thought a good employment for Sunday. [7] I then went out to my worthy friend Sir Alexander Dick, and having made out a requisition to the Sheriff of Edinburghshire for a meeting to address His Majesty, I got him with great zeal to sign it, having informed him that the Arniston family had a delicacy as to beginning the matter, as it might look like supporting their relation. But they would promote it. I dined with him. Found Miss Semple at tea at my house. The children said divine lessons.

MONDAY 8 MARCH. (Writing the 31.) Had Mr. Lawrie running

[5] Form of *wigs*, buns or small cakes made of fine flour.

[6] These anecdotes have not been recovered.

[7] He sent to the printer for the *Life of Johnson* the copy (now at Yale) of the letter to Dr. Hope made by Lawrie, his clerk, but signed and annotated by Boswell himself. He described Johnson as having been seized this winter with a "spasmodic asthma" which had confined him to the house for about three months. He was also suffering from "oedematous tumours" on his legs and thighs. The physicians, all of whom held chairs in the faculty of medicine in the University of Edinburgh, were obviously reluctant to make particular diagnoses from a second-hand report. They approved the use of diuretics to relieve the fluid which both Drs. Monro and Cullen feared was in Johnson's breast as well as in his limbs (a sign of congestive heart failure). Cullen candidly approved laudanum (Johnson was also taking "syrup of poppies") as the only way of rendering "tolerably easy" a life which he despaired of saving (10 March 1784); if Johnson was to live another winter he must certainly pass it abroad in a mild climate. Boswell reported the physicians' letters selectively to Johnson. Their original replies are all at Yale.

about all day among the Edinburghshire freeholders to get the requisition for an Address signed; and after getting a sufficient number, sent it to the Lord President. An advertisement for it appeared in tonight's papers. It was curious how *I* managed all this. Not one freeholder knew of another, or from whence the application came, except Sir Alexander Dick and Young Arniston. The Laird of Logan and Mr. John Boswell at Ayr dined with us. Dr. Hope called on me when I was out. I waited on him in the evening and he gave me a very good letter to Dr. Brocklesby about Dr. Johnson.

TUESDAY 9 MARCH. (Writing the 31.) Clerk Matthew and Grange dined with us, and Captain John Webster supped. I was sleepy.

WEDNESDAY 10 MARCH. (Writing the 31.) The Laird of Fairlie and Mr. John Boswell, Ayr, dined. I drank tea at Mr. Robert Boswell's, where I had not been all the winter. I regretted this inwardly, while my heart warmed to my dear uncle's descendants. Treesbanks was with me. He then accompanied me while I visited Lady Auchinleck.

THURSDAY 11 MARCH. (Writing the 31.) The Session rose. I was in excellent spirits. I attended the meeting for the Edinburghshire Address, and had the satisfaction to see it carried by a great majority.[8] I in the very time of the meeting indulged a metaphysical speculation on cause and effect, Liberty and Necessity, being *sure* that *I* was the *secret cause* of all that was now doing; and that though the honest freeholders did not know it, they were in reality moved by *me*. Miss Semple, Lady Hannah Maitland, and two Miss Gavins were with us at tea. I had formed a pleasing idea of Lady Hannah Maitland,[1] and I found it true. I was then for the first time at Corri's concert or academy for his scholars,[2] and heard Veronica sing —— admirably. I was delighted. She had played before I came in.

FRIDAY 12 MARCH. (Writing the 31.) Was to go to Auchinleck next day and from thence to London, which kept me in a state of some agitation. There was an unhappy renewal of the domestic disturbance, which vexed me exceedingly. My wife and I were at Barnard's ball, where our daughters are scholars.

SATURDAY 13 MARCH. (Writing the 31.) The Laird of Logan and I went west together post. My parting with my valuable spouse was not dreary, as my mind was animated with various interesting objects. Logan's continual flow of ideas, no matter what, entertained me all the

[8]Alexander Fraser Tytler, later Lord Woodhouselee, wrote the Address, which is in a strain of conventional eulogy.

[1]The daughter of James Maitland, seventh Earl of Lauderdale. She was married the next year to the seventh Marquess of Tweeddale.

[2]The concert on 26 February 1784 was given by Corri himself.

way. My chaise was waiting for me at Cumnock, where I drank tea, Messrs. John Boswell and James Johnston with me, and got home about eleven. Little James was up. I *enjoyed existence* at this excellent *home*.

SUNDAY 14 MARCH. (Writing the 31.) All the three Auchinleck children were at my bedside before I rose, and all happy to see me. Mr. Millar and Sandy went with me in the chaise to the church. I was quite comfortable.

MONDAY 15 MARCH. (Writing the 31.) Walked about with James Bruce and settled several matters. I visited John Colvin[3] in his ninetieth year.

TUESDAY 16 MARCH. (Writing the 31.) Sandy and I rode over and visited the Rev. Mr. George Reid. In the afternoon received some rents and settled other matters. The weather was so excessively cold that I resolved not to go in the fly the Carlisle road, as it went all night, but thought I might get a companion at Edinburgh.

WEDNESDAY 17 MARCH. (Writing the 31.) As I had come west on purpose to support a loyal Address to the King from our county, I had been at great pains preparing one. I believe I wrote six or seven copies, and corrected so late as this very morning of the day on which we were to meet.[4] I did not apprehend there would be an opposition regularly formed, and therefore was not at much pains to send notice to my good friends to attend. However, that there might be a decent number, I gave notice to Craigdarroch, Wallacetown, Dernconner, Duncanziemuir, Friendlesshead, Bennals, all of whom attended.[5] I also wrote to Mr. Bruce Campbell, who came. I wrote to Netherplace[6] that, as there had always been a good understanding (or some such expres-

[3] A slip of the pen for Colvill.
[4] The Address duly appeared in the official *London Gazette*, 3 April 1784. The last paragraph reads as follows: "Permit us, Sire, to say that a loyal Address from the extensive district of Ayrshire may claim particular consideration, because it is one of those western shires of Scotland, which, in times very different from Your Majesty's benignant reign, resisted tyranny in one branch of the Constitution, undismayed by the risk of life and fortune [it was a centre of armed opposition to the efforts of the Crown to re-establish episcopacy]. Trusting that we inherit the firmness and intrepidity of our forefathers, we are equally ready to resist tyranny in another branch. Our principles are uniform to withstand encroachment in whatever quarter, and maintain the just balance of our admirable monarchy, limited by progressive wisdom and spirit to a full consistency with rational freedom."
[5] Craigdarroch at this time was probably Andrew Howatson of Craigdarroch. Boswell's other friends were William Wallace of Wallacetown, John Lennox of Dernconner, John Reid of Duncanziemuir, William Ronald of Bennals, a farm in Tarbolton, and John Mitchell, all neighbouring small lairds. Mitchell was a vassal of Boswell's.
[6] William Campbell of Netherplace.

sion) between his family and mine, I hoped it would be continued, and that he would come to Ayr upon this occasion and give his honest voice for the side he thought in the right. He did not come, nor did he send me an answer. I was at first inclined to be angry with him. But I made allowance for his *rustic inefficiency*, and hoped to make him better. It was a fine morning; so instead of taking my chaise as I had ordered, I rode to Ayr. I overtook upon the road Craigdarroch, Wallacetown, and Duncanziemuir, and had a cordial ride along with them. When I got to Ayr, I discovered that there was a considerable opposition; and I afterwards learnt that the Laird of Fairlie, *supposing* that Lord Eglinton was still for the Coalition ministry, or more properly speaking, for the Duke of Portland, and would be against the Address, had sent expresses and endeavoured to collect forces against it. Colonel Montgomerie's answer, which Sundrum read to me from a letter the Colonel wrote to him, was honourable and spirited: that he was to tell Fairlie "he thought he paid the Earl a sufficient compliment when he stayed away. But no man in Europe should make him come down and oppose the Address." I never in my life felt myself better than I was today. I recalled to my mind all the ideas of the consequence of county meetings and of the credit of the family of Auchinleck which I had acquired from my father in my early years, and I superadded the monarchical principles which I had acquired from Dr. Johnson. The account which I sent to the newspapers will remain as a record of what passed this day.[7] I was quite happy upon my success, but by no means insolent. I dined at the King's Arms with Lord Loudoun, etc., twelve in all, and was quite hearty, though I drank only water coloured with toast. I then drank tea at John Boswell's, and went at night to Lady Crawford's. Nobody there but her Ladyship, Lady Mary, Lord Crawford and his brother, and Mr. Crawford, the factor. I played whist and won, and passed the evening most agreeably. I assisted Lord Crawford in writing letters, as preses of the county, to Mr. Pitt and Sir Adam Fergusson.[8]

[7] The *Edinburgh Evening Courant* published a short account on 20 March, with additions on the 24th, but the *Edinburgh Advertiser* for 23 March reported his speeches with great fulness. The London newspapers also carried reports, the *Public Advertiser* on 25 March and the *Whitehall Evening Post* on the 30th. It appears that Boswell really was the most prominent speaker on the occasion. Every measure he advocated was adopted by a vote of at least two to one, and though several copies of addresses were presented, it was his strong and partisan statement that was accepted. Both the *Courant* (24 March) and the *Advertiser* (26 March) also published an address "To the Real Freeholders of the County of Ayr," signed by Boswell, in which he announced his intention to offer himself as candidate for the county in the coming election if Colonel Montgomerie did not stand.

[8] It was Lord Crawford who was preses. Boswell had moved the vote of thanks to Pitt "for the magnanimity with which he has supported the constitutional cause of the

THURSDAY 18 MARCH. (Writing the 31.) After breakfast, at which John Boswell, who had brought out the Address and the vote of thanks to Mr. Pitt, was present, I with reluctance as usual quitted Rozelle. I called on Sundrum, who rode with me a good way into the Trabboch. I got home to dinner, and found Sir John Whitefoord, who had received accounts of what passed yesterday by express, had come this forenoon with the Hon. Andrew Erskine to hear particulars from myself. Also that Lord Dumfries's house-clerk, who had been present at the meeting, had brought the news of it to Cumnock, and it had spread around with animation. I felt myself just what I could wish to be, except that I had not actual employment from the King. I settled several more pieces of business, and had a comfortable afternoon. Every evening that I have been here there has been regular family worship, except the first, when it was too late; and Mr. Millar has been a good companion to me.

FRIDAY 19 MARCH. (Writing the 31.) I set out for Edinburgh in my own chaise; and as I drove up the avenue with my son Sandy, who took a drive with me to the head of it, I spoke of the beauty of Auchinleck, and at the same time calmly reminded him how inconsiderable everything upon this earth was compared with heaven. The sun shone bright, and I thought the rays of religion beamed on his young mind. I dined at Douglas Mill, and at night went to Carnwath,[9] where I was very well lodged, and read old magazines.

SATURDAY 20 MARCH. (Writing the 31.) Set out at six, and got to Edinburgh early in the forenoon. It was the preparation day before the Sacrament. I went to the New Church in the afternoon. Was busy with several things in the evening, as I was resolved to set out for London on Monday, that I might at any rate be present at the general meeting of the County of York to address His Majesty. I was quite happy to be again with my dear wife.

SUNDAY 21 MARCH. (Writing the 31.) I received the Sacrament in the New Church with a decent devotion. Dr. Hope sent me a most refreshing letter from Dr. Brocklesby that Dr. Johnson was wonderfully relieved. I waited on Dr. Hope in the evening and talked more about Dr. Johnson's health. Found the Doctor a most humane, worthy man. I had before this had a letter from Dr. Cullen concerning Dr. Johnson,

---

KING and PEOPLE against a violent faction." The Hon. Patrick Boyle then moved a vote of thanks to Sir Adam Fergusson "for his conduct in Parliament." Boswell succeeded in getting this amended so "that the thanks should be only for the present session," because Sir Adam had "supported Lord North's administration, and voted for the *accursed American war*" (*Edinburgh Advertiser*, 23 March 1784).

[9] The next town on the direct coaching-route (the "new road") from Ayr to Edinburgh.

and Dr. Monro had made an apology for delay, and promised to send me one.[1] I was a good deal agitated tonight. There had unfortunately been another fit of the domestic disturbance. I had delayed fixing as long as I could in hopes of getting a partner in a post-chaise. At eleven I engaged a seat in the diligence by Berwick. My wife's accuracy in having all my things ready was admirable.

[EDITORIAL NOTE. The fully written journal breaks off at this point, with a heading for 22 March but no entry. The record is continued to 8 April by some very rough jottings which Boswell made on a loose leaf.]

MONDAY 22 MARCH. Away for London. Berwick night. Mr. Aitcheson.[2] All alone inn; uneasy.

TUESDAY 23 MARCH. Do not remember who with me.[3] Loftus's, good house, Mordieu's also. Dr. Hall with you at Loftus's (Leighton there), and supped Mordieu's.[4] Inn, uneasy, waked with note that Mr. Dundas was down, so dissolution.[5]

WEDNESDAY 24 MARCH. Remember only Rev. Mr. Joy from Smeaton, keen for Address. George Inn, York; bad tonight. Called Mr. Cayley. Supped with Mr. Joy.[6]

THURSDAY 25 MARCH. Headache, burnt brandy. Breakfasted York Tavern. Met Mr. Duncombe and Mr. Wyvill. Mr. Slater Milnes and you took to each other.[7] At Castle gate decent clergyman: Mr. Mason![8] Introduced to him. Got good place. Was full of English feelings.

[1] All these letters are reported above, 7 March 1784, n. 7.
[2] The Rev. James Aitcheson, a Presbyterian minister in Berwick with whom Temple had business dealings, apparently in connexion with his father's estate. Later this year Temple asked Boswell to procure him a presentation to a living in Scotland.
[3] Substituted for, "All alone, except part of the way, old soldier."
[4] Boswell is now at Newcastle. Dr. John Hall, physician, and John Leighton, surgeon, had cared for Lt. John Boswell while he lived there.
[5] The Parliament was formally dissolved by a speech from the throne, 24 March 1784, to take effect next day, but Dundas would have known of the Ministry's plans some time before. Boswell went on to York, the route to London, but with the immediate plan of attending the meeting called to address the King.
[6] Both clergymen: the Rev. William Cayley, rector of Thorpe and canon of York, and the Rev. Thomas Joy, vicar of Grinton. Boswell had known Cayley since 1776.
[7] Henry Duncombe was M.P. for Yorkshire, Richard Slater Milnes M.P. for the City of York. Christopher Wyvill, Secretary of the Yorkshire Association, was no doubt largely responsible for the present meeting.
[8] This is Boswell's first meeting with the Rev. William Mason, canon of York, friend of his friend Temple and the poet Gray, correspondent of Horace Walpole, and poet

[From the *Edinburgh Evening Courant*, 31 March 1784.]

To the Printer of the *Edinburgh Evening Courant.*

S<small>IR</small>,—In justice to the very respectable freeholders of the County of York, of whose proceedings, at their late meeting to address His Majesty, a confused account has been given in some of the newspapers, I think it my duty to send you a short authentic state, signed with my name, as I was present during the whole; and having been most obligingly permitted to have a seat very near to the High Sheriff, had an opportunity of seeing and hearing to the greatest advantage.

Mr. Danby, the Sheriff, having, at the requisition of above one hundred freeholders, called the meeting by public advertisements a long time before, the utmost exertions were made by the adherents of the *Coalition* to prevent the Address; and when it is considered that the *Duke of Devonshire, Lord John Cavendish, The Earl of Carlisle, The Earl of Surrey, Earl Fitzwilliam, Sir Thomas Dundas,* etc. etc. were all in opposition, and were all present, the independency of spirit with which a numerous body of English yeomanry supported the Address was a noble instance of the popular freedom of England, thus described by Dr. Goldsmith,

> Where ev'n the peasant boasts these rights to scan,
> And learns to venerate himself as man.[9]

Soon may the time come when this shall be said of Scotland!

No hall being large enough to contain the freeholders who appeared upon this occasion, to the number of about *seven thousand*, the meeting was held in the Castle yard, against the wall of which was erected a kind of throne, with a canopy of wood, for the High Sheriff. From this throne was a gradation of seats for persons of distinction, and in front was placed upon the ground a long table or rather stage of boards, on each side of which were rows of forms, which accommodated people who got in first—the rest stood in the large extent of the yard. The Castle gate was opened at half past ten, when we rushed in, and the business began without delay. Every man who spoke, be his rank what it would, was obliged to mount upon the boards, and from thence harangue the audience as far as his voice could reach. The debate was kept up with ability and spirit on both sides for upwards of six hours,

---

whose works Boswell had admired from early youth. In 1775 Boswell had written him a very civil letter and had received a reply which he justly described as arrogant and ill-humoured. He now reported to Temple his "being agreeably surprised with the agreeable manners of Mr. Mason; that he and I have taken to one another admirably" (26 March 1784, Register of Letters).

[9]*The Traveller; or, A Prospect of Society,* ll. 333–334, slightly altered.

and, notwithstanding the immensity of the multitude, I do declare there was as much order preserved as in the House of Commons. At last, indeed, *Lord John Cavendish* was not suffered to speak, though he made several attempts. This I imputed partly to the lateness of the hour and the severity of the weather, there being a cold east wind and showers of sleet, and many of the freeholders being impatient to return to their habitations, some of them twenty miles off, and partly to regret and indignation felt by the generous Yorkshiremen, that this amiable and once very popular nobleman should now appear as an abettor of a party which they dreaded and detested.[1] There was therefore such a roar for *the question*, that my Lord John was obliged to desist. The sense of the meeting was then taken in the usual mode by *a show of hands*, when it was evident that there was a very great majority for the Address; it seemed *five to one*. And the High Sheriff might then have declared the majority, but some of the Coalitionists, disappointed and exasperated, made a desperate effort to annihilate the glorious success by insisting for a *division*, to which the High Sheriff, with too much diffidence, as I humbly thought, consented. Upon which there ensued a scene of mobbing and tumult; for, as it was not distinctly known which side of the Castle yard was to be occupied by the one party and which by the other, there was a fluctuation like that of the sea in a storm; and besides, a rabble of all sorts pressed in amongst the freeholders. The Sheriff, therefore, very properly said, that this *had produced nothing but confusion*, but that *his own decided opinion* was, that there was a great majority; and he accordingly signed the Address of the County, and transmitted it to London.

The result of this day was of vast consequence in the present conflict of parties. The County of York, for extent of territory, the number and riches of its inhabitants, is a kingdom of itself. It is the county which has distinguished itself most conspicuously for constitutional liberty, and it was very unjustly supposed of the Yorkshiremen, as of other friends of freedom, that they would oppose the King when the *House of Commons* was disregarded; but the honest Yorkshiremen were not to be gulled by *sounds* contrary to *sense*. They *knew* that a majority of the House of Commons had violently attempted to assume the executive power, which would have destroyed our Constitution. They knew that the King had, with a conscientious firmness, resisted those attempts, for which all gratitude was due from His Majesty's faithful

[1] He was Member for York from 1768 to the dissolution, and Chancellor of the Exchequer in Rockingham's second administration, March to July 1782, and under Portland, April to December 1783. Boswell had been in company with Cavendish at The Hague, 1764.

subjects. The gentlemen of the *Yorkshire Association*, in particular, declared that they were happy in having an opportunity this day of vindicating themselves from the charge of maintaining republican principles. They had, it is true, asserted the rights of the people. They had resisted the *undue influence* of the Crown; but now, when its *just prerogative* was attacked, they should be the foremost to defend it.

I took pretty large notes of the speeches upon this memorable occasion. I send you one of them, and, if it is found agreeable, may send more.[2] I shall only add, that I would willingly have gone a thousand miles to have been present at the Yorkshire meeting, and witnessed such an union of *loyalty* and *freedom,* to both of which I am warmly attached. I am, Sir, your most humble servant,

JAMES BOSWELL.

Dined with freeholders, drank wine moderately. Evening, tea York Tavern. Mason said of Lord Effingham, "If no such thing as toast, most valuable man."[3] Hesitation whether to go to London or return.[4]

FRIDAY 26 MARCH. Breakfasted Cayley with Mr. Mason, etc. He made me dictate to old ———, a printer.[5] He went away. I dined Cayley's with Morritt, near Greta Bridge, and Robison, a clergyman.[6] Also coffee. Called Old Wyvill. Very cold.

SATURDAY 27 MARCH. Returned to Newcastle. Got good bed.

SUNDAY 28 MARCH. Called Dr. Hall; agreed to be with him evening. Got Neil Gillies and went to places of worship. Catholics: one locked, one over. A little in Presbyterian, a little in St. ——— Church. Then Subscription Room. Good second breakfast. Read my address to Ayrshire freeholders, and *Critical Review* on my *Letter [to the People*

[2] The speech of Samuel Buck, Recorder of Leeds, who opened the debate at the meeting, follows Boswell's letter to the *Courant* and runs to about a column.

[3] The landlord of an inn at Sheffield had told Boswell that Effingham "would sit and get drunk with cutlers" (Journal, 25 September 1777). Horace Walpole called him "a rough soldier of no sound sense" (*Last Journals,* ed. A. F. Steuart, 1910, i. 439), but Effingham had been Treasurer of the Household, was this year made Master of the Mint, and in 1789 became Governor of Jamaica. His seat, New Grange, was in Yorkshire.

[4] He still did not know whether Colonel Montgomerie would stand for Parliament.

[5] Perhaps the letter printed above reporting the meeting 25 March 1784. It also appeared in the *Edinburgh Advertiser* 2 April, with a sequel 6 April 1784.

[6] John Sawrey Morritt of Rokeby, father of the Morritt who was one of Sir Walter Scott's favourite correspondents. There are several possibilities for "Robison." An interesting one would be the Rev. William Robinson, Mrs. Elizabeth Montagu's brother and a great friend of Gray.

of Scotland].⁷ Very comfortable. Old Jonathan Forbes marked me as a visitor.⁸ Then St. Nicholas's Church.⁹ Then dined inn. Coffee and tea Dr. Hall's. Called Miss Silvertop at Mr. Dun's. Mr. Leighton not in, but saw son. Mrs. Atkins not in. Supped Dr. Hall's with Mr. Leighton. Some wine cordially. Hopes of Parliament.

MONDAY 29 MARCH. Got to Edinburgh, Mr. Lawrie and Grange with me. House seemed *dereliction*, but was firm.¹ Alarmed that Sir Adam Fergusson had Lord Eglinton's interest. Called Mr. Dundas, engaged.

[EDITORIAL NOTE. The politics of Ayrshire were unusually complicated. Two candidates had the support of one or more of the Ayrshire peers, which was necessary for election: Eglinton and Cassillis supported Colonel Hugh Montgomerie, and Glencairn and Dumfries supported John "Fish" Craufurd of Auchenames. Besides Boswell, another "independent" appeared in the person of Sir John Whitefoord. Neither had the slightest chance of being put forward by Henry Dundas, who was restored to his post as Treasurer of the Navy and more powerful than ever. His candidate was Sir Adam Fergusson. Craufurd's hopes were unrealistic (he was a friend of Fox), and he withdrew after making a futile attempt to bargain with Montgomerie for future support. Dundas made a deal to support Eglinton's candidate for one parliament with the understanding that Eglinton would support his for the next. Fergusson therefore withdrew, leaving Montgomerie unopposed, but Dundas had no intention of losing so valuable a henchman even for one parliament. Since the death of Sir Lawrence Dundas he had had the City of Edinburgh in his pocket. For decency's sake he allowed James Hunter Blair, Sir William Forbes's partner, to be returned, but in the following August replaced him by Fergusson, Hunter Blair vacating his seat on the ground that his professional duties made his attendance in London impracticable. He was at once elected Lord Provost. Boswell had no inkling at this time of the high-handed scheme to bring in Sir Adam in any case.]

⁷A highly favourable review which refers to Boswell as having "always distinguished himself by an attachment to public liberty" (January 1784, lvii. 74).
⁸Forbes was an old army officer, captain of a company of invalids quartered at Sheerness, and deputy-governor of Clifford's Fort, near Tynemouth.
⁹Now the cathedral, distinguished particularly by its crown tower, which inspired the tower of St. Giles's, Edinburgh.
¹"My house seemed deserted." Mrs. Boswell, with the two children remaining in Edinburgh, had gone on to Auchinleck.

TUESDAY 30 MARCH. Breakfasted well. Then Mr. Dundas, a levee. Taken in to him. Found him very agreeable. Breakfasted with him, Hunter Blair, etc. Ayrshire election all uncertain. Ran about forenoon as in London. Dined on beefsteaks home. Evening Col. James Stuart arrived and sent he was to sup at Fortune's. I went to bed.

WEDNESDAY 31 MARCH. Called Mr. Dundas. People with him. Went to call Colonel James, met him on bridge. Were lively and well. Altercation. BOSWELL. "Will preserve Crown." Walked with him to Castle. He said, "You don't look so cordial." BOSWELL. "No more difference than colour of coat."² Called Captain Webster's. Evening supped Surgeon Wood's.

THURSDAY 1 APRIL. Found Mr. Dundas, excellent conversation with him. Not gown yet, first *waste* of Opposition, etc., etc.³ Settled burgess of Edinburgh.⁴ Lord Provost asked to dine with Lord Provost, etc. Very lucky. Freedom of City proposed. Very jovial.⁵ Asked to Sir W. Forbes. But did not go as intoxicated a little and to go off early. Saw Lady Auchinleck, well. Was with Colonel James in street. Settled to see him at Auchinleck.

FRIDAY 2 APRIL. In fly home. M. M. met me at Cumnock, Mr. Dun and Old John Boswell. Most agreeable. But had *éclaircissement* of domestic disturbance. Was ashamed and clear. Poor Tiger ill.⁶

---

²Colonel Stuart (who until the dissolution had been M.P. for Plympton Erle) and Lord Mountstuart opposed Pitt's administration.

³Boswell had learned that Colonel Montgomerie *would* stand, and apparently asked Dundas to get him a judge's gown. "First waste of Opposition" is cryptic but presumably bears the same general sense as the advice Dundas gave Boswell later, 12 December 1784: "He said . . . I should first get something that I might carry to the bench with me." Perhaps: "First, pick up some office that will become vacant as the Opposition is plundered of its spoils."

⁴A consolation for patience, apparently. Boswell was enrolled a burgess of Edinburgh on 15 September 1784.

⁵The Lord Provost (John Grieve) invited him to attend the dinner at Walker's where the Magistrates and Town Council of Edinburgh honoured their Member of Parliament, Hunter Blair. He was returned again three days later. Other invited guests included Henry Dundas, Robert Dundas the Solicitor-General (son of the Lord President), Sir William Forbes, and Dr. Hugh Blair. Boswell sang a ballad of his own composition, *The Midlothian Address*, which made flattering reference to all three Dundases. He also put an account of the dinner, with one stanza of his song, into the *Edinburgh Advertiser* for 2 April.

⁶This mysterious domestic disturbance, for which Boswell had already expressed contrition, was reported above as first occurring on 20 February 1784; it was quieted next day, but recurred on 12 and 21 March 1784. Mrs. Boswell's *éclaircissement* perhaps brought Boswell up to date. For a possible explanation, see below, Editorial Note, 2 July 1784. We have no further information about Tiger. Perhaps a dog.

SATURDAY 3 APRIL. Away to Coilsfield. Not at home. Sundrum. Doonside. Bailie Neill's. John Boswell with me to Fairlie. Quite active and solid.

SUNDAY 4 APRIL. To Dreghorn Church. Lecture on James, Chapter [5], "effectual prayer." Sir Walter; promised not engage.[7] Bourtreehill. Back to dinner, Colonel Craufurd, excellent day.

MONDAY 5 APRIL. Breakfasted Dankeith with Sir William and Lady Betty.[8] He with me to Craufurdland. Truly antique. Tea Bruce Campbell. Home fine.

TUESDAY 6 APRIL. Berboth,[9] Colonel Hugh, etc., unwilling to engage different from where *heart* is.

WEDNESDAY 7 APRIL. Walked with Miss. Excellent conversation with Laird. Home by Ballochmyle. Sir John gone.[1]

THURSDAY 8 APRIL. At Willockston braes and walk round. Perfect good frame afternoon. Affectionate loving walk with M. M. Heard Burke Glasgow.[2] Resolved go.

SATURDAY 10 APRIL. Riding into Glasgow this morning from Kingswells, I attempted to pass a cart quickly upon a causeway near the Gorbals. My horse fell and threw me off before him, close by the track of the cart. *Providentially* (I *will* say) the horse which drew the cart, heavy-laden with sacks of meal, started a little to one side, so that while I lay on the ground the wheel next me missed my head by about an inch. It went over my hat, which had come off my head. The carter said "he *gaed blind*," so frightened was he. He told me he had never seen so narrow an escape in his life. My servant, Alexander Thomson,[3] gave me up as gone. I did not know of my danger till they informed me. It left a fright upon my imagination. I most sincerely returned thanks to Almighty GOD for my preservation. It was shocking to reflect how near I had been to a violent death, and how my dear wife and children might have been sadly afflicted by so unexpected a misfortune.[4]

[7] He got Sir Walter not to promise his vote for the present to any of the Ayrshire candidates for Parliament.

[8] Sir William Cuninghame of Caprington and his mother.

[9] The residence of John McAdam of Craigengillan. Boswell apparently found him inclined to support Colonel Montgomerie.

[1] Sir John Whitefoord.

[2] He was to be installed Lord Rector of the University of Glasgow, a dignity the *Public Advertiser* reported that he owed to his warm friend Adam Smith (23 December 1784). There is no note for 9 April 1784.

[3] This appears to be the only place in the journal where this servant is referred to by name. His name appears regularly with the entry of his wages in an Account of Expenses that Boswell kept from 17 June 1783 to 5 March 1784.

[4] "I shall solemnly commemorate this day with pious gratitude annually while I live.

When I got to the Saracen's Head Inn at Glasgow, where Mr. Burke was, I wrote a fair copy of the letter on the other side of this paper[5] and sealed it, intending to have made a waiter convey it to him, without letting him know that I was in the house. But as I walked upstairs, I met his servant, who knew me and asked if I would not go in to his master. I bid him first give Mr. Burke that letter.

[Boswell to Burke]

Glasgow, Saturday morning, 10 April 1784

MY DEAR SIR,—Your long silence, and particularly your not complying with my request to be informed of the time of your coming to Scotland, have made me apprehend it is possible you may have taken offence at my Tory zeal against a political system which you have supported. Yet I cannot easily believe that Edmund Burke is deficient in liberality of sentiment. You will please impute partly to my anxiety, partly to your neglect, that I have for a moment entertained a fear of what I should very much regret, for your sake as well as my own. I am grateful for your kindness. I love your virtues. I admire your talents. And on hearing of your arrival, I have hastened from my seat in the country to wait on you, to show you all the respect I can, and to entreat I may have the honour to see you at Auchinleck.

But if in this cursed strife, you "have ought against me," and will not be fully "reconciled" with me even in *this week*,[6] pray tell me frankly, that our difference may not be exposed to the profane, and that we may either not meet at all, or in your ever memorable words to the worthy Langton, "live pleasant." I am, my dear Sir, your faithful, obliged, humble servant.

No sooner had he read it than he came quickly into the parlour where I was, and approached me with all the good humour he ever showed at our meeting. We embraced complaisantly, and I said something of my apprehension, and of my joy that it was without foundation. He said, "What has made you go so mad of late? As to quarrelling with

---

'He took me from a fearful pit'" (Boswell's marginal note; the quotation is paraphrased from Psalms 40: 2). There is no indication in the journal that Boswell remembered this resolution. But the accident impressed him so strongly that two days later he wrote an abbreviated reminder of it: "Mem: providential escape 10 April 1784. Be calm and still (after communing with heart) at Auchinleck. ['Stand in awe and sin not: commune with your own heart upon your bed and be still': Psalms 4: 4.] Think of M. M. while blessed with so valuable a comfort."

[5] It is printed below.

[6] Passion Week. The quotations are from Matthew 5: 23–24.

you, that cannot happen; for as you observe as to Langton——" In
short he conveyed a compliment that my pleasantry was such that one
would be a loser by quarrelling with me. He said too, "As to telling you
when I should come to Scotland, I did not know myself till we were
dismissed. 'Deus nobis haec otia.' "[7] He invited me to breakfast with
him directly, as he was to go to the College at ten. In a little Lord
Maitland, who accompanied him, came to me, and was very polite and
affable. I went and joined them at breakfast. Lord Daer, Professor
Dalzel, Professor Dugald Stewart,[8] Professor Millar, and Dr. Adam
Smith were all of the party. I was a little flurried from the consciousness
of my being in the midst of opposition. But I conducted myself very
well. I had a curious feeling while I recollected that the first time I had
contemplated the character of Mr. Burke was at Glasgow, four-and-
twenty years ago, when I was a student of law there, and viewed him
like a planet in the heavens.[9] And now here he was actually Lord Rector
of that university, and sitting in the town, a reality almost as wonderful
to my mind as if some eminent man of a distant age had been before
my eyes. The feeling was heightened by reviving the thoughts which
I had *then* in company with Adam Smith, and those I had *now*. I believe
it is exceedingly rare to have the power of thus bringing together the
impressions of periods of time widely separated; for in general those
of an early period are obliterated when those of a period present but
long posterior to it are lively. I exulted in the soundness and comparatively[1] strength of mind of which I now was conscious.

About ten we walked to the College. I should wish to describe all
that passed minutely, but life is too short. Suffice it to say that Edmund
Burke looked exceedingly well in the Lord Rector's gown, and showed
that so great a literary honour sat very becomingly on one who had
no solemn appearance, but a pleasant air of genius. He made a speech
of a few sentences upon his being installed in . . .

[7]"The divinity [Augustus Caesar in Virgil's case, George III in Burke's] has provided
us with this leisure" (Virgil, *Eclogues*, i. 6, trans. H. R. Fairclough, Loeb ed., 1960).
[8]The only reference in the entire journal to the philosopher, which seems strange in
view of his great eminence and the fact that they became close neighbours when Stewart
bought Catrine in 1785. But in 1784 he was only thirty-one and had not yet been
appointed to the chair of moral philosophy in which he made his reputation. Boswell
left Edinburgh in 1786, and in any case would have been alienated soon after by
Stewart's sympathy with the principles of the French Revolution. In his *Elements of
Philosophy of the Human Mind* Stewart commended Boswell's ability as a teller of stories.
[9]He probably heard Adam Smith lecture on Burke's *Philosophical Inquiry into the Origin
of Our Ideas on the Sublime and Beautiful*, but he did not really read the book until much
later (18 July 1779).
[1]*Sic.* Boswell may have meant to write "comparative," or he may be using "comparatively" elliptically, in the sense of "comparatively speaking."

[EDITORIAL NOTE. The fully written journal breaks off here at the foot of a page, and perhaps was never carried further.[2] Boswell returned to Edinburgh on Monday the 12th, but that morning he wrote a note which survives in a rough draft, or a very hasty copy, headed "Left for Mr. Burke when I left Glasgow (he at Loch Lomond)." A memorandum in Boswell's hand follows the letter.]

[Boswell to Burke]

Glasgow, Monday morning, 12 April 1784

MY DEAR SIR,—Your admirable behaviour towards me at this time has made me exceedingly happy. It convinces me that our friendship "shall flourish in immortal youth unhurt amidst, etc. etc."[3] I am going to Edinburgh to meet my friend Colonel James Stuart and shall wait your arrival there. Since you could not now go to Auchinleck you will oblige me very much if you will indulge me with the honour of your presence under my roof in town and sup with me any night you are pleased to appoint by writing it on a slip of paper and sending it to me by post that I may engage some people whom you will like. I flatter myself that Lord Maitland will be of the party. I am more and more, my dear Sir, yours affectionately.

[MEMORANDUM.] If he comes, have Dr. Cullen and son, Sir William Forbes, Dalzel, Dundas, Colonel James, Lord Maitland, he, and you. *Nine* and *no more*. Perhaps [Adam] *Smith*.[4]

[Burke to Boswell]

[Glasgow, 15 April 1784]

MY DEAR SIR,—A thousand thanks for your kind invitation. I came very late last night, and go off very early (that is, at five) tomorrow

[2] Boswell preserved some rough notes on Burke's speech, the only memorial of it thus far known: "By much the greatest honour I ever received. On a very different principle from what honours usually [MS. apparently 'us.'] bestowed. If you have done right, done a very important act. Youth may see how endeavours, faithful indeed in public service but weak and imperfect, rewarded, etc."

[3] Addison, *Cato*, V. i. 29–31:

> But thou shalt flourish in immortal youth,
> Unhurt amidst the war of elements,
> The wrecks of matter, and the crush of worlds.

[4] The proposed guests not completely named are Dr. Cullen's eldest son, Robert Cullen, the advocate (later Lord Cullen), and Col. James Stuart. "Perhaps *Smith*" doubtless because Boswell thought him an "infidel," like Hume, and had even asked Johnson the year previous whether he should continue to associate with him (see above, 20 April 1783). The names of Dr. William Robertson and Dr. Hugh Blair were originally third and fourth on Boswell's list, but he later struck them through.

morning. I must therefore go to bed early and of course must deny myself the satisfaction of passing the evening with you. I am sincerely mortified at my disappointment. Yours ever most sincerely.

[EDITORIAL NOTE. On 18 April Boswell planned to go to Fife, where a superiority he had inherited from his father gave him a vote, to support the "good cause" in the election. He would probably have voted for Sir John Henderson, who was defeated by Robert Skene, the Coalition candidate. But some "alarm" sent him west again to Ayrshire that very day. In the latter part of the month he wrote a number of letters concerned with politics, and arranged to go south to keep the Easter term at the Temple commons. At the end of April he set out for London by way of Carlisle, Lancaster, Manchester, and Lichfield, where he made a pause of a day or two, probably to be present at Sunday service in the cathedral, certainly to flirt with the poet Anna Seward.[5] He had first noted her bright eyes (and "bad mouth"[5a]) when he and Johnson supped with her father, the Rev. Thomas Seward, canon of the cathedral, 24 March 1776. On this sojourn in Lichfield Boswell almost certainly stayed with David Garrick's elder brother, Peter, a wine-merchant, who had previously offered him a bed in his house. Fragments of dialogue with Peter Garrick, whom he once called "quite a London *narrateur*,"[6] are interspersed among Boswell's own aphorisms and verses in his notes of the journey to London. All this matter, probably intended for *Boswelliana*, is crowded together with a few notes made in London in the blank spaces of a letter which Boswell carried from Scotland. We present the observations below, although it is not always clear to whom they should be attributed. They have been given the order of Boswell's journey.]

A high road across a wild moor makes it look tame, gives it a civilized look. Like a collar on a dog.

[5] On 18 May he wrote to her, "I have been in a flutter ever since we parted. . . . Write to me without delay, and as a *token* enclose me a lock of that charming auburn hair I admired so much the delicious morning I was last with you. It will be a *talisman* against all temptation till I return to you." She rejected his advances firmly but offered him the affection of a sister. A lock of her hair (it is indeed auburn) tied with a bit of pink ribbon was found, however, in a letter she wrote to Boswell 20 June 1784. On the inside of the wrapper enclosing the lock is a signed set of verses in Miss Seward's hand:

> With spotless lilies, cull'd from friendship's bowers,
> That hide no thorns beneath their snowy flowers,
> By Boswell's hand be this light lock enwove,
> But never with the dangerous rose of love!

[5a] Boswell's own words, in his journal for 24 March 1776.
[6] Journal, 24 March 1776.

I make game of society in this transitory life, and of all its varieties, serious and comic. I frisk with women and with men too.[7]

For the ball at Ayr let Colonel Montgomerie send the bell. Since he bears the bell, let him send it about.[8]

A violent fellow's high spirits are *wash*.[9] They are not refined by distillation. He has no alembic in his head.

From Moffat to Lockerbie, Lieutenant. From Lockerbie to Carlisle, Jeanie Henderson, wife of John Trumbull, driver of the coach from the Bush[1] to Penrith. Both formerly at Clark's.[2] At Carlisle, Mr. Ewen, son of Bailie Ewen, baker, Glasgow. In the calico-printing line. Had been some time in London, boarded at the pastry-cook's, St. Paul's Churchyard. £40 per annum, first floor.

A little from Carlisle Mr. Thomas Richardson the famous cock-feeder joined. Lives at Keaston near Lancaster. At Penrith, Thomas Braithwaite, saddler.[3] Bruce can make a shilling go as far as eighteen-pence.[4] Richardson: feeds at Lancaster, York, Carlisle, Newcastle, Durham. Thirty guineas a main feeding, all expenses paid.[5] His father (of whom there is a print) followed the same business. But died a little after fifty, being also a huntsman and sitting late drinking with gents. "A man may take a glass at times. But to go a-drinking and sit up a-night and make a fool on oneself is very hurtful to the constitution. At least it is very hurtful to mine. Feeding great patience, sobriety, and nice feel. Difficult to get good stuff. Have gone ninety miles for a cock." Crossing. "May go on thirty years with their own blood."[6]

At Kendal, "Why two candles?" "Every man his *bird*." He laughed.[7] Curious fellow, at siege of Algiers in Spanish service. Loyalist in

---

[7] Our translation. The original is in French.

[8] "To bear the bell" means to win the prize, and clearly refers to Colonel Montgomerie's recent election to Parliament. We have found no record of a victory ball at Ayr or any use of a bell which would explain the pun.

[9] A watery fermented infusion.

[1] One of the principal inns at Carlisle.

[2] Also an inn at Carlisle, kept by William Clark.

[3] He wrote to Boswell in November 1786 asking him to get a soldier discharged, a feat which Boswell replied was not in his power.

[4] We are unable to identify the person against whom this sarcasm (probably Braithwaite's) was discharged.

[5] Skilled breeders (also called *feeders*) commanded fees of thirty to sixty guineas for conditioning cocks in the ten days before a main (or match). They guarded jealously the recipes and regimens by which the cocks were weighed in light three days before the fight and then raised to a maximum compatible with speed and aggressiveness.

[6] Breeders with good strains adopted the "in-and-in" system: they perpetuated the grand qualities by not crossing. Boswell put a query over "thirty."

[7] Probably two candles were set out for Boswell and Richardson, though they were sleeping in the same room. Richardson asked, "Why two?" and Boswell replied

America. Now settled, leather-dresser. "You have cast anchor." "I hope so. I wish to *ride*."[8] Tanner's daughter. Leather to leather.

At Kendal, Swainson's wine-cellar. Agent for the Sun Fire Office—Bardolph's fiery nose.[1]

We pick up any acquaintances in our early years as children pick up any stones. But as we advance to discern, and get valuable ones like pebbles,[2] we drop the coarse, both as loading us too much and as by their coarseness hurting the precious stones.

PETER GARRICK. "We all know what nectar is: raisin-wine. But as to ambrosia, I ain't sure whether strawberries and cream or fried onions." Asked to eat supper: "Excuse me. It would be *hornie* and *hoofie* all night."[3]

Peter Garrick said, "In this country we love strong wine, something that will strike *hard* upon the palate. I had some very old and with all the flavour, but smooth and mild. The colonel of a regiment who lay here, a countryman of yours who by his brother's death became a lord, said he did not like it. It wanted the hammer. If a man has not the devil of ambition or avarice and has done something, he may live very comfortably as one does here. Content is the great requisite." BOSWELL. "But that is against animated enterprise." GARRICK. "But in old age?" BOSWELL. "True. A man must then have his provision laid up. He must not have to forage."[4] GARRICK. "No. When a man is old that is too hard work." MISS ROGERS. "In *Vanity of Human Wishes*, the beggar; '*Increase his riches*' borders on a bull.[5] Malicious pleasure that so great a man should be catched in an error by so little a creature as I am."

---

with a proverbial expression which properly means "Every man prefers his own child" (*bird* = youngster, son, child), but with a pun, of course, on "bird" as "fighting cock."
[8] Lie at anchor.
[1] Joseph Swainson is listed in the *Universal British Directory* of this period as both wine-merchant and Sun Fire agent. Boswell suggests that a signboard showing Bardolph's head (*I Henry IV*) would advertise both of Swainson's occupations.
[2] Scotch pebbles are agates or other gems. Boswell spent many hours when he was at Auchinleck collecting them from streams such as the Lugar Water and the Dippol Burn.
[3] The Devil ("old Hornie" in Scots) would make mischief of his stomach.
[4] MS. "must not to have to forage."
[5] Lines 37–40:

> The needy traveller, secure and gay,
> Walks the wild heath, and sings his toil away.
> Does envy seize thee? crush th'upbraiding joy,
> Increase his riches and his peace destroy.

Miss Rogers (herself a poet, of Dronfield, Derbyshire) misquoted Johnson's verse, and thought it a bull, or a ludicrous contradiction in terms, because a beggar has no riches to increase. Boswell squeezed a correction alongside her remark: "It is not beggar—but *needy* traveller."

[BOSWELL]. "Young's *Night Thoughts* more images than any poem but *Hudibras*. Very different. But *there* similitude." MISS SEWARD. " 'For love, which scarce collective man' by some said to be indelicate." BOSWELL. "No, no. The context shows not.[6] It *might*. As Anacreon says, 'How *many* loves; Corinth one hundred, etc.' *That* 'scarce collective,' etc."[7]

I said to Primus Stiverson[8] once [of] Hugh Maxwell's black servant, then a waiter at the Bush Inn, Carlisle, "Poor fellow he has enough to do." "Yes, Sir" (said Primus). "I dare say he has both his hands and heart full."

Hayley makes the Duchess of Devonshire like a buoy on the tide of life. But she returns to her element and sinks again. She dives into cellars, etc. She is a diving *Belle*.[9]

[6] This line of Johnson's (*The Vanity of Human Wishes*, 361) occurs in a list of supplications to the deity which the poet declares to be legitimate. The complete line, which reads, "For love, which scarce collective man can fill," probably means, "[Pray] for a love so ample that all mankind can hardly exhaust its capacity." The critics Miss Seward refers to must have taken the line somehow as an appeal for sexual love, or at least have thought a sexual metaphor intended. See the note following this.

[7] To expand: "If this line stood alone, it well *might* be read, 'For a sexual appetite which the entire human race cannot satisfy.' Compare Anacreon's numbering of his loves: thirty-five at Athens, 'loves in bunches' at Corinth, two thousand altogether by the time Lesbos, Rhodes, Ionia, and Caria have been reckoned, with no mention of Egypt, Crete, India, and Bactria." Boswell is referring to the Anacreontic numbered xxxii in eighteenth-century editions, No. 14 in J. M. Edmonds's *Elegy and Iambus, with the Anacreontea*, Loeb ed., 1968, ii, *The Anacreontea*, pp. 34–37, but he seems actually to be quoting the paraphrase by Abraham Cowley, *The Account*, which we know he read aloud to his father in the spring of 1777. Lord Auchinleck, a good Greek scholar, was especially fond of Anacreon, and had in his library many texts of that poet, including some manuscripts.

[8] So the manuscript seems clearly to read, but Boswell's *r*'s and *n*'s are interchangeable. *Stivers* and *Stiverson* are both found currently in the United States though we do not find them in Scottish books of names. Hugh Maxwell was a Writer to the Signet and Boswell's cousin.

[9] William Hayley (patron briefly of the poet Blake) was the author of five *Plays of Three Acts Written for a Private Theatre*, which had been published recently. The dedication to the Duchess of Devonshire, dated 29 January 1784, includes the following lines:

> May thy light spirit, on the sea of life,
> Elude the rocks of care, the gusts of strife,
> And safely, as the never-sinking buoy,
> Float on th' unebbing flood of real joy!

Boswell, like members of the Court party, is disparaging the Duchess for her persuasive efforts to get out the popular vote for Charles Fox in the Westminster election, which ended 17 May. It was said that she entered "the most blackguard houses in Long Acre" (*Cornwallis Correspondence*, ed. Charles Ross, 1859, i. 166) and that she exchanged kisses for votes, a rumour she denied. The gossip drove her from town, but she returned at the request of the Duke of Portland to continue canvassing.

Too smooth a life is insipid. Cares *roughen* it. They make a Chinese ring.[1]

[EDITORIAL NOTE. Boswell arrived in London on 5 May and remained there or in the vicinity until 30 June. For no other of his spring jaunts do we possess such scanty memorials. The only continuous dated record for the period is a list that combines reminders of engagements with memoranda of activities already past. A few scattered journal entries and notes for journal, no part of this continuous list, also survive. We know that some papers have been lost, but it may be that Boswell was so busy enjoying himself he could find little time for journalizing and that what we have is nearly all the general record he ever made. For the long and intricate conversations which he reports in the *Life of Johnson* he must have had more notes, however, than the one specimen preserved (see below, 19 May 1784, n. 7). Till further notice we shall print the engagement list, eked out by such notes and journal as we possess (both following the dating-style "TUESDAY 11 MAY") interspersed with passages from the first draft of the manuscript of the *Life of Johnson* (dating-style "On Wednesday 5 May"). We have silently omitted from the engagement list entries that are more fully covered by some other record; and have also omitted from the draft of the *Life of Johnson* a few passages that were clearly written from the point of view of 1788. The latter omissions are indicated by ellipses. The first paragraph following was probably recovered entirely from memory.]

On Wednesday 5 May I arrived in London and next morning had the pleasure to find Dr. Johnson greatly recovered and having even a fresh look of *redintegration*.[2] I but just saw him, for a coach was waiting to carry him to Islington to the house of his friend the Rev. Mr. Strahan, where he went sometimes for the benefit of good air, which notwithstanding his having formerly laughed at the general opinion upon the subject, he now acknowledged was essentially different as to health in different places.

On Sunday 9 May I found Colonel Vallancey, the celebrated antiquarian and engineer of Ireland, with him. On Monday the 10 I dined with him at Mr. Paradise's, where was a large company: Mr. Bryant, Mr. Jodrell, Mr. Hawkins Browne, etc.[3]

[1] Or circle, such as contains the dualism of *yin* and *yang*, the first principle female, traditionally dark, negative, and evil, and the second principle male, bright, positive, and beneficent. Underneath the lines Boswell wrote "7 June." He was then in London, where he probably also wrote the pun about the Duchess of Devonshire.
[2] Restoration to perfect health. Boswell is quoting or imitating Johnson.
[3] Jacob Bryant, antiquary, best known for *A New System or an Analysis of Ancient Mythology,*

TUESDAY 11 MAY. Colonel Vallancey, eleven. Visits after. Dinner Mr. Hoole's.[4]

WEDNESDAY 12 MAY. King's Bench.[5] Dine Dr. Taylor's.[6]

On Thursday the 13 I dined with him at Mr. Jodrell's with another large company: the Bishop of Exeter,[1] Lord Monboddo, Mr. Murphy,[2] etc.

FRIDAY 14 MAY. Dine Mr. Sinclair.[3] Evening Ranelagh.

On Saturday 15 May I dined with him at Dr. Brocklesby's, where were Colonel Vallancey, Mr. Murphy, Mr. Devaynes, apothecary to the royal household, etc., etc. Of all these days and others on which I saw him, I have no memorials except the general recollection of his being copious and animated in conversation, and appearing to relish society as much as the youngest man. I find only these three small particulars. One, that when a person was mentioned who said he had lived fifty-one years in the world without having ten minutes of uneasiness, he exclaimed, "The man who says so lies. He attempts to impose on human credulity." Another, that when a gentleman of eminence in the literary world was violently censured for attacking people by anonymous paragraphs in newspapers,[4] he, from a spirit of contradiction, as I thought, took up his defence and said, "Come, come, this is not so terrible a crime. He means only to vex them a little. I do not say that I should do this. But there is a great difference. What is fit for Hephaestion[5] is not fit for Alexander." Another, that when I told him that a young and handsome lady of quality had said to me, "I should think to be praised by Dr. Johnson would make one a fool all one's life"; and that I answered, "Madam, I shall make him a fool today by repeating this

3 vols., 1774–1776; Richard Paul Jodrell, classical scholar; and Isaac Hawkins Browne the younger, editor of his father's poems, M.P. for Bridgnorth, and essayist.

[4] John Hoole, auditor in the East India House and man of letters, translator of Tasso and Ariosto.

[5] To hear the renewed proceedings in the case of Christopher Atkinson, corn-factor and M.P. for Hedon, who had sworn innocence to a charge of defrauding the Victualling Board and been found guilty of perjury. Sentence was postponed, but Atkinson was expelled from the Commons 4 December 1783. Boswell's friend John Lee was one of the counsel for the Crown and probably invited him to attend the hearing.

[6] Dr. John Taylor, a boyhood friend of Johnson's and prebendary of Westminster, appointed the previous month rector of St. Margaret's, Westminster.

[1] Dr. John Ross.

[2] Arthur Murphy, author, actor, and barrister.

[3] John Sinclair of Ulbster, agriculturist, created baronet in 1786. A voluminous writer (Boswell had helped revise his *Observations on the Scottish Dialect*), he is chiefly remembered now as the initiator of the *Statistical Account of Scotland*.

[4] George Steevens, the Shakespearean editor and intimate of Johnson.

[5] The boyhood friend and closest companion of Alexander the Great.

to him," he said, "I am too old to be made a fool, but if you say I am, I shall not deny it. I am much pleased with a compliment, especially from a pretty woman."[6]

On the evening of Saturday 15 May he was in fine spirits at our Essex Head Club.[7] JOHNSON. "I dined yesterday at Mrs. Garrick's with Mrs. Carter, Miss Hannah More,[8] and Miss Fanny Burney. Three such women are not to be found. I know not where I could find a fourth, except Mrs. Lennox, who is superior to them all."[9] BOSWELL. "What! Had you them all to yourself, Sir?" JOHNSON. "I had 'em all as much as they were had; but it might have been better had some more company been there." BOSWELL. "Might not Mrs. Montagu[1] have been a fourth?" JOHNSON. "Sir, Mrs. Montagu does not make a trade of her wit. But Mrs. Montagu is a very extraordinary woman. She has a constant stream of conversation, and it is always impregnated; it has always meaning." BOSWELL. "Mr. Burke has a constant stream of conversation." JOHNSON. "Yes, Sir; if you went by chance along with Burke under a shade[2] to shun a shower, you would say, 'This is an extraordinary man.' If Burke should go into a stable to see his horse dressed, the ostler would say, 'We have had an extraordinary man here.'" BOSWELL. "Foote[3] was a man who never failed in conversation. If he had gone into a stable—" JOHNSON. "Sir, if he had gone into a stable, the ostler would have said, 'Here has been a comical fellow,' but he would not have esteemed him." BOSWELL. "And the ostler would have answered him, would have given him as good as he brought, as the common saying is." JOHNSON. "Yes, Sir; and Foote would answer the ostler. When Burke does not descend to be merry, his conversation is very superior indeed. There is no proportion between the powers which he shows in serious talk and in jocularity. When he lets himself down, he is in the kennel."[4] . . .

[6] The "lady of quality," changed in revision to "countess," was possibly Lord Eglinton's second countess, Frances Twisden, whom he had married in 1783.
[7] Founded by Johnson the previous December to relieve his loneliness, it met three times weekly at the Essex Head, an inn near his house kept by a former servant of Henry Thrale.
[8] The great actor's widow; Elizabeth Carter, scholar and writer; and Hannah More, the dramatist, poet, and religious writer, who later founded the Sunday-school system.
[9] Mrs. Charlotte Lennox, *née* Ramsay, born in New York, where her father was Lieutenant-Governor. She earned her livelihood by her pen as novelist, dramatist, poet, translator, and for a short time, editor of the magazine *The Ladies' Museum*.
[1] Mrs. Elizabeth Montagu, author. Vivacious, learned, and witty, she was undisputed leader of the intellectual society of London for nearly fifty years.
[2] Dialectal for "shed"; Boswell corrected it to "shed" in revision. The word was probably his, not Johnson's.
[3] Samuel Foote, actor and dramatist.
[4] Gutter (the word is a variant of "channel").

Mr. Windham now said low to me that he differed from our great friend in this particular, for that Mr. Burke was often merry and very well. It would not have been right for either of us to have contradicted Johnson at this time in a society all of whom did not know and value Mr. Burke as much as we did. It might have occasioned something more rough, and at any rate would probably have checked the flow of Johnson's good humour. He called to us with a sudden air of exultation, as the thought started into his mind, "O gentlemen! I must tell you a very extraordinary thing. The Empress of Russia has ordered *The Rambler* to be translated into the Russian language. So I shall be read on the banks of the Volga.[5] Horace boasts that he should be read on the banks of the [Rhone]. Now, the Volga is farther from me than the [Rhone][6] was from Horace." BOSWELL. "You must certainly be pleased with this, Sir." JOHNSON. "I am pleased, Sir, to be sure. A man is pleased to find he has succeeded in that which he has endeavoured to do."

On Sunday 16 May I found him alone. He talked of Mrs. Thrale, and seemed much concerned. I could not imagine what disturbed him, for I had heard nothing to her disadvantage. He said, "Sir, she has done everything wrong since Thrale's bridle was off her neck. You must know there was an Italian singer ——" Here Dr. Douglas . . . was announced, and Johnson was interrupted in explaining himself to me. . . . Dr. Douglas's conversation was always very agreeable to Dr. Johnson. . . .[7] [He] upon this occasion corrected a mistake which is very common in Scotland: that the ecclesiastical discipline of the Church of England if duly enforced is insufficient to preserve the morals of the clergy, and that all delinquents may be screened by appealing to the Convocation, which is never authorized by the King to sit for dispatch of business; for the Convocation is not a court of judicature but like a parliament, to make canons and regulations as the time may require.[8] Johnson, talking of the fear of death, said, "Some people are not afraid because they look upon salvation as the effect of an absolute decree, and think they feel in themselves the marks of sanctification. Others, and those the most rational, in my opinion, look upon salvation as

[5] The Empress was Catherine the Great; Boswell, before he sent his manuscript to the press, added a footnote saying that the report was unfounded. It has since been shown that a few *Ramblers* and a truncated version of *Rasselas* had appeared in Russian as far back as 1764 and 1766.
[6] Boswell sent the manuscript of the *Life of Johnson* to the press with blanks for both mentions of the Rhone, filling the blanks in the proofs.
[7] Boswell later struck out this and the two preceding sentences. We have deleted a few words of the first draft that assume a date later than 1784.
[8] See below, 19 May 1784, p. 215, n. 6.

conditional; and as they never can be sure that they have complied with the conditions, they are afraid." Dine Duke of Montrose's.

On Monday 17 May I dined with him at Mr. Dilly's, where were Colonel Vallancey, Rev. Dr. Gibbons, Capell Lofft,[1] who though a most zealous Whig has a mind so cultivated with learning and knowledge and so much in exercise in the various exertions of literature and withal so much liberality that Dr. Johnson's stupendous abilities, though they did not frighten him, could not but excite his admiration. We had also Mr. Braithwaite of the Post-Office, that very amiable and friendly man, whose modest and unassuming good sense has been the companion of most of the wits of the age. Johnson was very quiescent today. I too; perhaps I was indolent. I find nothing more of him in my notes but that when I mentioned that I had seen in the King's Library[2] sixty-three copies of my favourite Thomas à Kempis, amongst which it was in eight languages, Latin, German, French, Italian, Spanish, English, Arabic, Armenian, he said he thought it unnecessary to collect many editions of a book which were all the same in the text. He would have all the translations and all the editions which differed in substance. He approved of the famous collection of editions of Horace by Douglas, who is said to have had a whole closet filled with them;[3] and he said every man should try to collect one book in that manner and present it to a public library.

TUESDAY 18 MAY. PARLIAMENT.[4] Dine with Preston.

On Tuesday 18[5] May, I found him going into a hackney-coach at the entry to his court. I accompanied him to Dr. Heberden's door, where he was to dine. I told him that the mob had called out as the King passed, "No Fox! No Fox!" which I did not like. He said, "They were right, Sir." I said, I thought not, for it seemed to be making Mr.

---

[1] Dr. Thomas Gibbons, a Nonconformist minister, had written *Memoirs* of Isaac Watts which Johnson had quoted with approval. Dilly's firm published a good deal of dissenting divinity. Capell Lofft, barrister, miscellaneous writer and translator, had praised Boswell in a poem entitled *The Praises of Poetry*, 1775; he lived to be pilloried in Byron's *English Bards and Scotch Reviewers*.

[2] Presumably during this visit to London, but we know nothing more of the matter.

[3] Dr. James Douglas, obstetrician and bibliophile, physician to Queen Caroline. He owned 557 volumes of Horace, which after his death were purchased by the Chevalier d'Éon. D'Éon's library was sold in 1813 and Douglas's collection dispersed.

[4] The first session of the new Parliament. Boswell was probably in the House of Lords (there is among the Boswell Papers a letter from his old friend, Sir John Dick, Comptroller of Accounts in the War Office, to Robert Quarme, Yeoman Usher of the House of Lords, 18 May 1784, directing Quarme to admit Boswell, "as I shall be sorry if he meets with any difficulty"). But he speaks three sentences later in the entry as though he had also been outside to witness the King's arrival.

[5] MS. "17," and the incorrect date appeared in the first edition of the *Life of Johnson*.

Fox the King's competitor. There being no audience, so that there could be no triumph in a victory, he fairly agreed with me. I said it might do very well if explained thus: "Let us have no Fox!" understanding it as a prayer to His Majesty not to appoint such a Minister.

WEDNESDAY 19 MAY. Convocation.[6]

On Wednesday 19 May I sat a part of the evening with him alone.[7] I mentioned a fine thought of Dr. Young's, that the death of our friends might be a consolation against the fear of death to ourselves, because we might have more friends in the other world than in this.[8] He perhaps felt this as a reflection upon his direful apprehension as to death, and said with heat, "How did he know *where* his friends were, or whether they would be his friends in the other world? How many friendships have you known formed upon principles of virtue? Most friendships are formed by caprice or chance, mere confederacies in vice or leagues in folly."[9] We talked of our worthy friend, Mr. Langton. He said, "I know not who will go to heaven if Langton does not. Sir, I could almost say, 'Sit anima mea cum Langtono.' "[1] I mentioned a very eminent friend as a virtuous man. JOHNSON. "Yes, Sir. But ——— has not the evangelical virtue of Langton. ———, I am afraid, would not scruple to pick up a wench."[2] He again insisted on one of our friends having

[6]"Wednesday 19 [May]. . . . Both houses of Convocation met in St. Paul's Cathedral and heard a sermon preached in Latin by the Rev. Dr. [William] Barford. The Archbishop of Canterbury [Dr. John Moore] pronounced the benediction, after which the archbishops, bishops, doctors of laws, etc., went to the Chapter House, where they were soon waited upon by the Lower House of Convocation, and signified their election of the Rev. Dr. [Cyril] Jackson for their prolocutor" (*Gentleman's Magazine*, 1784, liv. 383). Convocation, the assembly of the clergy of the realm, was summoned whenever a new parliament was summoned. After the activities described above, both houses addressed the Crown and Convocation was prorogued. As Dr. Douglas had remarked three days before, no licence from the Crown to proceed to business had been issued to Convocation since 1717.

[7]Undated notes for this conversation (perhaps the only notes Boswell had) appear in a blank space of the letter of Sir John Dick's mentioned above, 18 May 1784, n. 4. They read as follows: "How many friendships are formed upon principles of virtue? Mostly chance or caprice. Confederacies in vice and leagues in folly.—Langton a wrong-headed, absurd animal.—Chocolade well. It has substance, it has sweetness. But no spirit."

[8]"N.B. Having more friends in the other world than in this is *my* thought" (note by Boswell on the verso of the preceding leaf of the manuscript). He accordingly changed the passage to read, "I observed that the death . . ."; "How can a man know. . . ."

[9]"See if this be not a line in Young" (note by Boswell in the margin). He later struck out this direction, with no change in the text.

[1]"May my' soul be with Langton." A note by Boswell in the margin, "See if none of this be anywhere else," was later struck out with no change in the text.

[2]The blanks are in the first draft of the manuscript of the *Life of Johnson*, and so far

a ridiculous character.[3] "Sir," said he, "as an instance how wrong-headed he is, when I was ill, I desired he would tell me in what he thought my life was faulty. He brought me a sheet of paper on which he had written down all the texts of Scripture recommending charity, as if I had been defective in charity. And when I questioned him, what did this amount to? Why, that I sometimes contradicted people in conversation. Now, what harm does it do any man to be contradicted?" BOSWELL. "I suppose he meant the *manner* of doing it: roughly—and harshly." JOHNSON. "And who is the worse for that?" BOSWELL. "It hurts people of weak nerves." JOHNSON. "I know no such weak-nerved people." Here, though I did not choose to irritate him by pressing the subject farther in opposition to him, I could not help hinting that his censure was ill-founded, and that a conscientious friend, when thus asked as a confessor to tell a sick man what appeared to him amiss in his conduct, could not in a more gentle way admonish him. The texts chosen were. . . .[4] Mr. Burke, to whom I stated this, thought somewhat differently from me, and said, "It is well if when a man comes to die he has nothing heavier upon his conscience than having been a little rough in conversation." Certain it is that Johnson was highly offended at the time when the texts were presented to him, calling out to his friend in a loud and angry tone, "What is your drift, Sir?" Sir Joshua Reynolds pleasantly observed that it was a scene from a comedy to see the penitent get into a violent passion and labour[5] his confessor.

I mentioned to him this evening that one of our friends was not pleased with me for calling his conversation *chocolade*, which used to be very consolatory to me in a forenoon after having been elevated with the champagne of more impetuous talkers. JOHNSON. "I think, Sir, you express it very well when you call it chocolade. It has substance, it has sweetness, but it has no spirit."[6]

---

as we know, Boswell never positively identified this "very eminent friend." As Birkbeck Hill said, "eminent friend" in the *Life of Johnson* generally means Burke.

[3] "Will it not be better to tell it of Langton and sink the attack in strong terms?" (Note by Boswell in the margin.) He followed this suggestion, specifying Langton and reducing "ridiculous character" and "wrong-headed" to "want of judgement." He had already "sunk" Johnson's "strong terms" considerably. See above, n. 7.

[4] Boswell left a space of four lines or so blank for the references, which at the time he did not have or could not find. In the revision he struck out everything after ". . . weak-nerved people" and gave the texts ("[which] are now before me") in a leisurely footnote. The references are Matthew 5: 5, Ephesians 4: 1, 2, Colossians 3: 14, I Corinthians 13: 4, 5.

[5] Still current in the eighteenth century in the sense "belabour." Boswell changed it to "belabour" in the manuscript.

[6] This was probably Langton too, but nothing in the notes mentioned above in the

THURSDAY 20 MAY. Macklin's benefit.[7] Burke younger and Pole; Dr. Johnson.[8]

FRIDAY 21 MAY. Dine Mr. Dundas.[9] Apology Lord Galloway for not going to Delegates.[1]

SATURDAY 22 MAY. Dine Chelsea College.[2]

SUNDAY 23 MAY. Dine Lord Falmouth.[3]

MONDAY 24 MAY. Breakfast Osborn.[4] Parliament.[5]

TUESDAY 25 MAY. Club.[6] Supped Lord Eglinton's.

WEDNESDAY 26 MAY. Dined Sir J. Dick.[7] Evening, hour Lord Mountstuart's.

THURSDAY 27 MAY. Dine Sir Joshua Reynolds. Supped George's with W. Bosville.[8]

Editorial Note, p. 210, or in the manuscript of the *Life of Johnson* confirms that identification. Boswell cancelled the entire passage in revision.

[7] At Covent Garden this evening, Charles Macklin, actor, said to be eighty-seven years old, played for his own benefit the role of Sir Pertinax MacSycophant in his own play, *The Man of the World.*

[8] Richard Burke and a Polish gentleman supped with Boswell at General Paoli's. Dr. Johnson may have been of the company, or Boswell may have called on him that evening. The *Life of Johnson* has no entry for 21 May, but Boswell makes clear that he saw Johnson more than once between 19 May and 30 May though he failed to note the conversations.

[9] Henry Dundas.

[1] Galloway had probably asked Boswell to be a delegate in the General Election for one of the Wigtown Burghs which he controlled, and Boswell had declined the appointment.

[2] See above, 29 May 1783, p. 154.

[3] Boswell had entertained Falmouth (then Ensign George Evelyn Boscawen) in Edinburgh in 1776, on the recommendation of Mrs. Thrale. This is the first mention of him since in the existing journal.

[4] John Osborn, brother of Sir George Osborn, Bt. Boswell met him in Marseilles in 1765 and had renewed the acquaintance in London in 1781.

[5] On this, the first business day of the new Parliament, the House plunged at once into sharp party debate on the Administration's conduct in the late Westminster election. Admiral Lord Hood (Administration candidate) headed the poll, and Fox had a small lead over the second Administration candidate, Sir Cecil Wray. Wray demanded a scrutiny, whereupon the High Sheriff (Thomas Cobbett) announced himself unable to make a return until the results of the scrutiny should be known. John Lee, Lord North, and Fox moved today that the High Bailiff should have returned Hood and Fox, leaving the question of a scrutiny to a committee of the House of Commons; and they openly maintained (what was certainly the case) that the Bailiff's action had been a ploy of the Administration to keep Fox out of Parliament, at least for some months. But Pitt and other leaders of Government spoke against the motion and got it disposed of by moving the previous question.

[6] The Literary Club. Members present: Banks, Boswell, Richard Burke, Colman, Fordyce, Hamilton, Johnson, Malone, and Shipley.

[7] Sir John Dick. See above, 18 May 1784, n. 4, and below, 8 May 1785, n. 6.

[8] Boswell's new "Chief," the eldest son of the late Godfrey Bosville. He had been a

FRIDAY 28 MAY. Morning Mr. Ward's.[9] Dine home.[1]

SATURDAY 29 MAY. Dine Chelsea College. General Hale observed strong memory Charles II. Then, glorious and immortal [memory]. "A jump," said I.[2] ADAM.[3] "Jump from winter to summer. Strange such a jump without a *spring*." SIR GEORGE HOWARD. "Pardon Stuarts' prerogative; had it from Tudors. But angry for bad use of it." BOSWELL. "Poor Stuarts, Bailiffs of Westminster."[4] Sir George Howard's Latin toast. "That clear," said somebody. "Ay," said I in lawyer-style. "We need not call *witnesses*." "But," said William Grenville, "*testes*."[5] I said a man should gradually supply old friends, as his cellar. General Hale drank health of man he had often read with pleasure. Now seen and much obliged for pleasant conversation.[6] Talking of some part of the finishing of one of Sir Lawrence Dundas's houses being gilt, Robert Adam said, "I gilt that pill."[7] "What connexion with a pill," said I,

---

lieutenant in the Coldstream Guards, but was now retired from the army and living the life of a *bon vivant* in London.

[9] William Ward, later third Viscount Dudley and Ward of Dudley, M.P. for Worcester. He was married to William Bosville's beautiful sister Julia.

[1] At Paoli's, now No. 1 Upper Seymour Street, Portman Square. Among four "Memorabilia Paoli" he had recorded the previous day is the pointed observation that "Mankind as individuals are cunning; as a multitude they are drunkards. Take care of them. If you are a pleasant bottle companion, they will not employ you as a lawyer; they will not trust you with their property. But they will give their voice to make you a minister of state."

[2] Lt.-Gen. Bernard Hale, Lt.-Governor of Chelsea Hospital, remarked that Charles II, the founder of the Hospital, had a powerful memory (one of the natural endowments for which Lord Halifax praised him). Following this "observation," the traditional Revolution toast to William III ("To the glorious and immortal memory") was proposed. Boswell remarked the "jump," that is, the discontinuity in the succession of ideas, but what is more important, the historically significant leap from Charles II to William III.

[3] Robert Adam, the architect.

[4] They got the blame for the political manoeuvres of others, like the Bailiff in the contested Westminster election. See above, 24 May 1784, n. 5.

[5] The youngest son of George Grenville (1712–1770), statesman, and himself later Baron Grenville and Prime Minister, he was at this time, in his twenty-fifth year, M.P. for Buckinghamshire, Paymaster General of the Forces, and chief secretary to his brother, Earl Temple, the Viceroy of Ireland. His off-colour jest (*testis* in Latin means both "witness" and "testicle") might seem less pointless if we had the text of Sir George Howard's toast. Grenville had won a prize for Latin verse at Oxford.

[6] He drank Boswell's health as the author of *An Account of Corsica*, now met for the first time.

[7] Adam had enlarged and renovated Dundas's house at Moor Park, Herts., between 1763 and 1766 at a cost of £9,077.5s.11¾d., which included £200 "to Norman for gilding" (Arthur T. Bolton, *The Architecture of Robert and James Adam*, 1922, ii. 346). Pills were literally wrapped in gold or silver leaf (a practice adopted from the mediaeval Arabs) well into the nineteenth century, not only because the metal rendered them

"unless *High German Doctor?*" They applauded. I could not find the meaning. "No matter," said Young Burke. "Say it and people will see the meaning."

SUNDAY 30 MAY. General Oglethorpe, chocolade.[1] I said, "People now *hot*. Let Pitt *strike* 'em. He may mould 'em as he pleases." He would not agree. Portuguese Chapel. Then in Pall Mall met Ulbster and Lord Balgonie. Visited Sir Robert Herries.[2] "Trade like economy. Not saving, so not venturing, but proper combining of chances."[3] Then Burke, more than an hour. Much pleasantry.

I mentioned Wilberforce catching Lord Fitzwilliam. "Don't talk to me of them. Villains, etc. We shall beat Bill. What! Are men to be governed by laws, by pieces of paper, when villains are in power?" Quite wild.[4]

Burke said House of Commons as good as it could be. "Men drawn out of bags, as samples. Very good way to take 'em professionally. There would be the same lawyers, the same soldiers as now. Charters; say chatter.

"Wilkes has played his cards as well as any man. First people, then King. First got the fruit of the underwood, then royal oak itself." I said, "First the brambles." "Hops and haws," said Burke. "But what of oak?" said I. "Why acorns for such a distiller's swine?"[5]

---

tasteless but also because of the medicinal properties it was thought to possess. Adam's pun may allude both to the extraordinary charges the gilding made palatable and to the benefits it conferred on an old and unattractive house, which was built originally by Cardinal Wolsey and recased and largely rebuilt earlier in the eighteenth century.

[1] The General breakfasted with Boswell at Paoli's.

[2] A banker in a London house that bore his name. He was knighted in 1774.

[3] "Trade is more like the orderly management of the resources of a community or an estate than it is like saving, which implies complete avoidance of risks. It is the proper combining of chances."

[4] William Wilberforce, a close friend and ally of Pitt, had surprised Lord Fitzwilliam, Burke's patron since the death of Rockingham, by forcing him to withdraw his candidates for Yorkshire at the General Election the previous month. Boswell's remark provoked Burke, as he knew it would, into a wild denunciation of Pitt's supporters and his forthcoming East India Bill. Burke's emotional instability had been the subject of discussion since at least the previous year (see entry above, p. 153); that apart, he was outraged by his party's débâcle nationwide. One hundred and sixty Members of Parliament ("Fox's Martyrs") had failed to be returned to their seats largely on the issue of the Fox-Burke East India Bill.

[5] Wilkes's father, Israel Wilkes, was a prosperous malt-distiller. Burke makes this the ground for a second tier of puns: "hops and haws" instead of the expected "hips and haws" (fruits of the wild rose and hawthorn berries), and Boswell continues the play with "distiller's swine." Swine-culture was a subsidiary activity of malt-distillers: they fed the exhausted wash to swine kept on the premises, and likewise fattened the pigs which country farmers drove into London and other cities. The practice led to lucrative

Dine brother's. Hoole's.[6] Placid.[7] SIR JAMES JOHNSTONE.[8] "Arguments when fee'd." I. "All courts."[9] DR. JOHNSON. "Testimony and argument. Boyle[1] fine thought. Strength of hand."

I have preserved no more of his conversation at the times when I saw him during the next of this month till Sunday the 30th, when I met him in the evening at Mr. Hoole's, where there was a large company both of ladies and gentlemen. Sir James Johnstone happened to say that he paid no regard to the arguments of counsel at the bar of the House of Commons, because they were paid for speaking. JOHNSON. "Nay, Sir, argument is argument. You cannot help paying regard to their arguments if they are good. If it were testimony, you may disregard it if you know that it is purchased. There is a beautiful image in Bacon upon this subject: testimony is an arrow shot from a long-bow; the force of it depends on the strength of the hand that draws it. Argument is an arrow from a cross-bow, which has equal force though shot by a child."

He had now a great desire to go to Oxford as his first jaunt after his illness. We had talked of it for some days, and I had promised to accompany him. He was impatient and fretful tonight because I did not at once agree to go with him on Thursday. When I considered how ill he had been, and what allowance should be made for the influence of sickness upon his temper, I resolved to indulge him, however inconvenient it might be. I had omitted to attend the first days of the Commemoration of Handel in Westminster Abbey. The third and last was to be on the following Saturday, and it was then believed that there would [not] be again an opportunity of hearing that very magnificent

---

victualling contracts for the Navy. Wilkes's political position was now correct from the King's point of view, but we do not know what "acorns" he received from the Crown at this period. His most recent substantial place, the City Chamberlainship (1779), did not come from the Crown.

[6] Apparently a change of plans, for the engagement list for this day reads, "Dine brother's. Evening Richmond Lodge." We print in full Boswell's journal-note of the evening at Hoole's, following it with the entry for 30 May from the first draft of the manuscript of the *Life of Johnson*. This arrangement enables the reader to see how few hints Boswell needed for recovering a Johnsonian conversation.

[7] Presumably, "Dr. Johnson was placid."

[8] M.P. for the Dumfries Burghs.

[9] Boswell dropped out his own share in this conversation when he wrote it up for the *Life of Johnson*. He presumably said something like, "In all courts counsel are fee'd for speaking. Would you pay no regard to them anywhere?"

[1] This name (the Hon. Robert Boyle, 1627–1691, natural philosopher and chemist, author of "Boyle's Law") is cramped and blotted in the manuscript. When Boswell wrote the draft of the *Life of Johnson*, he misread it as "Bacon," and as "Bacon" it appeared in the first three editions of the *Life*.

musical performance in which upwards of ———[2] exerted their talents. I thought it hard to lose this, but I was willing to make the sacrifice for the quiet and complacency of Johnson. However, Sir Joshua Reynolds, who then thought that I certainly should not lose it, suggested an expedient, which was that I should go with Johnson to Oxford on Thursday, and having seen him safe there, return to town on Friday, be at the Commemoration on Saturday, and go again to him afterwards. This, Sir Joshua thought he could not take amiss, but must rather consider it as paying him a great compliment to go to Oxford purposely to attend him.

MONDAY 31 MAY. Rochester.[3]

TUESDAY 1 JUNE. Chatham.

WEDNESDAY 2 JUNE. *London Magazine* dinner.[4] Walked with brother. Woodfall's. Dempster's.

THURSDAY 3 JUNE. Had passed a restless, but not uneasy night. Was full of fondness of M. M.

[EDITORIAL NOTE. He had probably received one or both of the letters below, which are not entered in the very faulty Register of Letters for this period.]

[Margaret Boswell to Boswell]

Auchinleck, 26 May 1784

A THOUSAND THANKS TO YOU, my dearest Mr. Boswell, for all your letters, which are great comforts to me, and what I stand much in need of. You will have received intelligence by this time of your brother's arrival.[5] He is really the most disagreeable companion I ever lived with. He has not one grain of compliance in his disposition. He will not accommodate himself to any one domestic rule. At dinner he never

---

[2] Left blank in the manuscript. There were 525 performers. Boswell cancelled nearly a page of his draft here, no doubt thinking he was talking too much about himself.

[3] A trip to visit Bennet Langton and his family. Boswell's admittedly sparse records record no meeting with Langton in London this spring.

[4] A business dinner with the other partners of the *London Magazine*.

[5] Boswell had instructed John to go from Moffat to Auchinleck. On 24 May 1784 James Bruce, Boswell's overseer, wrote to him, "Your brother came here by the Ayr diligence Friday last. He looks ill, but seems sensible, making inquiry about everything. Observes much alteration in the Place, plantings, etc. But is still in that dull, stum [silent, dumb] way. I wish you had been here to introduce him, as your lady's brisk way will, I am afraid, not suit him. And she's anxious to please his taste if it was known. He takes no notice of Miss Young or Mr. Millar. Your lady and children only he speaks to. The misses is vastly fond about him."

arrives till after we are all obliged to sit down and begin, and then his sullen pride is shocked that he is not waited for, as if he was something above the common. At tea, supper, and at breakfast, all the same. Last night he would not come to prayers, and the day before would not kneel, and little Jamie said, "Mama, that man stood all the time of big prayers as if it had been the little ones" (meaning the grace). I trust in God you will give him no encouragement to pitch his tent here, otherwise adieu to every comfort! Mr. Millar and Miss Young are quite confounded, and I cannot help being ashamed.

In my last, I wrote you about Sandy; he still continues better, and I would gladly flatter myself, with care and attention, accompanied with God's blessing, he may soon get quite well. I have had him out in the chaise for some days past every day and he does not complain. Your brother rides your horse, I may say, all day, and mounts and dismounts perhaps ten times in a mile. I see him now moving in a slow, solemn manner up the avenue.

In your letter on a certain subject you desire me not to oppose you. I never had any desire to do it. I only wish you to be perfectly settled in your own mind and convinced of the propriety of quitting your country and profession, for in that case England or anywhere is equally the same to me, so put me quite out of the question; and if *you* resolve, I am already prepared in my heart to follow you or accompany you, where I have not to sail.[6] But my weak lungs and seasickness forbid that method of transporting myself.

I am sorry for poor Davie.[7] I shall write him soon. I shall be anxious till I hear how you and Mr. Pitt behaved to each other.[8] I think you

[6] Mrs. Boswell is repeating the pledge, echoing Ruth, that she made in accepting Boswell's proposal of marriage fifteen years before: "My heart determines my choice. May the Almighty grant His blessing and protection, and we need not be afraid; His provision extends over all the earth, so that wherever you go, I shall willingly accompany you and hope to be happy."

[7] At the turn of the year T. D. had submitted to propriety and the pressure of the lady's friends and reluctantly married Miss Anne Catherine Green, whom he had known about a year. As he had foreseen, the marriage suffered financial strain, for his last years in Spain were unprofitable, he had little business in London, and his wife brought with her only a meagre provision. Henry Dundas's promise to Lord Auchinleck that he would get his youngest son a place was not fulfilled until 1791, when T. D. was appointed a clerk in the Navy Pay Office. He prospered thereafter, but his wife was mentally ill at least in the later years. There were two children.

[8] Boswell had evidently informed his wife that he had arranged a meeting with the Prime Minister on the strength of their correspondence over the *Letter to the People of Scotland* (see above, 9 February 1784, n. 1). A letter to Pitt written a year later, 25 May 1785, indicates that Boswell sought a conference with him then. No answer has been recovered. One would expect that if either meeting had taken place some mention of so impressive an event would occur even in the scanty records that survive for these

should tell Mr. Dundas your plan of practice at the English bar. I have not yet gone to see Lady Crawford. I could not think of leaving Sandy.

I hear nothing new to write you. I am amazed you do not get my letters, for I have wrote you frequently since you left us. We had Mr. Auld one day at dinner, and Mr. Bruce Campbell was here yesterday. He was very friendly; he came upon hearing there was a roup of wood, but it was only a small parcel. Adieu. The children offer you their duty and long for your return. They have cleaned out the bell-house in order to keep the King's birthday,[9] and they propose dressing it all up with flowers and spending the day in the most loyal manner. You can imagine the two girls laid themselves up yesterday with downright hard labour to get all things prepared for this joyful occasion. It never struck them to do this before; it looks as if it was a disease over the land, and young and old infected by it.

I have wrote to your brother[1] and send it for your perusal. If you approve of it, pray seal it and deliver it to him. Write me whether you are to come here or go straight to Edinburgh. Your brother[2] says you tell him you are to be down the 12th of June. He conversed a little this evening. As he did not come to tea till an hour after the rest had done so, he and I had a tête-à-tête.

I must now conclude with assuring you how sincerely I am your ever faithful and affectionate

M. B.

Respectful compliments to General Paoli, and kind love to worthy Sir Charles Preston when you see him. I wish Captain Robert would come down and take a fancy to Lady M. Lindsay and she for him.[3]

Auchinleck, 29 May 1784

I AM SORRY I MENTIONED your brother's sullen manner, lest it should vex you or cause you write to him, which would make him worse. I therefore entreat you will take no notice of it to him and let him just do as he pleases till you return, and when present, you may by some gentle method try to bring him right.

---

periods. Boswell later complained bitterly about Pitt's disregard of his political services to the King and his party.

[9] Celebrated 4 June 1784 (see below, p. 228, n. 5). There is now no bell on Auchinleck House or its offices, but there may have been in the eighteenth century. It was housed, perhaps, in one of the four pavilions, each topped by a lantern, which are attached to the mansion by sweeping brick walls.

[1] David.

[2] John.

[3] The matchmaking dreams were disappointed. Lady Mary Lindsay, who became a somewhat eccentric recluse, died unmarried in 1833.

I went to Lady Crawford's yesterday and found her Ladyship quite well and Lady Mary vastly better and looking charmingly. She told me she had a vast inclination to write you (as Lord and Lady Dalhousie, attended by Baron Stewart, were gone to Earl David's) that there were Lords in this house.[4] I wish you would write to either Lady Crawford or her and give them any little agreeable intelligence you can pick up to amuse them in their rural abode. They go to the sea-bathing beginning of next week. They have a sad story about Lord Pembroke in this country, and find it comes from the Mures: that he set off with an opera-girl and left poor Lady Pembroke and his dying daughter, the most amiable, beautiful girl that ever was seen. I cannot think it is possible, otherwise I should look upon him as the greatest monster of inhumanity that is in existence.[5] If it is true, I hope you will have no connexion with him, as I really think he is a disgrace to human nature who is void of the feelings of affection and humanity.

Your brother did not dine with the family yesterday nor sup, as I was not at home. He cannot bear the *teachers* of either sex. Indeed I was a good deal disgusted myself to find upon my return that the children had not got one single lesson of any one branch of education, but the *two* had spent their day in amusing each other. You may believe I was not silent nor not very sweet upon this occasion. It showed me how little confidence I had to place in a certain person's attention when under a necessity of trusting to her.[6] Indeed I believe they are upon the whole not doing much to the purpose. Veronica is falling off miserably in her singing; Sandy is still continuing pretty easy.

You will see that patronage has prevailed.[7] I am really vexed about John Boswell's affair. I advised him to say nothing of his having got

[4] Lady Mary was apparently making jocose reference to the fact that her brother, George Lindsay-Crawford, the twenty-second Earl of Crawford, was absent in London, like Boswell. "Earl David" was the Earl of Cassillis.

[5] The scandal seems to have been true. Horace Walpole, identifying Lady Charlotte Herbert, wrote on one of his letters, "Only daughter of Henry, Earl of Pembroke; her father and mother had carried her to Nice for a consumption, of which she died [at Aix-en-Provence, 21 April]—but the Earl had fallen in love with an Italian female dancer or singer, and was gone with her to Florence" (*Correspondence*, ed. W. S. Lewis, xxv. 497 n. 5). On 24 June 1784 Boswell wrote to the Countess of Crawford, "Alleviation of Lord Pembroke's late amour" (Register of Letters).

[6] Miss Young.

[7] On 25 May 1784 the General Assembly rejected an overture (formal proposal) of the synod of Glasgow and Ayr praying that the Assembly apply to Parliament to revive the Act of 1690, which established Presbyterianism, abolished patronage, and transferred the right of presentation to heritors and elders. That settlement had been undermined by the oath of allegiance and abjuration tacked on to the Toleration Act of 1712. A motion to continue the law of patronage as it stood was passed on 26 May, thus underscoring the continued control of the "Moderates" in the General Assembly.

it, but I find he and Old Knockroon have blazed it about everywhere. I cannot think the commission can ever be of any use to him, as it has been procured upon a false information of the present incumbent's death.[8] Write Lady C. when you see Lord Crawford, and pray let us know how Lord Eglinton does.[9] I thank you most sincerely for all letters; they are my comfort in my solitude. Your children are all pretty well and offer you their kind love. Remember me where it will be acceptable. Adieu, and believe me, with sincerest affection, my dearest Mr. Boswell, your ever faithful

M. BOSWELL.

Hastened to Dr. Johnson's, as I was to accompany him to Oxford—his first jaunt after his severe illness which confined him so long. I found him calmly philosophical. I told him that Sir James Lowther's introduction into the House of Lords had made my mouth water;[1] and I expatiated warmly on the dignity of a British peerage. He bid me consider the transient nature of all human honours. I said that would produce indifference. "But," said he, "if you allow your mind to be too much heated with desire for a British peerage, you will wish to obtain it 'per fas aut nefas.' "[2]

We talked of Langton's inefficiency. He repeated from Dryden some lines which I shall find: How the bold impious get. The conscientious wait till the prize is gone.[3] He said Langton taught his son himself to save money. He would send him to Parr if he could do it

[8] At Boswell's request, Henry Dundas had obtained the office of clerk to the Justices of Peace for the shire of Ayr for Knockroon on Knockroon's report that the incumbent had died. It soon appeared, however, that the late incumbent had been succeeded by his son, probably through the terms of the father's commission. Knockroon, in reporting a vacancy, had given the deceased his son's name. Mrs. Boswell seems to have thought this misstatement of the facts deliberate.

[9] Lady Crawford had been Eglinton's mother-in-law. See above, 10 September 1783, n. 8.

[1] It had taken place the day previous, Wednesday 2 June, scarcely the event one would expect Boswell to omit from his list of activities. We know that he was present from his letter of 8 July 1784 to his friend Temple (see below). Lowther was rewarded with what G. E. Cokayne calls a shower of peerages (Baron Lowther, Baron of the Barony of Kendal, Baron of the Barony of Burgh, Viscount of Lonsdale, Viscount of Lowther, Earl of Lonsdale) for having given Pitt his first seat in Parliament.

[2] "Right or wrong" (Livy, VI. xiv. 10).

[3] *Aureng-Zebe*, II. 508–513, Aureng-Zebe to the Emperor:

> The world is made for the bold impious man;
> Who stops at nothing, seizes all he can.
> Justice to merit does weak aid afford;
> She trusts her balance, and neglects her sword.
> Virtue is nice to take what's not her own;
> And, while she long consults, the prize is gone.

for nothing. I spoke of Langton's uncle, whom I had seen at Rochester.[4] The Doctor said he was a good man. All the three brothers were good men. Virtuous men and virtuous the same way; they wore the same livery, the same colour of virtue. He then made a striking remark: "Virtue almost never produces friendship. Good men and bad are not enemies. They are not embittered by contest. The thing is not disputed between them. Enmity takes place between men who are good different ways." There is a depth and justness of observation in this remark.[5]

Mrs. Desmoulins made tea to us. The Oxford post-coach stopped at Bolt Court to take us up. Frank had gone off early in the heavy coach. The other two passengers were a widow, Mrs. Beresford, and Miss Beresford, her daughter, the first a very sensible, polite lady, the second a genteel, pleasing young creature.[6] As we passed through Leicester Square I pointed to Sir Joshua Reynolds's house and said, "There lives our friend."[7] "Ay, Sir," said the Doctor, "there lives a very great man." I am sorry I do not recollect the particulars of the Doctor's conversation. But it was so striking that Mrs. Beresford asked me in a whisper if this was the celebrated Doctor Johnson. She had read his *name* at the coach-office. I told her it was. Miss Beresford said to me, "Every sentence he speaks is an essay." I was delighted to observe the immediate effect of his wonderful genius.[8] She amused herself in the coach with knotting. He would not allow it any merit. "Next to mere idleness," said he, "I think knotting is to be reckoned in the scale of insignificance; though I once attempted to learn knotting. Dempster's sister"[9] (looking to me) "attempted to teach me it, but I made no progress."

At the inn[1] where we dined he was exceedingly dissatisfied with some roast mutton which we had for dinner. The ladies, I saw, wondered to see the great philosopher whose wisdom and wit they had been admiring all the way get into a downright passion for such a cause. He

[4]Samuel Langton. His other uncle, Peregrine, was dead.
[5]Boswell omitted it and all the preceding conversation from the *Life of Johnson*, probably so that he could pick up the Oxford theme and carry the narrative forward swiftly.
[6]Mrs. Beresford and her daughter were Americans, as Boswell reported in the *Life of Johnson*, and Mr. Beresford, who owned extensive estates in England, was a member of the Continental Congress. ("Widow" was a mistake; Richard Beresford lived to 1803.)
[7]At No. 47, on the west side, where he lived until his death.
[8]The leaf of journal ends here. We continue with the first draft of the manuscript of the *Life of Johnson*.
[9]Jean, who kept house for Dempster in his earlier years in London.
[1]Boswell left a blank here in the first draft, apparently intending to fill it with the name of the stage when he remembered it. In the revision he settled for "the inn."

scolded the waiter, saying, "It is as bad as bad can be. It is ill-fed, ill-killed, and ill-dressed."

He stood the journey very well, and seemed to feel himself elevated as he approached Oxford, that venerable seat of learning, orthodoxy, and Toryism. Frank came in the heavy coach in readiness to attend him, and we were received with the most polite hospitality at the house of Dr. Adams, Master of Pembroke College, who had given us a kind invitation. Before we were set down, I communicated to Johnson my having engaged to return to London for the reason I have mentioned, but that I would hasten down to him again. Sir Joshua Reynolds had guessed right, for he was much pleased that I had made this journey merely to keep him company. He was easy and placid at Dr. Adams's with his excellent old friend, Mrs. and Miss Adams, and Mrs. Kennicott, widow of the learned Hebrean, who was here on a visit. He soon dispatched the inquiries which were made about his illness and recovery by a short narrative, and then assuming a gay air and repeating from Swift,

> Nor think on our approaching ills
> Nor talk of spectacles and pills. [2]

Bishop Newton having been mentioned, Johnson, recollecting what is said of him in that prelate's memoirs of his own life, thus made his retort: "Tom knew he should be dead before what he said of me should be printed. He durst not have printed it while he was alive." [3] DR. ADAMS. "I believe his *Dissertation on the Prophecies* is his great work." JOHNSON. "Why, Sir, it was Tom's great work, but how far it is great or how much of it was Tom's is another question. I fancy a considerable part of it was borrowed." DR. ADAMS. "He was a very successful man." JOHNSON. "I don't think so, Sir. Tom did not get high. He was late of getting what he did get, and he did not get it by the best means. I believe he was a mighty gross flatterer."

I set off for London in the night, so as to be at Court next day, being the King's birthday. . . . [4]

[2] *Stella's Birthday, 1726–1727*, ll. 5–6. Boswell's note surprisingly reads "spectres and pills."

[3] Thomas Newton, Bishop of Bristol and Dean of St. Paul's, some five years older than Johnson, was, like Johnson, a native of Lichfield. In his posthumous *Account of His Own Life*, 1782, he had accused Johnson of displaying malevolence, spleen, and ill humour in his *Lives of the Poets*.

[4] For the remainder of this sentence, see below, Editorial Note.

FRIDAY 4 JUNE. Up all night. Returned London. Levee. Drawing-room.[5] Dined Sir George [Osborn].[6]

SATURDAY 5 JUNE. Breakfast Sir Joshua. *Messiah*.

[EDITORIAL NOTE. The last sentence of Boswell's first draft of the manuscript of the *Life of Johnson* for 3 June 1784 (see above) ended ". . . and being fully rewarded for my trouble by hearing *The Messiah* in Westminster Abbey, the impression of which was such that I resolved I never would go again lest it should be effaced." Yet the one leaf of notes that he left (or at least that we possess) for 5 June says little of music and consists entirely of lively remarks of his own made as he was waiting for the music to begin. For a more informative account of the event we turn to the diary of another member of his party, Miss Mary Hamilton, granddaughter of Lord Archibald Hamilton (he was a younger son of the third Duke of Hamilton) and niece of Sir William Hamilton, Minister Plenipotentiary to the Court of Naples. She and Boswell had family connexions and many friends in common (Sir William Hamilton was a member of The Club, and Boswell had known him since 1765), but on her own testimony they first met on this day. A young lady of twenty-eight, she had served for five years as assistant sub-governess in the royal nursery (the Prince of Wales at the age of sixteen had made her the object of a violent infatuation), was a correspondent of Horace Walpole, and was on terms of intimacy with Mrs. Garrick, Mrs. Vesey, Elizabeth Carter, Hannah More, Fanny Burney, Mrs. Delaney, Mrs. Montagu, Mrs. Boscawen, and others. She wrote: "June 5 was the day of the Handel Celebration and performance of *The Messiah* at the Abbey. Got up at six. At a quarter before nine Dr. Burney and Miss Palmer came for me in Dr. Burney's coach. Sir Joshua Reynolds and Mr. Boswell followed in Sir Joshua's chariot. . . .[7] We got in without any difficulty. The lower part was already filled with people, but Dr. Burney got us the proper seats for hearing the music. Sir Joshua introduced me to Mr. Boswell (the Mr. Boswell who wrote the

[5] "Being His Majesty's birthday, the same was observed at Court with uncommon magnificence. The King was dressed in plain uncut velvet, but the Queen was exceedingly brilliant and appeared in high spirits. The whole Court seemed to outdo each other in magnificence and dress. And in the City there was the most splendid display of illuminations and other demonstrations of loyalty that has been known for many years" (*Gentleman's Magazine*, June 1784, liv. 472).
[6] Reading not certain. The name is cramped into the edge of the paper, and there appears to have been some over-writing.
[7] This omission and the next were made by the editors of Miss Hamilton's diary in publishing it. We know nothing about the nature of the omitted passages, but assume that the editors considered them trivial.

HENRY HOME, LORD KAMES (1696–1782), colleague of Boswell's father on the bench in the Courts of Session and of Justiciary, friend and mentor of Boswell himself. This portrait, painted by David Martin in 1794, twelve years after Kames's death, shows him in the scarlet robe of a Lord of Justiciary. It now hangs in the Scottish National Portrait Gallery, Edinburgh.

HENRY DUNDAS, FIRST VISCOUNT MELVILLE (1742–1811), member of a famous legal family and classmate of Boswell's at the University of Edinburgh. He entered Parliament in 1771 and became the most powerful of Scottish political managers. The portrait, by John Rising, is in the Scottish National Portrait Gallery, on loan from His Grace the Duke of Buccleuch and Queensberry, K. T.

THE WRECK OF THE *Centaur*. Engraving by Thomas Gaugain, 1784, after a painting by James Northcote. It shows Captain John Inglefield and eleven members of his crew escaping from the *Centaur*, which foundered in a hurricane off the coast of Newfoundland in September 1782.

SAMUEL JOHNSON, LL.D. (1709–1784). This portrait, painted some time between 1782 and 1784, is the last of the five known portraits that Reynolds painted of Johnson over the years. It was painted for his old friend, Dr. Taylor of Ashbourne, and is now hanging in the Quaker Collection at Haverford College, Pennsylvania.

ANNA SEWARD (1742–1809), poet, "The Swan of Lichfield," and friend of Southey and Scott. The portrait, by Romney, was begun in 1782 and finished in 1788, when she presented it to her father. Boswell flirted with her on his visits to Lichfield; a lock of her auburn hair is among his Papers at Yale.

JOHN LEE (?1733–1793), lawyer and politician, self-declared "enemy to the influence of the Crown." Coarse and abusive in manner, he was nevertheless respected for his honesty and integrity both in Parliament and at the bar. Boswell, though he differed with him on most issues, knew "few men I would go farther to serve than Jack Lee." The portrait, by Reynolds, was painted in 1786.

EDMOND MALONE (1741–1812), editor of Shakespeare and book collector. He was of invaluable help to Boswell in bringing out the *Tour to the Hebrides* in 1785 and the *Life of Johnson* in 1791. The portrait, by Reynolds, was painted in 1778.

V. Lunardi Esq.ʳ Mᵐ Sage G. Biggin Esq.ʳ

THE AERIAL TRAVELLERS. Engraving by F. Bartolozzi, 1785, after a painting by J. F. Rigaud. Vincenzo Lunardi, the leading aeronaut of the day, is shown (waving his hat) with his companions Mrs. Sage and Mr. Biggin. The ballooning craze was at its height in Britain in 1784 and 1785.

JAMES BOSWELL (1740–1795). Boswell asked Reynolds to paint his portrait in June 1785, in anticipation of his being called to the English bar the following year. He promised to pay him out of his first fees as a barrister, but the debt was still unpaid in 1791, when the *Life of Johnson* was published. It was dedicated to Reynolds, who shortly afterwards made Boswell a present not only of this portrait but also of the portrait of Johnson that was reproduced as frontispiece to the *Life*.

history of Corsica). From nine to twelve passed away very agreeably in conversation with Miss Palmer and these three sensible men and in remarking the countenances of the company. . . . Mr. Boswell is one of those people with whom one instantly feels acquainted. We conversed together with as much ease and pleasantry as if we had been intimate a long time. . . . I was so delighted that I thought myself in the heavenly regions; 513 performers, the harmony so unbroken that it was like the fall of waters from one source, imperceptibly blended. The spectacle too was sublime. So universal a silence. So great a number of people. . . . It was over at four o'clock" (*Mary Hamilton . . . at Court and at Home*, ed. Elizabeth and Florence Anson, 1925, pp. 190–191).]

SATURDAY 5 JUNE. In Westminster Abbey I said I was perpetually falling in love, though I was as fond of my wife as any man.[8] She could not complain. I was always willing to prefer her when she was fond of me; and when she was indifferent, it was better I should be fond of others than allow my fondness to grow cold and perhaps irrecoverable. The fire might become quite dead. If I had a good cook and often had no dinners at home, I should not wish him to be idle and lose his talent by want of use. No, let him go to my lord Duke, the Earl, and as many employers as he could find. I should like very well to hear him say, "I had the honour to give very great satisfaction to his Grace or to his Lordship." But he must give me the preference. He must say, "I would serve your honour rather than any man in the world, whenever you have occasion for me."

I told how harshly Dr. Johnson had treated Langton for delicately telling him his fault. Yet the Doctor said to me he sent for him as his *confessor* and his confidant.[9] Sir Joshua said it was a scene for the stage— begging a friend fairly to tell one's faults, and then to be violent against him. I said, "Strange usage for a penitent to a confessor." Said Sir Joshua, "To give him a blue eye." Said I, "You have *clenched* it" (alluding to boxing). I said, "Dr. Johnson's harsh attacks on his friends arise from uneasiness within. There is an insurrection aboard. His loud explosions are guns of distress."

I mentioned Dr. Douglas at the Bishop of Chester's saying, "*One* other glass, if your Lordship pleases," with his sly glistening look. Said Sir Joshua, "Squinting, with one eye fixed on the bottle, one on the Bishop." Said I to Miss Hamilton, "Sir Joshua completes a saying. He

[8]The remark was no doubt prefaced by an extravagant assurance to the company that he had fallen in love with Miss Hamilton.
[9]See above, 19 May 1784.

is like a jeweller. You bring him a diamond. He cuts it, and makes it much more brilliant. Look at it now."

I said to Dr. Arnold the figures in the glass window looked like come down to join chorus—to meet half-way.[1] He repeated from Dryden, "He raised a mortal," etc.[2]

SUNDAY 6 JUNE. Petersham Church. Bassoon and flute. Good sermon on Trinity.[3]

[EDITORIAL NOTE. Boswell wrote to Dr. Adams from London on Monday 7 June saying that he had postponed his return to Oxford because John Osborn, formerly British Minister at Dresden, had arranged a dinner for Tuesday 8 June and had invited Gen. Robert Boyd, General Paoli, and others "*to meet me. I could not with propriety or indeed in gratitude refuse to accept of an invitation so polite. I trust you will satisfy your pupil that I have done right, though I shall be two days more absent from college than I might have been.*"[4] After 5 June 1784 there survive only two brief and disjointed scraps of anything like journal actually written during this London jaunt. It is probable that we have lost another leaf on which Boswell listed his engagements to the end of the month, afterwards adding a few very brief journal notes under some of the dates, but there is no compelling evidence that anything else is missing. Boswell wrote up for the *Life of Johnson* dated conversations for 9–16, 22–25, 27–30 June, but it is our impression that the "notes" and "memorandums" he occasionally mentions need have been no more extensive than those in the leaf of engagements which we have for 11 May–6 June. Since these are the last conversations

[1]Samuel Arnold, Mus.D., was one of the assistant-directors of the Commemoration. He had charge of one side of the chorus. The performers were tiered up against the great west window.

[2]*Alexander's Feast*, ll. 169–170:

> He [Timotheus] raised a mortal to the skies;
> She [St. Cecilia] drew an angel down.

[3]A puzzling entry. It probably means that Boswell has made a week-end visit to the Stuarts at Richmond Lodge and that on Sunday 6 June (Trinity Sunday in 1784) he attended divine service in the nearby church of Petersham. It seems strange, however, that he should have recorded the church but not the name of his hosts. The combination of bassoon and flute may have struck him as odd (or interesting) enough to deserve a note.

[4]Among some notes otherwise recording bits of conversation at Oxford, 11–[13] June 1784, Boswell has noted a remark perhaps made at this dinner of Osborn's: "When I laughed at a poor joke of my own, General Paoli said I was like the Corybantes making a noise to hide the infant Jupiter." The Corybantes (modern authorities prefer the Curetes) danced around the new-born Zeus and drowned his cries by clashing their weapons against their shields, thus saving him from being devoured by his father, Kronos.

Boswell ever had with Johnson, we follow with the entire series as they
appear in the first version of the manuscript of the *Life of Johnson*.
Passages that have been omitted because they clearly have the ring of
1788 are indicated by ellipses. It is a great pity that Boswell did not
make out of this visit with Johnson to Dr. Adams at Oxford, 3, 9–16
June 1784, a full and spirited journal in the style of the Ashbourne
journal (he and Johnson at Dr. Taylor's in Ashbourne), 10–27 September 1777.]

I was to have been at Oxford again in one day, but was detained
till Wednesday [9 June], when I was happy to find myself again in the
same circle at Pembroke College, with the comfortable prospect of
making some stay. Johnson welcomed my return with more than ordinary glee: "How d'ye do, my friend?" Such slight touches, which
render a picture vivid, shall never be omitted by me, let cold and dry
critics cavil as they will.

He talked with great regard of the Hon. Archibald Campbell, whose
character he had given at the Duke of Argyll's table when we were at
Inveraray,[5] but he added, "I never knew a nonjuror who could
reason.". . .

On Thursday 10 June, while we were at breakfast, the 37 volume
of the *Gentleman's Magazine* was brought, that he might look at the
"Apotheosis of Milton," which had been ascribed to him. He declared
it was not his. He believed it to be Guthrie's. In the volume he pointed
out the following passage from Savage's *Wanderer*, saying, "These are
fine verses. If," said he, "I had written with hostility of Warburton in
my Shakespeare, I should have quoted these lines:

> Here Learning, blinded first and then beguiled,
> Looks dark as Ignorance, as Fancy wild.[6]

You see they'd have fitted him to a T" (smiling). DR. ADAMS. "But you
did not write against Warburton." JOHNSON. "No, Sir. I treated him
with great respect, both in my Preface and in my notes." DR. ADAMS.
"I remember I carried a message to you from him. He said he knew

---

[5] Journal, 25 October 1773.
[6] Instead of "the 37th volume of the *Gentleman's Magazine*," Boswell should have
written "the volume of the *Gentleman's Magazine* for 1737," and even then he would
have been only partially accurate. "The Apotheosis of Milton," a prose vision, was
printed serially in the *Gentleman's Magazine* for 1738 and 1739 where it breaks off
unconcluded, but an excerpt from Savage's *Wanderer* containing the couplet which
Johnson signalized (ii. 169–70) did appear in the volume of the *Gentleman's Magazine*
for 1737 (vii. 310). Boswell probably trusted to his memory for the couplet, for he has
one word wrong: "Fancy" should be "Frenzy."

nobody who was acquainted with you but myself and Hawkins Browne;[7] and he begged I would tell you that he honoured you much for your letter to Lord Chesterfield, which was written with a proper spirit."

Mrs. Kennicott spoke of her brother, who had given up good preferments in the Church of England on his conversion to the Roman Catholic faith.[8] Johnson, who felt conscientiousness as warmly as man could do, said with fervency, "GOD bless him." She observed, as a confirmation of Dr. Johnson's opinion in favour of the present age as not worse than former ones, that her brother assured her there was now less infidelity on the Continent than there had been; Voltaire and Rousseau were less read. I asserted from good authority that Hume was certainly less read. JOHNSON. "All infidel writers drop into oblivion when personal connexions and the floridness of novelty are gone, though there is a foolish fellow who by thinking to be witty upon them may bring them again into notice. He has been a college joker and does not consider that what is a joke in a college will not do in the world. To such writers in favour of religion I would apply a part of a poem which I remember to have seen in some old magazine:

> Henceforth be quiet and agree,
>   Each kiss his empty brother;
> Religion scorns a foe like thee,
>   But dreads a friend like t'other.[9]

The point is well, though the expression is not correct. *One*, and not *thee*, should be opposed to *t'other*."

On the Roman Catholic religion he said, "There is one side on which a good man might be persuaded to embrace it. A good man of a timorous disposition, in great doubt of his acceptance with GOD, and pretty credulous, might be glad to be of a church where there are so many helps to heaven. I would be a papist if I could. I have fear enough, but an obstinate rationality prevents me. I shall never be a papist unless on the near approach of death, for which I have a very great fear. I wonder that all women are not papists." BOSWELL. "They are not more afraid of death than men are." JOHNSON. "Because they are less wicked." DR. ADAMS. "They are more pious." JOHNSON. "No,

[7] The elder, poet and wit, a somewhat older schoolfellow of Johnson's in the grammar-school of Lichfield. Johnson had a very high opinion of his conversation.

[8] The Rev. George Chamberlayne; his ordination in the Roman Catholic Church was recent.

[9] Boswell quoted the stanza from memory, but before sending his copy to the printer found the poem in the *Foundling Hospital for Wit*, 1749. The lines actually run: "Peace, coxcombs, peace, and both agree;/ N[ash], kiss thy empty brother;/ Religion laughs at foes like thee/ And dreads a friend like t'other."

hang 'em, they are not more pious. A wicked fellow is the most pious when he takes to it. He'll beat you all at piety." He argued in defence of some of the peculiar tenets of the Church of Rome. As to giving only the bread to the laity, he said, "They may think what was merely ritual might be altered from considerations of conveniency; and I think they are as well warranted to make this alteration as we are to baptize by sprinkling." As to the invocation of saints, he said, "Though I do not think it warranted, it appears to me that 'the communion of saints' in the Creed means communion with 'the saints in heaven' as connected with 'the Holy Catholic Church.' " He admitted the influence of evil spirits upon our minds, and said, "Nobody who believes the New Testament can deny this." I brought a volume of Dr. Hurd the Bishop of Worcester's sermons and read from one of them upon this text: "Resist the Devil and he will flee from you" (James 4: 7). I was happy to bring so judicious and elegant authority for a doctrine which, I know not why, should in this world of imperfect knowledge, and therefore of wonder and mystery, be contested by some with an unaccountable assurance.

After dinner, when one of us talked of there being a great enmity between Whig and Tory, JOHNSON. "Why, not much I think, unless when they come in competition with each other. There is none when they are only common acquaintance, none when they are of different sexes. A Tory will marry into a Whig family, and a Whig into a Tory family, without any reluctance. But indeed in a matter of much more concern than political tenets, and that is religion, men and women do not concern themselves much about difference of opinion. And ladies set no value on the moral character of men who pay their addresses to them: the greatest profligate will be as well received as the man of the greatest virtue, and this by a very good woman, by a woman who says her prayers three times a day." Our ladies endeavoured to defend their sex from this charge, but he roared them down. "No, a lady will take Jonathan Wild as readily as St. Austin[1] if he has threepence more; and what is worse, her parents will give her. Women have a perpetual envy of our vices. They are less vicious than we, not from choice, but because we restrain them. They are the slaves of order and fashion. Their virtue is of more consequence to us than our own, so far as this world is concerned."

Dr. Wall, physician at Oxford, drank tea with us. Johnson had always a peculiar pleasure in the company of physicians, which was certainly not lessened by the conversation of this learned, ingenious,

[1]St. Augustine. Jonathan Wild, the notorious leader of a gang of thieves, was hanged at Tyburn in 1725.

and pleasing gentleman. Johnson said, "It is wonderful how little good Radcliffe's travelling-fellowships have done.[2] I know nothing that has been imported by them. Yet many additions to our medical knowledge might be got in foreign countries. Inoculation, for instance, has saved more lives than war destroys. And the cures performed by the bark have been very numerous.[3] But it is in vain to send our travelling physicians to France and Italy and Germany, for all that is known there is known here. I'd send them out of Christendom. I'd send them among barbarous nations."

On Friday eleventh June we talked at breakfast of prayers. JOHNSON. "I know of no good prayers but those in the *Book of Common Prayer.*" DR. ADAMS (in a very earnest manner). "I wish, Sir, you would compose some family prayers." JOHNSON. "I will not compose prayers for you, Sir, because you can do it for yourself. But I have thought of getting together all the books of prayers which I could, selecting those which I thought the best, putting out passages, inserting others, adding some prayers of my own, and prefixing a discourse on prayer." We all gathered about him upon this, and two or three of us at a time joined in pressing him to execute the plan. He seemed to be a little displeased at our importunity, and in agitation said, "Do not talk thus of what is so awful. I know not what time GOD will allow me in this world. There are many things which I wish to do." Some of us persisted, and Dr. Adams said, "I never was more serious about anything in my life." JOHNSON. "Let me alone! Let me alone! I am overpowered!" And then he put his hands upon his face and reclined for some time upon the table.

I mentioned Jeremy Taylor's using in his forms of prayer "I am the chief of sinners" and other such self-contemning expressions. "Now," said I, "this cannot be done with truth by every man. I myself cannot say that I am the worst of men. I *will* not say so." JOHNSON. "A man may know that physically he is not the worst man, but morally he may be so. Law, in his *Serious Call*, observes that 'every man knows something worse of himself than he is sure of in others.'[4] You may not

---

[2] Dr. John Radcliffe, 1650–1714, who made the greatest fortune by medical practice of any London physician of his day, left by his will property to endow two fellowships of £600 each yearly. The Radcliffe fellowships could be held for ten years, for at least half of which time the Fellows were bound to travel overseas for their professional improvement.

[3] Inoculation for smallpox was brought to England from Turkey by Lady Mary Wortley Montagu in 1718. "The bark" (Peruvian bark, quinine), a specific for malaria, was introduced into Europe in the early seventeenth century from Peru, where it was already in use.

[4] William Law, *A Serious Call to a Devout and Holy Life*, 1729, ch. 23, p. 474 (paraphrased).

have committed such crimes as some men have done, but you do not know against what degree of light they have sinned. Besides, Sir, 'the chief of sinners' is a mode of expression for 'I am a great sinner.' So St. Paul, speaking of our Saviour's having died to save sinners, says, 'of whom I am the chief,'[5] yet he certainly did not think himself so bad as Judas Iscariot." BOSWELL. "But, Sir, Taylor means it literally, for he founds a conceit upon it: 'Lord, thou wilt not leave thy *chief* work undone.' "[6] JOHNSON. "I do not approve of figurative expressions in addressing the Supreme Being, and I never use them. Taylor gives a very good advice: 'Never lie in your prayers; never confess more than you really believe; never promise more than you mean to perform.' "[7] I recollected this in his *Golden Grove*, but his *example* for prayer contradicts his *precept*.

Dr. Johnson warmly contended with me that Taylor in this treatise did not hold the *real presence* in the Sacrament. But I pointed out to him this passage.[8]

He and I went in Dr. Adams's coach to dine with Dr. Nowell, Principal of St. Mary's Hall, at his beautiful villa at Iffley, on the banks of the Isis, about two miles from Oxford. While we were upon the road, I had the resolution to ask him whether he thought that the roughness of his manner had been an advantage or not, and if he would not have done more good if he had been more gentle. I proceeded to answer myself thus: "Perhaps it has been of advantage, as it has given weight to what you said. You could not perhaps have talked with such authority without it." JOHNSON. "No, Sir. I have done more good as I am. Obscenity and impiety have always been repressed in my company." BOSWELL. "True, Sir; and that is more than can be said of every bishop. Greater liberties have been taken in the presence of a bishop, though a very good man, from his being milder, and therefore not commanding such awe. But many people who might have profited by your conversation have been frightened away. Langton has told me that he has often been frightened to talk to you." JOHNSON. "Sir, he need not have been frightened if he had anything rational to say. If he had not, it was better he did not talk." . . .

[5] I Timothy 1: 15.
[6] The point at issue is discussed in Discourse 12 of the *Great Exemplar*, but like Hill-Powell, we cannot identify the quotation as Boswell gives it.
[7] Jeremy Taylor, *Works*, 1850–1859, vii. 622 (paraphrased).
[8] Boswell, as usual, left the passage to be supplied. He later added a sign-post referring to the verso of the preceding leaf: "Take it in"; that is, "Set the passage as marked in the volume I am sending along with the copy." He continued on the same verso, "He then yielded; and I could not but call to mind our conversation upon this mysterious subject . . ." but at that point decided to cancel the whole paragraph.

We were well entertained and very happy at Dr. Nowell's, where was a very agreeable company. When we drank "Church and King" after dinner and I thought of Dr. Nowell, Dr. Johnson, and myself sitting together, it seemed the very perfection of Toryism.[9] I relished the old port and hugged myself.

We talked of a certain clergyman of extraordinary character, who by exerting particular talents and displaying uncommon intrepidity had raised himself to wealth and splendour.[1] I maintained that merit of every sort was entitled to reward. JOHNSON. "Sir, I will not allow this man to have merit. No, Sir, what he has is rather the contrary. I will indeed allow him courage, and on this account we so far give him credit. We have more respect for a man who robs boldly on the highway than for a fellow who jumps out of a ditch and knocks you down. Courage is a quality so necessary for maintaining virtue that it is always respected, even when it is associated with vice."

I complained of the gross abuse which was become fashionable in the House of Commons, and said that if the Members must attack each other personally in debate, it should be done more genteelly. JOHNSON. "No, Sir. That would be much more dangerous. Abuse does not last when there is no vehicle of wit or delicacy, no subtle conveyance. The difference between one mode of abuse and the other is as between being bruised by a club and wounded by a poisoned arrow."[2] . . .

On Saturday twelfth June there drank tea with us at Dr. Adams's Mr. John Henderson, student of Pembroke College, celebrated for his wonderful acquirements in mystical and other abstruse and curious learning, as also the Rev. Herbert Croft, who, I am afraid, was somewhat hurt at Dr. Johnson's not being highly pleased with some family dis-

[9] At St. Margaret's, Westminster, on 30 January 1772, Dr. Thomas Nowell had preached before the Speaker and four other Members of the House of Commons the fast sermon appointed for the anniversary of the execution of Charles I. The usual vote of thanks was passed by the House the next day, but on 25 February the entry of the vote was ordered to be expunged. When the sermon was printed, the Members found that it compared George III to Charles I and likened themselves and the public of the day to the rebellious subjects of Charles I.

[1] The Rev. Henry Bate, later Bate Dudley and a baronet. He edited the *Morning Post*, fought duels, and was gaoled for a libel on the Duke of Richmond.

[2] Boswell had, among other notes, a dated note for this much of the present paragraph on a scrap of paper with writing on both sides headed "Boswelliana" (changed from "Johnsoniana"). We print it to show how little Boswell felt himself tied down by the exact words of his first records when he came to give them literary finish. To Boswell an original diary note was a hint for remembering, not a fixed authority. "At Dr. Nowell's, 11 June 1784, I complained of the gross abuse in the House of Commons, and said it should be more genteelly done. 'Sir,' said Dr. Johnson, 'it would be worse. It does not last when there is no vehicle of wit or delicacy. The difference is between being bruised by a club or wounded by a poisoned arrow.' "

courses which he had printed.[3] They were in a style somewhat of familiarity, such as addressing his manservant by name and mentioning his playing on the fiddle. Johnson could not approve of any mixture of levity in religious exercises. I have no note of this evening's conversation except this fragment.[4] When I mentioned Thomas Lord Lyttelton's vision, the prediction of the time of his death and its exact fulfilment, JOHNSON. "It is the most extraordinary thing that has happened in my day. I heard it with my own ears from his uncle, Lord Westcote.[5] I am so glad to have evidence of the spiritual world that I am willing to believe it." DR. ADAMS (who had no superstition). "You have evidence enough, good evidence, which needs not such support." JOHNSON. "I like to have more." He repeated the story of Parson Ford's ghost, and how his wife believed it. "But then," said he, "we do not know the character of the waiter to whose information she trusted."[6]

Mr. Henderson, with whom I had sauntered in the venerable walks of Merton College and found a very extensive and firm divine, supped with us. Dr. Johnson surprised him not a little by acknowledging with a look of horror that he was much oppressed by the fear of death.

[3] *A Brother's Advice to His Sisters*, 1775.

[4] No such note is among the Boswell Papers at Yale. It may have been a brief addition to the entry for 12 June in the lost list of engagements we postulate (above, Editorial Note following 6 June 1784).

[5] Thomas Lord Lyttelton, known from his extraordinary sexual licence as "the wicked Lord Lyttelton," died in 1779 at the age of thirty-five. There are various versions of the vision and the fulfilment of the prophecy; Lord Westcote's is preserved in a document written by him on 13 February 1780 and allowed by a later Lord Lyttelton to be printed in *Notes and Queries*, 21 November 1874 (5th Ser., ii. 401–402). According to this account, Lord Lyttelton, at breakfast on Thursday 25 November 1779, told four female guests in his house in London (all apparently his concubines) that he had dreamed the night before that "he was in a room which a bird flew into, which appearance was suddenly changed into that of a woman dressed in white, who bade him prepare to die; to which he answered, 'I hope not soon, not in two months'; she replied, 'Yes, in three days.'" On Saturday, the 27th, with the women and two male companions, he went down to Pitt Place, his house near Epsom. That evening, having said he was very well and believed he should "bilk the ghost," he went cheerfully to his bedchamber, where he gave directions for his breakfast, but as his servant was undressing him, he "put his hand to his side, sunk back, and immediately expired without a groan."

[6] The Rev. Cornelius Ford, a profligate parson, was Johnson's first cousin. According to the story which Johnson had told Boswell on 12 May 1778, Ford's ghost appeared twice in the cellar of a Turkish bath in Covent Garden to a waiter, who had not heard of Ford's death. When he was told that Ford was dead, he "took a fever" and lay ill for some time. "When he recovered, said he had a message to deliver to some women from Ford. But he was not to tell what or to whom. Walked out. He was followed, but somewhere about St. Paul's they lost him. He came back and said he had delivered the message, and the women said, 'Then we are all undone'" (Journal, and the *Life of Johnson*).

Amiable Dr. Adams suggested that GOD was infinitely good. JOHNSON. "That He is infinitely good as far as the perfection of His nature will allow, I certainly believe; but it is necessary for good upon the whole that individuals should be punished. As to an *individual* therefore, He is *not* infinitely good; and as I cannot be sure that I have fulfilled the conditions on which salvation is granted, I am afraid I may be one of those who shall be damned" (looking down dismally). DR. ADAMS. "What do you mean by 'damned'?" JOHNSON (passionate and loud). "Sent to hell, and punished everlastingly." DR. ADAMS. "I don't believe that." JOHNSON. "Do you believe that some will be punished at all?" DR. ADAMS. "Being excluded from heaven will be a punishment, yet there may be no great positive suffering." JOHNSON. "Well; but if you admit any degree of punishment, there is an end of your argument for infinite goodness simply considered; for infinite goodness would have no punishment at all. There is not infinite goodness physically considered; morally there is." BOSWELL. "But may not a man attain to such a degree of hope as not to be uneasy from the fear of death?" JOHNSON. "A man may have such a degree of hope as to keep him quiet. You see I am not quiet from the vehemence with which I talk. But I do not despair." MRS. ADAMS. "You seem, Sir, to forget the merits of our Redeemer." JOHNSON. "Madam, I do not forget the merits of my Redeemer. But my Redeemer has said that He will set some on His right hand and some on His left." He was in gloomy agitation and said, "I'll have no more on't." . . . I now thanked GOD that my mind was calm and placid while I considered my "latter end";[7] and Dr. Adams, to whom I expressed it, agreed with me that I could not be more sure of being right were I in great fear than I was at present.

From the subject of death we passed to discourse of life, whether it was upon the whole more happy or miserable. Johnson was decidedly for the misery. In confirmation of which I maintained that no man would choose to lead over again that life which he had experienced. Johnson exclaimed, "I would not lead my life over again though an archangel should request it." This is an inquiry often made, and there being cause for it is at least a proof that much misery presses upon human feelings, for those who are conscious of a felicity of existence would never hesitate to accept of a repetition of it. I have met with very few who would. I heard Mr. Burke one day make use of a very ingenious and plausible argument. "Every man," said he, "would lead his life over again, for every man is willing to go on and take an addition to his life, which as he grows older he has no reason to think will be better, or even so good as, what has preceded." I believe however the

[7]The phrase occurs in several books of the Old Testament.

truth is that there is a deceiving hope that the next part of life will be free from the pains and anxieties and sorrows which we have already felt. We are for wise purposes "condemned to Hope's delusive mine," as Johnson finely says.[8] And I may also quote Dryden, equally philosophical and poetical:[9]

> When I consider life, 'tis all a cheat;
> Yet, fool'd with hope, men favour the deceit;
> Trust on, and think tomorrow will repay:
> Tomorrow's falser than the former day;
> Lies worse; and while it says we shall be blessed
> With some new joys, cuts off what we possessed.
> Strange cozenage! None would live past years again,
> Yet all hope pleasure in what yet remain;
> And from the dregs of life, think to receive
> What the first sprightly running could not give.[1]

On Sunday 13[2] June our philosopher was calm at breakfast. There was something exceedingly pleasing in our leading a college life with no restraint and with superior elegance, having the company of ladies. Mrs. Kennicott related a lively saying of Dr. Johnson to Miss Hannah More, who said to him she wondered that Milton, who had written *Paradise Lost*, should write such poor sonnets: "Milton had a genius that could cut a colossus from a rock, but could not carve heads upon cherry-stones."[3]

[8] The first line of Johnson's verses *On the Death of Dr. Robert Levett*. See above, 21 March 1783.

[9] In the first draft Boswell quoted the last two lines of this excerpt imperfectly from memory, and left a blank space above for the rest. At some time later he copied the entire passage on the verso of the preceding leaf, connecting it by a sign-post to the word "poetical."

[1] *Aureng-Zebe*, IV. 33–42, Aureng-Zebe to Nourmahal.

[2] "11" in the first draft.

[3] This anecdote is also recorded in the leaf of "Boswelliana" mentioned on p. 236, n. 2; though undated, it was clearly written at the same time as the entries dated 11 and 13 June 1784. It gives a rather better version of Johnson's reply (" 'No wonder at all, child', said Dr. Johnson . . ."), but does not inform the reader that Boswell had the anecdote at second hand from Mrs. Kennicott. In the same leaf is a remark dated "Oxford, 13 June," unassigned but probably made by Johnson: "Soame Jenyns told me of Duke of Grafton to a parson: 'I have heard one thing in your sermon I hope never to hear again: clock strike twice.' " In the margin of the leaf is another anecdote which probably followed immediately on that same day: "Mrs. Kennicott was present at the Bishop of Chester's when a gentleman (she did not remember who) came up to Mr. Jenyns in a circle and complimented him on his disquisition 'Argument for Pre-existent State.' 'Oldest thing [I can remember] keys rattling in my mother's pocket three months before I was born.' " Soame Jenyns's *Disquisitions on Several Subjects* (No. 3 of which is "On a Pre-existent State") had appeared in 1782.

We talked of the casuistical question whether it was allowable at any time to depart from truth. JOHNSON. "The general rule is, truth should never be violated, because it is of the utmost importance to the comfort of life that we should have a full security by mutual faith; and occasional inconveniencies should be suffered that we may preserve it. There are, however, exceptions. If a murderer should ask you which way a man is gone, you may tell him what is not true, because you are under a previous obligation not to betray a man to a murderer." BOSWELL. "Supposing it to be true[4] that Mr. ———— really wrote Junius and were asked if he did, might he deny it?" JOHNSON. "I don't know what to say to this. If you were *sure* that Mr. ———— wrote Junius, would you, if he denied it, think as well of him afterwards? Yet it may be urged that what a man has no right to ask you may refuse to communicate; and there is no other mode of preserving a secret, and an important secret, the discovery of which may be very hurtful to you, but a flat denial; for if you are silent or hesitate or evade, it will be held a confession. But stay, Sir; here is another case. Suppose Mr. ———— had told me that he had written Junius and I were asked if he had, I should think myself at liberty to deny it because under a previous promise express or implied to conceal it. Now, what I should do for Mr. ————, may I not do for myself? But I deny the lawfulness of telling a lie to a sick man for fear of alarming him. You have no business with consequences. You are to tell the truth. Besides, you are not sure what effect your telling him that he is in danger may have. It may increase his distemper, and that may cure him. Of all lying, I have the greatest abhorrence at this, because I believe it has been frequently practised on myself."[5] . . .

Dr. Johnson, in repeating the fine verses to Pope in the notes to *The Dunciad*, [where they are] called "amiable verses," instead of "one established fame" said "one unclouded fame," which he thought better and supposed was the reading in former editions. But I suppose it is a flash of his own genius. He praised the verses highly.[6] Miss Seward, who admired them much, begged I would ask Dr. Johnson who wrote them.[7] He told me they were written by one Lewis, an undermaster

[4] The first draft of the MS. has "untrue," no doubt a slip of the pen.

[5] The paragraph that follows is printed from an undated memorandum in the leaf of "Boswelliana" which we have had occasion to mention before. (See above, p. 236, n. 2.) Boswell passed over it in the first draft of the *Life of Johnson*, but at some later time inserted it at the end of the entry for Sunday 13 June.

[6] The anonymously published verses (four four-line stanzas) appeared in *The Dunciad*, 1743, ii. 142, an edition to which others besides Pope contributed annotation. Boswell was right about the line in question.

[7] Miss Seward no doubt gave him the commission when he called on her in Lichfield, April 1784, and it was as a result of Boswell's putting her question to Johnson that Johnson repeated the verses in the first place.

or teacher in Westminster School who published a *Miscellany* in which *Grongar Hill*[8] first came out. It is strange that such fine verses should appear without the author's name.

On Monday 14 and Tuesday 15 June Dr. Johnson and I dined, on one of them[9] with Mr. Mickle, translator of *The Lusiad*, at Wheatley, a very pretty place a few miles from Oxford, and on the other with Dr. Wetherell, Master of University College, Dr. Adams being with us. I have no memorial of either day except a slight pleasantry as we went to Mr. Mickle's: "Now, Sir, if Mickle have sense, he will give us a large dish of peas. We have been eating them with teaspoons at Oxford." There happened to be a very large dish of them, upon which I jogged him and he laughed. The other *leaf* which must *not wither*[1] was his going from Dr. Wetherell's to visit his old friend, Mr. Parker the bookseller, and when he returned to us saying, "I have been to see poor Sack Parker, who is very ill indeed. I find he has married his maid. He has done right. She had lived with him many years in great confidence, and they had mingled minds. I do not think he could have found any wife that would have made him so happy. The woman was very attentive and civil to me. She pressed me to fix a day for dining with them and to say what I liked, and she would get it for me. Poor Sack! He is very ill, indeed. We parted as never to meet again. It has quite broke me down."[2] This pathetic account was strangely diversified with a grave and earnest defence of a man's marrying his maid which one could not but feel as ludicrous.

In the morning of Tuesday 15 June, while we sat at Dr. Adams's, we talked of a printed letter from Herbert Croft to a young gentleman who had been his pupil, in which he advised him to read to the end whatever books he should begin to read. JOHNSON. "This is a strange advice surely. You may as well resolve that if you get acquainted with a man to keep to him for life. A book may be good for nothing. Or there may be only one thing in it worth knowing. Are we to read it all through? These voyages—"(pointing to the three large volumes of voyages to the South Sea which were just come out)[3] "who will read them through? A man had better work his way before the mast than read 'em through. They will be eaten by rats and mice before they're

[8]A landscape poem by John Dyer (?1700–1758), much admired in its time. Editors of the *Life of Johnson* have found Johnson's report on its initial publication only roughly accurate.

[9]Interlinear addition, "I forget which." This rather counts *against* the supposition that when Boswell drafted the *Life of Johnson* he had before him a dated engagement list for 7–30 June 1784. We still think he did, and assume some ambiguity at this point.

[1]Psalms 1: 3.

[2]As it happened, "poor" Sackville Parker outlived both Johnson and Boswell.

[3]*A Voyage to the Pacific Ocean*, vols. i and ii by James Cook, vol. iii by James King.

read through. There can be little entertainment in such voyages. One set of savages is like another." BOSWELL. "I do not think the people of Otaheite can be reckoned savages." JOHNSON. "Don't cant about savages." BOSWELL. "They have the art of navigation." JOHNSON. "A dog or a cat can swim." BOSWELL. "They carve very ingeniously." JOHNSON. "A cat can scratch and a child with a nail can scratch." I perceived this was none of the "mollia tempora fandi,"[4] so desisted.

Upon his mentioning that when he came to college he wrote his first exercise twice over, but never did so again, MISS ADAMS. "I suppose, Sir, you could not make them better." JOHNSON. "Yes, Madam, to be sure I could make them better. Thought is always better than no thought." MISS ADAMS. "Why, Sir, do you think you could make your *Ramblers* better?" JOHNSON. "To be sure I could." BOSWELL. "I'll lay you cannot." JOHNSON. "But I will, Sir, if I choose. I shall make the best of 'em you shall pick out better." BOSWELL. "But you may add to them. I will not allow of that." JOHNSON. "Nay, Sir, there are three ways of making them better: putting out, adding, or correcting."

The following conversation passed between him and a gentleman who was about to be called to the bar.[5] Being asked if a very extensive acquaintance in London which was very valuable and of great advantage to a man at large might not be prejudicial to a lawyer by preventing him from giving sufficient attention to business, JOHNSON. "Sir, you will attend to business as business lays hold of you. You may see your friends as much as you do now. You may dine at a club every day and sup with one of the members every night. And you may be as much at public places as one who has seen them all would wish to be. But you must take care to attend constantly in Westminster Hall, both to mind your business, as it is almost all learnt there (for nobody reads now), and to show that you want to have business. And you must not be too often seen at public places, that those who wish to get the fees you get may not have it to say, 'He is always at the playhouse or Ranelagh, and never to be found in his chambers.' I have nothing particular to say to you. All this I should say to anyone. I should have said it to Lord Thurlow twenty years ago." . . .

[EDITORIAL NOTE. The leaf of "Boswelliana" we have had to refer to so frequently (see above, p. 236, n. 2) contains four memorandums of

---

[4] "Mollissima fandi/tempora: The happiest seasons for speech" (Virgil, *Aeneid*, iv. 293–294).
[5] Revised for publication to "between him and me on the subject of my trying my fortune at the English bar," what one would have found, of course, in the journal, if there had been one. This is a rare reversal of Boswell's usual practice in presenting himself in the *Life of Johnson*.

Johnson's or Boswell's talk on this visit which it seems impossible to date.]

When I told Dr. Johnson that Dr. Adams told me that he was a gay and frolicsome fellow when first at Oxford, the Doctor said, "I was rude[6] and violent. It was bitterness which they mistook for frolic. I was miserably poor, and I thought to fight my way by my literature and wit; so I disregarded all power and all authority."

Fear of death. For one without it from hope, five hundred from negligence.[7]

Habit of calm *retenue* acquired at Oxford.[8]

[When I once asked him whether a person whose name I have now forgotten] studied hard, "No, I don't believe he studied hard. I never knew a man who studied hard. I conclude from the effects that men have studied hard, as Bentley and Clarke."[9]

[EDITORIAL NOTE. Boswell might have defended himself for not keeping a really full journal of this quiet week he spent in daily company with Johnson (see above, p. 231) by pointing out that he spent much of the time when he was not with Johnson questioning Adams and recording Adams's recollections of Johnson's earlier years. We present his notes as being matter he might have incorporated in a journal if he had been keeping one. They are here arranged chronologically, not in the order in which he jotted them down. Some repetition in the notes has been eliminated and the transitions adjusted by conflation.]

[31 October 1728.] Dr. Adams remembers his father bringing him to college, and was present the first evening, when he was introduced to Jorden, his tutor. The mighty cub! His father told he was a good scholar and a poet and wrote Latin verses. He appeared strange to them; behaved modestly and sat silent till upon something he struck in and quoted Macrobius. How they wondered a schoolboy should

---

[6] *Sic.* When Boswell transcribed this passage into the manuscript of the *Life of Johnson* (end of the year 1729), he misread his own hand and gave the word as "mad."

[7] Fear of death is a reiterated topic in the *Life of Johnson*, but if Boswell used this dictum anywhere in it, we have been unable to find it. The *idea* occurs in a conversation with Boswell and Mrs. Knowles on 15 April 1778.

[8] This is perhaps more likely to have been a note of a remark by Boswell, not Johnson. Boswell was fond of the French word *retenue* (self-control); Johnson, we think, would hardly have used it.

[9] Boswell introduced this fine bit into the account he gave of Johnson's reading, *Life of Johnson*, end of the year 1729.

know Macrobius! It was about the last day of October. [1] It was near the 5 of November, which was then kept as a great day at Pembroke. Exercises were given in. Johnson failed. [2] I [3] am sorry for it; a poem by him on the Gunpowder Plot would have been sublime. He gave in an excuse titled "Somnium," [3a] a common thought that the Muse came to him and said it did not become him to write on such high subjects as politics, but should confine himself to humbler themes. But it was in Virgilian verse. Then Jorden set him as a task to translate *The Messiah*, which was done in two months after he came to college. He loved and respected Jorden, not for his literature: "But," said he, "whenever he gets a young man for his pupil, he was his son."

[1748.] Dr. Adams found him at his Dictionary. "This is a great work, Sir. How can you get all the etymologies?" "Why, there is a shelf with Junius and Skinner and others, and there is a Welsh gentleman who has published a collection of Welsh proverbs would help him [4] with the Welsh." [5] "But, Sir, how can you do this in three years?" "Yes, Sir, I can do it in three years." "But French Academy of forty took forty years." "Why, Sir, thus it is. This is the proportion. Let me see: 40 times 40 is 1,600. As 3 to 1,600 is the proportion of an Englishman to a Frenchman."

[1749.] Dr. Adams told me he was present the first night when *Irene* was acted. There were catcalls whistling before the curtain drew up, which was alarming. The prologue soothed the audience. The play went off tolerably till it came to the conclusion, when Mrs. Pritchard was to be strangled upon the stage, and was to speak two lines with the bowstring round her neck. They cried out, "Murder, murder!" She several times attempted to speak, but in vain. At last she was obliged to go off the stage alive. [6] Dr. Adams believes it was altered afterwards.

[1754.] Dr. Adams told me Warburton spoke well of the *Dictionary* and desired the Doctor would tell Johnson he honoured him for the spirit with which he refused to dedicate to Lord Chesterfield and for his letter to him. Dr. Adams told Johnson he was sorry he had written

[1] Johnson was in fact entered a commoner of Pembroke College, Oxford, on 31 October 1728.
[2] Neglected to perform the exercise.
[3] Boswell speaking in his own person.
[3a] "A Dream."
[4] *Read* me. The notes show in other places that Boswell was writing at great speed.
[5] Thomas Richards, who in 1753 brought out *Antiquae Linguae Brittanicae Thesaurus*, to which are prefixed a *Welsh Grammar* and a collection of British proverbs.
[6] There is a rough note for this in the leaf of "Boswelliana": "[Dr. Adams] present first night of *Irene*. Catcalls. Then 'Murder! murder!' and Mrs. Pritchard obliged go off alive."

such a letter. "Sir," said Johnson, "he is the proudest man that ever existed." "No, Sir," said Dr. Adams. "I know a prouder man that exists now, and that is yourself." "But," said Johnson, "my pride was defensive."

Dr. Adams mentioned to Dodsley that he was sorry Dr. Johnson had written his letter to Lord Chesterfield. Dodsley said he was very sorry, too, for that he had a property in the *Dictionary* to which Lord Chesterfield's patronage might be of consequence. He then told Dr. Adams that Lord Chesterfield had shown him the letter. "I should have imagined," said Dr. Adams, "Lord Chesterfield would have concealed that letter." "Poh!" said Dodsley, "do you think a letter from Johnson could hurt Lord Chesterfield? Not at all, Sir. It lay upon his table where anybody might see it. He read it to me, said, 'This man has great powers,' pointed out the severest passages, and observed how well they were expressed. His Lordship said he was unjustly blamed. If Johnson had been ever refused access, it must have been from something in his appearance. But his Lordship would have turned off the best servant he ever had if he had known he had denied him to Johnson. As to not inquiring after him for years, he had inquired but could not find out where he was. Besides, he said it was Johnson's business to inquire after him. He said also he did not know that Johnson's tragedy *Irene* was brought on the stage.[7]

When Dr. Adams first spoke to Dr. Johnson of his letter to Lord Chesterfield, there was somebody present. Dr. Johnson took him into the next room and repeated it from beginning to end.

Dr. Adams in the year [1755] visited Dr. Johnson at his house in Gough Square. He found the parlour floor covered with parcels of foreign journals and English reviews, and he told Dr. Adams he meant to undertake a review. "How, Sir," said Dr. Adams, "can you think of doing it alone? All branches of knowledge must be considered in it. Do you know mathematics? Do you know natural history?" Dr. Johnson answered, "I must do as well as I can. My chief purpose is to give my countrymen a view of what is doing in literature upon the Continent, and I shall have in a good measure the choice of my subjects." Dr. Adams suggested it would be better for him to do the reverse, and having a high esteem for Dr. Maty, he then mentioned that he had just laid aside his *Bibliothèque britannique* and Dr. Johnson might do well to take his assistance. [The] Doctor flew into a passion[8] and said,

[7] In the *Life of Johnson* Boswell did not allow Chesterfield to state his defence as here given but paraphrases it with an unfavourable introduction ("We may judge of the flimsiness of his defence").

[8] Alternative reading, "was angry."

"Damn Maty, little dirty-faced dog! I'll throw him into the Thames!" Dr. Johnson never executed this scheme of a review.

In the year 1766 he was dreadfully afflicted with low spirits. Dr. Adams called at his house. Mrs. Williams said nobody had been admitted to him for some days but Mr. Langton. But he would see Dr. Adams. He found Mr. Langton with him. He looked miserable; his lips moved, though he was not speaking; he could not sit long at a time, was quite restless, sometimes walked up and down the room, sometimes into the next room and returned immediately. He said to Dr. Adams, "I would suffer a limb to be amputated to recover my spirits."[9]

On Wednesday 16th June we returned to London in the post-coach. There was nobody in the post-coach with us but a gentleman's servant, who, when he observed Dr. Johnson reading Euripides in Greek, said, "I would pay for many dinners to be able to read that book." He was not well today and said very little. He expressed some displeasure at me for not observing sufficiently the various objects upon the road. "If I had your eyes, Sir," said he, "I should count the passengers." It was wonderful how well he could observe with his imperfect eyesight, owing to *attention*, which I believe may be *acquired*.

[Margaret Boswell to Boswell][1]

Auchinleck, 8 June 1784

I NO SOONER SEND OFF A LETTER to you on the subject of *emigrating* than I turn uneasy lest it should stagger you in your *resolution* and by that means deprive you of your present pleasing ideas. I therefore beg that you will always consider anything I have written or may in future write only as hints thrown out for you to consider on or not as you think proper. I was disappointed at not hearing from you last night, as you had mentioned your being low-spirited. You was sure it would make me anxious to know if you was better, and also the cause.

James Bruce would write you about your sale of woods, etc. I hear no more about the tenant Bruce Campbell spoke of to Braehead.[2] David Reaside from Stewarton was looking at it, as he says he does not know but he is to leave Mr. Hunter Blair's farm of Robertland, as he had wrote him to that purpose. He said if that was the case, he would give £50 yearly for a tack, but as I think it an unfriendly thing to entice

---

[9] We return to the first draft of the *Life of Johnson*.

[1] This letter was probably awaiting his return to London.

[2] That is, a new tenant *for* Braehead, which Boswell had allowed the widow of James Chalmers ("Fingland") to retain, although the tack (lease) ended with his death 4 April 1783. Boswell had also agreed that Mrs. Chalmers might possess without charge during her lifetime a house that her husband had built at Braehead. Andrew Arnot succeeded Mrs. Chalmers as tenant.

away either a servant or tenant, I advised him to remain where he was, as I alleged the Stewarton people were not fond of any other place. He seemed, however, very anxious that you should let it without telling him. I think Mr. Blair should not part with him for a trifle, as he is an honest, industrious creature. He was so surprised and pleased with Veronica's music that he begged I would allow him to make an annual visit for the pleasures of hearing her.

As to Mrs. Chalmers's claim in equity, I think she has none.[3] She and her family have possessed a farm for twenty-eight or twenty-nine years, from which they have had a profit of near £50 per annum, and upon which they have built houses to the value, I shall suppose, of £300. Your father gave them wood (Mr. Auld informs me), so *that* is to be deducted. They have worn out your land, and she has taken every advantage that law could give her upon these different considerations. I said nothing to James Bruce till you come yourself. My idea of equity in this affair is, she should be preferred as a tenant if she gives the value of the land, and I would give her, nor no person, a tack of it without binding her hand and foot with regard to managing the ground. She has ploughed the holms[4] after allowing them only two years' rest. D. Reaside says he thinks them in no way inferior to the Lainshaw holms, which after seven years' rest gave £5 sterling per acre for ploughing. She had proposed to pick your ground and give you at the rate of fifteen shillings per acre for what she should choose, and this J. Bruce seemed to think was a *reasonable* offer.

I wish you would write about your servant, whether he is to come to Auchinleck or remain in Edinburgh on board-wages. I would think if you remain in London till July, he had better come west, and Thomas Edmondson will do if you go to Edinburgh, or you may take your own servant from this.[5]

Sandy continues pretty easy; he is surprised you are not coming home, and begs I will desire you to come soon. Phemie is not well today. Mr. John is also complaining. He set out for his evening's ride and did not return till near twelve o'clock at night; but nobody knows where he goes, or dare ask. I wish he may not get drink, as that and the heat will most certainly do him harm. Adieu; God bless and preserve you to your ever faithful and affectionate

M. BOSWELL.

[3] Boswell and she were now negotiating her claims to reimbursement for long-term investments in the farm, and the continued rental of a dozen or so acres.
[4] Low or bottom lands.
[5] Boswell's servant arrived at Auchinleck ten days later, 18 June 1784. He is almost surely still Alexander Thomson. Thomas Edmondson, Boswell's servant between 1766 and 1769, was now keeper of Parliament House, but he occasionally helped out when the Court of Session rose.

[EDITORIAL NOTE. The "journal" (manuscript draft of the *Life of Johnson*) is resumed immediately after Johnson and Boswell returned from Oxford by post-coach Wednesday 16 June.]

For some time after he returned to London from this excursion I saw him frequently, but have preserved no memorandums till Tuesday 22nd June, when I dined with him at THE LITERARY CLUB. . . . There were present [the Bishop of St. Asaph, Lord Eliot, Lord Palmerston, Dr. Fordyce, and Mr. Malone.][6] He looked ill but had such a manly fortitude that he did not trouble the company with melancholy complaints. They all showed evident marks of kind concern about him with which he was much pleased, and he exerted himself to be as entertaining as his indisposition allowed him breath to be. Here I must again regret my neglect in recording.

The anxiety of his friends for preserving so valuable a life as long as human means might be supposed to have influence made them plan for him a retreat from the severity of a British winter to the mild climate of Italy. This scheme was at last brought to a very serious resolution at General Paoli's, where some of us had often talked of it. It was considered that he would be exceedingly helpless and dull were he to go alone, and therefore it was concerted that he should be accompanied by Mr. Sastres the Italian master, who we were persuaded would wait on him with a very affectionate attention, and who very readily agreed to go.[7] One essential matter however we understood was necessary to be previously settled, which was obtaining from the King such an addition to Johnson's pension as would be sufficient to put him in a situation to defray the expense in a manner becoming the first literary character of a great nation and, independent of all his other merits, the author of the DICTIONARY OF THE ENGLISH LANGUAGE. The person to whom I above all others thought I should apply to negotiate this business was Lord Thurlow, Lord High Chancellor of Great Britain, but I first consulted with Sir Joshua Reynolds, who perfectly agreed with me. I

[6]Names filled in at the time of revision. Boswell presumably consulted the Minute-Book of The Club.

[7]This entire sentence is cancelled in the draft and "Mr. Sastres" and "master" are heavily scored and written over in a determined effort to make them illegible. Why Boswell wished to conceal Sastres's generous involvement in the scheme is not apparent. Boswell tells us nothing whatever about Sastres, but it is clear that he was a close and valued friend of Johnson's in the latter years of his life. Johnson in his will left him five pounds "to be laid out in books of piety for his own use" (*Life of Johnson*, 8–9 December 1784).

therefore, though personally very little known to his Lordship, wrote to him as follows: To the Lord High Chancellor. (Take it in.)[8]

Here then was a ticket in the lottery of royal favour which I put into the wheel for him; and while the effect of it was to be progressively discovered I continued to see him without any difference in my behaviour, but exactly as if nothing of the sort had been done.[9]

On Wednesday 23rd June, I visited him in the forenoon, after having witnessed the shocking sight of fifteen men executed before Newgate.[1] I said to him that I was sure that human life was not machinery, that is to say, a chain of fatality planned and directed by the Supreme Being, as it had in it so much wickedness and misery, such instances of both as that by which my mind was now clouded. Were it machinery, it would be better than it is in these respects, though less noble, as not being a system of moral government. He agreed with me, and added, "The smallpox can less be accounted for than an execution, upon the supposition of machinery; for we are sure it comes without a fault. But, Sir, as to the doctrine of Necessity, no man believes it. If a man should give me arguments that I do not see, though I could not answer them, should I believe that I do not see?" Talking of the religious discipline proper for unhappy convicts, he said, "Sir, an ordinary clergyman will probably not impress their minds sufficiently. They should be attended by a Methodist preacher or a popish priest.". . .

On Thursday June 24[2] I dined with him at Mr. Dilly's, where were the Rev. Mr. Knox, master of Tunbridge School, Mr. Smith, rector of Southill, Dr. Beattie, Mr. Pinkerton, and the Rev. Dr. Mayo of Wellclose

[8]On review Boswell decided to paraphrase: ". . . wrote to him, stating the case and requesting his good offices for Dr. Johnson. I mentioned that I was obliged to set out for Scotland on Monday the 28, so that if his Lordship should have any commands for me respecting this pious negotiation, he would be pleased to send them before that time; but Sir Joshua Reynolds would gladly give all attention to it."

[9]The entry for Thursday 24 June originally followed this in the first draft of the manuscript of the *Life of Johnson*, but while Boswell was still at work on the narrative for June 1784, he by some means or other recalled a meeting with Johnson on Wednesday 23 June and went back and entered it on the verso of the preceding leaf.

[1]"Wednesday 23. This day fifteen of the malefactors on whom sentence of death had been pronounced in April last were executed on the scaffold erected for that purpose before Newgate. Such a number of unhappy wretches all at once launched into eternity for crimes committed against the laws of their country brought an amazing concourse of people into the Old Bailey, but happily they dispersed quietly without doing any other mischief than emptying the pockets of some of the spectators" (*Gentleman's Magazine*, June 1784, liv. 474).

[2]Originally "Friday 25 June." If when he wrote this Boswell had a list of his engagements from 7 June, it must have been defective or ambiguous at this point.

Square. At my desire Old Mr. Sheridan was invited, as I was earnest to have Johnson and him brought together again by chance, that a reconciliation might be effected. Mr. Sheridan came early, and having learnt that Dr. Johnson was to be there, went off; so I found with sincere regret that my friendly intentions were hopeless. I have no note of what passed this day except Johnson's quickness, who when Dr. Beattie observed that he had chanced to see both No. 1 and No. 1000 of the hackney-coaches, the first and the last, "Why, Sir, there is an equal chance for one's seeing those two numbers as any other two." He was clearly right, yet the seeing of the two extremes could not but strike one in a stronger manner than the sight of any other two numbers in the indiscriminate course of numbers. Though I have neglected to preserve his conversation of this day, I believe it was from it that Mr. Knox formed the notion of it which he has exhibited in his *Winter Evening's Amusements*.

On Friday 25 June I dined with him at General Paoli's, where he says in one of his letters to Mrs. Thrale, "I love to dine."[3] There were a variety of dishes much to his taste, of all which he seemed to me to eat so much that I was afraid he might be hurt by it; and I whispered to the General my fear and begged he might not encourage it. "Alas!" said the General, "see how very ill he looks; he can live but a very short time. Would you refuse any slight gratifications to a man under sentence of death? There is a human[4] custom in Italy by which persons in that melancholy situation are indulged with having whatever they like to eat and drink, even with expensive elegancies."

I showed him some verses on Lichfield which I had that day received from Miss Seward, and had the pleasure to hear him approve of them. He confirmed to me the truth of a high compliment which I had been told he had paid to that lady when she mentioned to him *The Colombiade*, an epic poem by Mme. du Boccage: "Madam, there is not in it any description equal to yours of the sea round the North Pole[5] in your ode on the death of Captain Cook."

On Sunday 27 June I found him rather better than he had been on Friday. I mentioned to him a young man who was going out to Jamaica with his wife and children in expectation of being provided

[3] 1 May 1783 (*Letters of Samuel Johnson*, ed. R. W. Chapman, 1952, iii. 22).

[4] Boswell's printer substituted the older spelling "humane," which since 1700 has been more commonly used for this sense of the word.

[5] As G. B. Hill points out, it was the sea around the *South* Pole that Miss Seward described, and the poem was an *elegy* not an *ode*. The mistakes were no doubt Boswell's and are surprising. Even if he had not read the poem, he must have known that Cook had no connexion with the Arctic and that the title of his second book was *A Voyage towards the South Pole*.

for by two of her brothers, a clergyman and a physician.[6] JOHNSON. "It is a wild scheme, Sir, unless he has a positive and deliberate invitation. There was a young woman who used to come about me who had a cousin in Barbados, who in a letter to her desired she would come out to that island, and expatiated on the good circumstances in which she was there. The poor girl went. Her cousin was much surprised and asked her why she came. 'Because,' said she, 'you invited me.' 'Not I,' answered the cousin. The letter then was produced. 'I see it is true,' said she, 'that I did invite you, but I did not think you'd come.' They lodged her in an outhouse, where she passed her time miserably, and as soon as she had an opportunity, she returned to England. Always tell this when you hear of people going abroad to relations upon a notion of being well received. Here the clergyman spends all he gets, and the physician does not know how much he is to get."

I had some hopes that he would have accompanied me a part of the way to Scotland, that he might have had the benefit of air at a distance from London in a friend's house. But in this I was disappointed, for Dr. Taylor, to whom I had written at his desire to know if his house, which he was repairing, would be in readiness, wrote to me that it would not; and a lady who used to express much regard for him, and to whom I therefore wrote of myself suggesting that his being under her roof might be much for the benefit of his health, fairly gave me to understand that she would not choose to have such a guest.[7]

We this day dined at Sir Joshua Reynolds's with General Paoli, Lord Eliot, Dr. Beattie, and some more company. Talking of Lord Chesterfield, JOHNSON. "His manner was exquisitely elegant, and he had more knowledge than I expected." BOSWELL. "Did you find, Sir, his conversation to be superior?" JOHNSON. "Sir, in the conversation I had with him, I had the best right to superiority, for it was upon philology and literature." Lord Eliot, who had travelled along with Mr. Stanhope, Lord Chesterfield's natural son, justly observed that it was strange that a man who showed he had so much affection for his son as Lord Chesterfield did by writing so many of those letters to him, almost all

---

[6] This was Boswell's clerk, John Lawrie. It is our impression that he did not emigrate.
[7] Mrs. Cobb, of the Friary, Lichfield. Boswell wrote on 11 June saying that he wanted to get Johnson to Lichfield until Dr. Taylor's house should be ready, and that Johnson (as Mrs. Cobb knew) was not "quite easy under the roof of a certain person [his stepdaughter, Lucy Porter]. . . . I presume then to hint that an invitation to your house might be very comfortable to him, and if he should not accept, it would at least make a certain person more desirous to accommodate him agreeably." Mrs. Cobb (13 June) returned a polite but firm reply: "It would not be perfectly convenient to me to receive Dr. Johnson, nor do I think Mrs. Porter would be pleased by my giving him an invitation."

of them when he was Secretary of State,[8] should endeavour to make his son a rascal. His Lordship told us that Foote had intended to bring on the stage a father who had thus tutored his son, and the son an honest man to everyone else, but practising his father's maxims upon him and cheating him. JOHNSON. "I am much pleased with this design, but I think there was no necessity for making the son honest at all. No, he should be a consummate rogue; the contrast between honesty and knavery would be the stronger. It should be contrived so that the father should be the only sufferer by the son's villainy, and thus there would be poetical justice."

An addition to our company came after we went up to the drawing-room. Dr. Johnson seemed to rise in spirits as his audience increased. He said he was for Lord Orford's pictures and Sir Ashton Lever's museum being purchased by the public, because both the money and the pictures and curiosities would remain in Britain, whereas if they were sold abroad, the nation got indeed some money, but lost the pictures and curiosities, which it would be desirable we should have as models of taste and natural history. The only question was that as the nation was much in want of money, whether it would not be better to take a large price from a foreign state.[9]

He entered upon a curious discussion of the difference between intuition and sagacity, how one was immediate in its effect, the other required a circuitous process; one was as it were the *eye*, the other the *nose* of the mind; and then quoted from Dryden. . . .[1]

A gentleman[2] present took up the argument against him and with some reason maintained that we never think of the *nose of the mind*, not

---

[8] Not so. Lord Chesterfield was Secretary of State only from November 1746 to February 1748. His letters to his son run from 1738 to 1768.

[9] By handling the Houghton Collection and Lever's Museum together, Johnson (or Boswell) gives the impression that both were still available for purchase for the nation. The Houghton Collection had been sold in 1779 by the third Earl of Orford (Sir Robert Walpole's grandson) to Catherine of Russia for £40,555. Lever's Museum, a general collection of natural objects and savage weapons and costumes, was at this time being shown in Leicester House, Leicester Square, London. Valued at £53,000, it had been offered in 1783 to the British Museum for a moderate sum, but the trustees declined to purchase it. In 1788 Lever got permission to dispose of it by a lottery. It was dispersed by auction in 1806.

[1] Boswell left a blank for the quotation, and wrote in the margin, "See a passage in which *sagacious hound* comes in." He either failed to locate the passage (probably "Nor wanted horns to inspire sagacious hounds," *The Cock and the Fox*, l. 752) or on finding it thought it not particularly illuminating: in revision he struck out the reference to Dryden.

[2] Almost certainly Young Burke. The second edition of the *Life of Johnson* reads "Mr. * * * * *" below, where we have "Mr. _____ ." In the third edition Boswell inserted "young" before "gentleman."

adverting that though that phrase seems strange to us as very unusual, it is truly not more forced than Hamlet's "in my *mind's eye*, Horatio." He persisted much too long, and appeared to Johnson as putting himself forward as his antagonist with a flippant vanity. Upon which he called to him angrily, "What is it you are contending for, if you *be* contending?" And afterwards, imagining that the gentleman retorted upon him with a kind of smart drollery, he said, "Mr. ———, ridicule is not your talent. You have here neither intuition nor sagacity." The gentleman protested that he had intended no improper freedom, but had the greatest respect for Dr. Johnson. After a short pause, during which we were somewhat uneasy, JOHNSON. "Give me your hand. You was too tedious and I was too short." MR. ———. "Sir, I am honoured by your attention in any way." JOHNSON. "Come, Sir, let us have no more of it. We offended one another by our contention. We shall offend the company by our compliments."

He this day said he should wish much to go to Italy, and that he dreaded next winter in England. I said nothing, but enjoyed a secret satisfaction in thinking that I had taken the most likely way to get him to Italy in a proper way.

On Monday 28 June I had the honour to receive from the Lord Chancellor the following letter.[3]

This letter gave me an elevated satisfaction which has been seldom equalled in the course of the events of my life. I next day went and showed it to Sir Joshua Reynolds, who was exceedingly pleased with it, and in the warmth of his friendly joy said that he himself would undertake that Mr. Sastres[4] should have a pension of eighty pounds for his life. He thought that I should now communicate the negotiation to Dr. Johnson, who might afterwards complain if the success with which it had now been honoured should be too long concealed from him. I intended to set out for Scotland next morning, but he cordially insisted that I should stay another day, that Johnson and I might dine with him, that we three might talk of his going to Italy and "have it all out." I hastened to Johnson and was told by him that he was rather better today. BOSWELL. "I am really anxious about you, Sir, and particularly that you should go to Italy for the winter, which I believe is your own wish." JOHNSON. "It is, Sir." BOSWELL. "You have no objection but the money." JOHNSON. "Why no, Sir." BOSWELL. "Why then, Sir,

[3]Printed in the *Life of Johnson*. Thurlow expressed warm approval of Boswell's suggestion and said he would press it as far as he could. "It would be a reflection on us all if such a man should perish for want of the means to take care of his health" (28 June 1784).
[4]The name is again heavily scored (not merely struck) out, but this time the last five letters are clearly discernible. See above, 22 June 1784, n. 7.

suppose the King should give you the money? I have reason to think he will." JOHNSON. "Why should you think so?" BOSWELL. "You are not to be angry with me." JOHNSON. "No." BOSWELL. "Why then I will tell you fairly what I have done. I have applied to the Lord Chancellor." He listened with much attention while I communicated to him what had passed, then warmly called out, "This is taking prodigious pains about a man." "O Sir," said I, with most sincere affection, "your friends would do everything." He paused, grew more and more agitated, till tears started into his eyes, and he exclaimed with much emotion, "GOD bless you all." I was so affected that I also shed tears. After a little while he renewed his grateful benediction, "GOD bless you all for JESUS CHRIST's sake." We remained for some time unable to speak. He got up suddenly and quitted the room *attendri*.[5] He stayed out a short time till he had recovered his firmness, and I should suppose till he had offered up his solemn thanks at the throne of grace. We had a very little conversation, as I was in a hurry to be in the Court of Exchequer to hear the great cause of Sutton and Johnstone.[6] I secured him for Sir Joshua Reynolds's next day. . . .

On Wednesday 30 June he and I had the friendly confidential dinner with Sir Joshua Reynolds, nobody being present but ourselves. . . . Both Sir Joshua and I were so sanguine in our expectations, knowing the very high esteem which the Sovereign had expressed for him, that we expatiated with confidence on the large provision which we were sure would be made for him, conjecturing whether it would be a donation at once or an augmentation of his pension, or both. He himself yielded so much to our enthusiasm as to suppose it not impossible that our hopes might in one way or other be realized. He declared that he would rather have his pension doubled than a grant of a thousand pounds, "for," said he, "though probably I may not live to receive as much as a thousand pounds, a man would have the consciousness that he should be for the rest of his life in splendour." Considering what a moderate proportion six hundred pounds a year bears to innumerable fortunes in this country, it is shocking to think

[5] "Quite melted in tenderness" (reading of the first edition of the *Life of Johnson*).
[6] Cmdre. George Johnstone had arrested Evelyn Sutton, captain of the *Isis*, after a battle with the French in the bay at Port Praya, Cape Verde, 16 April 1781, and charged him with failure to pursue the enemy, though the *Isis* was crippled. He also denied Sutton a court martial and kept him imprisoned. Sutton was acquitted by a court martial on his return to England and brought action against Johnstone for false and malicious arrest. A special jury awarded him £5,000 at a trial in the Guildhall which began 19 July 1784, and another special jury raised the sum to £6,000. The verdict was appealed and in 1786 reversed by Lords Mansfield and Loughborough, but it was reconfirmed by the House of Lords. Johnstone died in 1787 and Sutton never got his money.

that a man so truly great should think it splendour. As an instance of extraordinary generosity of friendship, he told us that Dr. Brocklesby had offered him a hundred a year for his life. A tear started into his eye as he spoke this in a faltering tone. Dr. Brocklesby told me that Johnson said he would accept of no such bounty but from the King.

We endeavoured to flatter his imagination with agreeable prospects of happiness in Italy. "Nay," said he, "I must not expect that. Were I going to Italy to see fine pictures, like Sir Joshua, or to run after women, like Boswell, I might to be sure have pleasure in Italy. But when a man goes to Italy merely to feel how he breathes the air, he can enjoy very little."

Talking of various enjoyments, I argued that a refinement of taste was a disadvantage, as they who had attained to it were seldomer pleased than such as had no nice discrimination and were therefore satisfied with almost everything that comes in their way. JOHNSON. "Nay, Sir, be as perfect as you can in every way."

Sir Joshua Reynolds's coach was to set us both down. When we came to the entry of Bolt Court, he asked me if I would not go in with him. I declined it from an apprehension that my spirits would sink. We bade adieu to each other affectionately in the carriage. When he had got down upon the foot-pavement, he called out, "Fare you well!" and without looking back sprung away with a kind of pathetic briskness (if I may use that expression), which seemed to indicate a struggle to conceal uneasiness, and was to me a foreboding of our long, long separation. I remained one day longer in town to have the chance of talking over my negotiation with the Lord Chancellor, but the multiplicity of his important business did not allow of this. So I left the business in the hands of Sir Joshua Reynolds.

[EDITORIAL NOTE. Sir Joshua was a benevolent man, but Johnson lamented Boswell's departure. "They that have your kindness may want your ardour," he wrote to him 26 July 1784. "In the meantime I am very feeble, and very dejected." Thurlow finally did call on Reynolds, who in turn reported to Boswell 2 September 1784 that the application was unsuccessful, but that the Lord Chancellor had invited Johnson to draw on him for five or six hundred pounds. Johnson gratefully declined the offer at once on the ground that his health was so much improved as to make it unnecessary. He also acknowledged the official rejection with inimitable candour and dignity. Boswell printed the letter in the *Life of Johnson* from an original draft in Johnson's hand, and added a postscript: "Upon this unexpected failure I abstain from presuming to make any remarks or to offer any conjectures." He had extracted an admission from Thurlow on 26 February 1786 that the

King himself was informed of Johnson's wish for an addition to his pension but did not grant it.

On 2 July 1784 Boswell set out for Scotland, having waited in London as long as he could for Lawrie to arrive and conclude arrangements for his emigration. His pocket almanac for 1784 (now in the Hyde Collection) contains the following characteristic note: "2 July 1784. Travelled from London to Coventry with Mr. John Willday, an eminent hatter at Atherston, Warwickshire. Has sold 13,000 of them in a year. —Points of similarity which he said a man might travel all his life and not find: wife Montgomerie. Her family consumptive though she not. Five children. A governess, Miss Cropley from Mrs. Stevenson's, London; well looked, fine bosom, elegant in dress, uses many perfumes; fond of admiration; writes many letters; teaches French and music; is a little harsh to his daughters. A pretty maid who opens the window shutters every morning." (Perhaps the "domestic disturbance" which Boswell chronicled so mysteriously early in the year concerned *his* daughter's governess, Miss Young, or *his* pretty maid?[6a]) On 6 July Boswell arrived at Doncaster.]

[Boswell to Temple]

Doncaster, 6 July 1784

MY DEAR TEMPLE,—Thus far on my way to Scotland I am waiting at an inn till the coach from London to Carlisle comes up to carry me on. I arrived at Lichfield on Friday, and was elegantly and hospitably entertained at the Rev. Mr. Seward's, who lives in the Bishop's Palace. He is a canon of that cathedral, far advanced in years, much of a gentleman, having travelled with a son of the Grafton family,[7] and been besides in a great deal of high company; and he is one of the writers in Dodsley's *Collection*, of *The Female Right to Literature*, etc.[8] His charming daughter has established that right in brilliant characters. Though not now a *girl*, she is still beautiful. Her eyes are exquisite,

[6a]See above, 20 February, 12 and 21 March, and 2 April 1784.
[7]He was travelling-tutor to Lord Charles Fitzroy, fourth son of the second Duke of Grafton, who died in his twenty-first year while he and Seward were on tour in Italy, 1739.
[8]*The Female Right to Literature, in a Letter to a Young Lady, from Florence* and four other poems by the Rev. Thomas Seward were published anonymously and in sequence in Robert Dodsley's *A Collection of Poems by Several Hands*, 2nd ed., 1748, ii. 296–307. *The Female Right to Literature* is a review made from East to West of

> The coward insults of that tyrant, man.
> Self-prais'd, and grasping at despotic pow'r,
> He looks on slav'ry as the female dow'r;
> To Nature's boon ascribes what force has giv'n,
> And usurpation deems the gift of Heav'n (ii. 296, ll. 14–18).

her *embonpoint* delightful, her sensibility melting. Think of your friend (you know him well) reclined upon a sofa with her while she read to him some of the finest passages of her *Louisa*.[9] How enchanting! Many moments of felicity have I enjoyed. Let me be thankful. Maupertuis thinks that human life should not be taken as a whole but as moments of good and of evil, the latter of which he is of opinion predominates.[1] I fear it is true as to men of delicate and keen sensations. But Dr. Johnson at a choice dinner at Sir Joshua's the day before I left London, just we three, asserted that though a man should have more pain than pleasure from having his faculties finer and more improved, he should not wish they were duller. "Be as perfect as you can," said he, "be the consequences what they may."[2] A noble thought! But the question is if *perfection* be not referable to *happiness*? And were there not hope of a more perfect world, would it not be an advantage to be less feeling in every respect than either you or I am in this? But there *is* hope of a world where we shall be happy in proportion to our refined faculties. My dear friend! From the first dawn of our intimacy, from our worshipping in Porter's Chapel[3] on Christmas Day, all through life religion has been our chief object, however smaller objects coming close to us may have at times obscured our view of it.

Allow me to say that I think both you and myself exceedingly selfish. We are perpetually thinking of our own enjoyments, our own cares, and perpetually writing to one another of them. Nor can either of us allow that the other has much reason to complain. Yet I am conscious at present that my uneasiness at not being able to get your son out to India is truly sincere.[4] A letter from Hawkins, earnest on the subject, overtook me at Lichfield. I answered it, owned I wondered that we had met so seldom in London, told him my applications had been in vain but perhaps his interest as a Member of Parliament might prevail. And

[9] Boswell's long and fulsome review of her verse-novel, heavy with quotation from its most "poetical" passages, had appeared in the *Public Advertiser* 3 June 1784. He has hardly warmed to his subject in the first paragraph: "Lichfield has in our time been highly distinguished by genius. *Thence* came *Garrick—thence* came *Johnson*. . . and *there* resides *Miss Seward*, by whose poetry every reader of sensibility and taste is charmed."
[1] Pierre-Louis-Moreau de Maupertuis, French mathematician, astronomer, and philosopher, *Essai de philosophie morale*, published 1749. Boswell's statement is almost a direct translation from the *Oeuvres*, 1756, i. 197 and 203.
[2] See above, 30 June 1784, p. 255.
[3] The Church of England chapel in Carrubber's Close, Edinburgh. See above, 25 December 1782, n. 7.
[4] Temple, who had eight living children and an annual income from all sources of about £500, was trying to place his eldest son and namesake (Boswell's godson) in a more promising situation than the ensigncy in the army which seemed likely to be his lot. A tall and handsome youth of sixteen, young William showed a gift for languages.

I loved him for the concern he took for our worthy friend. Hawkins may perhaps be a tolerably good man. I shall not break with him. [5]

I did not hear that Wyvill was in London. I wrote an apology to Claxton for not having waited on him and his lady, told him of my resolution to transplant myself to the English bar, and that we should meet.

I breakfasted and dined with *Jack Lee* the day but one before I set out. Found him hearty and friendly in advising me as to what I am to read to have as much English law as will be necessary for me to begin with. I am not to go to a Special Pleader. [6] It would cost me a considerable sum of money and be a servitude ill-suited to my time of life. I am to acquire *elements* and *forms* [7] by private study. It is amazing with what avidity I read to fit me for trying what I wish for so much. Lord Graham observed to me very well that people who act by the advice of others act but by halves and never do much. But when a man acts from himself he proceeds with all his might. Let us see if my *resolution* (which after years of wavering came at once upon me with wonderful power) will make me an eminent barrister. I am *sure* from what I have already done upon many public occasions that in all jury trials, where popular declamation is of consequence, I shall be distinguished. General Paoli, who is truly a wise as well as a good man, counsels me to depend upon myself and not to court others. "Be always armed," said he. "Show that you have abilities. They will apply to you." I am to be at his house all winter.

When you have read Lord Melcombe's diary you will see that I do right to make him a beacon, for he was continually courting statesmen. In a life of him in the *European Magazine* it is justly remarked that his great fault was not having a proper respect for himself, which made his talents and fortune and rank in life of less consequence than they might have been. [8] "Memento," said I to myself.

[5] Why Boswell should have contemplated a break with Christopher Hawkins we do not know. Temple thought Hawkins "not the most amiable of companions" (From Temple, 26 October 1784), complaining of his peevishness and narrow mind, but agreed that he had many good qualities.
[6] A member of an inn of court who drew pleadings, civil or criminal, and wrote opinions upon statements submitted to him, though he was not admitted to the bar.
[7] Basic principles of the law and the appropriate formal procedures.
[8] The diary of George Bubb Dodington (1691–1762), representative of an old Somerset family, M.P., and successively Lord Lieutenant of Somerset, Lord of the Treasury, and Treasurer of the Navy, had only recently been published, and refreshed memories of his place-hunting from 1749 to 1761. Dodington courted and was used by Sir Robert Walpole, Frederick, Prince of Wales, the Duke of Argyll, Pelham, the Duke of Newcastle, Lord Halifax, and Lord Bute, in whose administration he was created Baron Melcombe of Melcombe Regis, in Dorset. The severe appraisal of him which appeared

Carlisle, 8 July

Here I am, after a hard journey. I was obliged to travel as an outside passenger[9] for above a hundred miles, the coach being full and my day for being home having been fixed, so that my not coming would have alarmed my wife painfully. And certainly I should be most unwilling that she should suffer any uneasiness, for her constant and generous affection is highly to be valued. I have found at the post-office here a charming letter from her. I hope to be with her and our dear children tomorrow. Carlisle pleases me peculiarly. It was the first English town I ever saw, and here for the first time my soul was raised to heaven by the solemn devotion of a cathedral.[1] I view it now as a town where I shall be every autumn upon the Northern Circuit. Now that I am *resolved* to try my fortune at the English bar you and all my friends must encourage me, as Dr. Johnson *mirabile dictu*! does in his powerful manner. He tells me, "If you only take care not to exceed your income, you cannot be wrong. You have every chance in your favour. You will *certainly* improve your mind, and you *may* improve your fortune." You cannot imagine with what firmness I am prepared to live in London upon a small scale for some time, and after having entertained (I may splendidly) the first company at my table, to entertain none at all. Burke says this is very manly. What a triumph shall I have if I acquire wealth and grandeur to the ancient family of Auchinleck. The difficulties are to keep the family seat in good repair, to be once a year there for some months with my family, the travelling expenses amounting to £120 annually, to get my debts kept quiet and gradually cleared off. To restrain my eagerness for variety of scenes, to conduct myself with prudence. But strict economy will, I trust, do a great deal, and a determined attendance on Westminster Hall, and a course of study and practice of the English law will give me a desirable steadiness. Your visits to *town* will be cordials to me. But remember you must make full allowance for the difference between your feeble and my robust constitution. I must, however, have a philosophical resolution not to be cast down though I should have no practice. Of this I am aware as a thing possible. My retreat to the bench in Scotland will, I trust, be secured. Did I mention to you that I talked over my

---

in the *European Magazine* for June 1784 ends with the statement that "Lord Melcombe now stands distinguished only as a miracle of servility, mean compliance, and political prostitution" (v. 407).
[9] In a seat outside the coach, at half price, an innovation introduced after 1750, when roads became smoother.
[1] When Boswell was seventeen and made a jaunt to Carlisle from Moffat, the modest spa where he had been sent to recover from a severe depression.

scheme fairly to the King, and that His Majesty was graciously pleased to listen to me, and talked of it afterwards to the Lord in Waiting?[2] I think my pretensions to employment as a lawyer of fifteen years' good practice in Scotland in all questions of the law of that country should be strong.

It has occurred to me that if it be possible to get your son sent to India Dundas can do it; and as I really believe he is a generous fellow, a handsome letter to him such as you can well write, as an old college companion might probably have some effect.[3] You *must* congratulate him on his elevation and consequence in the State. You may do it very honestly. I need say no more but that you may mention that the young man is my godson. Direct to the Rt. Hon. Henry Dundas, M.P., etc., etc., London.

Are you to publish anything next winter? I am sorry that your elegant productions are not more popular. I wish you were more in the world.[4] Could I but see you in a dignified station here or in York! For after all, it is probable the latter part of my life will be spent in the North.

If you cannot succeed as to India I would have William put into a corps in America. General Vaughan[5] can assist you with his advice.

Pray get a strong-box made and put all my letters into it by themselves. I will do the same as to yours and bring them to London. We have put all our thoughts so freely into our letters that it would be shocking if they were to be read by others. Let us have a meeting and a general review and selection of them.

Would you were here with me today. I could talk to you and listen to you alternately from morning to night. It is unpleasant to me to go to Edinburgh for the remainder of this Summer Session and be stared at and talked to with Scottish familiarity concerning my change of

[2] The only memorial of attendance at Court in Boswell's scanty spring journal is the brief entry for 4 June 1784, above. So far as we know the conversation is unreported.
[3] Temple, Dundas, and Boswell were students at the University of Edinburgh in the same years.
[4] Temple's own plaint in the letters sent to Boswell from his remote vicarage in Cornwall. Serious and scholarly, but without driving energy, Temple pined for learned company and access to a university library.
[5] Sir John Vaughan, a veteran soldier, M.P. for Berwick, and Temple's cousin once removed. (His brother, Wilmot Vaughan, fourth Viscount Lisbourne, had presented Temple to his first living, Mamhead, near Exeter.) General Vaughan offered young William a place as ensign in his own regiment (for which Temple was to give £400, at considerable sacrifice), and he joined the 46th at Cork, March 1785. But in August he suddenly returned from Ireland with a "dropsical complaint," and after seventeen months of an alternately swelling and wasting illness, with two remissions, he died, 4 January 1787.

situation. "Nunc animis opus, Aenea, nunc pectore firmo."[6] I shall say little. The great consolation is my permanent consequence as Baron of Auchinleck, which is believed to be of much more value than I know it to be. What pleasure shall I feel when I am free from debt! May I not indulge the ambitious hope of being a *Baron* indeed, of being created by my Sovereign *Baron Boswell of Auchinleck in the County of Ayr.* I *have* indulged that hope ever since I saw Sir James Lowther introduced into the House of Lords.[7] "Segnius irritant animum," etc.[8]

I read some of my *Hypochondriacks* to Dr. Johnson, and he said, "Sir, these are very fine things; the language is excellent, the reasoning good, and there is great application of learning. I may say to you what my wife said to me after I had published four or five of my *Ramblers.* 'I thought very well of you before. But I did not expect anything equal to this.' I would have you publish them in a volume and put your name to them." Now my *priest!* what say you? He is to revise them, and then I shall bring them forth in two or perhaps three elegant volumes.[9]

You may now have franks enough from Hawkins. So write very often. Let us not wait for answers. I am ever most affectionately yours,

J. B.

[Boswell to Temple]

Edinburgh, 20 July 1784

MY DEAR TEMPLE,—All is sadly changed. I was three nights comfortably well with my family at Auchinleck. Then my wife accompanied me to Edinburgh,[1] where I was no sooner arrived than at once, as if plunged into a dreary vapour, my fine spirits were extinguished and I became as low and as miserable as ever. There certainly never was a mind so *local* as mine. How strange, how weak, how unfortunate is it that this my *native city* and my *countrymen* should affect me with such wretchedness. I have been harassed by the arguments of relations and friends against my animated scheme of going to the English bar. I have lost all heart for it. My happiness when last in London seems a delirium. I cannot account for it. I have at that time thought of English law as of an *end* without perceiving the *means;* for upon endeavouring to

[6]"Now, Aeneas, thou needest thy courage, now thy stout heart!" (Virgil, *Aeneid,* vi. 261, trans. H. R. Fairclough, Loeb ed., 1960.)
[7]2 June 1784 (see above, 3 June 1784, p. 225, n. 1).
[8]"Segnius irritant animos demissa per aurem/quam quae sunt oculis subiecta fidelibus: Less vividly is the mind stirred by what finds entrance through the ears than by what is brought before the trusty eyes" (Horace, *Ars Poetica,* ll. 180–181, trans. H. R. Fairclough, Loeb ed., 1961).
[9]See above, 10 January 1784, n. 5.
[1]They arrived 12 July 1784.

acquire it I perceive myself incapable of the task, at least I imagine so. Then upon making out a State of My Affairs I find my debts amount to so large a sum that the interest of them and a moderate annual appropriation of rents for a sinking-fund will leave me no more than what will maintain my family in Scotland, but would by no means support it in London unless I could submit to live in penurious privacy, which my wife with her admirable good sense observes would deprive me of all the felicity which London now yields me. That when I go thither at present as a gentleman of fortune I am on a footing with the first people, easy, independent, gay. But were I settled as a man of business, labouring uphill and anxious for practice, my situation would be quite different. Add to all this, the weakness of her lungs renders her very unfit to live in the smoke of London. Last night she had a return of spitting of blood. In short, my friend, I tell you *in confidence* I am *satisfied* that my airy scheme will not do. And moreover, that if I cannot obtain an office from His Majesty I must drag on a life of difficulties.

I entreat of you to comfort me. Say nothing to any human being of my having altered my resolution. But let it remain as a matter in *agitation* against which they who wish me well in this country are endeavouring to persuade me.

But alas! what is to become of my ambition? What of my love of England, where I am *absolutely certain* that I *enjoy life*, whereas *here* it is *insipid*, nay, *disgusting*. Oh, could I but have the *perfugium*[2] in study which you have! The coarse vulgarity all around me is as shocking to me as it used to be to Sir John Pringle. Dr. Blair accosted me with a vile tone, "*Hoo did you leave Sawmuel?*" What *right* have I to be so nicely delicate?

It is curious to think that at this moment probably you are envying the high spirits which my last letter exhibited. And *now* what am I? Pray burn this as soon as you have answered it with your elegant kindness. May I not get into Parliament for a few sessions? Colonel Hugh Montgomerie would gladly give me his seat for Ayrshire could he get a place. My dear friend, I am ever most affectionately yours,

JAMES BOSWELL.

22 July. I am rather better and my scheme revives. Oh, would but *rex meus* patronize me!

[EDITORIAL NOTE. On 13 August 1784 Boswell returned to Auchinleck, where he remained until 10 November. His scanty correspondence and the Register of Letters reveal that the four months

[2] Refuge.

following his return to Scotland were clearly spent in a state of indecision and extreme misery about his desire to try his fortunes at the English bar.]

FRIDAY 12 NOVEMBER. (Writing 14.) Awaked with the first *image* my mind has produced for a long time. "My spirits," thought I, "are worse now than ever. Formerly I could appear gay, though inwardly sad. Now I cannot. The garrison is now so weak that not only is there not a sufficient complement of men within it, but it cannot even furnish as many as to make a show upon the walls." I visited Lord Rockville. Then attended the Court of Session. Was quite hypochondriac. Called on my brother John. He drank tea with us, which added to my sadness. Was roused a little by Mr. Walter Ross talking with me of the affairs of Ross the patentee, to whom I wrote tonight.[3] I had received a letter from Dr. Johnson last night that the dropsy increased upon him. I was callous by reiteration of misery. Tonight I wrote a short letter to him in a kind of despair. My valuable spouse made me keep it.[4]

SATURDAY 13 NOVEMBER. (Writing 16.) Was exceedingly ill. Visited, after the Court of Session rose, Mr. George Wallace, Lord Advocate,[5] Lord Henderland. In the evening was able to write to my brother David and Mr. Dilly. My brother John dined and drank tea drearily.

SUNDAY 14 NOVEMBER. (Writing 16.) A wet day. Heard Dr. Blair forenoon. Afternoon read a good part of *Hamlet*, to interest me in a melancholy character. Mr. Sibthorpe[6] supped with us. I was quite low.

MONDAY 15 NOVEMBER. (Writing 16.) Visited Lord Provost (Hunter Blair),[7] Lady Auchinleck, and Commissioner Cochrane. Was very unhappy. My wife and I were in town by ourselves for some time. I drank tea at Lord Rockville's; grew a little better. He seemed rec-

[3] "Royal Ross," an actor as well as a manager, and an old acquaintance (see above, 22 March 1783, n. 4), had been living in extreme poverty, ruined by extravagance and a broken leg. Boswell informed him in his letter that he could draw on Walter Ross, Writer to the Signet and the actor's nephew, for £50. For some years before his death, Ross was sustained by an annual gift of £60 from another benefactor, who was subsequently discovered to be Adm. Samuel Parrington.
[4] He probably suppressed it and later wrote a less despairing one. The Register of Letters for 19 November reads "Dr. Samuel Johnson, of my sad illness."
[5] Ilay Campbell, who had succeeded Henry Erskine in the office on the fall of the Portland ministry.
[6] A second cousin from County Down, studying at the University of Edinburgh by Boswell's arrangement.
[7] He had been elected at Michaelmas, 29 September 1784. Sir William Forbes wrote that his partner had little knowledge of books but great knowledge of the world and of men.

onciled to my attempting the English bar. But I shrunk from it now with the horror of timid indolence. I read his session papers in the evening, which engaged my attention; and insensibly I was relieved and felt myself so as I had not been for four months. I was convinced that occupation is absolutely necessary for me.

TUESDAY 16 NOVEMBER. (Writing 19.) Visited Lord President and drank some tea with him at breakfast. Was displeased with his vulgar jocularity amidst a number of young advocates. My mind continued better. James Donaldson the bookseller drank tea with us. Law papers again amused me.

WEDNESDAY 17 NOVEMBER. (Writing the 19.) Still continued better.

THURSDAY 18 NOVEMBER. (Writing 19.) I walked to Leith with Mr. Allan Maconochie. His uncouth communication of various knowledge was wearisome to me. But I envied him for the knowledge.[8] Miss Susie Dunlop drank tea with us. Her gaiety pleased me. Captain Wemyss of Unthank came after tea and was introduced by her.[9] I went over to Lord Rockville by invitation a little before nine and had a friendly conversation, in which he seemed not averse to my trying the English bar, though he rather wished I should be soon a judge with him. I eat some cold meat and took a little *eau de noyau*[1] and was wonderfully cheerful.

FRIDAY 19 NOVEMBER. (Writing the 22.) After the Court of Session rose, met the Hon. Andrew Erskine on the street and walked with him to St. Anne's Yards[2] discoursing of the wretchedness of hypochondria. I was animated by hearing him talk rationally of it, as of a *fact* inexplicable like many others.

SATURDAY 20 NOVEMBER. (Writing 22.) I fairly sat out the Court of Session every day this week, and having read all the papers, was amused, but did not find myself strong enough to launch into society. Visited Mr. John Spottiswoode, now in Edinburgh.[3] Mr. Sibthorpe and the young Campbells dined with us. —— ——.

[8] Maconochie, eight years younger than Boswell, was Regius Professor of Public Law in the University of Edinburgh from the age of thirty-one and a man of wide-ranging curiosity and learning. The exuberant exercise of his mind and a need to impress listeners with the singularity of his views vexed his contemporaries.

[9] Her mother, Mrs. Frances Ann Dunlop of Dunlop, was the favourite correspondent of Robert Burns, who often mentioned Susan in his letters. Captain Wemyss appears to have been on the half pay in the 87th Foot at this time.

[1] A liqueur made of brandy flavoured with the stones of fruits.

[2] A park adjacent to Holyrood Palace on the south.

[3] A Scotsman practising law in London. He had several times engaged Boswell to plead cases before the House of Lords.

SUNDAY 21 NOVEMBER. (Writing 22.) Was at New Church forenoon and afternoon, with little edification. In the evening read some
of Heylyn's *Lectures*[4] and *The Rambler* to my wife, and was wonderfully
well.

MONDAY 22 NOVEMBER. (Writing 24.) My wife was so good as to
walk out to Lady Colville's with me to breakfast. I was greatly better,
and had some good talk with the Hon. Andrew. He and I walked into
town together, my wife having gone with Lady Colville in her coach.
In the evening Veronica and Phemie and their governess and Miss
Jeanie Campbell came.

TUESDAY 23 NOVEMBER. (Writing 24.) I was not quite so well. Mr.
Spottiswoode, solicitor in London, etc., supped with us. I drank a glass
or two of wine and some punch, which I had not done for some time.

WEDNESDAY 24 NOVEMBER. (Writing 28.) Went to the Grassmar-
ket after dinner and looked at horses with Lord Rockville.[5] Then went
home with him and drank some wine cordially. Thought I had a cold,
so bathed my feet and went to bed early.

THURSDAY 25 NOVEMBER. (Writing 28.) Dictated two law papers
wonderfully well. Mr. James Loch had drank tea with us one afternoon.
This was the anniversary of my marriage. I sincerely approved of my
choice after fifteen years.[6]

FRIDAY 26 NOVEMBER. (Writing 28.) Had a visit one of these days
of Gen. Archibald Campbell, late Governor of Jamaica,[7] but was sadly
out of spirits.

SATURDAY 27 NOVEMBER. (Writing the 30.) Heard pleadings before the Court of Justiciary upon a trial for perjury for taking the trust
oath.[8] Lord Lyle,[9] etc., dined with us. I eat and drank more than usual,

[4] John Heylyn (?1685–1759), the "Mystic Doctor." His *Theological Lectures at Westminster
Abbey* were first published in 1749.
[5] The chief county market for horses and cattle since the charter granted by James III
in 1477.
[6] There is here a symbol somewhat resembling a P or a flower with a curved stem.
[7] A popular hero of the American war (he led the successful expedition against Sa-
vannah), he was Governor of Jamaica 1782–1784 and Boswell's legal client for many
years.
[8] Alexander Penrose Cumming of Altyre, leader of the Moray Association (formed in
1783 by the independent freeholders of Elginshire to abolish nominal qualifications)
and defeated candidate for Moray in the General Election of 1784, brought actions of
perjury against three voters who held no landed property in the county. The defendant
today was the Rev. Mr. William Leslie, minister of St. Andrew's-Lhanbryd parish. The
matter of false swearing to the Oath of Trust and Possession had long been agitated in
the newspapers, and the court was "exceedingly crowded, and many noblemen and
gentlemen of distinction present" (*Edinburgh Advertiser,* 26–30 November 1784). The
trial was continued to 30 November 1784 (see below).
[9] Sir Walter Montgomerie-Cuninghame. He claimed the peerage, which had been

and was a little disturbed. Played a great deal at draughts, my only amusement at present.

SUNDAY 28 NOVEMBER. (Writing the 30.) Heard Dr. Blair in the forenoon and Mr. Hardy (his first sermon as minister of the New Church)[1] in the afternoon. Was not as I could wish. Visited Captain and Mrs. Mingay shortly. Sat a good while with Lord Rockville, who was ill of a cold. In the forenoon Provost Hunter Blair had visited us.

MONDAY 29 NOVEMBER. (Writing the 30.) Walked out and visited worthy Sir Alexander Dick, and was revived somewhat. Lord Lyle gave me some concern at present, his manners were so agreeable and his affairs so perplexed. My brother John dined and drank tea with us. I conversed a good deal with him pretty cheerfully.

TUESDAY 30 NOVEMBER. (Writing 2 December.) Heard Maclaurin plead very well upon the trust oath.[2] Afternoon with my daughters saw procession of Freemasons. It did not strike me as usual.[3]

WEDNESDAY 1 DECEMBER. (Writing the 2.) One afternoon lately Surgeon Wood drank tea with us, and as I was troubled with scorbutic complaints,[4] especially on my head, he advised me to take flour of brimstone and honey, and have my head shaved. I have taken his advice, and this night I again submitted to the razor, which was a kind of change to my existence. I was still by no means well. Lord Rockville called and supped with us, which cheered me somewhat.

---

dormant since the death of the last heir male around 1551, as representative of the daughter of the last Lord Lyle, who had married Sir Niel Montgomerie of Lainshaw. Sir Walter's vote as Lord Lyle had been refused at the election of Representative Peers the previous May. A petition in 1790 to the House of Lords was tabled.

[1] The Rev. Thomas Hardy, minister of Ballingry, was called to the New Church 30 April 1784 and admitted 25 November. An eloquent preacher with an active and vigorous mind, he was in 1786 appointed Professor of Ecclesiastical History in the University of Edinburgh, where the degree of D.D. was conferred upon him two years later. He was unanimously elected Moderator of the General Assembly in May 1793 and appointed a chaplain in ordinary to His Majesty and a dean of the Chapel Royal in October of the same year.

[2] He was arguing the preliminary point for Cumming, whether he had a right to prosecute. The *Edinburgh Advertiser* described his pleading (continued the next day) as "replete with law knowledge, ingenuity, and wit" (30 November–3 December 1784), but Alexander Wight, Solicitor-General, replied with great ability, and the Court ordered printed Informations to be given in. Leslie finally stood trial for perjury before an assize; on 25 November 1785 he was found not guilty.

[3] The feast of St. Andrew, patron saint of Scotland, was celebrated with an annual procession by the Freemasons of Edinburgh. They marched from Parliament House, where they elected the officers of the Grand Lodge, to a feast and entertainment in New Assembly Close. Boswell led his lodge as Master in 1774 and 1775, and was elected Depute Grand Master in 1777.

[4] A skin rash.

THURSDAY 2 DECEMBER. (Writing 9.) Nothing to mark.

FRIDAY 3 DECEMBER. (Writing 9.) My wife had asked Sir Andrew Cathcart to spend the evening with us, which luckily obliged me to rouse myself to a capacity of entertaining company. We had Lord Rockville and Lady Dumfries, etc., etc., and I played cards and was a lively companion, though by no means *content*, as the French say. Lady Colville and Lady Anne Erskine had drank tea with us, which did me good. As it was the first time the Knight of Carleton, the ancient Mair of Carrick,[5] had been in my house, my heart warmed and I drank a good deal too much.

SATURDAY 4 DECEMBER. (Writing 10.) Awaked very ill and continued so all day in bed. Luckily had no causes in the Court of Session. Rose at night. Was alarmed somewhat on account of Lord Lyle and his brother David having been apprehended by a Justiciary warrant, David having beat a Glasgow merchant and he and Lord Lyle and Henry having deforced a messenger and party.[6] David made his escape. Lord Lyle found bail.

SUNDAY 5 DECEMBER. (Writing 10.) Was pretty well. Heard Mr. Hardy in the forenoon and Dr. Blair in the afternoon. In the evening read one of Mr. Walker's sermons. ——.

MONDAY 6 DECEMBER. (Writing 10.) Nothing to mark.

TUESDAY 7 DECEMBER. (Writing 10.) Nothing to mark but that my mind was easier.[7]

WEDNESDAY 8 DECEMBER. (Writing 10.) Nothing to mark. One of these days I had a visit of Sir William Forbes, but could not relish his society as I do when quite well.

THURSDAY 9 DECEMBER. (Writing 10.) These three days I have regularly visited my brother John, who was ill of a cold. He was calmly social. I had been sketching a letter to Mr. Henry Dundas, entreating

[5] Sir Andrew Cathcart, Bt., of Killochan Castle, had inherited the estate and the title upon the death of his brother in March of this year. A "mair (mayor) of fee" was an officer having delegated judicial or executive functions who held his office as a heritable possession. Sir Andrew's ancestor, the first of the Cathcarts of Carleton, became mair of fee of Carrick (the southernmost of the three districts of Ayrshire) by charter in 1485.

[6] That is, they forcibly prevented a messenger-at-arms (his name was Govan) from performing his official duty, perhaps the execution of an attachment for a debt due to the "Glasgow merchant." Boswell wrote to T. D. Boswell to get Henry Cuninghame, who had fled to London, to join his brothers in posting security of £100 to answer Govan's claim for damages and expenses. Henry sailed soon after for the East Indies with some money which Boswell advanced him on assignment of his allowance. He died there in 1790.

[7] He wrote to Dr. Brocklesby this day inquiring anxiously about the state of Johnson's health.

his counsel what to do in the present situation of my affairs and ambitious restlessness. But I could not please myself. Lord Rockville called
before dinner and told me he had dined in his company the day before,
and they had some conversation about me. Mr. Dundas said my pamphlet on Fox's East India Bill was excellent. That the Ministry felt it.
And that if anything of two or three hundred a year had fallen then,
he believed I would have got it. Lord Rockville kindly said, "Has he
not the same merit yet?" Lord Rockville told my wife privately that my
jocularity was against me in my claim for a judge's place, as also my
openly declaring my antipathies to many people. He was very desirous
I should have a more sedate behaviour. This was very friendly. He told
her Mr. Dundas told him he had received a letter from her on the
subject of my settling in London. That he did not like to write, because
it was a very delicate matter, for if he dissuaded me from my project,
I might afterwards reproach him and say he had prevented me from
rising in life. He said he would call and speak with her on the subject.
This did not satisfy her. She thought he ought at least to have acknowledged receipt of her letter. I was discouraged to think that my merits
were so coldly considered; and I indulged a kind of satisfaction in
discontent, and earnestly wished for an opportunity to treat the world
with disdain. In short, I was not at all as I could wish, but yet better
than if sunk in listless melancholy. My wife rationally said I would be
the better to have an agreeable company at my house one evening
every week, and that it was a duty I owed to my family to keep up an
intercourse with genteel people who might be friends to my children.
She said that by keeping myself abstracted, I saw people's faults;
whereas if I would mix with them, I would find they were better than
I now thought them. All this was very proper. But my indolence, joined
with the sadness of disappointed eagerness for distinction, made me
live almost entirely without society at Edinburgh. I had today at dinner
Mr. French of the High School, to converse as to the course my son
Sandy should follow to keep equal with his class.[8] I was tolerably tranquil. In the evening I revised the accounts of my father's trust, with
the vouchers. His death was a gloomy, dejecting thought. How vain
is human life!

FRIDAY 10 DECEMBER. (Writing 18.) Nothing to mark.

SATURDAY 11 DECEMBER. (Writing 18.) I was pretty well, and in
the evening went to the Duchess of Gordon's rout.

[8]Sandy had been left at Auchinleck, probably because of the inguinal hernia from
which he suffered. James French, master at the High School, was a brother-in-law of
John Witherspoon, President of the New Jersey College (later Princeton) and a signer
of the Declaration of Independence.

SUNDAY 12 DECEMBER. (Writing 18.) Mr. Henry Dundas had appointed with me to breakfast with him this morning to have a confidential conversation. I considered that taking measures to establish myself in life was a work of necessity for myself and mercy for my family, and therefore might be done on Sunday. After breakfasting with his sister and daughters, we retired to his room, where we talked, I think more than an hour. The import of what he said was this: that when he approved of my going directly to settle in London and try the English bar, he took it for granted I had £1,000 or £1,200 a year to spend, so that I could maintain my family in London. But as I had now informed him I had not above £500 a year to spend, his opinion was different. That he would not give me a rash advice, but would think seriously, and talk with Mr. Pitt, with the Attorney-General, and with the Chancellor,[9] and see whether I could get an office of some hundreds a year, or could be assured of immediate practice; either of which was indispensably necessary to make my settling in London rational. He said no man ever got good by pleading poverty; but I should give out that though a man of fortune, I had not a fortune that could afford a large expense. He said he could not find fault with my wishing to be in a wider sphere than in Scotland, for if an office of £10,000 a year should be created for him on condition of his being quiet here, he would not accept of it. (My imagination suggested this idea, and he eagerly adopted it.) He owned that the bar here was not what it has been; and he said he would not have me go to the bench for some time, at any rate, for that there would be an end of me (or some such phrase). He said I could then get no additional office; and I should first get something that I might carry to the bench with me. He gave me his hand and promised he would be in earnest to assist me; told me he had read my East India *Letter* at a Cabinet dinner; and if any office of some hundreds a year had then fallen, I should have had it. He told me he had a note of mine concerning my friend Johnston, and if an opportunity offered, would do for him.[1] He also said he had been active to get my brother David an office, as he had pledged himself to my father. He told Lord Carmarthen, "It was a deathbed promise and I must fulfil it."[2] I left him quite animated and full of

[9]Richard Pepper Arden was Attorney-General and Lord Thurlow Lord Chancellor.
[1]This must be the letter which Boswell informed Grange on 12 September 1784 he was going to write "earnestly" about him as well as himself. He had been soliciting Dundas since 1782 for some office for Grange, whose legal practice was limited and whose small estate was encumbered by family debts. In the spring of this year he was nominated to a half-share in the clerkship to the Justices of Ayr, but there was a prior claim to the appointment.
[2]He did, at last, in 1791, when David was appointed a clerk in the Navy Pay Office.

manly hope, and saw no desponding objections. My wife thought all this might be artful, to keep me off from interfering with his numerous claimants of a seat on the bench. But I thought him sincere. We shall see. He promised to write me fully from London. I shall send him a memorial.[3] I was in such agitation I could not settle. Wished to dine and drink wine with Sir W. Forbes. But having met Lord Lyle, walked with him to the Abbey and King's Park, and then dined at a tavern with him and his brother David, who was in hiding from a caption.[4] I was to give good advice. Drank rather too much. Not a well-spent Sunday.

MONDAY 13 DECEMBER. (Writing 19.) The father of William Spence, a matross[5] indicted for destroying a distillery at Ford, had solicited me so anxiously to appear for his son this day in the Court of Justiciary that though my mind was not as it should be, I could not resist. I acquitted myself very well; boldly opposed the sanguinary keenness of the Court, and gave a good charge to the jury. I had the satisfaction to be informed in the evening by a note from Mr. Jollie, one of their number, that the verdict was *not guilty*.[6] This gave me an agreeable agitation. ———.

TUESDAY 14 DECEMBER. (Writing 19.) When Spence was acquitted, I made him come home with me. The mob huzzaed and accompanied us to the head of James's Court. I had told him in the morning that he was safe. I gave him a glass of wine, and a good admonition to keep out of mobs again. Lord Rockville came and joined. I insisted that his Lordship and I should dine together, either at my house or his, as I was in high spirits. He made me dine with him. We were cordial.

[3] There is no record of such a memorial, or of the promised letter from Dundas. Boswell wrote to him 1 March 1785 soliciting the vacant office of Knight Mareschal of Scotland; Dundas replied on 30 March that he had not forgotten the conversation recorded above, but he declined to make the appointment, and firmly discouraged Boswell from leaving his home "to embark on other pursuits here equally precarious and uninviting."

[4] Arrest by judicial process.

[5] An artilleryman next in rank below the gunner.

[6] Spence was accused of having been an active member of a riotous mob which on 7 June 1784 burned to the ground the distillery of Alexander Reid at Ford, a village about ten miles south-east of Edinburgh. This was one of several violent outbursts occurring about the same time. The rioters believed that in a time of great scarcity (in August and September the *Public Advertiser* was reporting famine in Scotland) the distillers were using huge quantities of all kinds of grain and even of potatoes, turnips, and carrots, thus inflating prices. The Lord Advocate (Ilay Campbell) prosecuted the case in person, and the Lord Justice Clerk gave a charge to find Spence guilty. In his *Letter to the People of Scotland* (1785) Boswell exults over the independence of the jury.

WEDNESDAY 15 DECEMBER. (Writing 19.) I enjoyed the credit of bringing off Spence,[7] and continued to attend the Court of Session assiduously. I sat a good while with Sir W. Forbes. I drank tea at Mr. Robert Boswell's.

THURSDAY 16 DECEMBER. (Writing 19.) Lady Colville was to have dined with Lord Rockville, and I was engaged to meet her. She could not come, being indisposed, but I kept my appointment, and we were cordial. His nephew, Mr. George Gordon, was with us.

FRIDAY 17 DECEMBER. (Writing 19.) This must be ever remembered as a melancholy day, for it brought me the dismal news of my great and good friend, Dr. Samuel Johnson. His physician, Dr. Brocklesby, favoured me with a very full letter dated on Monday the 13, the night of his death. I was stunned, and in a kind of amaze. I had company engaged to sup with us; and as it might have appeared vain affectation to forbid their coming, I received them and behaved with much ease, and said nothing of the dismal news but to worthy Sir William Forbes, just as he was going away. I did not shed tears. I was not tenderly affected. My feeling was just one large expanse of stupor. I knew that I should afterwards have sorer sensations.[8] ——.

SATURDAY 18 DECEMBER. (Writing 19.) I mentioned Dr. Johnson's death to Mr. George Wallace, Mr. Nairne, Mr. Maclaurin, and Lord Hailes. He said, "I wish everyone were as well prepared for the great change as he was." I sat again some time with Sir William Forbes and talked of this sad event. My mind had for some days been unexpectedly vigorous, so that I could bear more than when relaxed by melancholy. My resolution was to honour his memory by doing as much as I could to fulfil his noble precepts of religion and morality. I prayed to GOD that now my much respected friend was gone, I might be a follower of him who I trusted was now by faith and patience inheriting the promises. But it gave me concern that I was conscious of a deadness of spiritual feeling, and indeed a cold indifference as to the awful subject of religion, having just a sort of superficial speculation that I might take my chance with a careless hope of mercy. This, I believe, is the state of most people, even of those who have had the ordinary religious education. I was desirous to be better. I went in the afternoon and paid a visit to old M. Dupont, whom I found wonderfully entire in mind, though quite feeble in body. He was reading the prophet

[7] He deserved it: the newspapers report a long list of rioters who were imprisoned, and to the end of the summer many others were still being prosecuted successfully.
[8] "I not only revered but loved Dr. Johnson, so that his loss is particularly afflicting to me. I feel it more now than at first" (from the postscript of Boswell's reply to Dr. Brocklesby, written the next day).

Ezekiel in Arabic. I was humbled to think how little I applied to literature. I also visited Miss Scott, who had been ill of a fever. I had a message from her last night that she had been ill and that M. Dupont was very weak. So I went to wait on them. I was consoled to think that I continued the attention which my father showed to them. In the evening I read two accounts of Dr. Johnson's death in the *Public Advertiser* and *London Chronicle*.[1] And I had a letter from Mr. Dilly mentioning it, and in the true spirit of *the trade* wanting to know if I could have an octavo volume of 400 pages of his conversations ready by February. I had had a letter from him lately suggesting that I might be the editor of all his works and write his life. I answered him that I had a large collection of materials for his life, but would write it deliberately.[2] I was now uneasy to think that there would be considerable expectations from me of memoirs of my illustrious friend, but that habits of indolence and dejection of spirit would probably hinder me from laudable exertion. I wished I could write now as when I wrote my *Account of Corsica*. But I hoped I should do better than I at first apprehended.

SUNDAY 19 DECEMBER. (Writing the 28.) Was at the Old English Chapel in the forenoon and the New in the afternoon. Captain and Mrs. Mingay drank tea with us. Dr. Johnson's death filled me with a kind of amazement.

MONDAY 20 DECEMBER. (Writing 28.) I recollect nothing except making a motion in Exchequer for the first time. It was for the Laird of Logan. Also attended a meeting of the Faculty of Advocates.

TUESDAY 21 DECEMBER. (Writing 28.) I recollect nothing.

WEDNESDAY 22 DECEMBER. (Writing 28.) I recollect nothing.

THURSDAY 23 DECEMBER. (Writing 28.) My worthy friend Lord Rockville asked me to his family dinner with Lady Colville. I was in such sad spirits I could not go, but did not dine at all, and walked in the Greyfriars churchyard.[3] The weather was severe.

[1] The author of the second article wrote that he had known Johnson intimately for over forty years, and "can with justice say, he never knew a man who possessed more benevolence, more friendship, or had a purer heart." The writer may have been the publisher of the *London Chronicle*, William Strahan, who began to print Johnson's *Dictionary* about 1748–1749.

[2] Dilly's suggestion was made before Johnson's death; Boswell's restrained reply was sent 7 December 1784. But Dilly was persistent: on 16 December Boswell received a letter "about an edition of Johnson," on the 18th the request that he "hasten" to publish the volume of conversations, and on the 20th the suggestion that he announce his intention to publish the life of Dr. Johnson (Register of Letters). Boswell responded 23 December (see the note following this one).

[3] He also sent five letters, among them one requesting particulars concerning Dr. Johnson from Sir Joshua Reynolds, and another informing Dilly that in the spring he

FRIDAY 24 DECEMBER. (Writing 28.) The Court of Session rose for the Christmas vacation. I was quite dull.

SATURDAY 25 DECEMBER. (Writing 28.) The holy festival of Christmas could not dissipate the dreary clouds which hung upon my mind. It vexed me much that my old and confidential friend John Johnston of Grange, who had dined cordially with me every Christmas since ever I had a house, was not come to town. He had been ill, and the weather was rigid. But I was really angry that he had now failed to be with me. It seemed that this was an extraordinary year. Dr. Johnson was gone. Grange was absent. My chief satisfaction was a kind of obstinate firmness which despair makes us feel. I went to Mr. Wight's in the forenoon to consider a Submission to him and me by Craigengillan and his brother David concerning the extent of heirship movables, a question never decided by the Court of Session.[4] I was sufficiently clear-headed. But my heart and imagination were dreary. I took my two daughters Veronica and Phemie to the New English Chapel. They were charmed with the evening service. I was cold and unhappy. Our three youngest children being in the country was a great want of pleasing variety.

SUNDAY 26 DECEMBER. (Writing 28.) Heard Dr. Blair in the forenoon and Mr. Hardy in the afternoon, with little profit. Drank tea at Lady Auchinleck's, and then paid a visit to Old Lady Wallace. Grew somewhat better. Was convinced that I require a succession of different company. Mr. Nairne supped with us.

MONDAY 27 DECEMBER. (Writing 28.) I had been supinely lazy in the morning for a long time. Today for the first time I made Sandy Walker, my clerk, come at seven, when I rose and fell to dictating a Memorial for Dr. Hall of Newcastle in an action for the freight of a ship.[5] I laboured all day and finished the paper to my mind.

---

would publish his tour of the Hebrides with Johnson, "a good prelude to my large work, his life. Will he go halves in an edition?" (Register of Letters).

[4] Boswell and Wight were the arbiters in a dispute between David McAdam, heir to the landed estate of his brother Quintin, and his younger brothers, John and James, who had inherited the movable effects (furnishings, livestock, and equipment). John and James challenged some of the movable articles that David had claimed on the legal principle that protected an heir from succeeding to a dismantled property. In a Decreet filed 28 December 1784 the arbiters rejected some of David's claims ("six mahogany chairs and an elbow chair, five rubbers and five towels . . . a smoothing iron, Fielding's works . . . one score of sheep"), but they also allowed him items he had not requested ("one pair blankets, a Bible, one dozen of bottles, and further, the best bridle, saddle, and whole other furniture for a riding-horse if any such was in the defunct's possession").

[5] Boswell had engaged Walker by letter from London on 26 June. Dr. Hall, who had a private sanatorium in Newcastle, also owned a commercial ship, the *Morning Star*.

TUESDAY 28 DECEMBER. (Writing 29.) Revised a long Memorial, altered it a little, and made several additions so as to form Answers for my friend Dempster to a Petition against him in the Court of Session by Watson of Turin.[6] Went to drink tea with Mr. George Wallace. But he had company at dinner. Drank tea with Mr. James Donaldson, bookseller. Mr. Mercer, wine-merchant, was there. I was somewhat cheered by conversation. Here I read Dr. Johnson's will in an English newspaper.[7] His death still made an impression of amazement upon my mind. I could not fully believe it. My *imagination* was not convinced. I was a little uneasy that I was not mentioned in his will amongst other friends who had books left them "as a token of remembrance." But I considered that I had several books in a present from him, and many more valuable tokens.[8] I resolved however to make the most of my connexion with him in an honourable way.

[EDITORIAL NOTE. The fully written journal breaks off at this point, but a "review" written in the same notebook covers the period from 30 December 1784 to 24 March 1785. The marginal dates that are not furnished by the journal are derived from Boswell's Book of Company and his Register of Letters.]

He had taken an action against Charles and Robert Falls, merchants in Dunbar, to collect the balance of charges for transporting a cargo of grain from Libau (now Liepája, Latvia), on the Baltic Sea, to Liverpool. The defendants claimed a deduction from the stipulated freight on the ground that the cargo was delivered six weeks late, when the price of corn was fallen. See below, 14 March 1785, for the outcome.

[6] A renewed attempt to enjoin George Dempster to restore a dam on Restennet, a small loch entirely on Dempster's property but the chief source of water for an ancient mill of which Watson was proprietor. Watson argued traditional usage, Dempster that Watson had been granted only an indulgence. The real point at issue seems to have been that Dempster wished to prevent the washing away of marl (a valuable soil-conditioner) from his lake, whereas Watson, by continuing the overflow, wished to reduce competition with marl-dragging on a loch of his own. The Lords reaffirmed their interlocutor favouring Dempster.

[7] It was printed in both the *London Chronicle* and the *St. James's Chronicle* for 23–25 December and in the *Public Advertiser* 26 December 1784.

[8] Among those "tokens" was a quantity of the original copy of the *Lives of the Poets*. Dr. Brocklesby wrote Boswell a long letter 27 December 1784 describing Johnson as "so agitated till the day I pronounced he could not live [three days before his death], that he forgot to mention in his will made in that time of perplexity the names of Boswell, Strahan, Murphy, etc., whom he loved sincerely but forgot their mention. But I know he loved and respected you sincerely." In the *Life of Johnson* Boswell pointed out that such intimate friends as Dr. Adams, Dr. Taylor, Charles Burney, and Edmund Hector were also omitted from the codicil in which the small memorials were listed. According to John Hoole, who was present and recording the major provisions of the will, Johnson dictated them to Sir John Hawkins, under pressure from Hawkins, when he was suffering so acutely from asthma that he could scarcely speak.

1785

I went to Auchinleck by myself on the 30 of December 1784, found my three youngest children well, was attracted by country affairs, and instantaneously was relieved of that wretchedness which had depressed me. My son Sandy slept with me. I received my rents due at Whitsunday, except some arrears. It was hard frost, and I had for the first time a trial of the diversion of *curling*, or playing with stones upon the ice,[9] which diverted me much. I abstained from visiting, except going to Fairlie, where I received from the Laird very full instructions as to the management of my estate, and to Eglinton as a due honour to my wife's Chief;[1] to Sir Walter Montgomerie, Lord Lyle's, as her nephew; and to Sir John Whitefoord's in my way home, to dine with him for the last time at Ballochmyle.[2] I dined one day at Mr. Dun's when I received my village rents in the room off the aisle[3] at the kirk and had the bellman for my attendant. I was highly satisfied with Sandy's progress in Latin, and Mr. Millar was a good companion to me. By Fairlie's advice I engaged Mr. Bruce Campbell for a gratuity of ten guineas yearly to survey my farms with attention, to see if the tenants complied with the obligations in their leases, and to assist me in letting farms.

[9] It is strange that Boswell had never before played this ancient Scottish game, which in the eighteenth century was so popular that forty-two curling societies were formed in various parts of Scotland, including three in Ayrshire.
[1] The first of the Lainshaw family, Niel Montgomerie (d. 1547), was a younger son of Hugh, first Earl of Eglinton.
[2] The estate had been sold to Claud Alexander, who made a fortune in India. Whitefoord was ruined by the failure of Douglas, Heron, and Company in 1773, and ultimately lost all his properties.
[3] Boswell spelled this word "ail" and underlined it, as though he doubted the spelling. The word "aisle," which by etymology means "wing," was (and is) in common use in Scotland to designate a lateral wing to a church used as a family burial-place. The Boswell vault was actually under the floor of the church, but the aisle covered the stairs going down to the vault and perhaps contained a family loft opening into the church. As this passage indicates, there was also in or attached to the aisle a room with a fireplace, probably furnished like a small parlour, where the kirk-session could meet or the laird collect his rents. The Boswell aisle was replaced in the nineteenth century by the structure now known as "the Boswell Mausoleum," a tomb for Sir James Boswell and his family.

Fairlie gave me an estimate of my arable land at 10/- for three years, 12/- for three more, and 14/- for the remaining twelve years of an eighteen years' lease. By this I perceived that in seven years my rent would upon an average be tripled. The thought was elevating.[4] But I doubted if I should have resolution to make my tenants agree to the terms; and I was not sure but they were too high. I resolved however to insist upon them in all my farms where there were no tenants, as Dernlaw, Turnerhill, etc., and I thought I might relax them somewhat where the tenants were anxious to continue. I had a consolatory kind of sensation from the act of receiving my rents in person. I had no great company with me, but only a few good people with whom I was not upon ceremony, and my living was plainly and soberly hospitable. I had Mr. Halbert, the parish schoolmaster, twice at dinner, and had the merit of pushing him to bring forward his statute money accounts to the present year.[5] Family prayers every evening composed my mind.

13 JAN.   I returned to Edinburgh on the 13 January. Mr. Millar accompanied me to Douglas Mill. My good spirits continued. I found Grange returned from the country, by no means in good health and spirits. I did him good by my company. During this month and February (till the 23 of that month, on which I am now writing), I had upon the whole a pretty good life, though not quite as I could wish; for I could not apply to the writing out of my *Tour to the Hebrides in Company with Samuel Johnson, LL.D.*, as I hoped I might do.[6] Fortunately

[4] Boswell's figures indicate that at the time of writing he was receiving an average annual rent of 4s. 8d. per acre. That he followed up Fairlie's recommendations is probably shown by a letter he wrote to Bruce Campbell 24 January 1786 objecting "that the offers for Martinshill, Dickston, etc. are too low, and showing my understanding of their value" (Register of Letters).

[5] "Statute money" was money paid in exchange for work on the roads in Ayrshire that by an act of 1669 was required of all "tenants, cottars, and other labouring men" six days annually. As one might expect, the statute was ineffectual, and the roads were so inadequate that by petition of several large landowners an act for turnpike roads and commuted statute labour was passed in 1766–1767. A County Board of Road Trustees was inaugurated to administer the money and co-ordinate the improvements. Halbert was session-clerk as well as schoolmaster, and also kept the registers for marriages, baptisms, and deaths. Those, too, he kept erratically (see Journal, 2 September 1780). Yet the same Mr. Halbert was the author of an original and ingenious treatise called *The Practical Figurer, or An Improved System of Arithmetic*, published 1789.

[6] An account in Boswell's hand dated Sunday 6 February 1785 and endorsed "My

for me, Mr. Baron Gordon and Dr. Blair, to the first of whom
I read a good deal of my original MS. in the forenoon of
Monday the 21 and to the latter in the afternoon, confirmed   21 FEB.
me in thinking that it might be printed with little variation;
so (writing 27 February) I resolved that I would set myself
down quietly in London and get the work executed easily.

I had been several times at Lady Colville's, and often at
Lord Rockville's; had dined at Lord Stonefield's, Lady Auchinleck's, Balmuto's, and some other houses, and on 23 Feb-   23 FEB.
ruary took an occasional family dinner with Mrs. McAdam,
where I drank wine enough to be heated;[7] then drank tea
with Dr. Blair and sat with him till nine o'clock upon literary
discourse and a little upon religion. He freely owned he did
not believe the eternity of punishment. I dined one day with
Commissioner Cochrane cordially. My practice in the Court
of Session, though not very lucrative, made a creditable appearance. But my wish for "being a spoke in the great wheel,"
as Jack Lee expressed it to me, made me restless. I had not
many company to dine and sup with us. But had some. The
state of my affairs disturbed me a good deal. But Sir William
Forbes obligingly proposed I should give him and Company

---

dream in the night between 5 and 6 February 1785" reveals that he had been haunted
by Johnson's death and was anxious about his own. "Last night I dreamt that I was
with my much respected friend, Dr. Johnson. I saw him distinctly, sitting in a chair
opposite to me in his usual dress. He talked something which I do not perfectly recollect
about his library not being in such order as he could have wished, and gave as a reason
his being hurried as death approached. He then said in a solemn tone, 'It is an aweful
thing to die.' I was fully sensible that he had died some time before, yet had not the
sensation of horror as if in the presence of a ghost. I said to him, 'There, Sir, is the
difference between us. You have got that happily over.' I then felt myself tenderly
affected, and tears came into my eyes, and clasping my hands together, I addressed
him earnestly. 'My dear Sir! pray for me.' This dream made a deep and pleasing
impression on my mind. I this morning invoked him to pray for me if he heard me
and could be of influence. He did not absolutely disapprove of invoking departed
saints. God grant us a happy meeting!" (Original in the possession of Mr. Jonathan
T. Isham.) The reference to Johnson's disorderly library may have been an unconscious
attempt to explain the omission of Boswell's name from the list of friends to whom
Johnson had willed a book (see above, 28 December 1784). For Johnson on the invocation of saints, see above, 10 June 1784. That un-Protestant practice had previously
brought Boswell tranquillity after painful bereavements, as when he prayed to his
mother 28 January 1766 "like most solemn Catholic to saint" and to his young son
David 30 March 1777.

[7] There is some confusion here, for Boswell later says that on this day he dined with
Walter Campbell of Shawfield and supped at Hamilton of Grange's.

security on my house in St. Andrew's Square[8] for my debt to them, making £1,400; and if I paid the interest regularly, I might clear off the principal at my leisure. This was a relief to me.

22 FEB. On Tuesday Sir Philip and Lady Ainslie and Baron Gordon supped with us. There had been a coldness between Maclaurin and me, as I had disapproved of his deserting Mr. Dundas when he was turned out of office.[9] I expostulated with him, and we got into tolerable terms again. I dined with him one day at Mr. Mackintosh the advocate's, a good rational social day; more like a London day than any I have had for

23 FEB. a long time. On Wednesday I dined jovially at Shawfield's

24 FEB. and supped at Hamilton of Grange's. Was so ill on Thursday morning that I was obliged to return home from the Court of Session in the forenoon and go to bed again for some time.

25 FEB. On Friday was still a little uneasy from having taken too much

26 FEB. wine on Wednesday. On Saturday the Laird of Fairlie dined with us, and he and I had some good conversation on improving my estate. We prevailed on him to stay the evening, and got his niece, Mrs. McAdam, and her three children to come and sup with him, as did Miss Macredie and Grange. It was a most cheerful evening. I had dined once with Grange at Sir Alexander Dick's. Before that, Captain Dick and Captain Trevelyan of the Guards,[1] son of Sir John Trevelyan, had dined with me and been very joyous. The two young rogues sat on and drank wine freely, and I could not raise them. Indeed, I was not unwilling to sit. At Sir Alexander's we had another hearty day, which pleased both Grange and me at the time, though I felt it a little incongruous with the classical temperance of Prestonfield. Drinking may be had in a thousand places. Classical elegance is rare. The Saturday after, I had Dick and Trevelyan and a Colonel Henderson from Jamaica,[2] who was at Sir A. Dick's that day, to dine at my house; also Mr. George Wallace. We did not drink to excess. I do not recollect much more of my life this winter.

---

[8] The house in the New Town which his father had purchased shortly before his death in 1782. Lady Auchinleck had the liferent.

[9] He had resigned as First Lord of the Treasury when the Fox-North Coalition came in, April 1783, and was dismissed as Lord Advocate August 1783.

[1] Capt. George Trevelyan (he was actually ensign at this time) later took orders and rose to be archdeacon of Taunton, canon of Wells, and rector of Nettlecombe. His son, Sir Charles Edward Trevelyan, married Macaulay's sister, and their son, Sir George Otto, was Macaulay's biographer.

[2] Unidentified.

I had upon the whole tolerable spirits. But I did not perceive myself improving, and no wonder, for I read almost nothing but law papers.

There was a great deal of writing about my life of Dr. Johnson in the *St. James's Chronicle*. I was highly praised[3] and thought it proper to write in that paper declaring that since 18 JAN. Dr. Johnson's death I had not sent a single paragraph concerning him, nor should send one that was not signed with my name. I begged that the writer of such praise as animated my mind to its best exertions would have the generosity to avow himself publicly, or at least would let me know privately to whom I was obliged. I had a letter from Mr. Baldwin, the 29 JAN. printer, acquainting me it was Mr. Steevens, who united with Dr. Johnson in an edition of Shakespeare.[4] I wrote to Mr. 21 JAN. Hector at Birmingham, Dr. Adams at Oxford, and Miss Seward for materials for Dr. Johnson's life, and got good packets from all of them.[5] Such attention to me was truly flattering.

Colonel Montgomerie was one night in Edinburgh in his way to London. We drank only a bottle of old Madeira in negus. He had at the time of last election said to Sir John Whitefoord he could not be for him, for he would be for me were he not to be Member himself. I sounded him to discover what return I might expect for my most generous friendly

[3] "To Mr. Boswell the public will be indebted on the subject of our author's life for genuine and ample information as well as entertainment. He has been happy in resources that were obvious to none but himself. He was acquainted with the *mollia fandi tempora* and improved them to the best advantage. His playful importunities and anxious solicitations were alike prevalent with Johnson. If he failed once in an enquiry, he renewed it at a more lucky hour, and seldom retired without the intelligence he sought. During his long association with the Doctor in England, as well as throughout his Hebridean tour, he may be pronounced to have lost no opportunity of search respecting the past occurrences of our author's life, or his sentiments relative to men and literature; nor will it be suspected by those who are acquainted with Mr. Boswell's active mind that his curiosity permitted one circumstance to escape him that might illustrate the habits or exalt the character of the sage whom he respected almost to adoration." The paragraph appeared in a collection of Johnsoniana in the issue for 8–11 January 1785.

[4] He had revised Johnson's edition in 1773. Boswell's letter to the *St. James's Chronicle* was written 18 January 1785 and printed in the issue for 22–25 January.

[5] He received them on various dates in February. The surgeon Edmund Hector, a Lichfield schoolfellow, had invited Johnson to live with him at Birmingham in 1732, and there introduced him to "Tetty," later Mrs. Johnson. Boswell first collected information from Adams and Hector when he accompanied Johnson on a jaunt to Oxford, Birmingham, and Lichfield in March 1776. He later changed his mind about the value of Anna Seward's contributions.

keenness for him. My wife had with her usual penetration assured me that he would not be for me, but would be for one of his own brothers. I expressed to him my wish to be in Parliament. He said he wished I was. I asked if he could get a good office, would he go out of Parliament? He said he would not choose to do it. "But," said I, "supposing you to become Earl of Eglinton, would you support me as a candidate for the county?" He said he could not say.[6] In short, I perceived that I had indulged a fallacious notion of his having a reciprocal wish for my obtaining what I was so happy he had at last obtained. It hurt me a good deal. I resolved to stand upon my own legs and exert myself to secure if possible a respectable share of the independent interest of the county, by which in the midst of contending parties I might perhaps be successful. My wife observed very justly that Colonel Montgomerie would be much more inclined to oblige people who lived in his own style than me who avoided much visiting and entertaining.

I one forenoon paid a visit to Miss Gray, and we talked of Sir John Pringle. The Laird of Fairlie dined, stayed the evening, and supped with us on Saturday 26 February, and

26 FEB.

5 MAR. he supped with us on 5 March, together with Matthew Dickie. I had been at Prestonfield with Fairlie in the forenoon. I was at this time hurried with a variety of business in the Court of Session, though it was observed by many of my brethren at the bar that there was much less business in the Court this winter than had been formerly. I had one evening played at whist and brag[7] at Lord Rockville's, and sat late, and felt the feverish fretfulness of gaming, though I did not lose much. I had attended regularly Signor Corri's concerts for his scholars, at which my two daughters sung and played wonderfully well; and I had been at Dunn's assemblies twice,[8] once with my wife, who dressed better this winter and went more into company than she used to do. Such is, as far as I now recollect

[6]Colonel Montgomerie vacated his seat in 1789, when he was appointed Baggage-Master and Inspector of Roads in North Britain at £500 a year. In the special election that followed he did not support Boswell, who was certain only of three nominal votes created by his father, and of his own.

[7]An old card game resembling poker.

[8]On 1 February he attended the regular subscription assembly, which was held at Dunn's Hotel at least once a week, and on 15 February the special celebration of "Fastens Even" (Shrove Tuesday). His record of expenditures also shows that he attended the annual dinner of Mundell's scholars on 22 January.

(6 March), the state of my life for what part of this year is now over. My faith and piety were quiet and constant, though not vigorous. I suppose I am too nicely anxious for a dignified course of existence. Mine is, I dare say, better than that of most of those of my rank. Yet I am sadly dissatisfied.

    I have now (12 March) six days more to review. I had really upon the whole good spirits, and wrote well for the Court of Session. On Sunday I heard Dr. Blair in the forenoon, sat a good part of the afternoon at Grange's with him and the Hon. Andrew Erskine, and drank tea at Commissioner Cochrane's from regard to relationship and old acquaintance, though he had not acted well by me with my father.[9] On Monday I laboured hard all day dictating a long Petition for Janet Buchanan for marriage or damages against the Laird of Macnab.[1] On Tuesday Clerk Matthew and Grange dined with me, and Grange and I went to Schetky's concert and heard the music in *Macbeth* well performed.[2] On Wednesday I dined at Mr. Matthew Dickie's with the Laird of Fairlie, and my wife and I supped at Dr. Blair's very agreeably. On Thursday the Hon. Andrew Erskine, Grange, and I dined at Fortune's to revive old acquaintance. We were very cordial, but I pushed the bottle too much. We drank two bottles of port apiece. But I was not much the worse for it. On Friday I dined at Lord Rockville's (a party made about three weeks ago to be very merry) with Harry Erskine, Maclaurin, Cullen, Baron Gordon, Lord Eskgrove, Lord Swinton,

6 MAR.

6 MAR.

7 MAR.

8 MAR.

9 MAR.

10 MAR.

11 MAR.

[9] Cochrane had offended him by joining with Lady Auchinleck, John Stobie, and Claud Boswell in "a secret combined exertion" to make Lord Auchinleck buy a house in the New Town (Journal, 23 January 1782).

[1] Janet Buchanan alleged marriage with the Laird by mutual declaration (no more was necessary in Scotland for a valid marriage) 2 November 1781; her son Francis Macnab was born 20 August 1782. She lost her process in 1786, after Boswell had moved to London. An anecdote concerning Boswell and the trial of this Laird of Macnab was among the notes (now in the Yale University Library) which Sir Walter Scott sent in letters to Croker when Croker was editing Boswell's *Life of Johnson* but which he did not use because it was one of several which Scott said "may be written though not printed." The text is printed in the Centenary Edition of Scott's *Letters*, ed. H. C. Grierson, xii. (1937), 478–479.

[2] Johann Schetky, a well-known composer and cellist descended from an ancient Transylvanian family, settled in Edinburgh in 1772. He was a friend of Robert Burns, at whose request he set to music his song, "Clarinda, mistress of my soul." The instrumental and vocal music to *Macbeth*, which was popular since the beginning of the century and was once attributed to Purcell, is now believed to have been composed by the singer Richard Leveridge.

Mr. John Anstruther; and Lord Haddo was added to the party by his coming to town accidentally.[3] The party did not do so well as we expected till Cullen's mimicry made us laugh immoderately. But it was not "the feast of reason and the flow of soul."[4] There was too much law topics and not enough of variety and wit. I was checked too by thinking that it was the night of Barnard's ball, where both Lord Rockville and I had children dancing, yet we did not go to it. There was a great deal of wine drank. I in particular indulged in it, and challenged Lord Haddo to cordial bumpers, and when the company broke up about twelve, he and I sat by ourselves, had a little table in a corner by the fire, and took an additional dose. Then we joined the ladies and several of the gentlemen who stayed, and we played brag till about two in the morning. I was so much intoxicated that I knew very little of what went on, and after I came home was exceedingly ill, which I con-

12 MAR. tinued to be next day, and did not get up till past four in the afternoon. I was really vexed, and in a horrid state of relaxation. It shocked me too that I did not recollect what had passed, so that I might have perhaps behaved absurdly; and as I had borrowed of Lord Haddo to play at brag, I could not be sure how much I had lost. I thought I recollected owing Lord Haddo just a guinea. But as my wife well observed, I was in his power for whatever sum he might name.

13 MAR. I grew a little better at night. On Sunday I visited Lord Rockville, and found my loss at play did not exceed a guinea and a half. I think I was at the New Church part of the day. I drank tea with Lord Eskgrove by appointment. Instead of

14 MAR. going to Auchinleck on Monday as I intended, I stayed and dictated a law paper for April boxes,[5] which I saw in print; as also the greatest part of the Case for Mercer of Lethendy in his appeal to the House of Lords for more damages on account of John Duff, his servant, having been adjudged as a recruit;[6] as also the greatest part of a Reclaiming Petition for Dr. Hall, most of which was copied verbatim from my

[3] Anstruther, younger son of Sir John Anstruther of Anstruther, was a Scots advocate, English barrister, and M.P. for the Anstruther Easter Burghs; George Gordon, styled Lord Haddo, was the son and heir of the third Earl of Aberdeen.
[4] Pope, *First Satire of the Second Book of Horace*, l. 128.
[5] During vacations, legal papers could be filed or "boxed" on specified days.
[6] See above, 30 April 1783, and below, 8 June 1785.

Memorial for him.[7] I had a satisfaction in getting business
thus dispatched.

On ——— my wife and I went to Auchinleck. Next day   16 MAR.
we went to Rozelle, where we had an excellent day and night,   17 MAR.
and next day Knockroon went with us to Auchinleck. Our   18 MAR.
three youngest children were well and lively by having been
all winter in the country. On Saturday Mr. Hamilton of   19 MAR.
Grange, who was going with me to London, and Mr. Reid
Cunninghame of Auchenharvie came to dinner, and stayed
till Monday, when Grange and I set out. Knockroon infeft   21 MAR.
me upon Willockshill, my new purchase, and wrote an heritable bond to the Rev. Dr. Andrew Mitchell for the price of
it.[8] I this day at last did what I had delayed too long. I made   19 MAR.
a settlement upon my wife and children as allowed by the
entail of Auchinleck.[9] It was a great comfort to me to have
this done. I thought I might now die in peace. I felt some
regret in leaving Auchinleck. Mr. Bruce Campbell met me
on the road to the church on Sunday, heard sermon, as did   20 MAR.

[7] See above, 27 December 1784. Boswell had argued that the charter-party (a contract
between ship-owners and merchants for safe delivery of a cargo) did not specify a
time-limit but called only for "expeditious" delivery, and that despite repairs, problems
in loading, bad weather, and ill winds, the *Morning Star* got back faster than other
ships. But on 19 February 1785 Lord Kennet reduced the charges more than £1
sterling per last (eighty bushels) of grain, to the rate generally effective when the
Morning Star actually sailed from Newcastle for the Baltic. The "Reclaiming Petition"
was an appeal against the interlocutor to the entire Court of Session. Three months
later the Court adhered to the Lord Ordinary's decision. Boswell advised Dr. Hall that
the sum at issue did not warrant an appeal to the House of Lords, but offered to assist
him without fee if he was determined to try it.
[8] Boswell had tried in vain to persuade his father to purchase Willockshill, a farm about
half a mile north of Auchinleck House which belonged to Lord Loudoun. It is characteristic of him that at a time when he was in despair because the state of his finances
made emigration to London impracticable he should have gone into debt to increase
his landed holdings. It is also ironic that the former minister of Muirkirk (the "Andro'
gowk"—cuckoo or fool—of Burns's *The Kirk's Alarm*) had money to invest while the
Laird of Auchinleck had none.
[9] The original document, in Boswell's hand except for the date, is in the Register House
in Edinburgh. In it he grants his wife the liferent of specified lands amounting in
yearly value to not more than one quarter of the free rent of the estate "after deduction
of public burthens." He also settled annuities of £150 on James, his second son, and
of £100 on each of his daughters. In a codicil of 12 October 1791 Boswell annulled
a clause which reduced the daughters' annuities by half when they married. The
settlement was witnessed by Hamilton of Grange and Knockroon.

Grange. Auchenharvie, and Knockroon, and dined with us;
but Bruce went home at night. Mr. Hamilton and I had a

22-24
MAR.
very good journey. We got to Lancaster on Tuesday, and
stayed there two days to see the assizes. Judge Willes was
exceedingly civil to me, as I have ever found him, and had
me and my companion to dine with him both days.[1] On

23 MAR.
Wednesday evening we were entertained at supper by the
counsel.[2]

[EDITORIAL NOTE. The London journal which follows, like that for
1783 and the fragment of 1784, is a mixture of notes and fully written
journal. But it differs in being continuous and practically complete,
and only in a few stretches are the notes reduced to mere lists of names
and engagements. The material is of such biographical interest that
it has seemed best to present it exactly and in full, though this procedure
results again in a more crabbed style and a heavier load of annotation
than had been thought proper for this edition generally. The journal
overlaps the "review" above at the beginning, but in neither record
does Boswell mention that he slept at Carlisle the first night out. That
information heads another poignant memorandum:

Carlisle, in the night between the 21 and 22 March 1785, dreamt
I was sitting with Dr. Johnson. Did not recollect he was dead, but
thought he had been very ill, and wondered to see him looking very
well. I said to him, "You are very well, Sir." He called out in a forcible
pathetic tone, "O no!" He said, "I have written the letter to Paoli which
you desired." He then expressed himself towards me in the most obliging manner, saying he would do all in his power (or words to that
purpose) to show his affection and respect, and seemed to search his
mind for variety of good words.[2a]]

[1] Boswell had disapproved of Judge Willes's levity when he first observed him in court
22 August 1778, but within a few days he came to respect his knowledge and his
accuracy. The two men took to each other quickly.
[2] Boswell printed a bit of mealtime byplay with John Lee in the *Public Advertiser*
13 May 1785, introducing it with a characteristic observation: "Nothing can be more
liberal than the social connexion between Mr. Lee and Mr. Boswell, after the latter
hung up the former in his last year's letter in defence of *chartered rights*: fair public
contests should never interfere with private good humour."
[2a] From a small notebook of Boswell's once in the possession of Professor Chauncey B.
Tinker but now missing.

Left Auchinleck, Monday 21 March. Arrived at Lancaster on Tuesday 22. Dined with Judge Willes 23 and 24, and 24 lay at Preston. 25 at Manchester. 26 at Lichfield.[3] 27 received the Holy Sacrament in Lichfield Cathedral. 28 lay at Birmingham.

WEDNESDAY 30 MARCH. Arrived in London.

THURSDAY 31 MARCH. Mr. Hamilton dined with us at Mr. Dilly's.

FRIDAY 1 APRIL. I dined at Lord Eglinton's with Lord Advocate, etc. Much wine. All night in strange state. Not home[4] till seven in morning on Saturday 2. Dined that day at Mr. Thomas Gordon's.

SUNDAY 3 APRIL. Bavarian Chapel. Dined home, Major Arabin,[5] etc.

MONDAY 4 APRIL. Dined home.

TUESDAY 5 APRIL. Ditto.

WEDNESDAY 6 APRIL. Ditto.

THURSDAY 7 APRIL. Dined Piazza with Sir Charles Preston, and saw *Macbeth* with him.[6]

FRIDAY 8 APRIL. Dined home.

SATURDAY 9 APRIL. Ditto.

SUNDAY 10 APRIL. Brother breakfasted. Warm weather began. Calm forenoon. Dined Macbride's;[7] Mr. Western, Mrs., and Miss. Supped Lord Eglinton's. Very ill that night and Monday 11. Dined Sir Joshua Reynolds's with Mrs. Siddons.[8] Supped with Seward.

TUESDAY 12 APRIL. In all forenoon. Dined Club. House of Commons a little. Home early.

[3] He called on Anna Seward and her father and may have slept at their house. She appears to have given him at this meeting the additional anecdotes about Johnson which he had solicited 15 February 1785.

[4] General Paoli's.

[5] William John Arabin of the 2nd Troop of Horse Guards. Now in his thirty-fourth year, he rose steadily to the rank of general in the army in 1814.

[6] There is an error here in dating. Boswell's record of expenditures shows three shillings for a ticket to *Macbeth* Thursday 31 March 1785, when the play was indeed performed at Drury Lane (Mrs. Siddons as Lady Macbeth and Kemble as Macbeth for the first time). It was next staged Tuesday 19 April 1785, with William Smith, the original Macbeth, restored. In the MS. all the notes up to 26 April are written in one unbroken paragraph, probably at the same time.

[7] Capt. (later Adm.) John Macbride, an Irish cousin of Mrs. Boswell. He had played a prominent role in the relief of Gibraltar in 1780 and was renowned for the capture of formidable French and Dutch privateers. Macbride was returned to Parliament for Plymouth in 1784.

[8] His first recorded meeting with the great actress, who sat for Reynolds several times. He had painted her portrait as the Tragic Muse in 1783.

WEDNESDAY 13 APRIL. Richmond Lodge.[9]

THURSDAY 14 APRIL. Home.

FRIDAY 15 APRIL. Somerset Coffee-house with Macbride. Welsh Club; Admiral Lloyd, etc.

SATURDAY 16 APRIL. Dempster's; his brother the *Ganges*, fine fellow.[1] Whist and potter[2] evening.

SUNDAY 17 APRIL. Brother with Major Green.[3] Temple commons. Brocklesby a little. Paradise's; Langton, Mrs. Cosway,[4] Lord Sandys.

MONDAY 18 APRIL. Reform Parliament.[5] Could not get in, and was not desirous. Dined Brocklesby; Devaynes,[6] etc. Tho. Davies a little.[7] Supped Lord Eglinton's; two bottles claret. Home ill.

TUESDAY 19 APRIL. Early out; brandy. Banks.[8] Breakfasted Shepherd and read d'Ankerville's papers. Breakfasted there.[9] Then Mr. Almack;[1] quite intoxicated. Sir Charles Preston; Westminster double.[2] Brandy; wild glow. Miss Palmer. Both Burkes came a little. Dined Aubrey's, Wilkes, Hutton (head of Moravians), etc. Great day. Mrs. Cosway's; music. Supped Lord Eglinton's again; two bottles claret. Quite sober.

---

[9] To visit the Stuarts.

[1] Dempster's half-brother, John Hamilton Dempster, now in command of the *Ganges*, an East Indiaman. He was drowned when the *Earl Talbot* was lost with all on board in 1800.

[2] Trifling talk.

[3] T. D. Boswell's brother-in-law, later a baronet and a general.

[4] This may have been Boswell's first meeting with Maria Cecilia Louisa Hadfield Cosway, the beautiful and well-known miniaturist, with whom he immediately established terms of intimacy. Born and raised in Italy (her mother was Italian), she was brought to England to study art and became a close friend of General Paoli.

[5] Pitt's motion for reform was made and defeated.

[6] John Devaynes, the King's apothecary (general medical practitioner) and a member of the Essex Head Club. He attended Boswell in his last illness.

[7] Boswell's last recorded meeting with Davies, who died at his house in Russell Street, Covent Garden, 5 May 1785.

[8] Sir Joseph Banks.

[9] D'Ankerville later reappears as a dinner-guest at Paoli's. Who he was and what his papers were remain mysterious. "Shepherd" is probably the Market Coffee-house in Shepherd's Market, Mayfair. The second notice of breakfast is an interlinear addition.

[1] Probably William Almack, barrister, son of the founder of Almack's Club, which survives as Brooks's.

[2] The manuscript is clear, but the meaning is not. It may signify a sexual encounter. Boswell was also in Westminster when he met "Polly Wilson," who appears in the notes for journal 25 and 26 April, below.

WEDNESDAY 20 APRIL. General ill from disturbance. Resolved no more. Lay all forenoon.

THURSDAY 21 APRIL. Dined Colonel Erskine. Opera; *Robin Gray.*[3] Birsled[4] peas Mrs. Sinclair's. George Wallace's. Spottiswoode's.

FRIDAY 22 APRIL. Dined Mr. Osborn's. Evening Mrs. Buller.

SATURDAY 23 APRIL. Dined Mr. Langton's.

SUNDAY 24 APRIL. Duke of Montrose; Lady Graham. Duchess, old china.[5] Evening Miss Monckton.

MONDAY 25 APRIL. Breakfasted Mrs. Cosway. On guard with Lord Cathcart, etc.[6] Mrs. Cosway's; Miss Hervey.[7] Supped Guard. Polly Wilson.

TUESDAY 26 APRIL. Horse Guards review. Lord Ossory. Polly Wilson. Dr. Smith. House of Commons committees. Jack Lee. Home with him, and Paley's book.[8] Colonel Hamilton. Club. Supped Seward.

WEDNESDAY 27 APRIL. Dined Devaynes. Essex Head Club. Dilly's, after being at Betts's and fixing with Smith to see execution.[9]

THURSDAY 28 APRIL. Up between five and six. Smith ready. Almost shrunk in Newgate. Mr. Herne and Mr. Young, under-sheriffs. Mr. Akerman. Grew well. Saw the nineteen pass close to me in review.[1]

[3] A popular ballet performed with a new set of Caledonian reels after the first act of the opera *Arteserse* at the King's Theatre in the Haymarket.

[4] Parched, roasted dry (Scots).

[5] She was now in her sixty-eighth year. Her daughter-in-law, Lady Graham, a bride of only one month, died in childbirth the next year.

[6] That is, he joined him on guard-duty and dined with him at the officers' mess ("etc."). Cathcart was a lieutenant-colonel in the Coldstream Guards.

[7] Perhaps Elizabeth, the only child of the Hon. William Hervey and one of Johnson's favourites.

[8] The *Principles of Moral and Political Philosophy*, published this year. Boswell later purchased a copy (see Appendix A, 12 September 1785).

[9] Betts was the proprietor of the Queen's Arms in St. Paul's Churchyard. "Smith" ("Dr. Smith" in the preceding entry) is probably the headmaster of Westminster School, whom Boswell consulted in 1772 on the cause of his client John Hastie, the abusive schoolmaster. Boswell was almost certainly Smith's guest at the school 3 May 1785 (see below, p. 289).

[1] None of the prisoners had been convicted of a crime that would now be capital. One was found guilty of having counterfeited stamps, another of forging a will; three had returned from transportation before the expiration of their terms. The remainder were charged with thefts ranging from "a looking-glass, a surtout coat, and a pair of velvet breeches" to ten thousand dollars and forty watches. The *London Chronicle* observed that "they were mostly very young, and to all appearance seemed very penitent" (26–28 April 1785).

Then on roof. Not shocked. Townshend the thief-taker.[1a] Mrs. Knowles's. H. Baldwin's. To Richmond Lodge. Miss Monckton there. Comfortable day.

FRIDAY 29 APRIL. Fine sail from Putney. Dined Malone's; Mr. Palmer, Mrs. Byng, and Miss Forrests.[2] Most agreeable day. Sat with him till two in morning, full of bar scheme, and encouraged.

SATURDAY 30 APRIL. In almost all forenoon writing *Tour*. Dined Solicitor-General.[3] But a dull day, yet content. Then Dilly's; with Baldwin and fixed printing *Tour*. "You must *feed* the press." "Alas! dinners, etc. I *feed myself*." Jack Dilly here. Resolved now, pamphlet against diminishing Lords of Session.[4]

SUNDAY 1 MAY. Breakfasted Forbes, vastly well. Advised me to frame Dr. Johnson's letter,[5] and if asked reason why come to London, take them into next room: "*There* are my reasons." Chapel, Moorfields, truly devout. Good sermon on prayer from Irish priest. Then walked Mile End. Coaches to Woodford.[6] Most hearty day. Grindall told three instances of making selves eunuchs which he *knew*: young Quaker in

[1a] John Townshend or Townsend, whose career as a Bow-Street officer spanned more than fifty years. He was later chief officer of the Bow-Street police and a great favourite of George IV as well as George III.

[2] Edmond Malone, scholar, critic, and editor; probably the Rev. John Palmer, Sir Joshua Reynolds's nephew; and the three daughters of Cmdre. Arthur Forrest. Bridget Forrest was married to John Byng, Commissioner of Stamps, author of the travel-diaries, later (for a fortnight only) fifth Viscount Torrington.

[3] Robert Dundas, son of the Lord President.

[4] Four days earlier, Ilay Campbell had introduced a bill into the House of Commons to reduce the number of the Lords of Session from fifteen to ten and to increase the salaries of the diminished court. The bill was actually Henry Dundas's, whom Boswell should have conciliated in every way if he was really serious in his suit for political preferment. But he was outraged by all innovation, particularly as regarded English guarantees to Scotland, and the sense of having truckled to Dundas rankled. He threw prudence to the winds and wrote the most extravagant of all his publications, calling Dundas "Harry the Ninth" and airing his grievance over the Ayrshire election. But he also argued to the point that the law would be delayed by reducing a court already overburdened with cases, and that increasing the salaries of fewer judges would make their appointments altogether an object of political preferment. Written in the first person and with great fervour, the *Letter to the People of Scotland* (1785) is both a patriotic document and a calculated effort to win the independent interest (see above, 21 January 1785, p. 280) for the seat in Parliament that Boswell announced he would seek at the next election.

[5] Consenting to Boswell's settling in London and reviewing the advantages, which Boswell extracted from the letter (dated 11 July 1784) and published in the *Life of Johnson*.

[6] He walked to Robert Preston's city house at Mile End and from there went in a series of coaches to the house at Woodford which Preston had inherited from Charles Foulis, director of the Sun Fire Office.

London Hospital, from false religion; a ——— because he would have no more children; a German jeweller, despairing love for his landlady. "You bitch, you shall have it one way or other"; threw it at her.

MONDAY 2 MAY. Up well. Wrote part of pamphlet against diminishing Lords of Session. Cried Bob: "He's fit for anything." To town in his chaise with *gong*.[7] Alarmed all the Poultry[8] with it. Wrote so much *Hebrides Tour*. Went to Baldwin's with the *copy*, and had it fairly put to the press. Dined Lord Ossory's (first time); Lord Palmerston, Sir Joshua, Col. James Erskine, Andrew Stuart (had not been in his company these sixteen years).[9] Resolved not to be sulky but good-humoured, and was so. A. S. said I had asked Lord Mansfield if he had read something. "Your *Letters*," said I. "It is not true. I did not, upon my honour. But since you have mentioned the subject, I will tell you. I introduced them. Observed if he winced. If he was hurt. He did not wince. He was not hurt. They were *telum imbelle*."[1] Lady Ossory was truly courteous; spoke much of her expectations of my account of Dr. Johnson. Said her daughter, Lady Anne, was asked to dine at her grandmother's.[2] Excused herself because Mr. Boswell was to dine. Her grandmother sent back word if she had known Mr. Boswell there, would not have asked her. "There!" said Sir Joshua. "There's something to write down." Was brilliant. In Sir Joshua's coach with Lord Ossory to Brooke's[3] door. Then I to Spottiswoode's and steadily revised Mercer's Case.[4]

TUESDAY 3 MAY. In a good part of the forenoon. Then to Westminster School. Heard many boys deliver themes. Dined in the Hall.[5] Sat next the apprentice of Mr. Harman, an eminent attorney. Dr.

[7] A large Chinese gong promised him by Foulis and transmitted by Preston. See below, 2 June 1785.

[8] Where Dilly's house was located.

[9] In his *Letter to the People of Scotland* Boswell managed to refer to this dinner and to praise both Palmerston and Ossory. Andrew Stuart was the Duke of Hamilton's agent in the Douglas Cause, and conducted it with great keenness and ability.

[1] "A harmless weapon" (Virgil, *Aeneid*, ii. 554). In the appeal to the House of Lords both Thurlow (Douglas's counsel) and Mansfield made severe reflections on Stuart's conduct. He fought a duel with Thurlow, and published a series of *Letters to the Right Honourable Lord Mansfield* accusing him of partiality. The letters were much admired, and were frequently compared in point of style with the contemporary invective of Junius. Boswell conducted his experiment on Lord Mansfield 11 April 1773.

[2] Lady Ossory was Anne Liddell, divorced wife of the Duke of Grafton, and one of Horace Walpole's favourite correspondents. Her mother was Lady Ravensworth.

[3] Probably Brooks's Club. Lord Ossory was a Whig.

[4] Spottiswoode was the solicitor (agent) in the appeal to the House of Lords.

[5] It was the day of the annual election dinner, when the "major candidates" were chosen for Christ Church, Oxford, and Trinity College, Cambridge.

Jackson[6] denied he had claret, but showed some afterwards. Said I: "Mr. Harman, if you had him in Westminster Hall, you'd cross-question him." "I'm sure you would," said he. I told him I was coming there. He drank success to me in Westminster Hall. (*Mem.*: This accidental meeting may be of use.) Then heard boys deliver epigrams. Found Dr. Taylor. Made friendship with him.[7]

WEDNESDAY 4 MAY. Dined Dilly's with Matra,[8] Engraver Strange,[9] Mr. Murray from Maryland, etc. Was excellent company.

THURSDAY 5 MAY. Dined Douglas's; Lord Ancram, Colonel Wemyss, Young Townshend. Wemyss and I two bottles each champagne. Was quite intoxicated. Brought home by Wemyss.

FRIDAY 6 MAY. Was in agitation but not ill. Breakfasted Jack Lee and had brandy. Very cordial. Dined with Dr. Taylor of Westminster tête-à-tête, and he dictated a great deal about Dr. Johnson, which I wrote down. Invited me to come again to Ashbourne. I was quite at *home* in *England*. Mrs. Sally[1] made tea. I insisted on it, as 'tis the custom, and besides, I like her. Stayed till half past ten. Seward's a little.

SATURDAY 7 MAY. Dined at Langton's. There was there a young officer of the navy who recounted sea actions in which he had been. Langton said, "I drink it in greedily." *I'd* as soon have heard an attorney recount twenty suits. I eat *well* and drank *some*. Then we had a conversazione in the drawing-room. I was quite happy to meet Mrs. Garrick again. Made her shake hands. Miss Hannah More and I had much chat. She liked Colley Cibber's saying of good pickings in old age,[2] and said, "I take it *you'll* have good pickings." I talked a little with Mrs. Carter, Miss Streatfield, Mrs. and Miss Ord (Bigge's relations)[3]. Sir J.

[6]The Dean of Christ Church and a former Westminster scholar.

[7]Boswell first met Taylor, prebendary of Westminster and Dr. Johnson's Lichfield schoolfellow and lifelong friend, when he accompanied Johnson on a visit to Taylor's Ashbourne residence, March 1776. He was cultivating his friendship now for reasons that appear below, 6 May 1785.

[8]James Maria Matra, consul to the Canaries, and "father" of Australia. His far-sighted "Proposal for Establishing a Settlement in New South Wales" by the voluntary migration of loyalist refugees from America was laid before the Coalition government the previous summer. Under pressure, Matra added provisions for transported criminals, who should be reclaimed by outright grants of acreage for farming. Though his plan was rejected, it led to the proposal for a penal colony which Pitt's government adopted.

[9]Robert Strange, a Scots Jacobite, the outstanding British engraver of the century. He was knighted by King George III in 1787 after engraving West's painting, "The Apotheosis of the Royal Children."

[1]Sarah Vigras, Dr. Taylor's servant.

[2]Reported to Boswell by Sir John Pringle, 21 March 1781.

[3]Sophia Streatfield, a beauty and a scholar, one of the circle the Thrales had gathered at Streatham; Mrs. Anna Ord, a widow from Newcastle, and her daughter Charlotte,

Hawkins and I did very well. Stood in a corner and talked grave and earnest. He accounted for Johnson's fear of death: "I have read his diary. I wish I had not read so much. He had strong amorous passions." BOSWELL. "But he did not indulge them?" HAWKINS. "I have said enough."[4] Then Sir Joseph Banks's. Evening company. Did not make much of it. But respectable.

SUNDAY 8 MAY. Breakfasted Serjeant Bolton[5] who advised me as a friend to take next winter in Westminster Hall and be used to them a little. For if I should come upon them directly from Scotland, 'twould be like Macbeth. My letter against diminishing Lords of Session was now printing. Repeated some of it to Bolton, which he thought very eloquent. Then Sardinian Chapel. Was fully devout. Admired very much a charming woman; "God bless you." "Dieu vous bénisse." Kitty Abbot, chambermaid. Dined Sir J. Dick's; General Paoli, Gentili, Sir Matthew White Ridley,[6] Lady and sister and brother, two Trevelyans. I took much to Sir Matthew, and prepared him against Court of Session job.[7] He spoke violently against Dundas, and said he'd be quoted as a precedent to justify a total disregard of public spirit. I drank a great deal. Told Sir J. Dick tête-à-tête of my *Letter*. He applauded my standing on my own legs, and thought Dundas insolent. Supped Captain Macbride's.[8] Was quite cordial with him. Prepared him fully for my

---

staunch friends of the Burneys. Mrs. Ord's other surviving daughter, Jemima, was the wife of Thomas Charles Bigge, of Benton House, near Newcastle. Boswell had made his acquaintance during his tour of Italy in 1765.

[4] In his biography of Johnson (1787) Hawkins implied that Johnson's sexual desires overcame his scruples when he came to London and associated with Richard Savage. Boswell tendered the same explanation for Johnson's harsh self-judgement and his great fear of death, though more delicately, in the last pages of his *Life of Johnson*. He also had read surreptitiously in Johnson's diary, in 1773, but whatever he had learned, this conversation with Hawkins and a conference with him "upon a delicate question" on 8 July 1786, again at Langton's, explain with reasonable certainty the coincidence of their views. They probably agreed at their second meeting to mention Johnson's licentiousness guardedly, without authority, so that information taken from his diary, which Johnson had recovered from Hawkins and burned, should not be used against him.

[5] James Clayton Bolton, serjeant-at-law, one of a superior order of barristers from which the Common Law judges were chosen until 1873.

[6] Dick, comptroller of accounts in the War Office, while consul at Leghorn had been intermediary in the early correspondence between Boswell and General Paoli. He also collected both manuscript and printed materials for *An Account of Corsica*. Grateful for his help, Boswell had encouraged him in the assumption of a dormant baronetcy to which his claims were at best dubious. Ridley was M.P. for Newcastle-upon-Tyne.

[7] Job: public business carried through with a view to improper private gain.

[8] Paragraphs on both Sir Matthew White Ridley ("that stately, that pleasing Northumbrian") and Macbride ("that brave Irishman, the cousin of my wife, and the friend of my heart") were worked into the *Letter*.

Letter, and said I did not care how it was taken. But I begged he would be kind enough to be my friend in the field if Dundas or any of them should challenge me. He readily agreed, saying, however, he knew nothing of these affairs. But he said, "He won't challenge you." I drank pretty well here too, and nodded. When I got home I felt firm, having my mind made up.

MONDAY 9 MAY. Working hard at my *Letter* and attending press. Dined home; d'Ankerville, brother T. D., etc., there. I think lay Dilly's. Yes.

TUESDAY 10 MAY. Breakfasted Dr. William Scott, amiable and friendly. He said I had come up last year with all Scotland at my heels. Encouraged me to Westminster Hall.[9] Thought my *Letter* eloquent. Worked hard at Baldwin's. Was half-way to our Literary Club. But thought I'd cancel all in my *Letter* about *myself*. So returned and ordered sheet to be cancelled. Unpleasing uncertainty.[1] *Loder* the compositor an accurate, obliging man. Took a lobster and porter in Butcher Row. The only dreary day this time in London. Mrs. Bosville's a little, a rout; Sir Thomas Blackett there, etc., etc.

WEDNESDAY 11 MAY. Hard at Baldwin's and Dilly's. Took a share of Dilly's family dinner. Was at Essex Head Club; Dr. Brocklesby, ——— Wyatt. "Duke of Richmond," said Brocklesby, "has none of the amiable weaknesses."[2] Wyatt told us he gives his brother £50 a year only to spend a few days with him and talk of architecture.[3]

THURSDAY 12 MAY. Breakfasted with Tom Tyers. Was quite rapt into literature. N.B. His little maid curtsied simply. *Letter* goes on. Dined at Dr. Orme's, my vassal in Glassmount, by invitation of his

[9] Scott himself had been admitted to the bar after achieving renown as Camden Reader in Ancient History at Oxford. His allusion to Boswell's following is surely to the Address to the King from Ayrshire which Boswell managed and carried up to London. Scott may also have learned that Boswell was instrumental in getting addresses presented by the burgh of Culross and the county of Midlothian.

[1] He cancelled pages 9–16 and ended by cancelling pages 17–24 as well. The manuscript of the *Letter*, which is in the Hyde Collection, also discloses that Boswell later revised the contents of these two half-sheets and restored most of the matter to the pamphlet at pages 51–62 and 93–94. Among the topics are his friendship with the Dundas family and the Earl of Eglinton, his love for his wife, Margaret Boswell, and the details of his financial differences with Sir Adam Fergusson. The final matter, an avowal of political independence and integrity, introduces the long personal conclusion to the pamphlet, where Boswell asks that he be allowed to "indulge a little more" his "own *egotism* and *vanity*," and includes a footnote on his genealogy extending over three pages.

[2] He was accused of domestic parsimony and of cowardice. Brocklesby may be implying that the weaknesses of Richmond's great-grandfather, King Charles II, *were* amiable.

[3] James Wyatt, renowned architect and member of the Essex Head Club. His brother Joseph also practised architecture.

brother Alexander.[4] A Mr. Colquhoun, formerly in the army, son of Provost Colquhoun of Edinburgh, there. A most excellent day. Superior and vassal admirably kept up, and Mrs. Orme, a Highgate lady, entered quite into the spirit of it. I said to her, "There was *one* right, Madam, the superior had: *mercheta mulierum*. But it is too late now."[5] A deal of wine drank. And *Sandy* confirmed the *principles* of my *Letter*. Told me a fine anecdote of ―――― at the Union proposing we should have no Members, but trust the generous English. Tea. Then wandered. Foot of Ludgate Hill, Dean's Court, Old Bailey, ysteB htimS. Pleasing and honest. Dilly's night. Had in *St. James's* short letter to people of Scotland: "Hear at large soon."[6]

FRIDAY 13 MAY. Morning twice with ys.[7] Then Dilly's a minute. Then breakfasted Molly Knowles, fine. Tea with her. Then White Hart Court, Quakers' Meeting, a great day with them.[8] One man and two women preached very well. I took out my last night *St. James's Chronicle* letter to look at. A stiff Quaker rebuked me: "'Tis unseemly to read at Meeting. I never saw such a thing before." I said I forgot a word, which disturbed me. Then Batson's. Met there a decent man who proved to be unfortunate Mr. James, Fordyce's partner.[1] He took me

[4]David Orme, M.D., was "man-midwife extraordinary" to the City of London Lying-in Hospital. He appears to have held Glassmount in Fife, of which Old James Boswell had purchased the superiority in 1733. Boswell and Alexander ("Sandy") Orme, Writer to the Signet, had been acquainted at least since January 1768.

[5]The ancient Scottish privilege of the "first night" granted the lord of the manor or a baron on a vassal's marriage. The custom gave way to a monetary payment on the marriage of a tenant, but even that feudal tax was now generally extinct.

[6]"To the People of Scotland: I rejoice to find you are roused by the alarming attempt to *infringe the articles of the Union*, and introduce a *most pernicious innovation* by obtaining an Act of Parliament to alter the *Constitution* of the *College of Justice* by diminishing the number of the *Lords of Session* in order to give them larger salaries. I feared you were torpid. Having called to you with so much success last year to oppose Mr. *Fox's East India Bill*, I resolved to call to you again on this momentous occasion. My friends and countrymen, be not afraid. I am *upon the spot*. I am *upon the watch*. The Bill *shall not pass* without a spirited appeal to the justice and honour of the Commons of Great Britain. Collect your minds. Be calm, but be firm. You shall hear from me at large a few days hence" (*St. James's Chronicle*, 12 May 1785).

[7]Again Betsy Smith.

[8]That is, an important day to the Friends. Boswell was at the regular sixthday-morning Meeting, which was swelled by country Friends who had already arrived for the London Yearly Meeting, the assembly for church affairs of the Society of Friends in Great Britain. It began at White Hart Court in Gracechurch Street Monday 16 May, and was preceded by the Meeting for Sufferings on Friday 13 May and the Yearly Meeting of ministers and elders Saturday 14 May.

[1]Batson's was a coffee-house next to the Royal Exchange in Cornhill. William James was ruined by the failure in 1772 of the banking-house Neal, James, Fordyce, and Down. Alexander Fordyce, the principal partner, had overplayed his hand in East India stock and absconded to France owing very large sums to his partners.

to Bethlehem Hospital, where I saw Lunardi ascend in his balloon. Was shocked and pleased.[2] Old acquaintance, Mr. White.[3] Pleasing ladies. Charming day. Looked at wards, both men and women. Pretty girl sung. I asked if she could [sing] "Maid of Bedlam." No. I sung part of it.[4] She could not be hurt. One said, "I'm incurable." One man Methodist. Dined Dr. Scott's; his lady, Mr. Palmer, Dr. Fisher.[5] Much drinking by me and Fisher. Scott said there was a great deal of phlogiston[6] in my *Letter*. Was intoxicated much. St. Paul's Churchyard, sung ballads with two women in red cloaks. Had pocket picked. Fell in street. Got home by help of two different worthy men, ――― and ―――.

SATURDAY 14 MAY. Tom Tyers breakfasted with us in fine spirits. Carried me in his coach to Bishop of St. Asaph's, where I sat a little with Mrs. and Miss Shipley, and then to Baldwin's to attend *Letter*. ys. Then Old Bailey. Judge Willes spied me and called me to bench and invited me to dinner. Baron Perryn and Recorder there. Willes very pleasant and Recorder also,[7] who told Foote's joke of "never saw a bit

[2]"Mr. Lunardi having been the first adventurer in the English atmosphere [15 September 1784], an invitation to attend his second voyage drew an amazing multitude on Friday to the Artillery Ground. The public had been induced to believe that a balloon of sufficient power to carry three persons with a proper apparatus and sufficient ballast would be launched into the air. The friends of Mr. Lunardi had been industrious in whispering the names and in giving a favourable impression of the talents of Mrs. Sage and Mr. Biggin, who were to return from an aerial tour to the Continent. . . . When the company, to the amount of four or five thousand in the Ground and eighty or a hundred thousand in the neighbourhood, were assembled, rumours of ill usage and dissension were propagated. It was seen by the preparations that the power of the balloon had been falsely estimated, and Lunardi getting into his car a little after one . . . he ascended, partly to fulfill his promise, partly to escape embarrassing interrogations. The wind being at south-east he was carried directly over London; . . . by disposing of his remaining ballast he with some difficulty proceeded to the ground at the end of Tottenham Court Road, from whence he and his balloon were conducted to the Pantheon. . . . The balloon was heavy from too many and clumsy precautions to prevent evaporation, and imputations have been cast on the process of filling it" (*St. James's Chronicle*, 12–14 May 1785). It should be said for Vincenzo Lunardi, secretary to the Neapolitan Ambassador in England, that he had achieved a very great height when he ascended over London the previous year.
[3]The steward of Bethlehem and Bridewell Hospitals.
[4]First stanza, from a copy with music published at London in 1772 (courtesy of the British Library):
    One morning very early, one morning in the spring,
    I heard a maid in Bedlam who mournfully did sing,
    Her chains she rattled on her hands, while sweetly thus sung she,
    I love my love, because I know my love loves me.
[5]John Fisher, LL.D., practised law in the ecclesiastical and admiralty courts.
[6]"A hypothetical substance or 'principle' supposed to exist in combination in all combustible bodies and to be disengaged in the process of combustion" (O.E.D.).
[7]*A Letter to the People of Scotland*, p. 82: "This letter was printed thus far (14 May 1785)

of Scotch beef; you send only bones." I said, "I'm well hardened; twenty years' acquaintance John Wilkes and Dr. Johnson." Scots pint came.[8] "*There now we* have it," [said] I. "Every dog has his day, Mr. Recorder."

[EDITORIAL NOTE. Boswell recorded one of Adair's more impressive anecdotes on a leaf which he headed "14 May 1785" and interleaved with the journal.]

Mr. Adair, Recorder of London, told me at the Sheriff's table at the Old Bailey that the King takes an important part himself when the report of the convicts under sentence of death is made to him in the Cabinet or select Council. As an instance, when the noted Patrick Madan's case was mentioned after his last condemnation,[9] His Majesty said, "Mr. Recorder, is not that an old acquaintance of yours?" "Yes, Sir," said the Recorder, "older than is to his credit." Said Lord Thurlow: "Mr. Recorder, don't you think the evidence on which he is convicted very slight, to say no worse?" "I do," said Adair. "What, Mr. Recorder," said the King, "do *you* think it not sufficient?" "I do, Sir," said Adair, "and there is not another of Your Majesty's subjects who would have been convicted upon it." "Well," said the King, "we do not sit here to try people's characters. He must not suffer. But what shall we do? He is a very bad man. We must not turn him loose upon the community." Said the Recorder: "Sir, since a jury has put him in Your Majesty's power, you do him no injustice when you save his life, though you send him to the coast of Africa"; and so was decreed.[1]

---

when I had the honour to dine in company with Mr. Justice Willes. . . ." Boswell then reports a pointed anecdote told by Willes on the obsequiousness of the nobility to Archibald, Duke of Argyll, for many years until his death in 1761 manager or "uncrowned King" of Scotland. Sir Richard Perryn was Baron of the Exchequer and James Adair, since 1779, Recorder of London (presiding judge at the Lord Mayor's Court of Record in Law and Equity).

[8] Equal to three English pints.

[9] Madan was sentenced to death at the Old Bailey December 1780 for stealing a collection of jewels, but the court later exercised the power granted the year previous to pardon felons if they accepted transportation to Africa for life. The ship carrying Madan was driven into the Cove of Cork (now Cobh), where he escaped, returned to London, and was apprehended. According to Madan, he had been left in Ireland because he could not be moved from sick-quarters ashore. There being no witnesses to his story, at the January Session 1782 Madan was remanded under his former sentence of death as having violated the conditions of his pardon.

[1] Madan was informed at the April Session 1782 that he would again be transported to Africa for life. There were continuing objections to such sentences in Parliament (Burke among the leaders) on the grounds that the tropical climate and native hostility meant certain death.

Time for court again approaching. "I hope we shall have a little more wine. Rather make a report of me to His Majesty than give me no more wine. Besides, Irish song: 'I will drink *wine* with thee, Robin *Adair.*'"² Court again in high glee. "My dear Lord Mayor,³ beg pardon for such familiarity, but I am so glad to see your Lordship. Ashamed some weeks in town. Make atonement by coming soon to Mansion House." *Hart* took great liking to me.⁴ He and I tea with counsel. Then home for nightcap to be with ys. Madly went to Lord Eglinton's and drank pint port and bottle claret. Stewart of Stair there. Went away. I had told going to ys. My Lord then in fine humour. I posted to Old Bailey; place occupied. Tried two inns.⁵ ys proposed friend, White-chapel. Walked briskly to it. *Three* then. Insisted she should repeat LORD's prayer. Strange mixture. Wondrous fondness.

SUNDAY 15 MAY. Up and got silver 2/- from ys. Dilly's and dressed, quite easy. Mansion House. Breakfasted Lord Mayor and Lady May-oress, etc. Then Lee. With him to Theophilus Lindsey's. Wonderfully good, but was frightened to be thrown loose.⁶ Dined home; brother, etc., and Signora Recha. Raved fine to her. To bed early; warm port and water, being quite sleepy and feverish.

MONDAY 16 MAY. Up wonderfully well. *Letter* going on. But some-thing not right appeared. Called ys and asked. Thought *not*. Dined home. Had walked in park with a Miss ———. Lord Eglinton and Wemyss saw it. Col. Erskine and I visited Shawfield.

TUESDAY 17 MAY. Dined Lord Eglinton's, chiefly an Ayrshire party. Got away not drunk and went straight to Baldwin's. Easily ac-cepted of a bed at his house. Drank only small beer and wine and water. Was elegantly lodged.

²An allusion not to the well-known ballad but to some earlier verses which were composed in Ireland in 1734 for the purpose of welcoming an Irish M.P. named Robert Adair to Puckstown, County Dublin.
³Richard Clark, former alderman, an attorney with a considerable practice, and a member of the Essex Head Club on Dr. Johnson's recommendation.
⁴The evidence is among Boswell's papers, endorsed in his hand "Spontaneous com-pliment": "From the small acquaintance of the man JH wishes to be better acquainted. This is plain honest dealing. I, John Hart, formerly alderman and also Sheriff of the City of London, now residing at No. 23, King Street, Bloomsbury, do give this spon-taneous testimony to you, James Boswell, Esquire, of Auchinleck, Ayrshire, as witness my hand at the court holden at the Old Bailey on the fourteenth of May in the year of our Lord one thousand seven hundred and eighty-five.—JOHN HART".
⁵Old Bailey, from which the Sessions House took its name, was a narrow street running between Ludgate Hill and Newgate Street, opposite Newgate Prison. It was a great collecting place for coaches and wagons, and there were many inns in the area.
⁶Boswell refers to the effect of the sermon at the Unitarian chapel in Essex Street, where Lindsey, a former Anglican clergyman, was minister and Jack Lee a member.

WEDNESDAY 18 MAY. Breakfasted Baldwin's, quite at home. House of Commons committee. Lord Advocate asked for my pamphlet. "Your Lordship shall have it. I am putting the lead to the ends of my *taws*.[7] The bill *shall* not pass." Dined home and drank only small beer. *Giuseppe*[8] advised medicinally.

THURSDAY 19 MAY. *Letter* went on. Was in *some* agitation as to a challenge. But roused my mind. Dined at home. Water. Spirits a little low.

FRIDAY 20 MAY. Resolved to be seen at Court recently before my *warm appearance*. Dressed in my scarlet suit. Looked like a baron, and was quite easy. Talked with Lord Cathcart, Major Arabin, Duke of Gordon, Lord Effingham, etc., etc., with a *perfect possession* of myself and *serene gaiety*. The Duke of Gordon, Lord Effingham, and I stood close by the door of the levee-room—on the outside, we being in the room before you enter *it*. The King with a truly benevolent, smiling countenance approached us. He asked Lord Effingham about a complaint which had distressed him a little, and asked if he took anything for it. My Lord said no. The King said, "You just let it work itself out." "I take a great deal of exercise," said the Earl. The King then talked of people being too fond of theories and adapting facts to them, whereas he thought it would be better first to get a collection of facts and then form a theory. He talked of balloons, and said he supposed experiments made in them could not be very exact, as the people must be so frightened that they could not give full attention. He told us a curious remark: that there is a point of time when the balloon gets so high, so far above the earth, that no noise is heard; and being in a quiet atmosphere, all is silence. "This," he said, "frightens them much. A very natural sensation." If quotation had been proper to Majesty, I should have mentioned Congreve's fine passage in the *Mourning Bride* upon the horror of stillness, so highly praised by Dr. Johnson.[9] But he was talking then to the Duke of Gordon, though Lord Effingham and I made part of the audience. I was not *quite sure* that the King recollected me. So was a little in a flutter *now*, as I should have been somewhat mortified if he had taken no notice of me. But I was soon relieved, for he said to me (without any "When did you come to town?" or such commonplace words), "Have you got balloons in the North?" "Sir," said I, "we have

[7] A leather strap with slit ends used for whipping schoolboys.
[8] General Paoli's valet.
[9] The dialogue concluding with Almeria's speech, "No, all is hush'd, and still as death.— 'Tis dreadful!" (II, i. 52–69). Johnson wrote in the "Life of Congreve," ¶ 34, that "if I were required to select from the whole mass of English poetry the most poetical paragraph, I know not what I could prefer" to that passage.

tried them, but have not succeeded, though I think we have as light heads there as the people here." The Duke of Gordon said they had tried a balloon at Aberdeen and done pretty well.[1] Lord Effingham said he would think himself safer above the sea than above the land; for a fall upon land would kill a man, whereas at sea he might have boats ready to pick him up. I then talked, I suppose rather too easily, to the King, for one should never begin a subject, but only answer: "Your Majesty knows that Mr. Windham has been up." "No," said he. "Dear me!" said I, "is it not known? He has been up, Sir." ("With Sadler of Oxford," said the Duke of Gordon.) "And Your Majesty was observing that they'd be so frightened in the balloon. Mr. Windham has assured me that he was not frightened, and that he has made very accurate observations, which he is to give us in print."[2] Here I certainly was not *in order*—to discover that the Sovereign had not heard of Windham's going up—that Majesty was ignorant of anything. (How angry Jack Lee was when I talked thus *Toryishly*!) And to exclaim, "Dear me!" was too *natural*. Yet the King did not seem at all displeased, but rather, I thought, liked to be entertained.

He then graciously asked me, "How do you go on with your account of your" (I think *great* or *old*) "friend?" "Sir," said I, "I am going first to give my *log-book*, my journal kept *de die in diem*,[3] of the curious journey which Dr. Johnson and I made through a remote part of *Your Majesty's dominions*, our Highlands and Islands" (thus connecting them with the King—throwing them into his bosom). "It will be more a journal of Dr. Johnson than of what I saw." I said, "Whenever it is finished, I shall take the liberty to present it to Your Majesty." The King gave a gracious nod. Said the King: "But when are we to have" (or "when are you to give") "your other work?" (meaning the *Life*). "Sir," said I, "Your Majesty a little ago remarked that people were sometimes in too great a hurry before they had collected facts. I mean to avoid that fault, and shall take time, as I intend to give a very full account of Dr. Johnson." KING. "There will be many before you." BOSWELL. "I wish first to see them all, Sir." KING. "There will be many foolish lives first. Do you make the best." BOSWELL. "I cannot presume

[1] After a number of frustrated attempts, James Tytler, Britain's first aeronaut, ascended over Edinburgh to a height of 350 feet 27 August 1784. An experiment with a small balloon had been conducted at Aberdeen in March of that year.

[2] Windham had flown over London with James Sadler, the aeronaut in whom George III came to take a special interest, 5 May 1785. Privately a vacillating man, Windham was so impressed with his own fearlessness on this occasion that he wrote in his *Diary*, "The experience . . . will warrant a degree of confidence more than I have ever hitherto indulged" (ed. Mrs. Henry Baring, 1866, p. 52).

[3] From day to day.

to say I can do that, Sir. But I shall do as well as I can." KING. "I believe you knew him more intimately than any man." BOSWELL. "He was very good to me, Sir. And I was very forward with him." In the course of the conversation he politely named *Dr. Johnson* to the Duke of Gordon and Lord Effingham, that they might know who was meant. KING. "I believe he was a very worthy man; a sincere Christian upon principle." BOSWELL. "He certainly was, Sir. And a great friend to subordination" (bowing respectfully to the Monarch), "in which he had great merit. As he used to say himself, 'I have great merit in this. For I hardly know who was my grandfather.' " KING. "There is one question concerning him to which I have never yet been able to get an answer, which is how he was so much master of the literature of his age, and yet for the last thirty or five-and-thirty years of his life was never known to study." BOSWELL. "Sir, he had the quickest apprehension and the most retentive memory of any man I suppose that ever lived. And he had a faculty of scooping out the substance of any book without reading it all through. He read very few books all through." (I think I said not above *five*, which was contracting too much.)

This was really a valuable conversation, and the King's gracious benignity refreshed the loyal flame in my bosom. Lord Howe[4] was at Court. I had not the honour of being known to him. But being anxious to get information for Auchenharvie and some more Saltcoats[5] people whether a Russian-built vessel of theirs could obtain a Mediterranean pass, I gently touched his Lordship on the arm and quietly made him fall back in the levee-room, into which I had now advanced. And thus I accosted him: "Lord Howe, will you give me leave to ask you a question? Does your Lordship recollect getting some oaks from Scotland?" LORD HOWE. "O, yes. Captain Fergusson was so good as to get me some." BOSWELL. "My father, an old judge, was very happy in having that opportunity to send anything to your Lordship."[6] (He bowed genteelly.) "Pray, how do they grow?" LORD HOWE. "Why, Sir, I fancy our soil is not well fitted for them." BOSWELL. "I thought it had. For I have been told that in Nottinghamshire you have a clay soil and a

[4]Richard Howe, first Viscount Howe of Langar (the elder brother of Gen. Sir William Howe), Commander-in-Chief of the Navy in North America 1776–1778 and now First Lord of the Admiralty.
[5]A town above Ayr on the west coast of Scotland, an area rich in salt factories and coal mines. Robert Reid Cunninghame of Auchenharvie built the Saltcoats Canal in order to carry coal to Saltcoats harbour from the pits he had opened in the vicinity.
[6]On 30 November 1781 Boswell himself wrote from Edinburgh to James Bruce, overseer at Auchinleck, "to send greased eggs and young fowls, if cheap. To send woodcocks. Also a dozen or so of young oaks for Lord Howe" (Register of Letters). Captain Fergusson was probably John Fergusson of Greenvale, in Ayrshire.

wet climate, as we have in Ayrshire." LORD HOWE. "We have great varieties of soil." BOSWELL. "There is an Admiralty question, my Lord, as to which some neighbours of mine in the country are anxious to be informed, which is whether a Russia-built vessel, if British property and manned by British seamen, can get a Mediterranean pass. I have heard it said no, because we must encourage our own ship-building; so that if a foreign-built vessel is not either captured, or has undergone such a repair in Britain as to be in a manner British, that protection will not be granted." LORD HOWE. "I should think her being British property sufficient. But if you will state the case to the Admiralty, you shall have an answer." He was mildly courteous. I drove Major Arabin home in my hackney-coach. I was sorry to hear from him he was about to divorce his beautiful wife and to cut the throat of her gallant.[7] But my mind was now amazingly firm, and I was *prepared* for every event of life. I went to Baldwin's and revised more of my *Letter*. Dined quietly at home at the General's. Tea Dempster's. Dilly's at night.

SATURDAY 21 MAY. Early at Merchant Taylors' School. Detected Finch's shameful imposture.[8] Went as appointed at eleven to Sir Matthew White Ridley's, and begged he would present a petition for me against the bill for lessening the number of the Lords of Session. He obligingly agreed, and we revised it, he suggesting some alterations in form. Visited Mrs. Blair (the morning star).[9] Also Mr. Hawkins. Visited Mrs. Macbride. Sorry to find he was gone out of town for a fortnight, as his agreeing to go to the *field* with me if necessary had made me easy. Was uncertain to whom I should next apply. Visited Mrs. and Captain Bosville. Dined at home and was quiet the evening.

SUNDAY 22 MAY. Mr. Loch visited me. I was in great spirits, and he was satisfied I did right to come to English bar. In all forenoon and missed worship. Brother came, with whom I had refused to dine after engaging, and had asked him to the General's today. Yet I had sent

[7] Arabin got his divorce by Act of Parliament four years later. His wife's "gallant" at this time was Thomas Sutton, of Lincoln's Inn; later (in 1787) she is said to have lived in France and Italy with "a Mr. St. George." No throat-cutting is reported.

[8] This entry is an afterthought wedged between the date and the sentence which follows. Because it is written across the line underscoring the date, the name can be read either as "Tench" or "Finch." No persons named Tench were enrolled at Merchant Taylors' School or in the Company during the eighteenth century, and we have found no evidence that Boswell knew any of the eight Finches of appropriate date. Boswell presumably found that someone claiming to be an alumnus of the school was an impostor. "Shameful" might seem too strong a characterization of such a deception, but Finch (?Tench) may have been using the connexion as qualification for a considerable legal claim.

[9] Unidentified.

to General Oglethorpe I'd dine with him if at home, and was made welcome. He was not pleased. He walked with me to Sir M. Ridley's door, where I delivered a large well-written copy of my petition, to be in readiness. And then I proposed to take brother to Oglethorpe's, to which he agreed, and was very well received. Only we and a Yorkshire lady there. At tea were ladies, Hawkins Browne, Colonel Johnson (Irish) from America,[1] Mr. Baillie (Scotch) from India. My spirits sunk, as Oglethorpe talked it almost all himself. Brother accompanied me so far in Fleet Street, as I was going to Dilly's to publish my pamphlet calmly. Felt myself here comfortable as usual, yet with the full view of fighting, which did not disturb me.

MONDAY 23 MAY. General's a moment. Left word not home till Wednesday. Dined impromptu at brother's. Tea, Frank's wife,[2] Sadler's Wells.[3] Dilly's.

TUESDAY 24 MAY. Breakfasted Spottiswoode's with Robert Boswell. Pamphlet all ready. Dined Dilly, ham and cutlets. Lee for franks. Convener Ayrshire.[4] Waited. Then in chambers with him.[4a] Talked of people not taking real happiness. Called Milton, Hampden, etc., "Noble army of martyrs."[5] Saw him home. Mrs. Lee. In, pipe, one glass punch, and small beer. Good chat but rough Whiggism. Near twelve, franks. Too late; returned and he altered a day.[6] Sat a little more. Not so well, as a little jaded. Had seen Betsy ill, and called Weare[7] about hospital.

---

[1] The younger Browne (his father, the poet, had died in 1760); the colonel was doubtless Guy Johnson, American loyalist, son-in-law to Sir William Johnson and his successor as superintendent of Indian affairs in North America. He was associated with the operations of Joseph Brant (the Mohawk chief Thayendanegea), and is said to have claimed credit for inspiring the Wyoming massacre.

[2] Almost nothing is known of Francis Barber's wife, Elizabeth, except that she was white and kept a school in Lichfield after her husband's death in 1801. Boswell was probably trying to pick up Johnsoniana.

[3] A separate leaf with the following note was found among the Malahide Papers and is now at Yale: "Sadler's Wells, 23 May 1785. A fine bold fellow who went up to the gallery and beat a blackguard. James Andrew, carman, No. 13, Greenfield Street, off Thames Street. A comely, cheerful girl, Mrs. Sally Jones of Monmouthshire, uppermaid at Mr. Sheriff Hopkins's, Hatton Street."

[4] The meaning is obscure, but some reference must be intended to John Hamilton of Sundrum, who became Convener of Ayrshire at about this time.

[4a] With Lee.

[5] "Te Deum Laudamus," *The Book of Common Prayer.*

[6] A franked letter at this time was required to bear the full date of the letter in the Member's handwriting and to be posted that day.

[7] Identity uncertain. Dr. James Ware, a distinguished ophthalmic surgeon, had studied at St. Thomas's Hospital, where Betsy was admitted.

WEDNESDAY 25 MAY. Busy preparing presentation books and writing letters with them. Waited on Lord Mayor and got order for Betsy to St. Thomas Hospital, and obligation.[8] Robinson, Paternoster Row.[9] Went to her. She made difficulties, but said she'd go in a week. Mutton broth, Dr. Mayo. Had porter running over town with presents. A little agitated, as now out. Essex Club. George Wallace with us. Dilly's.

THURSDAY 26 MAY. Published.[1] Wrote *Hebrides* all forenoon. Dined Dr. Fisher's Commons; Stephenson rattling there, also Dr. Pretyman and Campbell.[2] Scott a little evening. Dilly's.

FRIDAY 27 MAY. My letters from General's came. Sir M. Ridley to know if present.[3] Hastened, not stirring. Breakfasted Sir J. Dick's. Sir M. not up. Uneasy. Away to Coghlan's, Charteris's, General's. Italian Marchese and *abate* from Signora Piozzi.[4] Then Sir M.; all well. Dilly's; mutton broth tête-à-tête. Visited Mr. Atkins, quite *lairdly*, quite as if walking in *Hern* on a sunny afternoon.[5] Tea Molly Knowles.

SATURDAY 28 MAY. In all day in night-gown and wrote *Hebrides*. David Cuninghame called for a little.

SUNDAY 29 MAY.[6] Breakfasted Chapter. Then Herne, Newgate

[8] That is, Boswell signed an obligation for her charges. He paid 10s. 6d. for her admission (see entry for 2 June 1785, Appendix A, p. 355).

[9] George Robinson the bookseller. Boswell was presumably arranging for him to sell copies of the *Letter to the People of Scotland*.

[1] And sold at half a crown, correctly so, Henry Erskine was reported to have said, "as no person with a whole crown would either write or read such a book" (letter signed "Ximenes," *Gentleman's Magazine*, 1785, lv. 682). Though never republished, the *Letter* had a large printing and aroused strong feeling. Extracts running to as much as thirteen paragraphs appeared in six issues of the *Public Advertiser* between 31 May and 17 June 1785, and the *Gentleman's Magazine*, the *Scots Magazine*, the *Critical Review*, the *Monthly Review*, and the *English Review* praised Boswell's patriotism, his arguments, and his humour. The *St. James's Chronicle* for Saturday 4 June 1785 found passages which showed that the writer had studied in the schools both of Johnson and of Burke.

[2] Doctors' Commons, of which Dr. David Stephenson was also a fellow, was primarily the lodging of doctors of Civil Law of Oxford and Cambridge, although other jurists might dwell there. The ecclesiastical and admiralty courts in which the doctors practised met in their hall. George Pretyman, D.D., at this time Pitt's private secretary, was appointed Bishop of Lincoln and Dean of St. Paul's in 1787. Mr. Campbell has not been identified.

[3] There is no record that the petition was ever presented. The bill for lessening the number of the Lords of Session had been withdrawn, but the Commons was still entertaining resolutions on the subject.

[4] Then travelling with her husband in Italy.

[5] Atkins, a Russia-merchant, was formerly proprietor of Hern, which had since become a part of the estate of Auchinleck.

[6] There is also a list of memoranda for the day: "Sunday 29 May. Call Herne, and go chapel *if he sends*. If not, St. Paul's. Call Strahan, Barrington, Irvine, Murray (Temple), Grange (Hamilton), Sir Thomas Blackett, Sydenham's (Frith Street), Dempster, Wood

Chapel. Much affected, though not tenderly.[7] Thought of *self* as perhaps dying. Then press-yard.[8] Then Betsy, and gave good advice. Then Strahan; Hole the surgeon there. Then made calls in Temple. Mr. J. Nichols[9] a little. Advised me write Johnson's *Life* first, then sell it, as I'd get three—nay, ten—times as much. Then visited Jack Lee to have it over.[1] "You're a very odd fellow. You'll raise enmities in so many people in Scotland, and Dundas will be angry and think it not right to laugh at him and call him 'Harry the Ninth' when you are on terms of friendship with him." I laughed it off on public and private. Temple commons. Sir J. Dick's, *tête-à-tête*.[2] Card from Sir G. Howard for archives revived me.[3] Then Pearson's;[4] porter, good talk, pretty garden. Asked sup; agreed. Wife uncouth at first, turned out well. Anxious to drive my name into them. His daughter. But —— when the candle entered, etc.[5] Colonel Chauvel. Mr. Wynne. Home to General's.

MONDAY 30 MAY. Breakfasted Malone and talked of duel. He advised military man. Lodged will with him.[6] To House of Commons

(Titchfield Street), Ross Mackye's. Take shirts, one *on*, one pocket, or both pocket. Home and dress calm, after seeing Malone, and have him to breakfast Monday. Go on strictly now with *Hebrides*. Talk to Sir J. Dick of music for Veronica. And think of *retainers* from him, etc. Commons begin today. Ask about them, and perhaps eat them [to complete another term at the Inner Temple]. Copy *Letter* for *Bosville*. After one week more, mercury pills. Home these three days, till Wednesday evening, Bucks. Thursday, St. Thomas. Commons and Mansion House." "Bucks" is explained below, 1 June 1785.
[7] By the sight of the condemned criminals who were to suffer on Wednesday.
[8] The assembly-place of criminals setting out for the gallows. So called because persons on trial who refused to plead had been pressed to death in this courtyard.
[9] The editor of the *Gentleman's Magazine*, printer of the *Lives of the Poets*, compiler of *Literary Anecdotes of the Eighteenth Century*, and a member of the Essex Head Club.
[1] He had asserted in the *Letter to the People of Scotland* that Lee, Fox, Burke, Wilkes, and Pitt would oppose the diminishing bill.
[2] Boswell's emphasis suggests that he did initiate a discussion with Dick about retainers when he was admitted to the English bar (see memoranda for the day, n. 6, above).
[3] A standing invitation to attend the anniversary dinner at Chelsea Hospital (see above, 29 May 1783, p. 154, n. 5 and p. 156, n. 5).
[4] Possibly Sir Richard Pearson, whom Boswell certainly dined with on 19 November 1793. He was in command of the *Serapis* in the memorable engagement with John Paul Jones's *Bonhomme Richard*, and was knighted for his behaviour, though he surrendered the ship. Jones is said to have remarked on hearing of this honour, "Should I have the good fortune to fall in with him again, I'll make a lord of him."
[5] Unexplained. Possibly memoranda of anecdotes.
[6] The original document, in Boswell's own hand, dated 28 May 1785 and written "while under the apprehension of some danger to my life, which however may prove a false alarm," is in the General Register House, Edinburgh. There is also a codicil, written

with Italian. Could not get in. Dined home quiet. Robert Boswell called in the afternoon, not having dined. Got him cold meat and wine. Went with him to Spottiswoode's, who had company, and then to House of Commons to find Bearcroft;[7] gone. His *Edinburgh forward vulgarity* quite disgusted me. Home at night.

TUESDAY 31 MAY. Home forenoon at *Hebrides*. Dined ———. Evening supped with Mrs. Baldwin tête-à-tête. Baldwin came home after supper. Lay at his house, ready for the execution next day.

WEDNESDAY 1 JUNE. Baldwin's man was lazy and let me sleep too long. By the time I got to the Old Bailey they were tying up the convicts, so that I could not talk with them as I intended. The good woman who keeps the Session House let me through to the back door of Newgate. But all were so engaged, they did not hear me knock. I was frightened a little by the echo of my feet as I returned. Then in the street, saw the *exit*.[8] George Ward struggled long. While they were yet hanging,

---

at Malone's and dated 30 May 1785, in which Boswell writes more legibly the names of those who are to receive mourning-rings, adds to the list the names of Paoli and Barnard, and requests "the prayers of all my pious friends for my departed soul, considering how reasonable it is to suppose that it may be detained some time in a middle state." He made no other will. He appointed literary executors (Malone, Forbes, and Temple) to review all his own papers and to publish more or less at their discretion. This provision, which afterwards had as its practical result the division of his papers and the Fettercairn litigation, was probably intended mainly to safeguard his Johnsonian materials and to ensure their publication if he died before completing the publication himself. He assigned all profits of publication to his children other than Alexander, his heir. In a second codicil to the will, dated 22 December 1785, he made Malone sole literary executor for the publication of the *Life of Johnson:* Malone was given unrestricted access to the materials in his journals, but Boswell trusted that he "would not divulge anything in the said volumes which ought to be concealed." The codicil became inoperative when Boswell himself published the *Life of Johnson* in 1791, but he made no change in his provision of literary executors, though he twice thereafter reviewed his settlements. It seems likely that he hoped that Malone, Forbes, and Temple would compile the book of travels on the Continent that he still had in mind to publish, perhaps even that they would extract some other book from his vast autobiographical record.

[7] Edward Bearcroft, K.C., M.P. for Hindon, and one of the leading barristers in England. He was counsel with Boswell in Mercer's appeal. See below, 8 June 1785, n. 7.

[8] On a separate sheet Boswell has given a list of the convicts and the crimes for which they suffered, as follows:

1 *George Ward* ⎫ assaulting a woman in Wigmore Street and taking
2 *Thomas Conner* ⎰ a basket of linens.
3 *George Mawley*: escaping twice from hulks [dismantled ships anchored in the Thames and used as prisons].
4 *Henry Wood*: robbing Humphry Stokes, highway, of metal watch.
5 *Thomas Bateman*: assaulting a woman, Fleet Street, and taking gold locket.
6 *Patrick Daley*: stealing bars of iron out of barge on Thames.

went to Betsy just by. Imagined the feelings of a desperate highwayman. Said to her, "I have got a shocking sight in my head. Take it out." Her pleasing vivacity *did* remove it. I then called a little at Dilly's. Breakfasted with Strahan; Mrs. Maxwell of Dundee, a daughter of Principal Wishart's,[9] with him. He seemed quite failed. Gave me a *little* about Dr. Johnson, and promised to look out some of his letters and notes. Sat some time at Nichols's, trying to find a quotation of Dr. Johnson's in Butler's *Remains*, but could not.[1] Wet day. Visited Dr. Gilbert Stuart. His bluntness did not please me, though his strong mind did.[2] Dined at commons; found I was now well known to Mr. Spinks, our under-treasurer. Sat next him with Mr. O'Ridzel,[3] an Irishman, a Mr. Elliot of Wells; very agreeable. Met David Cuninghame; took him to tea at Baldwin's. Sat a little with Dr. Scott, calm and well. Drank tea at Horn Tavern, and then was introduced by the landlord to the Royal Hanoverian Lodge of Bucks.[4] Was well entertained with singing, and sung "Mortals wisely," etc.[5] Home to Dilly's. Betsy and her companion called in coach, and I drove so far and then walked over London Bridge to St. Thomas's Hospital. Curious.

---

7 *Thomas Scott*: robbing W. Thompson, Whitechapel Road, of silver watch, etc.

8 *William Harding*: burglary in house of Robert Snow, and taking silver plate.

9 *John Hughes*: attacking James Braverling on highway in City of London and taking haberdashery.

10 *James Haywood*: burglary in house of John Veal, Whitechapel, and stealing gold pap-spoon, six silver tea-spoons, punch-ladle, and wearing-apparel.

[9] William Wishart, D.D., Principal of the University of Edinburgh, 1737–1753.

[1] The passage quoted by Dr. Johnson (at Cupar 18 August 1773) is in *The Character of the Assembly-man*, in Samuel Butler's *Remains*, but there is reason to believe that the real author of the work was Sir John Birkenhead.

[2] Stuart, born and educated at Edinburgh, was a learned but opinionated and disappointed man who wrote on any side. He was now a principal writer for the *English Review*, founded January 1783, and co-editor of articles in the *Political Herald and Review* against Henry Dundas and other members of the Pitt administration.

[3] Unidentified, but the spelling probably should be Rideal, Boswell's *z* being a Scots *z* with the value of *y*, as in Dalzell, Menzies.

[4] The Ancient and Honourable Society of Bucks is said to have been a spurious offshoot of Freemasonry. It was a convivial brotherhood which in 1770 had thirteen lodges meeting at various taverns in London, besides a few outside the metropolis. The Grand Master was called the Grand Buck; the members bore such designations as rangers, foresters, and keepers. Boswell's bill for admission has survived; it shows that he paid 5*s.* for "making" or initiation, 6*d.* for "quit rent," and 1*s.* 2*d.* for a "ticket."

[5] The opening words of an adaptation, called "The Advice," of the aria "Stringo al fine" from Handel's *Ezio*:

Mortals wisely live to measure
Life by the extent of joy.

THURSDAY 2 JUNE. Dined at Lord Mayor's and rung gong in Egyptian Hall.[6] Quite my early ideas of City of London. Sat by Mrs. ——, pleasing creature. Much singing. Wilkes. Away to Bearcroft's. Back again, tea.

FRIDAY 3 JUNE. Was almost all the forenoon with Malone revising *Hebrides*. Dined at home. D'Ankerville coarse today. *Aventuriers*.[7]

[EDITORIAL NOTE. The entry above marks the beginning of a literary collaboration so wholehearted and selfless that it deserves special notice. Malone was himself seeing an important work, a scholarly edition of Shakespeare, through the press, but the reader will no doubt observe how often Boswell worked on the *Tour to the Hebrides* with him and at his house and the easy sociability with which Malone kept Boswell at his task but diversified the routine. The journal only hints at the extent of Malone's contributions; the manuscript of the *Tour* shows his hand increasingly, and it is heavy in the proofs—not always to the advantage of the *Tour*, it should be added, because Malone's style was proper and Latinate where Boswell's was uninhibited and direct. Notes which survive from the few occasions that they worked apart also disclose that Malone's revisions were very particular, but they are evidence, on the other hand, that Boswell defended and retained many of his own readings.]

SATURDAY 4 JUNE. Laboured at revising *Hebrides* all the forenoon, calm. Dressed well. Malone and Tyers, whom I called *Tiresias* (first time he had heard it), dined. Very agreeable day. I went to Court in the evening and enjoyed the show.[8] Then Mrs. Cosway's. Then supped Mrs. Bosville's; Sir Thomas Blackett, Miss Mellish, etc. Quite cordial. But I could not sit up late, and went home at one.

[6]"The Lord Mayor, some days ago, had an agreeable party of musical friends to dine at the Mansion House. Mr. Boswell was of the company; and rung in the magnificent Egyptian Hall an instrument which his Lordship and all his guests but one had never heard before. This was a Chinese gong, or vibrating bell, which, when struck with a kind of baton having its end covered with a clew of cordage or some other soft stuff, produces a very noble sound, louder than that of the great bell of St. Paul's but more melodious. Mr. Boswell's gong is one of the largest and best that ever was brought to England." (*St. James's Chronicle*, 11–14 June 1785, obviously written by Boswell himself. He also wrote a rather silly *Ode on Mr. Boswell's Gong*, which was published in the *St. James's Chronicle* for 20–22 September 1785.) Charles Foulis had promised the gong to Boswell as a gift, but it was actually presented after Foulis's death, by his heir, Robert Preston.

[7]"Adventurers." Boswell is presumably expressing his opinion of d'Ankerville and others of Paoli's hangers-on.

[8]It was the King's birthday.

SUNDAY 5 JUNE. Bosville called, and was quite cordial and promised to settle my Yorkshire freehold, etc.[9] Dined Hawkins's, quite easy with his mother and sister. Wet night. Mrs. Macbride a little.

MONDAY 6 JUNE. Breakfasted Mrs. Harcourt. Dined commons. Mr. Addison (attorney) of Preston attentive and encouraging. Tea, brother. Baldwin's a little. Consultation Bearcroft's. Supped Spottiswoode.

[To His Majesty, King George the Third][1]

General Paoli's,
Portman Square, [London] 6 June 1785

SIR,—Your Majesty having convinced me by your inquiries at the levee that my *Journal of a Tour to the Hebrides* is not beneath the notice of my Sovereign, I with all humility presume to consult the King himself on a point of delicacy as to which the King alone can satisfy me.

I have several authentic curious anecdotes concerning that person who in 1745–1746 attempted to recover the throne upon which his ancestors sat. I wish to communicate them as they occur in the course of my publication. But I am at a loss how to design him. I have repeatedly taken the oath of abjuration, and the oath of allegiance to Your Majesty, whom may GOD long preserve. And I am clear that the right of the House of Stuart is extinguished. Yet I cannot help feeling that it would be an insult to an unfortunate man who must think very differently, and who is still alive, should I call him *Pretender*. May I not be permitted to call him *Prince Charles*?

Will Your Majesty condescend to signify to me your royal pleasure as to this? If I am not permitted to avoid what would hurt my tenderness for what even *has been* blood royal, I shall leave out those anecdotes. If I am permitted, I shall thus apologize for the designation:

"I do not call him *the Prince*, because I am satisfied that the right which his family had is extinguished. I do not call him *Pretender*, because I feel it as ungenerous to the representative of a great but unfortunate House who is still alive. And I am confident that the only Person who is entitled to take it amiss will liberally excuse my tenderness for what *has been* blood royal."

[9] In his *Letter to the People of Scotland* Boswell had asserted that his family was descended from the Bosvilles and announced that his "Chief," William Bosville, intended to let him have "a small bit of the old manor" as a freehold. Bosville firmly rebuffed all Boswell's efforts to purchase a rent-charge on his estate and informed him that he had no pretensions to be considered head of the ancient family of Boswells, which he understood to have sprung from the Boswells of Balmuto.

[1] From an unsigned draft.

I shall wait some days for a notification of Your Majesty's will. If I receive none, I shall take it for granted that Your Majesty disapproves of what I have ventured to suggest. Perhaps I am too presumptuous.[2] But I am descended from the Countess of Mar, sister of Lord Darnley.[3]

In all events I entreat Your Majesty may be assured that I ever am, with profound respect, Sir, Your Majesty's most faithful and most affectionate subject.

TUESDAY 7 JUNE. Dined Sir Joshua Reynolds and supped. (Metcalfe,[4] etc., dined.)

[Boswell to Reynolds]

London, 7 June 1785

MY DEAR SIR,—The debts which I contracted in my father's lifetime will not be cleared off by me for some years. I therefore think it unconscientious to indulge myself in any expensive article of elegant luxury. But in the mean time, you may die or I may die; and I should regret much that there should not be at Auchinleck my portrait painted by Sir Joshua Reynolds, with whom I have the felicity of living in social intimacy.

I have a proposal to make to you. I am for certain to be called to the English bar next February. Will you now do my picture, and the price shall be paid out of the first fees which I receive as a barrister in Westminster Hall. Or if that fund should fail, it shall be paid at any rate five years hence by myself or my representatives.[5]

If you are pleased to approve of this proposal your signifying your concurrence underneath upon two duplicates, one of which shall be

---

[2] Boswell's more usual spelling of adjectives in -*uous*, indicating a common eighteenth-century pronunciation concerning which dictionaries are strangely silent.

[3] A claim to cousinship, seven or eight times removed, with the King himself. Boswell's mother was a great-granddaughter of John Erskine, Earl of Mar, by his second countess, daughter of the first Duke of Lennox and first cousin once removed (not sister) to Lord Darnley, father of James VI and I. Boswell was an enthusiastic genealogist, but not always precise or accurate.

[4] The wealthy brewer and Member of Parliament whom Dr. Johnson had made trustee for the annuity to Francis Barber. He was an intimate friend of Sir Joshua.

[5] Reynolds's usual fee for a portrait of the size selected was one hundred guineas, but he seems to have halved it for Boswell. As late as 21 February 1791 Boswell showed a debt of £50 for the painting in a review of his affairs, but Reynolds forgave the debt at the time the *Life of Johnson* was published (it was dedicated to him), and Boswell then struck the entry through. Beneath the accounting he wrote, "Sir Joshua Reynolds handsomely and kindly made me a present of my picture." It now hangs in the National Portrait Gallery, London.

kept by each of us, will be a sufficient voucher of the obligation.[6]

I ever am with very sincere regard, my dear Sir, your faithful and affectionate, humble servant,

JAMES BOSWELL.

WEDNESDAY 8 JUNE. House of Lords.[7] Tea, Lady Grant. Last night of Essex Head Club. Finished Trinity commons by bread in < Hall. >

THURSDAY 9 JUNE. Dined home, brother with < me. > Supped Dr. Scott's; slept Baldwin's.

FRIDAY 10 JUNE. Dined Mr. Dilly's. Had seen Temple library. Wilkes, charming. Lay there.[8]

SATURDAY 11 JUNE. Up early; warm day. Walked to St. Thomas's. Strange scene. Was charitable.[1] Peggy Graves (got name afterwards), pretty nurse.

SUNDAY 12 JUNE. Dined Mr. Ward's and supped. A great deal of fine singing. Mrs. Campbell (Primate's[2] niece), Lady Burgoyne, Mr. Crowe of New College, Oxford. General invitation to dinner.

MONDAY 13 JUNE. Dined home.

TUESDAY 14 JUNE. Visited Bishop of London.[3] Dined Ward's, I having sent. Night, City; slept Baldwin's.

WEDNESDAY 15 JUNE. Home of Wedderburn and Professor Anderson[4] breakfasted with us. Court—great. Visited Mr. Barnard, invited to country-place.[5] Dined Coutts's; Sir John Eliot,[6] etc., Sir Joshua, etc. Supped Lord Eglinton. No awkwardness;[7] quite well.

[6]See below, 5 July 1785. On 10 September 1785 Reynolds wrote, "I agree to the above conditions" at the end of Boswell's letter and returned it to him. We print the text from Boswell's copy.

[7]Here, with a disappointing lack of detail, Boswell records the final action in the case of Mercer and Duff against the Perth Justices of the Peace. (See above, 30 April 1783 and 14 March 1785.) Bearcroft and Boswell argued against Ilay Campbell and Thomas Erskine and won a moral victory: they did not get the increased damages they were appealing for, but they kept the Lords from reversing the judgement of the Court of Session in Mercer's favour. Boswell received a fee of twenty guineas.

[8]At Dilly's. Wilkes was a guest at dinner.

[1]To the extent of 10s. 6d. (see below, Appendix A).

[2]Dr. John Moore's.

[3]Dr. Robert Lowth, poet and distinguished scholar of Hebrew.

[4]Patrick Home of Billie and Wedderburn, M.P. for Berwickshire, and John Anderson, Professor of Oriental Languages in the University of Glasgow since 1756 and of Natural Philosophy since 1760.

[5]Probably Bishop Barnard's son Andrew, who had a house at Wimbledon. He later married Lady Anne Lindsay.

[6]Thomas Coutts, banker to George III and founder with his brother of the modern banking-house of that name; and John Eliot, M.D., knighted in 1776, created baronet 1778, physician to the Prince of Wales. Both men were born and grew up in Edinburgh.

[7]Because of his criticism of Eglinton's politics in the *Letter to the People of Scotland*.

[EDITORIAL NOTE. Boswell's "great" day at Court received a separate fully written entry.]

G. R.

Wednesday 15 June 1785

I went to Court to the levee, in some anxiety to know whether the King would deign to give me any answer to the delicate question which I had presumed to put in a letter to His Majesty as to the designation of an unfortunate person in my *Tour to the Hebrides*. After talking a little with Colonel Bland and me together upon the usual topic of pleasant raillery upon horse-dealers, as if it were in vain for them to pretend to be honest, the King, who was then in the ———, contrived to get himself and me so much aside that nobody could hear us, and then he gave me an opportunity to renew my request, by saying, "How do you go on?" I answered, "I took the liberty to send something to Your Majesty. I hope you received it." KING. "Yes." BOSWELL. "I am come to receive Your Majesty's commands." His Majesty then, as if resolved to *prove* me—to know if I was truly in earnest—said, "I never before was questioned as to this designation." This he said with such an air, and made such a pause, that it was a wonder I was not disconcerted. I felt myself quite firm, and I considered that I had gone too far to retreat without a solution of the difficulty if it could possibly be obtained. I replied, "I dare say not, Sir. But I entreat to know Your Majesty's pleasure." His Majesty *proved* me once more. He said, "What do you think? How do you feel yourself?" Here I was at a loss to be certain whether His Majesty meant to put a simple question as to the manner in which I was affected upon the subject, or if the import of his words might not be, "What do you think of such an extraordinary application to your sovereign? How should you feel to be thus pressed yourself?" I made a profound bow and respectfully answered, "That, Sir, I have already stated in writing to Your Majesty." The trial was now over. The King found I was a man. He stepped a little forward, and inclining towards me with a benignant smile equal to that of any of Correggio's angels, he said, "I think and I feel as you do." My heart glowed with emotion, and I felt an admiration and affection for my king such as a warm royalist alone can imagine. "Sir," said I, "I did suppose that Your Majesty's liberality of mind would make Your Majesty give the answer you have done. Then, Sir, I may do as I have proposed?" KING. "But what designation do you mean to give?" BOSWELL. "Why, Sir, 'Prince Charles' I think is the common expression." His Majesty appearing to hesitate or demur, I proceeded, "Or shall it be 'the grandson of King James the Second'?" KING. "Yes." BOSWELL. "Then I have Your Majesty's permission to call him so?" KING. "You have. To tell you the truth" (I *think* he said, by way of a familiar preface, but am *sure* of what follows), "I do not think it a matter of consequence to my family how they are called; for after the abdication, the change of religion, and other circumstances, I think there can be no question as to the right." BOSWELL. "Certainly not, Sir. I am quite clear as to that. My difficulty is merely from sentiment. 'Pretender' may be a *parliamentary* expression, but it is not a *gentlemanly* expression; and, Sir, allow me to inform you that I am his cousin in the seventh degree."

This very remarkable conversation, in which GEORGE III did great honour to himself in the opinion of all to whom I related it, and even in that of some of those most prejudiced against him, took up a considerable time, during which Lord Sydney, Mr. Dundas, Mr. Grenville, and many more stood at a distance, and were no doubt amazed what it could mean.[8]

[EDITORIAL NOTE. Another account of Boswell's interview with the King is preserved in a document in an unidentified hand headed "Extract of a letter from the Hon. Vice-Adm. Sir Alexander Cochrane, G.C.B., to Sir J. C. Hippisley, Bt., dated Murdostoun 10 July 1819."[9] Though writing thirty-five years after the event, Cochrane confirms Boswell's account to an extraordinary degree. There are discrepancies, of course, but the reader will no doubt feel that where such differences occur Boswell's account has the feeling of greater authenticity. The extract is printed, we believe for the first time, by the kind permission of the Osborn Collection, Yale University.]

I was at a levee at St. James's when the good old King in going round the circle spoke to your humble servant, who stood next to Mr. Boswell, who on making his bow was asked by His Majesty

[8] Boswell incorporated phrases from the conversation and from his letter to the King in a footnote to the *Tour to the Hebrides* at the point where Charles Edward is first mentioned ("the grandson of the unfortunate King James the Second"), 13 September 1773. In this footnote Boswell also justified his referring thereafter to "Prince Charles Edward," disregarding what was evidently the King's real wish. Bennet Langton later told Boswell that his questioning had put King George in a bad humour. "He asked me how he should name the Pretender. I did not care how" (Journal, 23 April 1788).
[9] Cochrane, Knight Grand Cross of the Order of the Bath, was a distinguished naval officer appointed to command the North American station in 1814 and raised to admiral August 1819. He was a younger son of Boswell's great-uncle, Thomas Cochrane, eighth Earl of Dundonald, consequently first cousin to Boswell's mother, though eighteen years Boswell's junior. Sir John Coxe Hippisley was a diplomat, officer of the East India Company, and M.P. Murdostoun is a seat in Lanarkshire.

when he meant to publish the life of Dr. Johnson,[1] to which Mr. Boswell replied that it must depend upon His Majesty. "How so?" said the King. Boswell replied that he was come to that part where he must speak of the Pretender, and Pretender he could not call him, for it would be an insult to an unfortunate Prince, "Your Majesty's eighth cousin and my eighth cousin too." Upon which the King said he by no means would wish that anything should be said that could give offence, and was walking away, when Boswell with his left hand took the King by the right elbow and fairly brought him round, saying at the same time, "Suppose, Sir, we call him the grandson of the unfortunate James the Second," to which the King replied, "Very good, very good indeed, Mr. Boswell," and immediately proceeded to speak to other persons in the circle.

The above I distinctly heard, and I think the late Lord Melville[2] must have heard it also as he was close on my right hand.

THURSDAY 16 JUNE. To Murphy's; not in. Breakfasted Serjeant Walker. To Westminster; Lee well.[3] Rachel.[4] Baldwin's. Dilly's. Dined Strange's; sweet Miss Douglas. Whist, etc. Gordon.[5]

FRIDAY 17 JUNE. Dined Blackwall on a great turtle. Lay Dilly's.

SATURDAY 18 JUNE. Preston, etc., dined here, Sir Charles going next day.

SUNDAY 19 JUNE. Too late for Sir J. Dick's. Putney, eel, etc., comfortable, and Richmond Lodge.

MONDAY 20 JUNE. All day Sir J. Dick's and Richmond Park. Sir J. Eliot. Drank too freely. Mrs. Stuart had gone to London in the morning.

TUESDAY 21 JUNE. To town; too late for museum.[6] Sir J. Banks a little. Club. Dr. Warren: "Intoxication is the good of wine. Children and savages dislike *taste* till they feel *effect*."[7] Walked in *Park*; madness. St. Martin's Lane. Supped Lord Eglinton's.

[1] An obvious error for something like "the account of your tour through Scotland with Dr. Johnson."
[2] Henry Dundas, who died in 1811.
[3] Speaking before the court at Westminster Hall.
[4] Unidentified.
[5] Miss Douglas is probably Joanna, heiress of William Douglas of Garvaldfoot, Peeblesshire, and Gordon is Strange's friend, Alexander Gordon, Principal of the Scots College, Paris. Boswell lost eight shillings at play.
[6] Probably the British Museum, for which it was necessary to secure a ticket of admission naming a day and hour.
[7] The itemized bill for The Club dinner, amounting to £9. 5s. 2d. ("£1. 4s. each") is

WEDNESDAY 22 JUNE. Ill. Lay till one. Coffee in bed. Went to Malone and corrected well. Dined home. In sad fear of new disorder. Went to Westminster, but could not find *hesterna nox*.[8] By water to Blackfriars. Rejoicing toll off.[9] Home quiet.

THURSDAY 23 JUNE. Home.

FRIDAY 24 JUNE. Court and home. King only asked about what time I should be in the North this year. (A hint this.) I said, "Not till what I am engaged in be finished."

[From the *St. James's Chronicle*, 2–5 July 1785.]

At the Court at St. James's, June 24, 1785, the following Address was presented to the King by James Boswell, Esq., being introduced by the Lord in Waiting. It was most graciously received, and Mr. Boswell had afterwards the honour to kiss His Majesty's hand.

To the King's Most Excellent Majesty.

The humble Address of the Tenants and others residing upon the estate of James Boswell, Esq., of Auchinleck, Ayrshire.

MAY IT PLEASE YOUR MAJESTY,—We, who though in an humble station, are not the least faithful of Your Majesty's subjects, beg leave to approach the throne, with anxious concern, yet relying upon Your Majesty's paternal goodness to all your people.

We, Sir, live far distant from the seat of Government; we are very unskilled in state affairs; we are not represented in Parliament; and we do not complain: because what we do not understand we trust will be wisely settled by those who do; and when there is any real grievance we know we have a right to make our complaints be heard, by address, petition, or remonstrance.

Being informed that an attempt is now making in Parliament to lessen the number of the Lords of Session, which even we can discern to be contrary to the Articles of the Union between England and Scotland, in which it is covenanted that the Court of Session shall remain in all time coming as then constituted; and as our Presbyterian religious

---

at Yale. The other members present were Lord Palmerston, Sir Joshua Reynolds, Sir Charles Bunbury, Malone, Langton, and Burney. Dr. Warren, physician to the King, was admitted to The Club the previous December. Boswell engaged him for his own family, and Warren attended him in his last illness.

[8] He could not find the girl he had picked up "last night."

[9] "Yesterday at noon the committee of Blackfriars Bridge ordered the gates and toll-houses to be taken down, and people immediately passed free of toll" (*Morning Chronicle*, 23 June 1785).

establishment which our forefathers secured by their blood, and which is very dear to us, is in the same manner guarded by those Articles, we cannot but be alarmed to a distressful degree when there is the appearance of danger that they may be violated.

Our worldly goods, Sir, are but scanty. But we can with industry support ourselves with contentment, under an indulgent family upon whose estate our lines have fallen,[1] and upon which some of us can trace our predecessors for many generations. It would be hard if our religious comfort should be disturbed.

We therefore do humbly beseech Your Majesty to take such measures as to the King in his great wisdom shall seem meet, to prevent what we greatly fear.

Our prayers, Sir, shall never cease to be offered to the Most High, by whom Kings reign, for His best blessings upon Your Majesty's person, family, and government, that we may lead a quiet and peaceable life in all godliness and honesty.

Signed by two hundred and eighty-nine men all fit to bear arms in defence of their King and country.

The above Address was transmitted to Mr. Boswell by Mr. Millar, assistant preacher at Auchinleck, with the following letter:

Auchinleck, June 6, 1785.

SIR,—I send you an Address to the King from the tenants and others residing upon your estate, showing their disapprobation and utter dislike of the attempt making in Parliament to diminish the number of the Lords of Session in Scotland, which they beg you will present if you see it necessary. They are encouraged to this measure by the candid attention of the Sovereign to the voice of his people upon a former occasion;[2] and they are happy that your sentiments, Sir, correspond with theirs, that all innovations of our excellent Constitution ought to be warmly opposed by every friend to our country.

On account of the quiet and happy life which their fathers led under your ancestors, and which they themselves enjoy under you, they consider it as their duty and do feel it their pleasure to be ever at your disposal, being confident that they and their country in general shall always have in you a fast friend. I am, Sir, your most obedient and very humble servant,

ALEXANDER MILLAR.[3]

[1] Psalms 16: 6: "The lines are fallen unto me in pleasant places."
[2] The loyal Address from Ayrshire on the East India Bill, Boswell's own composition. See above, 17 March 1784.
[3] The Rev. Mr. Millar collected the tenants' signatures at Boswell's direction, but Boswell

SATURDAY 25 JUNE. Mr. Gentili and I breakfasted Miss Wilkes, Capt. E. Thompson. *Jack* read "Lord Effingham in shades."[4] Sailed to St. Thomas's. Mr. Ward's. Vauxhall.

SUNDAY 26 JUNE.[5] Captain Grant's.

MONDAY 27 JUNE. Sir J. Eliot's. Mrs. Cosway's.

TUESDAY 28 JUNE. Malone all morning. Dined home, Hamilton of Grange and T. D. Was taken ill in street; feverish, cold, and sore. Home and to bed.

WEDNESDAY 29 JUNE. Not well yet. (Good accounts from Court of Session.)[6] But visited Mrs. and Miss Douglas. Heard music. Showed them Mrs. Cosway's; not in. Baldwin's a little. Dined Dr. Brocklesby at three, who had asked me in the street to take my commons with him. Only his sister and a child. Dull a little till he brought me sixteen letters from Dr. Johnson. Visited my brother a little. Drank tea with Mr. Tyers, who said, "You fill my mind." Then a dreary visit to Tom Davies's widow. Then home, and early to bed.

THURSDAY 30 JUNE.[7] Long with Malone. Not well at all yet. Went

---

himself appears to have written both the Address and the letter of transmittal. They were also printed in the *Public Advertiser* 6 July, the *London Chronicle* 5–7 July, and the *Morning Chronicle* 8 July 1785. We have silently corrected three errors in the text of the Address from instructions which Boswell sent Robert Boswell to assure that it was reprinted accurately in the Edinburgh newspapers.

[4] Wilkes's own composition, formally entitled "Remarks of the Earl of Effingham on a Late Excursion to Elysium," a lengthy, unpublished *jeu d'esprit* playing on the canard circulated in London about the disappearance of Lord Effingham (Wilkes's intimate friend) in the first days of the Gordon Riots. Effingham, who resigned from the army at the outbreak of the American war rather than fight his own countrymen, was a chief target of the charge that peers in opposition to the Ministry had fomented and participated in the riots. It was alleged that he was killed in the fierce fighting at Blackfriars Bridge 6 June 1780 and his body thrown into the Thames by members of his own party. Eighteen months later he reappeared in the House of Lords and reported that he had been at his seat, Grange Hall, in Yorkshire. Tongue in cheek, Wilkes "proved" that the noble Earl had indeed been killed at the bridge but was now returned to life. He also related how Effingham had passed his time below, a witty and suggestive satire on politics, religion, and Effingham's *penchant* for women and wine. Wilkes read his fantasy to the Society of Beef Steaks in 1782, the delighted Earl in the audience. The manuscript, which Lord Effingham endorsed with a witty slur against the King and the people, is now in the British Library.

[5] The expense account shows that he worshipped at the Portuguese Chapel, where he gave a porter 2*s.* 6*d.* (see below, Appendix A).

[6] Adam Neill, the Edinburgh printer, had sold in two days the fifty copies of the pamphlet that Boswell first sent him and he now requested an additional fifty copies. On 1 July Neill reported that he had sold off the second shipment directly.

[7] General Oglethorpe died on this day, aged at least eighty-seven. The *Gentleman's Magazine* reported that he had retained "his understanding, his eyesight (reading

to Hayward[8] and consulted calm. Dilly's, and had mutton broth and reviews[9] and physic; quite at home. Read some in Rutty's *Diary*.[1] Felt myself as usual good and regular here.

FRIDAY 1 JULY. Physic had from break of day kept me in brisk operation. Breakfasted well. Wrote all forenoon to Bishops of Killaloe and Dromore and Mr. Cooper Walker.[2] Then called Woodfall, who showed me an abusive letter against me, signed "An Ayrshireman," which he was unwilling to insert, but said, "I believe I *must*." I desired to read it, and having read it, said, *"Insert it*. It is very stupid and very erroneous."[3] Said he: "A public man is fair game." Said I: *"Certainly."*

I then came to Baldwin's a little and revised the press. I was quite relieved of fever. I got home *just in time*. Found Mrs. and Miss Douglas, M. del Campo, the Spanish Minister, Conte Carloucci and Conte Piazza, two Cremona noblemen,[4] Mr. and Mrs. Cosway, ———. All went on well. After dinner we had M. d'Ageno, Genoese Minister.[5] And a choice concert: Borghi, young Bartolozzi, Dantz (violins), Smith (bass), Tenducci and Mrs. Cosway (singers).[6] My sweet Miss Douglas was quite enchanted, and her mother was delighted to see all this and behold

without spectacles), his hearing, and the use of his limbs till within two or three days of his death" (July 1785, lv. 517). Boswell had last called on him on 22 May 1785.
[8]Perhaps John Heawood, a surgeon in Southwark.
[9]The reviews appeared at the very end of the month in which they were dated. The *Letter to the People of Scotland* was reviewed in the *Monthly Review*, the *Critical Review*, the *English Review*, and the *Scots Magazine* for June.
[1]The spiritual diary and soliloquies of Dr. John Rutty, physician, writer, and ardent member of the Society of Friends. An abstemious man, he recorded his efforts to deny all excesses and left directions in his will that the diary be published posthumously. Boswell reported in the *Life of Johnson* that Johnson had laughed at Rutty's self-condemnation, particularly his serious regret over occasional instances of "swinishness in eating and doggedness of temper." "It did not occur to him that many passages in his own diary might be as much a sport to 'wicked wits,'" Boswell had added, but he did not print that statement (MS. *Life of Johnson*, 19 September 1777).
[2]All requests for Johnson material. Walker, an Irish antiquary and literary historian, had offered to collect Johnson's private letters among the Dublin literati.
[3]See below, 14 July 1785.
[4]"Carloucci" is not further identified, but the name should probably have been spelled "Colucci."
[5]The Genoese had long since withdrawn from Corsica, but d'Ageno might still not have been welcome at Paoli's except for a break with his government, which tried to relieve him in 1781 of the charge he had held since 1760. The British government refused to acknowledge his dismissal or to recognize his successor.
[6]Gaetano Bartolozzi, son of Francesco, the popular engraver, was himself an engraver who devoted most of his time to music. "Dantz" is William Dance, a first violinist and the leader of the orchestra at the King's Theatre since 1775; so far as we know, Boswell employs this spelling nowhere else (see above, 30 March 1783). Tenducci is the famous Drury Lane castrato (he sang soprano in *The Messiah*) described in *Humphry Clinker*.

her daughter so happy. After the ladies went, we had . . . .⁷ A pleasing day.

SATURDAY 2 JULY. Breakfasted Malone, as there was to be a party to Richmond. Bad day, so put it off. Windham breakfasted with us. Then Malone and I corrected all forenoon. Dined with the ladies,⁸ as did Windham. Then Malone and I walked to Westminster and fixed boat. I visited Mrs. and Miss Douglas.

SUNDAY 3 JULY. Portuguese Chapel a little. Then Malone's; boat gone off. So he and I and ladies in coach, and Courtenay and Windham to follow.⁹ Met Mrs. Stuart, who suggested King Henry's Mound¹ and sent dessert. Quite pleasant. Tea at Castle Inn.² Stuart's night.

MONDAY 4 JULY. Mrs. Stuart took me in landau four miles. I then walked. Called Mrs. Douglas. Dined home. Then Baldwin's about my book. Home, dressed. Mrs. and Miss Douglas to Mrs. Cosway's. Charming. I sat much by my girl. Talked to Mrs. Abington,³ and was introduced to her. Home with ladies, who were to go for France next morning. Supped Lord Eglinton's; Col. Fullarton there. Missed my second volume of Hebrides journal.

TUESDAY 5 JULY. Up at six to be in time. Breakfasted with ladies. Miss read Italian; mother wondered. I said, "I'd make her sing in a week." Adieu.⁴ Then Sir Joshua's, who began my picture. I sat in uncertainty as to book being found, yet hoping. Then Murphy a little. Then Baldwin's; no book. Was agitated. Malone's; no book. Miserable. Searched all at home in vain. . . .⁵ At last Giacomo Pietro told me Joseph had seen it lying in parlour. Great, great relief. Had sent apology to

⁷MS. defective. Perhaps six or seven letters are missing.
⁸Probably Malone's sisters, Henrietta and Catherine, and the wife of his brother Richard, with whom Boswell had tea 6 July 1785, below.
⁹This is the first reference in the journal to John Courtenay, who was to become one of Boswell's closest friends. He was an Irishman, the nephew of Lord Bute, and a bold and witty Member of the House of Commons. The friendship with Boswell was based purely on personal liking, for as Boswell grew more conservative, Courtenay became more radical. He supported the Fox-North Coalition, opposed the slave trade, advocated a thorough-going reform of Parliament, and sympathized ardently with the French revolutionists.
¹On the grounds of Pembroke Lodge in Richmond Park.
²A fine house with a lawn running down to the river and a garden in front, one of the two most fashionable Richmond inns of the period.
³The flower-girl who had become queen of comedy at Drury Lane and was now acting at Covent Garden.
⁴Nothing further is heard in the journal of this sweet Miss Douglas. On 15 July 1785 she sent Boswell a letter in French and Italian from Boulogne and he replied in kind. She was married in Paris, 3 March 1786, to Sir William Dick of Prestonfield, son of Boswell's old friend, Sir Alexander Dick.
⁵MS. defective. Perhaps a dozen letters are missing.

Sir Joshua for not returning to sit this forenoon as I promised. Met him at Club. He and I tête-à-tête: a bottle of port and a bottle of claret. [6] Vastly well. I had told him I was going to the execution next morning, Shaw, once Burke's servant, being to suffer. Sir Joshua was drawn to it, and said he'd go. I undertook to arrange it all for him. We drank tea with Miss Palmer, and then I went to Mr. Herne's and sent a note to Sir Joshua to be at his house half past five at latest. I went to Dilly's; he in the country.

WEDNESDAY 6 JULY. Up early. Sir Joshua was before me at Mr. Herne's with his coach, which drove us to Newgate. Convicts were in chapel. We heard singing. Then we saw irons knocked off, and man beckon them to a room where they were pinioned. Shaw said (at first when kept waiting) with a sigh, "I wish they were come." (I have given a particular account in the *Public Advertiser*.)

[From the *Public Advertiser*, 7 July 1785]
Execution Intelligence.

Peter Shaw, one of the five convicts who suffered yesterday for having robbed Mr. Stanhope's house, persisted to the last in denying that he had set fire to it. [7] He behaved with a manly composure, and said it was the happiest day of his life; it was but going to heaven a little sooner, only he regretted his wife and children. He had been some time servant to Mr. Burke, of whom he spoke to Mr. Boswell with great regard: "He is a worthy good gentleman—God Almighty prosper him. [8] His brother, out of his own generosity, came to the court, and gave me a character." Shaw was a tall, handsome fellow, a native of Ireland; his long hair hung flowing down his back, and his manners were much above those of an ordinary servant. He never once changed countenance or showed either fear or affectation. One very extraordinary circumstance marked his possessing himself perfectly: while he stood under the fatal tree and the awful moment was approaching, he observed Sir Joshua Reynolds and Mr. Boswell, two friends of his old master, Mr. Burke, placed by Mr. Sheriff Boydell; upon which he turned round, and with a steady but modest look made them a graceful bow.

Ivemay and Horey, the two highwaymen of yesterday's sad group,

[6] The bill for dinner amounted to 14*s*. each: they drank cider and strong beer in addition to port and claret (see below, Appendix A).
[7] He admitted only to stealing goods and money valued at more than £58 from Francis Stanhope's house in Curzon Street, Mayfair.
[8] It may be only coincidence that Burke's house at Beaconsfield was reported robbed the previous autumn.

were good-looking young men, especially the former. When they came upon the scaffold Horey addressed himself to the people, saying, "Let *us* be an example; take warning by us." "Ay" (added Ivemay), "here's warning enough for you all."[1]

The ceremony of knocking off their irons just before taking the convicts out to execution is the most striking circumstance of the whole. Horey affected a little too much spirit upon that occasion, for he called to his companion, "My boy, let's be glad we are *free* again." A momentary freedom, for in a minute after he was pinioned. It, however, put one in mind of Marcus, in Addison's *Cato*:

> Good morrow, Portius; let us now embrace;
> Once more embrace whilst yet we both are *free*.[2]

A number of Italian noblemen and gentlemen saw the execution yesterday from a window, and we are sorry witnessed a superstition as weak as any in their own country—no less than four diseased persons, who had themselves rubbed with the sweaty hands of malefactors in the agonies of death, and believed this would cure them.

[EDITORIAL NOTE. "Execution Intelligence," as printed in the *Public Advertiser*, actually began with the following paragraph: "While a great concourse of spectators were assembled, the first person who appeared upon the scaffold yesterday morning was Mr. Boswell. *That* was nothing extraordinary, but it was surprising when he was followed by Sir Joshua Reynolds.—'Evil communications corrupt good manners.'[2a]—It is strange how that hard Scot should have prevailed on the amiable painter to attend so shocking a spectacle." Boswell cannot have written that paragraph and must have been stunned when he read it. The printer apparently grouped paragraphs of different authorship under Boswell's heading or a heading of his own choice. To be sure, Boswell was given to advertising his own eccentricities, but he would not have accused himself of being hard-hearted, nor would he have subjected Sir Joshua to public rebuke. Among Reynolds's papers was found what appears to be the draft of a letter assuring Boswell that he was grateful to him for securing his presence at the execution and defending himself and others for attending. The paragraph so incongruously affixed to Boswell's report is important as marking the beginning in the news-

[1] They were executed for robbing Edward Gray of his watch and some money. Of the remaining two convicts, Joseph Brown suffered for stealing goods worth £2 from a dwelling in Hampton, and Robert Jackson for forging a letter of attorney in order to receive the prize-money of a seaman lately of H.M.S. *Carysfort*.
[2] I. ii. 5-6. In line 1 *read* once *for* now.
[2a] I Corinthians 15: 33.

papers of really malignant reflections on Boswell. For these he could no doubt blame the liberties he had taken in his *Letter to the People of Scotland*.]

Sir Joshua and I saw the machinery perfectly. We breakfasted with Mr. Boydell, saw all his drawings, and Mary, his niece, was justly vain of *her* collection.[3] Then Mr. Boydell, Sir Joshua, and I saw the flying-fish-balloon.[4] Then I went to St. Thomas's; Betsy gone to her lodgings. I followed and met her in the Old Bailey, looking wonderfully well. But she frankly told me she would not take a place; she would rather resume her former life. I said, "You are a pleasing, honest creature, but the most profligate being I ever knew." I made her take my arm, and we walked about Blackfriars Bridge and Doctors Commons, and I went home and sat a little with her. All my arguments were in vain. She said she'd be her own mistress. Said I: "At the mercy of every brutal ruffian." She said masters and mistresses had bad tempers. Said I: "What have many of the men that you must submit to?" I told her I was ashamed, but I loved her. I was vexed at such an instance of depravity. But it was curious. It verified Reynolds's maxim that human nature loves *gaming*; agitation, uncertainty. I called at Lee's. He was to go to the Circuit next morning. Went to Guildhall; heard him plead and settled to dine with him, which I did. Just he and I and Mrs. Lee, vastly well. After dinner Dr. Price came in. He and I began to stagger[5] as to Pitt. Lee had said the evil of life seemed to him almost nothing; told me a curious remark of Sir George Savile's on reasoning being influenced by our passions. "If a worthy friend, a heavy man, hung by a piece of small whip-cord, you think it will hold and hang him; if the same whip-cord is put round the waist of your child, and he's hung on a rock to gather samphire, you think it will break and he'll be dashed in pieces." I engaged to see him at his house at Stanthorpe.[6] I sat a little with Mrs. Strange. Mrs. Malone's[7] tea. Home, gloomy somewhat.

[3]John Boydell, alderman since 1782, Sheriff of London in 1785, Lord Mayor 1790–1791, was an engraver and publisher of prints.

[4]Probably a small experimental balloon not intended to carry passengers, but nothing has been found about it.

[5]To doubt or waver in their opinions. Boswell's interlocutor is Dr. Richard Price, the nonconformist minister, writer on moral philosophy, economics and politics, and friend of Franklin and Priestley. Boswell later called him "obnoxious" because Price shared Priestley's zeal for the French Revolution (see *Life of Johnson*, September 1783, the long intrusive note on Dr. Priestley).

[6]Old variant form of Staindrop, Co. Durham.

[7]Mrs. Richard Malone. Her husband had been created Lord Sunderlin 30 June 1785, but apparently the patent had not yet arrived. See below, 9 and 10 July 1785.

THURSDAY 7 JULY. Another rural party; Courtenay and the ladies in coach, Malone and I in chaise. Went and saw Strawberry Hill,[8] Hampton Court, dined in Bushey Park in the air, saw Pope's grotto.[9] Tea Brentford. Home about twelve. Vastly well.

FRIDAY 8 JULY. Breakfasted with Sir Joshua, and sat again for picture. Baldwin's some time. Dined Ward's with Topham and Andrews, and drank tea cordial. He and she[1] were going for a little to Nottingham.

SATURDAY 9 JULY. Called on Courtenay to see if we went to General Dalrymple's.[2] Breakfasted Dempster. Baldwin's a little. Brother's a little. Quite calm. Was to have dined tête-à-tête with Malone and corrected all the afternoon. But Courtenay called, and he asked him, and he sent a couple of bottles of burgundy, and we were quite pleasant and had coffee and tea after. Then Malone and I corrected. Then had some port and water, etc., when his brother arrived, now Lord Sunderlin.

SUNDAY 10 JULY. Hamilton of Grange breakfasted with us, and then consulted me as to a proposed marriage for his sister.[3] I advised caution and inquiry. Then called Malone; at his brother's. Went there, and on *knee* did obeisance to *my Lady*. Then home with Malone and heard Jephson's recollection of Dr. Johnson's letter to Lord Chesterfield,[4] and plan for publishing Goldsmith's poetical works with a life by the Bishop of Dromore.[5] Then away to Kew Bridge in stage. Met brother by appointment at Richmond Green, he being on a visit to a lady near Brentford. We walked through Richmond Gardens to Colo-

---

[8] Walpole's Company Book records that tickets to visit the house had been issued to "Mr. Malone and three."

[9] At Twickenham. Bushey Park is the large royal park noted for tame deer and the triple avenue (over a mile long) of horse-chestnuts and lime-trees planted by William III as an approach to Hampton Court Palace from the north.

[1] Mr. and Mrs. Ward. Edward Topham and Miles Peter Andrews were writers of plays and men-about-town.

[2] Maj.-Gen. (later General) William Dalrymple, M.P. for the Wigtown Burghs. They dined with him 31 July 1785, below.

[3] Probably Joana, who in April 1786 married Edward McCormick, advocate, later Sheriff of Ayrshire.

[4] Robert Jephson, the dramatist, a schoolfellow of Malone. Evidently Boswell did not know at this time that Langton had a copy of the letter which Johnson had dictated to Baretti and later corrected in his own hand. He secured that text on 12 July 1785 (see below).

[5] The "Percy Memoir" or Life of Goldsmith, based on materials which the Bishop had shown Boswell 28 March 1775, was published finally in the *Miscellaneous Works* of 1801. Percy contributed to the Memoir, but it was written chiefly by the Rev. Thomas Campbell.

nel James's lodge, and dined; Colonel Fothringham and lady there. Brother went away early. We drank some claret, but not to excess, and the Colonel and I went to tea; Lady Greenwich and Lady Mary Coke there.[6] The Colonel[7] sent for me and *lectured* me as a friend on having had an Address from my tenants, which might have done well enough after a number of others, but was now like Lord G. Gordon.[8] I however think well of it. He and Mrs. Stuart walked a little with me. It was dark and weary on Ham Common. Coach, Fulham. Found at General's "lobster night," as Pope says.[9] Many gentlemen and Maria Cosway came a little. Fine after walk.

MONDAY 11 JULY. The press had stopped a little for want of copy. Went to Malone and brought forward some. Dined Chelsea College, instead of 29 May (Anniversary) as room new-painted. Sir George Howard and I at head of table in armchairs. Did not riot. Tea with Lady Effingham.[1] Lively with Lady Mary Coke. General Trapaud carried me home. Then to Mrs. Cosway's; music. Introduced to Mrs. Cowley.[2] Then Lord Eglinton's. Supper over; he sulky. Drank bottle of claret.

TUESDAY 12 JULY. Somewhat disturbed by heat and headache. Worked with Malone. Dined worthy Langton *en famille*, quiet and comfortable. Got letter to Lord Chesterfield.[3] Walked by Willow Walk and Millbank. Home calm, he accompanying me to top of St. James's

[6] Daughters of John, second Duke of Argyll. Lady Mary Coke, the widow since 1753 of Edward, Viscount Coke, son of the Earl of Leicester, was now in her fifty-ninth year. She had been intimate with Edward Augustus, Duke of York (the brother of George III), to whom, she alleged, she had been secretly married. This is Boswell's first reference to her since his journal of 1763 (where she may be the "Lady Mirabel" whom he knew a great deal better than he ostensibly knew Lady Mary) and the journal of 1764. The published portion of her voluminous and useful diary makes no references to Boswell.

[7] Stuart.

[8] Gordon was notorious as a presenter of petitions, among them the petition of the Protestant Association which precipitated the anti-Catholic riots of 1780. On 7 February 1785 he brought one before the Commons to repeal the tax on the products of Scottish weavers, who had threatened insurrection because of desperate financial conditions.

[9] *A Farewell to London,* ll. 45–46:

> Luxurious lobster-nights, farewell,
> For sober, studious days!

[1] Her first appearance in the journal. We have not learned how Boswell came to know Lady Effingham well enough to be invited to tea. He was in company with Lord Effingham at Court 20 May 1785, above, but the other allusions to him in the journal are second-hand.

[2] Hannah Cowley, the dramatist.

[3] See above, 10 July 1785, n. 4.

Street. Spottiswoode's a little. On coming home, found a letter from M. M. on my duelling,[4] which touched my heart like a celestial flash.

WEDNESDAY 13 JULY. Dined at home. Was busy drawing up abstract of Prince Charles's history while in the Hebrides.[5] Drank tea at Mrs. Bosville's; Lord Macdonald there.[6] Felt some compunction for having trimmed him in my Hebridean tour. Evening quiet at home.

THURSDAY 14 JULY. Worked with Malone. (Royal Ross found me first, and I was kindly to him.) Called Sir Joshua and asked if he dined at home and had no company. "Only Mr. W. Eliot."[7] I was to come. Baldwin's. Dinner and tea Sir Joshua. Evening Paradise's; talked with Mr. Horne Tooke.[8]

[From the *Public Advertiser*, 14 July 1785]

To James Boswell, Esq.

Ayr, 13 June 1785

SIR,—I have had your pamphlet addressed to the people of Scotland sent me, and I have glanced over this incoherent rhapsody, in which you have involved many men and much matter. Lord G. Gordon and you seem to think it is well for this country that you are both *on the spot*,[9] that you may remonstrate to Parliament. You both seem to run the same race; but from the regard I had for your worthy father I wish that your petulant vanity and violent versatility did not mark you out so conspicuously an object of contempt and ridicule. Was there ever such consummate, empty arrogance seen in any mortal as in your assuming to yourself the merit of overturning Mr. Fox's India bill by your writing against it? I dare say there are not five men in England,

---

[4] Not recovered.

[5] Boswell brought together all the anecdotes in his Hebridean journal concerning Charles Edward and combined them with a "paper of information" sent to him by John MacLeod of Raasay. He entered this abstract in the published *Tour* at 13 September 1773, after the account of Johnson's meeting with Flora Macdonald on the Isle of Skye.

[6] Mrs. Diana Wentworth Bosville, the widow of Godfrey Bosville, was Lord Macdonald's mother-in-law. Boswell had himself once thought of marrying her daughter Elizabeth Diana, but, like Johnson, he was appalled by her dulness when they were the guests of the Macdonalds at Armadale in 1773.

[7] William Eliot, the youngest son of Reynolds's friend and patron, Edward, Lord Eliot.

[8] The famous "Parson Horne," clergyman, philologist, and agitator for Wilkes, the Americans, and Parliamentary reform. He founded the Constitutional Society to support the bill of rights in 1771.

[9] The italicized phrase is from Boswell's letter to the *St. James's Chronicle* of 12 May 1785 (see above, p. 293, n. 6).

out of the circle of your own acquaintance, who ever heard of your writing on the subject.

Some things you say against lessening the number of the Scotch judges seem to be reasonable. I have not heard the arguments of the other side; but I know that by trusting to one another business has been slabbered over in a most slovenly manner too often in the Court of Session. Your panegyric upon Mr. Dempster is the best part of your pamphlet,[1] as every man in both kingdoms will join in the eulogy, but your rage against his very particular friend, the Member for Edinburgh, seems to boil over with a most unwarrantable impetuosity. You say he has occasioned you great vexation, and you wonder at the citizens of Edinburgh having chosen him for their Member; but I fancy it is no difficult matter to account for these things. Sir Adam Fergusson from his earliest days displayed uncommon talents, and has all his life been as remarkable for a steady, uniform discretion as you have been for a want of it, which is saying a great deal, James, and is perhaps one cause of your vexation. The citizens of Edinburgh have known him from his infancy; they admired his abilities at a very early period, when his pleadings in the Douglas Cause first gave rise to the sentiment which almost universally prevails at present, notwithstanding the decision.[2] They have seen in him a most exemplary conduct; and knowing that he possesses talents for the duties of a Member in Parliament superior to the united abilities of all who have been the Members for Edinburgh to my knowledge these forty years, they naturally applaud the choice of their magistrates.

The gentlemen in our county, to their shame be it said, were long most disgracefully led by a contending aristocracy, but at last they resolved to shake off the servile yoke and choose a Member independent of the peerage.[3] A coalition of the contending peers who had long contended against each other was formed to defeat this purpose; but the excellent character of Sir Adam Fergusson had gained him the good-will and affection of all the independent gentlemen of the county, who united cordially in electing him to be the Member; and no man stood forth with a more manly spirit to assist in the discomfiture of that coalition than your truly wise and worthy father, whose memory

[1]"My amiable and honourable friend Dempster, that *rara avis* of the Scottish breed, who has sat in Parliament almost as long as our present most gracious Sovereign has sat upon the throne, and has shown himself uniformly independent, uniformly benevolent . . ." (*Letter to the People of Scotland*, 1785, p. 15).

[2]Fergusson was counsel for the Duke of Hamilton. He compiled the huge Memorial, besides pleading viva voce.

[3]In the General Election of 1774.

will be dear to all of us who knew him, notwithstanding your insinuations.[4] You ought to remember that he has left you a good estate, though your indiscretion compelled him to let you know that it was not entailed.

I have no objection to your being Mayor of Garratt[5] in England, but I have ten thousand to your being a Lord of Session in Scotland; and you never shall have my vote for your being the representative of our county in Parliament. I am yours, etc.,

                                        AN AYRSHIREMAN.[6]

FRIDAY 15 JULY. Had Royal Ross at breakfast. Helped him to draw up an advertisement for his being Master of Ceremonies at Bristol.[7] It was a very wet day. Went to Malone's and got a good deal done. General Paoli and I dined at Mr. Ross Mackye's; Earl of Eglinton and Lord Elphinstone there.[8] It was curiously striking to me to be thus with my father's companion, born in 1708.[1] Drank rather too much. He and I tea.

SATURDAY 16 JULY. Was somewhat disturbed by last night's wine, and my health was not yet as it should be. Did something with Malone. Dined at Lord Sunderlin's on venison; only Malone and ladies. Sir Michael Cromie came and was with us some time after dinner. A genteel man. Drank rather too much claret. Played whist and lost.[2] Stayed supper. Waited on General Murray (Atholl) about his father.[3]

[4] Boswell had criticized Dundas in the *Letter* for persuading Lord Auchinleck in 1774 to create nominal and fictitious votes, which he abhorred, for Fergusson. The charge missed the mark only technically: Lord Auchinleck's new votes did not mature in time for the election.

[5] A burlesque office. After each general election in England the president or "mayor" of the citizens' association of the tiny hamlet of Garratt in south London was chosen at a hilarious election satirizing the conventions and corruption of real politics. The shrewd publicans in the environs made up a purse to finance the event, and Foote (author of the farce, *The Mayor of Garratt*), Garrick, and Wilkes are reputed to have written addresses for the candidates. Tens of thousands of fun-seekers choked the various roads from London and all the approaches to the polling-places.

[6] Unidentified; doubtless one of the "independent gentlemen" in the county.

[7] We have not found the advertisement. Ross had just come from Bath, where according to the *Public Advertiser* of 14 July 1785 he was "pretty certain of succeeding to the Mastership of the Ceremonies." Nothing appears to have come of either of his efforts.

[8] Both Representative Peers, and Governor and Lt.-Governor of Edinburgh Castle respectively.

[1] John Ross Mackye (see above, 26 March 1783 and n. 3).

[2] Sir Michael was M.P. for Ballyshannon. Boswell lost £1. 5s.

[3] The proofs of the *Tour to the Hebrides* contain a passage on p. 229 in which Prince Charles blamed the loss at Culloden on the refractory conduct of his principal general,

SUNDAY 17 JULY. Breakfasted at home. Worshipped in the Portuguese Chapel. Was some time with Malone. Eat an olio[4] with T. D.; Major Green there. Came to Hyde Park at seven and walked an hour, expecting a lady, from a note—probably a trick. However weather not fine. But I thought in such cases of enchantment, "Fair is foul and foul is fair."[5] Home quiet.

MONDAY 18 JULY. Breakfasted Dempster with Malone. Dined home. Evening Dilly's. Fine mountain.

TUESDAY 19 JULY. Calm in forenoon. Visited Mrs. Knowles. Wet day. Dined Langton's; Paradise, Taylor (a Greek teacher), Shaw the Erse Man.[6] Wearied and went away soon. A little dreary. Called Burney's; company there and I not dressed. Sir Joshua's. Most fortunate; found him still at table with Miss Palmer, Burke, and Metcalfe. He and Metcalfe were to set out for Holland next day. I talked of Shaw's execution. Burke said . . .[7]

WEDNESDAY 20 JULY. Breakfasted by appointment with Atholl General Murray. Atholl porridge.[8] Was shown electrical experiments. A little frightened, but stood them well enough. Malone's. Visited Lord Eglinton and Lady Macartney.[9] Dined Mrs. and Thomas Bosville; the Gascoignes there, and a Mr. Mason. Drank rather too briskly. Malone's; corrected and supped.

THURSDAY 21 JULY. Malone's.

FRIDAY 22 JULY. Went to Pott;[1] declared free from infection. In great joy went to Malone's; breakfasted and corrected a little. At twelve

---

Lord George Murray. Boswell wrote in the margin, "This paragraph I settled with General Murray, son of Lord George," undoubtedly on the occasion here recorded. In the printed text Charles Edward reflects more cautiously on the conduct of the battle and Murray's name is not mentioned. Boswell identifies Lt.-Gen. James Murray as "Atholl"—he was brother of the third Duke of Atholl, uncle of the fourth, and former commander of the Atholl Highlanders—in order to distinguish him from the Gen. James Murray who had been Governor of Quebec and of Minorca.

[4] A hodgepodge.

[5] *Macbeth*, I. i. 11.

[6] The Rev. William Shaw, whose *Memoirs* of Dr. Johnson appeared this year. Johnson had written "Proposals" for Shaw's *Analysis of the Gaelic Language*. The Greek teacher is Thomas Taylor, the Platonist.

[7] The entry was never completed. Sir Joshua made a short visit to Brussels, then in the Netherlands, to purchase paintings for himself and for the Duke of Rutland. He purchased five Rubenses, three Van Dycks, and other paintings in private hands.

[8] Whisky, honey, and oatmeal.

[9] Jane Stuart Macartney, the second daughter of Lord Bute.

[1] Percival Pott, the distinguished surgeon whose writings revolutionized English practice. "Pott's fracture" was named from him. He had treated Boswell for venereal infections in 1768 and 1769.

old John Ross Mackye came with a chaise and drove me to Richmond Lodge. Pleasant to think of his travelling with my father. Quite well with Colonel James and his lady. Drank cheerfully.

SATURDAY 23 JULY. Got Colonel's mare and had his son Jack[2] to accompany me on his little mare. Rode to Lady Di Beauclerk's; not at home. Cambridge's;[3] not at home. Then Wallings, the Duke of Montrose's butler, came up to me and showed me the Duke's villa close by. Went and visited him.[4] Tea from Lady Graham. Found Jack a fine, sensible boy and a good scholar. Lord Eglinton came to dinner at the Lodge. We had a jovial day. Old Johnnie Ross sung many a French song. At night the Colonel came into my room and sat cordially. I told him if I had been *challenged* on account of my pamphlet, I should have asked him to be my second. Would he not have gone out with me? "Yes," said he, "and made you behave damned well, too." We shook hands, and he promised if ever I should have an affair of that kind, he would be with me. He appeared a steady friend. He advised me to answer a letter in the *Public Advertiser* signed "An Ayrshireman."

SUNDAY 24 JULY. Up early. Rode the Colonel's mare to East Sheen. Had tea there, and got a seat in Richmond coach to town. Breakfasted at the General's on chocolade, sponge-biscuits, and tea, as always on Sundays. High mass at Portuguese Chapel. Then Malone and revised some. Dined General's; not many at table. Evening sat with Dempster awhile. Then met Dilly at Hamilton of Grange's, and supped Strahan;[5] his landlord and a Lieutenant Snodgrass with us. Home with Dilly.

MONDAY 25 JULY. After good coffee, visited Mrs. Knowles. Then wrote answer to the letter signed "An Ayrshireman." Baldwin's a little. Malone's and revised. Dined at home.

TUESDAY 26 JULY. General drove me in his chariot to Woodfall's, where I corrected the proof of my answer to the letter signed "An Ayrshireman." Then he set me down at Malone's, where I was to dine. We revised some. Then Lord Sunderlin, Windham, Courtenay dined. Hamilton, being taken ill, could not come. A very pleasant day. Malone and I revised at night and sat till two in the morning.

[2] Colonel Stuart's eldest son, now twelve years old.

[3] The villa of Richard Owen Cambridge situated in the meadows opposite Richmond Hill (see above, 26 March 1783, n. 5).

[4] A kindly act. The Duke, totally blind for over thirty years, was now very deaf and had lost the use of his legs. The Duchess was paralytic, and they were bereft of their only daughter, Lady Lucy, the wife of Archibald Douglas of Douglas, who had died at the age of twenty-eight.

[5] William Strahan had died a fortnight before and was succeeded in the business by his son Andrew, probably the Strahan with whom Boswell supped. His brother George, a clergyman, lived in Islington, but he could have had a residence in London.

WEDNESDAY 27 JULY. Hamilton of Grange breakfasted with us. Malone was busy today with his Shakespeare.[6] So I could not get any of his time. Went to Baldwin's a little. Also to Woodfall's, and got some copies (slips) of my answer.

[From the *Public Advertiser*, 27 July 1785]

For the *Public Advertiser*
Mr. Boswell's Answer to a letter in this paper
signed AN AYRSHIREMAN[7]

Upper Seymour Street,
Portman Square No. 1, 25 July 1785

When a gentleman puts his name to what he publishes he is not obliged to take notice of anonymous attacks. This is my general rule, and it was my intention to have allowed the letter signed AN AYR-SHIREMAN to have died away like other spawn of ill nature, of which the press is too prolific. But an honourable friend, whose opinion I greatly respect, having advised me to make an answer to it I submit what follows to all impartial readers. I cannot however but think it is very disagreeable to be thus disturbed in the course of my present labours for the instruction and entertainment of the world—to be obliged to descend from recording the wisdom and wit of DR. JOHNSON to a contest about *Sir Adam Fergusson*.

I shall certainly however abstain from saying one word in reply to the personal scurrility of this writer, who either thinks, or affects to think, that my pamphlet shows a "*rage*" against Sir Adam Fergusson. He little knows me if he is in earnest. I can assure him that *parcere subiectis*[8] is a constant maxim of my conduct; and that, in consideration of what I supposed Sir Adam Fergusson's feeling to be upon his dismission from even the *appearance* of so proud a situation as being Member for the great County of Ayr (*real* Member I never allowed him to be), I anxiously studied to express myself with as much delicacy as I possibly could, consistently with my patriotic wish to rouse my countrymen against the late audacious attempt upon the Court of Session and with my views as his competitor at the next General Election for the County of Ayr. Rancour I abhor, and wish on all occasions to preserve good humour. But it is perfectly fair to undeceive gentlemen who may be misled by notions of "spirited resistance to *aristocracy*."

[6]His edition of the plays was announced in 1783 and published in 1790.
[7]See above, 14 July 1785.
[8]To spare the humbled (see above, 17 May 1783, n. 8).

This writer says that "the gentlemen in our county resolved to shake off the servile yoke, and choose a Member independent of the *peerage*"; and he adds that "*all the independent gentlemen* of the county united cordially in electing Sir Adam Fergusson to be the Member."[1]

The whole of this, whether proceeding from gross ignorance or intentional falsehood, I do positively contradict; and as Sir Adam Fergusson is *upon the spot*[2] as well as I am I appeal to *himself* if the *fact* be not as I shall here state it.

Sir Adam Fergusson was supported by the interest of *three peers*. Colonel Montgomerie was also supported by the interest of *three peers*. For Sir Adam Fergusson were the Duke of Hamilton, the Earl of Glencairn, and the Earl of Dumfries. For Colonel Montgomerie were the Earl of Eglinton, the Earl of Cassillis, and the Earl of Loudoun. The first three peers prevailed and made Sir Adam Fergusson Member by throwing into his scale a number of those *superiority votes* which the County of Ayr has declared to be *nominal and fictitious*, while Colonel Montgomerie had a *considerable majority of real votes*, that is to say, of those gentlemen who have real landed property in the county.

Was *this* an election *independent of the peerage*? Did *all* the independent gentlemen cordially unite in electing Sir Adam Fergusson? What a shameful misrepresentation of the truth has this writer attempted to impose upon the public!

But farther—when the last General Election approached, two of the *peers* who supported Sir Adam Fergusson, viz. the Earls of Glencairn and Dumfries, declared for Mr. Craufurd, a first cousin of the Countess of Dumfries. *Where* were all the independent gentlemen *then* who we are told had so cordially united for Sir Adam Fergusson? Did Sir Adam Fergusson trust to such imaginary interest? Did he stand forth with *them* "resolved to shake off the *servile yoke*?" *I say No*. And I *ask* if he did not form a *coalition* with the Earl of *Eglinton*, with that very *peer* against whose interest he had so violently struggled with the aid of Sir John Whitefoord, the family of Dunlop, and others. I *ask* if he did not *bind* himself by an *agreement* to support for the whole of this Parliament *any* candidate whom that *peer* should name upon *condition* that that *peer* should support him for the next Parliament?

If I am misinformed as to the whole or any part of these political transactions I shall be very glad to make every acknowledgement that a gentleman ought to do. But if the plain and direct questions which

[1] In the election of 1774.
[2] Boswell deliberately repeats the phrase from his letter to the *St. James's Chronicle* 14 May 1785 which "An Ayrshireman" had mocked in the *Public Advertiser* 14 July 1785 (see above, p. 323).

I have now put are *not answered* in the *negative*, I must be permitted to think that this anonymous writer, who so impudently and invidiously snarls at a decision in which a MANSFIELD and a CAMDEN united,[3] is not a writer who will do me any injury, either with my country in general, or with the worthy gentlemen of Ayrshire in particular.

There is one other circumstance in this letter at once so base and so absurd that I know not well what to say to it; yet I cannot pass it in silence. Having mentioned my honoured father, he says, "whose memory will be dear to all of us who knew him *notwithstanding your insinuations*." What does he mean by *my* insinuations? No son ever respected a father more, though we had some unhappy differences with which this writer has no business, and though (as has happened to men of the finest minds) evil influence was ungenerously practised upon him in the decline of his life. That he made a great addition to the estate of Auchinleck, enriched and adorned it, and built an elegant house, I and my posterity will ever gratefully remember. But it is *not true* that he ever told me the estate was not entailed. He was too much of a *gentleman*, too much of an *old baron*, to talk so unhandsomely to his son and heir. Besides, *he and I both knew* that the estate *was* entailed upon me by different settlements which he could not defeat but by selling it; and rather than do that, I have no doubt he was Roman enough to have sacrificed his life, for no man had a steadier regard for the principle of family.

JAMES BOSWELL.

[EDITORIAL NOTE. The journal for Wednesday 27 July is resumed.]

Took brother home to dinner. I had met Akerman, who told me he was every night at the Globe Tavern, Fleet Street, as one of the "Friends round the Globe." I asked to be one. He engaged to introduce me. Called at Betsy's. Found she had gone, they could not tell whither. In the evening, brother and I walked calm to Temple Bar. Then to Globe, that I might not be tardy in getting into Akerman's club. He introduced me, Glover (formerly Torrington) in chair, and I was unanimously

---

[3] Lord Mansfield and Charles Pratt, Baron Camden, Lord Chancellor from 1766 to 1770, were such notorious opponents that their united support of Archibald Douglas in the Douglas Cause was celebrated in contemporary engravings. Their differences are symbolized by the Wilkes trial, which Mansfield prosecuted zealously. Camden, then Chief Justice of the Court of Common Pleas, won popular favour by deciding against the legality of general warrants, granting Wilkes a habeas corpus returnable the same day, and releasing him from the Tower on the grounds of Parliamentary privilege.

chosen.[3a] Comfortable sociality. Akerman talked well of the cares and dangers of his important office, which he had held above thirty years, having succeeded his father. He had never been from London above one night at a time, and very few nights (I think not above fifteen). He complained of Sheriff Taylor much, and of the tap being abolished in Newgate by Act of Parliament.[4] The consequence was that the prisoners got worse liquor and not less, and the gaol is disturbed by numbers of people bringing liquor; and more opportunities are got of bringing in instruments to the prisoners for making their escape. He used to pay —— a year for porter. It was so good that people used to send and get a pot as a great favour. He got £400 a year by the tap, out of which he gave £200 a year to poor prisoners. It hurts him that he has it not in his power now to relieve them as formerly. Much noise has been made as to the great emoluments of his office. If they were so great, he would have retired long ago from an office of such anxiety. Debtors may escape, and he be liable for what they owe. Convicts often attempt violence. He told me he had two sets of a good account of remarkable convicts, in four volumes, and he would make me a present of a set.[5] He said he was at the Globe almost every night, and drank either a bottle of port or three sixpenny-bowls of brandy and water. He never was drunk. He drank nothing at dinner but small beer or a little drop of spirits. When any complaint was made of his turnkeys' being rough, he uses to say, "I cannot get a man who has had an university education to be a turnkey." My mind was somewhat agitated with apprehension of a challenge from Sir Adam Fergusson. But I was *resolved*. Thinking of Newgate and violent deaths hardened me. I recalled the notions of my youth about that great gaol, the *Beggar's Opera*, etc. He told me he had now above 470 prisoners. I liked to hear him express some sense of religion. In opposition to Dornford's attack on him for not going to chapel, he said he preferred going somewhere else than among the

[3a] And so announced in the *London Chronicle*, 4 August 1785. Glover is almost certainly William Frederick Glover, the convivial booksellers' hack described above, 19 April 1783, n. 9, and Torrington probably the president of the club, who had stepped down from the chair to second Akerman's nomination. He remains unidentified. If he were George Byng, fourth Viscount Torrington, Boswell would have prefaced his name with a title.

[4] Sir Robert Taylor, architect (see above, 12 May 1783, n. 9), and Sheriff of London 1782–1783, was author of the act forbidding gaolers to sell liquors to the prisoners, which had gone into force 24 June 1785 with "the warmest support of Lord Mansfield and Lord Loughborough" (*Public Advertiser*, 20 July 1785).

[5] *The Annals of Newgate*, by the Rev. John Villette, Ordinary of Newgate, and others, 1776.

wretches, that he might not be disturbed in his devotions.[6] He said in his opinion, whenever a man's weight is upon the rope, he feels nothing, though there is an appearance of struggling. Glover came and shook hands with me, talked of our having met at Shakespeare's Jubilee, and of his having read with pleasure my *Letter* on the Court of Session. It is wonderful how many have read it. I came home about twelve. While with Akerman I thought of being counsel at Old Bailey.

THURSDAY 28 JULY. Wrote some letters, and then went to Malone at two. He said I should dine with him, and we would eat and drink and revise for hours. Unfortunately I had engaged myself to go to Astley's with the General and Mrs. Cosway.[6a] However, we had our quiet dinner most comfortably, and revised till six, when the General came in his coach and took me up, and then we took up Mrs. Cosway and Miss Charlotte, her sister. I was much entertained at Astley's. Lord and Lady Melbourne,[7] Lady Dungannon, and Lord William Gordon sat before us in the same box. Dr. William Scott sat near me in the next box, and we talked together. Cosway himself was with us. He walked both to and from. We passed the evening at Cosway's rather insipidly.

FRIDAY 29 JULY. At Malone's. Dined at Courtenay's, a choice company: Windham, Dempster, Colonel Erskine, Malone, Burke, Courtenay, and myself. It was a delightful day.[7a] We had admirable

---

[6] The last five of ten letters criticizing the administration of the prisons which Josiah Dornford, member of the Common Council of London, had addressed to the Council under a pseudonym were publicly acknowledged and printed in the *Morning Chronicle* 15 May to 2 August 1784. In the seventh letter, part 1 (22 May 1784), "Fidelio" charged Richard Akerman with economic exploitation of the prisoners, recommended that the keeper be paid only a salary, and asked, "And does the keeper himself and the prisoners constantly attend the divine service? I fear not." Akerman refuted the charges *seriatim* in the *Morning Chronicle* for 16 December and the *Public Advertiser* for 17 December 1784, and declared that "he does attend divine service, whenever it is convenient to him."

[6a] Astley's was a very popular equestrian circus or exhibition at which the proprietor was himself the leading performer. Boswell wrote a note to Mrs. Cosway in Italian, asking what time he and Paoli should accompany her to see Astley, "who, unlike you, makes dogs resemble human beings, while you (if I may revert to English) *treat men like dogs*" (To Maria Cosway, 28 July [1785]).

[7] Lady Melbourne, mother of the future Prime Minister, was later the mother-in-law of Lady Caroline Lamb (who was born in this year) and the recipient of Byron's confidences.

[7a] "Many a dull dinner is announced in the newspapers given *to divers of the nobility* by temporary statesmen. How much superior was 'the feast of reason and the flow of soul' at Mr. Courtenay's table last week? There sat Mr. Courtenay himself— Mr. Windham—Mr. Malone—Colonel Erskine—Mr. Dempster—Mr. Boswell— Mr. Burke!" (*Public Advertiser*, 4 August 1785).

burgundy and claret and excellent conversation. We saw no ladies, but had coffee and tea in the drawing-room. I told my transaction with the King concerning Prince Charles. Burke allowed that His Majesty showed feeling and the spirit of a gentleman. Erskine said, "It is plain he would have liked better to be the grandson of James the Second than of George the Second." Dempster said with sly pleasantry, "Why don't you write oftener to him, Boswell?" Dempster told us that at the meetings of East India directors, anyone who was five minutes too late paid a crown, and it was wonderful what an influence this crown had even upon very rich men. Burke said that was the *influence of the crown.*[8] I do not recollect the conversation, but it was highly pleasing at the time. At tea Burke gave us an admirable dissertation on a good conjugal life, which made an impression on me. He showed that it was a great bond of society, and that we must not expect a continuation of the fervour of love, but be satisfied with a calm friendship. He said a husband would come to be as little disgusted with little indelicacies about his wife as with his own; and he declared it as his opinion that keeping separate beds was a certain sign of corruption. A woman in that case never went to bed to her husband but with a gross purpose; whereas if she slept with him constantly, that might happen or not, as inclination prompted.

SATURDAY 30 JULY. At Malone's. Dined at Windham's: Courtenay, Malone, Burke, Beresford[9] and his son there. Another good day. But I have nothing to record. In the evening Windham, Courtenay, Malone, young Beresford, and I walked out, sauntered awhile, and then eat cold meat and drank negus at the Prince of Wales's Coffeehouse, Conduit Street.

SUNDAY 31 JULY. In Portman Chapel a moment, devout after breakfast at home. Then had post-chaise and took up Courtenay, and he and I drove to Thrale's house at Streatham to General Dalrymple's,[10] who had obligingly offered to show me what he supposed were notes by Dr. Johnson upon books in Thrale's library. They proved to be not his. By the way Courtenay and I had good conversation. He said (though I fear a sceptic) that he thought it might be urged in favour of a future state that all men had a hope of it, and yet the belief was

[8] An allusion to the famous resolution which John Dunning introduced in the Commons 6 April 1780: "that the influence of the Crown has increased, is increasing, and ought to be diminished."

[9] John Beresford, Member for Waterford in the Irish Commons and the virtual manager of Irish affairs from the time Pitt became Prime Minister until 1802.

[10] Dalrymple succeeded Lord Shelburne as tenant at Streatham while the Piozzis were in Italy.

not clear, because that would make us do nothing in this life. He said all that was required in an ordinary duel was only to show that a man can risk his life. It is not necessary to make a man who has abused you retract what he has said. We had a pleasant saunter and a hearty dinner at Dalrymple's. I liked him well. At night I drove to Dilly's and had excellent cold roast beef and mountain Malaga with him and Braithwaite.

MONDAY 1 AUGUST. After breakfast, Baldwin's a little; Malone's a little. Dined home. Was restless. Walked to Dilly's; supped. Then Globe with Akerman. Then home.

TUESDAY 2 AUGUST. Malone's. General said something about those whom I opposed in writing sending to *inquire* after me. My *nerves* were bad today. I dined at home. Went at night to Dilly's. Was uneasy.

WEDNESDAY 3 AUGUST. A very wet day. Malone's a minute and fixed to be with him at night. Sent to Ward's to know if he dined at home; welcomed. Evening Malone's and revised a good deal.

THURSDAY 4 AUGUST. Breakfasted with the Governor of Madras.[1] He was politely kind. Told him of my restless ambition. He promised if he saw a good opening for me in India, to let me know.[2]

FRIDAY 5 AUGUST. The General, Coti, Masseria, and I breakfasted at T. D.'s. Malone at Windsor. I went to Langton's at three and shared his family dinner. He walked with me to Piccadilly, where I got into Richmond coach. Reached the Lodge before nine; Mr. and Mrs. Hale and Ross Mackye there. Colonel and I sat till two over punch. He was truly cordial.

SATURDAY 6 AUGUST. Went on back of phaeton, talking to Mrs. Stuart and Mrs. Hale, to Putney. Then boat to Chelsea. Home. Ward had a card lying for me to dine with him. Malone's awhile. Then Ward's, most comfortable. *Felt* that with such connexions all things, even quarrels, appear not distressing. Evening Globe with Akerman. Bottle of port. Too hard living, this.

SUNDAY 7 AUGUST. Breakfasted home. Portuguese Chapel. Malone's a little. Governor of Madras, and went to Woodford[3] and dined with Preston; a number of people. A most joyous day. Evening Malone's though a good deal intoxicated. Lord Sunderlin and the ladies there, and Mr. and Mrs. Byng. Supped.

[1] Gen. Sir Archibald Campbell, who was appointed successor to Lord Macartney 9 March 1785 and arrived at Madras 6 April 1786.
[2] There is nothing at Yale suggesting that he tried to place Boswell in India, from which he himself returned in poor health after only three years' service.
[3] Possibly, "Governor of Madras and [I] went to Woodford."

MONDAY 8 AUGUST. Malone's a little. Dined Ward's and went to the Haymarket Theatre with him, etc., and saw with much pleasure the new comedy, *I'll Tell You What.*[4] Sat in the first row of a stage-box in my scarlet coat, between Hon. Mrs. Ward and Hon. Mrs. Shirley.[5] Wondered to feel myself perfectly easy and fashionable. Lord Macdonald was in the box. I felt remorse for having printed so much severity against him; resolved to cancel a leaf and spare him.[6] Supped at Ward's.

TUESDAY 9 AUGUST. Home calm till twelve, when the Hon. Mr. Shirley called, and he and I walked out beyond Paddington and visited John William Ward, our friend's child, this being his birthday on which he entered his fifth year.[7] Found Mrs. Ward there, and returned with her in the coach. We had a grand birthday dinner at Ward's; Wilkes there and Mrs. Bosville and both her sons. Stayed the evening: cards, music, supper. Mrs. Ward told me I was a great favourite of Mr. Ward's. In the morning came a card to me, same hand and seal with invitation to Hyde Park:[8] Mrs. *Stewart's* compliments, begging to see me, No. 47, Devonshire Street, Bloomsbury, any day between two and five. I went this very day, and as I suspected, found—Mrs. Rudd.[9] She looked as well as ever and was exceedingly agreeable. Wanted an introduction

[4] By Elizabeth Inchbald. It opened 4 August 1785 and went to twenty nights in this season.

[5] Frances Ward Shirley, the wife of Washington Shirley (later eighth Earl Ferrers) and cousin of the Hon. William Ward.

[6] Boswell did cancel leaf M4 of the *Tour to the Hebrides* (p. 168), deleting Johnson's remark on 4 September 1773 that Lord Macdonald had "no more the notions of a chief than an attorney who has twenty houses in a street and considers how much he can make of them." But the first edition contained many other severities, including charges that Macdonald was a mean host and that he drove large numbers of tenants to emigration because of rack-rents. The cancelled passage was restored, moreover, under the date 3 November 1773 as "the character of a rapacious Highland chief."

[7] Later fourth Viscount Dudley and Ward of Dudley and first Earl Dudley and Secretary of State for Foreign Affairs under Canning. His father maintained a separate establishment for him, allowed him neither playmates nor sports, and developed his precocious talents by a series of tutors. He was generally undistinguished, however, shy, and given to rehearsing publicly what he intended to say to others, using two voices, one gruff and one shrill. A wit remarked that this was "Lord Dudley conversing with Lord Ward" (*Memoirs, Journal, and Correspondence of Thomas Moore*, ed. Lord John Russell, 1854, v. 203).

[8] See above, 17 July 1785.

[9] Margaret Caroline Rudd, the celebrated courtesan and adventuress. Boswell had interviewed her and been enchanted, despite considerable wariness, in April 1776, three months after she had been acquitted of the charge of forgery. Her accomplices, the Perreau brothers, were executed.

to Mr. Dundas to recommend her to the Lord Chancellor, that his Lordship's influence might make a man do her justice with whom she had lived six years, and had now separated from him.[1] I advised her to go directly to the Chancellor herself. She begged to see me sometimes, and that I would *not forget her*. It was a romantic scene.

WEDNESDAY 10 AUGUST. Malone was busy with his Shakespeare. So we did not *sit* upon my *Tour*. I breakfasted with Sir Joshua Reynolds tête-à-tête and heard an account of his late jaunt to the Continent.[2] Sat awhile with my brother T. D. and engaged him to dine with us. Visited Miss Derby, also Dilly. T. D. dined at General's with us. I was pretty calm. Supped Dempster's.

THURSDAY 11 AUGUST. Malone devoted the whole of this day to me, that we might get forward with my *Tour*. I breakfasted, dined, drank tea, and supped with him, and sat till near two in the morning. Yet we did not get a great deal winnowed, there was so very much chaff in that portion of it.

FRIDAY 12 AUGUST. Met Wilkes in Piccadilly. He invited me to dine with him at his country-house at Kensington Gore, where he keeps Mrs. Arnold, a lady whom he met with eight years ago at Bath, and has had ever since. I was a little at Malone's and at Baldwin's, and then went to Wilkes's. His house was all elegance: an exquisite collection both of prints and china, and an extraordinary number of large mirrors.[3] The woman seemed decent enough. A maidservant attended us, and we had a very pretty dinner, with Madeira, mountain, port, and afterwards coffee and gunpowder tea.[4] It was a gay, social scene, but I drank rather too much, and when I got to town, wandered about in the mob looking at illuminations for the Prince of Wales's birthday, and had my pocket picked of some silver and a key. Went to Sir Joshua Reynolds's and sat some time with him and Miss Palmer.

SATURDAY 13 AUGUST. Awaked feverish and vexed. Breakfasted with Dempster and grew pretty well. At Malone's awhile. Dined Dilly's

[1] Unidentified, and there is no evidence that his name was Stewart. Mrs. Rudd seems to have been capitalizing on her ancestry. Her mother was the natural daughter of a Major W. Stewart, who, according to her own account, was of the family of Ballymoran in Ireland, cadets of the Stewarts of Garlies in Scotland. If her father indeed was a Stewart of Ballymoran, then, like Boswell, she could claim cousinship with the sovereign through Lady Marie Stuart, Countess of Mar and daughter of the Duke of Lennox.
[2] See above, 19 July 1785 and n. 7.
[3] The house was Lilliputian, according to Wilkes's biographer, Horace Bleackley, and had six long windows in the small parlour and mirrors lining the walls everywhere because Wilkes liked a bright room even when the shutters were drawn. He bequeathed the house and its contents to Amelia Arnold.
[4] A fine kind of green tea, each leaf of which is rolled up so that it has a granular appearance.

with Braithwaite, Hatter Sharp, Dr. Thomson of Kensington,[5] Rev. Mr. Jones. Evening at Globe; Akerman not there till I was gone. Returned to Dilly's, and he and I were by ourselves quiet.

SUNDAY 14 AUGUST. Visited Mrs. Knowles a moment after breakfast. Then to St. Paul's and attended service well. Still kept a degree of heated imagination as to uncertainty of life—which however is indeed the *true* feeling if we think—and had no *fear* of consequences, but a sort of thoughtless, *risking* frame. Then visited Mrs. Rudd, who was elegantly dressed; said she had an independency and would not form another connexion unless it were very agreeable. I promised to visit her again. Dined at home, a good number with us. Was worn out with too hard living. After dinner was somewhat dreary and restless. Lay down on bed and slumbered. Up and played whist. Mrs. Cosway came and played on the pianoforte and sung. I grew easier, bathed feet, and went early to bed and drank capillaire.[6]

MONDAY 15 AUGUST. Breakfasted with Sir Joshua and sat to him. Dined at Malone's with General Paoli, Sir Joshua Reynolds, Mr. Byng. Malone said Johnson had made an era in the English language. Everybody wrote a higher style now, even Christie in advertisements.[7] After coffee and tea, he and I sat and revised *Tour* till late.

TUESDAY 16 AUGUST. Some time with Malone. Visited Mr. Villette.[8] Dined at home. Went to Dilly's at night to be ready to attend the execution next day.

WEDNESDAY 17 AUGUST. Was not called soon enough. It struck six when I was in Paternoster Row. With difficulty (by holding up my stick, as some sagacious man advised me) got the crowd to make way for me till I got to the door of Newgate, where Mr. Akerman saw me and took me in. Saw some of the unhappy men's irons knocked off, and some of them pinioned. There were seven men and one woman.[1]

[5] An ordained minister of the Church of Scotland who resigned his charge and became a prolific booksellers' hack in London. He seems also to have kept an academy at his house at Kensington Gravel Pits. Richard Sharp, a hat-manufacturer in the company that bore his name, was commonly styled "Conversation Sharp" because of his great gifts for social talk.

[6] A once-fashionable drink, an infusion of the maidenhair fern, sometimes flavoured with orange-flowers, to which a great many medicinal properties were ascribed. Johnson poured it into port. Boswell used it for a hangover cure, and sometimes, as here, to avoid wine.

[7] James Christie the auctioneer, founder of the well-known company.

[8] In the *Life of Johnson* Boswell praised his "earnest and humane exhortations" to the inmates of Newgate, and nudged the Court and the City to reward him with preferment for his "extraordinary diligence" on behalf of the prisoners (23 June 1784).

[1] She was Elizabeth Taylor, the sister of Martin Taylor, who suffered with her. They had been convicted of "a burglary in the house of Mr. Samuel Hooker, at Highgate,

Guthrie, a grenadier,[2] told me he was born at Dysart and served his time to a shoemaker at Aberdour. As he could not reach his pocket (his hands being tied), he asked me to give him a book out of it (the *Common Devotions of Newgate*), which I did. He and Morris, another grenadier, were in terrible agitation, and I was much shocked and had a dreary impression of the dismal fate which may attend men. There was a vast crowd,[3] and a prodigious heavy rain fell. I was quite unnerved. I stayed and saw them all cut down, carried into Newgate, and stretched dead upon a table. I made Guthrie's cap be pulled up and looked at his face, which was neither black nor distorted. The quick transition from life to death struck me. I breakfasted at Baldwin's. Was very uneasy. Visited Chelmsford.[4] A little with Malone. Walked in the street with Lord Townshend; all would not dissipate. Dined at home; *canonico* from Naples brought Italy quite before me. Drank a great deal of wine. Malone had promised me all the evening to revise. I went between six and seven, but was not very fit for the task. However, we went on till one in the morning, when I came home dismal.

THURSDAY 18 AUGUST. A very little with Malone. Dined at Sir Joshua Reynolds's with Malone, General Paoli, Langton, etc. A good day enough. Home quietly at night.

[EDITORIAL NOTE. The entries for 19–26 August 1785 are missing. Boswell's expense account shows that on the 20th he had visited "Mr. Barnard" at his country-place, an invitation tendered 15 June 1785, almost certainly by Bishop Barnard's son Andrew, of Wimbledon (see above, p. 309 and n. 5). The costs of a jaunt to Streatham were recorded the 23rd of August, and a return from Hampstead on the 25th. Rough notes for the journal begin again with the 27th.]

SATURDAY 27 AUGUST. Barnard's.

---

and stealing lace, ribbons, etc. . . . The brother and sister kissed each other several times, both before and after the prayers upon the scaffold, and they went out of the world hand in hand, in which state they remained till they were cut down" (*London Chronicle*, 16–18 August 1785).
[2] Convicted of assault and robbery.
[3] "The crowd was as great as ever known on the like occasion, and many of both sexes lost their shoes and buckles, cloaks, hats, etc., through the pressure of the populace. . . . At four this morning it is supposed curiosity had drawn more than a thousand people into the Old Bailey" (*London Chronicle*, 16–18 August 1785).
[4] This cannot be taken literally, for Chelmsford was a day's journey from London, and Boswell remarked later in his journal (26 July 1786) that he had not visited it since 1763. The allusion is probably to a woman from Chelmsford, possibly Betsy Smith.

SUNDAY 28 AUGUST. Portuguese [Chapel]. Richmond, Sir Joshua.[5] Colonel Stuart's.[6] "... a good, pleasant boy. Never having been accustomed to refuse himself anything, he has gone on on all occasions: 'I will have this woman'; but by taking such gratifications he loses what is more valuable: the consequence which he should have in his country from his rank, fortune, and talents. He is conscious he is not the great Earl of Pembroke." This was a very instructive lecture to me. Sir Joshua also talked of Mrs. Rudd, and said that if a man were known to have a connexion with her, it would sink him. "You," said he, "are known not to be formally accurate" (or some such phrase) "in your conduct. But it would ruin you should you be known to have such a connexion." I did not see why this should appear so peculiarly bad. He had a good image as to Lord Pembroke: "Were it not that he has a great title, he would sink. His coronet, as if made of cork, keeps his head swimming above water." I am very lucky in my intimacy with this eminent man. It is truly enviable. At Colonel Stuart's I found Lady Lonsdale, who talked away very well, as I thought. The Colonel and I were social as usual, and Mrs. Stuart was charming.

MONDAY 29 AUGUST. Colonel Stuart's. Night Malone.

TUESDAY 30 AUGUST. Braithwaite's. Dilly's night.

WEDNESDAY 31 AUGUST. Brocklesby's. Malone's.

THURSDAY 1 SEPTEMBER. Ward's with General, etc. Weary. Supped; revived.

FRIDAY 2 SEPTEMBER. Home. Malone's tea, etc.

SATURDAY 3 SEPTEMBER. Mrs. Bosville's. Globe. Langton's. Parade.[7]

[5] They went in Sir Joshua's coach to Wick House, his country retreat on Richmond Hill, near the park and overlooking the Thames. It is now a residence for nurses.

[6] There was once a fully written entry for this day, but only the last page of it has been recovered. Boswell is with Sir Joshua, who is talking pointedly about Boswell's friend, Lord Pembroke.

[7] The procession of the Lord Mayor and principal aldermen to open Bartholomew Fair. "Saturday being Bartholomew Fair day, it was, according to annual custom, ushered in by Lady Holland's mob, accompanied with a charming band of music, consisting of marrow-bones and cleavers, tin kettles, etc., etc., much to the gratification of the inhabitants about Smithfield: great preparations were then made for the reception of the Lord Mayor, the sheriffs, and other City officers, who, after regaling themselves with a cool tankard at Mr. Akerman's, made their appearance in the fair about one o'clock to authorize *mimic* fools to make *real* ones of the gaping spectators. The proclamation being read, and the Lord Mayor retiring, he was saluted by a flourish of trumpets, drums, rattles, salt-boxes, and other delightful musical instruments. ... There were wild beasts from all parts of the world roaring—puppets squeaking— sausages frying—kings and queens raving—pickpockets diving—roundabouts twirl-

SUNDAY 4 SEPTEMBER. Holy Sacrament. Ward's dinner. Home supper. Sacrament Sunday.[8]

MONDAY 5 SEPTEMBER. Dined Baldwin's, supped Malone's. Letter Temple, serious.[9]

TUESDAY 6 SEPTEMBER. Breakfasted Dempster. A *little* sunk from hard drinking. Dined and supped Malone's.

WEDNESDAY 7 SEPTEMBER. Early out. Breakfasted Malone; revised. Charming day and fine spirits. Dempster a moment. Sauntered with Paradise and Seward. Dined Sir Joshua's with Sir John and Lady Doyly and several more from Bengal. Malone and Dr. Burney. Malone's; supped and revised till two in the morning. Yet (*memorabile!*) home before the General.

THURSDAY 8 SEPTEMBER. *Finished revise* with Malone at Baldwin's. Dined and supped Malone.

FRIDAY 9 SEPTEMBER. Breakfasted Dempster. *Chelmsford.*[1] Dined home. Tea Malone. Supped Dempster's.

SATURDAY 10 SEPTEMBER. Breakfasted Sir Joshua and had picture finished. M. C. S.;[2] told her honestly not in circumstances. " 'Tis tantalizing." "Come and see me sometimes and you shall not be tantalized.[3] Should like to have a child between you and me; curious being. It would find its way in the world." Dined Ward's; cards and lost.[4] Malone's. Romantic history.[5]

SUNDAY 11 SEPTEMBER. Wet at times. Malone's. Bavarian Chapel,

---

ing—hackney-coaches and poor horses driving—and all Smithfield alive-O. The learned horse paid his obedience to the company, as did about a score of monkeys—several *beautiful young* ladies of forty—Punches—Pantaloons—Harlequins—Columbines—three giants—a dwarf—and a giantess" (*London Chronicle*, 3–6 September 1785).

[8] He probably means that it was Sacrament Sunday at Auchinleck. See above, 28 August 1783, p. 161, n. 7.

[9] Boswell's letters to Temple for this period are lost, and the Register of Letters is imperfect. The letter in question is probably one which Temple wrote to him on 31 August 1785 lecturing him on his manner of life, especially for associating with Mrs. Rudd.

[1] See above, 17 August 1785, p. 338, n. 4.

[2] Margaret Caroline Rudd, now "Mrs. Stewart."

[3] There are no quotation marks in the manuscript, and what follows may have been said by Boswell.

[4] Twelve shillings.

[5] Presumably an allusion to Malone's unfulfilled love affairs, to which he made veiled reference in later correspondence with Boswell. Susanna Spencer went mad (Malone was contributing £100 annually to her support), and Sara Loveday had summarily rejected him.

low *missa*. Langton's to dine, but he did not come in, so home. Evening Malone's.

MONDAY 12 SEPTEMBER. Went to Langton's to dine, but accounts came of Lady Rothes's[6] death, so home to General's. Then walked to Richmond Lodge. Colonel not at home. Good advice.

TUESDAY 13 SEPTEMBER. Mrs. Stuart brought me in coach to Putney, and I sailed to Blackfriars. Then Malone a little. General got account of his nephew's death.[7] I wished not to disturb him. Dined at Sir Joshua's with Malone; Salt of the Temple, Commissioner Agar,[8] Dr. Brocklesby, Metcalfe. An excellent social day. Sir Joshua said, "We have had many pleasant together." I drank too much. Metcalfe, Malone, and I stayed supper. I fell asleep. Away to Dilly's; he in the country. But I got in.

WEDNESDAY 14 SEPTEMBER. A little confused by yesterday's excess. But lemonade and coffee made me well. Saw Cadell in his shop for the first time.[9] Malone's. He and I and Wilkes dined at Dilly's. A pleasant day. Malone stayed oysters. I walked with him to Catherine Street. Sauntered, but under vow.[1] Back to Dilly's.

THURSDAY 15 SEPTEMBER. A very wet morning. It faired, and Dilly and I walked to bookbinder's and Baldwin's. Then Old Bailey some time. Dined with Lord Mayor, judges, etc. Lord Mayor drank Court of Session. Tea Malone's and revised. Back to Dilly's. Intended to go next day to Claxton's.[2]

FRIDAY 16 SEPTEMBER. Poor Dilly had been disturbed by me last night, and was disconcerted. An addition to my *Tour* (defending faculty of writing conversations) occurred to me.[3] So I stayed in town and Malone and I laboured as usual. Dined at General's. Evening Malone's.

SATURDAY 17 SEPTEMBER. Busy at printing-house hurrying the press. Dined Malone's tête-à-tête and passed the evening.

[6] Boswell should have written "Lady Haddington." She was Langton's mother-in-law.
[7] Paoli is known to have had two nephews, but both were living later in the century. Most likely Pasquale Fondacci, the husband of his sister's daughter.
[8] Samuel Salt, the chief character in Charles Lamb's "Old Benchers of the Inner Temple," and Welbore Ellis Agar, Commissioner of Customs. Lamb's father was Salt's clerk and confidential servant; his mother was Salt's housekeeper. Charles Lamb was born in Crown Office Row in chambers belonging to Salt, and spent the first seven years of his life there. It was Salt who procured him his appointment as clerk in the India House.
[9] Thomas Cadell, successor to Andrew Millar, partner of William Strahan, and one of the leading publishers of London. He now appears in the journal for the first time.
[1] A line has been drawn through "Street . . . vow," perhaps by Boswell.
[2] His estate was at Shirley, near Croydon.
[3] The concluding paragraphs of the book.

SUNDAY 18 SEPTEMBER. Breakfasted home. Walked to Dilly's. Did not find him at home, but found him at Mr. Davies's, near Queen Square.[4] Malone's a little. Dined Mr. Ward's with Andrews. Too much wine. Then General's with Madama Cosway, etc.

MONDAY 19 SEPTEMBER. Not in good spirits. Had a return of hypochondria. Malone's forenoon. Dined Cosway's with General and several foreigners. Was *ennuyé*. Away to Malone's and complained. Could still maintain desperation. Dilly's at night to go next day to Claxton's.

TUESDAY 20 SEPTEMBER. At nine in Croydon coach. Good comfortable day with worthy Claxton, his wife, and old Mrs. Bedford, her mother. At night Malone's and found the end sheet, etc., of my *Tour*.

WEDNESDAY 21 SEPTEMBER. Breakfasted home pretty well. Went to the levee. The King asked me when I went north. I said, "On Saturday, Sir. My book has detained me longer than I expected. But tomorrow is *coronation* day with me too. 'Finis coronat opus.'[5] It will then be finished. Your Majesty will[6] have it tomorrow evening."[7] I then went to Malone's and settled my title-page. Then to Baldwin's; gave all my directions so as to have four books tonight for Sir Joshua, Dr. Brocklesby, Dempster, Langton, all of whom Malone had kindly asked to meet me at his house at dinner next day to be impanelled on the *Tour*. I then hastened to Preston's in Lime Street and dined with him hearty in the midst of captains of ships, etc. Drank too much. Then to Dilly's; wrote to wife and Squire Dilly that I had fixed Saturday for setting out.

THURSDAY 22 SEPTEMBER. Dined at Malone's with the *jury* on my *Tour*, who applauded it much. Had my baggage with me, and drove to Dilly's at night, having bid a cordial adieu to my kind and elegant friend Malone.

FRIDAY 23 SEPTEMBER. My brother T. D. breakfasted with us. I went to the other end of the town to view my room calmly and see if

[4]Probably William Davies, who held an important position in the employ of Thomas Cadell. Boswell spent almost all the week with members of the book trade.
[5]"The end crowns the work." George III was crowned on 22 September 1761.
[6]The MS. has the alternative "shall" written above the line, and Boswell may indeed have meant the auxiliary verb to express determination. A Scotsman, he never mastered the intricate and largely artificial "rules" of southern literary English for "shall" and "will." His native idiom, like the present-day American vernacular, used "will" in all three persons to express simple futurity ("I will see" instead of "I shall see"). Malone, in the revision of the *Tour*, had been coaching him on English usage, with the result merely of making him suspect that every "will" ought to be "shall."
[7]The book was first advertised in the newspapers Monday 26 September and published Saturday 1 October 1785.

anything was forgot.[8] Once more saw Malone. Paid a few visits. T. D. dined with me at Dilly's. Evening wrote letters and notes about presentation copies of my *Tour*. Sat up too late, as I was to set out early next morning.

SATURDAY 24 SEPTEMBER. Rose between five and six. Got into the Bedford coach at six. Stopped at Shefford, where Mr. Dilly's[8a] horses and boy came, and I rode to Southill. He at Ware, so I dined and drank tea with his sister, and he came home at night. We were hearty.

SUNDAY 25 SEPTEMBER. A very wet day. He and I went in his chaise to Chicksands, Sir George Osborn's, a complete fine old abbacy. Morning service most decent in his family chapel. But I thought he should sometimes go to the parish church for a good example. We could not get out to walk. Dined and drank tea. Back to Southill at night.

MONDAY 26 SEPTEMBER. Miss Dilly went with me in the Squire's chaise to Biggleswade. Visited Farmer Rudd and Rev. Mr. Gibson. Got into Newcastle coach. Grantham at night. Horrid stories of punishment of Negroes in Jamaica.[9]

TUESDAY 27 SEPTEMBER. Came out at Doncaster. Visited Mrs. Boswelle. Her son married and from home. She a Boswell born and fond of the name.[1] Took seat in retour-chaise to Wakefield to go Sir Thomas Wentworth Blackett's. Heard he was at Harrogate. Took chaise to Leeds. Found Carlisle coach did not come till next afternoon. Stayed all night, a little dreary alone.

WEDNESDAY 28 SEPTEMBER. Called on Buck, the Recorder; gone to some distance. A gentleman agreed to take a post-chaise with me to Harrogate. We discovered ourselves to each other. He Mr. Dunn, secretary to the present Speaker, formerly secretary to Lord Grantley in that capacity, and now a kind of steward for him.[2] We dined at the *Salutation*[3] ordinary. He went to Lord Grantley's, and I drank tea and

---

[8] That is, he went to General Paoli's in Portman Square. He had given the servants six guineas in tips the previous day (see below, Appendix A).

[8a] Squire Dilly's.

[9] The *Gentleman's Magazine* for April of this year prints a story of a "new Negro" in Jamaica who ran amok and killed three other slaves. After a mock trial he was "burnt alive ... with all the excruciating circumstances of horror that could be devised."

[1] She and her husband were probably descendants of Nicholas Boswelle, of Doncaster (d. 1692), who had several children, including John Boswelle, of Doncaster.

[2] Fletcher Norton, in 1782 created Lord Grantley, was Speaker of the House of Commons 1770–1780. His seat at Grantley was about seven miles north of Harrogate. The "present Speaker" of the House was Charles Wolfran Cornwall.

[3] One of the four principal inns of the village of Upper Harrogate.

played whist and supped with the company. A Lady Danvers said they admitted strangers of good appearance passing, but not people in stage-machines. When the Carlisle coach came, I walked into the room boldly and announced that I went in it.

[EDITORIAL NOTE. The journal breaks off here at the foot of a full page. Boswell's complicated and strenuous itinerary (Bedford coach to Shefford, Newcastle coach to Doncaster, post-chaise to Leeds, post-chaise to Harrogate, Carlisle coach) was laid out not merely to give him a week-end with Squire Dilly at Southill, Bedfordshire, but also to allow him to pay a visit to Counsellor John Lee at his country-house at Staindrop, County Durham, near Bishop Auckland. Boswell was delighted by Lee's invitation because he admired Lee professionally and personally and hoped to get help from him if he came to the English bar, as Lee had encouraged him to do. For three days, beginning 28 September 1785, he proclaimed their connexion in the *Public Advertiser* by a string of paragraphs transmitted through Charles Dilly.

"A prodigious noise was lately made in England by some people about the fantastical French authoress *Madame* Genlis.[4] Honest Boswell said upon this, 'Come, come. Let me have MONSIEUR *Jeun Lee*' (precisely the same French pronunciation of the name of his friend Mr. *John Lee*)."

"Mr. Boswell has *at last* quitted the metropolis for a little while, and is gone down to the country-seat of *his friend Jack Lee*" (29 September 1785).

"It is *true* Mr. Boswell *has* quitted the metropolis for a little while, and is to visit his friend Counsellor Lee at Staindrop, but he is gone to his own country-seat at Auchinleck to settle leases and other private business" (30 September 1785).[5]

[4] Stéphanie-Félicité Ducrest de Saint-Aubin de Genlis, author and educational theorist (indebted in part to Rousseau), the wife of Charles-Alexis Brulart, Comte de Genlis, mistress of the Duc de Chartres and "governor" to his children. She arrived in London about 25 June and returned to Paris 27 July 1785. Her works already ran to seventeen volumes, and three of her major publications had been translated into English.

[5] From Dilly, 5 October 1785: "Having a desire you should come forward to the bar of our courts with great reputation, I wish most sincerely—and I hope you will not suppose it from any other motive than for your welfare—I do therefore wish you would let alone writing paragraphs about yourself. The three you sent from Southill in my own judgement should not have appeared, but as you gave such charge about them I sent the order to Mr. Woodfall, who inserted accordingly. He told me himself he was hurt to see such paragraphs. They have been noticed and ridiculed, I am told, in the *Public Herald*."

Boswell appears to have enjoyed the pleasures of Lee's company only briefly: a letter from his host dated 3 October 1785 alludes to a "late short visit." On the same day that Lee wrote, Boswell arrived home at Auchinleck.[6]

By that time (1 October) the *Tour to the Hebrides* was published and exciting a widespread response. Public expectation had been raised high by a long course of newspaper notices. The applause of the jury of friends which Malone had impanelled at dinner on Thursday 22 September was probably as whole-hearted as it was sincere; the occasion was not one for small reservations. But the book was now going before the wide jury of the general reading public, where reservations were not likely to be muted or suppressed. *An Account of Corsica*, a book which had enjoyed a remarkably friendly reception from the reviewers, had appeared so far back as 1768; the extravagancies of the second *Letter to the People of Scotland* were more likely to set the tone.

One thing was certain: people found the book compulsively readable. The whole impression of 1,500 copies was sold out by 17 October, that is, in little more than two weeks. A second and a third edition were published within the year. Voluminous extracts were printed serially in the newspapers and magazines, and all through 1785–1786 the *Journal of a Tour to the Hebrides* was given more space in reviews and letters to the editor than any other book. Yet the general character of the reception was vigorous applause alternating with strident disapproval of the same subject matter. Reviewers, while they were entertained, were disquieted and baffled by Boswell's lack of reticence and his method of characterization by minute detail—what he later called his giving of a "Flemish picture." To such critics the *Tour* had on principle to be condemned as a farrago, a torrent of indiscriminate minutiae. Contemporaries of a great innovative work, they recoiled from its revolutionary feature: familiar and ignoble detail controlled by a presiding impression of magnanimity, goodness, and compassion.

From the first Boswell's really objectionable egotisms made him the butt of a good deal of coarse and ill-tempered raillery. He had himself to blame for this. Malone had cordially accepted all the exploitation of self in the manuscript that served a structural purpose, but had strongly urged him to suppress gratuitous self-advertisement. The personal intrusions were especially noxious to critics because they treated the book as Johnsonian memoirs despite its explicit title. The

[6]The Boswell manuscripts at Yale contain the greater part of an expense account for the London jaunt just concluded. It furnishes so illuminating a supplement to the journal that it is printed entire in Appendix A.

virtues of the *Tour* as a travel book were almost completely ignored. Criticism of the *Journal of a Tour to the Hebrides* therefore anticipated criticism of the *Life of Johnson*; indeed, without identifying dates one might sometimes be confused as to which book was being discussed.]

[From the *Public Advertiser*, 6 October 1785]

Extract of a letter from Bagshot, 2 October 1785.

"I have read today about a hundred pages of Boswell's journey to the Hebrides. It *entertains the party;* and I find in it, as I expected, all the qualities it was recommended to us for. Its speciality pleases me much . . . and [I] am much obliged to Boswell for the pains he has taken."

[From the *Morning Herald*, 19 October 1785]

"And Bozzy—last not least with his biography—to Bozzy the only recommendation we can give, or he can want, is to blot and abbreviate."

[From the *Public Advertiser*, 24 October 1785]

"Boswell and Johnson, says a correspondent, put him in mind of Pope and Bolingbroke. Others resemble them to Lunardi and his balloon, and say he avails himself of the learned Doctor's *gas*, to give himself a short-lived elevation above his natural element, but as this gradually evaporates and loses its force, the dead weight attached to the literary car must speedily fall into its native obscurity.—Q."

[From the *St. James's Chronicle*, 25 October 1785]

"To the Printer of the *St. James's Chronicle*. Sir, . . . Whether you, Mr. Baldwin, your editor, or an unknown correspondent has reviewed Mr. Boswell's late publication I cannot say, but it determined me to buy the book, and having read it, I am perfectly satisfied that my money was well bestowed, and has made me impatient to see the Life of his fellow-traveller, which, I doubt not, will be written with the same spirit and adorned with the same truths with which the *Tour* is so strongly marked. To see a North Briton warmly attached to his native soil, yet above concealing the little blemishes which mark it or which characterize some of its inhabitants, is candid, manly, and becoming the bosom friend of Dr. Johnson. And though I have read all the Doctor's writings with pleasure, and I hope with profit also, he stands much higher in my estimation now than ever. His books only proved how much he knew and how well he could convey his knowledge to others; but Mr. Boswell has made me personally acquainted with a man to whom I was before a stranger; he has drawn his picture better than Sir Joshua could have drawn it.—M. M."

[From the *Critical Review*, November 1785]

"It is not easy to distinguish the different feelings and sentiments with which we read the 'memorabilia' before us. The original dictator is nearer to Socrates than his reporter to Xenophon; and, instead of a calm pleasing light, which generally illuminates every intricate question, we successively pass from the most illiberal sarcasms, and the most trifling vanity, to judicious remarks, and the most interesting conversations. . . . Perhaps there has not occurred a fairer object of criticism than this journal. The author deserves all our attention; the different parts of it are of very dissimilar merit. . . . Indeed, though we are occasionally disgusted by the circumstances before mentioned, we are frequently entertained, often instructed, and almost always interested.

"The peculiarities of Johnson, those little drawbacks, which bring literary eminence nearer to the common rank, are generally mentioned. We delight in them, because they are apologies for ourselves, in a degree, greater in proportion as we rank below the 'rover through the Hebrides.' Johnson's bigotry deserves a severer reprehension: he would not hear Robertson preach, because he would not countenance a Presbyterian assembly; though he would have heard him preach from a tree. . . . Sometimes the most trifling conversations are preserved with a care which should only have distinguished useful and ingenious ones.

"We cannot easily leave Johnson, but his companion will not forgive us if we pass him without notice; and why should we omit to mention him, whose vivacity has confessedly enlivened the didactic gravity of the literary Colossus—whose good-humoured vanity generally pleases? Excuse us, Mr. Boswell; though we sometimes smile *at* your volubility, yet we go with you cheerfully along. Life has too many grave paths; let us catch the fluttering butterfly occasionally in the flowery meadows: he will not detain us long, and may deceive the length, sometimes the tediousness of the way.

"Mr. Boswell has drawn his own and Dr. Johnson's character: the last is delineated with much strength, and coloured with justness; the former is drawn from the heart. . . . The egotisms of the journalist are numerous: he apologizes for them, and says they are related rather as 'keys to what is valuable belonging to others, than for their own sake.' This is a plausible excuse; but unluckily when these keys are examined, we often find no locks. The reporter rather resembles the chamberlain of an inn in ruins; the badge of office is preserved, the keys are numerous, but nothing valuable is discovered on applying them.

"But it is now time to leave Dr. Johnson and his journalist: in spite of the errors which we have so freely pointed out, in spite of a few Scotticisms, which the journalist, with all his anxiety to write 'high English,' has not been able to detect, in spite of a few laughable attempts to palliate Johnson's errors, we must recommend this journal as a pleasant, lively, and sometimes useful companion."[7]

[From the *English Review*, November 1785]

"A blind and undistinguishing admiration is among the characteristics of weak and frivolous minds. There are men who venerate their fellow creatures as if they were gods; who pay homage even to their weaknesses and follies . . . ; and who seek for distinction by appearing in their train. These reflections, which obtrude themselves upon us, we express with reluctance and regret, as we wish to think well of Mr. Boswell, and are content to place to the account of early impressions his present excess of veneration.

"But allowing to Dr. Johnson all the merit which his warmest admirers ascribe to him, was it meritorious, was it right or justifiable in Mr. Boswell to record and to publish his prejudices, his follies and whims, his weaknesses, his vices? . . . It was counteracting, we should imagine, his design, which, if we mistake not, was to hold up Dr. Johnson in the most respectable light. . . . We cannot, however, but observe how derogatory it would have been to the fame and character of Socrates, and indeed, how injurious to the cause of virtue, had Xenophon haunted that great moral teacher in all his retreats, gaping after everything he said and did, and published all his infirmities to the world . . . Mr. Boswell provides fuel for that passion for minutiae, for trifling anecdotes, which takes place of all nobler views and pursuits.

"Yet amidst the trifles and trash with which our author has filled his volume, we meet with not a little of solid and manly observations on men, books, and things; and we should have laid the blame of those trifles and that trash wholly on Mr. Boswell, if it did not appear that he was in the habit of reading his diary to his gigantic companion, who did not discountenance, but was flattered and pleased with it.

"In this journal there is not a little egotism relating wholly to Mr. Boswell himself, which in a man who appears very good-natured, and is certainly an agreeable trifler, we readily excuse. But we hope that

[7] lx. 337–345 *passim*.

Mrs. Boswell has often given her husband more essential tokens of complaisance and affection than by changing her bed-chamber for one night to accommodate Dr. Johnson. Yet our author celebrates this act of hospitality in the highest strains of panegyric.

"On the whole, this is a very entertaining journal; but it does by no means tend to exalt the fame either of its subject or of its author."[8]

[From the *European Magazine and London Review*, December 1785]

"This title-page promises much information and much entertainment; and the work, particularly in the latter, amply gratifies the candid reader's expectation. . . . The journal of a tour to the Hebrides with such a man as the late Dr. Samuel Johnson cannot fail, if faithfully executed, to contain many particulars curious and interesting to philosophical minds. . . . We are introduced by anecdotes to a familiar acquaintance with characters which otherwise could only be the objects of distant and indistinct admiration. It is to the writings of the learned that we must apply for an estimate of their improvements and proficiency in science; but to read and discover the man—to form an idea of his virtues and vices—the liberality or narrowness of his sentiments— our best guide will always be found in genuine anecdotes;—and of the authenticity of those given by Mr. Boswell, besides their intrinsic evidences of veracity, none but those of a worse than capricious disposition can hesitate in his acquiescence. . . . Mr. Boswell's method of taking minutes from time to time on the spot gives the reader a satisfaction somewhat similar to that of a politician when he reads an agreeable piece of intelligence in the *London Gazette*.

"To give private conversations to the public is not the most pleasing task to true delicacy; and we think Mr. Boswell might have hit upon a better apology than that he has used. The observations and repartees of a Johnson, however delivered in small circles, were sure to be reported, and most probably with disadvantage and misconstruction; besides, in the sayings and opinions of such a man the public has a sort of property, and posterity will certainly be pleased with the knowledge of them. Something of this kind had certainly been better than our author's complimentary hint, that it cannot 'be imagined *he* would take the trouble to gather what grows on every hedge because he had collected such fruits as the *nonpareil* and the *bon chrétien*.'

"The work before us is a very proper and excellent guide and companion to the Doctor's celebrated tour. . . ."[9]

[8]vi. 370–374, 377–378 *passim*.
[9]viii. 448–450 *passim*.

"This journal, written with the approbation of Dr. Johnson and under his inspection, and which he declared to be a very exact picture of a portion of his life, has afforded us great variety of entertainment and instruction. It is an excellent commentary on the Doctor's own *Journey to the Western Isles*, contains some poetical pieces relative to it, and exhibits a series of his conversation, many literary anecdotes, and opinions of men and books, most of which, though delivered in common conversation, will abide the severest test of criticism: and to whose colloquial opinions, except Dr. Johnson's, could this elogium be given? This journal was composed during the actual performance of the tour, and must consequently be far more faithful than the details which are the result of recollection. Whilst we read this amusing, instructive, and edifying work, and reflect that it is not a selection of whatever was great or good in our illustrious biographer, but a plain and simple narrative of the ordinary business and manner of his life, we must be impressed with wonder and veneration. We behold the philosopher enforcing, by his own example, the precepts which he has taught; . . . and we here see him, with exemplary magnanimity of mind, suffering the occasional failings, and the little reprehensible peculiarities of his temper and character, to be recorded in the page which he knew was destined to the public, and would descend to posterity.

"If to the opinion of Mr. Boswell may be opposed the conjecture of those who only knew this great man through the medium of his writings, and whom only the voice of rumour has reached, we will venture to remark that the character drawn in the present performance does not give an entire and adequate idea of Dr. Johnson. Perhaps the great and leading feature of his mind was not learning, but religion; more attentive to the duties of the Christian than the avocations of the scholar, his first views were directed to that pious object. . . .

"But to return to the merits and business of the work now before us. It is, with some few exceptions, happily and vigorously written. The severity of criticism might occasionally detect some few errors of style. . . . But it would be not only uncandid but ungrateful to dwell on a few minute blemishes after the pleasure and profit we have received in the perusal of this work.—Mr. Boswell announces a Life of Dr. Johnson, for which we shall wait, not without impatience."[10]

---

[10] lv. 889–890 *passim*. The reviewer, "Mr. Urban," was undoubtedly John Nichols, editor of the *Gentleman's Magazine*.

APPENDIX A

Expense Accounts

Journey to London and in London

21 March–22 September 1785

			£	s.	d.
Had when I set out from Auchinleck			13	19	6
At Cumnock, D. Jamieson	–	1	–		
Toll	–	–	6		
Silk stockings, Lancaster	–	13	6		
Had on my arrival in London ...	–	10	–		
	1	5	–	1	5	–
Journey in all			12	14	6

Had on arrival, 10 /-. Got from brother 31 March, £4.

London Expense

		£	s.	d.
March 30.	Dinner, Swan with Two Necks[1] ...	–	2	3
	Porter	–	1	–
	Coach-helper	–	–	–¹⁄₂
	Sundries	–	1	1¹⁄₂
31.	Poor drummer	–	–	1
	Sundries	–	1	–
	Soup	–	–	6
	Gloves	–	1	2
	Ticket to *Macbeth*	–	3	–
		–	10	2

[1]An inn in Lad Lane, off Wood Street, just north of Cheapside; the booking-office and headquarters of coaches to the North.

	£	s.	d.
March 31. Brought forward [2]	–	10	2
April 1. Coach-hire	–	4	6
April 2. Sundries	–	2	6
Fruit	–	–	6
Sundries	–	1	–
Sundries	–	3	6
Post	–	–	1
	1	2	3
April 3. Sundries [3]	–	1	–
4. Sundries	–	1	–
Armour	–	–	8
Fruit	–	–	1
Post	–	–	2
5. Sundries	–	1	–
Brandy and water	–	–	6
Brandy and water	–	–	$2^1/_2$
Fruit	–	–	2
Sundries	–	1	–
6. Fruit	–	–	2
	1	8	$2^1/_2$
Naples soap [4]	–	9	–
	1	17	$2^1/_2$
April 6. Brought over	1	17	$2^1/_2$
Fines for absence, Essex Head Club	1	5	6
Club this evening	–	–	7
7. Dinner, Piazza	–	5	–
Oranges and playbill	–	–	5
Ticket, *Way to Keep Him,* Covent Garden [5]	–	3	–
Mending breeches	–	1	6
Postage	–	–	2
8. Sundries	–	2	–
Sundries	–	2	6
Coach-hire	–	1	–

[2] Each subtotal represents a page of Boswell's manuscript.
[3] Beginning with this entry in the manuscript there is an *x* after "sundries" for three successive days. The *x* on 4 April was afterwards heavily scored through.
[4] A soft soap made of olive oil and potash, sometimes used medicinally.
[5] A play by Arthur Murphy revived the month previous for the first time in five years. Johnson's favourite, Mrs. Abington, had the lead as Widow Belmour.

		£	s.	d.
	Spent with coachmen, etc. at Lewers's[6]	–	2	–
9.	Spent at Lewers's	–	1	6
	Sundries	–	1	–
	Sundries	–	1	9
	A hat	1	1	–
10.	Coach-hire	–	1	–
11.	Coach-hire	–	1	–
	Brandy	–	–	6
	Watchman	–	–	6
		5	10	$2^1/_2$
		[5	9	$1^1/_2$][6a]

		£	s.	d.
April 11.	Brought forward	5	10	$2^1/_2$
12.	Dinner, Club	–	15	6
	Subscription Dr. Johnson's monument[7]	2	2	–
	Sundries	–	2	–
13.	Sundries	–	2	–
14.	Sundries	–	2	–
15.	Dinner, Somerset[8]	–	8	–
	Sundries and brandy	–	6	–
16.	Washing and mending	–	2	9
	Ditto	–	4	6
18.	Davies's *Miscellanies*[9]	–	15	–
	Coach-hire	–	1	–
	Sundries	–	2	–
19.	Sundries	–	3	6
	Coach-hire	–	1	–
	2 pr. stockings	–	7	–
		9	4	$5^1/_2$
		[11	3	$4^1/_2$]

[6] Unidentified, but almost certainly a tavern or an inn.

[6a] Boswell's subtotals go astray with this page. The correct sums are given within brackets.

[7] A subscription of two guineas fixed by The Club for its members and the general public in order to raise in Westminster Abbey the monument to Johnson which had been sanctioned by the Dean and Chapter as early as 6 May 1785. Malone reported to Bishop Percy 28 September 1786 that there were as yet only two subscribers outside The Club, although the rate was low and the proposals were hung up for some months in the shops of three or four major booksellers.

[8] A coffee-house in the Strand.

[9] Thomas Davies's *Dramatic Miscellanies*, three volumes of critical observations on several

		£	s.	d.
April 19.	Brought forward	9	4	5¹/₂
26.	Dinner, Club	–	16	6
28.	Turnkey, Newgate	–	1	–
	Going to Richmond Lodge	–	1	6
29.	Returning from Richmond Lodge	–	1	–
	Sundries	–	1	–
	Coach-hire	–	1	–
30.	Coach-hire	–	1	–
May 1.	Going to Woodford	–	5	4
2.	Coach-hire	–	2	–
	Omitted, dues at Inner Temple ..	–	8	6
	Various expenses omitted	2	10	–
20.	Coach-hire	–	8	6
23.	Washings......................	1	1	6
24.	Ditto.........................	–	3	10
	Giuseppe's[1] bill	–	2	7
	James's[2] bill	–	1	6
		15	10	2¹/₂
		[17	10	1¹/₂]
May 24.	Brought forward	15	10	2¹/₂
25.	Stamp and paper for my Latter Will	–	5	2
	Porter carrying presentation			
	Letters to People of Scotland	–	5	–
27.	Veronica's nurse	1	1	–
	Medicines	–	2	–
29.	Collection, Newgate	–	–	6
	Several coach-hires	–	5	–
	Several Essex Head Clubs	–	4	4
30.	Washing	–	6	3
	Sculler on Thames	–	–	6
June 1.	Admission, Hanoverian Lodge of			
	Bucks and night's ticket	–	6	8

---

of Shakespeare's plays, with a review of the principal characters as represented by Garrick and other celebrated comedians, first published at London, by the author, in 1783–1784. A new edition was printed this year, 1785.
[1] Paoli's Corsican *valet de chambre.*
[2] Dilly's servant.

		£	s.	d.
2.	Admission, Betsy, to St. Thomas's	–	10	6
	Given	–	2	6
	Coach-hire	–	1	–
3.	Sulphurated pills	–	2	8
	Mercurial ditto	–	–	6
	Carry forward	19	4	$1^{1}/_{2}$
		[21	3	$8^{1}/_{2}$]
June 3.	Brought forward	19	4	$1^{1}/_{2}$
4.	Coach-hire	–	1	6
	Charity	–	–	$1^{1}/_{2}$
7.	Pair stockings	–	7	–
	Coach-hire	–	1	6
8.	Black silk stockings	–	14	–
	Coach-hire	–	2	–
	Johnsonian Club[3]	–	1	1
9.	Temple commons, etc., ending Trinity 1785	6	18	11
11.	Betsy, charity	–	10	6
13.	Print of balloon for Phemie	–	2	–
	Washings up to this date, when more linens given out	–	12	1
15.	Coach-hire	–	2	6
16.	Coach-hire	–	2	6
	Lost at whist	–	8	–
		27	17	10
		[31	7	5]
June 16.	Brought forward	27	17	10
17.	Coach-hire	–	1	–
	Half-subscription to print of Major Pierson's death[4]	1	11	6
	Sundries	–	3	–

[3] The Essex Head Club. See Journal, 8 June 1785.

[4] John Singleton Copley's most successful history painting, the scene during the battle with the French invaders in the market-place of St. Helier's, Jersey, 6 January 1781, in which the commander of the British militia, Major Francis Pierson of the 95th Regiment of Foot, fell in the moment of victory, aged twenty-four. John Boydell, the publisher and print-seller, had commissioned the painting for £800. When it was exhibited in the Great Room at No. 28, Haymarket in May 1784 it was accompanied

		£	s.	d.
18.	Coach-hire	–	2	–
19.	Dinner, Putney	–	4	–
	Coach-hire	–	1	–
21.	Dairymaid in Richmond Park	–	1	–
	Breakfast, Richmond	–	–	10
	Richmond stage to London	–	2	3
	Washing up to the 20th	–	6	–
	Bag for wig	–	4	6
	Letters	–	–	7
	Sundries	–	6	–
	Lord Coke, 2, 3, and 4 parts[5]	2	–	–
22.	Boat to Blackfriars	–	1	–
	Sundries	–	1	–
	Carry forward	33	3	6
		[36	13	1]
June 22.	Brought forward	33	3	6
23.	Lost at whist	–	10	–
	Orgeat at Smyrna[6]	–	–	6
24.	Coach-hire	–	3	–
25.	Coach-hire	–	1	–
	Vauxhall	–	9	–
26.	Coach-hire	–	4	–
	Porter, Portuguese Chapel	–	2	6
27.	Washing to this date	–	4	3
	Exchange on sleeve-buttons	–	1	9
	Perfumery at Boswell's[7]	–	2	8
30.	Coach-hire	–	1	–
July 3.	Jaunt to Richmond	–	5	–
5.	Dinner, Club	–	14	–
	Coach-hire	–	1	–

by a brochure advertising a proposal for an engraving by James Heath. Boswell's receipt for a half-subscription, dated 17 June 1785, is at Yale. The engraving was not published until 1796, a year after Boswell's death.

[5] *Institutes of the Law of England*, by Sir Edward Coke, published in four parts between 1628 and 1644 and reprinted frequently thereafter.

[6] A celebrated coffee-house of the time of Queen Anne, situated on the north side of Pall Mall adjacent to Marlborough House.

[7] William Boswell, perfumer in the Strand.

		£	s.	d.
6.	Execution	–	2	–
7.	Jaunt, Hampton Court	–	14	–
	Carry forward	36	19	4
		[40	8	9]
July 7.	Brought forward	36	19	4
8.	Music for Veronica	3	4	6
	Coach-hire	–	1	–
	To John Bruce, charity[8]	–	3	6
10.	Jaunt to Richmond Lodge	–	2	8
11.	Washing to this date	–	7	4
15.	Coach-hire	–	1	–
	Trifles	–	1	–
16.	John's bill for some weeks[9]	–	10	–
	Coach-hire	–	1	–
	Bark, etc.	–	3	10
	Lost at whist	1	5	–
	Given Richard Boswell's son[1]	–	1	–
18.	Interest to Mr. Dilly to March 1785[2]	10	–	–
	Letters	–	3	1
	Washing to this date	–	4	9
19.	Coach-hire	–	2	–
	Carry forward	53	11	–
		[57	0	5]

[8] Boswell's response to a letter for help from the son of John Bruce, Lord Auchinleck's old servant and late keeper in the Parliament House, Edinburgh. The younger Bruce, a cabinet-maker, had migrated to London with his family. In 1779 he sailed alone for America to improve his fortunes, but the ship was wrecked on a bar at Charleston, South Carolina, and he lost all his possessions. On working his way back to London he discovered that his wife had been informed that he was drowned, had sold all their furniture, and disappeared. He was now alone, unemployed, because he lacked working tools, and violently ill of a fever.
[9] A bill clearly for regular services from a person as yet unidentified (see also 8 August and 10 September 1785, below). Perhaps the barber (22 September, below).
[1] Unidentified.
[2] Dilly had made Boswell a loan of £200 2 March 1780 for a period of two years, but when it fell due he generously extended it, on request, to 1783, and apparently from year to year thereafter. Bowell paid the interest annually (his record is at Yale). On 26 October 1787 he incorporated the principal and a new loan of £300 in a promissory note to Dilly for £500. The entire sum was repaid in 1788.

		£	s.	d.
July 19.	Brought forward	53	11	–
22.	Mr. Pott, surgeon	1	1	–
24.	Returning from Richmond Park ..	–	3	–
25.	Washing to this date	–	4	8
	Tea, Chapter [Coffee-house]	–	–	8
	Coach-hire	–	1	–
	Children's books	–	3	8
	Omitted, Buller's *Nisi Prius* [3]	–	18	–
27.	Admission, etc., at Friends round the Globe	–	5	7
29.	Coach-hire	–	1	–
30.	Coach-hire	–	1	–
	Supper, Prince of Wales Coach-house	–	1	6
31.	Jaunt to General Dalrymple's with Mr. Courtenay	–	10	6
Aug. 1.	Medicines	–	4	–
	Globe	–	–	8
	Carry forward	56	19	3
		[60	16	8]
Aug. 1.	Brought forward	56	19	3
	Washing	–	4	–
3.	Coach-hire	–	1	–
4.	Hesiod, with Pasoris *Lexicon* [4]	–	7	–
6.	Jaunt, Richmond Lodge	–	3	3
	Globe	–	2	8
	Pamphlets, Col. J. Stuart	–	3	–
7.	Coach-hire	–	1	–
8.	Washing to this date	–	4	1
	John's bill	–	4	1
	Ticket to play	–	5	–
11.	Ribbon, Norfolk Sally	–	2	3
	Dr. Johnson's *Prayers*, etc. [5]	–	3	6

[3] *An Introduction to the Law Relative to Trials at Nisi Prius,* a compilation made by the learned second judge of the King's Bench, Francis Buller. First published in England in 1772, the book ran to many editions.

[4] A revised edition, published 1772, of the Works of Hesiod, with an "Index Vocabulorum," Greek into Latin, by Georgius Pasor.

[5] *Prayers and Meditations, composed by Samuel Johnson, LL.D.*, published from his manuscripts by George Strahan, 1785.

		£	s.	d.
13.	Globe	–	–	8
14.	Seat, St. Paul's	–	–	6
	Carry forward	59	1	3
		[62	18	8]
Aug. 14.	Brought forward	59	1	3
15.	Washing	–	4	3
20.	Horse to London, returning from Mr. Barnard's	–	1	–
	Globe	–	–	8
21.	Coach-hire	–	2	–
22.	Washing	–	5	6
	Letters	–	1	–
	Two keys for black case	–	2	–
23.	Globe	–	–	8
	Porter with message	–	–	6
	Omitted, jaunt to Streatham	–	10	–
25.	Returning from Hampstead	–	1	–
27.	Coach-hire	–	1	–
28.	Fare to Kew Green	–	1	6
29.	Colonel Stuart's coachman and footman	–	2	–
	Fare in retour-chaise[6]	–	1	–
	Carry forward	60	15	4
		[64	12	9]
Aug. 29.	Brought forward	60	15	4
	Washing	–	4	3
	Washing silk waistcoat	–	1	6
Sept. 3.	Globe	–	1	11
4.	Charity, Westminster Abbey	–	1	–
5.	Washing	–	4	6
	Coach-hire	–	1	–
	Omitted, watchman	–	1	–
	Post, letters	–	–	4
	Omitted, three lost cards[7]	–	12	6

[6] A carriage hired for a return journey at reduced rates which had been specifically hired for the outward journey by another party.
[7] Three losses at cards.

		£	s.	d.
7.	Cutting crest for my *Tour* [7a]	–	5	–
	Two hieroglyphic Bibles [8]	–	2	–
8.	Gold bosom-pin	–	5	–
	Coach-hire	–	1	–
10.	Lost at cards	–	12	–
	John's bill	–	2	6
12.	Key to my bureau [9]	1	1	–
	Lavender-water	–	1	–
	Jaunt to Richmond Lodge	–	3	6
	Carry	64	16	4
		[68	13	9]
Sept. 12.	Brought forward	64	16	4
	Washing	–	4	4
	Cleaning, etc., a silk waistcoat	–	2	6
	A patent lock for my bureau	1	1	–
	Paley's *Philosophy*	1	1	–
13.	Venison for General	–	13	–
	Going and coming, Richmond Lodge	–	3	–
15.	Printed linen	2	12	6
22.	Bureau	7	7	–
	Waters, stationer	1	2	–
	Miles, hatter	1	4	–

[7a] The woodcut made for the title-page from a professionally executed sketch probably drawn by James Cummyng, herald-painter. The motto "Vraye Foy" is displayed in a banner unfurled above a hooded hawk; beneath the hawk Boswell has added his own initials in a large and interlaced script.

[8] Copies of either the second or third edition (1784, 1785) of *A Curious Hieroglyphic Bible*, select passages from the Old and New Testaments in which pictures replaced key words, in order (to quote the subtitle) "to familiarize tender age, in a pleasing and diverting manner, with early ideas of the Holy Scriptures." The first work of this kind in English, it ran to twenty editions by the early nineteenth century. Thomas Bewick, the engraver, executed some if not all of the cuts.

[9] Boswell spent a total of nine guineas, a considerable sum, for this locked bureau, or writing-desk (see entries below, 12 and 22 September). He kept it at General Paoli's, his London home, and in a codicil to his will explained that it contained two additional keys: one to a drawer in the bureau which held several parcels of materials for writing the *Life of Johnson*; the other to a trunk he had left at Charles Dilly's which contained many volumes of his journal and from which Johnsonian passages might be excerpted. On 22 December 1785 Boswell gave the key to the bureau to Edmond Malone (see above, 30 May 1785, n. 6).

	£	s.	d.
Hartshorne and Lyde for hats, ribbons, and fans	3	12	–
Lady's riding-hat	1	–	–
Gold band	–	7	6
Things for children	–	5	–
Carry over	85	10	8
	[89	8	7]
Sept. 22. Brought forward	85	10	8
Washing in City	–	13	10
Loder,[1] extra	2	2	–
Warehouseman	–	2	6
City barber's lads	–	2	6
Coach-hire	–	2	–
Account with Mr. Dilly[2]	12	15	9
Greatcoat, Mr. Dilly's shopman, I having lost his	2	6	6
Mr. Dilly's maid	1	1	–
General Paoli's servants	6	6	–
Mr. Dilly's maid	1	1	–
Footman	–	10	6
Apprentice	–	2	6
	112	16	9
	[116	14	8]
Journey home	12	12	
(Forgotten 22.)[3]	125	8	9
	[129	6	8]

Expense, London, 1785

	£	s.	d.
Brought from Auchinleck	13	19	6
By draft on Sir Robert Herries	26	–	–

[1] Baldwin's compositor.

[2] The first itemized account with Dilly for which records exist at Yale was drawn up in 1786. It is for books, postage, and small sums of cash, doubtless the kinds of purchases and loans for which Boswell made payment on this day.

[3] This sum is the difference between the figure opposite, £125. 8s. 9d., the total of Boswell's recorded expenditures, and his parallel computation (below), which showed in fact that he had spent £147. 10s. 6d. during the late London jaunt.

	£	s.	d.
Appeal, Mercer	21	–	–
Paid by David Cuninghame	30	–	–
Borrowed of Sir John Dick	60	–	–
	150	19	6
Brought home	3	9	–
	147	10	6
On return home:			
Collection, Auchinleck Church	1	1	–
Account, Saddler Roger	4	4	–

APPENDIX B

Glossary of Legal Terms

BOX. To lodge a printed copy of a petition or answers to the Court of Session in the box of each judge.

CESSIO BONORUM. A total surrender by a debtor of his whole property, on oath, in favour of his creditors, so that he may escape perpetual imprisonment.

CURATOR. A legal guardian of females between twelve and twenty-one and males between fourteen and twenty-one.

DECERN. To decree or adjudge.

DECREET ARBITRAL. The judgement of an arbiter in a private judicial proceeding.

DEFENDER. The defendant or respondent.

DUPLY. A second reply; a defender's rejoinder to a pursuer's reply.

FEU. A holding for which the vassal makes a return in grain or in money rather than in military service. In practice, a long-term lease.

HEIRSHIP MOVABLES. Movable property which the law withholds from the executor or nearest of kin and assigns to the heir so that he might not succeed to a dismantled house and lands.

HERITABLE SECURITY. Security in land, or whatever is connected with land, for the interest and principal of a loan.

INFEFTMENT. Investiture in heritable property.

INFORMATION. A written pleading ordered by the Lord Ordinary when he takes a cause to report to the Inner House.

INTERLOCUTOR. The judgement of the court, or of the Lord Ordinary, which, unless reclaimed or appealed, has the effect of deciding the cause.

LIBEL. Generally speaking, the part of the indictment stating the grounds of the charge on which a civil or criminal prosecution takes place. As a verb, to institute proceedings by filing a libel, or complaint.

MEMORIAL. A statement of facts drawn up to be submitted for counsel's opinion. Also, an advocate's brief.

MINUTE. A notice of intention presented to the court by a party to a suit.

PETITION. An application to the judge stating the cause and the judgements that have been pronounced and requesting an alteration of the judgement.

363

POINDING (*pronounced* pīnding). The process by which a creditor seizes a debtor's property so as to become vested with the title and right of sale or appropriation in satisfaction of his debt.

PRECOGNITION. The preliminary examination of possible witnesses in order to ascertain the evidence which they can give at the trial.

PROCESS. Writs and forms by which a party is brought into court and by which the action is carried on to a conclusion.

PURSUER. The plaintiff or prosecutor.

RATIO DECIDENDI. The ground of decision, that is, the point in a cause which determines the judgement.

RECLAIMING PETITION. A written pleading stating the grounds on which a judgement of the Lord Ordinary or whole court is expected to be altered.

REDUCTION. An action to rescind or annul.

REPRESENTATION. A written pleading presented to the Lord Ordinary when his judgement is brought under review.

SUBMISSION, DEED OF. A contract by which the parties in a dispute agree to submit the disputed matters to arbitration.

TRUST OATH. A long and detailed oath which could be put to a freeholder presenting himself to vote at an election for a Member of Parliament for a county, stating that his title to his estate was "not nominal or fictitious, created . . . in order to enable me to vote for a member to serve in Parliament, but that the same is a true and real estate in me, for my own use and benefit, and for the use of no other person whatsoever."

TUTOR. A legal guardian of girls under twelve and of boys under fourteen.

DOCUMENTATION and BIBLIOGRAPHY

A. The manuscripts and printed documents from which the text is made are numerous and varied, chiefly because of substantial gaps in Boswell's journals for 1783 and 1784. A few leaves of the manuscript have deteriorated, others have been lost or removed by censors. But it also appears that Boswell kept his journal erratically and sometimes neglected it entirely for sustained periods from early spring through mid-November 1784. Where the text fails, we have substituted, if possible, other Boswellian documents that report his activities (rough notes, letters, extracts from newspapers) or matter that he might have recorded in missing or unwritten journal: the interviews with Lord Kames which Boswell preserved apart for a biography, Johnsonian anecdotes that he took down hurriedly from Dr. Adams, and the conversations from the first draft of the *Life of Johnson* at which he himself was present. Occasionally we have supplemented the journal with the report of another author. All the manuscripts in section A are at Yale and are printed in full in this book unless notice is given otherwise. Documents printed for the first time, in whole or in part, are signalized at A7, 11, 12, 16, 20, 21, and 22.

1. "Notes and Journal of My Wife's Illness and of My Own Life from 22 June to 11 November 1782 Inclusive": 11 quarto and 2 octavo leaves, unpaged, 26 sides written on, loose, but enclosed in a wrapper endorsed by Boswell as quoted. We begin with 30 August 1782. The account of Margaret Boswell's illness up to 30 August is summarized for this volume in the Sketch of Boswell's Life; after that date Boswell gradually expanded the entries, until by 9 October he was keeping a regular journal of his own activities. The shift to ordinary journal is marked by larger quarto leaves. The two octavo leaves, which contain the entries for 29 October to 11 November, were mainly written at Boswell's request by Alexander Millar, assistant minister at Auchinleck. The entries for 9 to 11 November are in Boswell's hand.

2. Journal in Edinburgh, 11 November 1782: 2 unpaged leaves, 3 sides written on, following a blank leaf in the quarto notebook with leather spine and marbled paper-board covers which contains the fully written journal for 12 June to 28 August 1782.

3. Journal in Edinburgh, 1 to 25 December 1782: 6 unpaged quarto leaves, 12 sides written on, loose.

4. Notes for Journal at Auchinleck, 27 to 31 December 1782: 1 octavo leaf, 1 side written on, loose.

5. Journal at Auchinleck and in Edinburgh, 1 January to 13 March 1783: a partly filled quarto notebook with leather spine, red marbled paper-board covers, and 44 numbered pages. This notebook also contains the journals in Scotland beginning 1 August 1783, 12 November 1784, and 30 December 1784, numbers 8, 13 and 14, below.

6. Journal in London, 14 March to 4 April 1783: quarto notebook, bound in vellum, 54 leaves (64 sides written on) numbered 1–54, 35–41, 41–43, although the content is continuous. Pp. 39–41 of the first series are missing, and the numbering does not include three versos on which Boswell has written additional notes. There are four blank leaves at the end of the notebook.

7. Journal in London, 10 April to 30 May 1783: rough notes and fully written journal, 43 leaves of various sizes, 76 sides written on, loose. There are entries for the following dates only: 10, 19 to 21, 28-30 April; 1, 8, 11, 12, 15, 17, 18, 22, 23, 29, 30 May. The entries for 28 April and 17 and 23 May are fragmentary or damaged, and the notes for 11 May are so abbreviated that we have summarized them in editorial narrative. For 10 April there are two entries: rough notes, and a Paper Apart, an expansion of the notes which Boswell revised for the manuscript of the *Life of Johnson,* to come in at p. 882. For Easter Sunday, 20 April, there are three entries: memoranda and a collection of Boswelliana written on two sides of a portion of the cover in which a letter to Boswell was enclosed; a Paper Apart, one quarto leaf written on both sides, a fully written account of the conversation at Dr. Johnson's which Boswell edited for the manuscript of the *Life of Johnson,* to come in at p. 894; and a complete and independent document written on five sides of three quarto leaves and headed "Extraordinary Johnsoniana—*Tacenda.*" There are also three entries for 21 April: memoranda, journal, and an expansion of the journal made on a separate occasion. The entry for 10 April, the entire record for 20 April (the Paper Apart as first written), and the memoranda written on both sides of an octavo leaf at Southill 30 May 1783 are printed for the first time.

8. Journal in Scotland, 1 August 1783 to 21 March 1784: fully written journal, 77 pages, originally numbered 51–134, in the same quarto notebook as A5, above, following four blank leaves. P. 88 is a blank, and pp. 75–80 (three leaves) are missing. 8 August to 11 November 1783 is covered by a "Review." There is a heading for 22 March 1784, but no entry.

9. Notes for Journal in Yorkshire and Scotland, 22 March to 8 April 1784: 1 quarto leaf, both sides written on, loose.

10. Journal and Notes for Journal in Glasgow, 10 and 12 April 1784: rough notes and fully written journal recorded on the outside of a letter from John Lawrie (Boswell's clerk), on a fair copy of the letter to Burke dated 10 April 1784, and on a leaf which also contains a draft of the letter to Burke dated 12 April 1784. 4 quarto and 1 octavo leaves, 10 sides written on, loose. We have printed only the fully written journal, 10 April, and drawn upon the other matter for editorial narrative.

11. Observations and Notes made on the way to London and in London, April to June 1784: recorded on a letter to Boswell from John Nornaville, Charles Dilly's clerk; 2 quarto leaves, 4 sides written on. Published for the first time.

12. Journal and Notes for Journal in London, Rochester, and Oxford, 11 May to 6 June and 11–13, 15 June 1784: a list of engagements interspersed with memoranda of both intended and past activities; also rough notes, fully written journal, and "Boswelliana" (changed from "Johnsoniana"); 7 unpaged leaves of various sizes, 13 sides written on, loose. Except for the journal for 3 and 5 June, all published for the first time.

13. Journal in Edinburgh, 12 November to 28 December 1784: fully written journal, 20 quarto pages, numbered 141–160, following the Journal in Scotland, 1 August 1783 to 21 March 1784, after three blank leaves in the notebook (see A5, above).

14. Journal in Scotland, 30 December 1784 to 24 March 1785: a "Review"; fully written journal, 13 quarto pages, numbered 161–173, following the journal above after one blank leaf in the notebook (see A5, above).

15. Journal and Notes for Journal in London, 21 March to [28] September 1785: rough notes, fully written journal, and Papers Apart, 34 unpaged leaves of various sizes, 58 sides written on, loose. The entries for 19 to 26 August, if ever written, are missing, and the fully written entry for 28 August is fragmentary.

16. "Materials for Writing the Life of Lord Kames," 18 November to 22 December 1782: 3 folio, 24 quarto leaves, 43 sides written on, loose. Boswell's record of interviews with Lord Kames in the final months of his life. The entries for 29 November, 3, 4, 5 December and the two leaves (4 sides) added to the entry for 10 December 1782 are printed for the first time. Where bits of the interviews with Lord Kames duplicate the journal proper one of the versions has been silently expunged.

17. Mock covenant drawn by James Bruce, overseer at Auchinleck, nominating his infant grandson to the succession as gardener and overseer, 3 May 1783: 1 quarto leaf, 1 side written on, signed; enclosed

in a letter from Bruce to Boswell dated 5 May 1783.

18.   Conversation with King George III, 15 June 1785: 2 unpaged quarto leaves, 4 sides written on, loose.

19.   Johnsoniana related by the Rev. Dr. William Adams, Oxford, June 1784: 7 quarto leaves, 9 sides written on, loose. One instance of repetition in the notes has been eliminated and the transition adjusted by conflation in the entry dated 1755. Incorporated in the *Life of Johnson* at the years the incidents occurred.

20.   Manuscript of the *Life of Johnson* as first drafted by Boswell, narrative for the dates 12, 18, 28 April, and 17, 19 or 21, 26 May 1783; 5, 6, 9, 10, 13, 15–19, 30 May, and 3, 9–16, 22–25, 27–30 June 1784. In all, 79 quarto leaves, 81 sides written on, loose, at the stage of the first draft numbered on the rectos 882-899, 908-910, 924-981 and apparently blank on the versos except for p. 923, an undated interpolation at 5 May 1784, and p. 967, a full report for 23 June 1784. The entry for 12 April 1783 is a Paper Apart keyed to p. 882 of the main draft, 2 quarto leaves, 3 sides written on, loose. All printed for the first time.

21.   Eleven letters: Boswell to Edmund Burke, 10 April 1784, 2 quarto leaves, written on recto of first leaf only (fully written journal on the other three sides), copy by Boswell, unsigned; Boswell to Edmund Burke, 12 April 1784, 1 quarto leaf, 1 side written on, rough draft or copy by Boswell, unsigned; Burke to Boswell, 15 April 1784, 1 quarto leaf, 1 side written on; Margaret Boswell to Boswell, 26, 29 May and 8 June 1784, printed from typescripts made under the direction of Geoffrey Scott, the first editor of the *Private Papers of James Boswell from Malahide Castle in the Collection of Lt.-Colonel Ralph Heyward Isham*. The manuscripts from which the typescripts were made disappeared from the fireproof safe where Isham had kept them, and Isham assumed that Scott, who was then working on them, had lost them on the Long Island Railroad while carrying them between Isham's residence and the house in New York where he was living; Boswell to the Rev. William Johnson Temple, 6 and 8 July 1784, 4 quarto leaves, 8 sides written on (the portion for 8 July begins on side 4), signed "J. B."; Boswell to Temple, 20 July 1784, 2 quarto leaves, 4 sides written on, signed; Boswell to George III, 6 June 1785, 2 quarto leaves, 4 sides written on, a draft, unsigned; Boswell to Sir Joshua Reynolds, 7 June 1785, 2 quarto leaves, 2 sides written on, signed, and endorsed in Boswell's hand, "Agreement with Sir Joshua Reynolds, 1785"; "Extract of a letter from the Hon. Vice-Adm. Sir Alexander Inglis Cochrane, G.C.B., to Sir J. C. Hippisley, Bt., dated Murdiston 10 July 1819": 1 quarto leaf, 2 sides written on in an unknown hand: Cochrane's version of No.

18 above. In the Osborn Collection, Yale University. So far as we know, printed for the first time.

22. Expense Account, Journey to London and in London, [21] March to 22 September 1785: 12 leaves of various sizes (2 of them blank), 17 sides written on; side 17 written on the verso of a wrapper addressed to Boswell in Lord Hailes's hand. The entries to 19 April 1785 are printed for the first time.

23. Extracts from newspapers: *Edinburgh Evening Courant,* 31 March 1784, signed letter from Boswell on the meeting at Yorkshire to address the King; *St. James's Chronicle,* 5 July 1785, the Address to the King from the tenants and others residing at Auchinleck (presented at Court by Boswell 24 June 1785), and the letter of transmittal from the Rev. Alexander Millar, dated 6 June 1785; *Public Advertiser,* 7 July 1785, "Execution Intelligence," account of the execution of Peter Shaw and others, unsigned article by Boswell; *Public Advertiser,* 14 July 1785, letter addressed to Boswell denouncing the *Letter to the People of Scotland* (1785) and signed "An Ayrshireman"; *Public Advertiser,* 27 July 1785, Boswell's reply to "An Ayrshireman," signed.

B.   Other Boswellian documents, as follows, have been drawn upon for editorial links and for annotation. They, too, are at Yale unless notice is given to the contrary. Matter printed for the first time, in whole or in part, is signalized at B1, 3, 5, 6, and 7.

1. Memoranda, 4 and 5 May 1783: 1 quarto leaf, a programme of activities headed "Domenica" (Sunday) written on the one side; other matter on the second side. Printed for the first time.

2. Pocket almanac for 1784: the Hyde Collection.

3. "My dream in the night between 5 and 6 February 1785," a dream about Samuel Johnson recorded in Boswell's hand and dated 6 February 1785: 1 quarto leaf, both sides written on. In the collection of Jonathan Isham. Printed for the first time.

4. Memorandum, Carlisle, a dream about Samuel Johnson in the night between 21 and 22 March 1785: from a notebook of Boswell's once in the possession of Professor Chauncey Brewster Tinker but now missing.

5. Upwards of 500 letters which Boswell sent or received, 30 August 1782 to 5 October 1785. For 17 of these from Johnson, and 4 to him by Boswell, no manuscripts are known to exist except a long and anxious letter, now at Yale, which Boswell wrote from Auchinleck 1 October 1782. It may be assumed that whenever we cite or quote from this unrecovered correspondence our sources are the texts in the *Life*

of Johnson. More than 60 miscellaneous letters sent and received are also known only from printed texts or are in collections other than Yale's. When quotation is made from a manuscript in the latter group its present location is stated. The remainder of the 500 letters are at Yale, and are for the most part unpublished. Boswell's letters are mainly drafts or copies made by him or his clerk, as one would expect. The Register of Letters, which except for periodic lapses in letters received, was kept systematically "Post Successionem" to 29 November 1782, and again 1 January 1783 to 2 May 1785, and provides summaries of correspondence not now known to exist.

6. Legal documents, manuscript and printed. Continuing the practice of *Boswell in Extremes* and *Boswell, Laird of Auchinleck,* we provide somewhat fuller annotation of Boswell's legal causes than was attempted in the earlier volumes. We have obtained from the Advocates' and the Signet Libraries, Edinburgh, photocopies and microfilm copies of printed papers by Boswell and others in Douglas of Garallan v. Alexanders and Moir; Macmikin (Mrs. Jane Ferguson) v. McDowall and Company; Hall v. Falls; and Dempster v. Watson of Turin. From the Scottish Record Office we have obtained photocopies of the processes, the College of Physicians v. Hunter and the Submission and Decreet Arbitral for McAdam of Craigengillan and his brothers. The S.R.O. also furnished photocopies of the testamentary documents mentioned in this volume: Boswell's will, two codicils to it, the disposition of liferent to his wife, and the settlement of annuities on his children. The House of Lords provided photocopies of the processes, Mercer and Duff v. the Perthshire Justices and Macmikin v. McDowall and Company. Dr. Jean Munro, researcher in Edinburgh, sent us extracts from the Minute Book of the Court of Session containing the Decreets for the Edinburgh and Dumfries Fly v. Dalziel and Malcolm v. Malcolm. By searching the Signet Library Session Papers and the records of the Justiciary Court she also furnished information for the note on Cumming v. Leslie. Dr. A. L. Murray, Assistant Keeper of the Scottish Record Office, obtained the information from the Murray of Murraythwaite Papers which enabled us to write the note on Bryden v. Murray. Except for the testamentary documents, all these legal reports are made available to the general reader for the first time.

7. Various miscellaneous documents: expense accounts and financial statements, the Book of Company and Liquors at Auchinleck (Hyde Collection), the estate journal kept by James Bruce, Boswell's overseer, memoranda and Boswelliana, manuscript verses, letters and paragraphs published in the newspapers, Johnsoniana collected for the *Life of Johnson,* Margaret Boswell's catalogue of the library at Au-

chinleck (1783), the *Catalogue* of the auction of that library, 1893, etc. Many of these extracts are printed for the first time.

C. A selected bibliography, printed works by Boswell and others. The major finding tools for Boswellian research are F. A. Pottle, *The Literary Career of James Boswell,* Clarendon Press, 1929, 1965, 1967; the article on Boswell by Professor Pottle in the *New Cambridge Bibliography of English Literature,* Cambridge University Press, 1971; the catalogue of the Collection of Lt.-Colonel Ralph Heyward Isham as it stood at the end of 1930 (*Private Papers of James Boswell from Malahide Castle,* by F. A. Pottle and Marion S. Pottle, Oxford University Press, New York, 1931); and *A Catalogue of Papers Relating to Boswell . . . Found at Fetter-cairn House,* by C. Colleer Abbott, Clarendon Press, 1936.

Boswell's journal was edited by Geoffrey Scott and F. A. Pottle and published without annotation in the eighteen volumes of *Private Papers of James Boswell from Malahide Castle in the Collection of Lt.-Colonel Ralph H. Isham,* 1928–1934, an expensive, privately printed edition limited to 570 sets. The Yale-McGraw-Hill trade edition initiated in 1950 is the first to make this matter available to the general reader. (The eleven volumes of journal now in print are listed on p. [i].) Most of the journal printed in *Boswell: The Applause of the Jury* appeared first in the fifteenth and sixteenth volumes of Isham's *Private Papers.* The two volumes which will complete the Yale-McGraw-Hill trade edition are in progress, but until they are printed the Isham edition still furnishes the only printed text for the journal after 3 October 1785.

Professor Chauncey Brewster Tinker's *Letters of James Boswell,* 2 vols., Clarendon Press, 1924, is still the only printed general collection. It contains 22 letters from Boswell for our period; 2 of them are derived from the *Life of Johnson.* The great majority of the letters from late summer 1782 to autumn 1785 now known to exist will appear in a chronological volume of Yale's Research Edition of Boswell's Correspondence, which is published by both McGraw-Hill and Heinemann. Of the three volumes now in print *The Correspondence of James Boswell and John Johnston of Grange,* edited by R. S. Walker, 1966, contains 7 letters for the period by and to Boswell; *The Correspondence and Other Papers of James Boswell Relating to the Making of the "Life of Johnson,"* edited by Marshall Waingrow, 1969, contains 42 letters, 2 of them first printed by Tinker and 2 others elsewhere; and *The Correspondence of James Boswell with Certain Members of The Club,* edited by C. N. Fifer, 1976, contains 38 letters by and to Boswell, 4 of them first printed by Tinker and 8 others elsewhere.

The *Life of Johnson,* edited by R. W. Chapman, with introduction by C. B. Tinker, was printed complete in one volume, with Boswell's notes and others, by the Oxford University Press, 1953. A third edition of Chapman, corrected by David Fleeman, was published in 1970. Scholars use the edition of the *Life of Johnson* by G. B. Hill, 6 vols., Clarendon Press, 1887, revised by L. F. Powell, 1934–1964. The fifth volume of this edition is Boswell's *Journal of a Tour to the Hebrides with Samuel Johnson,* the text as published by Boswell himself in 1785 and 1786. The text of the Hebridean journal as actually written by Boswell on the tour was edited by F. A. Pottle and C. H. Bennett and published in 1936 by the Viking Press and William Heinemann, Ltd.; a new impression with additional notes by F. A. Pottle appeared in 1962 with the imprint of the McGraw-Hill Book Company and in 1963 with that of William Heinemann, Ltd.

The entire series of Boswell's *Hypochondriack* essays, to which we make frequent reference, has been reprinted by Margery Bailey, in two volumes with extensive annotation, 1928, and in *Boswell's Column,* one volume with reduced annotation, 1951. The essays appeared in the *London Magazine* during Boswell's lifetime, but they were never before collected, though Boswell had begun to revise them for that purpose. Neither of the political pamphlets he wrote in 1783 and 1785 has been republished. *A Letter to the People of Scotland on the Present State of the Nation,* printed at Edinburgh December 1783 and reprinted in London for Charles Dilly January 1784, is rare; *A Letter to the People of Scotland on . . . Diminishing the Number of the Lords of Session,* published by Dilly May 1785, is found in a larger number of university and public libraries, though it, too, is not readily available.

Of the innumerable works of reference upon which we have drawn for editorial links and annotation we call particular attention to *The Letters of Samuel Johnson,* edited by R. W. Chapman, 3 vols., Clarendon Press, 1952; *The Diaries of William Johnston Temple,* edited by Lewis Bettany, 1929, which furnished evidence of Boswell's activities when his own records for May and early June 1783 failed us; and to *Mary Hamilton . . . at Court and at Home,* edited by Elizabeth and Florence Anson, 1925, the source of the charming report on Boswell by a member of the party with which he attended the historic performance of the *Messiah* in Westminster Abbey 5 June 1784.

I. S. L.

INDEX

This is in general an index of proper names with an analysis of actions, opinions, and personal relationships under the important names. Abbreviations used are D. (Duke), M. (Marquess), E. (Earl), V. (Viscount), B. (Baron), Bt. (Baronet), W.S. (Writer to the Signet), JB (James Boswell), SJ (Samuel Johnson).

Abbot, Kitty, chambermaid, 291
Aberdeen, 124n.9
Aberdeen, University of, 124n.9
Aberdein, Robert, advocate, 126, 138–139
Abington, Frances, actress, 317 and n.3
Adair, James, Recorder of London, 294 and n.7, 295
Adair, Robert, Irish M.P., 296n.2
Adam, John, of Blair-Adam, 138n.4
Adam, Robert, architect, 126n.7, 218 and nn.3, 7
Adam, William, M.P., 138n.4
Adams, Sarah (Hunt), wife of William Adams, 227
Adams, Sarah (Mrs. Hyatt), dau. of following, 227, 242
Adams, William, Master of Pembroke College, Oxford, 227, 230, 231–233, 234, 236, 238, 241, 243–246, 274n.8, 279 and n.5
Addison, John, attorney, 307
Addison, Joseph, 148n.1; *Cato*, 205 and n.3, 319 and n.2
Adventurer, 139
"Advice, The" (song), 305n.5
Advocates, Faculty of, 18 and n.1, 58 and nn.7, 1, 66n.1, 161n.6, 172–173, 272
Advocates' Library, 41, 60, 68, 172
Affleck, Robert, preacher, 29 and n.7
Agar, Welbore Ellis, Commissioner of Customs, 341 and n.8
Ageno, Francesco Maria d', Genoese Minister to Great Britain, 316 and n.5
Aiken, Robert, "writer," 168
Ainslie, Sir Philip, 40, 170
Aisley Park, 114, 115
Aitcheson, Rev. James, of Berwick, 196 and n.2
Aitken, Mrs. Edward (Mrs. Atkins), Newcastle, 200
Akerman, Richard, Keeper of Newgate, 287, 330–332, 332n.6, 334, 337–338, 339n.7
Albany, Charlotte Stuart, Duchess of, 27n.8
Alexander, Claud, of Ballochmyle, 275n.2
Alexander, Robert, 61n.5
Alexander, William, 61n.5
Allerdean (farm), 159

Almack, William, barrister, 286 and n.1
Alva (James Erskine), Lord (Lord Barjarg), 7n.8, 43, 55, 68,
American colonies (American Revolution), British officers in, 8n.1, 49n.4, 145n.1, 161n.5, 265n.7, 299n.4; Commons censures articles of peace with, 76n.8; JB on "accursed American war," 174n.8, 194n.8; visitors from, 226n.6, 301 and n.1; English sympathizers with, 315n.4, 323n.8
Anacreon, 209 and n.7
Ancram, William Ker, *styled* Lord, *later* 6th M. of Lothian, 190
Anderson, Andrew, solicitor, 147
Anderson, John, Professor at Glasgow, 309 and n.4
Anderson, William, W.S., Remembrancer of Exchequer, 55
Andrew, James, carman, 301n.3
Andrews, Miles Peter, dramatist, 321 and n.1, 342
Angus, Earls of, 140
Ankerville (David Ross), Lord, 89, 93
Ankerville, M. d', in London, 286 and n.9, 292, 306 and n.7
Anstruther, Sir John, of Anstruther, Bt., 282n.3
Anstruther, John, M.P., son of preceding, 282 and n.3
Anthropomorphites (Christian sect), 38 and n.3
"Apotheosis of Milton," 231 and n.6
"Apotheosis of the Royal Children, The" (painting), 290n.9
Arabin, Henrietta, (Molyneux), wife of following, 300 and n.7
Arabin, Maj. William John, 285 and n.5, 297, 300 and n.7
Arcot, Nawab of, 159, 190
Arden, Richard Pepper, Attorney-General, 269 and n.9
Argyll, Archibald Campbell, 1st D. of, 63n.2
Argyll, Archibald Campbell, 3rd D. of, 23 and n.9, 144–145, 258n.8, 294n.7
Argyll, John Campbell, 2nd D. of, 322n.6

Boswell, James, II. 2 *(cont.)*:

185*n*.1; fear of death reiterated topic in, 243*n*.7; second and third editions, 252*n*.2; SJ's letters, 185*n*.1, 255; solicits material for, from Hector, Adams, Miss Seward, 279 *and n*.5; Croker edited, 281*n*.1; J. Nichols advises JB to write before *Tour,* 303, disavows writing about, in newspaper, 279 *and n*.5; explains SJ's harsh self-judgement and fear of death, 291*n*.4; will write slowly, 298–299; Malone sole literary executor for, 303*n*.6; praises Villette, 337*n*.8; reference to, in text, 110, 128; reference to, in notes, 6*n*.5, 58*n*.8, 59*n*.2, 63*n*.3, 68*n*.3, 74*n*.1, 75*n*.4, 81*n*.7, 82*n*.1, 100*nn*.6, 9, 101*n*.5, 108*n*.6, 111*n*.8, 114*n*.3, 123*n*.7, 128*n*.6, 138*n*.2, 141*n*.6, 152*n*.1, 176*n*.2, 179*n*.1, 191*n*.7, 213*n*.6, 214*n*.5, 215*n*.2, 216*n*.6, 217*n*.8, 220*nn*.6, 9, 1, 226*nn*.5, 6, 241*n*.8, 243*nn*.6, 9, 248*n*.7, 253*n*.3, 254*n*.5, 274*n*.8, 288*n*.5, 316*n*.1, 320*n*.5; mentioned, 97, 346, 350

3. *Other works: Account of Corsica,* 24*n*.3, 77*n*.2, 133, 218*n*.6, 272, 291*n*.6, 345; early verses, 67*n*.5; *Journal of a Tour to the Hebrides,* dedicated to Malone, 24*n*.3, JB reads original journal to Kames, 32, as prelude to SJ's life, 272*n*.3, printing of, 288, 289, 298, 302 *and n*.6, 304, 317, 322, 341, 342 *and nn*.4, 7; 345, revises with Malone, 306–342, Prince Charles, 307–308, 310–311, 311*n*.8, 323 *and n*.5, proofs of, 325*n*.3, treatment of Macdonald in, 323, 335 *and n*.6, jury of friends on, 342, published, 342*nn*.4, 7, 345, presentation copies of, 343, reaction to, 345–346, crest for, 360 *and n*.7a, mentioned, 44*n*.7, 95*n*.4, 276–277; *Laird o' Glenlee,* 163*n*.1; *Letter to the People of Scotland on the State of the Nation* (1783), writes, 173–174, JB asks Dilly to reprint, 175*n*.1, applause for, 176 *and n*.3, 178, 181, effect on future fortunes, 175, 177–178, and Pitt, 184–185, 185*n*.1, 222*n*.8, review of, 199–200, 200*n*.7, distributed, 175 *and n*.1, and Mountstuart, 177, mentioned, 178, 186; *Letter to the People of Scotland* (1785), writes, 288 *and n*.4, 289, in press,

Boswell, James, II. 3 *(cont.)*:

291–292, 294*n*.7, 296, 297, fears challenge over, 292, 297, 303 *and n*.6; revisions in, 292*n*.1, 300; phlogiston in, 294 *and n*.6; published, 301, 302 *and nn*.9,1; raises enemies by, 303 *and n*.1; letter from "An Ayrshireman" attacks, 323–325; extravagancies of, 345, mentioned, 181*n*.3, 270*n*.6, 292*n*.1, 307*n*.9, 309*n*.7, 332; *No Abolition of Slavery* (1791), 81*n*.8; *Ode by Dr. Samuel Johnson to Mrs. Thrale upon Their Supposed Approaching Nuptials* (1788), 81*n*.8; *Ode on Mr. Boswell's Gong,* 306*n*.6; prologue for Lady Houston's *Coquettes,* 178*n*.8; prologue to *Earl of Essex,* 78*n*.4; review of Anna Seward's *Louisa,* 257*n*.9; "To the Real Freeholders of the County of Ayr," 193 *and n*.4, 194*n*.7; *Verses on Thomas Barnard's Promotion to the See of Killaloe* (a draft), 59*n*.2

4. *Periodical items:* "Rampager," 86*n*.4; account of Hunter Blair dinner, *Edinburgh Advertiser,* 201*n*.5; short letter to the people of Scotland, *St. James's Chronicle,* 293 *and n*.6, 323*n*.9; letter signed "An Ayrshireman" and answer to, 313, 323–325, 327, 328–330; paragraphs about JB and Lee, *Public Advertiser,* 344 *and n*.4

5. *Journal:* published as *Boswell, Laird of Auchinleck,* 4, 98*n*.2; separate journal on Mrs. Boswell's health, 4; entries written by Millar, 14*n*.8; entries from Kames materials substituted for, 16–17, 31–33; lapses in, 46*n*.1, 97, 134, 139, 142*n*.7, 149, 151, 338, 339*n*.6; on writing journal of so insipid a life, 53; uses to review his life, 68*n*.3; really private, 82*n*.3; if neglects, cannot bring up journal accurately, 84; pages removed, 88*n*.4, 171; omits material from, 98*n*.3; *Life of Johnson* material substituted for, 99–106, 109–110, 111*n*.7 (*and see* II. 2 in this entry); writes in, 106*n*.5, 138; alterations in, 107*n*.2, 341*n*.1; memoranda and expansion of journal printed as journal, 113, 158–159, 196, 205–210, 274–284; programme of activities substituted for, 128; Temple's diary material substituted for, 129, 134, 146, 149, 151; his book

Boyle, Hon. Patrick, son of 2nd E. of Glasgow, 194*n*.8

Boyle, Hon. Robert, natural philosopher, 220 *and n*.1

Brackenhill (Auchinleck farm), 8, 12

Bradshaw, William, writer, 98*n*.2

Braehead (Auchinleck farm), 6*n*.9, 246 *and n*.2

Braithwaite, Daniel, of the Post-Office, 84 *and n*.6, 214, 334, 337, 339

Braithwaite, Thomas, saddler, 207 *and n*.3

Brant, Joseph, Mohawk chief. *See* Thayendanegea

Braxfield (Robert Macqueen), Lord, 11*n*.2, 21, 64 *and n*.6

Brentford, 321

Brigend Mill, 47

British Museum, 133 *and n*.1, 146

Brocklesby, Richard, M.D., at Reynolds's, 341; on SJ's health, 184, 267*n*.7, 271 *and n*.8, 274*n*.8; dines at Malone's, 211; offers SJ annuity, 255; JB visits, dines with, 286, 315, 339; applauds *Tour*, 342; mentioned, 192, 195, 292 *and n*.2

Brome, Richard, *Jovial Crew*, 132*n*.5

Brooke, Henry, *Earl of Essex*, 78*n*.4

Brown, John, M.D. (Joannes Bruno), 55 *and n*.1, 184; *Elementa Medicinae*, 55*n*.1

Brown, Joseph, convict, 319*n*.1

Browne, Isaac Hawkins, the elder, poet, 232 *and n*.7, 301*n*.1

Browne, Isaac Hawkins, the younger, essayist, 210 *and n*.3, 301 *and n*.1

Bruce (ident. uncertain), 207 *and n*.4

Bruce, Alexander, advocate (d. 1729), 18 *and n*.9; *Decisions of the Lords of Council and Session*, 18*nn*.9, 1, 33*n*.1

Bruce, Alexander, son of James Bruce, 135

Bruce, Bell. *See* Bruce, Isobel (next entry)

Bruce, Isobel ("Bell"), nurse and housekeeper for the Boswells, 135, 168–169, 168*n*.5

Bruce, Isobel, petition of, 34

Bruce, James, overseer at Auchinleck, ident., 7*n*.7; views estate with JB, 7, 12, 47, 50, 193; correspondence with JB, 62, 80, 83, 97, 134, 135, 221*n*.5, 299*n*.6; collects rents, 176; mentioned, 186*n*.6, 246, 247

Bruce, James, grandson of James Bruce, overseer, 135

Bruce, Jean, dau. of James Bruce, overseer, 135

Bruce, John, 357 *and n*.8

Bruce, Rebecca, dau. of James Bruce, overseer, 135

Brunonian system, 55*n*.1

Brussels, 326*n*.7

Bryant, Jacob, antiquary, *A New System or an Analysis of Ancient Mythology*, 210 *and n*.3

Bryden, Rev. William, minister of Dalton, 184 *and n*.9

Buccleuch, Henry Scott, 3rd D. of, 145 *and n*.3

Buchan, David Steuart Erskine, 11th E. of, 58*n*.9

Buchanan, Janet, 281 *and n*.1

Buck, Samuel, Recorder of Leeds, 199*n*.2, 343

Buckingham, George Nugent-Temple-Grenville, 1st M. of, 177

Bucks, Ancient and Honourable Society of, 302*n*.6, 305 *and n*.4

Buller, Francis, *Nisi Prius*, 358 *and n*.3

Buller, Mary (Coxe), wife of James Buller, 91, 287

Bullock, Col. John, 107 *and n*.10

Bunbury, Sir Thomas Charles, Bt., 312*n*.7

Burgh, Thomas, of Chapelizod, 154 *and n*.6, 155

Burgh, William, D.C.L., 154 *and n*.6, 158–159

Burgoyne (Charlotte Frances Johnstone), Lady, wife of Lt.-Gen. Sir John Burgoyne, Bt., 309

Burke, Edmund, ident., 75*n*.3; letters from JB, 160*n*.4, 170*n*.8, 203, 205; letters to JB, 162 *and n*.8a, 205–206; JB calls on, visits, breakfasts with, 75, 76, 86–87, 89–90, 91, 93, 96, 115–116, 126–127, 154–155, 203–204, 219 *and n*.4; Paymaster of Forces, 76*n*.1, 93*n*.8, 153 *and n*.3, 154 *and n*.5; treasurer of Chelsea College, 154*n*.5, invites JB to, 154 *and n*.5, 155–157; mock-epitaph on, 87*n*.8; Kenyon on, 88; on JB, 10*n*.9, 89–90, 116, 259; on Chatham, 90; H. Dundas on, 94; W.G. Hamilton early patron of, 95*n*.5; advice for JB, 108 *and n*.9, 157, 158; on SJ, 112, 216; his estate (Gregories), 113 *and n*.3a, 116, 318*n*.8; JB on, 115–116, 146, 212–213; on Pitt, 116; SJ on, 118 *and n*.2, 146, 212–213, 215*n*.2; makes puns, 122 *and n*.3, 219 *and n*.5; JB introduces Temple and Hawkins to, 129; and Powell, 153 *and n*.3; laughs at Delany's *King David*, 155; JB asks help of, 160*n*.4, complains to,